WORDS OF FIRE

Words of FIRE

AN ANTHOLOGY OF
African-American Feminist Thought

BEVERLY GUY-SHEFTALL

THE NEW PRESS
NEW YORK

Library of Congress Catalog Card Number 95-69570
ISBN 1-56584-256-1

Published in the United States by The New Press, New York
Distributed by W. W. Norton & Company, Inc., New York

Established in 1990 as a major alternative to the large, commercial publishing houses, The New Press
is the first full-scale nonprofit American book publisher outside of the university presses. The Press is
operated editorially in the public interest, rather than for private gain; it is committed to publishing in
innovative ways works of educational, cultural, and community value that, despite their intellectual
merits, might not normally be commercially viable. The New Press's editorial offices are located at the
City University of New York.

Book design by Charles Nix
Production management by Kim Waymer
Printed in the United States of America

9 8 7 6 5 4

FOR...

Maria Stewart, Anna Julia Cooper, Nannie Burroughs, Pauli Murray, and Audre Lorde—who showed us the way

the sister-writers in **Theorizing Black Feminisms**

the SAGE editorial group

all the students at Spelman

my mother, Ernestine—who stays in my heart

all my sister-friends, especially Paula

and most especially for my sister Francine who helps me see rainbows

Contents

Chapter Two
Triumph and Tribulation: Defining Black Womanhood, 1920–1957

Chapter Three
Civil Rights and Women's Liberation: Racial/Sexual Politics in the Angry Decades

CHAPTER FOUR

Beyond the Margins: Black Women Claiming Feminism

CHAPTER FIVE
The Body Politic: Sexuality, Violence, and Reproduction

CHAPTER SIX
Reading the Academy

CHAPTER SEVEN
Discourses of Resistance:
Interrogating Black Nationalist Ideologies

Preface

The intellectual history of a people or nation constitutes to a great degree the very heart of its life. To find this history, we search the fountainhead of its language, its customs, its religion, and its politics expressed by tongue or pen, its folklore, and its songs.

— GERTRUDE BUSTILL MOSSELL, 1894

The history of American feminism has been primarily a narrative about the heroic deeds of white women. In Miriam Schneir's *Feminism: The Essential Historical Writings* (1972), which focuses on "first-wave" feminism, Sojourner Truth is the only black woman from the mid-nineteenth century to the 1920s who helped to create the conditions that made "second-wave" or modern feminism possible. The chapter on "Men as Feminists" did not include Frederick Douglass (he is included in the chapter on "An American Woman's Movement") and William E. B. Du Bois, two of the most outspoken women's rights advocates in the nineteenth century. In Schneir's subsequent volume, *Feminism in Our Time: The Essential Writings, World War II to the Present* (1994), black women are more visible, but the old framework remains unchallenged. In her brief description of the circumstances that precipitated the first organized women's movement in 1848 at Seneca Falls, New York, black women are absent, slavery is not mentioned, and generalizations about American womanhood clearly refer only to a particular class of white women. Elizabeth Cady Stanton and Susan B. Anthony are invoked, predictably, as the quintessential feminists.

Words of Fire: An Anthology of African American Feminist Thought documents the presence of a continuous feminist intellectual tradition in the nonfictional prose of African American women going back to the early nineteenth century when abolition and suffrage were urgent political issues. It is a rewriting of the familiar narrative of American feminism and a retelling of African American intellectual history. It is deliberately incomplete and includes mostly previously published essays.

Because black women scholars (primarily) have documented over the past two decades the existence of a black women's literary tradition[1] and generated a substantial body of work in the area of black feminist literary studies,[2] many discussions of black feminism focus narrowly on the imaginative literature of black women, particularly fiction.[3] For several reasons I have omitted from this collection fiction, poetry, and literary criticism, though black feminist perspectives certainly inform much of this work, particularly since the 1960s. The literature of contemporary black women is more accessible because of a tremendous outpouring of publications heralding what some scholars call a black women's literary renaissance. As literary critic Cheryl Wall indicates, "over the past two decades, Afro-American women have written themselves into the national consciousness. Their work is widely read, frequently taught, and increasingly the object of critical inquiry" (Wall, 1). Literary critic Deborah McDowell's edited *Black Women Writers* series (Beacon Press), the thirty-volume series, *The Schomburg Library of Nineteenth-Century Black Women Writers* (1988), edited by Henry Louis Gates, Jr., as well as other reclamation projects, also make available a broad range of writing by black women in the nineteenth and early twentieth centuries.

I have also not included pioneering critical essays in black feminist literary studies such as Mary Helen Washington's "Black Women Image Makers: Their Fiction Becomes Our Reality," June Jordan's "On Richard Wright and Zora Neale Hurston: Notes Towards a Balancing of Love and Hate,"[4] Barbara Smith's "Toward a Black Feminist Criticism," Deborah McDowell's "New Directions for Black Feminist Criticism," Alice Walker's "In Search of Our Mothers' Gardens," Barbara Christian's "A Race for Theory," and many more whose focus is primarily the creative expression of African American women.[5]

I use the term "feminist" to capture the emancipatory vision and acts of resistance among a diverse group of African American women who attempt in their writings to articulate their understanding of the complex nature of black womanhood, the interlocking nature of the oppressions black women suffer, and the necessity of sustained struggle in their quest for self-definition, the liberation of black people, and gender equality. Some also express solidarity with other women and people of color engaged in local and global struggles for liberation. Cheryl Wall names these impulses "critical self-consciousness about our positionality, defined as it is by race, gender, class, and ideology."[6] bell hooks describes this kind of "theorizing" on the part of black women, including herself, coming from our "lived" experience of critical thinking, reflection, and analysis. Selections were chosen not because the authors self-identify as feminists or are being defined by me as feminists; some may even reject this terminology altogether. I concur with bell hooks who reminds us that "we can act [or write] in feminist resistance without ever using the word 'feminism'."[7] The women included here are also not a monolithic band with similar world views or the same conceptions of "feminism."[8] They have different family configurations and class backgrounds, widely divergent political views, and diverse disciplinary perspectives. Sometimes their feminist discourse is autobiographical, controversial, visionary, understated and subtle, but more often it is hard-hitting and strident. Some authors are passionate and angry, others more cautious and indirect. There are familiar figures—Sojourner Truth, Shirley Chisholm, Angela Davis—and not so familiar ones—Julia Foote, Amy Jacques Garvey, and Mary Ann Weathers. They have multiple identities, several voices, and different battles to engage. They are academics, activists, artists, community organizers, mothers. They are race women, socialists, communists, Christians, atheists, lesbian and straight, traditional and radical. They share a collective history of oppression and a commitment to improving the lives of black women, especially, and the world in which we live.

The anthology has both a chronological and thematic organization with headnotes preceding each selection which include commentary about the author and the significance of the text. A broad range of issues is discussed —the moral integrity of black women, lynching, poverty, institutionalized racism and sexism, the racism of white women, the sexism of black men, education, black families, male/female relationships, economics, reproductive freedom, sexual and family violence, sexuality, heterosexism, the Civil Rights movement, black nationalism, women's liberation struggles nationally and internationally, and female genital mutilation.

The first four chapters trace the development of black feminist thought from Maria Stewart, writing in the 1830s, through the emergence of black feminist theorizing in the 1970s and 1980s, and the final three chapters focus on a particular theme. Chapter 1, "Beginnings: In Defense of Our Race and Sex, 1831–1900," includes the writings of a number of nineteenth-century "race women" who are also early feminists, though they would not have used this terminology. These foremothers include a number of women whose voices are not here—Josephine St. Pierre Ruffin, Fannie Barrier Williams, Mary Shadd Cary, and Sarah Remond, to name a few. They all reveal a sensitivity to race and gender issues, though they tend not to question their culturally prescribed roles as wives and mothers. They demand equal access to education, the removal of barriers which would prohibit their work in the public domain, and a greater voice in the political arena. They also acknowledge the extraordinary accomplishments of black women in a variety of professions, despite restrictive cultural attitudes within and without the black community.

Chapter 2, "Triumph and Tribulation: Defining Black Womanhood, 1920–1957," covers the first half of the twentieth century, a time during which the patriarchal gender conventions that characterized the post-Reconstruction or Progressive era became more entrenched. These readings attempt to define the complex nature of the black female experience; name in very explicit terms the nature of the oppression which black women continued to experience; and articulate strategies of resistance which made possible the emergence of a "new Negro woman" less hemmed in by outmoded gender definitions and unbridled racism. This section also illustrates bell hooks's assertion that "the production of feminist theory is complex, that it is less the individual practice than we often think, and usually emerges from engagement with collective sources."[9] We see the influence of the Stewart-Truth generation and the impact of feminist struggles throughout the world on the thinking, for example, of Amy Jacques Garvey and Lorraine Hansberry.

Chapter 3, "Civil Rights and Women's Liberation: Racial/Sexual Politics in the Angry Decades," documents the emergence of what we would now call contemporary black feminism, which is traceable in large part to the frustrations of black women in the male-dominant Civil Rights and black nationalist movements of the sixties. We revisit the dilemmas that black women also faced during the nineteenth century with respect to alliances with white women more committed to the eradication of sexism than they were to ending racism. I hasten to add, however, that while the "second-wave" women's movement was dominated by white women, black women were significant participants, though largely unacknowledged, in the development of the modern women's movement, despite their experience of racism within mainstream feminist organizations.[10]

Chapter 4, "Beyond the Margins: Black Women Claiming Feminism," includes a small sampling of an enormous body of explicitly feminist discourse which was generated during the 1980s and demonstrates African American women's continuing commitment to the ideology of feminism broadly defined, as well as their critical role in the development of feminist theory, though they would be marginalized in this history as well.[11]

The remaining three chapters illuminate the contours of contemporary black feminism by focusing on three major themes—the body politic, the academy, and responses to black nationalism and mainstream white feminism. Chapter 5, "The Body Politic: On Sexuality, Violence, and Reproduction," probes a number of issues around which there has historically been considerable silence within the African American community for a number of reasons, not the least of which has been the desire to avoid airing "dirty linen" in a white supremacist society committed to perpetuating damaging racial stereotypes and disempowering entire groups.

Chapter 6, "Reading the Academy," underscores the historical connections African American women have made between learning and liberation; acknowledges their erasure within educational institutions; analyzes the development and impact of a new field of study called black women's studies or black feminist studies; and probes the plight of the black woman intellectual and the recent appropriation of African American women as literary and historical subjects by white feminists and black male scholars.

Chapter 7, "Discourses of Resistance: Interrogating Mainstream Feminism and Black Nationalism," foregrounds writings that explicitly challenge the hegemonic discourses of white, Western feminism because of its insensitivity to race and class, and of black nationalism, which has often been gender-blind, homophobic, and patriarchal in its worldview. Johnnetta Cole, president of Spelman College and author of *All American Women* (a widely used anthology in women's studies classes) and *Conversations: Straight Talk with America's Sister President,* has written a thoughtful epilogue about the importance of black women's maintaining connections to their feminist herstories.

Words of Fire is a highly selective collection of feminist essays by African American women some of which have appeared in a variety of places and are often difficult to retrieve, though some have been frequently anthologized. In most cases, the entire text has been reprinted, and in a few cases the essay has been shortened. In order to keep the anthology to a reasonable size, it was necessary to exclude important essays such as Mae King's "Oppression and Power: The Unique Status of the Black Woman in the American Political System," Bonnie Thornton Dill's "Race, Class and Gender: Prospects for an All-Inclusive Sisterhood," Hortense Spillers's "Interstices: A Small Drama of Words," Joyce A. Joyce's "Black Woman Scholar, Critic, and Teacher: The Inextricable Relationship Among Race, Sex, and Class," Paulette Caldwell's "A Hair Piece: Perspectives on the Intersection of Race and Gender," Evelyn Brooks Higginbotham's "African American Women's History and the Metalanguage of Race," and Ann du Cille's "The Occult of True Black Womanhood: Critical Demeanor and Black Feminist Studies," to name only a few. In addition to excluding literary and cultural criticism, I also omitted highly specialized essays in academic disciplines/interdisciplines such as art history, film studies, classics, linguistics, jurisprudence, anthropology, and theology. I regret the absence, with one exception, of material on health and the sciences, though Evelyn White's *The Black Women's Health Book: Speaking for Ourselves* (1990) and *Wings of Gauze: Women of Color and the Experience of Health and Illness* (1993), provide excellent black feminist perspectives on a number of issues.

While this anthology is incomplete, it should achieve a number of objectives. It contributes to the retelling of American, African American, women's, and world history, and is instructive for black women and those wanting to understand the evolution of black feminist thought in the United States. In particular, it will be useful for black studies and women's studies curricula, especially in staple courses such as feminist theory and black women writers. It also helps to dismantle stereotypes about peoples of African descent, women, and particularly black women, where their intellects and sexualities are concerned. Moreover, it provides greater clarity about the impact and interface of racism, sexism, heterosexism, and classism on the lives of African American women, around whom swirl so many mythologies. These daring women also enable all of us to imagine a world in which race, gender, and class hierarchies are no longer viable. Finally, *Words of Fire* attests to the maturity of black feminist studies and its importance in the transformation of the American academy.

ENDNOTES

1. A small group of mainly black feminist scholars have been responsible for reconstructing the androcentric African American literary tradition by establishing the importance of black women's literature. See Helen Washington's "Black Women Image Makers," in *Black Eyed Susans: Classic Stories By and About Black Women* (Garden City, N.Y.: Doubleday/Anchor 1971) and *Invented Lives: Narratives of Black Women, 1860–1960* (New York: Doubleday, 1988); Barbara Christian, *Black Women Novelists: The Development of a Tradition, 1892–1976* (Westport, Conn.: Greenwood Press, 1980); Hazel Carby, *Reconstructing Womanhood: The Emergence of the Afro-American Woman Novelist* (New York: Oxford University Press, 1987); Deborah E. McDowell, *"The Changing Same": Black Women's Literature, Criticism, and Theory* (Bloomington: Indiana University Press, 1995). Early anthologies of black women's literature were also important: Roseann P. Bell, Bettye J. Parker, and Beverly Guy-Sheftall, eds., *Sturdy Black Bridges: Visions of Black Women in Literature* (New York: Doubleday, 1979); Pat Crutchfield Exum, ed., *Keeping the Faith* (Greenwich, Conn.: Fawcett, 1974); Barbara Smith, ed., *Home Girls: A Black Feminist Anthology* (New York: Kitchen Table, Women of Color Press, 1983); Mari Evans, *The Black Woman Writer, 1950–1989* (New York: Doubleday, 1984); Juliette Bowles, ed., *Frances, Zora and Lorraine: Essays and Interviews on Black Women and Writing* (Washington, D.C.: Howard University Press, 1979).

2. Landmark texts in black feminist literary criticism are Barbara Smith's "Toward a Black Feminist Criticism," *Conditions: Two* (1977): 27–28, followed by Deborah McDowell's "New Directions for Black Feminist Criticism," *Black American Literature Forum* (October 1980). See also: Barbara Christian, *Black Feminist Criticism: Perspectives on Black Women Writers* (New York: Pargamon Press, 1985), which critic Michele Wallace names "the Bible in the field of black feminist criticism" in *Invisibility Blues: From Pop to Theory* (London: Verso, 1990) 184; Gloria Wade-Gayles, *No Crystal Stair: Visions of Race and Sex in Black Women's Fiction* (New York: Pilgrim Press, 1984); Marjorie Pryse and Hortense J. Spillers, eds., *Conjuring: Black Women, Fiction and Literary Tradition* (Bloomington: Indiana University Press, 1985); Cheryl A. Wall, ed., *Changing Our Words: Essays on Criticism, Theory, and Writings by Black Women* (New Brunswick, N.J.: Rutgers University Press, 1989); Joanne M. Braxton, *Black Women Writing Autobiography: A Tradition Within a Tradition,* (Philadelphia: Temple University Press, 1989); Valerie Smith, *Self-Discovery and Authority in Afro-American Narrative* (Cambridge: Harvard University Press, 1987); Gloria T. Hull, *Color, Sex, and Poetry: Three Women Writers of the Harlem Renaissance* (Bloomington: Indiana University Press, 1987); Claudia Tate, *Domestic Allegories of Political Desire: The Black Heroine's Text at the Turn of the Century* (New York: Oxford University Press, 1992); and Karla Holloway, *Moorings and Metaphors: Figures of Culture and Gender in*

Black Women's Literature (New Brunswick, N.J.: Rutgers University Press, 1992). Feminist readings of black women writers have also been published by others, including Susan Willis, *Specifying: Black Women Writing the American Experience* (Madison: University of Wisconsin Press, 1987); Calvin Hernton, *The Sexual Mountain and Black Women Writers* (New York: Anchor 1987); Henry Louis Gates, Jr., ed., *Reading Black, Reading Feminist: A Critical Anthology* (New York: Penguin, 1990); Houston A. Baker, Jr., *Workings of the Spirit: The Poetics of Afro-American Women's Writing* (Chicago: University of Chicago Press, 1991); and most recently Madhu Dubey, *Black Women Novelists and the Nationalist Aesthetic* (Bloomington: Indiana University Press, 1994).

3. Exceptions include E. Frances White, "Listening to the Voices of Black Feminism," *Radical America* (1984): 7–25, which analyzes from a critical perspective the theoretical writing, excluding literary criticism, of contemporary black women since the 1970s on the themes of family, class, and sexuality; Wilson J. Moses, "Domestic Feminism, Conservatism, Sex Roles, and Black Women's Clubs, 1893–1896," *Journal of Social and Behavioral Sciences* 24 (Fall 1897): 166–177, in which he uses the phrase "genteel domestic feminism" to characterize the work of late-nineteenth-century black clubwomen, who, for the most part, accepted Victorian sexual values and the notion that women have the responsibility of upgrading the morality of home and family by toiling within the "women's sphere." More typical is the approach taken by Linda Perkins in "Black Women and Racial 'Uplift' Prior to Emancipation," *The Black Woman Cross-Culturally,* ed. Filomina Steady (Cambridge: Scheckman Publishing, 1981), in which she employs a race-focused analysis in her discussion of the activist work of nineteenth-century black women.

4. The Washington and Jordan essays which appeared in the August 1974 issue of *Black World* signalled the importance of black women writers in the cultural history of African Americans and provided a catalyst for the development of black feminist criticism.

5. Ann duCille identifies such works as "the founding texts of contemporary black feminist studies," in "The Occult of True Black Womanhood: Critical Demeanor and Black Feminist Studies," *Signs* 19: 3 (1994): 591–629.

6. Wall, 1. She chronicles "the community of Black women writing" beginning with Toni Cade's *The Black Woman* (New York: Signet 1970) and marks a "few transformative moments in the development of black feminist criticism beginning with the work of critic Mary Helen Washington, which became more self-conscious with Barbara Smith's 1977 landmark essay, "Toward a Black Feminist Criticism." She also locates Alice Walker's "In Search of Our Mothers' Gardens," *Ms.* (May 1974), 64–70, in this tradition because it "posits a theory of black female creativity and defines a tradition of black women's art" (5).

7. bell hooks, "Out of the Academy and into the Streets," in *Getting There: The Movement Toward Gender Equality,* ed. Diana Wells (New York: Carroll & Graf Publishers, 1994), 192–193. A longer version of this essay appeared as "Theory as Liberatory Practice," *Yale Journal of Law and Feminism* 4: 1, 1–12.

8. For a discussion of the history of the use of the French terms "feminisme" and "feministe" in the 1880s and eventually the English term "feminism" in the early 1900s, see Nancy Cott's *The Grounding of Modern Feminism* (New York: Yale University Press, 1987) in her chapter on "The Birth of Feminism." Cott prefers not to use the term "feminism" in her discussions of the nineteenth-century women's rights or suffrage movement and alludes to a December 1909 article in the *American Suffragette,* "Suffragism Not Feminism," in which some American women distanced themselves from what they perceived to be radical terminology. Cott indicates that it was around 1913 that American women embraced the term "feminism," which marked a "new phase in thinking about women's emancipation" (15).

9. hooks, *Getting There,* 193.

10. See Flora Davis, *Moving the Mountain: The Women's Movement Since 1960* (New York: Simon & Schuster, 1991) though she, unfortunately, does not always identify women racially.

11. Three early anthologies of contemporary feminism—Joanne Cooke et al.'s *The New Women: An Anthology of Women's Liberation* (1970), Robin Morgan's *Sisterhood Is Powerful: An Anthology of Writings from the Women's Liberation Movement* (1970), and Deborah Babcox and Madeline Belkin's *Liberation Now! Writings from the Women's Liberation Movement* (1970) pay some token attention to black women. They all include Frances Beale's "Double Jeopardy: To Be Black and Female." Morgan's book includes a section on women in the black liberation movement, and a long essay by Flo Kennedy, a civil rights lawyer, a member of The Feminists, and one of the founding members of the National Organization for Women (NOW). "Liberation Now!" contains a section on "caste, class, and race" and "sisters in revolution," which includes an essay by an African woman.

Selections

Margaret Walker Alexander, "Black Women in Academia," *How I Wrote Jubilee* (New York: Feminist Press, 1990).

Sadie T. M. Alexander, "Negro Women in Our Economic Life," *Opportunity* (July 1930): 201–203.

Frances Beale, "Double Jeopardy: To Be Black and Female," *The Black Woman,* ed. Toni Cade (New York: Signet, 1970).

Shirley Chisholm, "Facing the Abortion Question," *Unbought and Unbossed* (Boston: Houghton Mifflin, 1970), 127–136.

Cheryl Clarke, "Lesbianism: An Act of Resistance," *This Bridge Called My Back,* ed. Cherríe Moraga and Gloria Anzaldúa (Watertown, MA: Persephone Press), 128–137.

Pearl Cleage "What Can I Say," *Atlanta Tribune,* June 1994.

Patricia Hill Collins, "The Social Construction of Black Feminist Thought," *Signs* 14 (August 1989): 745–773.

The Combahee River Collective, "A Black Feminist Statement," *All the Women Are White, All the Blacks Are Men, But Some of Us Are Brave: Black Women's Studies,* ed. Gloria T. Hull, Patricia Bell Scott, and Barbara Smith (New York: Feminist Press, 1982).

Anna Julia Cooper, *A Voice from the South by a Black Woman of the South* (Xenia, OH: Aldine Printing House, 1892).

Angela Davis, "Reflections on the Black Woman's Role in the Community of Slaves," *Black Scholar* 3 (December 1971): 2–15.

Alice Dunbar-Nelson, "The Negro Woman and the Ballot," *Messenger* IX (April 1927).

Julia A. J. Foote, "Women in the Gospel," *A Brand Plucked from the Fire: An Autobiographical Sketch* (Cleveland, OH: Lauer and Yost, 1886).

Amy Jacques Garvey, "The Role of Women in Liberation Struggles," *Massachusetts Review* (Winter/Spring 1972): 109–112.

———, "Women as Leaders," *The Negro World,* October 25, 1925.

———, "No Sex in Brains and Ability," *The Negro World,* December 27, 1924.

Paula Giddings, "The Last Taboo," *Race-ing Justice, En-gendering Power: Essays on Anita Hill, Clarence Thomas, and the Construction of Social Reality,* ed. Toni Morrison (New York: Pantheon Books, 1992), 441–465.

Jacquelyn Grant, "Black Theology and the Black Woman," *Black Theology: A Documentary History, 1966–1979,* ed. S. Welmore and J. Cone (Maryknoll, NY: Orbis, 1979).

Patricia Haden, Donna Middleton, and Patricia Robinson, "A Historical and Critical Essay for Black Women," *Voices of the New Feminism,* ed. Mary L. Thompson (Boston: Beacon Press, 1970), 316–324.

Evelynn Hammonds, "Missing Persons: African American Women, AIDS, and the History of Disease," *Radical America* 20 (1986): 7–23.

Lorraine Hansberry, "Simone de Beauvoir and *The Second Sex:* An American Commentary," unpublished manuscript. Lorraine Hansberry Archives, Croton-on-Hudson, New York.

Frances E. W. Harper, "Woman's Political Future," *World's Congress of Representative Women,* ed. May Wright Sewall (Chicago: Rand, McNally and Co., 1894), 433–437.

Elizabeth Higginbotham, "Designing an Inclusive Curriculum: Bringing All Women into the Core," *Women's Studies Quarterly* 18 (Spring/Summer 1990): 7–23.

Darlene Clark Hine, "Rape and the Inner Lives of Black Women in the Middle West: Preliminary Thoughts on the Culture of Dissemblance," *Signs* 14 (August 1988): 912–920.

bell hooks, "Black Women: Shaping Feminist Theory," *Feminist Theory: From Margin to Center* (Boston: South End Press, 1984).

Claudia Jones, "An End to the Neglect of the Problems of the Negro Woman," *Political Affairs,* 1947, reprinted in Buzz Johnson's *I Think of My*

Mother: Notes on the Life and Times of Claudia Jones (London: Karia Press, 1985).

June Jordan, "A New Politics of Sexuality," *Technical Difficulties* (New York: Pantheon, 1992), 181–193.

Gloria Joseph, "Black Feminist Pedagogy and Schooling in Capitalist White America," *Bowles and Gintes Revisited: Correspondence and Contradiction in Educational Theory,* ed. Mike Cole (London and New York: Falmer, 1988).

Florynce Kennedy, "A Comparative Study: Accentuating the Similarities of the Societal Position of Women and Negroes," *Color Me Flo: My Hard Life and Good Times* (Englewood Cliffs, NJ: Prentice-Hall, 1976).

Deborah K. King, "Multiple Jeopardy, Multiple Consciousness: The Context of a Black Feminist Ideology," *Signs* 14 (Autumn 1988): 42–72.

Linda La Rue, "The Black Movement and Women's Liberation," *Black Scholar* 1 (May 1970): 36–42.

Audre Lorde, "Age, Race, Class, and Sex: Women Redefining Difference," *Sister Outsider* (Trumansburg, NY: Crossing Press, 1984).

Elise Johnson McDougald, "The Double Task: The Struggle of Negro Women for Sex and Race Emancipation," *Survey Graphic* LIII (October 1924–March 1925): 689–691.

N. F. Mossell, *The Work of the Afro-American Woman* (Philadelphia: George S. Ferguson, 1894).

Pauli Murray, "The Liberation of Black Women," *Voices of the New Feminism,* ed. Mary Lou Thompson (Boston: Beacon Press, 1970), 87–102.

Barbara Omolade, "Hearts of Darkness," *Powers of Desire: The Politics of Sexuality,* ed. Ann Snitow, Christine Stansell, and Sharon Thompson (New York: Monthly Review Press, 1983), 350–367.

Barbara Ransby and Tracye Matthews, "Black Popular Culture and the Transcendence of Patriarchal Illusions," *Race and Class* 35: No. 1 (1993): 57–68.

Marilyn Richardson, ed., *Maria W. Stewart, America's First Black Woman Political Writer: Essays and Speeches* (Bloomington: Indiana University Press, 1987).

Beth Richie, "Battered Black Women: A Challenge for the Black Community," *Black Scholar* 16 (March/April 1985): 40–44.

Barbara Smith, "Some Home Truths on the Contemporary Black Feminist Movement," *Black Scholar* 16 (March/April 1985): 4–13.

Mary Church Terrell, "The Progress of Colored Women," *Voice of the Negro* (July 1904): 291–294.

Pauline Terrelonge, "Feminist Consciousness and Black Women," *Women: A Feminist Perspective,* ed. Jo Freeman (Palo Alto, CA: Mayfield, 1984).

Sojourner Truth, "When Woman Gets Her Rights Man Will Be Right," *Major Speeches by Negroes in the U.S., 1797–1971,* ed. Eric Foner (New York: Simon and Schuster, 1972), 345–346.

Alice Walker, "In the Closet of the Soul," *Living by the Word* (New York: Harcourt Brace Jovanovich, 1988).

Michele Wallace, "Anger in Isolation: A Black Feminist's Search for Sisterhood," *Invisibility Blues* (London: Verso, 1990). First published in *Village Voice* 28 (July 28, 1975): 6–7.

Mary Ann Weathers, "An Argument for Black Women's Liberation as a Revolutionary Force," *Voices of the New Feminism,* ed. Mary Lou Thompson (Boston: Beacon Press, 1970), 303–307.

Ida Wells-Barnett, "Lynch Law in America," *Arena* (January 1990), 15–24.

E. Frances White, "Africa on My Mind: Gender, Counterdiscourse and African American Nationalism," *Journal of Women's History* 2 (Spring 1990): 73–97.

Acknowledgments

This project has had both a long and short history. I have been reading and collecting, on a sustained basis, the writings of African American women since I joined the English Department at Spelman College in 1971. *Sturdy Black Bridges: Visions of Black Women in Literature* (Doubleday, 1979) —co-edited by my deceased and beloved colleague, Roseann P. Bell, and friend Bettye J. Parker—was the first flowering of my passion for the wisdom, too often buried, of black women. My involvement with *SAGE: A Scholarly Journal on Black Women* and my many years of work on the doctoral dissertation *Daughters of Sorrow: Attitudes Toward Black Women, 1880–1920* (Carlson, 1990) confirmed what I had discovered during the lengthy evolution of my first publishing effort which was that black women have struggled against racism *and* sexism and many other "isms" during our involuntary sojourn in this country and that these courageous efforts have been ignored, misinterpreted, or maligned. I and many others name this work, among other descriptors, "feminist," though I'm not bothered if others prefer different labels. Keeping this in mind, I would first of all like to thank all those sister-writers, especially the contributors to this anthology, who have validated our existence in the world.

Words of Fire also has another, less complicated history. Several years ago a colleague and I started compiling feminist essays by black women going back to Maria Stewart which we planned to publish when we could get around to it, but we never did. Eventually Dawn Davis, editor at The New Press, contacted me about publishing with them and since I liked what they were doing, I agreed to reconceptualize and complete this first collection of readings on the evolution of feminist thought among African American women. I am grateful to my colleague for encouraging me to complete the project. I am also pleased that Dawn was persistent and allowed me the freedom to proceed. Her editorial judgment has been invaluable and I owe her a big thanks for helping me to fulfill one of my dreams. I would also like to acknowledge the cooperation of two friends.

Jewell Gresham Nemiroff granted me permission to include Lorraine Hansberry's unpublished essay on Simone de Beauvoir's *The Second Sex*. This gesture of friendship I am deeply grateful for. I would also like to thank Professor Margaret Wilkerson, Lorraine Hansberry's biographer, for agreeing to edit the unfinished essay on very short notice and for writing an eloquent introduction. I would like to thank as well Professor Ula Taylor for helping me to select from the numerous editorials which Amy Jacques Garvey wrote and for writing an introduction.

And finally I want to remember my own mother—the first feminist I ever knew. She encouraged me to live freely, be independent, sit on my own bottom, develop my intellect, treasure friendships with women, and recognize a good man when I saw one.

Introduction

THE EVOLUTION OF FEMINIST CONSCIOUSNESS AMONG AFRICAN AMERICAN WOMEN

*... black women both shape the world and are shaped by it. ...
[they] create their own black feminist theory. They come to feminist
theory and practice out of the oppression they experience as people
who are poor and black and women. ... black feminism has evolved
historically over centuries, outside traditional white feminine roles,
white social institutions, and white feminist cultural theory.*

— KESHO YVONNE SCOTT, *The Habit of Surviving*

The struggle for black women's liberation that began to emerge in the
mid-1960s is a continuation of both intellectual and activist traditions
whose seeds were sown during slavery and flowered during the antislavery
fervor of the 1830s. When a small group of free black "feminist-abolitionists" in the North surfaced during the early nineteenth century, among
whom were Maria Stewart, Sojourner Truth, and Frances E. W. Harper,
the history of African American feminism began.[1] Their involvement in
abolitionist and other reform movements as lecturers, writers, and journalists—traditionally male domains—met with resistance and violated the
Victorian ethic of "true womanhood," which stressed piety, chastity, submissiveness, and domesticity (Welter, 151).*

The argument that African American women confront both a "woman
question and a race problem" (Cooper, 134) captures the essence of black
feminist thought in the nineteenth century and would reverberate among
intellectuals, journalists, activists, writers, educators, artists, and community
leaders, both male and female, for generations. While feminist perspectives
have been a persistent and important component of the African American
literary and intellectual traditions for generations, scholars have focused
primarily on its racial overtones.[2] This tendency to ignore long years of

---

* Barbara Welter, "The Cult of True Womanhood," *American Quarterly* 18 (Summer
1966), 151.

political struggle aimed at eradicating the multiple oppressions that black women experience resulted in erroneous notions about the relevance of feminism to the black community during the second wave of the women's movement. Rewriting black history using gender as one category of analysis should render obsolete the notion that feminist thinking is alien to African American women or that they have been misguided imitators of white women. An analysis of the feminist activism of black women also suggests the necessity of reconceptualizing women's issues to include poverty, racism, imperialism, lynching, welfare, economic exploitation, sterilization abuse, decent housing, and a host of other concerns that generations of black women foregrounded.

While black feminism is not a monolithic, static ideology, and there is considerable diversity among African American feminists, certain premises are constant: 1) Black women experience a special kind of oppression and suffering in this country which is racist, sexist, and classist because of their dual racial and gender identity and their limited access to economic resources; 2) This "triple jeopardy" has meant that the problems, concerns, and needs of black women are different in many ways from those of both white women and black men; 3) Black women must struggle for black liberation *and* gender equality simultaneously; 4) There is no inherent contradiction in the struggle to eradicate sexism and racism as well as the other "isms" which plague the human community, such as classism and heterosexism; 5) Black women's commitment to the liberation of blacks and women is profoundly rooted in their lived experience.

Discussions about the evolution of feminist consciousness[3] among African American women usually begin with abolitionist Sojourner Truth (less often with abolitionist Maria Stewart), since the catalyst for the emergence of women's rights in the mid-nineteenth century was the movement to eradicate slavery. There is certainly little disagreement among historians about the link between women's rights and abolition: "It was in the abolition movement that women first learned to organize, to hold public meetings, to conduct petition campaigns. For a quarter of a century the two movements, to free the slave and liberate the woman, nourished and strengthened one another" (Flexner, 41).

It was the horrendous circumstances that enslaved African women endured since 1619, not the abolition movement, that inspired their first yearnings for freedom and rebellious spirit. They resisted beatings, involuntary breeding, sexual exploitation by white masters, family separation, debilitating work schedules, bad living conditions, and even bringing into the world children who would be slaves. A few of their life stories called attention to the peculiar plight of black women and their strategies for resistance.[4] In her antebellum autobiography, *Incidents in the Life of a Slave Girl: Written by Herself* (1861), Harriet Jacobs publicized her sexual vulnerability and stated unequivocally that "slavery is terrible for men; but it is far more terrible for women. Superadded to the burden common to all, *they* have wrongs, and sufferings, and mortifications peculiarly their own" (Yellin, 77). Covert use of contraceptives, the practice of abortion, and desperate attempts to control the fate of their children, including occasionally infanticide, provided some slave women a measure of control over their bodies and their reproductive capacity. The most well-documented case of infanticide concerns Margaret Garner, who escaped slavery in Kentucky in 1856, and during her capture in Cincinnati killed her baby daughter rather than have her returned to her master. This saga inspired Toni Morrison's award-winning novel, *Beloved,* which was published in 1987.

Manifestations of black women's race and gender consciousness are also found in the single-sex, self-help organizations which free Northern black women formed in the early 1800s because it was difficult for them to become leaders in organizations with black men, or because they were denied membership in white women's groups. It was also easier for black women to attend to their own political, cultural, and intellectual agendas with the establishment of separate literary, debating, abolitionist, or other reform organizations. Located primarily in the northeast, one of the earliest of these organizations was the Afric-American Female Intelligence Society of Boston, founded in 1831. In 1832, free women of color were also responsible for organizing the first female abolitionist group, the Salem Massachusetts Female Antislavery Society, a year before the founding in Philadelphia of the all-male American Anti-Slavery Society (AAS), the most prominent abolitionist organization. The racially mixed Philadelphia Female Anti-Slavery Society, also founded in 1833, emerged because the AAS prohibited female membership. Though ignored by historians attempting to document the development of feminism in the mid-nineteenth century, black women's self-help, abolitionist, and other reform activities also contributed to a climate of discontent which foreshadowed the historic women's rights gathering at Seneca Falls in 1848.

In 1832, Maria W. Stewart (1803–1879), a free black from Connecticut with abolitionist and feminist impulses, delivered four public lectures in Boston, the first one before the Afric-American Female Intelligence Society. She was probably the first black woman to speak publicly in defense of women's rights, though she is remembered primarily as the first American-born woman of any race to lecture publicly about political matters to racially mixed audiences of women and men. Though she spoke on a variety of issues relevant to the black community—literacy, abolition, economic empowerment, and racial unity—she admonished black women in particular to break free from stifling gender definitions and reach their fullest potential by pursuing formal education and careers, especially teaching, outside the home. She was also adamant that black women assume leadership roles. These were all familiar themes in what we now label a black feminist agenda during the nineteenth century. Passionate in her defense of black womanhood, she queried: "How long shall the fair daughters of Africa be compelled to bury their minds and talents beneath a load of iron pots and kettles? . . . Possess the spirit of independence. . . . Sue for your rights and privileges" (Richardson, 38).

Discouraged by criticism from black men about her inappropriate female behavior (political activism and lecturing in public), Stewart left the lecture circuit a year later in 1833, but not without defending womanhood in the most glowing terms by alluding to historical and biblical precedents of women leaders and scholars. She also warned against a paradoxical problem which would plague the black community for generations—preaching against prejudice in the white community but being discriminatory in its own backyard.

During the 1830s and 1840s, other American women, like Stewart, began lecturing against slavery and discovered that they had to defend their right to speak in public, which motivated them to demand their own emancipation. In 1840, the mostly white male American delegates to the World's Anti-Slavery Convention arrived in London to find the women delegates among them excluded from participation. While seated in the gallery behind a curtain with the rest of the women, Elizabeth Cady Stanton and Lucretia Mott felt the striking similarity between themselves, as white women, and black slaves, a common theme in early white feminist discourse. During ten frustrating days, they became friends and agreed to hold a women's right convention on their return to America. Eight years later, the Seneca Falls convention, most of whose participants were white female abolitionists, was held in New York; this convention signaled the beginning of the United States women's movement. Frederick Douglass, prominent abolitionist and women's rights advocate, was the lone black in attendance.

While Frederick Douglass believed the antislavery movement was helping to empower women, he understood the need for an independent, organized movement to achieve equal rights for women. On July 14, 1848, his *North Star* carried the announcement of the Seneca Falls Convention. A constant reminder to readers of his commitment to the rights of women was the newspaper's slogan—"Right is of No Sex." At Seneca Falls, when it appeared that Elizabeth Cady Stanton's resolution for woman suffrage was headed for defeat, Douglass at a critical juncture asked for the floor and delivered an eloquent plea on behalf of women's suffrage. The resolution was then put to vote and carried by a small margin.

Serious involvement on the part of black women in the "first-wave" women's rights movement is manifest in the life of Sojourner Truth, the most revered black feminist-abolitionist. Though she could neither read nor write, we know of the details of her life because she dictated her autobiography to a friend. Truth, whose slave name was Isabella, was born around 1773, having been brought as a child with her parents from Africa and sold as a slave in the state of New York. At age nine, she was sold away from her parents to John Nealy for $100 and sold twice more before she was twelve years old. Her last master, John Dumont, raped her, and later married her to an older slave, Thomas, by whom she had several children. Although slavery was ended by law in New York in 1817, her master delayed her emancipation; she was finally freed by another master in 1827. For a number of years she worked in New York City as a domestic, the major source of work for black women in the North during this period. Feeling called by God, she left New York in 1843, abandoned her slave name, Isabella, became an itinerant preacher, and attended many antislavery gatherings.

In 1850, she attended the second women's right convention in Salem, Ohio (as did Douglass), and spoke at the third women's rights convention, in Worcester, Massachusetts. Her legendary, but now controversial, "Ain't I a Woman" speech, delivered at the Akron, Ohio, women's rights convention in 1851, is an eloquent statement of black feminist thought because of the implicit links it makes between race and gender in the lives of black women. Truth also reminds her audience that poor black women, whose experiences are radically different from those of white women, must be considered in notions about womanhood.[5]

In 1866, following the Civil War, Douglass and Charles Remond were among the vice presidents chosen for the newly formed Equal Rights Association (ERA) after the American Anti-Slavery Society disbanded. Later in the year at an Albany meeting, Douglass warned the ERA that it was in danger of becoming a women's right association only. At the first annual meeting of the ERA in 1867, Sojourner Truth addressed women's rights again, but worried that the freedom of black men was getting more attention than black women's liberation. Two years later, a major split occurred in the women's movement over woman suffrage. At the proceedings of the ERA meeting in New York in 1869, the famous debate between Frederick Douglas and white feminists occurred during which he argued for the greater urgency of race over gender. He believed it was the Negro's hour, and women's rights could wait since linking woman suffrage to Negro suffrage at this point would seriously reduce the chances of securing the ballot for black men, and for black (males), Douglass reiterated, the ballot was urgent. When asked whether this was true for black women as well, he quickly responded, "Yes, yes, yes . . . but not because she is a woman, but because she is black (Foner, 87)." Frances E. W. Harper, a prominent black feminist-abolitionist, supported Douglass, while Sojourner

Truth supported white suffragists, believing that if black men got the vote they would dominate black women.

Following this meeting, Stanton and Anthony organized the women-only National Woman Suffrage Association (NWSA) because they believed male leaders had betrayed their interests. In 1869 in Cleveland, the American Woman Suffrage Association (AWSA) was organized with Lucy Stone as chair. By the fall of 1873, even though the Fifteenth Amendment granted black male suffrage and excluded women from voting, white women were anxious to reconcile their differences with Douglass. Peace was finally restored with black abolitionists at the 1876 convention of NWSA, during which Douglass was told that he was needed in the continuing struggle for women's rights. Though he was still somewhat bitter about the racism which surfaced during the battle over the Fifteenth Amendment, he announced that he was willing to work for women's emancipation and became a familiar figure at women's rights conventions again.

An examination of the extraordinary saga of black women journalists during this period provides another perspective on their feminist vision. Mary Shadd Cary (1823–1893), born in Delaware to abolitionist parents, was the first black female newspaper editor in North America. Her pioneering publishing efforts in the 1850s mark the beginning of black women's leadership roles in the male-dominated field of journalism. She migrated to Canada with her brother after the passage of the Fugitive Slave Act in 1850 and a year later solicited the help of Samuel Ringgold Ward, abolitionist and fugitive slave, in the founding of their own abolitionist newspaper, the *Provincial Freeman,* which would also be a publishing outlet for other black women whom she encouraged to write. Its motto was "Self-Reliance Is the True Road to Independence" which was consistent with her ideas about black female empowerment.

After the death of her husband, she returned to the United States in 1863, started a school for black children in Washington, D.C., and joined the antislavery lecture circuit. She also became the first black woman lawyer in the United States, graduating from Howard Law School in 1870. In 1880, she founded the Colored Women's Progressive Franchise Association in Washington, D.C., one of the earliest women's rights organizations for African American women. Though gaining suffrage for black women was the major objective, the Association's twenty-point agenda included broadening occupations for black women and establishing newspapers that black women would control.

The black women's club movement, which emerged on the national level in the 1890s as did white women's clubs, must be reconceptualized as a manifestation of middle-class black women's race *and* gender obligations, though scholars locate it primarily within the context of self-help and racial uplift. During the 1870s, middle-class white women, freed from the drudgery of housework because of advances in technology, the availability of immigrant domestics, and access to education and leisure, organized clubs for themselves for the purpose of self- and community improvement. Sorosis and the New England Women's Club were among the first of these local organizations, but they quickly proliferated throughout the country, and by 1890 the largely white General Federation of Women's Clubs was founded as an umbrella entity. Black women's clubs emerged not only because white women's clubs prohibited their membership, except in New England, but because they had a unique set of issues—defending black womanhood, uplifting the masses, and improving family life, to name a few.

Five years after the General Federation of Women's Clubs was organized, the first national convention of black women's clubs took place in Boston in 1895. The specific catalyst was a letter that Florence Belgarnie, an officer of the Anti-Lynching Committee in London, received from John Jacks, an American newspaper editor. Angry over Belgarnie's antilynching activities, which had been encouraged by Ida Wells Barnett's antilynching crusade in England, Jacks wrote her a letter defending the white South and maligning black women for their immorality. In turn, Belgarnie sent a copy of the letter to Josephine St. Pierre Ruffin, a black member of the largely white New England Women's Club and founder, in 1893, of the New Era Club for black women. Later she distributed the letter to numerous black women's clubs and called for a national conference in Boston in 1895, which resulted in the formation of the National Federation of Afro-American Women.

When this historic gathering of black clubwomen occurred, a number of items were on the agenda—temperance, higher education, home life, morality, and education for girls and boys—however, it was also clear that black female empowerment for individual and race advancement was the overriding objective:

> ... we need to talk over not only those things which are of vital importance to us as women, but also the things that are of especial interest to us as *colored* women ... what *we* especially can do in the moral education of the race ... our mental elevation and physical development ... how to make the most of our own ... limited opportunities ... (*Women's Era,* September 1895, 2).

An important goal of the meeting was vindicating the honor of black women and denouncing Jacks. In 1896, the National Association of Colored Women (NACW) was formed as a result of a merger between the Federation and Mary Church Terrell's National League of Colored Women of Washington, D.C.

A pivotal moment in black women's publishing history and the coming of age politically for clubwomen occurred with the founding of *Women's*

Era. In 1890, Josephine St. Pierre Ruffin organized the New Era Club in Boston and initiated its journal, which eventually became the official organ of the NACW. The first issue came out March 24, 1894, and twenty-four issues were published through 1897. Since it was founded, edited, and published by suffragist Ruffin, it is not surprising to find in the publication a strong advocacy of woman suffrage, especially for black women.

The front page of the first issue carried a portrait and feature article on the women's rights leader Lucy Stone. The first issue also contained an article on the closing meetings of the New England Woman Suffrage Association, of which Ruffin was a member. There was also strong advocacy for black women entering the public arena in order to solve their unique problems. An awareness of the dilemma that black women faced as a result of the "double jeopardy" of race and gender is apparent throughout *Women's Era,* the most significant outlet for the expression of their political views and aspirations during the Progressive era.

In 1892, clubwoman and educator Anna Julia Cooper published *A Voice from the South by a Black Woman of the South,* the first book-length feminist analysis of the condition of African Americans. Cooper was born a slave during the Civil War, in Raleigh, North Carolina. At the age of eight, she attended St. Augustine's Normal School and eventually became a teacher there. An early manifestation of her sensitivity to sexism was her protesting female students' exclusion from Greek classes, which were only open to male theology students. She boldly appealed to the principal and was finally granted permission to enroll as the lone female. Her experiences with respect to male privilege at St. Augustine awakened in her a sensitivity to the urgent need for gender equality in the educational arena.

Cooper's collection of essays, many of which were speeches delivered to black organizations, is also a progressive discussion of the oppressed status of black women. Not content with simply describing their plight, she argued that black women needed to speak out for themselves and stop allowing others, including black men, to speak for them. Commenting on black women's unique status, she advanced the argument of "double jeopardy," since black women experienced both gender and race problems.

A strong advocate for black women's liberation, Cooper was especially concerned about the accessibility of higher education for black women. She also felt that elevating the status of black women would uplift the entire black race, a persistent theme in the writings of Josephine St. Pierre Ruffin and Mary Church Terrell (the first president of NACW), both of whom consistently espoused feminist ideas in their speeches and articles. Cooper was critical of black men who were unsupportive of black female equality, and she frequently spoke at black male gatherings about the importance of women in the struggle for racial uplift. In fact, she believed that women, because of their special qualities and moral values, should be in the forefront of the fight for racial equality. Though she was aware of the double burden of race and gender which was particular to black women, she also felt that black women shared many problems with black males, because of racial oppression, that white women did not share with their men. Cooper also analyzed relationships between black men and women and the problematic nature of those relationships—an analysis that links her to contemporary black feminists.

The next generation of clubwomen would continue and expand the work that Ruffin and Cooper initiated. NACW member Nannie Burroughs (1879–1961), who had Mary Church Terrell and Anna Julia Cooper for teachers and role models at M Street High School in Washington, D.C., worked for the race and for women within a religious context. One of the founders of the Women's Convention, an auxiliary group of the National Baptist Convention and the largest membership organization of black women in the United States, she attended the founding meeting in 1900 in Richmond, Virginia, and spoke when she was only twenty-one on "How the Sisters Are Hindered from Helping." This feminist critique of sexism within the church catapulted her into national prominence.[6] A strong advocate for woman suffrage, she also criticized the church for failing to assist in the political development of women, and argued in the *Crisis* (August 1915), the official organ for the National Association for the Advancement of Colored People (NAACP), that the vote would enable women to fight male dominance. In 1909, she founded the National Training School for Women and Girls in Washington, D.C., which stressed industrial education because she wanted to prepare black women for employment in areas that were open to them.

A few years later, in 1914, the outbreak of World War I precipitated a number of advocacy efforts for the many working women who were leaving domestic service in the South for jobs in northern industry. These included the founding of the Women Wage Earners Association in Washington, D.C., by clubwomen such as Mary Church Terrell and Julia F. Coleman, and efforts to unionize black women workers. After the War ended in 1918, black women found themselves in desperate straits economically given their loss of jobs after the men returned home from Europe. Nannie Burroughs's concern for the plight of black working-class women, particularly domestic servants, resulted in her organizing the National Association of Wage Earners, in 1920. Her intense feelings of racial pride were also manifested in her rejection of white standards of beauty, and she accused her sisters of "color phobia" if they used hair straighteners and skin bleachers. After the Nineteenth Amendment was passed in 1919, she worked with the NACW to mobilize black women voters and in 1924 became president of the National League of Republican Colored Women.

During this same period, the International Council of Women of the

Darker Races (which sometimes met in Washington, D.C., at Nannie Burroughs's school) was spawned by the racial uplift impulses and the international educational projects of the black women's club movement. Organized by several club women in 1924, most notably Margaret Murray Washington, founder of the Tuskegee Woman's Club and President of NACW from 1914–1918, its purpose was to study the history of peoples of color throughout the world and disseminate knowledge about them for the purpose of engendering racial pride. Study groups, which were called Committees of Seven, were also formed to infuse public school curricula with material on blacks (a precursor of Black Studies) and other people of color and field trips were organized to gain firsthand experience of other cultures.

The council also studied the situation of women and children of color internationally. Like Cooper, who mentioned Muslim harems and the Chinese practice of foot binding on the first page of *A Voice from the South,* council members were aware of the differential experiences of women because of their travel to international conferences. Washington taught a course at Tuskegee Institute on the condition and status of women throughout the world. The Pan-African Congress, which stressed the unity of all African peoples, was organized in 1919 in Paris by William E. B. Du Bois, a strong supporter of black women's liberation. Cooper, who spoke on "The Negro Problem in America," was one of only two black women to address this international gathering of people of African descent. The council also cosponsored with the Chicago Women's Club a fund-raising activity to support Pan-Africanist feminist Adelaide Casely-Hayford's efforts to build a school in Sierra Leone. She was married to a prominent Ghanaian lawyer who edited *Gold Coast Leader,* a leading Pan-Africanist publication. This work of the council is reminiscent of more recent attempts by black feminist activists to learn about and establish linkages with women of color internationally and to struggle for the elimination of sexism and racism globally. In 1960, for example, African American women attended the First Conference of African Women and Women of African Descent held in Accra, Ghana, in July 1960.

A frequently overlooked aspect of black women's activism during this period, especially within the context of Pan-Africanism or nationalism, was their battle against gender oppression, though black liberation would be their major priority. In 1925, Elise McDougald, Harlem teacher and journalist, discussed the economic plight of a particular class of African American Women. She also acknowledged that black women's "feminist efforts are directed chiefly toward the realization of the equality of the races, the sex struggle assuming a subordinate place" (McDougald, "The Double Task: The Struggle of Negro Women for Sex and Race Emancipation" *Survey Graphic* LIII [October 1924–March 1925].) This granting of greater urgency to racial concerns was predictable given the pervasiveness of white supremacy.

The feminist–Pan-Africanist views of Amy Jacques Garvey (1896–1973), Marcus Garvey's second wife, are especially important to consider during this period because of their potential impact on thousands of working class urban blacks involved with the most powerful nationalist organization in the United States—the Universal Negro Improvement Association (UNIA), which her husband founded in Jamaica in 1914 with his first wife, Amy Ashwood.[7] As a young man, Marcus was outraged by the exploitation of blacks in the Caribbean. A trip to London in 1912 brought him in contact with Africans who inspired him to struggle against colonialism. When he returned to Jamaica, he organized the UNIA for the promotion of racial solidarity and self-determination among African peoples through-out the world. From the beginning, women were crucial in the hierarchy of the organization, and women's issues were discussed, among them the question of whether a woman's intellect was as highly developed as a man's. Scholars of the Garvey movement also agree that a distinguishing characteristic of the UNIA was the opportunity it provided for black women's political development.

As editor from 1924–1927 of the Women's Page of the *Negro World,* the UNIA's weekly newspaper, Amy Jacques Garvey wrote passionately in "Our Women and What They Think" about the evils of imperialism, racism, capitalism, and the interlocking race, class, and gender oppression that black and other women experienced globally, particularly in colonial contexts. She believed the women's movement was one of the most signifi-cant struggles in human history, and that the emancipation of women was imperative. She called for women to participate in all spheres of public life despite their important duties as wives and mothers. She also felt that women were central to the success of black liberation struggles both in the United States and abroad, and she urged them to struggle against imperial-ist domination as well as their own oppression within their communities.

Echoing Sojourner Truth and Anna Julia Cooper, she espoused a femi-nist vision of the world in which women would set things right: "You [men] had your day at the helm of the world, and a pretty mess you have made of it . . . and perhaps women's rule will usher in the era of real brotherhood, when national and racial lines will disappear, leaving man-kind in peace and harmony one with another" (Garvey, *Negro World,* 1926, 5). She also had a special warning for black men: ". . . watch your step! Ethiopia's queens will reign again and her Amazons protect her shores and people. Strengthen your shaking knees and move forward, or we will displace you and lead on to victory and glory" (Lerner, 579). Concerned about the status of women globally, particularly in Asia and Africa, she applauded Egyptian women's removal of the veil and women's political gains in India, Russia, and China. A "training ground for black feminists of the 1930s," both in the United States and Jamaica (Lewis and Bryan, 82), the UNIA deserves a place in the history of black feminism in the diaspora.

Despite the decline in black fertility rates since the turn of the century, advocating for birth control was another black feminist agenda item during the 1920s and 1930s.[8] It is important to point out that the covert use among slave women of contraceptives and abortifacients was perhaps the earliest manifestation of black women's exercising reproductive freedom, a major demand of contemporary feminists. Having fewer children was a deliberate choice of some women to enhance their family's standard of living as well as a strategy espoused in the black press for ensuring the community's economic well-being, particularly during the Depression. Black women also had a feminist perspective on excessive childbearing, linking it to burdensome physical and mental problems, and were also concerned about sterilization abuse. On a national level, Margaret Sanger, prominent white birth control crusader, launched a major campaign in 1915 to legalize the dissemination of information about birth control methods and founded the American Birth Control League in 1921.[9] The Women's Political Association of Harlem, founded in 1918 and concerned about all aspects of black women's leadership, was the first black organization to advocate birth control, though numerous birth control clinics appeared nationwide in the black community from 1925–1945. The Association also supported Sanger's desire to establish a birth control clinic in Harlem. In September 1919 Sanger's *Birth Control Review* published a special issue on "The New Emancipation: The Negroes' Need for Birth Control, as Seen by Themselves." This issue included the work of black women writers—a feminist play by Mary Burrill, *They That Sit in Darkness,* which dramatizes the tragedy of too many children, and a short story, "The Closing Door," by Angelina Weld Grimké, the niece of the white Grimké sisters who were famous feminist-abolitionists.

The two most important civil rights organizations in the black community—the National Urban League and the NAACP—supported the use of birth control because they believed that smaller families were more viable economically. This issue sparked controversy, however, within certain circles as nationalist concerns about racial extinction and traditional male views about women's primary role as mothers clashed with feminist demands for sexual autonomy among black women. There was a range of attitudes among black leaders on this issue. Marcus Garvey felt that contraceptives were retarding the growth of the race. Sociologist and Pan-Africanist William E. B. Du Bois, one of the founders of the NAACP, argued in "The Damnation of Women" (1925) that women must be free to choose motherhood, and he repeated this progressive stance in "Black Folks and Birth Control" in the June 1932 issue of *Birth Control Review.*

Concern for black working women also fueled black women's activism during the 1940s and the aftermath of World War II. Because of the labor shortage with men at war, thousands of black women left the rural South again and migrated to the North for better jobs in industry. The promise of a better life remained elusive, however, since they were relegated to the most menial, hazardous, low-paying factory jobs. Poor living conditions in crowded urban settings, job discrimination, the absence of child care facilities, and segregated, substandard housing produced a climate ripe for agitation.

One of the most radical voices during this era was Claudia Jones, whose family had migrated to Harlem from Trinidad in 1924. Economic hardship during the Depression caused her to drop out of school and get a factory job. At age eighteen, she joined the Young Communist League along with many other working-class Harlemites during the 1930s. During the 1940s, she became one of the most outspoken black Communists on the issue of women's rights; in a 1947 issue of *Political Affairs,* a Communist Party journal, she argued that black women, "as workers, as Negroes, and as women," were "the most oppressed stratum of the whole population" (Jones, 4). In her passionate analysis of the situation of black women historically, the plight of the contemporary worker, and the struggles of militant "Negro women" for peace, civil rights, and economic justice, she anticipated a sophisticated black feminist discourse which was a generation away. Though she applauded women in organizations such as the National Association of Negro Women and trade unionists, she chastised the latter for being insensitive to the misery and urgent needs of domestic workers who were unprotected by labor legislation. She also made an insightful connection between the sexist treatment of black domestics and the dehumanizing treatment of black women in general. Reminiscent of Cooper and other nineteenth-century black women feminist-abolitionists, she exposed the racism of white women and reminded them that it was in their own self-interest to work for black women's liberation "inasmuch as the super exploitation and oppression of Negro women tends to depress the standards of all women" (Jones, 12). Her prophetic call for the women's movement to embrace an antiracist agenda anticipated similar pleas by black feminists two generations later. "A developing consciousness on the woman question today . . . must not fail to recognize that the Negro question . . . is *prior* to, and not equal to, the woman question; that only to the extent that we fight all chauvinist expressions and actions as regards the Negro people, and [the] right for the full equality of the Negro people, can women as a whole advance their struggle for equal rights" (Jones, 15).

In the 1960s, black feminist struggle came to the forefront in a more sustained manner and among a larger group, mainly as a result of the failure of the Civil Rights and women's rights movements to address the particular concerns of black women. Heightened consciousness about the confluence of racism and sexism in their lives was one result of their experiences with male chauvinism within the Civil Rights movement. In her autobiography, *The Trumpet Sounds* (1964), Anna Arnold Hedgeman describes her feelings about the male-dominant civil rights leadership and her experiences as the only woman on the planning committee for the 1963 March on Washington. When she discovered the omission of women as speakers on the program, she was appalled and wrote a letter to director A. Philip Randolph in which she alluded to black women's important roles in the Civil Rights movement. She also argued that "since the 'Big Six' [civil rights leaders] [had] not given women the quality of participation which they [had] earned through the years," (Hedgeman, 179), it was even more imperative that black women be allowed to speak. The outcome, according to Hedgeman, was that on the day of the March the wives of the civil rights leaders and a few other black women were asked to sit on the dais, Daisy Bates was asked to say a few words, and Rosa Parks was presented, but didn't speak. Hedgeman's response that historic day was one of disappointment: "We grinned, some of us, as we recognized anew that Negro women are second-class citizens in the same way that white women are in our culture" (Hedgeman, 180).

In 1964, Mary King and Casey Hayden, white Student Non-Violent Coordinating Committee (SNCC) staffers, discussed the sexist treatment of women in SNCC in a position paper entitled "Women of the Movement," which they delivered at SNCC's Waveland Conference.[10] Ruby Doris Smith Robinson, SNCC executive secretary (1966), died of cancer a year later at age twenty-five, and Kathleen Cleaver, a former SNCC worker and Black Panther, believed Robinson's death was caused in part by overwork and "the constant struggles that she was subjected to because she was a woman" (Cleaver, 55). Similarly, Septima Clark, the Southern Christian Leadership Conference's (SCLC) director of education in 1961, criticized the sexism of SCLC in her autobiography *Ready From Within:* "... those men didn't have any faith in women, none whatsoever. They just thought that women were sex symbols and had no contributions to make ... I had a great feeling that Dr. King didn't think much of women either ..." (Crawford, 195–96). She also confronted King about his nondemocratic style of leadership and eventually joined the National Organization for Women (NOW) in 1968 because of its women's rights agenda.

The publication in 1970 of Toni Cade's *The Black Woman: An Anthology,* Shirley Chisholm's autobiography *Unbought and Unbossed,* Toni Morrison's *The Bluest Eye,* and Audre Lorde's *Cables to Rage* signaled a literary awakening among black women and the beginning of a clearly defined black women's liberation movement that would have priorities different from those of white feminists, and generate considerable debate, even hostility, within the black community. Cade's antiracist, antisexist, anti-imperialist agenda captures the essence of contemporary black feminism: conduct a comparative study of women's roles in the Third World; debunk myths of the black matriarch and "the evil black bitch"; study black women's history and honor woman warriors such as Harriet Tubman and Fannie Lou Hamer; do oral histories of ordinary black women (migrant workers, quilters, UNIA grandmothers); study sexuality; establish linkages with other women of color globally (Cade, 11).

The anthology includes SNCC activist Frances Beale's pioneering essay on the "double jeopardy" of black women, which highlights their sexual and economic exploitation, the inappropriateness of white models of womanhood, black male sexism, sterilization abuse of women of color globally, abortion rights, and Sojourner Truth's 1851 women's rights speech. Beale also voices her disapproval of black nationalist demands that women be subordinate to men and their assumption that women's most important contribution to the revolution is having babies: "To assign women the role of housekeeper and mother while men go forth into battle is a highly questionable doctrine to maintain" (Cade, 100).

In 1973, the National Black Feminist Organization (NBFO) would emerge in part as a reminder to the black liberation movement that "there can't be liberation for half the race"[11] Activist lawyer Flo Kennedy and Margaret Sloan decided to convene a small gathering of black feminists in May so that they could discuss their experiences within the racist women's movement, and what it meant to be black, female, and feminist. In their statement of purpose, they objected to the women's movement's being seen as white, and their involvement in it as disloyal to the race. Emphasizing black women's need for self-definition, they identified racism from without and sexism from within as destructive to the black community.

The National Black Feminist Organization officially began November 30, 1973, at an Eastern Regional Conference in New York City at the cathedral of St. John the Divine. This was a historic gathering of the first explicitly black feminist organization committed to the eradication of sexism, racism, and heterosexism. Workshops focused on a variety of issues—child care, the church, welfare, women's liberation, lesbianism, prisons, education, addiction, work, female sexuality, and domestic violence. Among those present were Shirley Chisholm, Alice Walker, Eleanor Holmes Norton, Flo Kennedy, and Margaret Sloan, NBFO's first and only president.[12]

A year after the founding meeting, the Boston chapter of NBFO decided to form a more radical organization, according to lesbian feminist writer Barbara Smith, and named itself in 1975 the Combahee River Collective after Harriet Tubman's "military campaign" in South Carolina (1863), which freed nearly 800 slaves. In 1977, after meeting informally for three years and doing intense consciousness-raising (the major strategy for feminist organizing in the 1970s), a black feminist lesbian manifesto was issued that foregrounded sexuality and asserted that "sexual politics under patriarchy is as pervasive in black women's lives as the politics of class and race" (Hull, Bell Scott, and Smith, 16). Emphasizing the "simultaneity" of racial, gender, heterosexist, and class oppression in the lives of black and other women of color, they affirmed their connection to an activist tradition among black women going back to the nineteenth century as well as to black liberation struggles of the 1960s. Despite the difficulty of sustaining a socialist black feminist organization with lesbian leadership for six years, they worked untiringly on a variety of "revolutionary" issues—reproductive rights, rape, prison reform, sterilization abuse, violence against women, health care, and racism within the white women's movement. They also understood the importance of coalition building and worked with other women of color, white feminists, and progressive men. Equally important was their breaking the silence about homophobia within the black community and providing lesbians and heterosexual women with opportunities to work together.

In 1975, Michele Wallace wrote an article for the *Village Voice* entitled "A Black Feminist's Search for Sisterhood," and precipitated an intense controversy within the black community when *Black Macho and the Myth of the Superwoman* appeared three years later. Wallace, a founding member of NBFO, critiqued black male sexism and the misogyny of black liberation struggles. Echoing Wallace, the August 27, 1979 issue of *Newsweek* chronicled a new black struggle that underscored intraracial tensions based on gender: "It's the newest wrinkle in the black experience in America—a growing distrust, if not antagonism, between black men and women that is tearing marriages apart and fracturing personal relationships." This "wake-up call" came on the heels of Ntozake Shange's award-winning Broadway play "For Colored Girls Who Have Considered Suicide/When the Rainbow is Enuf" (1976) and Wallace's polemic *Black Macho*, both of whom were demonized because of their negative assessments of black men.

The issue of sexual politics within the African American community became a hotly debated topic in journals such as *The Black Scholar, Freedomways,* and *Black Books Bulletin,* and provided the catalyst for the founding of a short-lived bimonthly magazine, *Black Male/Female Relationships* by sociologists Nathan and Julia Hare. *Black Scholar,* however, would provide the most extensive and sober treatment of the debate generated by Wallace's and Shange's controversial feminist writings. The April 1973 issue of *Black Scholar* on "Black Women's Liberation" led the way, followed by the March 1975 issue, "The Black Woman," the 1979 "Black Sexism Debate" issue, and the 1986 "Black Women and Feminism" issue. Robert Staples's essay "The Myth of Black Macho: A Response to Angry

Black Feminists," which appeared in the March/April 1979 issue, was a feminist-bashing response to Wallace and Shange, whom he accused of black male bashing; it stimulated a Readers' Forum in the subsequent May/June 1979 issue, in which the battle lines were drawn. Robert Chrisman's editorial for this special issue acknowledged in very strong terms the validity of the accusations, and called for a reconciliation between black men and women: "Black feminists have raised just criticisms of black male sexism. . . . We believe that the effort to clarify the nature of black male/female relationships is an important step in the process of reuniting our people and revitalizing the struggle against oppression. . . . the problems of black male/female relationships are neither new nor solely the creation of the white media."

A decade later, the controversy continued and grew more virulent; its most obvious manifestations were loud and angry litanies, especially among black professional men, about the portrayal of black male characters in the fiction of contemporary black women writers. Alice Walker's novel *The Color Purple* (1982) and Steven Spielberg's film adaptation sparked the most vitriolic responses. Shahrazad Ali's self-published *The Blackman's Guide to Understanding the Blackwoman* (1990) was one of the most disturbing publications during this decade-and-a-half-old family battle and is one of the most blatantly misogynist and racist texts to appear in print.

Black feminist writing proliferated during this period amid rancorous debate within the black community about the relevance of the contemporary white women's movement to black women. One of the most passionate defenders of feminist ideology to emerge, though she also delivered scathing critiques of white feminism, was bell hooks, whose pioneering monograph, *Ain't I a Woman: Black Women and Feminism* (1981) delineated the impact of sexism on the lives of black women; analyzed the devaluation of black womanhood, both historically and contemporaneously; and discussed the persistence of racism in the women's movement and the involvement of black women in struggles to achieve gender equality. The chapter on "Sexism and the Black Female Experience" advanced the new thesis that slavery, a reflection of a patriarchal *and* racist social order not only oppressed black men but also defeminized slave women. Over the next decade and a half, a substantial group of black feminist writers, among whom were Audre Lorde, Barbara Smith, Angela Davis, Alice Walker, Gloria Joseph, June Jordan, Ntozake Shange, Gloria Hull, Paula Giddings, and Barbara Christian, would redefine feminism as a broad political movement to end *all* forms of domination. In the words of hooks, ". . . feminism is not simply a struggle to end male chauvinism or a movement to ensure that women have equal rights with men; it is a commitment to eradicating the ideology of domination that permeates Western culture on various levels—sex, race, and class, to name a few—and a commitment to reorganizing

U.S. society so that the self-development of people can take precedence over imperialism, economic expansion, and material desires" (hooks, 1981, 194).

Reminiscent of the 1890s, writing, publishing, and organizing became a major preoccupation of black feminists during the 1980s, and heeding Cooper's words, black women were clearly speaking for themselves. Other groundbreaking texts were Barbara Christian's *Black Women Novelists* (1980); Angela Davis's *Women, Race, and Class* (1981); Filomina Chioma Steady's *The Black Woman Cross-Culturally* (1981); Hull, Bell Scott, and Smith's *All the Women Are White, All the Blacks are Men, But Some of Us Are Brave: Black Women's Studies* (1982); Paula Gidding's *When and Where I Enter: The Impact of Black Women on Sex and Race in America* (1984); Alice Walker's *In Search of Our Mothers' Gardens: Womanist Prose* (1983); Barbara Smith's *Home Girls: A Black Feminist Anthology* (1983); Audre Lorde's *Sister Outsider: Essays and Speeches* (1984); Deborah Gray White's *Ar'n't I a Woman?: Female Slaves in the Plantation South* (1985); and Hazel Carby's *Reconstructing Womanhood: The Emergence of the Afro-American Woman Novelist* (1987). Kitchen Table: Women of Color Press was founded in 1980 by Audre Lorde and Barbara Smith for the purpose of publishing mainly feminist women of color; its mission (see brochure) was also to provide a "political support network for feminists and lesbians of color as well." The first explicitly black feminist periodical devoted exclusively to the experiences of women of African decent in the United States and throughout the world was founded in 1984 in Atlanta, Georgia, and hosted by Spelman College's Women's Research and Resource Center, the first feminist institute on a historically black college campus. *SAGE: A Scholarly Journal on Black Women* would provide a major outlet for feminist perspectives on a variety of issues including mother-daughter relationships in the black community, health, science and technology, and the situation of women in rural Africa. During its founding conference in 1983, the National Black Women's Health Project, whose newsletter *Vital Signs* provides black feminist perspectives on health, attracted the largest group of black women ever to assemble on Spelman's campus.

Black feminist theory would come of age during the 1990s and move from the margins to the center of mainstream feminist discourse. Patricia Hill Collins's landmark *Black Feminist Thought* identified the fusion of activism and theory as its distinguishing characteristic, and analyzed its four core themes: the interlocking nature of race, class, and gender oppression in black women's personal, domestic, and work lives; the necessity of internalizing positive self-definitions and rejecting the denigrating, stereotypical, and controlling images (mammy, matriarch, welfare mother, whore) of others, both within and without the black community; and the need for active struggle to resist oppression and realize individual and group empowerment (Collins, 23, 32, 83–84). The Collins text would further establish, along with Toni Cade's *The Black Woman* and bell hooks's– *Ain't I a Woman,* a continuous black feminist intellectual tradition going back to the publication of Cooper's *A Voice from the South* a hundred years earlier.

Despite their commitment to ending sexism, however, some black women continued to be alienated by the term "feminist." Alice Walker's *In Search of Our Mothers' Gardens* (1983) provided the alternative term "womanist" as a more culturally appropriate label for black feminists or feminists of color. "Womanist" recalled a black folk expression of mothers admonishing their daughters to refrain from "womanish" behavior. According to Walker, a "womanist" prefers women's culture, is committed to the survival of the entire group, is serious, "loves struggle, *loves* the folk, and loves herself" (Walker, *In Search of Our Mothers' Gardens,* xi–xii). Inspired by Walker, scholars such as Cheryl Gilkes, Katie Cannon, Jacquelyn Grant, Delores Williams, Renita Weems, and Emily Townes, for example, self-identify as "womanist" theologians as a way of differentiating themselves from white feminist theologians.

President George Bush's 1991 nomination of Judge Clarence Thomas to the Supreme Court and Professor Anita Hill's subsequent allegations of sexual harassment, which resulted in televised hearings for three days in October, sparked perhaps the most profound intraracial tensions around sexual politics that the modern African American community had ever experienced. Despite Hill's allegations that Thomas had sexually harassed her while she worked under him at the Department of Education and the Equal Employment Opportunity Commission (EEOC), on October 16 the Senate confirmed, 52–48, Clarence Thomas as Associate Justice of the Supreme Court, replacing outgoing Thurgood Marshall.

A month later, a cogent statement opposing the racist and sexist treatment of Anita Hill appeared in the November 17, 1991, issue of the *New York Times* (A–53), "African American Women in Defense of Ourselves." Over 1,600 black women reminded the nation of Thomas's persistent failure, despite his own racial history and professional opportunities, to respond to the urgency of civil rights for disadvantaged groups. Furthermore, the statement called attention to a long history of sexual abuse and stereotyping of black women as "immoral, insatiable, perverse." The failure of Congress to take seriously Hill's sexual harassment charges was perceived as an attack on the collective character of black women (Chrisman and Allen, 292).

More than any other episode in recent memory, including the angry responses to *Black Macho, For Colored Girls,* and *The Color Purple,* the Thomas/Hill saga unmasked problematic gender attitudes within the black community and in some cases outright misogyny. Because Hill had violated a deeply held cultural taboo—that racial dirty linen shouldn't be aired in public—she came to epitomize black female treachery in breaking the silence about objectionable black male behavior. For over a decade, black women had been labeled traitors among some segments of the community because of their advocacy of feminism, which was associated with white women. Despite the criticism, however, contemporary black feminists, like their nineteenth-century counterparts, mobilized for struggle with the hope that eradicating the twin evils of racism and sexism would become a battle cry within the entire community. In the aftermath of the Thomas/Hill hearings, black women witnessed rancorous public dialogue about their character, which sparked the formation of a new feminist organization, African American Women in Defense of Ourselves.

In January 1994, the largest gathering of black feminist scholars and activists took place at the Massachusetts Institute of Technology (MIT) during a national conference entitled "Black Women in the Academy: Defending Our Name, 1894–1994." Ironically, nearly one hundred years after the historic gathering of clubwomen in Boston in 1895, over 2,000 mostly academic black women gathered again. Like black women in the 1890s, they found themselves under attack, much of which was generated by the Thomas/Hill hearings and the propaganda associated with welfare reform and "family values." In addition, two prominent black academic women with liberal politics, Johnnetta Cole and Lani Guinier (both of whom were keynoters at MIT), had been viciously attacked by the Right; as a result, both of them were abandoned as appointees of the Clinton administration. Twenty-five years earlier, Angela Davis (the third key-noter) had been fired from her faculty job at the University of California, Los Angeles, by Governor Ronald Reagan because of her political views and Communist Party membership.

Among other things, the MIT conference demonstrated the persistence of black women intellectuals' commitment to feminist discourse and action, despite the absence of common ground on a number of issues. A resolution was drafted and sent to President Clinton which, first of all, acknowledged the "complexity of social categories such as race, class, gender, and sexual orientation."[13] It called for a blue-ribbon panel on race relations in the United States; underscored the importance of research on black women that would promote the interests of the entire African American community; called for an examination of career advancement issues for women of color in higher education; and requested increased funding for community-based organizations serving poor black families and others in need, such as women in prison and people with AIDS. It also addressed international issues relating to Haiti, South Africa, Cuba, and Somalia. This document articulates the contours of contemporary black feminism and suggests a blueprint for the future.

As we approach the beginning of the twenty-first century, it is apparent that the lives of many women around the world have been unaffected by centuries-old struggles for gender equality. In most places, women are poorer than men, in some places, daughters are still valued less than sons, and a global epidemic of violence against women remains unchecked.

It is also the case that the promise of feminism—that females can live better lives with a wider range of choices and resources—is a reality for some women three decades after the beginning of the "second wave" of the United States women's movement even though poverty, racism, and heterosexual privilege remain deeply entrenched.

More of us, women and men, must heed the challenge set before us by bell hooks in her first book on black feminism: "Only a few black women have rekindled the spirit of feminist struggle that stirred the hearts and minds of our nineteenth century sisters. We, black women who advocate feminist ideology, are pioneers. We are clearing a path for ourselves and our sisters. We hope that as long as they see us reach our goal—no longer victimized, no longer unrecognized, no longer afraid—they will take courage and follow" *(Ain't I a Woman,* 196). The struggle continues.[14]

ENDNOTES

1. Blanche Glassman Hersh's *Slavery of Sex: Feminist-Abolitionists in America* (Urbana: University of Illinois Press, 1978) excludes black women abolitionists from her discussion of feminist-abolitionists (her terminology) because of her erroneous assessment of their minimal involvement in the first wave of the women's movement, which she describes as largely white. Jean Yellin and John Van Horne's collection of essays, *The Abolitionist Sisterhood* (Ithaca: Cornell University Press 1994), corrects Hersh's assumptions by including extensive discussions of women of African descent in their category of antislavery feminist, "that small circle of black and white American women who, in the 1830s and 1840s, initially banded together to remedy the public evils of slavery and racism and who ultimately struggled for equal rights for women as well as slaves" (3). Yellin and Van Horne also complicate the analysis by indicating that this group was diverse and included more traditional women who were not feminist.

2. See Shirley J. Yee's *Black Women Abolitionists: A Study in Activism, 1828–1860* (Knoxville: University of Tennessee Press, 1992) for an excellent analysis of the emergence of black feminism in the early nineteenth century.

3. Gerda Lerner's *The Creation of Feminist Consciousness: From the Middle Ages to Eighteen-Seventy* (New York: Oxford University Press 1993) documents the twelve-hundred-year struggle of women in the West to free their minds of patriarchal thinking, the roots of which can be found in institutionalized barriers to their intellectual development. Her brief discussion of African American women focuses on evangelists such as Sojourner Truth, whom she singles out as being "virtually alone among black women in the nineteenth century in staunchly combining the defense of her race with a defense of her sex" (106). Lerner also defines feminist consciousness as women's awareness that they belong to a subordinate group which has suffered because of societal constructs. As a result, they need to develop sisterly bonds with other women and work to change their subordinate status (274).

4. See Angela Davis's pioneering essay, "Reflections on the Black Woman's Role in the Community of Slaves," *Black Scholar* 3 (December 1971): 4–15, which

rewrites the history of slave resistance. Deborah Gray White's *Ar'n't I a Woman? Female Slaves in the Plantation South* (New York: W. W. Norton, 1985) also focuses on the black female slave experience.

5. Frances Dana Gage, a white abolitionist who chaired the historic meeting in Akron, is responsible for the details of this gathering, which focus on Truth's presence and what she did and said. The speech, which Gage is reputed to have recorded, appears in Elizabeth Cady Stanton's *History of Woman Suffrage,* 6 vols. (Rochester and New York, 1889–1992), 2: 193. See Nell Irvin Painter's "Difference, Slavery, and Memory: Sojourner Truth in Feminist Abolitionism," in *The Abolitionist Sisterhood,* eds. Yellin and Van Horne, and her "Sojourner Truth in Life and Memory," in *Gender and History* 2 (Spring 1990): 3–16, which raise doubts about Gage's version of the Sojourner Truth saga in Akron, Ohio.

6. See Evelyn Brooks Higginbotham's award-winning book *Righteous Discontent: The Women's Movement in the Black Baptist Church, 1880–1920* (Cambridge: Harvard University Press, 1993) for a discussion of the feminist theology of black Baptist women, Nannie Burroughs's struggles against racism and sexism, and the role of black women's organizations, such as the Women's Convention of the National Baptist Convention, in self-determination.

7. As is frequently the case with women married to prominent men, Amy Jacques Garvey has been largely overlooked in the scholarship on the Garvey movement. Exceptions are Mark D. Matthews, " 'Our Women and What They Think': Amy Jacques Garvey and *The Negro World,"* *Black Scholar* (May–June 1979): 2–13; " 'Always Leading Our Men in Service and Sacrifice': Amy Jacques Garvey, Feminist Black and Nationalist," *Gender and Society* 6 (September 1992): 346–375; and the work of Professor Ula Taylor. For discussions of women in the Garvey movement, see *Garvey: His Work and Impact,* eds. Rupert Lewis and Patrick Bryan (Trenton, N.J.: Africa World Press, 1991), which contains an essay by Tony Martin and Honor Ford Smith.

8. See Jessie M. Rodrique's "The Black Community and the Birth Control Movement," *Passion and Power: Sexuality in History,* eds. Kathy Peiss and Christina Simmons (Philadelphia: Temple University Press, 1989) for a discussion of the decline in fertility among blacks from the late nineteenth century to World War II (1880–1945), and a comprehensive analysis of the black community's considerable involvement with the issue of birth control from 1915 to 1945, though this has been overlooked in chronicles of the birth control movement in the United States.

9. See Angela Davis, *Women, Race, and Class* (New York: Random House, 1981) for a thoughtful analysis and critique of Margaret Sanger's racism.

10. Mary King, *Freedom Song: A Personal Story of the 1960s Civil Rights Movement* (New York: William Morrow, 1987), 567–569.

11. "Statement of Purpose," in *Feminism in Our Time,* ed. Miriam Schneir (New York: Vintage Books, 1994), 171–174.

12. See Beverly Davis, "To Seize the Moment: A Retrospective on the National Black Feminist Organization," *SAGE: A Scholarly Journal on Black Women* (Fall 1988): 43–46, for a detailed history of NBFO.

13. See *Black Scholar* 24 (Winter 1994): 6.

14. Portions of this introduction appear in my dissertation *Daughters of Sorrow: Attitudes Toward Black Women, 1880–1920* (Carlson, 1990) and "Remembering Sojourner Truth: On Black Feminism," *Catalyst* 1 (Fall 1986): 54–57.

CHAPTER ONE

Beginnings:
In Defense of Our Race
and Sex, 1831–1900

...for the sake of our own dignity, the dignity of our race, and the future good name of our children, it is "mete, right, and our bounded duty" to stand forth and declare ourselves and our principles, to teach an ignorant and suspicious world that our aims and interests are identical with those of all good aspiring women. Too long have we been silent under unjust and unholy charges; we cannot expect to have them removed until we disprove them through ourselves.

—JOSEPHINE ST. PIERRE RUFFIN, *The Women's Era*

The Negro woman "totes" more water; grows more corn; picks more cotton; washes more clothes; cooks more meals; nurses more babies; mammies more Nordics; supports more churches; does more race uplifting; serves as mudsills for more climbers; takes more punishment; does more forgiving; gets less protection and appreciation than do the women in any other civilized group in the world. She has been the economic and social slave of mankind.

—NANNIE BURROUGHS

INTRODUCTION

Like most students who attended public schools and colleges during the 1950s and 1960s, I learned very little about the involvement of African American women in struggles for the emancipation of blacks and women —so I did not read the words of any of the women who appear in this chapter as our feminist foremothers. Literary critic Mary Helen Washington, who initiated the movement to reclaim black women writers, asked a series of questions which Chapter 1, "Beginnings: In Defense of Our Race and Sex, 1831–1900," is intended to address: "Why is the fugitive slave, the fiery orator, the political activist, the abolitionist always represented as a black man? How does the heroic voice and heroic image of the black woman get suppressed in a culture that depended on her heroism for its survival?" (Washington, *Invented Lives,* xvii–xviii).

We must look back to the nineteenth century for answers to these questions. Reading Maria Stewart and Anna Julia Cooper, among others, tells us that black women themselves were aware of their own erasure from the annals of history. This is why they found it necessary to chronicle the achievements of their sister-activist-thinkers.

In order to reconstruct our black feminist intellectual tradition in the present, we must reinterpret familiar histories. The black women's club movement which blossomed in the 1890s as a project of racial uplift, according to traditional scholarship, was also the first feminist movement among African Americans. The struggles of club women to debunk stereotypes about their sexuality, to define black womanhood differently, and to work for their own empowerment are certainly the beginnings of a black women's liberation movement. As importantly, we must revisit the anti-lynching campaign of Ida Wells-Barnett, as historian Paula Giddings has done, and realize its importance as a precursor of the modern Civil Rights movement *and* the movement to liberate black women from a patriarchal, racist social order. The discourse on sexuality that Wells-Barnett generated in her brilliant analyses of the sexual politics of lynching makes her a race woman, to be sure, but she is much more, besides.

The feminist discourse here has been impacted by other discourses, particularly the Victorian "cult of true womanhood," which dictated that women embrace values such as piety, chastity, domesticity, and submissiveness. Women who embraced these values might be labeled "cultural feminists" because they did not reject altogether the gender prescriptions of their times. Though they espoused greater independence for women, they also insisted that enlightened wifehood and motherhood were appropriate aspirations.

What is clear is their understanding about the difficulties facing them because of their race and gender. Anna Julia Cooper admonished her brothers for their lack of enlightenment on the woman question and their internalization of conventional gender notions. ". . . [I]t strikes me as true that while our men seem thoroughly abreast of the times on almost every other subject, when they strike the woman question they drop back into sixteenth-century logic" (*A Voice from the South,* 75). She also urged married women to seek employment outside the home and develop their intellects, but hastened to add that marriage was not the only route to self-actualization.

I continue to wonder whether the black community would have distanced itself as much from women's liberation struggles in the 1970s if we had read the wise words—words afire—of our sister-ancestors, only a small group of whom appear in this chapter.

Maria Miller Stewart (1803–1879)

Maria Stewart, a free black from Hartford, Connecticut, may have been the first African American woman to speak in public about women's rights, particularly the plight of "daughters of Africa," whom she urged to develop their intellects, become teachers, combine family and work outside the home, oppose subservience to men, and participate fully in all aspects of community building. She also issued an unusual call for black women to build schools for themselves. In 1833, after a short career on the lecture circuit, she delivered a farewell speech to the black community, particularly ministers, in which she expressed resentment about its negative responses to her defiance of gender conventions as a public lecturer. This passionate defense of women's right to speak in public invokes biblical heroines and wise women throughout history.

"Religion and the Pure Principles of Morality, the Sure Foundation on Which We Must Build" appeared first as a pamphlet in 1831. Stewart's subsequent speeches, the first delivered before the Afric-American Female Intelligence Society in Boston in 1832, were reprinted in the Ladies Department of William Lloyd Garrison's abolitionist newspaper, *Liberator*. Her second speech, delivered at Boston's Franklin Hall before the New England Anti-Slavery Society on September 21, 1832, is historic because it was the first public lecture by an American woman of any race before a mixed audience of men and women, blacks and whites, and preceded by five years the Grimké sisters' more well-known antislavery speeches. Stewart stands at the beginning of an unbroken chain of black women activists whose commitment to the liberation of blacks and women defines their life's work. Stewart's biographer, Marilyn Richardson, captures her significance in the first published collection of Stewart's work: "Her original synthesis of religious, abolitionist, and feminist concerns places her squarely in the forefront of a black female activist and literary tradition only now beginning to be acknowledged as of integral significance to the understanding of the history of black thought and culture in America" (Richardson, xiv).

Religion and the Pure Principles of Morality, the Sure Foundation on Which We Must Build

*Productions from the Pen
of Mrs. Maria W. Steward [sic], Widow of the Late
James W. Steward, of Boston*

All the nations of the earth are crying out for liberty and equality. Away, away with tyranny and oppression! And shall Afric's sons be silent any longer? Far be it from me to recommend to you either to kill, burn, or destroy. But I would strongly recommend to you to improve your talents; let not one lie buried in the earth. Show forth your powers of mind. Prove to the world that

> Though black your skins as shades of night,
> your hearts are pure, your souls are white.

This is the land of freedom. The press is at liberty. Every man has a right to express his opinion. Many think, because your skins are tinged with a sable hue, that you are an inferior race of beings; but God does not consider you as such. He hath formed and fashioned you in his own glorious image, and hath bestowed upon you reason and strong powers of intellect. He hath made you to have dominion over the beasts of the field, the fowls of the air, and the fish of the sea. He hath crowned you with glory and honor; hath made you but a little lower than the angels; and according to the Constitution of these United States, he hath made all men free and equal. Then why should one worm say to another, "Keep you down there, while I sit up yonder; for I am better than thou?" It is not the color of the skin that makes the man, but it is the principles formed within the soul.

Many will suffer for pleading the cause of oppressed Africa, and I shall glory in being one of her martyrs; for I am firmly persuaded, that the God in whom I trust is able to protect me from the rage and malice of mine enemies, and from them that will rise up against me; and if there is no other way for me to escape, he is able to take me to himself, as he did the most noble, fearless, and undaunted David Walker.

Never Will Virtue, Knowledge, And True Politeness Begin To Flow, Till The Pure Principles Of Religion And Morality Are Put Into Force.

My Respected Friends,

I feel almost unable to address you; almost incompetent to perform the task; and at times I have felt ready to exclaim, O that my head were waters, and mine eyes a fountain of tears, that I might weep day and night for the transgressions of the daughters of my people. Truly, my heart's desire and prayer is, that Ethiopia might stretch forth her hands unto God. But we have a great work to do. Never, no, never will the chains of slavery and ignorance burst, till we become united as one, and cultivate among ourselves the pure principles of piety, morality, and virtue. I am sensible of my ignorance; but such knowledge as God has given to me, I impart to you. I am sensible of former prejudices; but it is high time for prejudices and animosities to cease from among us. I am sensible of exposing myself to calumny and reproach; but shall I, for fear of feeble man, who shall die, hold my peace? Shall I, for fear of scoffs and frowns, refrain my tongue? Ah, no! I speak as one that must give an account at the awful bar of God; I speak as a dying mortal to dying mortals. O, ye daughters of Africa, awake! Awake! Arise! No longer sleep nor slumber, but distinguish yourselves. Show forth to the world that ye are endowed with noble and exalted faculties. O, ye daughters of Africa! What have ye done to immortalize your names beyond the grave? What examples have ye set before the rising generation? What foundation have ye laid for generations yet unborn? Where are our union and love? And where is our sympathy, that weeps at another's woe, and hides the faults we see? And our daughters, where are they? Blushing in innocence and virtue? and our sons, do they bid fair to become crowns of glory to our hoary heads? Where is the parent who is conscious of having faithfully discharged his duty, and at the last awful day of account, shall be able to say, here, Lord, is thy poor, unworthy servant, and the children thou hast given me? And where are the children that will arise and call them blessed? Alas, O God! Forgive me if I speak amiss; the minds of our tender babes are tainted as soon as they are born; they go astray, as it were, from the womb. Where is the maiden who will blush at vulgarity? And where is the youth who has written upon his manly brow a thirst for knowledge; whose ambitious mind soars above trifles, and longs for the time to come, when he shall redress the wrongs of his father and plead the cause of his brethren? Did the daughters of our land possess a delicacy of manners, combined with gentleness and dignity; did their pure minds hold vice in abhorrence and contempt; did they frown when their ears were polluted with its vile accents, would not their influence become powerful? Would not our brethren fall in love with their virtues? Their souls would become fired with a holy zeal for freedom's cause. They would become ambitious to distinguish themselves. They would become proud to display their talents. Able advocates would arise in our defense. Knowledge would begin to flow, and the chains of slavery and ignorance would melt like wax before the flames. I am but a feeble instrument. I am but as one particle of the small dust of the earth. You may frown or smile. After I am dead, perhaps before, God will surely rise up those who will more powerfully and eloquently plead the cause of virtue and the pure principles of morality than I am able to do. O virtue! How sacred is thy name! How pure are thy principles! Who can find a virtuous woman? For her price is far above rubies. Blessed is the man who shall call her his wife; yea, happy is the child who shall call her mother. O woman, woman, would thou only strive to excel in merit and virtue; would thou only store thy mind with useful knowledge, great would be thine influence. Do you say you are too far advanced in life now to begin? You are not too far advanced to instil [sic] these principles into the minds of your tender infants. Let them by no means be neglected. Discharge your duty faithfully, in every point of view: leave the event with God. So shall your skirts become clear of their blood. . . .

I am of a strong opinion that the day on which we unite heart and soul, and turn our attention to knowledge and improvement, that day the hissing and reproach among the nations of the earth against us will cease. And even those who now point at us with the finger of scorn, will aid and befriend us. It is of no use for us to sit with our hands folded, hanging our heads like bulrushes, lamenting our wretched condition; but let us make a mighty effort, and arise, and if no one will promote or respect us, let us promote and respect ourselves.

The American ladies have the honor conferred on them, that by prudence and economy in their domestic concerns, and their unwearied attention in forming the minds and manners of their children, they laid the foundation of their becoming what they now are. The good women of Wethersfield, Conn., toiled in the blazing sun, year after year, weeding onions, then sold the seed and procured enough money to erect them a house of worship. And shall we not imitate their examples, as far as they are worthy of imitation? Why cannot we do something to distinguish ourselves, and contribute some of our hard earnings that would reflect honor upon our memories, and cause our children to arise and call us blessed? Shall it any longer be said of the daughters of Africa, they have no ambition, they have no force? By no means. Let every female heart become united, and let us raise a fund ourselves, and at the end of one year and a half, we might be able to lay the corner stone for the building of a High School, that the higher branches of knowledge might be enjoyed by us; and God would raise us up, and enough to aid us in our laudable designs. Let each one strive to excel in good housewifery, knowing that prudence and economy are the road to wealth. Let us not say we know this, or we know that, and practise nothing; but let us practise what we do know.

How long shall the fair daughters of Africa be compelled to bury their minds and talents beneath a load of iron pots and kettles? Until union, knowledge, and love begin to flow among us. How long shall a mean set of men flatter us with their smiles, and enrich themselves with our hard earnings, their wives' fingers sparkling with rings, and they themselves laughing at our folly? Until we begin to promote and patronize each other. Shall we be a by-word among the nations any longer? Shall they laugh us to scorn forever? Do you ask, what can we do? Unite and build a store of your own, if you cannot procure a license. Fill one side with dry goods, and the other with groceries. Do you ask where is the money? We have spent more than enough for nonsense to do what building we should want. We have never had an opportunity of displaying our talents; therefore, the world thinks we know nothing. And we have been possessed by far too mean and cowardly a disposition, though I highly disapprove of an insolent or impertinent one. Do you ask the disposition I would have you possess? Possess the spirit of independence. The Americans do, and why should not you? Possess the spirit of men, bold and enterprising, fearless and un-daunted. Sue for your rights and privileges. Know the reason that you cannot attain them. Weary them with your importunities. You can but die if you make the attempt, and we shall certainly die if you do not. The Americans have practised nothing but head-work these 200 years, and we have done their drudgery. And is it not high time for us to imitate their examples, and practise head-work too, and keep what we have got, and get what we can? We need never to think that anybody is going to feel interested for us, if we do not feel interested for ourselves. That day we, as a people, hearken unto the voice of the Lord, our God, and walk in his ways and ordinances, and become distinguished for our ease, elegance, and grace, combined with other virtues, that day the Lord will raise us up, and enough to aid and befriend us, and we shall begin to flourish. . . .

LECTURE DELIVERED
AT THE FRANKLIN HALL

Boston, September 21, 1832

Why sit ye here and die? If we say we will go to a foreign land, the famine and the pestilence are there, and there we shall die. If we sit here, we shall die. Come let us plead our cause before the whites: if they save us alive, we shall live—and if they kill us, we shall but die.

Methinks I heard a spiritual interrogation—"Who shall go forward, and take off the reproach that is cast upon the people of color? Shall it be a woman?" And my heart made this reply—"If it is thy will, be it even so, Lord Jesus!"

I have heard much respecting the horrors of slavery; but may Heaven forbid that the generality of my color throughout these United States should experience any more of its horrors than to be a servant of servants, or hewers of wood and drawers of water! Tell us no more of southern slavery; for with few exceptions, although I may be very erroneous in my opinion, yet I consider our condition but little better than that. Yet, after all, methinks there are no chains so galling as those that bind the soul, and exclude it from the vast field of useful and scientific knowledge. O, had I received the advantages of an early education, my ideas would, ere now, have expanded far and wide; but, alas! I possess nothing but moral capability—no teachings but the teachings of the Holy Spirit.

I have asked several individuals of my sex, who transact business for themselves, if providing our girls were to give them the most satisfactory references, they would not be willing to grant them an equal opportunity with others? Their reply has been—for their own part, they had no objection; but as it was not the custom, were they to take them into their employ, they would be in danger of losing the public patronage.

And such is the powerful force of prejudice. Let our girls possess whatever amiable qualities of soul they may; let their characters be fair and spotless as innocence itself; let their natural taste and ingenuity be what they may; it is impossible for scarce an individual of them to rise above the condition of servants. Ah! why is this cruel and unfeeling distinction? Is it merely because God has made our complexion to vary? If it be, O shame to soft, relenting humanity! "Tell it not in Gath! Publish it not in the streets of Askelon!" Yet, after all, methinks were the American free people of color to turn their attention more assiduously to moral worth and intellectual improvement, this would be the result: prejudice would gradually diminish, and the whites would be compelled to say, unloose those fetters!

> Though black their skins as shades of night
> Their hearts are pure, their souls are white.

Few white persons of either sex, who are calculated for anything else, are willing to spend their lives and bury their talents in performing mean, servile labor. And such is the horrible idea that I entertain respecting a life of servitude, that if I conceived of their [sic] being no possibility of my rising above the condition of servant, I would gladly hail death as a welcome messenger. O, horrible idea, indeed! to possess noble souls aspiring after high and honorable acquirements, yet confined by the chains of ignorance and poverty to lives of continual drudgery and toil. Neither do I know of any who have enriched themselves by spending their lives as house-domestics, washing windows, shaking carpets, brushing boots, or tending upon gentlemen's tables. I can but die for expressing my sentiments: and I am as willing to die by the sword as the pestilence; for I am a true born American; your blood flows in my veins, and your spirit fires my breast.

I observed a piece in the *Liberator* a few months since, stating that the colonizationists had published a work respecting us, asserting that we were lazy and idle. I confute them on that point. Take us generally as a people, we are neither lazy nor idle; and considering how little we have to excite or stimulate us, I am almost astonished that there are so many industrious and ambitious ones to be found; although I acknowledge, with extreme sorrow, that there are some who never were and never will be serviceable to society. And have you not a similar class among yourselves?

Again, it was asserted that we were "a ragged set, crying for liberty." I reply to it, the whites have so long and so loudly proclaimed the theme of equal rights and privileges, that our souls have caught the flame also, ragged as we are. As far as our merit deserves, we feel a common desire to rise above the condition of servants and drudges. I have learnt, by bitter experience, that continual hard labor deadens the energies of the soul, and benumbs the faculties of the mind; the ideas become confined, the mind barren, and, like the scorching sands of Arabia, produces nothing; or like the uncultivated soil, brings forth thorns and thistles.

Again, continual and hard labor irritates our tempers and sours our dispositions; the whole system becomes worn out with toil and fatigue; nature herself becomes almost exhausted, and we care but little whether we live or die. It is true, that the free people of color throughout these United States are neither bought nor sold, nor under the lash of the cruel driver; many obtain a comfortable support; but few, if any, have an opportunity of becoming rich and independent; and the enjoyments we most pursue are as unprofitable to us as the spider's web or the floating bubbles that vanish into air. As servants, we are respected; but let us presume to aspire any higher, our employer regards us no longer. And were it not that the King eternal has declared that Ethiopia shall stretch forth her hands unto God, I should indeed despair.

I do not consider it derogatory, my friends, for persons to live out to service. There are many whose inclination leads them to aspire no higher; and I would highly commend the performance of almost anything for an honest livelihood; but where constitutional strength is wanting, labor of this kind, in its mildest form, is painful. And doubtless many are the prayers that have ascended to Heaven from Afric's daughters for strength to perform their work. O, many are the tears that have been shed for the want of that strength! Most of our color have dragged out a miserable existence of servitude from the cradle to the grave. And what literary acquirement can be made, or useful knowledge derived, from either maps, books, or charts, by those who continually drudge from Monday morning until Sunday noon? O, ye fairer sisters, whose hands are never soiled, whose nerves and muscles are never strained, go learn by experience! Had we had the opportunity that you have had, to improve our moral and mental faculties, what would have hindered our intellects from being as bright, and our manners from being as dignified as yours? Had it been our lot to have been nursed in the lap of affluence and ease, and to have basked beneath the smiles and sunshine of fortune, should we not have naturally supposed that we were never made to toil? And why are not our forms as delicate, and our constitutions as slender, as yours? Is not the workmanship as curious and complete? Have pity upon us, have pity upon us, O ye who have hearts to feel for other's woes; for the hand of God has touched us. Owing to the disadvantages under which we labor, there are many flowers among us that are

> ... born to bloom unseen
> And waste their fragrance on the desert air.

My beloved brethren, as Christ has died in vain for those who will not accept his offered mercy, so will it be vain for the advocates of freedom to spend their breath in our behalf, unless with united hearts and souls you make some mighty efforts to raise your sons and daughters from the horrible state of servitude and degradation in which they are placed. It is upon you that woman depends; she can do but little besides using her influence; and it is for her sake and yours that I have come forward and made myself a hissing and a reproach among the people; for I am also one of the wretched and miserable daughters of the descendants of fallen Africa. Do you ask, why are you wretched and miserable? I reply, look at many of the most worthy and most interesting of us doomed to spend our lives in gentlemen's kitchens. Look at our young men, smart, active and energetic, with souls filled with ambitious fire; if they look forward, alas! What are their prospects? They can be nothing but the humblest laborers, on account of their dark complexions; hence many of them lose their ambition, and become worthless. Look at our middle-aged men, clad in their rusty plaids and coats; in winter, every cent they earn goes to buy their wood and pay their rents; the poor wives also toil beyond their strength, to help support their families. Look at our aged sires, whose heads are whitened with the frosts of seventy winters, with their old wood-saws on their backs. Alas, what keeps us so? Prejudice, ignorance, and poverty. But ah! methinks our oppression is soon to come to an end; yea, before the Majesty of heaven, our groans and cries have reached the ears of the lord of Sabaoth. As the prayers and tears of Christians will avail the finally impenitent nothing; neither will the prayers and tears of the friends of humanity avail us anything, unless we possess a spirit of virtuous emulation within our breasts. Did the pilgrims, when they first landed on these shores, quietly compose themselves and say, "The Britons have all the money and all the power, and we must continue their servants forever?" Did they sluggishly sigh and say, "Our lot is hard, the Indians own the soil, and we cannot cultivate it?" No; they first made powerful efforts to raise themselves, and then God raised up those illustrious patriots, WASHINGTON and LAFAYETTE, to assist and defend them. And, my brethren, have you made a powerful effort? Have you prayed the legislature for mercy's sake to grant you all the rights and privileges of free citizens, that your daughters may rise to that degree of respectability which true merit deserves, and your sons above the servile situations which most of them fill?

Sojourner Truth (1797–1883)

Sojourner Truth, born Isabella Baumfree as a slave in Ulster County, New York, was the person most responsible during the nineteenth century for linking abolition and women's rights, and demonstrating the reality of black women's gender and race identities. She attended her first women's rights convention in 1850 in Worcester, Massachusetts (Frederick Douglass was also present), and in 1851 delivered her legendary but now controversial "Ar'n't I A Woman" speech at the Akron, Ohio, women's rights gathering which was supposedly recorded by presiding officer Frances D. Gage and was subsequently published in Truth's *Narrative* (1875) and *History of Woman Suffrage* (vol. 1, 115–117), many years after the speech was supposedly delivered. Historian Nell Painter has written and lectured about the unreliability of Gage's account of Truth's famous speech and is presently completing a biography which will hopefully provide more clarity about the issue (See her "Soujourner Truth in Life and Memory: Writing the Biography of an American Exotic," in *Gender and History* 2 (Spring 1990): 3–16.). Carleton Mabee has also written extensively about the "famous Akron speech" (67–82). Since the speech is an important, though unsubstantiated, document in women's history, it belongs in this collection because of what it reveals about the involvement of black women in women's rights during the nineteenth century.

In the debates over black and woman suffrage surrounding the ratification of the Fourteenth Amendment, Truth sided with white feminists and opposed Douglass and other black abolitionists, including Frances Harper, who were against removing "male" from the amendment. Her 1867 speech delivered at the annual meeting of the American Equal Rights Association in New York articulates her fears about black men getting the vote and ignoring the plight of black women. Though she never learned to read or write, Sojourner Truth became a legendary figure in the annals of American feminism, an icon for contemporary feminists, and the link for black women to their activist foremothers.

Woman's Rights

1851

Wall, chilern, whar dar is so much racket dar must be somethin' out of kilter. I tink dat 'twixt de niggers of de Souf and de womin at de Norf, all talkin' 'bout rights, de white men will be in a fix pretty soon. But what's all dis here talkin' 'bout?

Dat man ober dar say dat womin needs to be helped into carriages and lifted ober ditches, and to hab de best place everywhar. Nobody eber helps me into carriages, or ober mud puddles, or gibs me any best place! And a'n't I a woman? Look at my arm! I have ploughed, and planted, and gathered into barns, and no man could head me! And a'n't I a woman? I could work as much and eat as much as a man—when I could get it—and bear de lash as well! And a'n't I a woman? I have borne thirteen chilern, and seen 'em mos' all sold off to slavery, and when I cried out with my mother's grief, none but Jesus heard me! And a'n't I a woman?

Den dey talks 'bout dis ting in de head; what dis dey call it? ("Intellect," whispered some one near.) Dat's it, honey. What dat got to do wid womin's rights or nigger's rights? If my cup won't hold but a pint, and yourn holds a quart, wouldn't ye be mean not to let me have my little half-measure full?

Den dat little man in black dar, he say women can't have as much rights as men, 'cause Christ wan't a woman! Whar did your Christ come from? Whar did your Christ come from? From God and a woman! Man had nothin' to do wid Him!

If de fust woman God ever made was strong enough to turn de world upside down all alone, dese women togedder (and she glanced her eye over the platform) ought to be able to turn it back, and get it right side up again! And now dey is asking to do it, de men better let 'em.

When Woman Gets Her Rights
Man Will Be Right

1867

My Friends, I am rejoiced that you are glad, but I don't know how you will feel when I get through. I come from another field—the country of the slave. They have got their rights—so much good luck. Now what is to be done about it? I feel that I have got as much responsibility as anybody else. I have as good rights as anybody. There is a great stir about colored men getting their rights, but not a word about the colored women; and if colored men get their rights, and not colored women get theirs, there will be a bad time about it. So I am for keeping the thing going while things are stirring; because if we wait till it is still, it will take a great while to get it going again. White women are a great deal smarter and know more than colored women, while colored women do not know scarcely anything. They go out washing, which is about as high as a colored woman gets, and their men go about idle, strutting up and down; and when the women come home, they ask for their money and take it all, and then scold because there is no food. I want you to consider on that, chil'n. I want women to have their rights. In the courts women have no right, no voice; nobody speaks for them. I wish woman to have her voice there among the pettifoggers. If it is not a fit place for women, it is unfit for men to be there. I am above eighty years old; it is about time for me to be going. But I suppose I am kept here because something remains for me to do; I suppose I am yet to help break the chain. I have done a great deal of work—as much as a man, but did not get so much pay. I used to work in the field and bind grain, keeping up with the cradler; but men never doing no more, got twice as much pay. So with the German women. They work in the field and do as much work, but do not get the pay. We do as much, we eat as much, we want as much. I suppose I am about the only colored woman that goes about to speak for the rights of the colored woman, I want to keep the thing stirring, now that the ice is broken. What we want is a little money. You men know that you get as much again as women when you write, or for what you do. When we get our rights, we shall not have to

[37]

come to you for money, for then we shall have money enough of our own. It is a good consolation to know that when we have got this we shall not be coming to you any more. You have been having our right so long, that you think, like a slaveholder, that you own us. I know that it is hard for one who has held the reins for so long to give up; it cuts like a knife. It will feel all better when it closes up again. I have been in Washington about three years, seeing about those colored people. Now colored men have a right to vote; and what I want is to have colored women have the right to vote. There ought to be equal rights more than ever, since colored people have got their freedom.

I know that it is hard for men to give up entirely. They must run in the old track. I was amused how men speak up for one another. They cannot bear that a woman should say anything about the man, but they will stand here and take up the time in man's cause. But we are going, tremble or no tremble. Men are trying to help us. I know that all—the spirit they have got; and they cannot help us much until some of the spirit is taken out of them that belongs among the women. Men have got their rights, and women has not got their rights. That is the trouble. When woman gets her rights man will be right. How beautiful that will be. Then it will be peace on earth and good will to men. But it cannot be until it be right ... It will come ... Yes, it will come quickly. It must come. And now when the waters is troubled, and now is the time to step into the pool. There is a great deal now with the minds, and now is the time to start forth ... The great fight was to keep the rights of the poor colored people. That made a great battle. And now I hope that this will be the last battle that will be in the world. Let us finish up so that there be no more fighting. I have faith in God and there is truth in humanity. Be strong women! Blush not! Tremble not! I want you to keep a good faith and good courage. And I am going round after I get my business settled and get more equality. People in the North, I am going round to lecture on human rights. I will shake every place I go to.

Frances Ellen Watkins Harper
(1825–1911)

Frances Harper, a free black from Baltimore, was a member of the Underground Railroad, one of the first black women to become a professional antislavery speaker, a board member of the Women's Christian Temperance Union, and founding member of the American Woman Suffrage Association. The "bronze muse" was one of the most popular and prolific nineteenth-century black writers, and is best known for her poetry, journalism, and eloquent oratory. In 1859, she became the first black woman to publish a short story, "The Two Offers," a feminist narrative serialized in the *Anglo-American,* which tells the story of two women, one who marries the wrong person and the other a writer who remains unmarried while pursuing the higher calling of racial uplift. Her poems, short stories, novel, essays, and letters, establish her place within a black female intellectual tradition largely ignored, until recently, in American and African American literary history. Her struggle against racism was waged within the women's rights movement as well. Though she worked closely with white suffragists, she exposed their insensitivity to race during the controversy surrounding the Fifteenth Amendment in a speech at the 1869 meeting of the American Equal Rights Association in which she acknowledged the more urgent need for black [male] suffrage: "When it was a question of race, she [Harper] let the lesser question of sex go. But the white women all go for sex, letting race occupy a minor position" (Stanton, *The History of Woman Suffrage,* 2; 391). She was also passionate about the special needs of black women and was present in Boston in 1896 at the historic meeting that led to the founding of the National Association of Colored Women, of which she was eventually elected vice president. "Woman's Political Future" was delivered in 1893 at the World's Congress of Representative Women at the Columbian Exposition in Chicago, and heralded the beginning of an era of emancipated womanhood in which women's intellectual and political power would be unleashed for a better world. Prof. Frances Smith Foster edited the first collection of Harper's work (*A Brighter Coming Day,* 1990) and discovered three of her short novels which appeared in *Christian Recorder* and were recently published.

Frances E. W. Harper }

WOMAN'S POLITICAL FUTURE

If before sin had cast its deepest shadows or sorrow had distilled its bitterest tears, it was true that it was not good for man to be alone, it is no less true, since the shadows have deepened and life's sorrows have increased, that the world has need of all the spiritual aid that woman can give for the social advancement and moral development of the human race. The tendency of the present age, with its restlessness, religious upheavals, failures, blunders, and crimes, is toward broader freedom, an increase of knowledge, the emancipation of thought, and a recognition of the brotherhood of man; in this movement woman, as the companion of man, must be a sharer. So close is the bond between man and woman that you can not raise one without lifting the other. The world can not move without woman's sharing in the movement, and to help give a right impetus to that movement is woman's highest privilege.

If the fifteenth century discovered America to the Old World, the nineteenth is discovering woman to herself. Little did Columbus imagine, when the New World broke upon his vision like a lovely gem in the coronet of the universe, the glorious possibilities of a land where the sun should be our engraver, the winged lightning our messenger, and steam our beast of burden. But as mind is more than matter, and the highest ideal always the true real, so to woman comes the opportunity to strive for richer and grander discoveries than ever gladdened the eye of the Genoese mariner.

Not the opportunity of discovering new worlds, but that of filling this old world with fairer and higher aims than the greed of gold and the lust of power, is hers. Through weary, wasting years men have destroyed, dashed in pieces, and overthrown, but to-day we stand on the threshold of woman's era, and woman's work is grandly constructive. In her hand are possibilities whose use or abuse must tell upon the political life of the nation, and send their influence for good or evil across the track of unborn ages.

As the saffron tints and crimson flushes of morn herald the coming day, so the social and political advancement which woman has already gained bears the promise of the rising of the full-orbed sun of emancipation. The result will be not to make home less happy, but society more holy; yet I do not think the mere extension of the ballot a panacea for all the ills of our national life. What we need to-day is not simply more voters, but better voters. To-day there are red-handed men in our republic, who walk un-whipped of justice, who richly deserve to exchange the ballot of the freeman for the wristlets of the felon; brutal and cowardly men, who torture, burn, and lynch their fellow-men, men whose defenselessness should be their best defense and their weakness an ensign of protection. More than the changing of institutions we need the development of a national conscience, and the upbuilding of national character. Men may boast of the aristocracy of blood, may glory in the aristocracy of talent, and be proud of the aristocracy of wealth, but there is one aristocracy which must ever outrank them all, and that is the aristocracy of character; and it is the women of a country who help to mold its character, and to influence if not determine its destiny; and in the political future of our nation woman will not have done what she could if she does not endeavor to have our republic stand foremost among the nations of the earth, wearing sobriety as a crown and righteousness as a garment and a girdle. In coming into her political estate woman will find a mass of illiteracy to be dispelled. If knowledge is power, ignorance is also power. The power that educates wickedness may manipulate and dash against the pillars of any state when they are undermined and honey-combed by injustice.

I envy neither the heart nor the head of any legislator who has been born to an inheritance of privileges, who has behind him ages of education, dominion, civilization, and Christianity, if he stands opposed to the passage of a national education bill, whose purpose is to secure education to the children of those who were born under the shadow of institutions which made it a crime to read.

To-day women hold in their hands influence and opportunity, and with these they have already opened doors which have been closed to others. By opening doors of labor woman has become a rival claimant for at least some of the wealth monopolized by her stronger brother. In the home she is the priestess, in society the queen, in literature she is a power, in legisla-tive halls law-makers have responded to her appeals, and for her sake have humanized and liberalized their laws. The press has felt the impress of her hand. In the pews of the church she constitutes the majority; the pulpit has welcomed her, and in the school she has the blessed privilege of teaching children and youth. To her is apparently coming the added responsibility of political power; and what she now possesses should only be the means of preparing her to use the coming power for the glory of God and the good of mankind; for power without righteousness is one of the most dangerous forces in the world.

Political life in our country has plowed in muddy channels, and needs the infusion of clearer and cleaner waters. I am not sure that women are naturally so much better than men that they will clear the stream by the virtue of their womanhood; it is not through sex but through character that the best influence of women upon the life of the nation must be exerted.

I do not believe in unrestricted and universal suffrage for either men or women. I believe in moral and educational tests. I do not believe that the most ignorant and brutal man is better prepared to add value to the strength and durability of the government than the most cultured, upright, and intelligent woman. I do not think that willful ignorance should swamp earnest intelligence at the ballot-box, nor that educated wickedness, violence, and fraud should cancel the votes of honest men. The unsteady hands of a drunkard can not cast the ballot of a freeman. The hands of lynchers are too red with blood to determine the political character of the government for even four short years. The ballot in the hands of woman means power added to influence. How well she will use that power I can not foretell. Great evils stare us in the face that need to be throttled by the combined power of an upright manhood and an enlightened womanhood; and I know that no nation can gain its full measure of enlightenment and happiness if one-half of it is free and the other half is fettered. China compressed the feet of her women and thereby retarded the steps of her men. The elements of a nation's weakness must ever be found at the hearthstone.

More than the increase of wealth, the power of armies, and the strength of fleets is the need of good homes, of good fathers, and good mothers. . . .

O women of America! into your hands God has pressed one of the sublimest opportunities that ever came into the hands of the women of any race or people. It is yours to create a healthy public sentiment; to demand justice, simple justice, as the right of every race; to brand with everlasting infamy the lawless and brutal cowardice that lynches, burns, and tortures your own countrymen.

To grapple with the evils which threaten to undermine the strength of the nation and to lay magazines of powder under the cribs of future generations is no child's play.

Let the hearts of the women of the world respond to the song of the herald angels of peace on earth and good will to men. Let them throb as one heart unified by the grand and holy purpose of uplifting the human race, and humanity will breathe freer, and the world grow brighter. With such a purpose Eden would spring up in our path, and Paradise be around our way. . . .

Anna Julia Cooper (1859?–1964)

Born in Raleigh, North Carolina, to a slave mother and her master, Anna Julia Cooper published the first book-length black feminist text, *A Voice from the South,* in 1892. This collection of essays provides a global perspective on racism, imperialism, and colonialism; praises black achievements; advocates black women's education; and critiques black male sexism and the racism of white women. Her feminist leanings were apparent at a young age, when she objected to sexist treatment which prohibited her from enrolling in Greek and other classes reserved for male ministerial students at St. Augustine's Normal School in North Carolina. Following her graduation from Oberlin College in 1884, she taught modern languages at Wilberforce University and, in 1887, began a long career at M St. High School in Washington, D.C. In 1900, she attended the first Pan-African Conference in London and presented a paper on "The Negro Problem in America." At age sixty-five, she completed the requirements for a doctorate at the Sorbonne, where she wrote a dissertation in French entitled "Slavery and the French Revolutionists, 1788–1805."

A Voice from the South espouses a cultural feminist position which posits that women, because of their inherent moral superiority, have the responsibility and capacity to reform the human race. In the chapter on "The Higher Education of Women," she argues that developing their intellects would render women self-reliant and economically independent, which would make them less dependent on marriage for physical support. Furthermore, she encourages women to expand their horizons and not to "look to sexual love as the one sensation capable of giving tone and relish, movement and vim, to the life she leads" (68–69). She was frustrated by black men who opposed higher education for women and made the insightful observation that "while our men seem thoroughly abreast of the times on almost every other subject, when they strike the woman question they drop back into sixteenth-century logic" (75). "The Status of Woman in America" captures the situation of African American women during the "woman's era" of the late nineteenth century.

Anna Julia Cooper }

The Status of Woman in America

To-day America counts her millionaires by the thousand; questions of tariff and questions of currency are the most vital ones agitating the public mind. In this period, when material prosperity and well-earned ease and luxury are assured facts from a national standpoint, woman's work and woman's influence are needed as never before; needed to bring a heart power into this money-getting, dollar-worshipping civilization; needed to bring a moral force into the utilitarian motives and interests of the time needed to stand for God and Home and Native Land *versus gain and greed and grasping selfishness.*

There can be no doubt that this fourth centenary of America's discovery which we celebrate at Chicago, strikes the keynote of another important transition in the history of this nation; and the prominence of woman in the management of its celebration is a fitting tribute to the part she is destined to play among the forces of the future. This is the first congressional recognition of woman in this country, and this Board of Lady Managers constitute the first women legally appointed by any government to act in a national capacity. This of itself marks the dawn of a new day.

Now the periods of discovery, of settlement, of developing resources and accumulating wealth have passed in rapid succession. Wealth in the nation as in the individual brings leisure, repose, reflection. The struggle with nature is over, the struggle with ideas begins. We stand then, it seems to me, in this last decade of the nineteenth century, just in the portals of a new and untried movement on a higher plain and in a grander strain than any the past has called forth. It does not require a prophet's eye to divine its trend and image its possibilities from the forces we see already at work around us; nor is it hard to guess what must be the status of woman's work under the new regime.

In the pioneer days her role was that of a camp-follower, an additional something to fight for and be burdened with, only repaying the anxiety and labor she called forth by her own incomparable gifts of sympathy and appreciative love; unable herself ordinarily to contend with the bear and the Indian, or to take active part in clearing the wilderness and constructing the home.

In the second or wealth-producing period her work is abreast of man's, complementing and supplementing; counteracting excessive tendencies, and mollifying over-rigorous proclivities.

In the era now about to dawn, her sentiments must strike the keynote and give the dominant tone. And this because of the nature of her contribution to the world.

Her kingdom is not over physical forces. Not by might, nor by power can she prevail. Her position must ever be inferior where strength of muscle creates leadership. If she follows the instincts of her nature, however, she must always stand for the conservation of those deeper moral forces which make for the happiness of homes and the righteousness of the country. In a reign of moral ideas she is easily queen.

There is to my mind no grander and surer prophecy of the new era and of woman's place in it, than the work already begun in the waning years of the nineteenth century by the WCTU [Women's Christian Temperance Union] in America, an organization which has even now reached not only national but international importance, and seems destined to permeate and purify the whole civilized world. It is the living embodiment of woman's activities and woman's ideas, and its extent and strength rightly prefigure her increasing power as a moral factor.

The colored woman of to-day occupies, one may say, a unique position in this country. In a period of itself transitional and unsettled, her status seems one of the least ascertainable and definitive of all the forces which make for our civilization. She is confronted by both a woman question and a race problem, and is as yet an unknown or an unacknowledged factor in both. While the women of the white race can with calm assurance enter upon the work they feel by nature appointed to do, while their men give loyal support and appreciative countenance to their efforts, recognizing in most avenues of usefulness the propriety and the need of woman's distinctive cooperation, the colored woman too often finds herself hampered and shamed by a less liberal sentiment and a more conservative attitude on the part of those for whose opinion she cares most. That this is not universally true I am glad to admit. There are to be found both intensely conservative white men and exceedingly liberal colored men. But as far as my experience goes the average man of our race is less frequently ready to admit the actual need among the sturdier forces of the world for woman's help or influence. That great social and economic questions await her interference, that she could throw any light on problems of national import, that her intermeddling could improve the management of school systems, or elevate the tone of public institutions, or humanize and sanctify the far-reaching influence of prisons and reformatories and improve the treatment of lunatics and imbeciles—that she has a word worth hearing on mooted questions in political economy, that she could contribute a suggestion on the relations of labor and capital, or offer a thought on honest money and honorable trade, I fear the majority of "Americans of the colored variety" are not yet prepared to concede. It may be that they do not yet see these questions in their right perspective, being absorbed in the immediate needs of their own political complications. A good deal depends on where we put the emphasis in this world; and our men are not perhaps to blame if they see everything colored by the light of those agitations in the midst of which they live and move and have their being. The part they have had to play in American history during the last twenty-five or thirty years has tended rather to exaggerate the importance of mere political advantage, as well as to set a fictitious valuation on those able to secure such advantage. It is the astute politician, the manager who can gain preferment for himself and his favorites, the demagogue known to stand in with the powers at the White House and consulted on the bestowal of government plums, whom we set in high places and denominate great. It is they who receive the hosannas of the multitude and are regarded as leaders of the people. The thinker and the doer, the man who solves the problem by enriching his country with an invention worth thousands or by a thought inestimable and precious is given neither bread nor a stone. He is too often left to die in obscurity and neglect even if spared in his life the bitterness of fanatical jealousies and detraction.

And yet politics, and surely American politics, is hardly a school for great minds. Sharpening rather than deepening, it develops the faculty of taking advantage of present emergencies rather than the insight to distinguish between the true and the false, the lasting and the ephemeral advantage. Highly cultivated selfishness rather than consecrated benevolence is its passport to success. Its votaries are never seers. At best they are but manipulators—often only jugglers. It is conducive neither to profound statesmanship nor to the higher type of manhood. Altruism is its *mauvais succès* and naturally enough it is indifferent to any factor which cannot be worked into its own immediate aims and purposes. As woman's influence as a political element is as yet nil in most of the commonwealths of our republic, it is not surprising that with those who place the emphasis on mere political capital she may yet seem almost a nonentity so far as it concerns the solution of great national or even racial perplexities.

There are those, however, who value the calm elevation of the thoughtful spectator who stands aloof from the heated scramble; and, above the turmoil and din of corruption and selfishness, can listen to the teachings of eternal truth and righteousness. There are even those who feel that the black man's unjust and unlawful exclusion temporarily from participation in the elective franchise in certain states is after all but a lesson "in the desert" fitted to develop in him insight and discrimination against the day of his own appointed time. One needs occasionally to stand aside from the hum and rush of human interests and passions to hear the voices of God. And it not unfrequently happens that the All-loving gives a great push to certain souls to thrust them out, as it were, from the distracting current for awhile to promote their discipline and growth, or to enrich them by communion and reflection. And similarly it may be woman's privilege from her peculiar coigne of vantage as a quiet observer, to whisper just the needed suggestion or the almost forgotten truth. The colored woman, then, should not be ignored because her bark is resting in the silent waters of the sheltered cove. She is watching the movements of the contestants none the less and is all the better qualified, perhaps, to weigh and judge and advise because not herself in the excitement of the race. Her voice, too, has always been heard in clear, unfaltering tones, ringing the changes on those deeper interests which make for permanent good. She is always sound and ortho-dox on questions affecting the well-being of her race. You do not find the colored woman selling her birthright for a mess of pottage. Nay, even after reason has retired from the contest, she has been known to cling blindly with the instinct of a turtle dove to those principles and policies which to her mind promise hope and safety for children yet unborn. It is notorious that ignorant black women in the South have actually left their husbands' homes and repudiated their support for what was understood by the wife to be race disloyalty, or "voting away," as she expresses it, the privileges of herself and little ones.

It is largely our women in the South to-day who keep the black men solid in the Republican party. The latter as they increase in intelligence and power of discrimination would be more apt to divide on local issues at any rate. They begin to see that the Grand Old Party regards the Negro's cause as an outgrown issue, and on Southern soil at least finds a too intimate acquaintanceship with him a somewhat unsavory recommendation. Then, too, their political wits have been sharpened to appreciate the fact that it is good policy to cultivate one's neighbors and not depend too much on a distant friend to fight one's home battles. But the black woman can never forget—however lukewarm the party may to-day appear—that it was a Republican president who struck the manacles from her own wrists and gave the possibilities of manhood to her helpless little ones; and to her mind a Democratic Negro is a traitor and a time-server. Talk as much as you like of venality and manipulation in the South, there are not many men, I can tell you, who would dare face a wife quivering in every fiber with the consciousness that her husband is a coward who could be paid to desert her deepest and dearest interests.

Not unfelt, then, if unproclaimed has been the work and influence of the colored women of America. Our list of chieftains in the service, though not long, is not inferior in strength and excellence, I dare believe, to any similar list which this country can produce.

Among the pioneers, Frances Watkins Harper could sing with prophetic exaltation in the darkest days, when as yet there was not a rift in the clouds overhanging her people:

> "Yes, Ethiopia shall stretch
> Her bleeding hands abroad;
> Her cry of agony shall reach the burning throne of God.
> Redeemed from dust and freed from chains,
>   Her sons shall lift their eyes,
> From cloud-capt hills and verdant plains
>   Shall shouts of triumph rise."

Among preachers of righteousness, an unanswerable silencer of cavilers and objectors, was Sojourner Truth, that unique and rugged genius who seemed carved out without hand or chisel from the solid mountain mass; and in pleasing contrast, Amanda Smith, sweetest of natural singers and pleaders in dulcet tones for the things of God and of His Christ.

Sarah Woodson Early and Martha Briggs, planting and watering in the school room, and giving off from their matchless and irresistible personality an impetus and inspiration which can never die so long as there lives and breathes a remote descendant of their disciples and friends.

Charlotte Forten Grimké, the gentle spirit whose verses and life link her so beautifully with America's great Quaker poet and loving reformer.

Hallie Quinn Brown, charming reader, earnest, effective lecturer and devoted worker of unflagging zeal and unquestioned power.

Fannie Jackson Coppin, the teacher and organizer, preeminent among women of whatever country or race in constructive and executive force.

These women represent all shades of belief and as many departments of activity; but they have one thing in common—their sympathy with the oppressed race in America and the consecration of their several talents in whatever line to the work of its deliverance and development.

Fifty years ago woman's activity according to orthodox definitions was on a pretty clearly cut "sphere," including primarily the kitchen and the nursery, and rescued from the barrenness of prison bars by the womanly mania for adorning every discoverable bit of china or canvass with forlorn looking cranes balanced idiotically on one foot. The woman of to-day finds herself in the presence of responsibilities which ramify through the profoundest and most varied interests of her country and race. Not one of the issues of this plodding, toiling, sinning, repenting, falling, aspiring humanity can afford to shut her out, or can deny the reality of her influence. No plan for renovating society, no scheme for purifying politics, no reform in church or in state, no moral, social, or economic question, no movement upward or downward in the human plane is lost on her. A man once said when told his house was afire: "Go tell my wife; I never meddle with household affairs." But no woman can possibly put herself or her sex outside any of the interests that affect humanity. All departments in the new era are to be hers, in the sense that her interests are in all and through all; and it is incumbent on her to keep intelligently and sympathetically *en rapport* with all the great movements of her time, that she may know on which side to throw the weight of her influence. She stands now at the gateway of this new era of American civilization. In her hands must be moulded the strength, the wit, the statesmanship, the morality, all the psychic force, the social and economic intercourse of that era. To be alive at such an epoch is a privilege, to be a woman then is sublime.

In this last decade of our century, changes of such moment are in progress, such new and alluring vistas are opening out before us, such original and radical suggestions for the adjustment of labor and capital, of government and the governed, of the family, the church, and the state, that to be a possible factor though an infinitesimal one in such a movement is pregnant with hope and weighty with responsibility. To be a woman in such an age carries with it a privilege and an opportunity never implied before. But to be a woman of the Negro race in America, and to be able to grasp the deep significance of the possibilities of the crisis, is to have a heritage, it seems to me, unique in the ages. In the first place, the race is young and full of the elasticity and hopefulness of youth. All its achievements are before it. It does not look on the masterly triumphs of nineteenth-century civilization with that *blasé* world-weary look which characterizes the old washed-out and worn-out races which have already, so to speak, seen their best days. . . .

Julia A. J. Foote (1823–1900)

Julia Foote, born in Schenectady, New York, to an African Methodist Episcopal (A.M.E.) Church family, was among a small group of women evangelists ("sisters of the spirit," according to William Andrews) in the nineteenth century who defied gender conventions by insisting on their right to preach. In 1894, against the wishes of her parents, husband, and minister, she became the first ordained deacon in the A.M.E. Church and the second woman to become an ordained elder in the church. Her spiritual autobiography, *A Brand Plucked from the Fire* (1879), like Jarena Lee's *Religious Experience and Journal* (1849) and Virginia W. Broughton's *Twenty Year's Experience of a Missionary* (1907), makes a feminist argument for Christianity's embrace of women evangelists like herself.

Later, the black church would continue to be a site of resistance on the part of feminist women. Nannie Burroughs (1879–1961), born in Virginia to former slaves, was a prominent clubwoman, educator, orator, religious, and women's rights leader, who devoted her life to various self-help initiatives for the race. One of the founders in 1900 of the Women's Convention Auxiliary of the National Baptist Convention, she delivered her inaugural speech in Richmond on "How the Sisters Are Hindered from Helping." An insightful analysis by historian Evelyn Brooks Higginbotham [in *Righteous Discontent: The Women's Movement in the Black Baptist Church, 1880–1920* (Cambridge: Harvard University Press, 1993)] of the feminist theology of black Baptist women includes a discussion of Burrough's campaign for gender equality within the Baptist church. She also discusses their indebtedness to Maria Stewart and disdain for black male sexism. Foote and Burroughs are important foremothers for a cadre of contemporary womanist theologians.

Julia A. J. Foote }

Women in the Gospel

Thirty years ago there could scarcely a person be found, in the churches, to sympathize with anyone who talked of Holiness. But, in my simplicity, I did think that a body of Christian ministers would understand my case and judge righteously. I was, however, disappointed.

It is no little thing to feel that every man's hand is against us, and ours against every man, as seemed to be the case with me at this time; yet how precious, if Jesus but be with us. In this severe trial I had constant access to God, and a clear consciousness that he heard me; yet I did not seem to have that plenitude of the Spirit that I had before.

Though I did not wish to pain anyone, neither could I please anyone only as I was led by the Holy Spirit. I saw, as never before, that the best men were liable to err, and that the only safe way was to fall on Christ, even though censure and reproach fell upon me for obeying His voice. Man's opinion weighed nothing with me, for my commission was from heaven, and my reward was with the Most High.

I could not believe that it was a short-lived impulse or spasmodic influence that impelled me to preach. I read that on the day of Pentecost was the Scripture fulfilled as found in Joel ii. 28, 29; and it certainly will not be denied that women as well as men were at that time filled with the Holy Ghost, because it is expressly stated that women were among those who continued in prayer and supplication, waiting for the fulfillment of the promise. Women and men are classed together, and if the power to preach the Gospel is short-lived and spasmodic in the case of women, it must be equally so in that of men; and if women have lost the gift of prophecy, so have men.

We are sometimes told that if a woman pretends to a Divine call, and thereon grounds the right to plead the cause of a crucified Redeemer in public, she will be believed when she shows credentials from heaven; that is, when she works a miracle. If it be necessary to prove one's right to preach the Gospel, I ask of my brethren to show me their credentials, or I can not believe in the propriety of their ministry.

But the bible puts an end to this strife when it says: "There is neither male nor female in Christ Jesus." Philip had four daughters that prophesied, or preached. Paul called Priscilla, as well as Aquila, his "helper," or, as in the Greek, his " fellow-laborer." Rom. xv. 3; 2 Cor. viii. 23; Phil. ii. 5; 1 Thess. iii. 2. The same word, which, in our common translation, is now rendered a "servant of the church," in speaking of Phebe (Rom. xix. 1.), is rendered "minister" when applied to Tychicus. Eph. vi. 21. When Paul said, "Help those women who labor with me in the Gospel," he certainly meant that they did more than to pour out tea. In the eleventh chapter of First Corinthians Paul gives directions, to men and women, how they should appear when they prophesy or pray in public assemblies; and he defines prophesying to be speaking to edification, exhortation, and comfort.

I may further remark that the conduct of holy women is recorded in Scripture, as an example to others of their sex. And in the early ages of Christianity many women were happy and glorious in martyrdom. How nobly, how heroically, too, in later ages, have women suffered persecution and death for the name of the Lord Jesus.

In looking over these facts, I could see no miracle wrought for those women more than in myself.

Though opposed, I went forth laboring for God, and He owned and blessed my labors, and has done so wherever I have been until this day. And while I walk obediently, I know He will, though hell may rage and vent its spite.

Gertrude Bustill Mossell
(1855–1948)

Gertrude Bustill Mossell, born in Philadelphia to a prominent free Quaker family, was an influential journalist and women's rights crusader. Her career as a journalist was influenced by her politically active abolitionist/feminist family which included Grace Bustill Douglass and her daughter Sarah Mapps Douglass, members of the Philadelphia Female Anti-Slavery Society. She was also the cousin of political activist Paul Robeson.

Her first column for T. Thomas Fortune's New York *Freeman* (December 1885) as editor of "Our Woman's Department" was "Woman's Suffrage" in which she indicated she would "promote true womanhood, especially that of the African race." She is best known for *The Work of the Afro-American Woman* (1894), which she wrote out of a desire to correct glaring omissions in American women's history and to affirm the noble womanhood of black women who were excluded from racist and classist concepts of "true women." This pioneering feminist history text also chronicled the achievements of black women in the professions (medicine, business, religion, education, and journalism), exposed black male sexism and white female racism, particularly their ostracism of black feminists, and celebrated black women writers.

"The Opposite Point of View" is a critique of traditional notions of marriage, which demand that wives be passive and submissive to their husbands. The best marriages, from her progressive vantage point, are ones in which wives possess a mind of their own and are equal partners. Joanne Braxton's assessment of this essay as "a radical statement on family life and marital relations," as well as a "valuable document of the sexual politics of black America" (Gates, *Schomburg Library,* xxxvi) locates Mossell within a clearly black feminist tradition. "A Lofty Study" called for women writers to have "a room of their own" long before the publication of Virginia Woolf's classic feminist essay, "A Room of One's Own" (1930). For an excellent discussion of Mossell, see Claudia Tate's *Domestic Allegories of Political Desire* (1992).

Gertrude Bustill Mossell }

The Opposite Point of View

Home is undoubtedly the cornerstone of our beloved Republic. Deep-planted in the heart of civilized humanity is the desire for a resting place that may be called by this name, around which may cluster life-long memories. Each member of a family after a place is secured, helps to contribute to the formation of the real and ideal home. Men's and women's desires concerning what shall constitute a home differ largely, sex counting for much, past environment for more. Man desires a place of rest from the cares and vexations of life, where peace and love shall abide, where he shall be greeted by the face of one willing to conform to his wishes and provide for his comfort and convenience—where little ones shall sweeten the struggle for existence and make the future full of bright dreams.

Woman desires to carry into effect the hopes that have grown with her growth, and strengthened with her strength from childhood days until maturity; love has made the path of life blend easily with the task that duty has marked out. . . .

Many wonder that so many people separate, my wonder is that so many remain together. Born in different places, reared differently, with different religious and political opinions, differing in temperament, in educational views, at every point, what wonder strife ensues. But we will consider in this paper the life of those who elect to remain together whether life is a flowery path or overgrown with briers and thorns. Now, first, here I must explain that I am about to look at the opposite side of a much-discussed question. The pendulum will swing in this paper in the opposite direction to the one generally taken.

The conservatives can take the median line with the pendulum at a standstill if they so desire. For several years, every paper or magazine that has fallen into our hands gave some such teaching as this: "The wife must always meet her husband with a smile." She must continue in the present and future married life to do a host of things for his comfort and convenience; the sure fate awaiting her failure to follow this advice being the loss of the husband's affection and the mortification of seeing it transferred to the keeping of a rival. She must stay at home, keep the house clean, prepare food properly, and care for her children, or he will frequent the saloon, go out at night, and spend his time unwisely at the least. These articles may be written by men or by women, but the moral is invariably pointed for the benefit of women; one rarely appearing by either sex for the benefit of men. This fact must certainly lead both men and women to suppose that women need this teaching most; now I differ from this view of the subject. In a life of some length and of close observation, having been since womanhood a part of professional life, both in teaching, preaching, and otherwise, where one receives the confidences of others, I have come to the conclusion that women need these teachings least.

I have seen the inside workings of many homes; I know there are many slatterns, many gossips, and poor cooks; many who are untrue to marital vows; but on the whole, according to their means, their opportunities for remaining at home, the irritating circumstances that surround them (and of our women especially), tempted by two races, they do well. After due deliberation and advisedly I repeat that they (remembering the past dreadful environment of slavery) do well. Man as often as woman gives the keynote to the home-life for the day; whether it shall be one of peace or strife. The wife may fill the house with sweet singing, have the children dressed and ready to give a joyful greeting to the father; the breakfast might be fit to tempt an epicure, and yet the whole be greeted surlily by one who considers wife and home but his rightful convenience. I may not be orthodox, but I venture to assert that keeping a clean house will not keep a man at home; to be sure it will not drive him out, but neither will it keep him in to a very large extent. And you, dear tender-hearted little darlings, that are being taught daily that it will, might as well know the truth now and not be crying your eyes out later.

Dear Willie can go out at night, yes, a little while even every night, and not be going to the bad nor failing to do his duty. Now let me tell you an open secret and look about you where you live and see if I am not right. The men that usually stay in at night are domestic in their nature, care little for the welfare or approval of the world at large, are not ambitious, are satisfied with being loved, care nothing for being honored. The men who used when single to kiss the babies, pet the cat, and fail to kick the dog where they visited are the men who remain at home most when married. A man who aspires to social preeminence, who is ambitious, or who acquires the reputation of being a man of judgment and knowledge, useful as a public man, will be often out at night even against his own desires, on legitimate business. By becoming a member of many organizations it may become necessary for him to spend most of his evenings out, sacrificing his own will to the will of the many. Again, men after working at daily drudgery come home to their families, eat the evening meal, hear the day's doings, read the paper, and then desire to meet with some masculine friends to discuss the topics of the day. The club, the church, the street corner, or a chum's business place may be the meeting place. Bad men go out for evil purposes; to be sure, many men, social by nature, are tempted by the allurements of the saloon and the chance of meeting their boon companions. But these men would do the same if they had no home, or whether it was clean or not. Wives should be kind, keep house beautifully, dress beautifully if they can; but after all this is accomplished their husbands will be away from home possibly quite as much for the above-given reasons. Women must not be blamed because they are not equal to the self-sacrifice of always meeting husbands with a smile, nor the wife blamed that she does not dress after marriage as she dressed before; childbirth and nursing, the care of the sick through sleepless, nightly vigils, the exactions and irritations incident to a life whose duties are made up of trifles and interruptions, and whose work of head and heart never ceases, make it an impossibility to put behind them at all times all cares and smile with burdened heart and weary feet and brain.

Small means, constant sacrifice for children prevent the replenishment of a fast dwindling wardrobe. Husbands and fathers usually buy what they *need*; at least most mothers and wives will not even do that while children need anything. The great inducement for a woman to fulfil these commands is that she may retain her husband's love and not forfeit her place to a rival. Suppose someone should tell a man, "Now you must smile at your wife always, in her presence never appear grumpy, dress her in the latest style, and so on, or else she will transfer her affections to the keeping of another." What would be his reply? We all know. And yet women need love to live and be happy, are supposed to be most susceptible to love and flattery, and men therefore ought to fear this fate most, and the daily record teaches the fact if the magazine writers fail to do so. A good husband will do his duty even if the wife fails, as so many wives are doing to-day with bad husbands. The man who wants to lead a reckless life, will complain of his wife's bad housekeeping, extravagance, the children's noise or, if not blessed with offspring, still complains that this fact makes home less interesting; but let me tell you, friend, it is all an excuse in nine cases out of ten. A husband's ill-doing is never taken as an excuse for a wife's turning bad, and why should a man be excused for doing wrong, if he has a bad wife? If he be the stronger-minded one, especially. If a husband is a true one in any sense of the word, his transference of the kiss at the door from the wife to the firstborn that runs before her to greet him will not cause even a sigh of regret.

Doing the best she can in all things will be appreciated by a true husband. The one remaining thought unmentioned is *temper,* the disposition to scold and nag. Now no man desires a scolding, nagging wife, and no child desires such a mother; but saints are rare and I don't believe that history past or present proves that saintly women have in the past or do now *gain men's love oftenest or hold it longest.* The two women, one white, another colored, that I sorrowed with over recreant husbands, were true, loving wives; one had just saved her small earnings toward buying the husband a birthday present and had unsuspectingly kissed good-bye the partner of his flight. The other clasped more lovingly the hand of the baby boy that most resembled him and only spoke of the facts as occasion required it in business concerning the property he had left behind; both men had found no fault with these wives, treated them kindly up to the last hour when they deserted them forever. Neither sugar nor pickles would be a good diet, but most of us could eat a greater quantity of pepper hash than of sugar after all. I believe that a woman who has a mind and will of her own will become monotonous to a less extent than one so continuously sweet and self-effacing; and I believe history proves it.

It may be humanity or masculinity's total depravity, but I believe more men tire of sweet women than even of scolds, and yet I do not desire to encourage the growth of this obnoxious creature. The desirable partner for a successful, peaceful married life is a woman of well-balanced temperament, who is known among her associates as one not given to what is often called fits of temper, and yet withal possessing a mind of her own....

Gertrude Bustill Mossell }

A LOFTY STUDY

In these days of universal scribbling, when almost everyone writes for fame or money, many people who are not reaping large pecuniary profits from their work do not feel justified in making any outlay to gratify the necessities of their labors in literature.

Everyone engaged in literary work, even if but to a limited extent, feels greatly the need of a quiet nook to write in. Each portion of the home seems to have its clearly defined use, that will prevent their achieving the desired result. A few weeks ago, in the course of my travels, I came across an excellent idea carried into practical operation, that had accomplished the much-desired result of a quiet spot for literary work, without the disarrangement of a single portion of the household economy. In calling at the house of a member of the Society of Friends, I was ushered first into the main library on the first floor. Not finding in it the article sought, the owner invited me to walk upstairs to an upper library. I continued my ascent until we reached the attic. This had been utilized in such a way that it formed a comfortable and acceptable study. I made a mental note of my surroundings. The room was a large sloping attic chamber. It contained two windows, one opening on a roof; another faced the door; a skylight had been cut directly overhead, in the middle of the room. Around the ceiling on the side that was not sloping ran a line of tiny closets with glass doors. Another side had open shelves. On the sloping side, drawers rose from the floor a convenient distance. The remaining corner had a desk built in the wall; it was large and substantial, containing many drawers. Two small portable tables were close at hand near the centre.

An easy chair, an old-fashioned sofa with a large square cushion for a pillow, completed the furniture of this unassuming study. Neatness, order, comfort reigned supreme. Not a sound from the busy street reached us. It was so quiet, so peaceful, the air was so fresh and pure, it seemed like living in a new atmosphere.

I just sat down and wondered why I had never thought of this very room for a study. Almost every family has an unused attic, dark, sloping, given up to odds and ends. Now let it be papered with a creamy paper, with narrow stripes, giving the impression of height; a crimson velvety border. Paint the woodwork a darker shade of yellow, hang a buff and crimson portière at the door. Put in an open grate; next widen the window-sills, and place on them boxes of flowering plants. Get an easy chair, a desk that suits your height, and place by its side a revolving bookcase, with the books most used in it. Let an adjustable lamp stand by its side, and with a nice old-fashioned sofa, well supplied with cushions, you will have a study that a queen might envy you. Bright, airy, cheerful, and almost noiseless, not easy of access to those who would come only to disturb, and far enough away to be cosy and inviting, conferring a certain privilege on the invited guest.

These suggestions can be improved upon, but the one central idea, a place to one's self without disturbing the household economy, would be gained.

Even when there is a library in the home, it is used by the whole family, and if the husband is literary in his tastes, he often desires to occupy it exclusively at the very time you have leisure, perhaps. Men are so often educated to work alone that even sympathetic companionship annoys. Very selfish, we say, but we often find it so—and therefore the necessity of a study of one's own.

If even this odd room cannot be utilized for your purposes, have at least your own corner in some cheerful room. A friend who edits a special department in a *weekly* has in her own chamber a desk with plenty of drawers and small separate compartments. The desk just fits in an alcove of the room, with a revolving-chair in front. What a satisfaction to put everything in order, turn the key, and feel that all is safe—no busy hands, no stray breeze can carry away or disarrange some choice idea kept for the future delectation of the public! Besides this, one who writes much generally finds that she can write best at some certain spot. Ideas come more rapidly, sentences take more lucid forms. Very often the least change from that position will break up the train of thought.

Mary Church Terrell (1863–1954)

Mary Church Terrell, born in Memphis, Tennessee, to a wealthy family, was a prominent club woman, race woman, lecturer, women's rights reformer, and teacher. She was educated at Oberlin College (1884) where she, unlike most females, took the gentlemen's course—four years of study in the classics. Against the wishes of her traditional father, she pursued a career after graduation that began with a teaching position at Wilberforce University (1885) and later the M St. High School in Washington, D.C. In 1892, she became president of the Colored Women's League in Washington, D.C., and was founding president of the National Association of Colored Women following the historic 1896 gathering in Boston of black club women. Terrell's 1898 speech to the mostly white National American Woman's Suffrage Association (reprinted in *Voice of the Negro* in 1904) emphasized the extraordinary intellectual and political achievements of black women only two generations away from slavery. She also spoke to the same group in 1900 on the "Justice of Woman Suffrage." Terrell was one among a few black women reformers with international connections, which her fluency in French and German facilitated. She was the only black woman present when she spoke at the 1904 Berlin International Congress of Women; she also spoke in 1919 at the International League for Peace and Freedom in Zurich, and in 1937 at the World Fellowship of Faiths in London. Major themes in her speeches and writing included black female empowerment, lynching, woman suffrage, and the glories of black history.

Mary Church Terrell }

THE PROGRESS OF COLORED WOMEN

"I expected to see a dozen clever colored women, but instead of twelve I saw two hundred. It was simply an eye opener." This is the way one white woman expressed herself, after she had attended a convention of colored women held in Chicago about four years ago. This sentiment was echoed by many other white women who assisted at the deliberations of the colored women on that occasion. These Chicagoans were no more surprised at the intelligence, culture, and taste in dress which the colored women displayed than white people of other cities. When the National Association of Colored Women held its biennial two years ago in Buffalo, New York, the logic, earnestness and common sense of the delegates were quite as much a nine days' wonder as it was in Chicago. "I hold myself above the pettiness of race prejudice, of course," said one of the best women journalists in the country, "but for all my liberal mindedness the four days session of this federation of colored women's clubs has been a revelation. It has been my lot, first and last to attend a good many conventions of women —'Mothers, Daughters,' and what not, and of them all, the sanest, the liveliest, the most practical was that of the colored women." And so quotation after quotation might be cited to prove that even the white people who think they know all about colored people and are perfectly just in their estimate of them are surprised when they have an ocular demonstration of the rapidity with which a large number of colored women has advanced. When one considers the obstacles encountered by colored women in their effort to educate and cultivate themselves, since they became free, the work they have accomplished and the progress they have made will bear favorable comparisons at least with that of their more fortunate sisters, from whom the opportunity of acquiring knowledge and the means of self culture have never been entirely withheld. Not only are colored women with ambition and aspiration handicapped on account of their sex, but they are almost everywhere baffled and mocked because of their race. Not only because they are women, but because they are colored women are discour-

agement and disappointment meeting them at every turn. But in spite of
the obstacles encountered, the progress made by colored women along
many lines appears like a veritable miracle of modern times, Forty years
ago for the great masses of colored women there was no such thing as
home. To-day in each and every section of the country there are hundreds
of homes among colored people, the mental and moral tone of which is as
high and as pure as can be found among the best people of any land. To
the women of the race may be attributed in large measure the refinement
and purity of the colored home. The immorality of colored women is a
theme upon which those who know little about them or those who maliciously misrepresent them love to descant. Foul aspersions upon the character of colored women are assiduously circulated by the press of certain
sections and especially by the direct descendants of those who in years past
were responsible for the moral degradation of their female slaves. And yet,
in spite of the fateful heritage of slavery, even though the safe guards
usually thrown around maidenly youth and innocence are in some sections
entirely withheld from colored girls. Statistics compiled by men not inclined
to falsify in favor of my race show that immorality among the colored
women of the United States is not so great as among women with similar
environment and temptations in Italy, Germany, Sweden, and France.

Scandals in the best colored society are exceedingly rare, while the progressive game of divorce and remarriage is practically unknown.

The intellectual progress of colored women has been marvelous. So great
has been their thirst for knowledge and so herculean their efforts to acquire
it that there are few colleges, universities, high, and normal schools in the
North, East, and West from which colored girls have not graduated with
honor. In Wellesley, Vassar, Ann Arbor, Cornell, and in Oberlin, my dear
alma mater, whose name will always be loved and whose praise will always
be sung as the first college in the country broad, just, and generous enough
to extend a cordial welcome to the Negro and to open its doors to women
on an equal footing with the men, colored girls by their splendid records
have forever settled the question of their capacity and worth. The instructors in these and other institutions cheerfully bear testimony to their intelligence, their diligence, and their success. As the brains of colored women
expanded, their hearts began to grow. No sooner had the heads of a favored
few been filled with knowledge than their hearts yearned to dispense blessings to the less fortunate of their race. With tireless energy and eager zeal
colored women have worked in every conceivable way to elevate their race.
Of the colored teachers engaged in instructing our youth it is probably no
exaggeration to say that fully eighty percent are women. In the backwoods,
remote from the civilization and comforts of the city and town colored
women may be found courageously battling with those evils which such
conditions always entail. Many a heroine of whom the world will never

hear has thus sacrificed her life to her race amid surroundings and in the face of privations which only martyrs can bear.

Through the medium of their societies in the church, beneficial organizations out of it, and clubs of various kinds, colored women are doing a vast amount of good. It is almost impossible to ascertain exactly what the Negro is doing in any field, for the records are so poorly kept. This is particularly true in the case of the women of the race. During the past forty years there is no doubt that colored women in their poverty have contributed large sums of money to charitable and educational institutions as well as to the foreign and home missionary work. Within the twenty-five years in which the educational work of the African Methodist Episcopal church has been systematized, the women of that organization have contributed at least five hundred thousand dollars to the cause of education. Dotted all over the country are charitable institutions for the aged, orphaned, and poor which have been established by colored women, just how many it is difficult to state, owing to the lack of statistics bearing on the progress, possessions, and prowess of colored women. Among the charitable institutions either founded, conducted, or supported by colored women, may be mentioned the Hale Infirmary of Montgomery, Alabama, the Carrie Steele Orphanage of Atlanta, the Reed Orphan Home of Covington, and the Haines Industrial School of Augusta, all three in the state of Georgia; a home for the aged of both races in New Bedford and St. Monica's home of Boston, in Massachusetts; Old Folks Home of Memphis, Tennessee, and the Colored Orphan's Home of Lexington, Kentucky, together with others which lack of space forbids me to mention. Mt. Meigs Institute is an excellent example of a work originated and carried into successful execution by a colored woman. The school was established for the benefit of colored people on the plantations in the black belt of Alabama. In the township of Mt. Meigs the population is practically all colored. Instruction given in this school is of the kind best suited to the needs of the people for whom it was established. Along with some scholastic training, girls are taught everything pertaining to the management of the home, while boys are taught practical farming, wheelwrighting, blacksmithing, and have some military training. Having started with almost nothing, at the end of eight years the trustees of the school owned nine acres of land and five buildings in which several thousand pupils had received instructions, all through the energy, the courage, and the sacrifice of one little woman.

Up to date, politics have been religiously eschewed by colored women, although questions affecting our legal status as a race is sometimes agitated by the most progressive class. In Louisiana and Tennessee colored women have several times petitioned the legislatures of their respective states to repel the obnoxious Jim Crow Car Laws. Against the Convict Lease System, whose atrocities have been so frequently exposed of late, colored women here and there in the South are waging a ceaseless war. So long as hundreds of their brothers and sisters, many of whom have committed no crime or misdemeanor whatever, are thrown into cells, whose cubic contents are less than those of a good size grave, to be overworked, under-fed, and only partially covered with vermin-infested rags, and so long as children are born to the women in these camps who breathe the polluted atmosphere of these dens of horror and vice from the time they utter their first cry in the world till they are released from their suffering by death, colored women who are working for the emancipation and elevation of their race know where their duty lies. By constant agitation of this painful and hideous subject, they hope to touch the conscience of the country, so that this stain upon its escutcheon shall be forever wiped away.

Alarmed at the rapidity with which the Negro is losing ground in the world of trade, some of the far-sighted women are trying to solve the labor question, so far as it concerns the women at least, by urging the establishment of Schools of Domestic Science wherever means therefor can be secured. Those who are interested in this particular work hope and believe that if colored women and girls are thoroughly trained in domestic service, the boycott which has undoubtedly been placed upon them in many sections of the country will be removed. With so few vocations open to the Negro and with the labor organizations increasingly hostile to him, the future of the boys and girls of the race appears to some of our women very foreboding and dark.

The cause of temperance has been eloquently espoused by two women, each of whom has been appointed National Superintendent of work among colored people by the Woman's Christian Temperance Union. In business, colored women have had signal success. There is in Alabama a large milling and cotton business belonging to and controlled by a colored woman who has sometimes as many as seventy-five men in her employ. Until a few years ago the principal ice plant of Nova Scotia was owned and managed by a colored woman, who sold it for a large amount. In the professions there are dentists and doctors, whose practice is lucrative and large. Ever since a book was published in 1773 entitled "Poems on Various Subjects, Religious and Moral by Phyllis Wheatley, Negro Servant of Mr. John Wheatley," of Boston, colored women have given abundant evidence of literary ability. In sculpture we are represented by a woman upon whose chisel Italy has set her seal of approval; in painting by one of Bougoureau's pupils; and in music by young women holding diplomas from the best conservatories in the land.

In short, to use a thought of the illustrious Frederick Douglass, if judged by the depths from which they have come, rather than by the heights to which those blessed with centuries of opportunities have attained, colored women need not hang their heads in shame. They are slowly but surely making their way up to the heights, wherever they can be scaled. In spite of handicaps and discouragements they are not losing heart. In a variety of ways they are rendering valiant service to their race. Lifting as they climb, onward and upward they go, struggling and striving and hoping that the buds and blossoms of their desires may burst into glorious fruition ere long. Seeking no favors because of their color nor charity because of their needs, they knock at the door of Justice and ask for an equal chance.

Ida Wells-Barnett (1862–1931)

Ida Wells-Barnett, the legendary anti-lynching crusader and militant journalist, was born to slave parents in Holly Springs, Mississippi, and became at age fourteen a teacher in Memphis to support her siblings after the untimely deaths of her parents during the yellow fever epidemic. After being fired from the public schools, she embarked on a journalism career and became editor and part owner of the *Memphis Free Speech* in 1892, the year three of her male friends were lynched. Her painstaking investigative reporting singled her out as the person most responsible at the turn of the century for enlightening the nation and the world about the powerful connection between lynching, patriarchy, racism, and cultural notions of white womanhood and black sexuality. Her inflammatory May 21, 1892, editorial in *Free Speech* suggested that white women voluntarily engaged in interracial sexual unions with black men, which aroused extreme hostility and rage among Southern white men. Wells's debunking of the myths of the chaste Southern white lady, the brute black male rapist, and the immoral black female reveals insightful analyses of the role of sexual and racial politics in constructions of black womanhood and manhood in the United States. A prominent club woman as well, she founded the first black woman suffrage organization, the Alpha Suffrage Club, in Chicago in 1893.

"Lynch Law in America," written in 1900, is a powerful critique of the institutionalized racism and sexism that render African American men and women vulnerable to previously unspeakable acts of violence.

Ida Wells-Barnett }

LYNCH LAW IN AMERICA

Our country's national crime is *lynching*. It is not the creature of an hour, the sudden outburst of uncontrolled fury, or the unspeakable brutality of an insane mob. It represents the cool, calculating deliberation of intelligent people who openly avow that there is an "unwritten law" that justifies them in putting human beings to death without complaint under oath, without trial by jury, without opportunity to make defense, and without right of appeal. The "unwritten law" first found excuse with the rough, rugged, and determined man who left the civilized centers of eastern States to seek for quick returns in the gold fields of the far West. Following in uncertain pursuit of continually eluding fortune, they dared the savagery of the Indians, the hardships of mountain travel, and the constant terror of border state outlaws. Naturally, they felt slight toleration for traitors in their own ranks. It was enough to fight the enemies from without; woe to the foe within! Far removed from and entirely without protection of the courts of civilized life, these fortune-seekers made laws to meet their varying emergencies. The thief who stole a horse, the bully who "jumped" a claim, was a common enemy. If caught he was promptly tried, and if found guilty was hanged to the tree under which the court convened.

Those were busy days of busy men. They had no time to give the prisoner a bill of exception or stay of execution. The only way a man had to secure a stay of execution was to behave himself. Judge Lynch was original in methods but exceedingly effective in procedure. He made the charge, impaneled the jurors, and directed the execution. When the court adjourned, the prisoner was dead. Thus lynch law held sway in the far West until civilization spread into the Territories and the orderly processes of law took its place. The emergency no longer existing, lynching gradually disappeared from the West.

But the spirit of mob procedure seemed to have fastened itself upon the lawless classes, and the grim process that at first was invoked to declare justice was made the excuse to wreak vengeance and cover crime. It next appeared in the South, where centuries of Anglo-Saxon civilization had made effective all the safeguards of court procedure. No emergency called for lynch law. It asserted its sway in defiance of law and in favor of anarchy. There it has flourished ever since, marking the thirty years of its existence with the inhuman butchery of more than ten thousand men, women, and children by shooting, drowning, hanging, and burning them alive. Not only this, but so potent is the force of example that the lynching mania has spread throughout the North and middle West. It is now no uncommon thing to read of lynchings north of Mason and Dixon's line, and those most responsible for this fashion gleefully point to these instances and assert that the North is no better than the South.

This is the work of the "unwritten law" about which so much is said, and in whose behest butchery is made a pastime and national savagery condoned. The first statute of this "unwritten law" was written in the blood of thousands of brave men who thought that a government that was good enough to create a citizenship was strong enough to protect it. Under the authority of a national law that gave every citizen the right to vote, the newly-made citizens chose to exercise their suffrage. But the reign of the national law was short-lived and illusionary. Hardly had the sentences dried upon the statute-books before one Southern State after another raised the cry against "negro domination" and proclaimed there was an "unwritten law" that justified any means to resist it.

The method then inaugurated was the outrages by the "red-shirt" bands of Louisiana, South Carolina, and other Southern States, which were succeeded by the Ku-Klux Klans. These advocates of the "unwritten law" boldly avowed their purpose to intimidate, suppress, and nullify the negro's right to vote. In support of its plans the Ku-Klux Klans, the "red-shirt," and similar organizations proceeded to beat, exile, and kill negroes until the purpose of their organization was accomplished and the supremacy of the "unwritten law" was effected. Thus lynchings began in the South, rapidly spreading into the various States until the national law was nullified and the reign of the "unwritten law" was supreme. Men were taken from their homes by "red-shirt" bands and stripped, beaten, and exiled; others were assassinated when their political prominence made them obnoxious to their political opponents; while the Ku-Klux barbarism of election days, reveling in the butchery of thousands of colored voters, furnished records in Congressional investigations that are a disgrace to civilization.

The alleged menace of universal suffrage having been avoided by the absolute suppression of the negro vote, the spirit of mob murder should have been satisfied and the butchery of negroes should have ceased. But men, women, and children were the victims of murder by individuals and murder by mobs, just as they had been when killed at the demands of the "unwritten law" to prevent "negro domination." Negroes were killed for disputing over terms of contracts with their employers. If a few barns were burned some colored man was killed to stop it. If a colored man resented the imposition of a white man and the two came to blows, the colored man had to die, either at the hands of the white man then and there or later at the hands of a mob that speedily gathered. If he showed a spirit of courageous manhood he was hanged for his pains, and the killing was justified by the declaration that he was a "saucy nigger." Colored women have been murdered because they refused to tell the mobs where relatives could be found for "lynching bees." Boys of fourteen years have been lynched by white representatives of American civilization. In fact, for all kinds of offenses—and for no offenses—from murders to misdemeanors, men and women are put to death without judge or jury; so that, although the political excuse was no longer necessary, the wholesale murder of human beings went on just the same. A new name was given to the killings and a new excuse was invented for so doing.

Again the aid of the "unwritten law" is invoked, and again it comes to the rescue. During the last ten years a new statute has been added to the "unwritten law." This statute proclaims that for certain crimes or alleged crimes no negro shall be allowed a trial; that no white woman shall be compelled to charge an assault under oath or to submit any such charge to the investigation of a court of law. The result is that many men have been put to death whose innocence was afterward established; and to-day, under this reign of the "unwritten law," no colored man, no matter what his reputation, is safe from lynching if a white woman, no matter what her standing or motive, cares to charge him with insult or assault.

It is considered a sufficient excuse and reasonable justification to put a prisoner to death under this "unwritten law" for the frequently repeated charge that these lynching horrors are necessary to prevent crimes against women. The sentiment of the country has been appealed to, in describing the isolated condition of white families in thickly populated negro districts; and the charge is made that these homes are in as great danger as if they were surrounded by wild beasts. And the world has accepted this theory without let or hindrance. In many cases there has been open expression that the fate meted out to the victim was only what he deserved. In many other instances there has been a silence that says more forcibly than words can proclaim it that it is right and proper that a human being should be seized by a mob and burned to death upon the unsworn and the uncorroborated charge of his accuser. No matter that our laws presume every man innocent until he is proved guilty; no matter that it leaves a certain class of individuals completely at the mercy of another class; no matter that it encourages those criminally disposed to blacken their faces and commit any crime in the calendar so long as they can throw suspicion on some negro, as is frequently done, and then lead a mob to take his life; no matter that mobs make a farce of the law and a mockery of justice; no matter that hundreds of boys are being hardened in crime and schooled in vice by the repetition of such scenes before their eyes—if a white woman declares herself insulted or assaulted, some life must pay the penalty, with all the horrors of the Spanish Inquisition and all the barbarism of the Middle Ages. The world looks on and says it is well.

Not only are two hundred men and women put to death annually, on the average, in this country by mobs, but these lives are taken with the greatest publicity. In many instances the leading citizens aid and abet by their presence when they do not participate, and the leading journals inflame the public mind to the lynching point with scare-head articles and offers of rewards. Whenever a burning is advertised to take place, the railroads run excursions, photographs are taken, and the same jubilee is indulged in that characterized the public hangings of one hundred years ago. There is, however, this difference: in those old days the multitude that stood by was permitted only to guy or jeer. The nineteenth-century lynching mob cuts off ears, toes, and fingers, strips off flesh, and distributes portions of the body as souvenirs among the crowd. If the leaders of the mob are so minded, coal-oil is poured over the body and the victim is then roasted to death. This has been done in Texarkana and Paris, Tex., in Bardswell, Ky., and in Newman, Ga. In Paris the officers of the law delivered the prisoner to the mob. The mayor gave the school children a holiday and the railroads ran excursion trains so that the people might see a human being burned to death. In Texarkana, the year before, men and boys amused themselves by cutting off strips of flesh and thrusting knives into their helpless victim. At Newman, Ga., of the present year, the mob tried every conceivable torture to compel the victim to cry out and confess, before they set fire to the faggots that burned him. But their trouble was all in vain—he never uttered a cry, and they could not make him confess.

This condition of affairs were brutal enough and horrible enough if it were true that lynchings occurred only because of the commission of crimes against women—as is constantly declared by ministers, editors, lawyers, teachers, statesmen, and even by women themselves. It has been to the interest of those who did the lynching to blacken the good name of the helpless and defenseless victims of their hate. For this reason they publish at every possible opportunity this excuse for lynching, hoping thereby not only to palliate their own crime but at the same time to prove the negro a moral monster and unworthy of the respect and sympathy of the civilized world. But this alleged reason adds to the deliberate injustice of the mob's work. Instead of lynchings being caused by assaults upon women, the statistics show that not one-third of the victims of lynchings are even charged with such crimes. The Chicago *Tribune*, which publishes annually lynching statistics, is authority for the following:

In 1892, when lynching reached high-water mark, there were 241 persons lynched. Of this number, 160 were of negro descent. Four of them were lynched in New York, Ohio, and Kansas; the remainder were murdered in the South. Five of this number were females. The charges for which they were lynched cover a wide range. They are as follows:

RAPE	46	ATTEMPTED RAPE	11
MURDER	58	SUSPECTED ROBBERY	4
RIOTING	3	LARCENY	1
RACE PREJUDICE	6	SELF-DEFENSE	1
NO CAUSE GIVEN	4	INSULTING WOMEN	2
INCENDIARISM	6	DESPERADOES	6
ROBBERY	6	FRAUD	1
ASSAULT & BATTERY	1	ATTEMPTED MURDER	2
NO OFFENSE STATED, BOY AND GIRL		2	

In the case of the boy and girl above referred to, their father, named Hastings, was accused of the murder of a white man. His fourteen-year-old daughter and sixteen-year-old son were hanged and their bodies filled with bullets; then the father was also lynched. This occurred in November, 1892, at Jonesville, La.

Indeed, the record for the last twenty years shows exactly the same or a smaller proportion who have been charged with this horrible crime. Quite a number of the one-third alleged cases of assault that have been personally investigated by the writer have shown that there was no foundation in fact for the charges; yet the claim is not made that there were no real culprits among them. The negro has been too long associated with the white man not to have copied his vices as well as his virtues. But the negro resents and utterly repudiates the efforts to blacken his good name by asserting that assaults upon women are peculiar to his race. The negro has suffered far more from the commission of this crime against the women of his race by white men than the white race has ever suffered through *his* crimes. Very scant notice is taken of the matter when this is the condition of affairs. What becomes a crime deserving capital punishment when the tables are turned is a matter of small moment when the negro woman is the accusing party.

But since the world has accepted this false and unjust statement; and the burden of proof has been placed upon the negro to vindicate his race. he is taking steps to do so. The Anti-Lynching Bureau of the National Afro-American Council is arranging to have every lynching investigated and publish the facts to the world, as has been done in the case of Sam Hose, who was burned alive last April at Newman, Ga. The detective's report showed that Hose killed Cranford, his employer, in self-defense, and that, while a mob was organizing to hunt Hose to punish him for killing a white man, not till twenty-four hours after the murder was the charge of rape, embellished with psychological and physical impossibilities, circulated. That gave an impetus to the hunt, and the Atlanta *Constitution*'s reward of $500 keyed the mob to the necessary burning and roasting pitch. Of five hundred newspaper clippings of that horrible affair, nine-tenths of them assumed Hose's guilt—simply because his murderers said so, and because it is the fashion to believe the negro peculiarly addicted to this species of crime. All the negro asks is justice—a fair and impartial trial in the courts of the country. That given, he will abide the result.

But this question affects the entire American nation, and from several points of view: First, on the ground of consistency. Our watchword has been "the land of the free and the home of the brave." Brave men do not gather by thousands to torture and murder a single individual, so gagged and bound he cannot make even feeble resistance or defense. Neither do brave men or women stand by and see such things done without compunction of conscience, nor read of them without protest. Our nation has been active and outspoken in its endeavors to right the wrongs of the Armenian Christian, the Russian Jew, and the Irish Home Ruler, the native women of India, the Siberian exile, and the Cuban patriot. Surely it should be the nation's duty to correct its own evils!

Second, on the ground of economy. To those who fail to be convinced from any other point of view touching this momentous question, a consideration of the economic phase might not be amiss. It is generally known that mobs in Louisiana, Colorado, Wyoming, and other States have lynched subjects of other countries. When their different governments demanded satisfaction, our country was forced to confess her inability to protect said subjects in the several States because of our State-rights doctrines, or in turn demand punishment of the lynchers. This confession, while humiliating in the extreme, was not satisfactory; and, while the United States cannot protect, she can pay. This she has done, and it is certain will have to do again in the case of the recent lynching of Italians in Louisiana. The United States already has paid in indemnities for lynching nearly a half million dollars.

Third, for the honor of Anglo-Saxon civilization. No scoffer at our boasted American civilization could say anything more harsh of it than does the American white man himself who says he is unable to protect the honor of his women without resort to such brutal, inhuman, and degrading exhibitions as characterize "lynching bees." No nation, savage or civilized, save only the United States of America, has confessed its inability to protect its women save by hanging, shooting, and burning alleged offenders.

Finally, for love of country. No American travels abroad without blushing for shame for his country on this subject. And whatever the excuse that passes current in the United States, it avails nothing abroad. With all the powers of government in control; with all laws made by white men, administered by white judges, jurors, prosecuting attorneys, and sheriffs; with every office of the executive department filled by white men—no excuse can be offered for exchanging the orderly administration of justice for barbarous lynchings and "unwritten laws." Our country should be placed speedily above the plane of confessing herself a failure at self-government. This cannot be until Americans of every section, of broadest patriotism and best and wisest citizenship, not only see the defect in our country's armor but take the necessary steps to remedy it. Although lynchings have steadily increased in number and barbarity during the last twenty years, there has been no single effort put forth by the many moral and philanthropic forces of the country to put a stop to this wholesale slaughter. Indeed, the silence and seeming condonation grow more marked as the years go by.

A few months ago the conscience of this country was shocked because, after a two-weeks trial, a French judicial tribunal pronounced Captain Dreyfus guilty. And yet, in our own land under our own flag, the writer can give day and detail of one thousand men, women, and children who during the last six years were put to death without trial before any tribunal on earth. Humiliating indeed, but altogether unanswerable, was the reply of the French press to our protest: "Stop your lynchings at home before you send your protests abroad."

CHAPTER TWO

Triumph and Tribulation: Defining Black Womanhood, 1920–1957

... who is more deserving of admiration than the black woman, she who has borne the rigors of slavery, the deprivations consequent on a pauperized race, and the indignities heaped upon a weak and defenseless people. Yet she has suffered all with fortitude, and stands ever ready to help in the onward march to freedom and power. Be not discouraged black women of the world, but push forward, regardless of the lack of appreciation shown you. A race must be saved, a country must be redeemed. . . .

—AMY JACQUES GARVEY, *Negro World*

INTRODUCTION

The period between 1920 and 1960 has frequently been interpreted as the "nadir" of feminist activity. With the passage of the Nineteenth Amendment in 1919, which granted women the right to vote, and the decline of major women's organizations, scholars argue that the feminist movement went into hibernation. Among African American women there is a different narrative. The New Negro Movement, to use Alain Locke's terminology, or the Harlem Renaissance (1917–1935), was characterized by an unprecedented outpouring of black women's creative energies. Zora Neale Hurston's feminist classic *Their Eyes Were Watching God* (1937) underscored the importance of black women's finding their own voices and liberating themselves from narrow conceptions of womanhood. A host of other women writers—Jessie Faucet, Nella Larsen, Angelina Weld Grimké, Georgia Douglas Johnson, Anne Spencer, Alice Dunbar-Nelson, Dorothy West, Gwendolyn Bennett, and Helene Johnson—joined the chorus and made visible the triumphs and tribulations of black women.

Elise Johnson McDougald captured the dualities of the black female experience in 1925—it seemed to have been both the best and worst of times. Professional women lived better lives while the masses of working women struggled to earn a decent living. While World War I had lured thousands of black women away from the kitchens of the South into better jobs in the industrial North, they were still relegated to the most menial, lowest-paying jobs. After the war ended in 1918, unemployment plagued them.

Black women's activism centered around passing a federal anti-lynching bill, unionizing themselves as workers, achieving economic independence, securing birth control, enhancing their educational status, and improving the working condition of domestics. Club women were also concerned about the global plight of women of color and infusing black history into school curricula. Educated women were aware of organized struggles for women's liberation worldwide after World War II and the reawakening of feminism as a rally cry. The publication of Simone de Beauvoir's *The Second Sex* (1949), in which she attempted to define the nature of womanhood, would energize feminists for generations. Her argument that "one is not born, but rather becomes a woman" through cultural conditioning impacted at least one African American feminist, Lorraine Hansberry, who wrote a long analysis which appears here in print for the first time.

The civil rights activism of women in the 1950s such as Anna Arnold Hedgeman, Ella Baker, Septima Clark, Jo Ann Robinson, Modjeska Simkins, and Daisy Bates generated a climate of discontent which anticipated the full-blown and transformative black liberation struggle of the 1960s, out of which emerged the "second-wave" women's movement.

Elise Johnson McDougald

Elise Johnson McDougald, journalist and teacher, wrote about the diverse lives of black women during the Harlem Renaissance in "The Double Task: The Struggle of Women for Sex and Race Emancipation," which appeared in *Survey Graphic,* Alain Locke's magazine, in 1925. Her delineation of four distinct categories of women reveals her sensitivity to class and to the oppression that plagues certain groups. This is also the first essay that names the double burden of racism and sexism that African American women face in the United States, though she indicates that they are more concerned with racial equality. She also discusses sexism within certain black families, and efforts on the part of black women in organizations to achieve racial empowerment despite the many obstacles they face.

Elise Johnson McDougald }

THE STRUGGLE OF NEGRO WOMEN FOR SEX AND RACE EMANCIPATION

Throughout the long years of history, woman has been the weather-vane, the indicator, showing in which direction the wind of destiny blows. Her status and development have augured now calm and stability, now swift currents of progress. What then is to be said of the Negro woman today?

In Harlem, more than anywhere else, the Negro woman is free from the cruder handicaps of primitive household hardships and the grosser forms of sex and race subjugation. Here she has considerable opportunity to measure her powers in the intellectual and industrial fields of the great city. Here the questions naturally arise: "What are her problems?" and "How is she solving them?"

To answer these questions, one must have in mind not any one Negro woman, but rather a colorful pageant of individuals, each differently endowed. Like the red and yellow of the tiger-lily, the skin of one is brilliant against the star-lit darkness of a racial sister. From grace to strength, they vary in infinite degree, with traces of the race's history left in physical and mental outline on each. With a discerning mind, one catches the multiform charm, beauty, and character of Negro women; and grasps the fact that their problem cannot be thought of in mass.

Because only a few have caught this vision, the attitude of mind of most New Yorkers causes the Negro woman serious difficulty. She is conscious that what is left of chivalry is not directed toward her. She realizes that the ideals of beauty, built up in the fine arts, exclude her almost entirely. Instead, the grotesque Aunt Jemimas of the street-car advertisements proclaim only an ability to serve, without grace or loveliness. Nor does the drama catch her finest spirit. She is most often used to provoke the mirthless laugh of ridicule; or to portray feminine viciousness or vulgarity not peculiar to Negroes. This is the shadow over her. To a race naturally sunny comes the twilight of self-doubt and a sense of personal inferiority. It cannot be denied that these are potent and detrimental influences, though not generally recognized because they are in the realm of the mental and spiritual. More apparent are the economic handicaps which follow her recent entrance into industry. It is conceded that she has special difficulties because of the poor working conditions and low wages of her men. It is not surprising that only the determined women forge ahead to results other than mere survival. The few who do prove their mettle stimulate one to a closer study of how this achievement is won in Harlem.

Better to visualize the Negro woman at her job, our vision of a host of individuals must once more resolve itself into groups on the basis of activity. First, comes a very small leisure group—the wives and daughters of men who are in business, in the professions and a few well-paid personal service occupations. Second, a most active and progressive group, the women in business and the professions. Third, the many women in the trades and industry. Fourth, a group weighty in numbers struggling on in domestic service, with an even less fortunate fringe of casual workers, fluctuating with the economic temper of the times.

Negro women are of a race which is free neither economically, socially, nor spiritually. Like women in general, but more particularly like those of other oppressed minorities, the Negro woman has been forced to submit to over-powering conditions. Pressure has been exerted upon her, both from without and within her group. Her emotional and sex life is a reflex of her economic station. The women of the working class will react, emotionally and sexually, similarly to the working-class women of other races. The Negro woman does not maintain any moral standard which may be as-signed chiefly to qualities of race, any more than a white woman does. Yet she has been singled out and advertised as having lower sex standards. Superficial critics who have had contact only with the lower grades of Negro women, claim that they are more immoral than other groups of women. This I deny. This is the sort of criticism which predicates of one race, to its detriment, that which is common to all races. Sex irregularities are not a matter of race, but of socio-economic conditions. Research shows that most of the African tribes from which the Negro sprang have strict codes for sex relations. There is no proof of inherent weakness in the ethnic group.

Gradually overcoming the habitual limits imposed upon her by slave masters, she increasingly seeks legal sanction for the consummation and dissolution of sex contracts. Contrary to popular belief, illegitimacy among Negroes is cause for shame and grief. When economic, social, and biological forces combined bring about unwed motherhood, the reaction is much the same as in families of other racial groups. Secrecy is maintained if possible. Generally the married aunt, or even the mother, claims that the illegitimate child is her own. The foundling asylum is seldom sought. Schooled in this kind of suffering in the days of slavery, Negro women often temper scorn with sympathy for weakness. Stigma does fall upon the unmarried mother, but perhaps in this matter the Negroes' attitude is nearer the modern enlightened ideal for the social treatment of the unfortunate. May this not be considered another contribution to America?

With all these forces at work, true sex equality has not been approximated. The ratio of opportunity in the sex, social, economic, and political spheres is about that which exists between white men and women. In the large, I would say that the Negro woman is the cultural equal of her man because she is generally kept in school longer. Negro boys, like white boys, are usually put to work to subsidize the family income. The growing economic independence of Negro working women is causing her to rebel against the domineering family attitude of the cruder working-class Negro man. The masses of Negro men are engaged in menial occupations throughout the working day. Their baffled and suppressed desires to determine their economic life are manifested in over-bearing domination at home. Working mothers are unable to instill different ideals in their sons. Conditions change slowly. Nevertheless, education and opportunity are modifying the spirit of the younger Negro men. Trained in modern schools of thought, they begin to show a wholesome attitude of fellowship and freedom for their women. The challenge to young Negro womanhood is to see clearly this trend and grasp the preferred comradeship with sincerity. In this matter of sex equality, Negro women have contributed few outstanding militants. Their feminist efforts are directed chiefly toward the realization of the equality of the races, the sex struggle assuming a subordinate place.

Obsessed with difficulties that might well compel individualism, the Negro woman has engaged in a considerable amount of organized action to meet group needs. She has evolved a federation of her clubs, embracing between eight and ten thousand women throughout the state of New York. Its chief function is to crystallize programs, prevent duplication of effort, and to sustain a member organization whose cause might otherwise fail. It is now firmly established, and is about to strive for conspicuous goals. In New York City, one association makes child welfare its name and special concern. Others, like the Utility Club, Utopia Neighborhood, Debutante's League, Sempre Fidelius, etc., raise money for old folks' homes, a shelter for delinquent girls, and fresh air camps for children. The Colored Branch of the Y.W.C.A. and the womens' organizations in the many churches, as well as in the beneficial lodges and associations, care for the needs of their members.

On the other hand, the educational welfare of the coming generation has become the chief concern of the national sororities of Negro college women. The first to be organized in the country, Alpha Kappa Alpha, has a systematized and continuous program of educational and vocational guidance for students of the high schools and colleges. The work of Lambda Chapter, which covers New York City and its suburbs, is outstanding. Its recent campaign gathered together nearly one hundred and fifty such students at a meeting to gain inspiration from the life-stories of successful Negro women in eight fields of endeavor. From the trained nurse, who began in the same schools as they, these girls drank in the tale of her rise to the executive position in the Harlem Health Information Bureau. A commercial artist showed how real talent had overcome the color line. The graduate physician was a living example of the modern opportunities in the newer fields of medicine open to women. The vocations as outlets for the creative instinct became attractive under the persuasion of the musician, the dressmaker, and the decorator. Similarly, Alpha Beta Chapter of the national Delta Sigma Theta Sorority recently devoted a week to work along similar lines. In such ways as these are the progressive and privileged groups of Negro women expressing their community and race consciousness.

We find the Negro woman, figuratively, struck in the face daily by contempt from the world about her. Within her soul, she knows little of peace and happiness. Through it all, she is courageously standing erect, developing within herself the moral strength to rise above and conquer false attitudes. She is maintaining her natural beauty and charm and improving her mind and opportunity. She is measuring up to the needs and demands of her family, community, and race, and radiating from Harlem a hope that is cherished by her sisters in less propitious circumstances throughout the land. The wind of the race's destiny stirs more briskly because of her striving.

Alice Dunbar-Nelson (1875–1935)

Alice Dunbar-Nelson, born in New Orleans, was a teacher, club woman, journalist, and writer, publishing her first book, *Violets and Other Tales,* in 1895. She is perhaps best known as a Harlem Renaissance poet and the wife (briefly) of poet Paul Lawrence Dunbar, with whom she had a stormy relationship. See Andrew Alexander's "The Dunbar Letters: The Tragic Love Affair of One of America's Greatest Poets," *Washington Post Magazine,* 28 June 1981. Dunbar's diary *Give Us Each Day* (1984), edited by literary critic Gloria T. Hull, is one of only two extant diaries by a nineteenth-century black woman and reveals an active black lesbian network, of which she was a part during the 1920s. Active in the black women's club movement and the national political arena, she was, in 1915, secretary of the National Association of Colored Women and field organizer for the Middle Atlantic states in the battle for woman suffrage. In 1920, she was also chair of the League of Colored Republican Women and, in 1922, was head of the Anti-Lynching Crusaders in Delaware, which fought for the passage of the Dyer federal Anti-Lynching Bill.

She wrote numerous short essays for her columns "From a Woman's Point of View" for the Pittsburgh *Courier* in 1926 and "As In a Looking Glass" for the Washington *Eagle* (1926–30). "The Negro Woman and the Ballot" appeared in *The Messenger* in 1927. See Gloria Hull's *Color, Sex and Poetry* for extensive discussions of three Harlem Renaissance writers—Dunbar-Nelson, Angelina Weld Grimké (1880–1956), and Georgia Douglas Johnson (1880–1966).

Alice Dunbar-Nelson }

The Negro Woman and the Ballot

It has been six years since the franchise as a national measure has been granted women. The Negro woman has had the ballot in conjunction with her white sister, and friend and foe alike are asking the question, What has she done with it?

Six years is a very short time in which to ask for results from any measure or condition, no matter how simple. In six years a human being is barely able to make itself intelligible to listeners; is a feeble, puny thing at best, with undeveloped understanding, no power of reasoning, with a slight contributory value to the human race, except in a sentimental fashion. Nations in six years are but the beginnings of an idea. It is barely possible to erect a structure of any permanent value in six years, and only the most ephemeral trees have reached any size in six years.

So perhaps it is hardly fair to ask with a cynic's sneer, What has the Negro woman done with the ballot since she has had it? But, since the question continues to be hurled at the woman, she must needs be nettled into reply.

To those colored women who worked, fought, spoke, sacrificed, traveled, pleaded, wept, cajoled, all but died for the right of suffrage for themselves and their peers, it seemed as if the ballot would be the great objective of life. That with its granting, all the economic, political, and social problems to which the race had been subject would be solved. They did not hesitate to say—those militantly gentle workers for the vote—that with the granting of the ballot the women would step into the dominant place, politically, of the race. That all the mistakes which the men had made would be rectified. The men have sold their birthright for a mess of pottage, said the women. Cheap political office and little political preferment had dazzled their eyes so that they could not see the great issues affecting the race. They had been fooled by specious lies, fair promises and large-sounding works. Pre-election promises had inflated their chests, so that they could not see the post-election failures at their feet.

And thus on and on during all the bitter campaign of votes for women.

One of the strange phases of the situation was the rather violent objection of the Negro man to the Negro woman's having the vote. Just what his objection racially was, he did not say, preferring to hide behind the grandiloquent platitude of his white political boss. He had probably not thought the matter through; if he had, remembering how precious the ballot was to the race, he would have hesitated at withholding its privilege from another one of his own people.

But all that is neither here nor there. The Negro woman got the vote along with some tens of million other women in the country. And has it made any appreciable difference in the status of the race? ... The Negro woman was going to be independent, she had averred. She came into the political game with a clean slate. No Civil War memories for her, and no deadening sense of gratitude to influence her vote. She would vote men and measures, not parties. She could scan each candidate's record and give him her support according to how he had stood in the past on the question of race. She owed no party allegiance. The name of Abraham Lincoln was not synonymous with her for blind G.O.P. allegiance. She would show the Negro man how to make his vote a power, and not a joke. She would break up the tradition that one could tell a black man's politics by the color of his skin.

And when she got the ballot she slipped quietly, safely, easily, and conservatively into the political party of her male relatives.

Which is to say, that with the exception of New York City, and a sporadic break here and there, she became a Republican. Not a conservative one, however. She was virulent and zealous. Prone to stop speaking to her friends who might disagree with her findings on the political issue, and vituperative in campaigns.

In other words the Negro woman has by and large been a disappointment in her handling of the ballot. She has added to the overhead charges of the political machinery, without solving racial problems.

One of two bright lights in the story hearten the reader. In the congressional campaign of 1922 the Negro woman cut adrift from party allegiance and took up the cudgel (if one may mix metaphors) for the cause of the Dyer Bill. The Anti-Lynching Crusaders, led by Mrs. Mary B. Talbot, found in several states—New Jersey, Delaware, and Michigan particularly —that its cause was involved in the congressional election. Sundry gentlemen had voted against the Dyer Bill in the House and had come up for re-election. They were properly castigated by being kept at home. The women's votes unquestionably had the deciding influence in the three states mentioned, and the campaign conducted by them was of a most commendable kind.

School bond issues here and there have been decided by the colored woman's votes—but so slight is the ripple on the smooth surface of conservatism that it has attracted no attention from the deadly monotony of the blind faith in the "Party of Massa Linkun."

As the younger generation becomes of age it is apt to be independent in thought and in act. But it is soon whipped into line by the elders, and by the promise of plums of preferment or of an amicable position in the community or of easy social relations—for we still persecute socially those who disagree with us politically. What is true of the men is true of the women. The very young is apt to let father, sweetheart, brother, or uncle decide her vote....

Whether women have been influenced and corrupted by their male relatives and friends is a moot question. Were I to judge by my personal experience I would say unquestionably so. I mean a personal experience with some hundreds of women in the North Atlantic, Middle Atlantic, and Middle Western States. High ideals are laughed at, and women confess with drooping wings how they have been scoffed at for working for nothing, for voting for nothing, for supporting a candidate before having first been "seen." In the face of this sinister influence it is difficult to see how the Negro woman could have been anything else but "just another vote."

All this is rather a gloomy presentment of a well-known situation. But it is not altogether hopeless. The fact that the Negro woman CAN be roused when something near and dear to her is touched and threatened is cheering. Then she throws off the influence of her male companion and strikes out for herself. Whatever the Negro may hope to gain for himself must be won at the ballot box, and quiet "going along" will never gain his end. When the Negro woman finds that the future of her children lies in her own hands—if she can be made to see this—she will strike off the political shackles she has allowed to be hung upon her, and win the economic freedom of her race.

Perhaps some Joan of Arc will lead the way.

Amy Jacques Garvey (1896–1973)

Ula Taylor

Amy Jacques Garvey, the second wife of Marcus Mosiah Garvey, the charismatic leader of the Universal Negro Improvement Association (UNIA), participated directly in the struggle to achieve the organization's goal—self-determination for black people around the world based on the doctrines of Pan-Africanism.

As a political activist, Amy Garvey is well-known for assisting and promoting her husband. However, equally important was Amy's call for black women to participate in the "race first" movement. Amy Garvey's woman's page, "Our Women and What They Think," published in the *Negro World,* the UNIA's weekly propaganda newspaper, promoted the notion that it was essential for black women to develop a political consciousness to "uplift" the race and ultimately "redeem" Africa.

Amy Garvey's editorials remind readers that she was not divorced from the historical legacy of the 1890s black club women. In fact, Amy helped to renew their feminist philosophies in the 1920s, adding to this body of thought the concept of black nationalism.

As had her predecessors, Amy Garvey advocated that black women be given every opportunity to develop intellectually. The educated woman was better equipped to raise productive children and negotiate her domestic environment and the public arena. Amy Garvey differed from the Progressive Era activists, however, because she urged black women to cultivate their womanhood not for integration into the mainstream but for a nationalist platform focused on the needs of the race.

Amy Garvey understood that a nationalist agenda required a general understanding of world affairs, particularly the activities of women whose statuses varied tremendously. Her writings covered a range of issues, reflecting her belief that it was essential for black women to place their

---

Ula Taylor is assistant professor in the Department of African American Studies at the University of California at Berkeley and wrote a dissertation entitled "The Veiled Garvey: The Life and Times of Amy Jacques Garvey."

activism in a global context. While Amy's editorials were diverse, her efforts to advance a feminist agenda were relentless. Her editorials challenged patriarchal privilege and the notion that women are intellectually inferior to men. She advocated that black women work in partnership with men in the worldwide liberation struggle. But, when it appeared that black men's political stance, or lack thereof, stifled the advancement of the race, she urged women to assume leadership roles.

In all of her editorials, Amy Garvey demonstrated not only her commitment to the Garvey philosophy, but also her belief that there were many ways that one could and should be active within one's communities. Her editorials are undeniably feminist in their emphasis on empowering women and expanding their roles and options in the world.

Amy Jacques Garvey }

Our Women Getting into the Larger Life

The worldwide movement for the enlargement of woman's sphere of usefulness is one of the most remarkable of the ages. In all countries and in all ages, men have arrogated to themselves the prerogative of regulating not only the domestic, but also the civic and economic life of women. In many countries, women were subject entirely to the whims and legislation of men. It is that way now in most Asiatic countries and among some of the tribes in Africa.

The recent upheaval in Turkey has carried with it condemnation of harem relations and the sanction of the family life as it has developed in Christian countries. Madam Kemal is the leader of the Turkish women for larger freedom in the ordering of their lives, but the innovation, which is bound to work for the betterment of men as well as women as the harem life is a blight on womanhood which degrades manhood as well, could only have been accomplished by the separation of Church and State, the Sultanate and the Caliphate, which amounts to negating the hitherto predominating influence of the Mohammedan religion in the affairs of State as of Church. However far the innovation will extend to other Moslem countries, and what influence, if any, it will have on the domestic life of the people of Asia and Africa, where the Mohammedan religion is strong, remains to be seen.

In Europe, average womanhood has been held at a very low valuation until it got into the recently developed currents of modern innovation, and the average still remains low, peasant life for the man and the woman and their children being of the lowest and hardest. Only in Great Britain has the movement for the larger and better life for women, by allowing them reasonable voice in making and enforcing the laws, made any appreciable headway.

The United States has gone further than any other nation in giving woman a share in making and enforcing the laws and in regulating her economic life to her advantage and not entirely to the advantage of man.

She is now given an equal part in political matters, and she is allowed a freedom in earning and controlling her earnings, which is a great improvement upon the former of old things. In social and personal matters, the American woman has attained to an independence and freedom which it will take centuries for the women of other nations to attain to.

Negro women of the United States share equally in the larger life which has come to women of other race groups, and she has met every test in the home, in bread winning, in church and social upbuilding, in charitable uplift work, and in the school room which could have been expected of her reasonably. She has yet to develop as active an interest in political affairs as the women of other race groups, but she is bound to grow in this as in other matters in which her interests are involved.

The women of the Universal Negro Improvement Association have shown an interest and a helpfulness so far-flung as to make it doubtful if the organization could have reached the high point of strength and effectiveness it has without them. To take woman and her sympathies and work out of the association would be like taking the wife out of the home of the husband. The women of the association are a tower of strength. They know it and glory in the fact, and their men are proud of them, and justly. The success of the Negro race thus far has been largely due to the sympathy and support which our women have given to the cause.

Our women are getting into the larger life, which has the womanhood of the world in its sweep. We are sure they will be equal to all of the demands made upon them in the future as in the past, and the demands are going to increase in volume and importance as we go along. It stands to reason.

Amy Jacques Garvey }

WOMEN AS LEADERS

The exigencies of this present age require that women take their places beside their men. White women are rallying all their forces and uniting regardless of national boundaries to save their race from destruction, and preserve its ideals for posterity.... White men have begun to realize that as women are the backbone of the home, so can they, by their economic experience and their aptitude for details, participate effectively in guiding the destiny of nation and race.

No line of endeavor remains closed for long to the modern woman. She agitates for equal opportunities and gets them; she makes good on the job and gains the respect of men who heretofore opposed her. She prefers to be a bread-winner than a half-starved wife at home. She is not afraid of hard work, and by being independent she gets more out of the present-day husband than her grandmother did in the good old days.

The women of the East, both yellow and black, are slowly but surely imitating the women of the Western world, and as the white women are bolstering up a decaying white civilization, even so women of the darker races are sallying forth to help their men establish a civilization according to their own standards, and to strive for world leadership.

Women of all climes and races have as great a part to play in the development of their particular group as the men. Some readers may not agree with us on this issue, but do they not mould the minds of their children the future men and women? Even before birth a mother can so direct her thoughts and conduct as to bring into the world either a genius or an idiot. Imagine the early years of contact between mother and child, when she directs his form of speech, and is responsible for his conduct and deportment. Many a man has risen from the depths of poverty and obscurity and made his mark in life because of the advices and councils of a good mother whose influence guided his footsteps throughout his life.

Women therefore are extending this holy influence outside the realms of the home, softening the ills of the world by their gracious and kindly contact.

Some men may argue that the home will be broken up and women will become coarse and lose their gentle appeal. We do not think so, because everything can be done with moderation. . . . The doll-baby type of woman is a thing of the past, and the wide-awake woman is forging ahead prepared for all emergencies, and ready to answer any call, even if it be to face the cannons on the battlefield.

New York has a woman Secretary of State. Two States have women Governors, and we would not be surprised if within the next ten years a woman graces the White House in Washington, D.C. Women are also filling diplomatic positions, and from time immemorial women have been used as spies to get information for their country.

White women have greater opportunities to display their ability because of the standing of both races, and due to the fact that black men are less appreciative of their women than white men. The former will more readily sing the praises of white women than their own; yet who is more deserving of admiration than the black woman, she who has borne the rigors of slavery, the deprivations consequent on a pauperized race, and the indignities heaped upon a weak and defenseless people? Yet she has suffered all with fortitude, and stands ever ready to help in the onward march to freedom and power.

Be not discouraged black women of the world, but push forward, regardless of the lack of appreciation shown you. A race must be saved, a country must be redeemed, and unless you strengthen the leadership of vacillating Negro men, we will remain marking time until the Yellow race gains leadership of the world, and we be forced to subserviency under them, or extermination.

We are tired of hearing Negro men say, "There is a better day coming," while they do nothing to usher in the day. We are becoming so impatient that we are getting in the front ranks, and serve notice on the world that we will brush aside the halting, cowardly Negro men, and with prayer on our lips and arms prepared for any fray, we will press on and on until victory is over.

Africa must be for Africans, and Negroes everywhere must be independent, God being our guide. Mr. Black man, watch your step! Ethiopia's queens will reign again, and her Amazons protect her shores and people. Strengthen your shaking knees, and move forward, or we will displace you and lead on to victory and to glory.

Sadie Tanner Mossell Alexander
(1898–1989)

Sadie Mossell Alexander, born in Philadelphia, was the granddaughter of Benjamin Tanner, editor of the *Christian Recorder* (1868–84) and founding editor of the *A.M.E. Church Review* (1884–88). She was the first African American to receive a doctorate in economics (University of Pennsylvania, 1921), but because of racism and sexism found it difficult to secure a suitable job upon graduation, so she worked as an actuary at North Carolina Mutual Life Insurance Company in Durham, North Carolina (1921–23). In 1927, after becoming the first African American to graduate from the University of Pennsylvania Law School, she joined a private law firm and became the first black woman to practice law in the state of Pennsylvania. "Negro Women in Our Economic Life," which appeared in *Opportunity* in 1930, discusses the economic plight of black women in the United States during the 1920s and 1930s.

Sadie T. M. Alexander }

Negro Women in Our Economic Life

Not even a cursory study of Negro women in our economic life can be assumed without first considering the changing position of all women in our economic life. One hears frequently the woman of today referred to as "the new woman," much as we write and speak of "the new Negro." In my opinion there is no more a new woman among us than there is a new Negro. What has changed and what is changing is not the woman. The change is in her status in a rapidly developing social order. The advent of the mechanical age, historically referred to as the Industrial Revolution, roughly marks the passing of one social and economic order and the dawn of another that is still in the process of unfolding its undetermined course. Under the old social and economic order, the family was the economic unit of production. Under these conditions the activities of women were recognized along with those of men as productive and the contribution of the wife was as valuable in the eyes of society as that of the husband. There was no difference in the economic function between men and women, in that they were jointly producers and consumers. But when, one after another, the traditional family activities were taken out of the home, the function of women in the home steadily lost its importance in production until it fell to a minimum, and emerged associated primarily with consumption. Production in the new economic order, where standards of value are money standards, became fundamentally a matter of creating a commodity or service which demands a money price. Modern industrial processes, having robbed the home of every vestige of its former economic function, left in the home to be performed by the woman only those services which are as "valueless" and "priceless" as air and water but not recognized as *valuable* in a price economy, where standards of value are money standards.

If, then, women were to answer the challenge of the new economy and place themselves again among the producers of the world, they must change their status from that of home makers to that of industrial workers and change their activities from valueless home duties to those that resulted in the production of goods that have a price-value. The answer of women to the challenge is shown by the increase in the number of women gainfully employed from 1,321,364 in 1870, when we first had census figures in which gainfully employed persons were separated by sex, to 7,306,844 in 1920.

We are principally interested in determining the extent to which Negro women have taken their places in this price economy and the effect, if any, their presence has had on our economic life. Work for wages has always been more widespread among Negro than among white women. In 1910, 54.7% of the 3,680,536 Negro women in the United States, ten years of age and over, were gainfully occupied while only 19.6% of the 30,769,641 white women of the same age group were gainfully employed. In 1920, 38.9% of the 4,043,763 Negro women, ten years of age and over, were gainfully employed as compared with 16.1% of the 36,279,013 white women of the same age group. The Negro women in 1910 were, however, principally confined to agricultural pursuits, domestic, and personal service. Only 67,937 Negro women, or 3.4% of the Negro women ten years of age and over gainfully employed, were among the 1,821,570 women employed in manufacture and mechanical industries; white women workers, on the other hand, during the same decade, came into the business and industrial world at a greater proportionate rate than even men. It was not until the Great War withdrew the men from industry that Negro women were found in any considerable numbers in manufacturing and mechanical industries. The 1920 Census shows that 104,983 Negro women, or 6.7% of the Negro women ten years of age and over gainfully employed, were among the 1,930,241 women employed in manufacturing and mechanical industries. This is an increase of almost 100% for Negro women in comparison to an increase of less than 1% of all women so employed.

There is no question but that this unprecedented increase in the number of Negro women in industry was due to demand for labor, because of the stress of war production and the reduction of available industrial labor supply resulting from the cessation of immigration and the withdrawal of 3,000,000 men from normal economic functions to war activities. That these women have been retained to a large degree is established by surveys made since 1920, principally in 1921, 1922, 1925, by the Women's Bureau of the United States Department of Labor. Their survey of Negro women employed in fifteen states, published in 1929, based on the study made in 1928, reports 17,134 Negro women employed in 682 establishments; an increase of nearly 1,000 over the 16,835 Negro women reported employed in the same industries in a similar survey published in 1922.

The wages of all women in industry have been found to be below that of men. It is not surprising, therefore, to find that the wages of Negro women, who are the marginal workers, should be not only lower than that of men employed in like pursuits, but also lower than that of white women. Any group that constitutes the marginal supply of labor will be paid less for their labor than those whose services are in constant and steady demand. Then, too, the labor turn-over among women is greater than that among men, due largely to family duties, physical handicaps, but principally to the fact that women do not consider their jobs as permanent. They have not developed a philosophy of work under which they regard the production of price-demanding commodities as their life work. They are constantly expecting when the children get out of the way, or their husbands obtain better jobs, that they will then stop work. The thought of working the rest of their lives is a foreign concept and never enters their minds. Hence, women are slow to organize in unions and men are slower to accept them. The Negro woman in addition has little if any factory training and therefore no factory sense. She must accept such opening wedges at such return as may be offered her.

Not only are the wages of Negro women lower than those of white women, but Negro women as a whole are confined to the simpler types of work, and are not engaged in highly skilled labor, although many of the occupations in which Negro women are found require care and a number require some skill. This, too, might be expected; for the industrial history of any highly organized community will show, that as members of a new and inexperienced nationality, sex, or race arrive at the doors of its industries, the occupations that open to them ordinarily are those vacated by an earlier stratum of workers who have moved on to more alluring places. All industrial workers, regardless of their racial identification, have started at the bottom of the round. The important thing is *the start*.

Although Negro women are not engaged as skilled, high priced workers, their presence in large numbers in industry during the past decade has had a marked effect on their status and on the economic life of the country.

To begin with, in the natural process of events in industry, the Negro women must eventually push on to more skilled, better paying jobs. Any other procedure would mean a waste of training, factory sense, and accumulated knowledge which the economies of big business must recognize.

Furthermore, the opportunity for participation in industrial pursuits by Negro women means a raising of the standard of living not only of Negro families but of all American families. The addition of this labor supply aids cheaper production, which in turn means more goods can be enjoyed by a large number of people. In a more direct sense it affects the Negro family, since another wage earner is added to the family. The derogatory effects of the mother being out of the home are over balanced by the increased family income, which makes possible the securing of at least the necessities of life and perhaps a few luxuries. If her services in the home are to be rated by the man as valueless consumption, the satisfaction which comes to the woman in realizing that she is a producer makes for peace and happiness, the chief requisites in any home.

The increased leisure that is enjoyed by women who have entered the industrial and manufacturing enterprises is giving rise to an improved educational and social standard among Negro women. Not many weeks ago, I was consulted by a colored woman sixty-two years of age, who had fallen in an unguarded, open manhole. Upon inquiry I learned that she and her witness were operators of machines in a dress factory and that they worked from 8:00 in the morning until 4:00 in the afternoon; that on the evening of the accident they were returning from night school where they had gone for a seven o'clock class to learn to be dress cutters, which would place them considerably higher up the wage scale. This is a typical example of the opportunity for economic and social advancement which the shorter hours enjoyed by industrial workers are making possible for Negro women who have industrial positions. Furthermore, the dignity of being a factory worker has resulted in Negro women thus engaged feeling a greater degree of self-respect and receiving opportunities for social intercourse and expression that as domestic servants were denied them.

The association between the various racial groups employed in a factory will prove an important factor in solving the laborer's problems. The real seat of racial friction is between the working groups, whose resistance to change in the economic status of a competing group invariably expresses itself in what we commonly define as race, or class prejudice. Could the great mass of white workers learn from industrial experience with Negro workers that they have a common purpose in life, the protection of their bargaining power, and that the sooner the untouched wealth of Negro labor is harnessed into this common purpose, the better can they bargain with capital; then and only then would industrial racial friction subside. Certainly the continued presence of Negro women in industry demonstrates that we have made progress toward reducing the resistance of white labor to Negro invasion of industry.

Surveying the field as a whole, we find over 100,000 Negro women employed in the manufacturing and mechanical industries of the United States in 1920, an increase of nearly 100% in the number so employed in 1910. This is a striking contrast to an increase of only 1/10 of 1% in all women so engaged during the decade. Without this additional labor supply it is doubtful that even scientific management could have carried mass production to such a degree that we should have had a period so marked in the magnitude of its productivity as to be called the "New Industrial Revolution." Within the two decades, during which Negro women have entered industry in large numbers, production has increased at such a rapid rate that economists have been forced to chance their theory of a deficit economy, based on the assumption that population would always press upon food supply, to a theory of surplus economy. While the labor of Negro women cannot be held as the efficient cause of the mass production, it is submitted that without this available labor supply, at a low price, mass production in many industries would not have been undertaken.

Negro families as well as all families have profited and suffered from the effects of a surplus economy. Mass productivity has multiplied the number and variety of stimuli which play upon the individual, resulting in not only high speed consumption but diversified consumption. The result is that individual interests and standards of conduct are conceived in terms of self-satisfaction without a stabilizing sense of group-responsibility. The Negro, the furthest down in the economic scale can least of all afford to succumb to these varied economic stimuli. If he is going to profit from the increased purchasing power, which the presence of Negro women in the productive enterprises has made possible, he must lead the way in harnessing the variety of his demands to the purchase of commodities representing the fundamental and durable satisfaction of life. Only in this way can we hope to promote the establishment of factors of stability in economic demand which will materially provide the basis of an economic balance in industry; which in turn will assure not only the continued presence of Negro women in industry, but stability of employment and constantly improving economic position for *all* workers.

Florynce "Flo" Kennedy (1916–   )

Flo Kennedy, born in Kansas City, Missouri, is an outspoken attorney, civil rights activist, and one of the few Black feminists in the radical wing of the women's movement at the beginning. She organized the Feminist Party (1971) which supported Shirley Chisholm's candidacy for President in 1972. A founding member of the National Organization for Women (NOW) in 1966 (she attended its first meeting in New York), she quickly became frustrated by its lukewarm positions, establishment orientation, and absence of a radical vision. She indicated in her autobiography, *Color Me Flo* (1976) that she "saw the importance of a feminist movement, and stayed in there because I wanted to do anything I could to keep it alive, but when I saw how retarded NOW was, I thought, 'My God, who needs this?'" (62). In 1968, she protested with Radical Women (organized in 1967 in New York) at the Atlantic City Miss America pageant during which feminists were labeled "bra burners," and in 1971 at the Coat Hanger Farewell Protest, a speak-out for abortion rights at St. Patrick's Cathedral. She was also a founder of the National Black Feminist Organization (NBFO) and delivered one of the keynote addresses at their first conference in New York City in 1975. In 1976 she coauthored with Diane Schulter one of the first books on abortion, *Abortion Rap,* which described the class action suit she filed to test New York's abortion laws. In her autobiography, *Color Me Flo,* she discusses the negative responses of black nationalist organizations to the New York law legalizing abortion in 1970, which was reminiscent of the 1967 Black Power Conference in Newark which argued that birth control and abortion were genocidal, a position with which she strongly disagrees.

Kennedy's early feminist consciousness is apparent in an undergraduate paper written for a sociology class at Columbia University in 1946 in which she analyzes links between institutionalized racism and sexism. The essay was included in her autobiography, *Color Me Flo: My Hard Life and Good Times* (1976).

Florynce Kennedy }

A COMPARATIVE STUDY:
ACCENTUATING THE SIMILARITIES OF
THE SOCIETAL POSITION OF WOMEN
AND NEGROES

The similarities of the societal positions of women and Negroes are fundamental rather than superficial. The obvious differences are accentuated by the fact that women are supposed to occupy a privileged position. No such pretense is usually made where the Negro is concerned, but a dispassionate consideration of the economic, sociological, historical, psychological, political, and even physiological aspects reveals some rather startling parallels.

The majority of both groups are generally dependent economically upon the dominant group. Great lengths are attained to insure these dependencies. The necessity for an F.E.P.C. (Fair Employment Practices Committee) in a "Democracy," and support clauses in divorce codes, which according to Hobhouse existed in pre-Christian societies, and which Monica Hunter, Naomi M. Griffen, Ruth Benedict, and Cora Du Bois refer to in their accounts of various primitive societies, may be accepted as proof of the excessive abuses prevalent.

More than any other aspect of culture, the economic factor determines cultural development and direction. The political and social implications of this fact are infinite. It is therefore of primary importance to examine carefully the means by which women as a group and Negroes as a group are rendered *hors de combat* by being deprived of economic equality and independence. The far-reaching effects of their economic incompetencies leave not the minutest detail of their lives unaffected.

Women and Negroes are less apt to be hired and more apt to be fired than a similarly equipped member of the currently dominant group. Exceptions are made for extraordinary competence or during emergencies such as wartime or political revolutions. Both women and Negroes command lower wages, and are usually confined to lower-bracket positions.

In times of economic stress working women and Negroes arouse the resentment of those of the dominant group who are unemployed. Thus a returned serviceman may be especially upset to find his job occupied by a woman or Negro. Without entering into a which-came-first-the-chicken-or-the-egg argument, it seems sufficient to point out that rivalry for jobs provides a source of serious friction.

Industry frequently adds insult to injury by exploiting the subordinate group to lower wage scales or break strikes. A dual purpose is served, since this divide-and-rule technique further alienates society from those women or Negroes thus exploited. It goes without saying that the disdain is directed not at the employer but at the tool.

Both groups are barred from many specialized fields. Prestige of a position tends to decline upon their entrance. The withholding of training and education precludes development of potentialities. Exclusion from intimate situations where powerful combines are made places a definite barrier in their path. Even those women or Negroes who have attained some prominence in a preferential field are only tolerated in exclusive clubs, at banquets, or on golf courses with equally distinguished members of the dominant group. In the isolated instance where such chummy relationships prevail, the adoption of patronage and subtle condescension saves the day for the dominants.

The preeminence of those exceptional among the weaker group is paradoxically viewed. Many conflicting theories and realizations are encountered: "Determination will win"..."The majority (e.g., of women or Negroes) are inferior; these are the exceptions that prove the rule"... (bosh)..."This woman has a masculine mind"...or..."This Negro has white blood"...what "Negro" hasn't?..."Women are getting all the best jobs"..."Negroes are 'taking over' the theatre"...

This magnifying of hard-won advancement makes it seem that a weak gnarled tree that pushes through the concrete in Brooklyn is a threat to miles of centuries-old forests which have flourished in fertile lands where the best of expert care has been lavished.

How are subordinate groups kept in subordination? Is their suppression a reflection of the will of all of the dominants? Do those who are submerged struggle to reach the level of their "betters"? If not, why not? How, if at all, are the submerged groups rewarded? How punished? Why do not the "superiors" crush them entirely? Women are much loved; Negroes are generally ignored, distrusted, pitied, or even disliked; do not these differences make any attempt to draw parallels seem a bit ridiculous?...

The psychological implications are vastly important in any consideration of personal-social relationships. The geographical, temperamental, financial, political, social, psychological, physiological, and historical are but a few of the most abstract factors which enter into every formula. For example: a customer is asking for a pound of butter...Alabama or New York? ...Humbly or peremptorily?...Mink coat or Union Square special?... New Deal and O.P.A. or Republicans and "free enterprise"?...Does the butcher read *P.M.* or the *Daily News?* Is he young or old? . . . a Coughlin-Bilbo fan or Henry Wallace devotee? . . . All generalizations ignore these variables. . . .

Social sanctions take many forms. There are written laws governing franchise, property, political participation, and legal articulation. Social legislation reflects the comparative insignificance of women and Negroes. Educational budgets and medical care for Negroes or women have long been unequal. In housing, Negro districts are invariably slumlike. The kitchen where the average housewife spends the majority of her time is often the least spacious, attractive, comfortable, or even practical room of the house. Overwork is the lot of most of the members of the subordinate groups. When their health suffers due to this insanitary environment, their poor health immediately becomes the "reason" for their exclusion from desirable endeavor or choice programs. . . .

The unwritten laws are often more convenient and certainly more difficult to combat. Some are rational; most are nonrational or irrational. Many paradoxes and inconsistencies exist. There are great discrepancies between theory and practice.

Nonsupport cases belie the exaltation of motherhood so often heard. Societal penalties and punishments are more severe for sex "transgressions" by women or Negroes. Both are regarded as evil and dangerous. The Christian and other religious influences, and the white southerner, are but two sources from which such ideas have come. Overemphasis of the potency of women and Negroes in personal-societal relations serves to place an almost insurmountable barrier between these groups whenever it is advantageous. Sex taboos do not prevent miscegenation, but usually guarantee secrecy and therefore minimize the possibilities for legalized union and familial solidarity. There's no denying that sex drives are frequently far more democratic than contemporary societal pretense.

Paradoxically, criminal action by women or Negroes may be approached with extraordinary leniency; depending upon the offense, a paternal we-don't-expect-much-of-you attitude is frequently encountered. A Negro who cohabits with a white southern woman is almost certainly doomed to die; a Negro who kills another Negro in a brawl may be rescued by his white employer. In rare conformance with the theory that they are the weaker sex, women may receive preferential treatment in criminal courts.

Indeed, so numerous are the devices employed to delineate and emphasize the desired role that it is difficult to account for the many digressions that exist. Fiction and nonfiction, movies (with silly Billy Burke and groveling Ingrid Bergman, shuffling Stepin Fetchit, and Mammy Louise Beavers as "typical" women and Negroes), radio, drama, myths and legends, gossip and rumor, implication and innuendo leave little to the average imagination as to what is acceptable to "society."

A passive woman or Negro is presented with a ready-made role. Choice may be made from a wide range of conceptualizations which are considered ideal and/or average. Individual distinctions are minimized. Accomplishment outside circumscribed areas is discouraged.

Clothing is designed to accentuate the societal roles which have been chosen for the weaker group. Any concerted attempted to emulate or imitate the dominant group in dress is frowned upon—or laughed at. Women in slacks or a well-dressed Negro in a small southern town may be subjected to numerous embarrassments.

Religious participation is encouraged. Futile, blind alley endeavor is sponsored. Docility, forbearance, reticence, faithfulness, blind loyalty, silent suffering, acceptance of the *status quo,* and recognition of the divine right of the dominants are dramatized and applauded by society. Eager for status, the subordinate group accepts the role assigned by the powers-that-be. *Hence comes the irony.*

The subordinates become the enthusiastic sponsors of the campaign for their own suppression!

Endless complexity results from the fact that the majority of a subordinate group, though rejecting the ignominious position, will accept and popularize the devices through which the suppression is maintained. . . .

Thus, the longer the history of an inferior position, the greater the necessity for a break with tradition. Little effort is required by either group to further the submergence of those chosen, once religion and the prescribed pattern are accepted. The program becomes self-perpetuating. The desire to be identified with the dominant group results in the least significant of the societal underlings becoming the unpaid guardians and champions of their exploiters' theories.

Rewards for conformance are spurious or superficial. Security and independence for the entire group are never expected or offered without a death struggle. The inevitability of the societal position is accepted by many of the most militant opposers to inequality.

Reforms are usually much too little and centuries too late. Reforms are at best not the result of intellectual conviction but of emotional effort. The recognitions of rights are considered concessions; sentimental reasons are offered to explain long-overdue justices. Progress results from struggle. Little fundamental change can be cited. Superficial progress has been merely a shifting of emphasis rather than an alteration of balance. Progress has seemed to some extent related to societal advancement.

Women and Negroes are but two of hundreds of groups within groups which occupy subordinate positions.

Foremost authorities to the contrary notwithstanding, I am convinced that the glorification—without qualification—of family life militates against the achievement of full equality for women. It would be interesting to see how many marriages would result without the church, *True Stories,* Myrna Loy, sex myths, and the *Ladies' Home Journal.* It would be more interesting to see how many monogamous marriages would endure if polygamy were legalized and popularized, and children's support were guaranteed by the states.

If women weren't coaxed and lured from industry and professions by societal cupids, those who are unsuited to marriage and breeding could direct their energies into other channels. Without pleading a case for a doctrine of individualism, it would seem that a recognition of the infinite variations among women and Negroes will lessen the occurrence of the every-girl-should-marry, women's-place-is-in-the-home philosophy as well as the more diabolical but no less effective keep-the-Negro-in-his-place attitude. Few societies at any cultural level provide for an acceptance of an independent life for large numbers of unmarried women. Emancipation for women and Negroes would seem to be contingent upon the emancipation of societal thought. This is, of course, question-begging at its worst, since there remains to be solved the problem of how to revolutionize the theories and thinking of "civilized" society.

If a study of this type has any value, it lies in the possible counteraction to the divide-and-rule technique which minority dominants invariably employ. Recognition of the similarity of their position can hasten the formation of alliances to combat the forces which advocate the suppression of many for the aggrandizement of the few.

The continuation of conscious or unconscious subordination of one group by another will hasten the coarsening of the moral fibre of society. Psychological maladjustments result from the difficulty of reconciling pretense with practice. Personal-social behavior is cramped when societal sanctions and taboos are at too great variance with logic and humanitarian proclivities.

Societal impoverishment inevitably results form policies of discrimination, segregation, and limitation. That such policies are absolutely necessary disproves the much-publicized contention that women and/or Negroes are "naturally" inferior. Bitterness and societal unrest arise out of attempts to exclude women and Negroes from full participation in societal endeavor.

No amount of segregation separates one unit of society from society as a whole. Thus, general societal health is ever contingent upon the health of its least significant member.

Exclusivistic tendencies deprive society of innumerable skills and contributions. The dissatisfied minorities within the subordinate groups provide an ever-present threat to societal peace. Need it again be necessary to call the attention of those who defend the *status quo* to the fact that it has never been a question of whether or not a subordinate group is capable of self-rule and equal right, but rather whether or not any group is worthy of the right to dominance and autocracy?

Claudia Jones (1915–1965)

Claudia Jones, born in Trinidad, migrated to Harlem in 1924, dropped out of school for a factory job following the premature death of her garment worker mother, and at age eighteen joined the Young Communist League. By 1940, she had become chair of their national council and a decade later was found guilty of being a Communist. Indicted in 1951 for violating the Smith Act, which forbade the teaching of Marxism, she was imprisoned in 1955 in the Federal Reformatory for Women and was deported to London, where she continued to struggle for radical causes. She wrote an essay prior to her legal problems entitled "An End to the Neglect of the Problems of Negro Women," which appeared in *Political Affairs* (1949) and chronicled the racist history of black women in the United States. Analyzing the situation of black women from a Marxist perspective, Jones calls for greater militancy on their parts since they remain the most oppressed class in the population. Like other radical activists, Jones has been invisible in black and women's history, which motivated her daughter, Buzz Johnson, to tell her mother's story (*"I Think of My Mother,"* 1985), particularly her struggles on behalf of black women burdened by racism, sexism, and poverty. Jones has been one of the few role models for contemporary black women who embrace socialism or communism, such as Angela Davis and Frances Beale.

Claudia Jones }

AN END TO THE NEGLECT OF THE PROBLEMS OF THE NEGRO WOMAN!

An outstanding feature of the present stage of the Negro liberation movement is the growth in the militant participation of Negro women in all aspects of the struggle for peace, civil rights, and economic security. Symptomatic of this new militancy is the fact that Negro women have become symbols of many present-day struggles of the Negro people This growth of militancy among Negro women has profound meaning, both for the Negro liberation movement and for the emerging anti-fascist, anti-imperialist coalition.

To understand this militancy correctly, to deepen and extend the role of Negro women in the struggle for peace and for all interests of the working class and the Negro people, means primarily to overcome the gross neglect of the special problems of Negro women. This neglect has too long permeated the ranks of the labor movement generally, of Left-progressives, and also of the Communist Party. The most serious assessment of these shortcomings by progressives, especially by Marxist-Leninists, is vitally necessary if we are to help accelerate this development and integrate Negro women in the progressive and labor movement and in our own Party.

The bourgeoisie is fearful of the militancy of the Negro woman, and for good reason. The capitalists know, far better than many progressives seem to know, that once Negro women undertake action, the militancy of the whole Negro people, and thus of the anti-imperialist coalition, is greatly enhanced.

Historically, the Negro woman has been the guardian, the protector, of the Negro family. From the days of the slave traders down to the present, the Negro woman has had the responsibility of caring for the needs of the family, of militantly shielding it from the blows of Jim-Crow insults, of rearing children in an atmosphere of lynch terror, segregation, and police brutality, and of fighting for an education for the children. The intensified oppression of the Negro people, which has been the hallmark of the post-war reactionary offensive, cannot therefore but lead to an acceleration of the militancy of the Negro woman. As mother, as Negro, and as worker, the Negro woman fights against the wiping out of the Negro family, against the Jim-Crow ghetto existence which destroys the health, morale, and very life of millions of her sisters, brothers, and children.

Viewed in this light, it is not accidental that the American bourgeoisie has intensified its oppression, not only of the Negro people in general, but of Negro women in particular. Nothing so exposes the drive to fascization in the nation as the callous attitude which the bourgeoisie displays and cultivates toward Negro women. The vaunted boast of the ideologist of Big Business that American women possess "the greatest equality" in the world is exposed in all its hypocrisy when one sees that in many parts of the world, particularly in the Soviet Union, the New Democracies, and the formerly oppressed land of China, women are attaining new heights of equality. But above all else, Wall Street's boast stops at the water's edge where Negro and working class women are concerned. Not equality, but degradation and super exploitation: this is the actual lot of Negro women!

Consider the hypocrisy of the Truman Administration, which boasts about "exporting democracy throughout the world" while the state of Georgia keeps a widowed Negro mother of twelve children under lock and key. Her crime? She defended her life and dignity—aided by her two sons —from the attacks of a "white supremacist." Or ponder the mute silence with which the Department of Justice has greeted Mrs. Amy Mallard, widowed Negro school teacher, since her husband was lynched in Georgia because he had bought a new Cadillac and become, in the opinion of the "white supremacists," "too uppity." Contrast this with the crocodile tears shed by the U.S. delegation to the United Nations for Cardinal Mindszenty, who collaborated with the enemies of the Hungarian People's Republic and sought to hinder the forward march to fuller democracy by the formerly oppressed workers and peasants of Hungary. Only recently, President Truman spoke solicitously in a Mother's Day Proclamation about the manifestation of "our love and reverence" for all mothers of the land. The so-called "love and reverence" for the mothers of the land by no means includes Negro mothers who, like Rosa Lee Ingram, Amy Mallard, the wives and mothers of the Trenton Six, or the other countless victims, dare to fight back against lynch law and "white supremacy" violence.

ECONOMIC HARDSHIPS

Very much to the contrary, Negro women—as workers, as Negroes, and as women—are the most oppressed stratum of the whole population.

In 1940, two out of every five Negro women, in contrast to two out of every eight white women, worked for a living. By virtue of their majority status among the Negro people, Negro women not only constitute the largest percentage of women heads of families, but are the main breadwinners of the Negro family. The large proportion of Negro women in the labor market is primarily a result of the low-scale earnings of Negro men. This disproportion also has its roots in the treatment and position of Negro women over the centuries.

Following emancipation, and persisting to the present day, a large percentage of Negro women—married as well as single—were forced to work for a living. But despite the shift in employment of Negro women from rural to urban areas, Negro women are still generally confined to the lowest-paying jobs. The Women's Bureau, U.S. Department of Labor, *Handbook of Facts for Women Workers* (1948, Bulletin 225), shows white women workers as having median earnings more than twice as high as those of non-white women, and non-white women workers (mainly Negro women) as earning less than $500 a year! In the rural South, the earnings of women are even less. In three large Northern industrial communities, the median income of white families ($1,720) is almost sixty percent higher than that of Negro families ($1,095). The super-exploitation of the Negro woman worker is thus revealed not only in that she receives, as woman, less than equal pay for equal work with men, but in that the majority of Negro women get less than half the pay of white women. Little wonder, then, that in Negro communities the conditions of ghetto-living—low salaries, high rents, high prices, etc.—virtually become an iron curtain hemming in the lives of Negro children and undermining their health and spirit! Little wonder that the maternity death rate for Negro women is triple that of white women! Little wonder that one out of every ten Negro children born in the United States does not grow to manhood or womanhood!

The low scale of earnings of the Negro woman is directly related to her almost complete exclusion from virtually all fields of work except the most menial and underpaid, namely, domestic service. Revealing are the following data given in the report of 1945, *Negro Women War Workers* (Women's Bureau, U.S. Department of Labor, Bulletin 205): Of a total seven and a half million Negro women, over a million are in domestic and personal service. The overwhelming bulk—about 918,000—of these women workers are employed in private families, and some 98,000 are employed as cooks, waitresses, and in like services in other than private homes. The remaining 60,000 workers in service trades are in miscellaneous personal service occupations (beauticians, boarding house and lodging-house keepers, charwomen, janitors, practical nurses, housekeepers, hostesses, and elevator operators).

The next largest number of Negro women workers are engaged in agricultural work. In 1940, about 245,000 were agricultural workers. Of them, some 128,000 were unpaid family workers.

Industrial and other workers numbered more than 96,000 of the Negro women reported. Thirty-six thousand of these women were in manufacturing, the chief groups being 11,300 in apparel and other fabricated textile products, 11,000 in tobacco manufactures, and 5,600 in food and related products.

Clerical and kindred workers in general numbered only 13,000. There were only 8,300 Negro women workers in civil service.

The rest of the Negro women who work for a living were distributed along the following lines: teachers, 50,000; nurses and student nurses, 6,700; social and welfare workers, 1,700; dentists, pharmacists, and veterinarians, 120; physicians and surgeons, 129; actresses, 200; authors, editors, and reporters, 100; lawyers and judges, 39; librarians, 400; and other categories likewise illustrating the large-scale exclusion of Negro women from the professions.

During the anti-Axis war, Negro women for the first time in history had an opportunity to utilize their skills and talents in occupations other than domestic and personal service. They became trail blazers in many fields. Since the end of the war, however, this has given way to growing unemployment, to the wholesale firing of Negro women, particularly in basic industry.

This process has been intensified with the development of the economic crisis. Today, Negro women are being forced back into domestic work in great numbers. In New York State, for example, this trend was officially confirmed recently when Edward Corsi, Commissioner of the State Labor Department, revealed that for the first time since the war, domestic help is readily obtainable. Corsi in effect admitted that Negro women are not voluntarily giving up jobs, but rather are being systematically pushed out of industry. Unemployment, which has always hit the Negro woman first and hardest, plus the high cost of living, is what compels Negro women to re-enter domestic service today. Accompanying this trend is an ideological campaign to make domestic work palatable. Daily newspaper advertisements which base their arguments on the claim that most domestic workers who apply for jobs through U.S.E.S. [United States Employment Service] "prefer this type of work to work in industry," are propagandizing the "virtues" of domestic work, especially of "sleep-in positions."

Inherently connected with the question of job opportunities where the Negro woman is concerned, is the special oppression she faces as Negro, as woman, and as worker. She is the victim of the white chauvinist stereotype as to where her place should be. In the film, radio, and press, the Negro woman is not pictured in her real role as breadwinner, mother, and protector of the family, but as a traditional "mammy" who puts the care of children and families of others above her own. This traditional stereotype of the Negro slave mother, which to this day appears in commercial advertisements, must be combatted and rejected as a device of the imperialists to perpetuate the white chauvinist ideology that Negro women are "backward," "inferior," and the "natural slaves" of others.

HISTORICAL ASPECTS

Actually, the history of the Negro woman shows that the Negro mother under slavery held a key position and played a dominant role in her own family grouping. This was due primarily to two factors: the conditions of slavery, under which marriage, as such, was non-existent, and the Negro's social status was derived from the mother and not the father; and the fact that most of the Negro people brought to these shores by the slave traders came from West Africa where the position of women, based on active participation in property control, was relatively higher in the family than that of European women.

Early historians of the slave trade recall the testimony of travelers indicating that the love of the African mother for her child was unsurpassed in any part of the world. There are numerous stories attesting to the self-sacrificial way in which East African mothers offered themselves to the slave traders in order to save their sons, and Hottentot women refused food during famines until after their children were fed.

It is impossible within the confines of this article to relate the terrible sufferings and degradation undergone by Negro mothers and Negro women generally under slavery. Subject to legalized rape by the slaveowners, confined to slave pens, forced to march for eight to fourteen hours with loads on their backs and to perform back-breaking work even during pregnancy, Negro women bore a burning hatred for slavery, and undertook a large share of the responsibility for defending and nurturing the Negro family.

The Negro mother was mistress in the slave cabin, and despite the interference of master or overseer, her wishes in regard to mating and in family matters were paramount. During and after slavery, Negro women had to support themselves and the children. Necessarily playing an important role in the economic and social life of her people, the Negro woman became schooled in self-reliance, in courageous and selfless action.*

There is documentary material of great interest which shows that Negro family life and the social and political consciousness of Negro men and women underwent important changes after emancipation. One freedman observed, during the Civil War, that many men were exceedingly jealous

---

* Today, in the rural sections of the South, especially on the remnants of the old plantations, one finds households where old grandmothers rule their daughters, sons, and grand-children with a matriarchal authority.

of their newly acquired authority in family relations and insisted upon a recognition of their superiority over women. After the Civil War, the slave rows were broken up and the tenant houses scattered all over the plantation in order that each family might carry on an independent existence. The new economic arrangement, the change in the mode of production, placed the Negro man in a position of authority in relation to his family. Purchase of homesteads also helped strengthen the authority of the male.

Thus, a former slave, who began life as a freedman on a "one-horse" farm, with his wife working as a laundress, but who later rented land and hired two men, recalls the pride which he felt because of his new status: "In my humble palace on a hill in the woods beneath the shade of towering pines and sturdy oaks, I felt as a king whose supreme commands were 'law and gospel' to my subjects."

One must see that a double motive was operative here. In regard to his wife and children, the Negro man was now enabled to assume economic and other authority over the family; but he also could fight against violation of women of his group where formerly he was powerless to interfere.

The founding of the Negro church, which from the outset was under the domination of men, also tended to confirm the man's authority in the family. Sanction for male ascendancy was found in the Bible, which for many was the highest authority in such matters.

Through these and other methods, the subordination of Negro women developed. In a few cases, instead of legally emancipating his wife and children, the husband permitted them to continue in their status of slaves. In many cases, state laws forbade a slave emancipated after a certain date to remain in the state. Therefore, the only way for many Negro wives and children to remain in the state was to become "enslaved" to their relatives. Many Negro owners of slaves were really relatives of their slaves.

In some cases, Negro women refused to become subject to the authority of the men. In defiance of the decisions of their husbands to live on the places of their former masters, many Negro women took their children and moved elsewhere.

NEGRO WOMEN IN MASS ORGANIZATIONS

This brief picture of some of the aspects of the history of the Negro woman, seen in the additional light of the fact that a high proportion of Negro women are obliged today to earn all or part of the bread of the family, helps us understand why Negro women play a most active part in the economic, social, and political life of the Negro community today. Approximately 2,500,000 Negro women are organized in social, political, and fraternal clubs and organizations. The most prominent of their organizations are the National Association of Negro women, the National Council of Negro

Women, the National Federation of Women's Clubs, the Women's Division of the Elks' Civil Liberties Committee, the National Association of Colored Beauticians, National Negro Business Women's League, and the National Association of Colored Graduate Nurses. Of these, the National Association of Negro Women, with 75,000 members, is the largest membership organization. There are numerous sororities, church women's committees of all denominations, as well as organizations among women of West Indian descent. In some areas, N.A.A.C.P. chapters have Women's Divisions, and recently the National Urban League established a Women's Division for the first time in history.

Negro women are the real active forces—the organizers and workers —in all the institutions and organizations of the Negro people. These organizations play a many-sided role, concerning themselves with all questions pertaining to the economic, political, and social life of the Negro people, and particularly of the Negro family. Many of these organizations are intimately concerned with the problems of Negro youth, in the form of providing and administering educational scholarships, giving assistance to schools and other institutions, and offering community service. The fight for higher education in order to break down Jim Crow in higher institutions, was symbolized last year, by the brilliant Negro woman student, Ada Louis Sipuel Fisher of Oklahoma. The disdainful attitudes which are sometimes expressed—that Negro women's organizations concern themselves *only* with "charity" work—must be exposed as of chauvinist derivation, however subtle, because while the same could be said of many organizations of white women, such attitudes fail to recognize the *special character* of the role of Negro women's organizations. This approach fails to recognize the special function which Negro women play in these organizations, which, over and above their particular function, seek to provide social services denied to Negro youth as a result of the Jim-Crow lynch system in the U.S.

THE NEGRO WOMAN WORKER

The negligible participation of Negro women in progressive and trade-union circles is thus all the more startling. In union after union, even in those unions where a large concentration of workers are Negro women, few Negro women are to be found as leaders or active workers. The outstanding exceptions to this are the Food and Tobacco Workers' Union and the United Office and Professional Workers' Union.

But why should these be exceptions? Negro women are among the most militant trade unionists. The sharecroppers' strikes of the '30s were sparkplugged by Negro women. Subject to the terror of the landlord and white supremacist, they waged magnificent battles together with Negro men and white progressives in that struggle of great tradition led by the Communist Party. Negro women played a magnificent part in the pre-C.I.O. days in strikes and other struggles, both as workers and as wives of workers, to win recognition of the principle of industrial unionism, in such industries as auto, packing, steel, etc. More recently, the militancy of Negro women unionists is shown in the strike of the packinghouse workers, and even more so, in the tobacco workers' strike—in which such leaders as Moranda Smith and Velma Hopkins emerged as outstanding trade unionists. The struggle of the tobacco workers led by Negro women later merged with the political action of Negro and white which led to the election of the first Negro in the South (in Winston-Salem, N.C.) since Reconstruction days.

It is incumbent on progressive unionists to realize that in the fight for equal rights for Negro workers, it is necessary to have a special approach to Negro women workers, who, far out of proportion to other women workers, are the main breadwinners in their families. The fight to retain the Negro woman in industry and to upgrade her on the job, is a major way of struggling for the basic and special interests of the Negro woman worker. Not to recognize this feature is to miss the special aspects of the effects of the growing economic crisis, which is penalizing Negro workers, particularly Negro women workers, with special severity.

THE DOMESTIC WORKER

One of the crassest manifestations of trade union neglect of the problems of the Negro woman worker has been the failure, not only to fight against relegation of the Negro woman to domestic and similar menial work, but to *organize* the domestic worker. It is merely lip-service for progressive unionists to speak of organizing the unorganized without turning their eyes to the serious plight of the domestic worker, who, unprotected by union standards, is also the victim of exclusion from all social and labor legislation. Only about one in ten of all Negro women workers is covered by present minimum-wage legislation, although about one-fourth of all such workers are to be found in states having minimum-wage laws. All of the arguments heretofore projected with regard to the real difficulties of organizing the domestic workers—such as the "casual" nature of their employment, the difficulties of organizing day workers, the problem of organizing people who work in individual households, etc.—must be overcome forthwith. There is a danger that Social-Democratic forces may enter this field to do their work of spreading disunity and demagogy, unless progressives act quickly.

The lot of the domestic worker is one of unbearable misery. Usually, she has no definition of tasks in the household where she works. Domestic workers may have "thrown in," in addition to cleaning and scrubbing, such tasks as washing windows, caring for the children, laundering, cooking, etc., and all at the lowest pay. The Negro domestic worker must suffer the additional indignity, in some areas, of having to seek work in virtual "slave markets" on the streets where bids are made, as from a slave block, for the hardiest workers. Many a domestic worker, on returning to her own household, must begin housework anew to keep her own family together.

Who was not enraged when it was revealed in California, in the heinous case of Dora Jones, that a Negro woman domestic was enslaved for more than forty years in "civilized" America? Her "employer" was given a minimum sentence of a few years and complained that the sentence was for "such a long period of time." But could Dora Jones, Negro domestic worker, be repaid for more than forty years of her life under such conditions of exploitation and degradation? And how many cases, partaking in varying degrees of the condition of Dora Jones, are still tolerated by progressives themselves!

Only recently, in the New York State Legislature, legislative proposals were made to "fingerprint" domestic workers. The Martinez Bill did not see the light of day, because the reactionaries were concentrating on other repressive legislative measures; but here we see clearly the imprint of the African "pass" system of British imperialism (and of the German Reich in relation to the Jewish people!) being attempted in relation to women domestic workers.

It is incumbent on the trade unions to assist the Domestic Workers' Union in every possible way to accomplish the task of organizing the exploited domestic workers, the majority of whom are Negro women. Simultaneously, a legislative fight for the inclusion of domestic workers under the benefits of the Social Security Law is vitally urgent and necessary. Here, too, recurrent questions regarding "administrative problems" of applying the law to domestic workers should be challenged and solutions found.

The continued relegation of Negro women to domestic work has helped to perpetuate and intensify chauvinism directed against all Negro women. Despite the fact that Negro women may be grandmothers or mothers, the use of the chauvinist term "girl" for adult Negro women is a common expression. The very economic relationship of Negro women to white women, which perpetuates "madam-maid" relationships, feeds chauvinist attitudes and makes it incumbent on white women progressives, and particularly Communists, to fight consciously against all manifestations of white chauvinism, open and subtle.

Chauvinism on the part of progressive white women is often expressed in their failure to have close ties of friendship with Negro women and to realize that this fight for equality of Negro women is in their own self-interest, inasmuch as the superexploitation and oppression of Negro women tends to depress the standards of all women. Too many progressives, and even some Communists, are still guilty of exploiting Negro domestic workers, of refusing to hire them through the Domestic Workers' Union (or of refusing to help in its expansion into those areas where it does not yet exist), and generally of participating in the vilification of "maids" when speaking to their bourgeois neighbors and their own families. Then, there is the expressed "concern" that the exploited Negro domestic worker does not "talk" to, or is not "friendly" with, her employer, or the habit of assuming that the duty of the white progressive employer is to "inform" the Negro woman of her exploitation and her oppression which she undoubtedly knows quite intimately. Persistent challenge to every chauvinist remark as concerns the Negro woman is vitally necessary, if we are to break down the understandable distrust on the part of Negro women who are repelled by the white chauvinism they often find expressed in progressive circles.

MANIFESTATIONS OF WHITE CHAUVINISM

Some of the crassest expressions of chauvinism are to be found at social affairs, where, all too often, white men and women and Negro men participate in dancing, but Negro women are neglected. The acceptance of white ruling-class standards of "desirability" for women (such as light skin), the failure to extend courtesy to Negro women and to integrate Negro women into organizational leadership, are other forms of chauvinism.

Another rabid aspect of the Jim-Crow oppression of the Negro woman is expressed in the numerous laws which are directed against her as regards property rights, inter-marriage (originally designed to prevent white men in the South from marrying Negro women)—and laws which hinder and deny the right of choice, not only to Negro women, but Negro and white men and women.

For white progressive women and men, and especially for Communists, the question of social relations with Negro men and women is above all a question of strictly adhering to social equality. This means ridding ourselves of the position which sometimes finds certain progressives and Communists fighting on the economic and political issues facing the Negro people, but "drawing the line" when it comes to social intercourse or inter-marriage. To place the question as a "personal" and not a political matter, when such questions arise, is to be guilty of the worst kind of Social-Democratic, bourgeois-liberal thinking as regards the Negro question in American life; it is to be guilty of imbibing the poisonous white-chauvinist "theories" of a Bilbo or a Rankin. Similarly, too, with regard to guaranteeing the "security" of children. This security will be enhanced only through the struggle for the liberation and equality of all nations and peoples, and not by shielding children from the knowledge of this struggle. This means ridding ourselves of the bourgeois-liberal attitudes which "permit" Negro and white children of progressives to play together at camps when young, but draw the line when the children reach teen-age and establish boy-girl relationships.

The bourgeois ideologists have not failed, of course, to develop a special ideological offensive aimed at degrading Negro women, as part and parcel of the general reactionary ideological offensive against women of "kitchen, church, and children." They cannot, however, with equanimity or credibility, speak of the Negro woman's "place" as in the home; for Negro women are in other peoples' kitchens. Hence, their task has been to intensify their theories of male "superiority" as regards the Negro woman by developing introspective attitudes which coincide with the "new school" of "psychological inferiority" of women. The whole intent of a host of articles, books, etc., has been to obscure the main responsibility for the oppression of Negro women by spreading the rotten bourgeois notion about a "battle of the sexes" and "ignoring" the fight of both Negro men and women—the whole Negro people—against their common oppressors, the white ruling class.

Chauvinist expressions also include paternalistic surprise when it is learned that Negroes are professional people. Negro professional women-workers are often confronted with such remarks as "Isn't your family proud of you?" Then, there is the reverse practice of inquiring of Negro women professionals whether "someone in the family" would like to take a job as a domestic worker.

The responsibility for overcoming these special forms of white chauvinism rests, not with the "subjectivity" of Negro women, as it is often put, but squarely on the shoulders of white men and white women. Negro men have a special responsibility particularly in relation to rooting out attitudes of male superiority as regards women in general. There is need to root out all "humanitarian" and patronizing attitudes toward Negro women. In one community, a leading Negro trade unionist, the treasurer of her Party section, would be told by a white progressive woman after every social function: "Let me have the money; something may happen to you." In another instance, a Negro domestic worker who wanted to join the Party was told by her employer, a Communist, that she was "too backward" and "wasn't ready" to join the Party. In yet another community, which since the war has been populated in the proportion of sixty percent Negro to forty percent white, white progressive mothers maneuvered to get their children out of the school in this community. To the credit of the initiative of the Party section organizer, a Negro woman, a struggle was begun which forced a change in arrangements which the school principal, yielding to the mothers' and to his own prejudices, had established. These arrangements involved a special class in which a few white children were isolated with "selected Negro kids" in what was termed an "experimental class in race relations."

These chauvinist attitudes, particularly as expressed toward the Negro woman, are undoubtedly an important reason for the grossly insufficient participation of Negro women in progressive organizations and in our Party as members and leaders.

The American bourgeoisie, we must remember, is aware of the present and even greater potential role of the masses of Negro women, and is therefore not loathe to throw plums to Negroes who betray their people and do the bidding of imperialism.

Faced with the exposure of their callous attitude to Negro women, faced with the growing protests against unpunished lynching and the legal lynchings "Northern style," Wall Street is giving a few token positions to Negro women. Thus, Anna Arnold Hedgeman, who played a key role in the Democratic National Negro Committee to Elect Truman, was rewarded with the appointment as Assistant to Federal Security Administrator Ewing. Thus, too, Governor Dewey appointed Irene Diggs to a high post in the New York State Administration.

Another straw in the wind showing attempts to whittle down the militancy of Negro women was the State Department's invitation to a representative of the National Council of Negro Women—the only Negro organization so designated—to witness the signing of the Atlantic Pact.

KEY ISSUES OF STRUGGLE

There are many key issues facing Negro women around which struggles can and must be waged.

But none so dramatizes the oppressed status of Negro womanhood as does the case of Rosa Lee Ingram, widowed Negro mother of fourteen children—two of them dead—who faces life imprisonment in a Georgia jail for the "crime" of defending herself from the indecent advances of a "white supremacist." The Ingram case illustrates the landless, Jim-Crow, oppressed status of the Negro family in America. It illumines particularly the degradation of Negro women today under American bourgeois democracy moving to fascism and war. It reflects the daily insults to which Negro women are subjected in public places, no matter what their class, status, or position. It exposes the hypocritical alibi of the lynchers of Negro manhood who have historically hidden behind the skirts of white women when they try to cover up their foul crimes with the "chivalry" of "protecting white womanhood." But white women, today, no less than their sisters in the abolitionist and suffrage movements, must rise to challenge this lie and the whole system of Negro oppression.

American history is rich in examples of the cost—to the democratic rights of both women and men—of failure to wage this fight. The suffragists, during their first jailings, were purposely placed on cots next to Negro prostitutes to "humiliate" them. They had the wisdom to understand that the intent was to make it so painful, that no woman would dare to fight for her rights if she had to face such consequences. But it was the historic shortcoming of the women's suffrage leaders, predominantly drawn as they were from the bourgeoisie and the petty-bourgeoisie, that they failed to link their own struggles to the struggles for the full democratic rights of the Negro people following emancipation.

A developing consciousness on the woman question today, therefore, must not fail to recognize that the Negro question in the United States is *prior* to, and not equal to, the woman question; that only to the extent that we fight all chauvinist expressions and actions as regards the Negro people and fight for the full equality of the Negro people, can women as a whole advance their struggle for equal rights. For the progressive women's movement, the Negro woman, who combines in her status the worker, the Negro, and the woman, is the vital link to this heightened political consciousness. To the extent, further, that the cause of the Negro woman worker is promoted, she will be enabled to take her rightful place in the Negro proletarian leadership of the national liberation movement, and by her active participation contribute to the entire American working class, whose historic mission is the achievement of a Socialist America—the final and full guarantee of woman's emancipation.

The fight for Rosa Lee Ingram's freedom is a challenge to all white women and to all progressive forces, who must begin to ask themselves: How long shall we allow this dastardly crime against all womenhood, against the Negro people, to go unchallenged! Rosa Lee Ingram's plight and that of her sisters also carries with it a challenge to progressive cultural workers to write and sing of the Negro woman in her full courage and dignity.

The recent establishment of the National Committee to Free the Ingram Family fulfills a need long felt since the early movement which forced commutation to life imprisonment of Mrs. Ingram's original sentence of execution. This National Committee, headed by Mary Church Terrell, a founder of the National Association of Colored Women, includes among its leaders such prominent women, Negro and white, as Therese Robinson, National Grand Directoress of the Civil Liberties Committee of the Elks, Ada B. Jackson, and Dr. Gene Weltfish.

One of the first steps of the Committee was the visit of a delegation of Negro and white citizens to this courageous, militant Negro mother imprisoned in a Georgia cell. The measure of support was so great that the Georgia authorities allowed the delegation to see her unimpeded. Since that time, however, in retaliation against the developing mass movement, the Georgia officials have moved Mrs. Ingram, who is suffering from a severe heart condition, to a worse penitentiary, at Reedsville.

Support to the work of this committee becomes a prime necessity for all progressives, particularly women. President Truman must be stripped of his pretense of "know-nothing" about the Ingram case. To free the Ingrams, support must be rallied for the success of the million-signatures campaign, and for U.N. action on the Ingram brief soon to be filed.

The struggle for jobs for Negro women is a prime issue. The growing economic crisis, with its mounting unemployment and wage-cuts and increasing evictions, is making its impact felt most heavily on the Negro masses. In one Negro community after another, Negro women, the last to be hired and the first to be fired, are the greatest sufferers from unemployment. Struggles must be developed to win jobs for Negro women in basic industry, in the white-collar occupations, in the communities, and in private utilities.

The successful campaign of the Communist Party in New York's East Side to win jobs for Negro women in the five-and-dime stores has led to the hiring of Negro women throughout the city, even in predominantly white communities. This campaign has extended to New England and must be waged elsewhere.

Close to fifteen government agencies do not hire Negroes at all. This policy gives official sanction to, and at the same time further encourages, the pervasive Jim-Crow policies of the capitalist exploiters. A campaign to win jobs for Negro women here would thus greatly advance the whole struggle for jobs for Negro men and women. In addition, it would have a telling effect in exposing the hypocrisy of the Truman Administration's "Civil Rights" program.

A strong fight will also have to be made against the growing practice of the United States Employment Service to shunt Negro women, despite their qualifications for other jobs, only into domestic and personal service work.

Where consciousness of the special role of Negro women exists, successful struggle can be initiated which will win the support of white workers. A recent example was the initiative taken by white Communist garment workers in a shop employing twenty-five Negro women where three machanics were idle. The issue of upgrading Negro women workers became a vital one. A boycott movement has been initiated and the machines stand unused as of this writing, the white workers refusing to adhere to strict seniority at the expense of Negro workers. Meanwhile, negotiations are continuing on this issue. Similarly, in a Packard U.A.W. local in Detroit, a fight for the maintenance of women in industry and for the upgrading of 750 women, the large majority of whom were Negro, was recently won.

THE STRUGGLE FOR PEACE

Winning the Negro women for the struggle for peace is decisive for all other struggles. Even during the anti-Axis war, Negro women had to weep for their soldier-sons, lynched while serving in a Jim-Crow army. Are they, therefore, not interested in the struggle for peace?

The efforts of the bipartisan war-makers to gain the support of the women's organizations in general, have influenced many Negro women's organizations, which, at their last annual conventions, adopted foreign-policy stands favoring the Marshall Plan and Truman Doctrine. Many of these organizations have worked with groups having outspoken anti-imperialist positions.

That there is profound peace sentiment among Negro women which can be mobilized for effective action is shown, not only in the magnificent response to the meetings of Eslande Goode Robeson, but also in the position announced last year by the oldest Negro women's organization, under the leadership of Mrs. Christine C. Smith, in urging a national mobilization of American Negro women in support of the United Nations. In this connection, it will be very fruitful to bring to our country a consciousness of the magnificent struggles of women in North Africa, who, though lacking in the most elementary material needs, have organized a strong movement for peace and thus stand united against a Third World War, with 81 million women in 57 nations, in the Women's International Democratic Federation.

Our Party, based on its Marxist-Leninist principles, stands foursquare on a program of full economic, political, and social equality for the Negro people and of equal rights for women. Who, more than the Negro woman, the most exploited and oppressed, belongs in our Party? Negro women can and must make an enormous contribution to the daily life and work of the Party. Concretely, this means prime responsibility lies with white men and women comrades. Negro men comrades, however, must participate in this task. Negro Communist women must everywhere now take their rightful place in Party leadership on all levels.

The strong capacities, militancy, and organizational talents of Negro women, can, if well utilized by our Party, be a powerful lever for bringing forward Negro workers—men and women—as the leading forces of the Negro people's liberation movement, for cementing Negro and white unity in the struggle against Wall Street imperialism, and for rooting the Party among the most exploited and oppressed sections of the working class and its allies.

In our Party clubs, we must conduct an intensive discussion of the role of the Negro women, so as to equip our Party membership with clear understanding for undertaking the necessary struggles in the shops and communities. We must end the practice, in which many Negro women who join our Party, and who, in their churches, communities, and fraternal groups are leaders of masses, with an invaluable mass experience to give to our Party, suddenly find themselves viewed in our clubs, not as leaders, but as people who have "to get their feet wet" organizationally. We must end this failure to create an atmosphere in our clubs in which new recruits—in this case Negro women—are confronted with the "silent treatment" or with attempts to "blueprint" them into a pattern. In addition to the white chauvinist implications in such approaches, these practices confuse the basic need for Marxist-Leninist understanding which our Party gives to all work-ers, and which enhances their political understanding, with chauvinist dis-dain for the organizational talents of new Negro members, or for the necessity to promote them into leadership.

To win the Negro women for full participation in the anti-fascist, anti-imperialist coalition, to bring her militancy and participation to even greater heights in the current and future struggles against Wall Street imperialism, progressives must acquire political consciousness as regards her special oppressed status.

It is this consciousness, accelerated by struggles, that will convince in-creasing thousands that only the Communist Party, as the vanguard of the working class, with its ultimate perspective of Socialism, can achieve for the Negro women—for the entire Negro people— the full equality and dignity of their stature in a Socialist society in which contributions to society are measured, not by national origin, or by color, but a society in which men and women contribute according to ability, and ultimately under Communism receive according to their needs.

Lorraine Hansberry (1930–1965)

Margaret B. Wilkerson

Lorraine Hansberry is best known for her prize-winning play, *A Raisin in the Sun,* which won the New York Drama Critics Circle Award in 1959, when she was only twenty-eight years old. The play, which captured the spirit of the Civil Rights movement, thrust her into the limelight as an articulate, talented writer frequently sought for interviews and commentary on theatre as well as the black struggle. When she died six years later at the age of thirty-four, she left behind a grieving public and a number of manuscripts and unfinished writing projects. During the next three decades, her literary executor and former husband, the late Robert Nemiroff, edited and released some of these works, among them: *To Be Young, Gifted and Black: Lorraine Hansberry in Her Own Words,* a compilation of her writings which toured as a stage production, was produced as a film, and was published in book form; excerpts from *All the Dark and Beautiful Warriors,* a semiautobiographical novel by Hansberry; several revised editions and production of *A Raisin in the Sun;* three of her plays—*Les Blancs, The Drinking Gourd,* and *What Use Are Flowers;* and other essays and poems. Jewell Nemiroff, current literary executor of the Hansberry estate, has continued his practice by releasing for publication other works, such as the original screenplay of *A Raisin in the Sun* and this unfinished essay.

"Simone de Beauvoir and *The Second Sex:* An American Commentary" is one of Hansberry's most revealing works. While the roles of the female characters in many of her published plays suggest her feminist views, they are frequently limited by the social constructions of the times in which they were first written or presented. For example, the women in *A Raisin in the Sun* and *The Sign in Sidney Brustein's Window* (the only plays produced during Hansberry's lifetime) are cast in fairly traditional roles of homemaker, domestic, or prostitute—the exception being Beneatha, the college student who aspires to be a physician and who is modeled on Hansberry at

Margaret B. Wilkerson is the former Chair of Black Studies at the University of California at Berkeley and is completing a biography of Lorraine Hansberry.

age twenty. They form the conventional circle of support for the male protagonists. At the same time, these women are ill at ease with or rebel against their circumscribed roles, although their resistance is not the central focus of the works; they are ultimately instrumental in the male protagonists' self-realization. Hansberry's feminist views are subtly expressed in these plays, a perception that has led feminist critics to wonder why Hansberry, a strong advocate for women's liberation, did not create a female protagonist in her major plays, and why in the case of two of her plays, she changed the protagonist from female to male.

While this essay does not fully answer such questions, it does give significant insight into Hansberry's views on the status of women. Hansberry read Simone de Beauvoir's ground-breaking book, *The Second Sex,* in 1953 or 1954, shortly after the English translation was released in the United States. She had just married Robert Nemiroff the year before and was beginning to pursue a writing career, having spent several years as associate editor of *Freedom,* Paul Robeson's newspaper. Revealing in this essay the effect of Beauvoir's work on her thinking, she describes herself as "the twenty-three-year-old woman writer closing the book thoughtfully after months of study and placing it in the most available spot on her 'reference' shelf, her fingers sensitive with awe, respect on the covers; her mind afire at last with ideas from France once again in history, *egalité, fraternité, liberté—pour tout le monde!*" It is worth noting that Hansberry wrote this commentary in 1957, the same year that she was completing her signal work, *A Raisin in the Sun.* And it is a sign of her times, the 1950s, that she was apparently one of few readers of either gender who paid close attention to Beauvoir's revolutionary analysis of "the woman question."

The essay was written for thinkers and readers from the Left and most likely would have been submitted to *Masses and Mainstream* or a similar publication. It is uncompromising in its critique of male supremacy wherever it appears, the concept of "a woman's place," and the failure of United States thinkers (particularly those of the Left) to take the book seriously enough to engage Beauvoir in a substantial and challenging dialogue. Women are not spared her criticism as Hansberry holds females responsible for much of the "confusion": "They have been born into a cultural heritage which has instructed them of a role to play without question and in the main they are willing to do so." Hansberry's condemnation of housework and homemaking as "drudgery" and a negation of women's potential to be producers rather than maintainers places her well beyond the 1950s discourse on and perception of women.

The essay is obviously unfinished and would undoubtedly have been revised and edited had Hansberry lived longer. It is published here essentially in its extant form in order to make available the feminist ideas of this extraordinary woman. The editorial revisions are limited primarily to punctuation and an occasional shifting of phrases for clarity. At the time of his death, Robert Nemiroff was editing a book of Hansberry's essays, which included this one; it is unclear at this time whether any of the word changes written on the manuscript are his or Hansberry's. None, however, seems to change substantially the import of the essay. What is published here represents approximately half of her intended outline.

The unfinished essay is published in its entirety rather than cut at some point of seeming completion, so that as much of her thought on this book and its important subject matter can be accessible. The Afterword, which is printed at the end of the essay, mentions the other topics she intended to cover as indicated by her outline.

This essay, with its brilliant, spirited observations, is a poignant reminder of the tremendous loss that Hansberry's death meant for intelligent, stimulating discourse on women. She had the courage and audacity to think independently and to express her views regardless of the controversy they might cause. Hers was and continues to be a persuasive voice that calls her readers to probe and examine their most sacrosanct notions. Future readings of Hansberry's work must take into account her perspective on women as revealed in this commentary on *The Second Sex*.

Lorraine Hansberry }

SIMONE DE BEAUVOIR AND *THE SECOND SEX:* An American Commentary

An Unfinished Essay-in-Progress

PRIMITIVE MAN: WOMAN, 1957

Four years have passed (eight since the French editions) since Simone de Beauvoir declared in the introduction of her book, *The Second Sex,* "What peculiarly signalizes the situation of woman is that she—a free and autonomous being like all human creatures—nevertheless finds herself living in a world where men compel her to assume the status of the Other." It is four years since those 732 pages of revolutionary treatment of the "woman question" exploded upon the consciousness of a fragment of American book readers. Four years and one waits.

We have had to endure since then the exhaustive, casual, ill-informed, and thoroughly irrelevant commentary from our acquaintances on the lady's personal life: her "affairs" with this or that famous Frenchman or American writer; unlimited debate as regards her marriage—or lack of it—to Jean-Paul Sartre; her alleged "lesbianism." And always from someone who "knows someone in Paris"—et al., ad nauseam.

One may well begin by suggesting that the fact of such gossip about one who does appear to be the leading woman intellectual of our time is in itself something of a tribute to the accuracy of the thesis embodied in the title of Mlle. Beauvoir's two volumes on the status of woman. Such is the nature of the question to which the author has addressed herself. It is impossible to conceive of any comparable volume of speculative fascination that could surround an equivalent male personality (the possible exception being that perhaps of homosexuality—which is also interesting). Tradition has accustomed us to assume that with regard to the writer, the artist, the theorist, the musician, the scientist—who is a man—that there are two aspects to his being: his work, which is important, and his personal life, which is really none of our business.

Beyond the absurdity of gossip itself, the immensity of the paradox overwhelms when one troubles to study the thought of Beauvoir. For instance, to discuss whether such a woman has chosen to "sanctify" her relationship to a man is to ignore a substantial part of her theories. While she does not attack marriage, she does not anywhere accept the traditional views of its sacred place in the scheme of human development. Therefore to discuss and "accuse" this woman of not respecting marriage is quite like accusing a communist of not "respecting" free enterprise.

This writer would suggest that *The Second Sex* may very well be the most important work of this century. And that, further, it is a victim of its own pertinence and greatness. Simone de Beauvoir has chosen to do what her subject historically demands; to treat of woman with the seriousness and dedication to complexity that any analysis of so astronomical a group as "half of humanity" would absolutely seem to warrant. However, it is in the face of her full acceptance of her self-set task that some of the most remarkable reactions appear to have developed toward the book.

(1) Innocence and ignorance of women themselves. The primary, negative attitude of legions of apparently intelligent women who are incapable of reading, let alone digesting, the heavy fabric of the writings. Women who therefore reflect what Beauvoir has shown to be their historical experience of utter intellectual impoverishment as a class. As a group they are unprepared and unable to accommodate a serious or profound discussion of their problems because of the very nature of their oppression. They cannot, therefore, be expected to assess in the manner of men even that which might herald their ultimate emergence or transcendence into liberty any more than I should imagine a slave prior to the Civil War could have understood intellectually the nature of his bondage. (This truth is hideously compounded, of course, in our own country, where the most devastating anti-equality myth of all is in the reign of our social order: the American myth of the *already* liberated American woman of all classes. And myth, we shall see, is what it is.)

(2) The overt hostility of the enemy. If women at this stage of history are incapable of appropriate assessment and use of the stuff of their delivery, the direct opposite is certainly true of their conscious foe. Within the ranks of the stalwarts of a male-dominated order there is little struggle to appreciate the ideas of *The Second Sex*. On the contrary, men, long adjusted to devastating argument, read it and properly attack it for its formidable solidity and undeniable brilliance.

(3) (It is not only fair but interesting to note the reverse: that among men dedicated to equality the book seemingly achieved respect and stature that many women have been unable to accord it.)

In connection with the first point I have seen clear thinking, crisp American types of women (women intolerant and contemptuous of the more blatant codes of a male supremacist universe) puzzling briefly and inadequately over the work and then dismissing it. There is the attractive, young unmarried scientist who is vague but feels the author talked too much about "sex" somehow; there is the married-new mother-engineer in her mid-twenties who has already contributed to the invention of breathtaking calculus machines but who was offended by the brutal and revolutionary discussions of motherhood and marriage—"All she seems to respect are career girls and lesbians." And so on until one wonders where the author might have begun.

These, however, are far from the sum total of feminine reaction to *The Second Sex*. To be sure, there was the playwright-actress who kept it open upon her backstage dressing table reading aloud between curtains to the feminine half of the cast and "indoctrinating" them, in the outraged and distressed opinion of the male director. There is the woman reviewer writing in the *Daily Worker* a shamefully brief and limited but nonetheless exuberant and intelligent review. There is the young, lovely blonde and vaguely literate secretary sitting in her apartment with the weighty thing propped upon her thighs, dictionary but inches away, forcing herself with passionate dedication to endure and, as far as possible, absorb seven hundred pages of what she describes as her "liberation." And then, of course, there is the twenty-three-year-old woman writer closing the book thoughtfully after months of study and placing it in the most available spot on her "reference" shelf, her fingers sensitive with awe, respect on the covers; her mind afire at last with ideas from France once again in history, *egalité, fraternité, liberté—pour tout le monde!*

Let us consider first of all the reception within the American Left, which will take little space, sadly enough. As with the Negro question it seems American Marxists, Communists in particular, have been far in advance in the western world in their *recognition* of the "woman question." (One modifies to "western" here because reports from and of China are gratifying if erratic and in some ways suspicious.) Certainly whatever foresight the American left may dare to credit itself with now might possibly include early misgivings about the realities of the experience of life for the Soviet woman. That she has been economically liberated (in Beauvoir's view also) seems no longer to be a question of conjecture. However, we have been obliged for years now to shift uncomfortably in our seats at those endless stories about small Soviet boys who demurred on becoming doctors when they should grow up because that was something or other thought of in their country as "woman's work." Granting the charm of the stories in our land where the medical profession's hostility to the female sex persists with an avidness that belongs to another century, we cannot help but wonder in which age of the socialist miracle will the concept of *anything* (beyond childbearing)[1] not be thought of as "woman's work." Similarly, this writer has never been impressed with the official photos from the USSR, which continue to show a representation in the officialdom of the nation in which there is no reflection at all of the fact that in that nation also half of the population are women.

As regards the theoretical bounty of literature on the question from the first socialist country in the world—one may search in vain for material of depth and stature. Pamphlets giving accounts of this or that experiment in child care, birth control, etc., do not miraculously supplant heavy theoretical work which would indicate a serious approach to the woman question in the Soviet Union. In fact, the dearth of such material seems but a primary indication of the state of the question within the Soviet Union. Moreover, who can be impressed by the reports of the primitive official attitude of urging women to become "seductive" again, which is paraded in our American press with what seems justifiable mirth, alongside of photographs of stoic-faced Russian women in the "new" fashions which would be assigned to memories of the corny thirties in our own over-fashion-conscious nation.

Adornment, decoration, have not lost their symbolism. Woman, the creature of seduction throughout her epochs of slavery, has sought to give the personal decorative arts some semblance of dignity beyond the obvious degrading truth, but it has only been a game. The profoundest discussion of this fact will be found in the pages of *The Second Sex,* where the writer brilliantly destroys all myths of woman's *choice* in becoming an ornament; and the charm of it is the photograph then on the dust jacket which presents a quite lovely brunette woman, in necklace and nail polish— Simone de Beauvoir. Nor need we despair for the promotion of beauty anywhere. Scent, jewelry, rouges have undoubtedly assumed some cultural identification with womanhood that, hopefully, will henceforth be independent of an association of the centuries of slavery which has been the lot of woman. Such a time does *not* exist, however, at the moment. And one longs to see official indictment against the fierce meaning of the "seductive" woman emerge from the Soviet Union before its women are humiliated by returning to the "way of women" in the eyes of the disparaging capitalist nations. There is implicit in the "return" the suggestion that woman liberated was a mistake. The rest of the world's women cannot afford that suggestion.

American Communists have possessed the leisure (their social programs in other areas have for obvious reasons been limited as far as the reality of action is concerned in recent years), and a not-to-be-underestimated impetus (in the form of a collection of what must be the most vigorous and insurgent women anywhere in the world—American women Communists) to lift the woman question beyond the ordinary sphere of the "battle-of-the-sexes"-type nonsense which is so tragically popular in our country. It is only conjecture, but one cannot help but feel that though the American woman is far from enjoying anything remotely akin to "equality" with men in her nation she is, subjectively speaking, possessed of a liberated attitude that must have a great deal to do with her historical experience in the New World. (Distinguished, however, from the rest of the "New World" excepting Canada perhaps, where the women of our America, chic and modern on the streets of Buenos Aires, Mexico City, and Rio de Janeiro, are nonetheless tied to a Latin and Catholic spirit of oppression that is horrifying to the most backward of the women of the United States.) We have been creatures of the frontier adventure; we have been the peasant girls off the ships from Ireland and Poland set loose in the industrial chaos of our social order; we have been even the black slave woman paradoxically assuming perhaps the most advanced internal freedom from a knowledge of the mythical nature of male superiority inherent in our experience as chattel. We have been the Jewish woman finding liberty in picket lines. We have not voted long, but we have a freedom in our gaits on the pavement that suggest almost an intuitive awareness of how that franchise was won. It is this multi-experienced class from which American Communist women must be drawn then, and it is they who have noisily, unscientifically, improperly, harmfully, hysterically, neurotically—and *heroically*—battled to place the question of the status of women in its proper place in the consideration of the most advanced thinking section of American political action and thought. That so much of the fight against "male supremacy" in the American Communist movement can be so negatively described is not the fault of women. It is the fault, as Beauvoir would insist, of situation.

Nor should this imply that there has not been a decisive acceptance and encouragement of advanced ideas from that part of the American Communist movement which is male. Indeed at this time within the Party there are attitudes and official programs which allow for special consideration of work with and for women.[2]

It was perhaps a mark of the insignificance in which the estate of woman is actually held that there did not appear, to my knowledge, a major work challenging the precepts of Simone de Beauvoir, either in our country or in Europe.[3] It would be a mistake to believe that the absence of any real negative furor is some indication that the American intelligentsia held out its arms with love to *The Second Sex*. It seems more intelligent to suppose that, on the contrary, the ideological struggle to maintain the male-dominated society felt no real threat in a work which was not going to ever reach those masses of women who might most effectively make use of it because:

(1) The overwhelming majority of American women (like the overwhelming majority of American men) do not read books, beyond a thin slicing who will forsake more popular materials occasionally in behalf of a "historical romance" or, less frequently, a contemporary "sensational" novel;

(2) That microscopic section of our people who might be called the American woman intellectual—or even embracing the middle class woman with enough intelligence (leisure she has) to read—were [not expecting] to find a volume purportedly dealing with *their* problems in the alien idiom of a scholar, a thinker, and an essayist. One feels (with all respect to the translator's intrusions or aids, as the case may be) that she is not less enamored of words than ideas, and we are a people, as oft noted elsewhere, who have grown accustomed to thought reduced on the tabloid sheet far below its least common denominator.

Still for all of that, a great woman has made a great study and written, qualifications aside for the moment, a *great* book. And the world will never be the same again.

It remains for the writer who can with superior theories attack and demolish the forlorn and difficult roots of some of the existentialist thought of Mlle. Beauvoir, where it needs attack and demolition, and hopefully such a writer will necessarily emerge from the ranks of those who embrace a more far-reaching historical materialist view of life than Simone de Beauvoir. Until then *The Second Sex* will remain beyond the vague and shabby criticism of dogmatists of all persuasive shades.

AN AMERICAN MYTH: "WE DON'T WEAR NO VEILS."

Surely for the students of the history of the development of the proletariat, there are few moments when the monumental haphazard of history can be more acutely felt than when one first learns that once workers, baffled and outraged at their clear oppression and desiring vengeance *somewhere,* first turned their fury *not* on the owners of the machines—but on the machines. Man—angry, frustrated, seeking his enemy, groping, attacking what *seems.* The picture comes to us of our ancestors bent over the fields in ancient times of famine, cursing and beating the earth with their fists.

It is a telling commentary on the nature of man's history that we have in due course learned not to attack our tools or the earth—but as regards the relationship between men and women (and, of course, between human and human) we yet see one another as the enemy.

Elsewhere can be read accounts and statistics of the truly primitive status of women in most of the world. It is, regardless of all other questions barring peace and liberation of the world's working classes and colonial peoples, the greatest social question existent; its depth and horrors and universality sometimes overlapping, even certain of those paramount issues mentioned above. Women, it cannot be said too loudly or too often, are half the human race and their condition sooner or later we must see as the more accurate measure of the distance we have come from the age of nothingness which was our beginning.

It would seem that the modern world has largely come to accept the woman of the United States as the symbol of the "free woman." Her reputation appears far more dramatic and expansive than that, for instance, of the Soviet woman, the reality of whose life might more justifiably claim the title, perhaps. Along with other almost mysterious stereotypes, the foreign attitude on the American woman always seems to have to do with her height; her *chic*ness (often, the stereotype insists, without real beauty); her angularity; and her freedom. The writer is reminded of a time in Buenos Aires when she was in the company of a young Argentinean woman lawyer who, though not out of her twenties, had circled the world a couple of times and was currently playing a major and politically important role in the peace movement of her nation. Preparing to make a meeting somewhere I drew on a suit jacket and tossed a shoulder strap bag across my shoulders and stood waiting for our departure in low-heeled plain pumps. At any time I should have considered the costume an unflattering one and to be explained by the chaotic nature of that visit to Argentina and by the necessities of shortly notified travel. I will not forget the eyes of the Argentine woman traveling the length of my frame (I am not a tall woman, really) and noting the outfit, and perhaps the stance, and saying aloud finally from the reaches of her shawls and earrings and long, flowing hair: *"Ah, la norteamericana típica!"* It was neither a compliment nor altogether an insult; it was a remark of wonder. Multitudes of United States women would have been offended by the association of my particular unattractive outfit of that afternoon with the *essence* of North American womanhood, and with good reason. Yet for all of it, there was a kernel of the recognition of a characteristic that is not without foundation. The tailored suit, the shoulder strap bag and the flat-heeled or low-heeled shoe is the mark of the fashion-indifferent woman who desires freedom and utility of movement and service in wearing apparel. It is the mark of women in the past who have believed they had something to do in the world other than "sit around and look pretty." It is not an empty stereotype in that such modes of costume have in the past been inextricably identified with the feminist; the woman professional; the radical woman; and, of course, the lesbian. Each of these classes of women have seen in fashion, ornament, its *true meaning* and have forcefully rejected it to the horror of both male and female society. The argument is far from over.

This writer, for instance, finds the drab, colorless garb of men as distasteful as any other outrage of arbitrary fashion and is inclined to feel that the decorative traditions of woman's wear, whatever their origins, lend a desirable and attractive quality to life, to existence—insofar as such fashions do not intrude on comfort, health, or safety.[4] However, to feel thus is not an excuse to disparage the truly advanced views of women who before and since George Sand have rebelled against the insanity of much of feminine attire; or not to take issue even with Simone de Beauvoir when she declares:

> When one fails to adhere to an accepted code, one becomes an insurgent. A woman who dresses in an outlandish manner lies when she affirms with an air of simplicity that she dresses to suit herself, nothing more. She knows perfectly well that to suit herself is to be outlandish . . . a woman who does not wish to appear eccentric will conform to the usual rules. It is injudicious to take a defiant attitude unless it is connected with positively effective action: it consumes more time and energy than it saves. A woman who has no wish to shock or to devaluate herself socially should live out her feminine situation in a feminine manner; and very often, for that matter, her professional success demands it.[5]

We may well consider this to be perhaps the most "reactionary" paragraph to be found in the pages of this book. It is well to remember that even though the author might herself demur or take offense at the description, Simone de Beauvoir is a soldier; it is a mistake not to see her as an angry woman because she has properly and successfully divorced herself from the "anti-man" precepts of her historical feminist forebears. As a soldier she is occasionally given to the *expediencies* of warfare. Whole chapters are given to the demolition of the myth of "the feminine," the social origins of this arbitrary phenomenon. Thus she willfully will accept concepts of dress and behavior for women in order to do battle with more fundamental areas of their oppression. However, if one may separate the argument for the moment from the matter of the woman question, we may consider that "insurgency" as such is hardly a destructive attitude in life— even keeping to the question of fashion. It seems in the matter of clothes that in the heat of summer a short trouser for men is clearly desirable to a long one, but at the outset of the popularity of the "Bermuda" short for men (in our eastern cities, at least) the occasional revolutionary who appeared on the streets in such apparel was the source of amusement, ridicule, and open contempt (places to which he could and cannot yet be admitted, though, needless to say, his "essentials" are well covered, if that is what society cares about!) Today it is not unfair to note that the legions of the formerly amused drop with relief and gratitude into these sensible kinds of apparel. This applies also to sandals, open shirts, etc.

Mlle. Beauvoir is actually careless rather than reactionary when she implies that the initial martyrs of a cause do not serve an essential and inexpendable purpose. If this writer prefers as a matter of perhaps misguided tastes certain of the more frivolous habits of feminine dress, it is but a matter of *taste* and not to be defended at the expense of those women, historical and contemporary, whose stouthearted campaign to dress as they please, now make it possible for this writer or Simone de Beauvoir to appear freely on the streets (at least, in the U.S.) in slacks, if the mood so compels us. It is another measure of freedom not to be discredited. It may be such an attitude which has lent itself to the flat-heeled, giant-striding stereotype of the American woman. In that sense, with all respect to the women of France and Latin America, the women of the United States have no cause to apologize for the stereotype. I have had the opportunity to see and live for short periods among women of Mexico, Argentina, Brazil, and good numbers from the Caribbean, and it may be said that at this moment in history the women of this country possess an objective circumstance of relative freedom which is unknown to other women in our hemisphere.[6]

Thus when one speaks comparatively of anything, the compared is liable to assume whatever dimensions its opposite does not possess. As long as an observer is able to report passages like the following speaking of our own times, it becomes clearer on what rests the celebrated "equality" allegedly enjoyed by the American woman:

> I recall seeing in a primitive village of Tunisia a subterranean cavern in which four women were squatting: the old one-eyed and toothless wife, her face horribly devastated, was cooking dough on a small brazier in the midst of an acrid smoke; two wives somewhat younger but almost as disfigured, were lulling children in their arms—one was giving suck. . . . As I left this gloomy cave . . . in the corridor leading upward toward the light of day I passed the male, dressed in white, well groomed, smiling, sunny. He was returning from the marketplace, where he had discussed world affairs with other men; he would pass some hours in this retreat of his at the heart of the vast universe to which he belonged from which he was not separated. For the withered old women, for the young wife doomed to the same rapid decay, there was no universe other than the smoky cave, whence they emerged only at night, silent and veiled.[7]

Not to even become involved in the variants on the place of woman which the world's religions may or may not alter to one degree or another as is the case with Islam or Christianity, Catholicism or Protestantism, etc., we may still suppose that woman condemned to stay indoors through the hours of light would have been of little use in helping to clear the American fields or sowing grain. Similarly today American journalists try to find a desperate amusement or frivolity in the fact of the liberation of the women of China from the most barbaric forms of their former oppression. They cannot see that, suspending the liability to "Communist sympathy" for a moment, a nation in fertile birth, or in a *renaissance,* be it young America or ancient China, cannot afford the traditional misuse, and therefore virtual uselessness *of half its people.* The frontier demands work, hard work, and a dedication to the future. There is not the time to clutter it with the worthlessness of the uselessness of women. Nothing could better indicate the *artificial* nature of their oppression to begin with. If the Communists of China have indeed ideologically elevated woman to a place of dignity which is beyond her mere economic status, this is hardly a point of jest, but one of the more inspiring developments of modern history.

I have remarked heavily upon the sociological roots of the comparative equality of American women because such sources are not to be confused as having come from some benevolent features of our principal religious ethic drawn as it was from the Judeo-Christian doctrines of the Mediterranean which set woman as firmly as ever in the encasement of subservient immanence.

Today in the United States our national attitude toward women and their place, or finding it, is one of frantic confusion. Women themselves are among the foremost promoters of the confusion. They have been born into a cultural heritage which has instructed them of a role to play without question and in the main they are willing to do so. And yet, therein hangs the problem: housework, "homemaking," are drudgery; it is inescapable, women flee it in one form or another. They do not always understand their own rebellion, or why they want to rebel or why *they* deprecate, more than anyone else really, what the rest of the nation will always insist, so long as it does not have to do it, is the "cornerstone" of our culture, the "key" to our civilization, and the "bedrock foundation" of our way of life. As for the housewife who has to endure it, she floods her afternoons with soap operas; buys a fantastic percentage of the pulp escapist literature that is produced in this country; eats too much for her health or figure; and invariably persists in exploding the entire myth day after day on the radios and television programs of America by shrugging a little, and saying, when asked, "And what do *you* do?"—*"Oh me, nothing—I'm just a housewife. . . ."*

The ripened confusion as regards what women "ought to do with themselves" (and as distinguished from the blatant undiluted male supremacist ideology found in another sphere to be discussed later) is typified by the mixed-up if clearly well-intentioned speech given by a woman, Agnes E. Meyer, at the 47th Annual Meeting of the American Home Economics Association in June, 1956.

After quoting Emerson's dubious and ambitious remark to the effect that "civilization" is "the power of good women," she spoke of the rebellion of women against "what seems" to them "the boredom of family responsibilities; others complain that not enough women have high positions in government and industry. . . ." She then proceeded (with only indirect justification, if any) to lay blame for much of woman's frustration at the door of the feminist movements of the past which, she declared, "taught women to see themselves as the *rivals* of men rather than as partners."[8] (Agnes

Meyer's emphasis.) Mrs. Meyer then summed up, unwittingly, in a single paragraph what amounts to the very essence of the confusion:

> It is one thing if women work because they must help support the family and other dependents or because they have a special contribution to make to society. It is quite another thing—it is socially undesirable—if society forces the mother to take a job in order that she may respect herself and gain the respect of others.

Somewhere it has escaped the attention of the most intelligent, active sections of American women, which Mrs. Meyer certainly belongs to, that there exists in the nature of "homemaking" an indestructible contradiction to usefulness. Housework, care of the family, is but humankind's necessity of function. *They are the things requisite to existence; to allowing oneself to do something else.* The human impulse, if we may believe the obvious in history is to *produce,* or to *transform* nature. Simone de Beauvoir speaks of it:

> The domestic labors that fell to her lot because they were reconcilable with the cares of maternity imprisoned her in repetition and immanence; they were repeated from day to day in an identical form, which was perpetuated almost without change from century to century; they produced nothing new. Man's case was radically different; he furnished support for the group . . . by means of acts that transcended his animal nature . . . To maintain, he created; he burst out of the present, he opened the future. This is the reason why fishing and hunting expeditions had a sacred character. Their successes were celebrated with festivals and triumph, and therein man gave recognition to his human estate. Today he still manifests this pride when he has built a dam or a skyscraper or an atomic pile. He has worked not merely to conserve the world as given; he has broken through its frontiers, he has laid down the foundations of a new future.

Then she is explicit:

> . . . in this he proved dramatically that life is not the supreme value for man, but on the contrary that it should be made to serve ends more important than itself. . . . It is not in giving life but in risking life that man is raised above the animal; that is why superiority has been accorded in humanity not to the sex that brings forth but to that which kills.[9]

From this we may consider the further remarks of Mrs. Meyer, "No wonder the average housewife is confused. She is no longer sure what society expects of her." Therein hangs the fallacy. It is all too clear that "society" in this instance would be all too willing to "expect," permit—in fact, demand—of woman that she stay quite where she was in the dark ages. It is woman herself who has wrought the changes in her condition: she has demonstrated and gone to jail; chained herself to the capitol gates of London and Washington for the right to vote, own property, and alter divorce laws. Failing that she has made the life of man miserable in pursuit of these and other goals. What, Beauvoir insists, woman desires is freedom. She is a subjective being like man and like man she must pursue her transcendence forever. This is the nature of the human race. The problem, then, is not that woman has strayed too far from "her place" but that she has not yet attained it; that her emergence into liberty is, thus far, incomplete, primitive even. She has gained the teasing expectation of self-fulfillment without the realization of it, because she is herself yet chained to an ailing social ideology which seeks always to deny her autonomy and more—to delude her into the belief that that which in fact imprisons her the more is somehow her fulfillment.

However, that woman is a creature of potentialities beyond those ordinarily prescribed for her does not today escape some of even her confused spokesmen. Mrs. Meyer in the same speech attacked the "insidious" attitude "which tempts women to . . . a preoccupation of glamor." Says she:

> I shall never forget a luncheon I attended some years ago in Washington in honor of Gabrielle Mistral, the distinguished Chilean poetess [sic][10] who won the Nobel Prize in 1946, and Lisa Meitner, the famous physicist who made valuable contributions to the development of the atom bomb. The faces of these two great women, worn by the furrows of deep thought and powerful character, were a shocking contrast to the surface beauty but robotlike similarity of the American women.

This last has been placed even more strongly than might seem necessary. But the sense of refutation of the shallow values imposed upon women is beautifully apparent. The wholesomeness of such a view is sharply contrasted with the tenor of the new (and not so new) male sex publications where the glorification of woman as sex object has reached a new and inglorious height. In these publications men are encouraged and even shown how to relegate an entire sex to the level of one long, endless, if one is to believe the fantasies (and one might add, boring), animal relationship.

This state of affairs unquestionably being the basis for much of our national neuroses it does not seem to occur to the overwhelming sections of American males that, in maintaining woman as Sex Object and/or Child Raiser, the fraternity of social relationships other than sex must necessarily suffer to the extent of creating what is in fact an impossible social arrangement—as indeed must the sexual relationship itself.

Woman like the Negro, the Jew, like colonial peoples, even in ignorance, is *incapable of accepting the role* with harmony. This is because it is an unnatural role which presupposes that she is something other than a human being possessed of the desire for transcendence. The station of woman is hardly one that she would assume by choice, any more than man would. It must necessarily be imposed on her—by force. It is therefore unnatural and unstable, not to say merely impermanent, which it most certainly is. A status not freely chosen or entered into by an individual or a group is necessarily one of oppression and the oppressed are by their nature (i.e., oppressed) forever in ferment and agitation against their condition and what they understand to be their oppressors. If not by overt rebellion or revolution, then in the thousand and one ways they will devise with and without consciousness to alter their condition. Woman, it may be said with some understatement to make the point, is oppressed.

Moreover, the nature of man is unique in the animal world. His sociality is such that once the hunter is at a certain stage of social organization he is incapable of hunting merely for his personal immediate hunger. He has already found in *his needs* the impetus, the need, to sustain others of his cave. Ultimately he must help to sustain the community because of his needs; because it is incumbent upon his needs that the community survive and even prosper, though the memory of a time without the community may yet exist in his mind. Similarly in a more sophisticated age when his ethic expands beyond his essential needs, his nature will require him by the same laws of the primitive past to satisfy the needs, *the spiritual needs, of his species.*

Thus in times past, woman, ignorant, inarticulate, has often found her most effective and telling champion among men. This is to suggest that if by some miracle women should not ever utter a single protest against their condition there would still exist among men those who could not endure in peace until her liberation had been achieved. Such we must always come to conclude is the nature of mankind, such is the glory of the human race of which the male is a magnificent half.

The housewife says "just a housewife" for all the reasons she would perhaps try to deny if she thought someone who was attacking housework and "homemaking" as drudgery was also attacking the cornerstone and key and bedrock foundation of her family, home, husband, nation, and world.

The ancient effort to glorify the care of the home into something which it is not and cannot be is one of the greatest assaults against womanhood. Women are, generally speaking, ignorant. Their views, their interpretations of almost anything will largely be drawn from what men have thought and believed and promoted in the world independent of them or any serious consultation with them. This will apply even to themselves. A society dictated and organized by men prescribes that women should not work outside the home because "they take the bread out of men's families' mouths." (One of the most remarkable arguments against anything I have ever heard.) And so, foremost among those shouting such an argument are always to be—women. Or, more to the immediate point, society tells woman from cradle to the grave that her husband, her home, her children will be the source of all rewards in life, the foundation of all true happiness. And women believe it and they plunge into marriages; wrap themselves in their husbands and their children—and continue to constitute one of the most neurotic sections, no doubt, of our entire population. Husband reveals himself as but a man, as men must, and they, being humans, are an inadequate, blustering, often pathetic lot, themselves struggling to keep abreast of the rigorous and pointless attitudes society has also set for them in this "man's world." And so beyond the second or third year, it is only the image of the myth which she married that woman can continue to lose herself in, to love.

Well, there are her children and they require much of her and she gives much—but they are only children. They are "the future of the race"; they are lovely; they are quick and bright and full of experiences for the observing adult—*but they are only children.* One may spend from fourteen to eighteen hours a day with a human being of five and the occasion simply will not arrive when one may discuss the meaning of strontium with that person. This is not a proper experience for the adult mind. As long as the threat exists one really ought to be discussing strontium—or, as a matter of fact, it would not be to the benefit of anyone if our public attitudes toward nursery schools had to rely on the intellectual spirit of five-year-olds—or for that matter, ten-year-olds.

AFTERWORD

Hansberry's commentary on *The Second Sex,* obviously unfinished, stops here. Her outline for this essay lists two additional, major subjects: "Man and Supremacy" and "Prospectus." Under the latter, she planned to address the question of biology and whether women are "wedded to the womb" forever. The last topic listed in her outline was simply "liberation."

ENDNOTES

1. This is far from a final statement on this question.

2. There will be many Communist women to read these remarks and shudder with a premature sense of betrayal. It will seem, out of the subjective experience of sensitive women, that I have, for the sake of ideally presenting a situation, grossly misstated the experience of the American Communist woman and movement. Let it suffice for the moment to insist that *we are speaking here merely in the general,* which, we feel, fact bears out.

3. Particularly in France itself where, if we may take Mlle. Beauvoir's word for it, the Revolution seems to have done little indeed for the lot of her countrywomen.

4. An article in the *N.Y. Post,* June 18, 1957, shows that the most important part of a woman's wardrobe depends on which industry is speaking. According to famous shoe designer J. Leon Touro, "Shoes are the most important, the most arresting, most sensuous part of a woman's outfit." Mr. Touro is the man who

first promoted what the *Post* properly calls "those dangerous to life and limb matchstick heels" which have become accepted style among U.S. women.

5. *The Second Sex,* 683.

6. A dispatch to the *New York Times* in June, 1957, tells us that the women of Paraguay expect to achieve suffrage, "very, very soon."

7. *The Second Sex,* 84.

8. It now begins to appear that the feminists are to be held responsible for every unattractive feature of woman's estate. In popular conversation and popular literature one can more easily conclude that women would have been better off without the feminists than with them. The tendency is to lay undue emphasis upon their wildest and most unfortunate exploits and attitudes and to remark not at all upon the meaning of the great role of historical feminism. It is idle to attack that which could not even have existed without a cause. What seems important is that if society found itself outraged by feminist fervor, it ought rather to have more speedily condemned that which gave rise to it: male supremacy. To the extent that the feminist leaders pronounced *man* rather than ideology as enemy they deserved correction; beyond that it is better to retain a deeply respectful and appreciative attitude of the role played by those great women and their great movement which moved humanity forward so decisively.

9. *The Second Sex,* 63–64.

10. Hansberry objected to this conceit, the feminization of professional work when performed by women, but she retained the term as part of this direct quote.

CHAPTER THREE

Civil Rights and Women's Liberation: Racial/Sexual Politics in the Angry Decades

Black liberation struggle must be re-visioned so that it is no longer equated with maleness. We need a revolutionary vision of black liberation, one that emerges from a feminist standpoint and addresses the collective plight of black people.

—BELL HOOKS, *Yearning*

From the outset black women encountered an America that denied their humanity, debased their femininity, and refused them self-possession. The acquisition of a measure of freedom and citizenship privileges would have to await a modern Civil Rights movement that they profoundly initiated and sustained.

—DARLENE CLARK HINE, *Lure and Loathing*

INTRODUCTION

The history of the Civil Rights and women's rights movements during the "angry decade" of the sixties has been well-documented. The role of African American women in these historic struggles remains less well known. Similarly, the history of the development of contemporary black feminism during this period has received little attention in chronicles of modern feminism, even ones published more recently, where the focus remains middle-class white women.

This chapter focuses on the experiences of black women activists during the sixties, their frustrations with civil rights and more radical organizations, and their embrace of feminism in the early seventies despite their experiences with racism inside the largely white women's movement. What is apparent from our revisiting the feminist writings of African American women during this critical juncture is that the women's movement would have attracted a broader cross-section of the female population had it taken seriously the insights of women of color. More than anything else, they were committed to societal transformations which would have enabled the poorest and most oppressed women to live better lives. After three decades of struggle this remains a dream deferred.

Frances Beale

Frances Beale, journalist and civil rights activist, was a founding member of SNCC's Black Women's Liberation Committee (New York coordinator) after returning in 1966 to the United States from Paris, where she had lived for six years. In 1970, she was director of the Black Women's Alliance, a feminist group associated with the Student Nonviolent Coordinating Committee (SNCC). "Double Jeopardy," first published in Robin Morgan's *Sisterhood Is Powerful* (1970), became the most anthologized essay in the early years of women's liberations publications. This now classic essay addressed the double burden of race and gender that black women confronted; dealt with issues of reproductive freedom for black women in a sanguine manner; articulated early on the necessity for the white women's liberation movement to be anti-imperialist and antiracist, a refrain that was repeated by many feminist women of color throughtout the 1970s and 1980s; and provided a revolutionary vision of a "new world" free of all oppressions, including capitalism. This essay, reminiscent of Elise McDougald's "The Struggle of Women for Sex and Race Emancipation" (1925), is also a manifesto for black women committed to eradicating the twin evils of racism and sexism.

Frances Beale }

Double Jeopardy:
To Be Black and Female

In attempting to analyze the situation of the black woman in America, one crashes abruptly into a solid wall of grave misconceptions, outright distortions of fact, and defensive attitudes on the part of many. The system of capitalism (and its afterbirth—racism) under which we all live has attempted by many devious ways and means to destroy the humanity of all people, and particularly the humanity of black people. This has meant an outrageous assault on every black man, woman, and child who resides in the United States.

In keeping with its goal of destroying the black race's will to resist its subjugation, capitalism found it necessary to create a situation where the black man found it impossible to find meaningful or productive employment. More often than not, he couldn't find work of any kind. And the black woman likewise was manipulated by the system, economically exploited, and physically assaulted. She could often find work in the white man's kitchen, however, and sometimes became the sole breadwinner of the family. This predicament has led to many psychological problems on the part of both man and woman and has contributed to the turmoil that we find in the black family structure.

Unfortunately, neither the black man nor the black woman understood the true nature of the forces working upon them. Many black women tended to accept the capitalist evaluation of manhood and womanhood and believed, in fact, that black men were shiftless and lazy, otherwise they would get a job and support their families as they ought to. Personal relationships between black men and women were thus torn asunder and one result has been the separation of man from wife, mother from child, etc.

America has defined the roles to which each individual should subscribe. It has defined "manhood" in terms of its own interests and "feminity" likewise. Therefore, an individual who has a good job, makes a lot of money, and drives a Cadillac is a real "man," and conversely, an individual who is lacking in these "qualities" is less of a man. The advertising media in this country continuously inform the American male of his need for indispensable signs of his virility—the brand of cigarettes that cowboys prefer, the whiskey that has a masculine tang, or the label of the jockstrap that athletes wear.

The ideal model that is projected for a woman is to be surrounded by hypocritical homage and estranged from all real work, spending idle hours primping and preening, obsessed with conspicuous consumption, and limiting life's functions to simply a sex role. We unqualitatively reject these respective models. A woman who stays at home caring for children and the house often leads an extremely sterile existence. She must lead her entire life as a satellite to her mate. He goes out into society and brings back a little piece of the world for her. His interests and his understanding of the world become her own and she cannot develop herself as an individual having been reduced to only a biological function. This kind of woman leads a parasitic existence that can aptly be described as legalized prostitution.

Furthermore it is idle dreaming to think of black women simply caring for their homes and children like the middle-class white model. Most black women have to work to help house, feed, and clothe their families. Black women make up a substantial percentage of the black working force, and this is true for the poorest black family as well as the so-called middle-class family.

Black women were never afforded any such phony luxuries. Though we have been browbeaten with this white image, the reality of the degrading and dehumanizing jobs that were relegated to us quickly dissipated this mirage of womanhood. The following excerpts from a speech that Sojourner Truth made at a women's rights convention in the nineteenth century show us how misleading and incomplete a life this model represents for us:

> ... Well, chilern, whar dar is so much racket dar must be something out o' kilter. I tink dat 'twixt de niggers of de Souf and de women at de Norf all a talkin' 'bout rights, de white men will be in a fix pretty soon. But what's all dis here talkin' 'bout? Dat man ober dar say dat women needs to be helped into carriages, and lifted ober ditches, and to have de best place every whar. Nobody ever help me into carriages, or ober mud puddles, or gives me any best places ... and ar'nt I a woman? Look at me! Look at my arm! ... I have plowed, and planted, and gathered into barns, and no man could head me— and ar'nt I a woman? I could work as much as a man (when I could get it), and bear de lash as well—and ar'nt I a woman? I have borne thirteen chilern and I seen 'em mos' all sold off into slavery, and when I cried out with a mother's grief, none but Jesus heard—and ar'nt I a woman?

Unfortunately, there seems to be some confusion in the movement today as to who has been oppressing whom. Since the advent of black power, the black male has exerted a more prominent leadership role in our struggle for justice in this country. He sees the system for what it really is for the most part, but where he rejects its values and mores on many issues, when it comes to women, he seems to take his guidelines from the pages of the *Ladies' Home Journal*. Certain black men are maintaining that they have been castrated by society but that black women somehow escaped this persecution and even contributed to this emasculation.

Let me state here and now that the black woman in America can justly be described as a "slave of a slave." By reducing the black man in America to such abject oppression, the black woman had no protector and was used, and is still being used in some cases, as the scapegoat for the evils that this horrendous system has perpetrated on black men. Her physical image has been maliciously maligned; she has been sexually molested and abused by the white colonizer; she has suffered the worse kind of economic exploitation, having been forced to serve as the white woman's maid and wet-nurse for white offspring while her own children were more often than not starving and neglected. It is the depth of degradation to be socially manipulated, physically raped, used to undermine your own household, and to be powerless to reverse this syndrome.

It is true that our husbands, fathers, brothers, and sons have been emasculated, lynched, and brutalized. They have suffered from the cruelest assault on mankind that the world has ever known. However, it is a gross distortion of fact to state that black women have oppressed black men. The capitalist system found it expedient to enslave and oppress them and proceeded to do so without consultation or the signing of any agreements with black women.

It must also be pointed out at this time that black women are not resentful of the rise to power of black men. We welcome it. We see in it the eventual liberation of all black people from this corrupt system of capitalism. Nevertheless, this does not mean that you have to negate one for the other. This kind of thinking is a product of miseducation; that it's either X or it's Y. It is fallacious reasoning that in order for the black man to be strong, the black woman has to be weak.

Those who are exerting their "manhood" by telling black women to step back into a domestic, submissive role are assuming a counterrevolutionary position. Black women likewise have been abused by the system, and we must begin talking about the elimination of all kinds of oppression. If we are talking about building a strong nation, capable of throwing off the yoke of capitalist oppression, then we are talking about the total involvement of every man, woman, and child, each with a highly developed political consciousness. We need our whole army out there dealing with the enemy and not half an army.

There are also some black women who feel that there is no more productive role in life than having and raising children. This attitude often reflects the conditioning of the society in which we live and is adopted from a bourgeois white model. Some young sisters who have never had to maintain a household and accept the confining role which this entails tend to romanticize (along with the help of a few brothers) this role of housewife and mother. Black women who have had to endure this kind of function are less apt to have these utopian visions.

Those who project in an intellectual manner how great and rewarding this role will be and who feel that the most important thing that they can contribute to the black nation is children are doing themselves a great injustice. This line of reasoning completely negates the contributions that black women have historically made to our struggle for liberation. These black women include Sojourner Truth, Harriet Tubman, Mary McLeod Bethune, and Fannie Lou Hamer, to name but a few.

We live in a highly industrialized society, and every member of the black nation must be as academically and technologically developed as possible. To wage a revolution, we need competent teachers, doctors, nurses, electronics experts, chemists, biologists, physicists, political scientists, and so on and so forth. Black women sitting at home reading bedtime stories to their children are just not going to make it.

ECONOMIC EXPLOITATION OF BLACK WOMEN

The economic system of capitalism finds it expedient to reduce women to a state of enslavement. They oftentimes serve as a scapegoat for the evils of this system. Much in the same way that the poor white cracker of the South, who is equally victimized, looks down upon blacks and contributes to the oppression of blacks, so, by giving to men a false feeling of superiority (at least in their own home or in their relationships with women), the oppression of women acts as an escape valve for capitalism. Men may be cruelly exploited and subjected to all sorts of dehumanizing tactics on the part of the ruling class, but they have someone who is below them—at least they're not women.

Women also represent a surplus labor supply, the control of which is absolutely necessary to the profitable functioning of capitalism. Women are systematically exploited by the system. They are paid less for the same work that men do, and jobs that are specifically relegated to women are low-paying and without the possibility of advancement. Statistics from the Women's Bureau of the United States Department of Labor show that in 1967 the wage scale for white women was even below that of black men; and the wage scale for nonwhite women was the lowest of all:

WHITE MALES	$6,704
NONWHITE MALES	$4,277
WHITE FEMALES	$3,991
NONWHITE FEMALES	$2,861

Those industries which employ mainly black women are the most exploitive in the country. Domestic and hospital workers are good examples of this oppression; the garment workers in New York City provide us with another view of this economic slavery. The International Ladies' Garment Workers Union (ILGWU), whose overwhelming membership consists of Black and Puerto Rican women, has a leadership that is nearly all lily-white and male. This leadership has been working in collusion with the ruling class and has completely sold its soul to the corporate structure.

To add insult to injury, the ILGWU has invested heavily in business enterprises in racist, apartheid South Africa—with union funds. Not only does this bought-off leadership contribute to our continued exploitation in this country by not truly representing the best interests of its membership, but it audaciously uses funds that black and Puerto Rican women have provided to support the economy of a vicious government that is engaged in the economic rape and murder of our black brothers and sisters in our Motherland, Africa.

The entire labor movement in the United States has suffered as a result of the superexploitation of black workers and women. The unions have historically been racist and chauvinistic. They have upheld racism in this country and have failed to fight the white skin privileges of white workers. They have failed to fight or even make an issue against the inequities in the hiring and pay of women workers. There has been virtually no struggle against either the racism of the white worker or the economic exploitation of the working woman, two factors that have consistently impeded the advancement of the real struggle against the ruling class.

This racist, chauvinistic, and manipulative use of black workers and women, especially black women, has been a severe cancer on the American labor scene. It therefore becomes essential for those who understand the workings of capitalism and imperialism to realize that the exploitation of black people and women works to everyone's disadvantage and that the liberation of these two groups is a stepping-stone to the liberation of all oppressed people in this country and around the world.

BEDROOM POLITICS

I have briefly discussed the economic and psychological manipulation of black women, but perhaps the most outlandish act of oppression in modern times is the current campaign to promote sterilization of nonwhite women in an attempt to maintain the population and power imbalance between the white haves and the nonwhite havenots.

These tactics are but another example of the many devious schemes that the ruling-class elite attempt to perpetrate on the black population in order to keep itself in control. It has recently come to our attention that a massive campaign for so-called birth control is presently being promoted not only in the underdeveloped nonwhite areas of the world, but also in black communities here in the United States. However, what the authorities in charge of these programs refer to as "birth control" is in fact nothing but a method of outright surgical genocide.

The United States has been sponsoring sterilization clinics in nonwhite countries, especially in India, where already some three million young men and boys in and around New Delhi have been sterilized in makeshift operating rooms set up by the American Peace Corps workers. Under these circumstances, it is understandable why certain countries view the Peace Corps not as a benevolent project, not as evidence of America's concern for underdeveloped areas, but rather as a threat to their very existence. This program could more aptly be named the Death Corps.

Vasectomy, which is performed on males and takes only six or seven minutes, is a relatively simple operation. The sterilization of a woman, on the other hand, is admittedly major surgery. This operation (salpingectomy)* must be performed in a hospital under general anesthesia. This method of "birth control" is a common procedure in Puerto Rico. Puerto Rico has long been used by the colonialist exploiter, the United States, as a huge experimental laboratory for medical research before allowing certain practices to be imported and used here. When the birth control pill was first being perfected, it was tried out on Puerto Rican women and selected black women (poor), using them as human guinea pigs, to evaluate its effect and its efficiency.

Salpingectomy has now become the commonest operation in Puerto Rico, commoner than an appendectomy or a tonsillectomy. It is so widespread that it is referred to simply as *la operacion. On the island, ten percent of the women between the ages of 15 and 45 have already been sterilized.*

And now, as previously occurred with the pill, this method has been imported into the United States. These sterilization clinics are cropping up around the country in the black and Puerto Rican communities. These so-called maternity clinics specifically outfitted to purge black women or men of their reproductive possibilities are appearing more and more in hospitals and clinics across the country.

---

* Salpingectomy: Through an abdominal incision, the surgeon cuts both fallopian tubes and ties off the separated ends, after which act there is no way for the egg to pass from the ovary to the womb.

A number of organizations have been formed to popularize the idea of sterilization, such as the Association for Voluntary Sterilization, and the Human Betterment (!!!?) Association for Voluntary Sterilization, Inc., which has its headquarters in New York City.

Threatened with the cut-off of relief funds, some black welfare women have been forced to accept this sterilization procedure in exchange for a continuation of welfare benefits. Black women are often afraid to permit any kind of necessary surgery because they know from bitter experience that they are more likely than not to come out of the hospital without their insides. (Both salpingectomies and hysterectomies are performed.)

We condemn this use of the black woman as a medical testing ground for the white middle class. Reports of the ill effects, including deaths, from the use of the birth control pill only started to come to light when the white privileged class began to be affected. These outrageous Nazi-like procedures on the part of medical researchers are but another manifestation of the totally amoral and dehumanizing brutality that the capitalist system perpetrates on black women. The sterilization experiments carried on in concentration camps some twenty-five years ago have been denounced the world over, but no one seems to get upset by the repetition of these same racist tactics today in the United States of America—land of the free and home of the brave. This campaign is as nefarious a program as Germany's gas chambers, and, in a long-term sense, as effective and with the same objective.

The rigid laws concerning abortions in this country are another vicious means of subjugation and, indirectly, of outright murder. Rich white women somehow manage to obtain these operations with little or no difficulty. It is the poor black and Puerto Rican woman who is at the mercy of the local butcher. Statistics show us that the nonwhite death rate at the hands of the unqualified abortionist is substantially higher than for white women. Nearly half of the childbearing deaths in New York City are attributed to abortion alone, and out of these, seventy-nine percent are among nonwhites and Puerto Rican women.

We are not saying that black women should not practice birth control. *Black women have the right and the responsibility to determine when it is in the interest of the struggle to have children or not to have them, and this right must not be relinquished to anyone.* It is also her right and responsibility to determine when it is in her own best interests to have children, how many she will have, and how far apart. The lack of the availability of safe birth control methods, the forced sterilization practices, and the inability to obtain legal abortions are all symptoms of a decadent society that jeopardizes the health of black women (and thereby the entire black race) in its attempts to control the very life processes of human beings. This is a symptom of a society that believes it has the right to bring political factors into the privacy of the bedchamber. The elimination of these horrendous conditions will free black women for full participation in the revolution, and, thereafter in the building of the new society.

RELATIONSHIP TO WHITE MOVEMENT

Much has been written recently about the white women's liberation movement in the United States, and the question arises whether there are any parallels between this struggle and the movement on the part of black women for total emanicpation. While there are certain comparisons that one can make, simply because we both live under the same exploitative system, there are certain differences, some of which are quite basic.

The white women's movement is far from being monolithic. Any white group that does not have an anti-imperialist and antiracist ideology has absolutely nothing in common with the black woman's struggle. In fact, some groups come to the incorrect conclusion that their oppression is due simply to male chauvinism. They therefore have an extremely antimale tone to their dissertations. Black people are engaged in a life-and-death struggle and the main emphasis of black women must be to combat the capitalist, racist exploitation of black people. While it is true that male chauvinism has become institutionalized in American society, one must always look for the main enemy—the fundamental cause of the female condition.

Another major differentiation is that the white women's liberation movement is basically middle class. Very few of these women suffer the extreme economic exploitation that most black women are subjected to day by day. This is the factor that is most crucial for us. It is not an intellectual persecution alone; it is not an intellectual outburst for us; it is quite real. We as black women have got to deal with the problems that the black masses deal with, for our problems in reality are one and the same.

If the white groups do not realize that they are in fact fighting capitalism and racism, we do not have common bonds. If they do not realize that the reasons for their condition lie in the system and not simply that men get a vicarious pleasure out of "consuming their bodies for exploitative reasons" (this kind of reasoning seems to be quite prevalent in certain white women's groups), then we cannot unite with them around common grievances or even discuss these groups in a serious manner because they're completely irrelevant to the black struggle.

THE NEW WORLD

The black community and black women especially must begin raising questions about the kind of society we wish to see established. We must note the ways in which capitalism oppresses us and then move to create institutions that will eliminate these destructive influences.

The new world that we are attempting to create must destroy oppression of any type. The value of this new system will be determined by the status of the person who was low man on the totem pole. Unless women in any enslaved nation are completely liberated, the change cannot really be called a revolution. If the black woman has to retreat to the position she occupied before the armed struggle, the whole movement and the whole struggle will have retreated in terms of truly freeing the colonized population.

A people's revolution that engages the participation of every member of the community, including man, woman, and child, brings about a certain transformation in the participants as a result of this participation. Once you have caught a glimpse of freedom or experienced a bit of self-determination, you can't go back to old routines that were established under a racist, capitalist regime. We must begin to understand that a revolution entails not only the willingness to lay our lives on the firing line and get killed. In some ways, this is an easy commitment to make. To die for the revolution is a one-shot deal; to live for the revolution means taking on the more difficult commitment of changing our day-to-day life patterns.

This will mean changing the traditional routines that we have established as a result of living in a totally corrupting society. It means changing how you relate to your wife, your husband, your parents, and your coworkers. If we are going to liberate ourselves as a people, it must be recognized that black women have very specific problems that have to be spoken to. We must be liberated along with the rest of the population. We cannot wait to start working on those problems until that great day in the future when the revolution somehow miraculously is accomplished.

To assign women the role of housekeeper and mother while men go forth into battle is a highly questionable doctrine for a revolutionary to maintain. Each individual must develop a high political consciousness in order to understand how this system enslaves us all and what actions we must take to bring about its total destruction. Those who consider themselves to be revolutionary must begin to deal with other revolutionaries as equals. And so far as I know, revolutionaries are not determined by sex.

Old people, young people, men and women, must take part in the struggle. To relegate women to purely supportive roles or to purely cultural considerations is dangerous doctrine to project. Unless black men who are preparing themselves for armed struggle understand that the society which we are trying to create is one in which the oppression of *all members* of that society is eliminated, then the revolution will have failed in its avowed purpose.

Given the mutual commitment of black men and black women alike to the liberation of our people and other oppressed peoples around the world, the total involvement of each individual is necessary. A revolutionary has the responsibility not only of toppling those that are now in a position of power, but of creating new institutions that will eliminate all forms of oppression. We must begin to rewrite our understanding of traditional personal relationships between man and woman.

All the resources that the black community can muster up must be channeled into the struggle. Black women must take an active part in bringing about the kind of society where our children, our loved ones, and each citizen can grow up and live as decent human beings, free from the pressures of racism and capitalist exploitation.

Mary Ann Weathers

Mary Ann Weathers's essay "An Argument for Black Women's Liberation as a Revolutionary Force" was included in the chapter on "Radical Feminism," which New York–based Leslie Tanner assembled for *Voices from Women's Liberation* (1970), one of the earliest publications from the newly emerging women's liberation movement. It had also been published in *No More Fun and Games* in 1969. Tanner's collection of papers were read and circulated in women's "consciousness raising" (CR) groups that met regularly on the Lower East Side in New York City and demonstrates an early strategy of the women's movement. CR, described in detail in Robin Morgan's *Sisterhood Is Powerful* (1979) began in 1966 among a small group of radical women (in the privacy and safety of their homes) who wanted to enable women to understand that the personal was indeed political, and that women's oppression was tied to the existence of a "sex class system" which needed to be dismantled. In the process of putting together *Voices,* Tanner became angered by the absence of women in history books and decided to include in her anthology feminist voices from the past; she included over thirty selections from the United States and England, and only one black voice, that of Sojourner Truth. The premise of the book was that all women are "sisters," despite class differences, because of their common experience of oppression. This major tenet of "second-wave" white feminism in the 1970s would be challenged by women of color and others.

Weathers's essay challenges the black liberation movement to embrace women's liberation which she hoped would be responsive to the needs of all oppressed people.

Mary Ann Weathers }

AN ARGUMENT FOR BLACK WOMEN'S LIBERATION AS A REVOLUTIONARY FORCE

"Nobody can fight your battles for you; you have to do it yourself." This will be the premise used for the time being for stating the case for black women's liberation, although certainly it is the least significant. Black women, at least the black women I have come in contact with in the movement, have been expounding all their energies in "liberating" black men (if you yourself are not free, how can you "liberate" someone else?). Consequently, the movement has practically come to a standstill. Not entirely due however to wasted energies, but adhering to basic false concepts rather than revolutionary principles, and at this stage of the game we should understand that if it is not revolutionary it is false.

We have found that women's liberation is an extremely emotional issue, as well as an explosive one. Black men are still parroting the master's prattle about male superiority. This now brings us to a very pertinent question: How can we seriously discuss reclaiming our African heritage—cultural living modes which clearly refute not only patriarchy and matriarchy, but our entire family structure as we know it. African tribes live communally where households, let alone heads of households, are nonexistent.

It is really disgusting to hear black women talk about giving black men their manhood—or allowing them to get it. This is degrading to other black women and thoroughly insulting to black men (or at least it should be). How can someone "give" one something as personal as one's adulthood? That's precisely like asking the beast for your freedom. We also chew the fat about standing behind our men. This forces me to the question: Are we women or leaning posts and props? It sounds as if we are saying if we come out from behind him, he'll fall down. To me, these are clearly maternal statements and should be closely examined.

Women's liberation should be considered as a strategy for an eventual tie-up with the entire revolutionary movement consisting of women, men, and children. We are now speaking of real revolution (armed). If you cannot accept this fact purely and without problems, examine your reactions closely. We are playing to win and so are they. Viet Nam is simply a matter of time and geography.

Another matter to be discussed is the liberation of children from a sick slave culture. Although we don't like to see it, we are still operating within the confines of the slave culture. Black women use their children for their own selfish needs of worth and love. We try to live our lives, which are too oppressing to bear, through our children and thereby destroy them in the process. Obviously the much acclaimed plaudits of the love of the black mother has some discrepancies. If we allow ourselves to run from the truth, we run the risk of spending another 400 years in self-destruction. Assuming of course the beast would tolerate us that long, and we know he wouldn't.

Women have fought with men, and we have died with men, in every revolution, more timely in Cuba, Algeria, China, and now in Viet Nam. If you notice, it is a woman heading the "Peace Talks" in Paris for the NLF [National Liberation Front]. What is wrong with black women? We are clearly the most oppressed and degraded minority in the world, let alone the country. Why can't we rightfully claim our place in the world?

Realizing fully what is being said, you should be warned that the opposition for liberation will come from everyplace, particularly from other women and from black men. Don't allow yourselves to be intimidated any longer with this nonsense about the "Matriarchy" of black women. Black women are not matriarchs, but we have been forced to live in abandonment and been used and abused. The myth of the matriarchy must stop, and we must not allow ourselves to be sledgehammered by it any longer—not if we are serious about change and ridding ourselves of the wickedness of this alien culture. Let it be clearly understood that black women's liberation is not antimale; any such sentiment or interpretation as such cannot be tolerated. It must be taken clearly for what it is—pro-human for all peoples.

The potential for such a movement is boundless. Whereas in the past only certain type black people have been attracted to the movement—younger people, radicals, and militants. The very poor, the middle class, older people, and women have not become aware or have not been able to translate their awareness into action. Women's liberation offers such a channel for these energies.

Even though middle-class black women may not have suffered the brutal suppression of poor black people, they most certainly have felt the scourge of the male-superiority-oriented society as women, and would be more prone to help in alleviating some of the conditions of our more oppressed sisters by teaching, raising awareness and consciousness, verbalizing the ills of women and this society, helping to establish communes.

Older women have a wealth of information and experience to offer and would be instrumental in closing the communications gap between the generations. To be black and to tolerate this jive about discounting people over thirty is madness.

Poor women have knowledge to teach us all. Who else in this society see more and are more realistic about ourselves and this society and about the faults that lie within our own people than our poor women? Who else could profit and benefit from a communal setting that could be established than these sisters? We must let the sisters know that we are capable, and some of us already do love them. We women must begin to unabashedly learn to use the word "love" for one another. We must stop the petty jealousies, the violence, that we black women have for so long perpetrated on one another about fighting over this man or the other. (Black men should have better sense than to encourage this kind of destructive behavior.) We must turn to ourselves and one another for strength and solace. Just think for a moment what it would be like if we got together and internalized our own 24-hour-a-day communal centers knowing our children would be safe and loved constantly. Not to mention what it would do for everyone's egos, especially the children's. Women should not have to be enslaved by this society's concept of motherhood through their children; and then the kids suffer through a mother's resentment of them by beatings, punishment, and rigid discipline. All one has to do is look at the statistics of black women who are rapidly filling the beast's mental institutions to know that the time for innovation and change and creative thinking is here. We cannot sit on our behinds waiting for someone else to do it for us. We must save ourselves.

We do not have to look at ourselves as someone's personal sex objects, maids, baby sitters, domestics, and the like in exchange for a man's attention. Men hold this power, along with that of the breadwinner, over our heads for these services, and that's all it is—servitude. In return we torture him, and fill him with insecurities about his manhood, and literally force him to "cat" and "mess around" bringing in all sorts of conflicts. This is not the way really human people live. This is whitey's thing. And we play the game with as much proficiency as he does.

If we are going to bring about a better world, where best to begin than with ourselves? We must rid ourselves of our own hang-ups, before we can begin to talk about the rest of the world and we mean the world and nothing short of just that. (Let's not kid ourselves.) We will be in a position soon of having to hook up with the rest of the oppressed peoples of the world who are involved in liberation just as we are, and we had better be ready to act.

All women suffer oppression, even white women, particularly poor white women, and especially Indian, Mexican, Puerto Rican, Oriental, and black American women whose oppression is tripled by any of the above mentioned. But we do have female's oppression in common. This means that we can begin to talk to other women with this common factor and start building links with them and thereby build and transform the revolutionary force we are now beginning to amass. This is what Dr. King was doing. We can no longer allow ourselves to be duped by the guise of racism. Any time the white man admits to something, you know he is trying to cover something else up. We are all being exploited, even the white middle class, by the few people in control of this entire world. And to keep the real issue clouded, he keeps us at one another's throats with this racism jive. Although whites are most certainly racist, we must understand that they have been programmed to think in these patterns to divert their attention. If they are busy fighting us, then they have no time to question the policies of the war being run by this government. With the way the elections went down, it is clear that they are as powerless as the rest of us. Make no question about it, folks, this fool knows what he is doing. This man is playing the death game for money and power, not because he doesn't like us. He couldn't care less one way or the other. But think for a moment if we all go together and just walk on out. Who would fight his wars, who would run his police state, who would work his factories, who would buy his products?

We women must start this thing rolling.

Linda La Rue

L inda La Rue discusses in "The Black Movement and Women's Liberation" (1970) the frustration of some blacks with the emergence of the
middle-class women's liberation movement, whose origins could be traced
to John F. Kennedy's Commission on the Status of Women (1961), which
Eleanor Roosevelt chaired; the publication of Betty Friedan's *The Feminine
Mystique* (1963); the addition of "sex" to Title VII of the 1964 Civil Rights
Act (to prevent job discrimination based on gender); and the founding, in
1966, of the National Organization for Women (NOW), whose first president, Betty Friedan was replaced in 1970 by a black woman, union organizer and civil rights activist Aileen Hernandez. Novelist Toni Morrison
also raised questions about the white-dominated women's movement in
"What the Black Woman Thinks About Women's Lib," (*New York Times
Magazine,* 22 August 1971). This distrust of white women, a legacy of
slavery, explained in part the ambivalence of many black women about the
emerging movement, in which they felt marginalized There was also a
belief that the women's movement had helped to eclipse the black movement, which was perceived to be in disarray in some circles. La Rue, a
graduate student in political science at Purdue University when she wrote
"The Black Movement," also objected to the analogy drawn in then current
feminist literature between the oppression of women and the oppression of
blacks.

Linda La Rue }

THE BLACK MOVEMENT AND WOMEN'S LIBERATION

Let us first discuss what common literature addresses as the "common oppression" of blacks and women. This is a tasty abstraction designed purposely or inadvertently to draw validity and seriousness to the women's movement through a universality of plight. Every movement worth its "revolutionary salt" makes these headliner generalities about "common oppression" with others—but let us state unequivocally that, with few exceptions, the American white woman has had a better opportunity to live a free and fulfilling life, both mentally and physically, than any other group in the United States, with the exception of her white husband. Thus, any attempt to analogize black oppression with the plight of the American white woman has the validity of comparing the neck of a hanging man with the hands of an amateur mountain climber with rope burns.

"Common oppression" is fine for rhetoric, but it does not reflect the actual distance between the oppression of the black man and woman who are unemployed, and the "oppression" of the American white woman who is "sick and tired" of *Playboy* foldouts, or of Christian Dior lowering hemlines or adding ruffles, or of Miss Clairol telling her that blondes have more fun.

Is there any logical comparison between the oppression of the black woman on welfare who has difficulty feeding her children and the discontent of the suburban mother who has the luxury to protest the washing of the dishes on which her family's full meal was consumed?

The surge of "common oppression" rhetoric and propaganda may lure the unsuspecting into an intellectual alliance with the goals of women's liberation, but it is not a wise alliance. It is not that women ought not to be liberated from the shackles of their present unfulfillment, but the depth, the extent, the intensity, the importance—indeed, the suffering and depravity of the *real* oppression blacks have experienced—can only be minimized in an alliance with women who heretofore have suffered little more than boredom, genteel repression, and dishpan hands.

For all the similarities and analogies drawn between the liberation of women and the liberation of blacks, the point remains that when white women received their voting rights, most blacks, male and female, had been systematically disenfranchised since Reconstruction. And even in 1970, when women's right of franchise is rarely questioned, it is still a less than common occurrence for blacks to vote in some areas of the South.

Tasteless analogies like abortion for oppressed middle-class and poor women idealistically assert that all women have the right to decide if and when they want children and thus fail to catch the flavor of the actual circumstances. Actual circumstances boil down to middle-class women deciding when it is convenient to have children, while poor women decide the prudence of bringing into a world of already scarce resources another mouth to feed. Neither their motives nor their objectives are the same. But current literature leads one to lumping the decisions of these two women under one generalization, when in fact the difference between the plights of these two women is as clear as the difference between being hungry and out of work, and skipping lunch and taking a day off.

If we are realisticallly candid with ourselves, we will accept the fact that despite our beloved rhetoric of Pan-Africanism, our vision of Third-World liberation, and perhaps our dreams of a world state of multi-racial humanism, most blacks and a good many who generally exempt themselves from categories still want the proverbial "piece of cake." American values are difficult to discard, for, unlike what more militant "brothers" would have us believe, Americanism does not end with the adoption of Afro hairstyles on pregnant women covered in long African robes.

Indeed, the fact that the independent black capitalism demonstrated by the black Muslims and illustrated in Nixon's speeches appeared for many blacks as the way out of the ghetto into the light lends a truthful vengeance to the maxim that perhaps blacks are nothing more than black Anglo-Saxons. Upon the rebirth of the liberation struggle in the sixties, a whole genre of "women's place" advocates immediately relegated black women to home and babies which is almost as ugly an expression of black Anglo-Saxonism as is Nixon's concept of "black capitalism."

The study of many developing areas and countries reflects at least an attempt to allow freedom of education and opportunity to women. Yet black Americans have not adopted developing areas' "new role" paradigm, but rather the Puritan-American status of "home and babies" which is advocated by the capitalist Muslims. This reflects either ingrained Americanism or the lack of the simplest imagination.

Several weeks ago, women's lib advocates demanded that a local women's magazine be "manned" by a woman editor. Other segments of the women's movement have carried on smaller campaigns in industry and business.

If white women have heretofore remained silent while white men maintained the better position and monopolized the opportunities by excluding blacks, can we really expect that white women, when put in direct competition for employment, will be any more openminded than their male counterparts when it comes to the hiring of black males and females in the same positions for which they are competing? From the standpoint of previous American social interaction, it does not seem logical that white females will not be tempted to take advantage of the fact that they are white in an economy that favors whites. It is entirely possible that women's liberation has developed a sudden attachment to the black liberation movement as a ploy to share the attention that it has taken blacks 400 years to generate. In short, it can be argued that women's liberation not only attached itself to the black movement, but did so with only marginal concern for black women and black liberation and with functional concern for the rights of white women.

The industrial demands of two world wars temporarily offset the racial limitations to mobility and allowed the possibility of blacks entering industry, as an important labor force, to be actualized. Similarly women have benefited from an expanded science and industrialization. Their biological limitation, successfully curbed by the pill and by automation, which makes stressing physical labor more the exception than the rule, has created an impressively large and available labor force of women.

The black labor force, never fully employed and always representing a substantial percentage of the unemployed in the American economy, will now be driven into greater unemployment as white women converge at every level on an already dwindling job market.

Ideally, we chanced to think of women's liberation as a promising beginning of the "oppressed rising everywhere" in the typically Marxian fashion that many blacks seem drawn to. Instead, the spectre of racism and inadequate education, job discrimination, and even greater unequal opportunity will be, more than ever before, a function of neither maleness nor femaleness, but of blackness.

This discussion has been primarily to ward off any unintelligent alliance of black people with white women in this new liberation movement, Rhetoric and anathema hurled at the right industrial complex, idealism that speaks of a final humanism, and denunciation of the system that makes competition a fact of life, do not mean that women's liberation has as its goal anyone else's liberation except its own.

It is time that definitions be made clear. Blacks are *oppressed,* and that means unreasonably burdened, unjustly, severely, rigorously, cruelly, and harshly fettered by white authority. White women, on the other hand, are only *suppressed,* and that means checked, restrained, excluded from conscious and overt activity. And there is a difference.

For some, the dangers of an unintelligent alliance with women's liberation will suggest female suppression as the only protection against a new economic threat. For others, a greater answer is needed, and required, before women's liberation can be seen in perspective.

To say that black women must be freed before the black movement can attain full revolutionary consciousness is meaningless because of its malleability. To say that black women must be freed from the unsatisfactory male-female role relationship that we adopted from whites as the paradigm of the good family has more meaning because it indicates the incompatibility of white role models with the goal of black liberation. If there is anything to be learned from the current women's lib agitation, it is that roles are not ascribed and inherent, but adopted and interchangeable in every respect except pregnancy, breast feeding, and the system generally employed to bring the two former into existence.

Role integration, which I will elaborate upon as the goal and the strength of the black family, is substantially different from the role "usurpation" of men by women. The fact that the roles of man and woman are deemed in American society as natural and divine leads to false ego attachments to these roles. During slavery and following Reconstruction, black men felt inferior for a great number of reasons, among them that they were unable to work in positions comparable to the ones to which black women were assigned. With these positions often went fringe benefits of extra food, clothes, and perhaps elementary reading and writing skills. Black women were in turn jealous of white women and felt inadequate and inferior, because paraded in front of them constantly was the white woman of luxury who had no need for work, who could, as Sojourner Trutrh pointed out, "be helped into carriages and lifted over ditches and . . . have the best place everywhere."

The resulting "respect" for women and the acceptance of the dominating role for men encouraged the myth of the immutability of these roles. The term "matriarchy" Frazier employed and Moynihan exploited was used to indicate a dastardly, unnatural role alteration, which could be blamed for inequality of opportunity, discrimination in hiring, and sundry other ills. It was as if "matriarchy" were transgression of divine law or natural law and thus would be punished until the proper hierarchy of man over woman was restored.

Black people have an obligation, as do white women, to recognize that the designation of "mother-head" and "father-head" does not imply inferiority of one and the superiority of the other. They are merely arbitrary role distinctions that vary from culture to culture and circumstance to circumstance.

Thus to quip, as has been popularly done, that the only place in the black movement for black women is prone is actually supporting a white role ideal, and it is a compliment neither to men nor to women to advocate sexual capitalism or sexual colonialism.

It seems incongruous that the black movement has sanctioned the involvement of women in the Algerian revolution, even though its revolutionary circumstances modified and often altered the common role models, but they have been duped into hating even their own slave grandmothers, who in not so admirable yet equally frightening and demanding circumstances also modified and altered the common role models of the black family. Fanon wrote in glorious terms about this role change:

> The unveiled Algerian woman, who assumed an increasingly important place in revolutionary action, developed her personality, discovered the exalting realm of responsibility.... This woman who, in the avenues of Algiers or of Constantine, would carry the grenades or the submachine gun charges, the woman who tomorrow would be outraged, violated, tortured, could not put herself back into her former state of mind and relive her behavior of the past.... [1]

Can it not be said that in slavery black women assumed an increasingly important place in the survival action and thus developed their personalities and sense of responsibility? And after being outraged, violated, and tortured, could she be expected to put herself back into her former state of mind and relive her behavior of the past?

The crux of this argument is essentially that blacks, since slavery and throughout their entire existence in America, have also been living in revolutionary circumstances and under revolutionary pressures. Simply because the black liberation struggle has taken 400 years to come to fruition does not mean that it is not every bit as dangerous or psychologically exhausting as the Algerian struggle. Any revolution calls upon the best in both its men and its women. This is why Moynihan's statements that "matriarchy" is a root *cause* of black problems is as unfounded as it is inane. He does not recognize the liberation struggle and the demands that it has made on the black family.

How unfortunate that blacks and whites have allowed the most trying and bitter experience in the history of black people to be interpreted as the beginning of an "unashamed plot" to usurp the very manhood of black men. But the myth was perpetuated, and thus what brought the alteration of roles in Algeria was distorted and systematically employed to separate black men and women in America.

> Black women take kindness for weakness. Leave them the least little opening and they will put you on the cross.... It would be like trying to pamper a cobra.... [2]

Unless we realize how thoroughly the American value of male superiority and female inferiority has permeated our relationships with one another, we can never appreciate the role it plays in perpetuating racism and keeping black people divided.

Most, but not all, American relationships are based on some type of "exclusive competition of the superior and the exclusive competition of the inferior." This means essentially that the poor, the uneducated, the deprived, and the minorities of the aforementioned groups compete among themselves for the same scarce resources and inferior opportunities, while the privileged, middle-class, educated, and select white minorities compete with one another for rather plentiful resources and superior opportunities for prestige and power. Competition among groups is rare, due to the fact that elements who qualify are almost invariably absorbed to some extent (note the black middle class) by the group to which they seek entry. We may well understand that there is only one equal relationship between man and woman, black and white, in America, and this equality is based on whether or not you can force your way into qualifying for the same resources.

But instead of attempting to modify this competitive definition within the black movement, many black males have affirmed it as a way of maintaining the closure of male monopolization of scarce benefits and making the "dominion of males" impenetrable to black females. This is, of course, very much the American way of exploitation.

The order of logic that makes it possible to pronounce, as did Dr. Robert Staples, that "Black women cannot be free qua women until all blacks attain their liberation,"[3] maintains, whether purposely or not, that black women will be able to separate their femaleness from their blackness, and thus they will be able to be free as blacks, if not free as women; or, that male freedom ought to come first; or, finally, that the freedom of black women and men and the freedom of black people as a whole are not one and the same.

Only with the concept of role integration can we hope to rise above the petty demarcations of human freedom that America is noted for and that are unfortunately inherent in Dr. Staples's remark. Role integration is the realization that:

- ego attachments to particular activities or traits must be abolished as a method of determining malehood and femalehood; that instead, ego attachments must be distributed to a wider variety of tasks and traits in order to weaken the power of one activity in determining self-worth, and

- the flexibility of a people in effecting role alternation and role integration has been a historically proven asset to the survival of any people—witness Israel, China, and Algeria.

Thus, the unwitting adoption and the knowing perpetuation of this American value reflects three interrelated situations:

- black people's growing sense of security and well-being and their failure to recognize the expanse of black problems;

- black people's over-identification with the dominant group, even though the survival of blacks in America is not assured; and

- black people's belief in the myth of "matriarchy" and their subsequent rejection of role integration as unnatural and unnecessary.

While the rhetoric of black power and the advocates of cultural nationalism laud black people for their ability to struggle under oppressive odds, they simultaneously seek to strip away or incapacitate the phenomenon of role integration—the very means by which blacks were able to survive! They seek to replace it with a weak, intractable role separation which would completely sap the strength of the black movement because it would inhibit the mobilization of both women and men. It was this ability to mobilize black men and black women that guaranteed survival during slavery.

The strength of role integration is sorely overlooked as blacks throw away the hot comb, the bleach cream, the lye, and yet insist on maintaining the worst of American values by placing the strength of black women in the traction of the white female status.

I would think black men would want a better status for their sister black women; indeed, black women would want a better status for themselves, rather than a warmed-over throne of women's inferiority, which white women are beginning to abandon.

Though most white women's lib advocates fail to realize the possibility, their subsequent liberation may spell a strengthening of the status quo values from which they sought liberation. Since more and more women will be participating in the decision-making process, those few women participating in the "struggle" will be outnumbered by the more traditional middle-class women. This means that the traditional women will be in a position to take advantage of new opportunities, which radical women's liberation has struggled to win. Voting studies now reflect that the traditional women, middle-class and above, tend to vote the same way as their husbands. Because blacks have dealt with these husbands in the effort to secure jobs, housing, and education, it does not seem likely that blacks will gain significantly from the open mobility of less tolerant women whose viewpoints differ little from those of their husbands.

If white radical thought has called upon the strength of all women to take a position of responsibility and power, can blacks afford to relegate black women to "home and babies" while white women reinforce the status quo?

The cry of black women's liberation is a cry against chaining very much needed labor and agitating forces to a role that once belonged to impotent, apolitical white women. Blacks speak lovingly of the vanguard and the importance of women in the struggle and yet fail to recognize that women have been assigned a new place, based on white-ascribed characteristics of women, rather than on their actual potential. The black movement needs its women in a position of struggle, not prone. The struggle blacks face is not taking place between knives and forks, at the washboard, or in the diaper pail. It is taking place on the labor market, at the polls, in government, in the protection of black communities, in local neighborhood power struggles, in housing, and in education.

Can blacks afford to be so unobservant of current events as to send their women to fight a nonexistent battle in a dishpan?

Even now, the black adoption of the white values of women has begun to show its effects on black women in distinctive ways. The black liberation movement has created a politicized, unliberated copy of white womanhood. Black women who participated in the struggle have failed to recognize, for the most part, the unique contradiction between renunciation of capitalistic competition and the acceptance of sexual colonialism. The failure of the black movement to resolve and deal with this dilemma has perpetuated the following attitudes in American politicized black women:

· The belief in the myth of matriarchy. The black woman has been made to feel ashamed of her strength, and so to redeem herself she has adopted from whites the belief that superiority and dominance of the male is the most "natural" and "normal" relationship. She consequently believes that black women ought to be suppressed in order to attain that "natural balance."

· Because the white women's role has been held up as an example to all black women, many black women feel inadequate and so ardently compete in "femininity" with white females for black males' attention. She further competes with black females in an attempt to be the "blackest and the most feminine," thereby superior to her fellow black sisters in appealing to black politicized men. She competes also with the apolitical black female in an attempt to keep black males from "regressing" back to females whom she feels have had more "practice" in the traditional role of white woman than has she.

· Finally, she emphasizes the traditional roles of women, such as housekeeping, children, supportive roles, and self-maintenance, but she politicizes these roles by calling them the roles of black women. She then adopts the attitude that her job and her life is to have more children which can be used in the vanguard of the black struggle.

· Black women, as the song "Black Pearl" relates, have been put up where they belong, but by American standards. Is it so inconceivable that the American value of respect and human relationships is distorted? It has taken the birth of women's liberation to bring the black movement back to its senses.

· The black woman is demanding a new set of female definitions and a recognition of herself as a citizen, companion, and confidante, not a matriarchal villain or a stepstool babymaker. Role integration advocates the complementary recognition of man and woman, not the competitive recognition of same.

The recent unabated controversy over the use of birth control in the black community is of grave importance here. Black people, even the "most liberated of mind," are still infused with ascribed inferiority of females and the natural superiority of males. These same values foster the idea of "good blood" in our children. If indeed there can be any black liberation, it must start with the recognition of contradictions like the following.

It gives a great many black males pride to speak, as Dr. Robert Staple does, of ". . . the role of the black woman in the black liberation struggle is an important one and cannot be forgotten. From her womb have come the revolutionary warriors of our time."[4]

How many potential revolutionary warriors stand abandoned in orphanages while blacks rhetorize disdain for birth control as a "trick of The Man" to halt the growth of black population? Why are there not more revolutionary couples adopting black children? Could it be that the American concept of "bastard," which is equivalent to inferior in our society, reflects black Anglo-Saxonism? Do blacks, like whites, discriminate against black babies because they do not represent "our own personal" image? Or do blacks, like the most racist of whites, require that a child be of their own blood before they can love that child or feed it? Does the vanguard of which Dr. Staples so reverently speaks recognize the existence of the term "bastard"?

Someone once suggested that the word "bastard" be deleted from the values of black people. Would it not be more revolutionary for blacks to advocate a five-year moratorium on black births until every black baby in an American orphanage was adopted by one or more black parents? Then blacks could really have a valid reason for continuing to give birth. Children would mean more than simply a role for black women to play or fuel for the legendary vanguard. Indeed, blacks would be able to tap the potenial of the existing children and could sensibly add more potential to the black struggle for liberation. To do this would be to do something no other civilization, modern of course, has ever done, and blacks would be allowing every black child to have a home and not just a plot in some understaffed children's penal farm. . . .

We can conclude that black women's liberation and black men's liberation is what we mean when we speak of the liberation of black people. I maintain that the true liberation of black people depends on their rejection of the inferiority of women, the rejection of competition as the only viable relationship between men, and their reaffirmation of respect for general human potential in whatever form—man, child, or woman—it is conceived.

ENDNOTES

1. Frantz Fanon, *A Dying Colonialism* (New York: Grove, 1965), 107.

2. Eldridge Cleaver, *Soul on Ice* (New York: McGraw-Hill, 1968), 158.

3. Robert Staples, "The Myth of the Black Matriarchy," *Black Scholar* (January/February 1970): 16.

4. Ibid.

Patricia Haden, Donna Middleton, and Patricia Robinson

"A Historical and Critical Essay for Black Women," written by Patricia Haden, Donna Middleton, and Patricia Robinson, appeared in Leslie Tanner's *Voices from Women's Liberation* (1970) in the chapter on "Radical Women." M. Rivka Polatnick's dissertation "Strategies for Women's Liberation: A Study of a Black and a White Group of the 1960s" (1985, being revised for publication), is the only source I've been able to locate which describes this radical group of mostly poor black women from Mt. Vernon and New Rochelle, New York, whose writings appeared (without descriptions of the authors) in early treatises on women's liberation. These women wrote about themselves in *Lessons from the Damned* in an essay entitled "The Revolt of Poor Black Women" (89–111).

Like Mary Weathers, who also appears in this chapter, these women were involved in the black liberation struggle of the 60s and became frustrated by black men's sexism and their romantic views of Africa. They argue, for example, that "it is a historical fact that our own feudal period in Africa was cruelly oppressive to black women and peasants." They also critique Western gender and race frameworks which assign women and African peoples an inferior place. Their revolutionary vision of a new world imagined the end of all race, gender, and class hierarchies.

A neglected topic in many histories of the radical phase of the women's movement is the involvement of black women such as Haden, Middleton, and Robinson, though Alice Echols's *Daring to Be Bad* (1989) attempts to correct these omissions. In this regard Cellestine Ware, a cofounder (with Shulamith Firestone and Anne Koedt) of New York Radical Feminists in 1969 (initially called the Stanton-Anthony Brigade) joined a small group of black feminists committed to radical social change. During the organization's six-month probationary period, which would insure the involvement of *radical* feminists only, potential members participated in intensive study of feminist literature and consciousness-raising in order to understand the pervasiveness of systemic gender oppression. This small group of black women, which also included Florynce Kennedy and Patricia Robinson (New York social worker and psychotherapist) were adamant about the connection between racism and sexism and were very conspicuous because of the small number of women of color in the early years of the women's liberation movement.

Patricia Haden, Donna Middleton, and Patricia Robinson }

A HISTORICAL AND CRITICAL ESSAY FOR BLACK WOMEN

PART I

It is time for the black woman to take a look at herself, not just individually and collectively, but historically, if she is to avoid sabotaging and delaying the black revolution. Taking a look at yourself is not simply good tactics; it is absolutely necessary at this time in the black movement when even black radical males are still so insecure about their identity and so full of revolutionary fantasies that they cannot reach out to the black woman in revolutionary love—to urge us to begin to liberate ourselves, to tell us the truth: "Black women, you are the most pressed down of us all. Rise up . . . or we as black men can never be free!"

No black man can or should even think he can liberate us. Black men do not have our economic, social, biologic, and historic outlook. We are placed by those who have historically formed and manipulated the values in this society—white males—at the very bottom of all these perspectives. There is so much scorn and fear of WOMEN, ANIMAL, and BLACK in this Western culture, and since we are all three, we are simply kept out of history. Except for certain "house women," history is made only by males. The word ANIMAL is used by most males to mean a hated and despicable condition, and anything that is hated is simultaneously feared. Black women get put down as "bitch dogs" and "pussies" by Western white and black men, especially those who so smugly overestimate their brain power flying from campus to campus rapping about reason and SOUL. Their heads blow out this intellectual and educated *spiel* on white and black power. They back it up, like males have always done down through written history, with Gods in their own image. What a comedown it is to these males that they so often have to slip away from Harlem and Wall Street— to take "a crap." And how they struggle against the fact that, like so many animals, they are born of the female, and from the moment of their leaving our dark wombs, they, like all animals, begin to die! Yet we black women in our deepest humanity love and need black men, so we hesitate to revolt against them and go for ourselves.

If we black women get a few of the goodies—and we have bought all that jive put down on us by our field-nigger families, who all our lifetime pushed and hustled to be just simple house niggers—our anger and frustration go underground. We don't dare to endanger what we have been conditioned to accept as making it—a little glass house full of TV crap. We become nervous-nagging-narrow-minded murderers of ourselves and our children. We turn our madness and frustrations into other channels— against other black women and against our oppressed white sisters. We even trip out on smokes. We psyche out on sex with some cat that is as hung-up as we are. Then we got the nerve to break into the bag of cleanliness, godliness, and "I'm better than you are, baby!"

If we are poor black women, one night in the streets we explode. That small razor cupped in our fingers slashes his hated black face, that face that reflects our own. We look at him and see ourselves for what we really are —traitors to ourselves as poor black women and traitors to him, our street-brother, because we let him get to where he's at now—not a man just a jive-time turkey. We did not confront him long ago because our minds were not "wrapped." But now we can hear, see, feel our mistakes through his actions against us, toward his children and his mother. Now he's going to try to prove himself a man—"walk that walk; talk that talk." He's still hanging on to his jive thing. He bops on the corner and raps that he's straight. "I'm coming to my people!" He's still out there *fucking* with his drugs and talking shit. We lunge and sink our knife deep into his chest to blot out this awful truth. His blood oozes and stops while ours gushes from between our legs. Nothing gets born. We just end up murderers of the future of our people.

If we feel ourselves to be college-educated and politically aware, we end up nothing but common opportunists, playing some role of some dreamed-up African Queen, like we "gonna" rule some black country somewhere with some dashiki cat, acting haughty and ending up a tripped out black king. It does not matter to us that it is a historical fact that our own feudal period in Africa was cruelly oppressive to black women and peasants; that in Africa this warring and exploitative period was only interrupted by the landing of the European colonialist and slave trader. The African chiefs and their clique had been selling troublesome relatives and competing tribesmen to Europeans, just as now three-fourths of the so-called African statesmen are wheeling and dealing to sell the riches of their land and the labor of their people under neocolonialism.

We want desperately to feel black, but we also need to feel superior to whitey. We want to take his place. We really want to take over his system and rule over and exploit *everyone*. We want to be black masters and missies and have white maids and big white houses. We want to go to college to get good jobs and bring our learning back to the people in the streets. We're jiving—we're going to college to be social workers, NAACPers, teachers, doctors, lawyers, to keep the minds of the poor messed up and confused. We're going to college to be a part of the system.

All of us caught in this white male-jive that was meant to keep us hooked, exploited, and oppressed groove on this big white world of male supremacy, this way-out white capitalism. We hold tight to that little capital, clothes, furniture, and bank account, because if we lose it we'd have to go back to that old feeling of "I ain't nothing." "I ain't nowhere!" We are scared to death of that "big dick," the military-industrial complex. But how we give all praise to its power and tell all our friends how you can't beat the man and his system!

PART II

Myths unite people and steer their culture. They are the dreams and hopes; they are the fears and confusions of people. They are found in their folk tales, customs, in their religious and economic systems. Myths are not about real people, but do express the movement of opposites which is contradiction. The deep thoughts and everyday attitudes of human beings are full of contradictions. Like electrical energy, these thoughts that may oppose each other at times, and may join together as one at other times, move whole peoples into action. They also keep a society steadily moving in one direction or keep it in general peace with itself and its neighbors.

The American Dream is a myth. If you trace it symbolically and historically, it is a long route away from the ANIMAL BODY, away from the LAND, away from the WOMAN, and away from BLACK to condensed wealth (which is capital, and in the American Dream is money, machines, and property), to the CITIES, to MAN, and to WHITE. It is now the historical time to examine this myth that has made dead things and their creators sacred and overvalued by us.

Black women in the United States are so systematically left out of this society that we do not have an important part in producing the products bought and sold in this economy. We are civil servants, domestic servants, and servants to our families. We have no Gods in our own image, even though South American women, through Catholicism, have the Black Madonna. We are separated from black men in the same way that white women have been separated from white men. But we are even less valued by white and black males because we are not white. The American Dream is white and male when examined symbolically. We are the exact opposite

—black and female—and therefore carry the stigma, almost religious in nature, of the spurned and scorned and feared outcast.

The Western world was built on much more than colonialism and imperialism. It was also built on a split in the minds of men that thoroughly separated male from female as well as the body from the mind. This mind-blowing phenomenon caused all things having to do with the animal body to be repressed unconsciously. It is a fact of the psyche that repressed feelings, like oppressed peoples, do not stay repressed. Repressed feeling, like living energy, struggle against the force of repression to rise to consciousness. Repression of feelings, which we have learned through the conditioning of myths, is unacceptable, is a constant struggle.

Oppression of unacceptable people—unacceptable to those who rule, reinforced by myths from their imagination—is also a constant struggle between those who oppress and those who are oppressed. The oppressed, like repressed feelings, struggle to rise into the open and freedom. This is an example of the movement of opposites and contradiction.

Men who controlled the making of myths and culture after the overthrow of women managed to banish women and what they had always symbolized to a psychic underworld—a chaotic hell of folktales and fables. ANIMALS, WOMEN, and BLACKS became the underground witches and demons in men's minds. Men's own feminine nature, inherent in their bisexuality, was denied by them. This mental split enabled the male to deny the fact that he was an animal, to struggle against the darkness and toward the light, and to lessen the fact of his dependence on women for his nourishment before and after birth.

Most important, he could deny his dependence on women for his very birth and life. He could now ripple his large muscles and dream of soaring one day to the heavens, where he could be in charge and therefore be worshiped as the God of Light and the Heavens—an Apollo. The woman's body, which receives, hosts, and gives forth the future of the species, is inherently powerful. Her body and power had to be overthrown and suppressed when the male felt overwhelmed by this power and responded with the desperate need to take power from the woman. His desperate need became a living force in his use of external power over others and in the repression of his own soft femininity.

Some thousands of years ago, the female was considered the Goddess of the Universe from which heaven and earth sprang. Certainly this myth conforms to basic reality—out of one comes two. The female births both the male and the female. The Adam and Eve myth that has for so long been an important part of black women's education through our part-time father—the Negro minister—and our devoutly religious black mothers, turns this basic reality on its head and into its opposite. The male gives birth through the magical intervention of an all-powerful male God. The rib of Adam is plucked out and made into woman by this powerful medicine man who resembles in action the African and Asian tribal priest. Indeed, this is a powerful myth, for it grants the role of man in human creation while at the same time utterly denying woman's role. Deep down we black women still believe this clever religious tale that puts us out of creation. The fact that we do exposes our terrible dependence on outside authority and our fear of trusting and thinking for ourselves.

Anthropologists have been able to trace the animal family to the first human family, and they observe that the male's only role early in human history was insemination. Then he drifted off, leaving the female to take care of herself during pregnancy, birth, and the nursing of the young. When men and women began to live together, what can be called culture began. But women controlled the first fruit or surplus, the child, by reason of its long need for protection before it could take care of itself.

This was concrete power over the child and the male in those places with a warm climate and readily available food and water. There was no real need for a male food gatherer, a hunter, in this Garden of Eden. When the male came to live with the female more often, parents and an extended family in a culture began. The children were molded and conditioned by all manner of rituals and folk stories. Their education kept them under control and made them ready to follow the customs and rules set up by parents—first by the female, then the male.

Today in the time of the cities, cybernetics, nuclear power, and space exploration, white men have developed a man-made body, the self-regulating machine. It can operate a whole series of machines and adjust itself much as our human brain is able to readjust to the needs of our body and to operate the human body. It can also do the mental and physical work of men's bodies. At last man has done away with the practical need for his own human form. Now he must turn his attention to the danger the woman's body has always posed to his rule. He struggles to perfect artificial insemination and a machine host for the human fetus. He concerns himself with the biological control of reproduction of the species. Those white males who rule the free world (capitalist world) understand that if they are to keep their rule over women and so-called lesser men, they must stop being dependent on their bodies and must perfect machines which they can control absolutely.

PART III

When any group must be controlled and used, their gods, their religion, their land, and their tools of survival must be taken away from them. These are all reflections of themselves and their inner being as well as practical means to living. This must be done by force at first.

In the days when all the forest was evergreen, before the parakeet painted the autumn leaves red with the color from his breast, before the giants wandered through the woods with their heads above the treetops; in the days when the sun and moon walked the earth as man and wife, and many of the great sleeping mountains were human beings; in those far-off days witchcraft was known only to the women on Onaland (Tierra del Fuego, South America). They kept their own particular lodge, which no man dared approach. The girls, as they neared womanhood, were instructed in the magic arts, learning how to bring sickness and even death to all those who displeased them.

The men lived in abject fear and subjugation. Certainly they had bows and arrows with which to supply the camp with meat, yet they asked, what use were such weapons against the witchcraft and sickness? This tyranny of the women grew from bad to worse until it occurred to the men that a dead witch was less dangerous than a live one. They conspired together to kill off all the women; and there ensued a great massacre, from which not one woman in human form escaped.

The legend goes on to describe how the men waited for the little girls to grow up so they could have wives. Meanwhile, they plotted how they would have their own lodge or secret society from which all women would forever be excluded. The lowly servant tasks would be performed only by women. They would be frightened into submission by means of demons drawn from men's minds.

This is only one of thousands of such legends taken from all parts of the world that indicate some great crisis did occur where leadership of society was taken away from the women by force. We blacks have a splendid oral tradition and respect for the history that comes to us through our older women. Much of their practical advice on how to doctor our children, make delicious dinners out of scraps the white world throws away, how to get meaning from our dreams, how they felt about the time of slavery, and how they overcame the master, have kept our spirits up. For those of us who want to break out of the subtle oppression of all black women, stories from the past have been used extensively in our research. We have begun to feel sure that before written history there was a great fear of women on the part of males and a sense of being oppressed by their inner and reproductive powers. "The Great Earth Mother" could bring forth life and inexplicably take it away. This was one kind of power—internal power. In all the folktales it could be overcome only through external power—force. It is possible that long ago there was a time when women were murdered in some massive genocide and their ancient God-like reflection destroyed along with their temples. Archaeologists have found such temples in Asia and northern Africa, along with statues of some female goddess. But it is better for women to make the historical connections about these remains, since black and white males still need to rule over us and cannot be depended upon to be free of male prejudice against women. It is enough for now that we note that men were determined at one time in the past to have external power over women, and her symbolic representative nature. . . .

Historical and political understanding of ourselves and our actual place in the American Dream is more important at this time than the gun. We black women look at our backwardness, our colossal ignorance and political confusion, and want to give up. We do not like ourselves or each other. Our contradictory feelings about our black brothers, who seem simultaneously to move forward and backward, are increased by their continual cautioning that we must not move on our own or we will divide the movement. About all that we will mess up will be their black study, black power, cultural nationalism hustle. Forget black capitalism, because when the master offers you his thing, you know it's over! There have been other movements in history when revolutionary males have appeared conservative, opportunistic, or just "stopped at the pass," and revolutionary women have always forged ahead of the males at this time to take the revolution to a deeper stage.

Black revolutionary women are going to be able to smash the last myths and illusions on which all the jive-male oppressive power depends. We are not alone anymore. This country no longer holds one well-armed united majority against an unarmed minority. . . . There is a whole bunch of brown and yellow poor folks out there in the world that the ruling middle-class of this country have used and abused, stolen from, and sold their shoddy goods to at way-out prices. They are fighting back now, taking over those United States companies that sucked their people and their land. They are putting out the United States Army and capitalist investors as they did in China and Cuba.

But a new stage of history really began when the poor Vietnamese men, women, and children beat up and killed a whole lot of white and black cats who had decided it was easier to fight little, brown, poverty-stricken people than fight the MAN. One-half of these courageous South Vietnamese NLF [National Liberation Front] fighters are women and children, and they have proved that no United States male, black or white, got what it takes to destroy a people who have decided in their guts to own themselves and their land. That is power United States males have forgotten, but not black women, especially those of us who are poor.

White males are only in the image of God and supernaturally powerful with unbeatable instruments of death, in our own "messed-over" minds— not in the revolutionary world beyond the borders of the United States. All that "Big Daddy" and "head of family" shit is possible because we play the game—ego-tripping black men and ourselves. If our minds are together, we can work, think, and decide everything for ourselves. It is only a cruel, capitalist system that digs money, property, and white broads more than it digs people, that forces us to be the dependents of men and wards of the state. We recognize that black males are frail human beings, born of women who love them, not for their "dick power" or their bread, but for their gentle, enduring, and powerful humanity.

It is important for black women to remind themselves occasionally that no black man gets born unless we permit it—even after we open our legs. That is the first, simple step to understanding the power that we have. The second is that all children belong to the women because only we know who the mother is. As to who the father is—well, we can decide that, too—any man we choose to say it is, and that neither the child nor MAN was made by God.

Third, we are going to have to put ourselves back to school, do our own research and analysis. We are going to have to argue with and teach one another, grow to respect and love one another. There are a lot of black chicks, field niggers wanting to be house niggers, who will fight very hard to keep this decaying system because of the few, petty privileges it gives them over poor black women. We will be disappointed to lose some house women who will have to revert to their class and who will go with the master, like they did during slavery. Finally, we are going to have to give the brothers a helping hand here and there because they will be uptight, not only with the enemy but with us. But at the same time we've got to do our own thing and get our own minds together.

All revolutionaries, regardless of sex, are the smashers of myths and the destroyers of illusion. They have always died and lived again to build new myths. They dare to dream of a utopia, a new kind of synthesis and equilibrium.

Pauli Murray (1910–1985)

Pauli Murray, lawyer, professor, ordained priest, civil rights activist, feminist, and writer, was born in Baltimore, Maryland, and a significant figure in the emergence of the modern women's movement. She was the only woman in her law school class at Howard University, the first African American to earn a doctorate in jurisprudence from Yale University Law School (1965), and the first black woman to be ordained an Episcopalian priest (1977). She was a member of President Kennedy's Commission on the Status of Women, where she joined a small but growing informal network of feminists. She was also involved in the struggle to pass Title VII of the landmark 1964 Civil Rights Act, which mandated equal employment opportunities for women. A founding member of the National Organization for Women in 1966, she remained a crusader for women's rights throughout her life. "Jane Crow and the Law," which appeared in the December 1965 issue of the *George Washington Law Review* and was coauthored with lawyer Mary O. Eastwood, was an early response to Title VII by feminist lawyers. Her essay "The Liberation of Black Women," which appeared in *Voices of the New Feminism* (1970), analyzed the double burden of racism and sexism that Black women suffer. She also coined the term "Jane Crow" to refer to institutional barriers and stereotypes that prevented black women from realizing their full potential. She also critiqued the black movement in the 1960s for not resisting patriarchal frameworks and for being essentially a "bid of black males to share power with white males in a continuing patriarchal society in which both black and white females are relegated to secondary status."

For additional information about Murray and her family see *Proud Shoes: The Story of an American Family* (1956) and her autobiography *Song in a Weary Throat* (1987).

Pauli Murray }

The Liberation of Black Women

Black women, historically, have been doubly victimized by the twin immoralities of Jim Crow and Jane Crow. Jane Crow refers to the entire range of assumptions, attitudes, stereotypes, customs, and arrangements that have robbed women of a positive self-concept and prevented them from participating fully in society as equals with men. Traditionally, racism and sexism in the United States have shared some common origins, displayed similar manifestations, reinforced one another, and are so deeply intertwined in the country's institutions that the successful outcome of the struggle against racism will depend in large part upon the simultaneous elimination of all discrimination based upon sex. Black women, faced with these dual barriers, have often found that sex bias is more formidable than racial bias. If anyone should ask a Negro woman in America what has been her greatest achievement, her honest answer would be, "I survived!"

Negro women have endured their double burden with remarkable strength and fortitude. With dignity they have shared with black men a partnership as members of an embattled group excluded from the normal protections of the society and engaged in a struggle for survival during nearly four centuries of a barbarous slave trade, two centuries of chattel slavery, and a century or more of illusive citizenship. Throughout this struggle, into which has been poured most of the resources and much of the genius of successive generations of American Negroes, these women have often carried a disproportionate share of responsibility for the black family as they strove to keep its integrity intact against a host of indignities to which it has been subjected. Black women have not only stood shoulder to shoulder with black men in every phase of the struggle, but they have often continued to stand firmly when their men were destroyed by it. Few blacks are unfamiliar with that heroic, if formidable, figure exhorting her children and grandchildren to overcome every obstacle and humiliation and to "Be somebody!"

In the battle for survival, Negro women developed a tradition of independence and self-reliance, characteristics that, according to the late Dr. E. Franklin Frazier, Negro sociologist, have "provided generally a pattern of equalitarian relationship between men and women in America." The historical factors that have fostered the black women's feeling of independence have been the economic necessity to earn a living to help support their families—if indeed they were not the sole breadwinners—and the need for the black community to draw heavily upon the resources of all of its members in order to survive.

Yet these survival values have often been distorted, and the qualities of strength and independence observable in many Negro women have been stereotyped as "female dominance" attributed to the "matriarchal" character of the Negro family developed during slavery and its aftermath. The popular conception is that because society has emasculated the black male, he has been unable to assume his economic role as head of the household, and the black woman's earning power has placed her in a dominant position. The black militant's cry for the retrieval of black manhood suggests an acceptance of this stereotype, an association of masculinity with male dominance, and a tendency to treat the values of self-reliance and independence as purely masculine traits. Thus, while blacks generally have recognized the fusion of white supremacy and male dominance (note the popular expressions "The Man" and "Mr. Charlie"), male spokesmen for Negro rights have sometimes pandered to sexism in their fight against racism. When nationally known civil rights leader James Farmer ran for Congress against Mrs. Shirley Chisholm in 1968, his campaign literature stressed the need for a "strong male image" and a "man's voice" in Washington.

If idealized values of masculinity and feminity are used as criteria, it would be hard to say whether the experience of slavery subjected the black male to any greater loss of his manhood than the black female of her womanhood. The chasm between the slave woman and her white counterpart (whose own enslavement was masked by her position as a symbol of high virtue and an object of chivalry) was as impassable as the gulf between the male slave and his arrogant white master. If black males suffered from real and psychological castration, black females bore the burden of real or psychological rape. Both situations involved the negation of the individual's personal integrity and attacked the foundations of one's sense of personal worth.

The history of slavery suggests that black men and women shared a rough equality of hardship and degradation. While the black woman's position as sex object and breeder may have given her temporarily greater leverage in dealing with her white master than the black male enjoyed, in the long run it denied her a positive image of herself. On the other hand, the very nature of slavery foreclosed certain conditions experienced by white women. The black woman had few expectations of economic dependence upon the male or of derivative status through marriage. She emerged from slavery without the illusions of a specially protected position as a woman or the possibilities of a parasitic existence as a woman. As Dr. Frazier observed, "Neither economic necessity nor tradition has instilled in her the spirit of subordination to masculine authority. Emancipation only tended to confirm in many cases the spirit of self-sufficiency, which slavery had taught."

Throughout the history of black America, its women have been in the forefront of the struggle for human rights. A century ago Harriet Tubman and Sojourner Truth were titans of the abolitionist movement. In the 1890s Ida B. Wells-Barnett carried on a one woman crusade against lynching. Mary McLeod Bethune and Mary Church Terrell symbolize the stalwart woman leaders of the first half of the twentieth century. At the age of ninety, Mrs. Terrell successfully challenged segregation in public places in the nation's capital through a Supreme Court decision in 1953.

In contemporary times we have Rosa Parks setting off the mass struggle for civil rights in the South by refusing to move to the back of the bus in Montgomery in 1955; Daisy Bates guiding the Little Rock Nine through a series of school desegregation crises in 1957–59; Gloria Richardson facing down the National Guard in Cambridge, Maryland, in the early sixties; or Coretta Scott King picking up the fallen standard of her slain husband to continue the fight. Not only these and many other women whose names are well known have given this great human effort its peculiar vitality, but also women in many communities whose names will never be known have revealed the courage and strength of the black woman in America. They are the mothers who stood in school yards of the South with their children, many times alone. One cannot help asking: "Would the black struggle have come this far without the indomitable determination of its women?"

Now that some attention is finally being given to the place of the Negro in American history, how much do we hear of the role of the Negro woman? Of the many books published on the Negro experience and the black revolution in recent times, to date not one has concerned itself with the struggles of black women and their contributions to history. Of approximately 800 full-length articles published in the *Journal of Negro History* since its inception in 1916, only six have dealt directly with the Negro woman. Only two have considered Negro women as a group: Carter G. Woodson's "The Negro Washerwoman: A Vanishing Figure" (14 *JNH*, 1930) and Jessie W. Pankhurst's "The Role of the Black Mammy in the Plantation Household" (28 *JNH*, 1938).

This historical neglect continues into the present. A significant feature of the civil rights revolution of the 1950s and 1960s was its inclusiveness born of the broad participation of men, women, and children without regard to age and sex. As indicated, school children often led by their mothers in the 1950s won worldwide acclaim for their courage in desegregating the schools. A black child can have no finer heritage to give a sense of "somebodiness" than the knowledge of having personally been part of the great sweep of history. (An older generation, for example, takes pride in the use of the term "Negro," having been part of a seventy-five-year effort to dignify the term by capitalizing it. Now some black militants with a woeful lack of historical perspective have allied themselves symbolically with white racists by downgrading the term to lowercase again.) Yet, despite the crucial role which Negro women have played in the struggle, in the great mass of magazine and newspaper print expended on the racial crisis, the aspirations of the black community have been articulated almost exclusively by black males. There has been very little public discussion of the problems, objectives, or concerns of black women.

Reading through much of the current literature on the black revolution, one is left with the impression that for all the rhetoric about self-determination, the main thrust of black militancy is a bid of black males to share power with white males in a continuing patriarchal society in which both black and white females are relegated to a secondary status. For example, *Ebony* magazine published a special issue on the Negro woman in 1966. Some of the articles attempted to delineate the contributions of Negro women as heroines in the civil rights battle in Dixie, in the building of the New South, in the arts and professions, and as intellectuals. The editors, however, felt it necessary to include a full-page editorial to counter the possible effect of the articles by women contributors. After paying tribute to the Negro woman's contributions in the past, the editorial reminded *Ebony*'s readers that "the past is behind us," that "the immediate goal of the Negro woman today should be the establishment of a strong family unit in which the father is the dominant person," and that the Negro woman would do well to follow the example of the Jewish mother "who pushed her husband to success, educated her male children first, and engineered good marriages for her daughters." The editors also declared that the career woman "should be willing to postpone her aspirations until her children, too, are old enough to be on their own," and, as if the point had not been made clear enough, suggested that if "the woman should, by any chance, make more money than her husband, the marriage could be in real trouble."

While not as blatantly Victorian as *Ebony,* other writers on black militancy have shown only slightly less myopia. In *Black Power and Urban Crisis*, Dr. Nathan Wright, chairman of the 1967 National Black Power Conference, made only three brief references to women: "the employment of female skills," "the beauty of black women," and housewives. His constant reference to Black Power was in terms of black males and black manhood. He appeared to be wholly unaware of the parallel struggles of women and youth for inclusion in decision making, for when he dealt with the reallocation of power, he noted that "the churches and housewives of America" are the most readily influential groups which can aid in this process.

In *Black Rage*, psychiatrists Greer and Cobbs devote a chapter to achieving womanhood. While they sympathetically describe the traumatic experience of self-depreciation which a black woman undergoes in a society in which the dominant standard of beauty is "the blond, blue-eyed, white-skinned girl with regular features," and make a telling point about the burden of the stereotype that Negro women are available to white men, they do not get beyond a framework in which the Negro woman is seen as a sex object. Emphasizing her concern with "feminine narcissism" and the need to be "lovable" and "attractive," they conclude: "Under the sign of discouragement and rejection which governs so much of her physical operation, she is inclined to organize her personal ambitions in terms of her achievements serving to compensate for other losses and hurts." Nowhere do the authors suggest that Negro women, like women generally, might be motivated to achieve as *persons*. Implied throughout the discussion is the sexuality of Negro females.

The ultimate expression of this bias is the statement attributed to a black militant male leader: "The position of the black woman should be prone." Thus, there appears to be a distinctly conservative and backward-looking view in much of what black males write today about black women, and many black women have been led to believe that the restoration of the black male to his lost manhood must take precedence over the claims of black women to equalitarian status. Consequently, there has been a tendency to acquiesce without vigorous protest to policies which emphasize the "underemployment" of the black male in relation to the black female and which encourage the upgrading and education of black male youth while all but ignoring the educational and training needs of black female youth, although the highest rates of unemployment today are among black female teenagers. A parallel tendency to concentrate on career and training opportunities primarily for black males is evident in government and industry.

As this article goes to press, further confirmation of a patriarchal view on the part of organizations dominated by black males is found in the BLACK DECLARATION OF INDEPENDENCE published as a full-page advertisement in the *New York Times* on July 3, 1970. Signed by members of the National Committee of Black Churchmen and presuming to speak "By Order and on Behalf of Black People," this document ignores both the personhood and the contributions of black women to the cause of human rights. The drafters show a shocking insensitivity to the revitalized women's rights/women's liberation movement which is beginning to capture the front pages of national newspapers and the mass media. It evidences a parochialism that has hardly moved beyond the eighteenth century in its thinking about women. Not only does it paraphrase the 1776 Declaration about the equality of "all Men" with a noticeable lack of imagination, but it also declares itself "in the Name of our good People and our own Black Heroes." Then follows a list of black males prominent in the historic struggle for liberation. The names of Harriet Tubman, Sojourner Truth, Mary McLeod Bethune, or Daisy Bates, or any other black women are conspicuous by their absence. If black male leaders of the Christian faith—who concededly have suffered much though denigration of their personhood and who are committed to the equality of all in the eyes of God—are callous to the indivisibility of human rights, who is to remember?

In the larger society, of course, black and white women share the common burden of discrimination based upon sex. The parallels between racism and sexism have been distinctive features of American society, and the movements to eliminate these two evils have often been allied and sometimes had interchangeable leadership. The beginnings of a women's rights movement in this country is linked with the abolitionist movement. In 1840, William Lloyd Garrison and Charles Remond, the latter a Negro, refused to be seated as delegates to the World Anti-Slavery Convention in London when they learned that women members of the American delegation had been excluded because of their sex and could sit only in the balcony and observe the proceedings. The seed of the Seneca Falls Convention of 1848, which marked the formal beginning of the women's rights struggle in the United States, was planted at that London conference. Frederick Douglass attended the Seneca Falls Convention and rigorously supported Elizabeth Cady Stanton's daring resolution on woman's suffrage. Except for a temporary defection during the controversy over adding "sex" to the Fifteenth Amendment, Douglass remained a staunch advocate of women's rights until his death in 1895. Sojourner Truth and other black women were also active in the movement for women's rights, as indicated earlier.

Despite the common interests of black and white women, however, the dichotomy of a racially segregated society which has become increasingly polarized has prevented them from cementing a natural alliance. Communication and cooperation have been hesitant, limited, and formal. In the past Negro women have tended to identify discrimination against them as primarily racial and have accorded high priority to the struggle for Negro rights. They have had little time or energy for consideration of women's rights. And, until recent years, their egalitarian position in the struggle seemed to justify such preoccupation.

As the drive for black empowerment continues, however, black women are becoming increasingly aware of a new development that creates for them a dilemma of competing identities and priorities. On the one hand, as Dr. Jeanne Noble has observed, "establishing 'black manhood' became a prime goal of black revolution," and black women began to realize "that black men wanted to determine the policy and progress of black people without female participation in decision making and leadership positions." On the other hand, a rising movement for women's liberation is challenging the concept of male dominance, which the black revolution appears to have embraced. Confronted with the multiple barriers of poverty, race, and sex, the quandary of black women is how best to distribute their energies among these issues and what strategies to pursue that will minimize conflicting interests and objectives.

Cognizant of the similarities between paternalism and racial arrogance, black women are nevertheless handicapped by the continuing stereotype of the black "matriarchy" and the demand that black women now step back and push black men into positions of leadership. They are made to feel disloyal to racial interests if they insist upon women's rights. Moreover, to the extent that racial polarization often accompanies the thrust for black power, black women find it increasingly difficult to make common cause with white women. These developments raise several questions. Are black women gaining or losing in the drive toward human rights? As the movement for women's liberation becomes increasingly a force to be reckoned with, are black women to take a backward step and sacrifice their egalitarian tradition? What are the alternatives to matriarchal dominance on the one hand or male supremacy on the other?

Much has been written in the past about the matriarchal character of Negro family life, the relatively favored position of Negro women, and the tensions and difficulties growing out of the assumptions that they are better educated and more able to obtain employment than Negro males. These assumptions require closer examination. It is true that according to reports of the Bureau of the Census, in March 1968 an estimated 278,000 nonwhite women had completed four or more years of college—86,000 more than male college graduates in the nonwhite population (Negro women constitute 93 percent of all nonwhite women), and that in March 1966 the median years of school completed by Negro females (10.1) was slightly higher than that for Negro males (9.4). It should be borne in mind that this is not unique to the black community. In the white population as well, females exceed males in median years of school completed (12.2 to 12.0) and do not begin to lag behind males until the college years. The significant fact is that the percentage of both sexes in the Negro population eighteen years of age and over in 1966 who had completed four years of college was roughly equivalent (males: 2.2 percent; females: 2.3 percent). When graduate training is taken into account, the proportion of Negro males with five or more years of college training (3.3 percent) moved ahead of the Negro females (3.2 percent). Moreover, 1966 figures show that a larger proportion of

Negro males (63 percent) than Negro females (57 percent) was enrolled in school and that this superiority continued into college enrollments (males 5 percent; females 4 percent). These 1966 figures reflect a concerted effort to broaden educational opportunities for Negro males manifested in recruitment policies and scholarship programs made available primarily to Negro male students. Though later statistics are not now available, this trend appears to have accelerated each year.

The assumption that Negro women have more education than Negro men also overlooks the possibility that the greater number of college-trained Negro women may correspond to the larger number of Negro women in the population. Of enormous importance to a consideration of Negro family life and the relation between the sexes is the startling fact of the excess of females over males. The Bureau of the Census estimated that in July 1968 there were 688,000 more Negro females than Negro males. Although census officials attribute this disparity to errors in counting a "floating" Negro male population, this excess has appeared in steadily increasing numbers in every census since 1860, but has received little analysis beyond periodic comment. Over the past century the reported ratio of black males to black females has decreased. In 1966, there were less than ninety-four black males to every one hundred females.

The numerical imbalance between the sexes in the black population is more dramatic than in any other group in the United States. Within the white population the excess of women shows up in the middle or later years. In the black population, however, the sex imbalance is present in every age group over fourteen and is greatest during the age when most marriages occur. In the twenty-five to forty-four age group, the percentage of males within the black population drops to 86.9 as compared to 96.9 for white males.

It is now generally known that females tend to be constitutionally stronger than males, that male babies are more fragile than female babies, that boys are harder to rear than girls, that the male death rate is slightly higher and life expectancy for males is shorter than that of females. Add to these general factors the special hardships to which the Negro minority is exposed—poverty, crowded living conditions, poor health, marginal jobs and minimum protection against hazards of accident and illness—and it becomes apparent that there is much in the American environment that is particularly hostile to the survival of the black male. But even if we discount these factors and accept the theory that the sex ratio is the result of errors in census counting, it is difficult to avoid the conclusion that a large number of black males have so few stable ties that they are not included as functioning units of the society. In either case formidable pressures are created for black women.

The explosive social implications of an excess of more than half a million black girls and women over fourteen years of age are obvious in a society in which the mass media intensify notions of glamour and expectations of romantic love and marriage, while at the same time there are many barriers against interracial marriages. When such marriages do take place, they are more likely to involve black males and white females, which tends to aggravate the issue. (No value judgment about interracial marriages is implied here. I am merely trying to describe a social dilemma.) The problem of an excess female population is a familiar one in countries which have experienced heavy male casualties during wars, but an excess female ethnic minority as an enclave within a larger population raises important social issues. To what extent are the tensions and conflicts traditionally associated with the matriarchal framework of Negro family life in reality due to this imbalance and the pressures it generates? Does this excess explain the active competition between Negro professional men and women seeking employment in markets which have limited or excluded Negroes? And does this competition intensify the stereotype of the matriarchal society and female dominance? What relationship is there between the high rate of illegitimacy among black women and the population figures we have described?

These figures suggest that the Negro woman's fate in the United States, while inextricably bound with that of the Negro male in one sense, transcends the issue of Negro rights. Equal opportunity for her must mean equal opportunity to compete for jobs and to find a mate in the total society. For as long as she is confined to an area in which she must compete fiercely for a mate, she will remain the object of sexual exploitation and the victim of all the social evils that such exploitation involves.

When we compare the position of the black woman to that of the white woman, we find that she remains single more often, bears more children, is in the labor market longer and in greater proportion, has less education, earns less, is widowed earlier, and carries a relatively heavier economic responsibility as family head than her white counterpart.

In 1966, black women represented one of every seven women workers, although Negroes generally constitute only 11 percent of the total population in the United States. Of the 3,105,000 black women eighteen years of age and over who were in the labor force, however, nearly half (48.2 percent) were either single, widowed, divorced, separated from their husbands, or had husbands absent for other reasons, as compared with 31.8 percent of white women in similar circumstances. Moreover, six of every ten black women were in household employment or other service jobs. Conversely, while 58.8 percent of all women workers held white-collar positions, only 23.2 percent of black women held such jobs.

As working wives, black women contribute a higher proportion to family income than do white women. Among nonwhite wives in 1965, 58 percent contributed 20 percent or more of the total family income, 43 percent contributed 30 percent or more and 27 percent contributed 40 percent or more. The comparable percentages for white wives were 56 percent, 40 percent, and 24 percent respectively.

Black working mothers are more heavily represented in the labor force than white mothers. In March 1966, nonwhite working mothers with children under eighteen years of age represented 48 percent of all nonwhite mothers with children this age as compared with 35 percent of white working mothers. Nonwhite working mothers also represented four of every ten of all nonwhite mothers of children under six years of age. Of the 12,300,000 children under fourteen years of age in February 1965 whose mothers worked, only 2 percent were provided group care in day-care centers. Adequate child care is an urgent need for working mothers generally, but it has particular significance for the high proportion of black working mothers of young children.

Black women also carry heavy responsibilities as family heads. In 1966, one-fourth of all black families were headed by a woman as compared with less than one-tenth of all white families. The economic disabilities of women generally are aggravated in the case of black women. Moreover, while all families headed by women are more vulnerable to poverty than husband-wife families, the black woman family head is doubly victimized. For example, the median wage or salary income of all women workers who were employed full-time the year round in 1967 was only 58 percent of that of all male workers, and the median earnings of white females was less than that of black males. The median wage of nonwhite women workers, however, was $3,268, or only 71 percent of the median income of white women workers. In 1965, one-third of all families headed by women lived in poverty, but 62 percent of the 1,132,000 nonwhite families with a female head were poor.

A significant factor in the low economic and social status of black women is their concentration at the bottom rung of the employment ladder. More than one-third of all nonwhite working women are employed as private household workers. The median wages of women private household workers who were employed full time the year round in 1968 was only $1,701. Furthermore, these workers are not covered by the federal minimum wage and hours law and are generally excluded from state wage and hours laws, unemployment compensation, and workmen's compensation.

The black woman is triply handicapped. She is heavily represented in nonunion employment and thus has few of the benefits to be derived from labor organization or social legislation. She is further victimized by discrimination because of race and sex. Although she has made great strides in recent decades in closing the educational gap, she still suffers from inadequate education and training. In 1966, only 71.1 percent of all Negro women had completed eight grades of elementary school compared to 88 percent of all white women. Only one-third (33.2 percent) of all Negro women had completed high school as compared with more than one-half of all white women (56.3). More than twice as many white women, proportionally, have completed college (7.2 percent) as black women (3.2 percent).

The notion of the favored economic position of the black female in relation to the black male is a myth. The 1966, median earnings of full-time year-round nonwhite female workers was only 65 percent of that of nonwhite males. The unemployment rate for adult nonwhite women (6.6) was higher than for their male counterparts (4.9). Among nonwhite teenagers, the unemployment rate for girls was 31.1 as compared with 21.2 for boys.

In the face of their multiple disadvantages, it seems clear that black women can neither postpone nor subordinate the fight against sex discrimination to the black revolution. Many of them must expect to be self-supporting and perhaps to support others for a considerable period or for life. In these circumstances, while efforts to raise educational and employment levels for black males will ease some of the economic and social burdens now carried by many black women, for a large and apparently growing minority these burdens will continue. As a matter of sheer survival black women have no alternative but to insist upon equal opportunities without regard to sex in training, education, and employment. Given their heavy family responsibilities, the outlook for their children will be bleak indeed unless they are encouraged in every way to develop their potential skills and earning power.

Because black women have an equal stake in women's liberation and black liberation, they are key figures at the juncture of these two movements. White women feminists are their natural allies in both causes. Their own liberation is linked with the issues that are stirring women today: adequate income maintenance and the elimination of poverty, repeal or reform of abortion laws, a national system of child-care centers, extension of labor standards to workers now excluded, cash maternity benefits as part of a system of social insurance, and the removal of all sex barriers to educational and employment opportunities at all levels. Black women have a special stake in the revolt against the treatment of women primarily as sex objects, for their own history has left them with the scars of the most brutal and degrading aspects of sexual exploitation.

The middle-class Negro woman is strategically placed by virtue of her tradition of independence and her long experience in civil rights and can play a creative role in strengthening the alliance between the black revolution and women's liberation. Her advantages of training and her values make it possible for her to communicate with her white counterparts, interpret the deepest feelings within the black community, and cooperate with white women on the basis of mutual concerns as women. The possibility of productive interchange between black and white women is greatly facilitated by the absence of power relationships, which separate black and white males as antagonists. By asserting a leadership role in the growing feminist movement, the black woman can help to keep it allied to the objectives of black liberation while simultaneously advancing the interests of all women.

The lesson of history that all human rights are indivisible and that the failure to adhere to this principle jeopardizes the rights of all is particularly applicable here. A built-in hazard of an aggressive ethnocentric movement that disregards the interests of other disadvantaged groups is that it will become parochial and ultimately self-defeating in the face of hostile reactions, dwindling allies, and mounting frustrations. As Dr. Caroline F. Ware has pointed out, perhaps the most essential instrument for combating the divisive effect of a black-only movement is the voice of black women insisting upon the unity of civil rights of women and Negroes as well as other minorities and excluded groups. Only a broad movement for human rights can prevent the black revolution from becoming isolated and can insure its ultimate success.

Beyond all the present conflict lies the important task of reconciliation of the races in America on the basis of genuine equality and human dignity. A powerful force in bringing about this result can be generated through the process of black and white women working together to achieve their common humanity.

Angela Davis (1944–   )

Angela Davis, born in Birmingham, Alabama, has been a relentless political activist involved in "local and global struggles for progressive social change" (Angela Davis, *Women, Culture, and Politics*, xiv) for over two decades. She has lent her radical voice as a consummate lecturer to a variety of urgent social issues—racism, economic justice, poverty, prison reform, women's liberation, particularly for women of color nationally and internationally, black liberation, welfare reform, reproductive freedom, sexual violence, health, child care, public education, apartheid, peace, and disarmament. Her landmark essay, "Reflections on the Black Woman's Role in the Community of Slaves," written while she was in prison on false charges of conspiracy and murder (she was acquitted in 1972), is an early example of black feminist discourse. Revisionist in approach, it debunks prevalent stereotypes about black women and unmasks androcentric biases in American history by calling attention to the scholarly neglect of the intellectual work and experiences of black women. She rejects, as well, the conventional African American history paradigm that posits black male experience as the norm and renders invisible, for example, black female resistance to slavery.

Angela Davis }

Reflections on the Black Woman's Role in the Community of Slaves

I

The paucity of literature on the black woman is outrageous on its face. But we must also contend with the fact that too many of these rare studies must claim as their signal achievement the reinforcement of fictitious clichés. They have given credence to grossly distorted categories through which the black woman continues to be perceived. In the words of Nathan and Julia Hare, " ... she has been labeled 'aggressive' or 'matriarchal' by white scholars and 'castrating female' by [some] blacks." (*Transaction*, November/December, 1970) Many have recently sought to remedy this situation. But for the time being, at least, we are still confronted with these reified images of ourselves. And for now, we must still assume the responsibility of shattering them.

Initially, I did not envision this paper as strictly confined to the era of slavery. Yet, as I began to think through the issue of the black matriarch, I came to the conclusion that it had to be refuted at its presumed historical inception.

The chief problem I encountered stemmed from the conditions of my incarceration: opportunities for researching the issue I wanted to explore were extremely limited. I chose, therefore, to entitle this piece "Reflections..." It does not pretend to be more than a collection of ideas that would constitute a starting point—a framework within which to conduct a rigorous reinvestigation of the black woman as she interacted with her people and with her oppressive environment during slavery.

I would like to dedicate these reflections to one of the most admirable black leaders to emerge from the ranks of our liberation movement—to George Jackson, whom I loved and respected in every way. As I came to know and love him, I saw him developing an acute sensitivity to the real problems facing black women and thus refining his ability to distinguish these from their mythical transpositions. George was uniquely aware of the need to extricate himself and other black men from the remnants of divisive and destructive myths purporting to represent the black woman. If his life had not been so precipitously and savagely extinguished, he would have surely accomplished a task he had already outlined some time ago: a systematic critique of his past misconceptions about black women and of their roots in the ideology of the established order. He wanted to appeal to other black men, still similarly disoriented, to likewise correct themselves through self-criticism. George viewed this obligation as a revolutionary duty, but also, and equally important, as an expression of his boundless love for all black women.

II

The matriarchal black woman has been repeatedly invoked as one of the fatal by-products of slavery. When the Moynihan Report consecrated this myth with Washington's stamp of approval, its spurious content and propagandistic mission should have become apparent. Yet even outside the established ideological apparatus, and also among black people, unfortunate references to the matriarchate can still be encountered. Occasionally, there is even acknowledgement of the "tangle of pathology" it supposedly engendered. (This black matriarchate, according to Moynihan et al., defines the roots of our oppression as a people.) An accurate portrait of the African woman in bondage must debunk the myth of the matriarchate. Such a portrait must simultaneously attempt to illuminate the historical matrix of her oppression and must evoke her varied, often heroic, responses to the slaveholder's domination.

Lingering beneath the notion of the black matriarch is an unspoken indictment of our female forebears as having actively assented to slavery. The notorious cliché, the "emasculating female," has its roots in the fallacious inference that, in playing a central part in the slave "family," the black woman related to the slaveholding class as collaborator. Nothing could be further from the truth. In the most fundamental sense, the slave system did not—and could not—engender and recognize a matriarchal family structure. Inherent in the very concept of the matriarchy is "power." It would have been exceedingly risky for the slaveholding class to openly acknowledge symbols of authority—female symbols no less than male. Such legitimized concentrations of authority might eventually unleash their "power" against the slave system itself.

The American brand of slavery strove toward a rigidified disorganization in family life, just as it had to proscribe all potential social structures within which black people might forge a collective and conscious existence.[1] Mothers and fathers were brutally separated; children, when they became of age, were branded and frequently severed from their mothers. That the mother was "the only legitimate parent of her child" did not therefore mean that she was even permitted to guide it to maturity.

Those who lived under a common roof were often unrelated through blood. Frederick Douglass, for instance, had no recollection of his father. He only vaguely recalled having seen his mother—and then on extremely rare occasions. Moreover, at the age of seven, he was forced to abandon the dwelling of his grandmother, of whom he would later say: "She was to me a mother and a father."[2] The strong personal bonds between immediate family members which oftentimes persisted despite coerced separation bore witness to the remarkable capacity of black people for resisting the disorder so violently imposed on their lives.

Where families were allowed to thrive, they were, for the most part, external fabrications serving the designs of an avaricious, profit-seeking slaveholder.

> The strong hand of the slave owner dominated the Negro family, which existed at his mercy and often at his own personal instigation. An ex-slave has told of getting married on one plantation: "When you married, you had to jump over a broom three times."[3]

This slave went on to describe the various ways in which his master forcibly coupled men and women with the aim of producing the maximum number of healthy child-slaves. In the words of John Henrik Clarke,

> The family as a functional entity was outlawed and permitted to exist only when it benefited the slave master. Maintenance of the slave family as a family unit benefited the slave owners only when, and to the extent that, such unions created new slaves who could be exploited.[4]

The designation of the black woman as a matriarch is a cruel misnomer. It is a misnomer because it implies stable kinship structures within which the mother exercises decisive authority. It is cruel because it ignores the profound traumas the black woman must have experienced when she had to surrender her childbearing to alien and predatory economic interests.

Even the broadest construction of the matriarch concept would not render it applicable to the black slave woman. But it should not be inferred that she therefore played no significant role in the community of slaves. Her indispensable efforts to ensure the survival of her people can hardly be contested. Even if she had done no more, her deeds would still be laudable. But her concern and struggles for physical survival, while clearly important, did not constitute her most outstanding contributions. It will be submitted that by virtue of the brutal force of circumstances, the black woman was assigned the mission of promoting the consciousness and practice of resistance. A great deal has been said about the black *man* and resistance, but very little about the unique relationship black women bore to the resistance struggles during slavery. To understand the part she played in developing and sharpening the thrust towards freedom, the broader meaning of slavery and of American slavery in particular must be explored.

Slavery is an ancient human institution. Of slave labor in its traditional form and of serfdom as well, Karl Marx had the following to say:

> The slave stands in absolutely no relation to the objective conditions of his labor; it is rather the *labor* itself, in the form of the slave as of the serf, which is placed in the category of *inorganic condition* of production alongside the other natural beings, e.g., cattle, or regarded as an appendage of the earth.[5]

The bondsman's existence as a natural condition of production is complemented and reinforced, according to Marx, by his membership in a social grouping which he perceives to be an extension of nature. Enmeshed in what appears to be a natural state of affairs, the attitude of the slave, to a greater or lesser degree, would be an acquiescence in his subjugation. Engels points out that, in Athens, the state could depend on a police force consisting entirely of slaves.[6]

The fabric of American slavery differed significantly from ancient slavery and feudalism. True, black people were forced to act as if they were "inorganic conditions of production." For slavery was "personality swallowed up in the sordid idea of property—manhood lost in chattelhood."[7] But there were no preexistent social structures or cultural dictates that might induce reconciliation to the circumstances of their bondage. On the contrary, Africans had been uprooted from their natural environment, their social relations, their culture. No legitimate sociocultural surroundings would be permitted to develop and flourish, for, in all likelihood, they would be utterly incompatible with the demands of slavery.

Yet another fact would militate against harmony and equilibrium in the slave's relation to his bondage: slavery was enclosed in a society otherwise characterized by "free" wage labor. Black men and women could always contrast their chains with the nominally free status of white working people. This was quite literally true in such cases where, like Frederick Douglass, they were contracted out as wage laborers. Unlike the "free" white men alongside whom they worked, they had no right to the meager wages they earned. Such were some of the many contradictions unloosed by the effort to forcibly inject slavery into the early stages of American capitalism.

The combination of a historically superseded slave labor system based almost exclusively on race and the drive to strip black people of all their social and cultural bonds would create a fateful rupture at the heart of the slave system itself. The slaves would not readily adopt fatalistic attitudes towards the conditions surrounding and ensnaring their lives. They were a people who had been violently thrust into a patently "unnatural" subjugation. If the slaveholders had not maintained an absolute monopoly of violence, if they had not been able to rely on large numbers of their fellow white men—indeed the entire ruling class as well as misled working people —to assist them in their terrorist machinations, slavery would have been far less feasible than it actually proved to be.

The magnitude and effects of the black people's defiant rejection of slavery have not yet been fully documented and illuminated. But there is more than ample evidence that they consistently refused to succumb to the all-encompassing dehumanization objectively demanded by the slave system. Comparatively recent studies have demonstrated that the few slave uprisings—too spectacular to be relegated to oblivion by the racism of ruling-class historians—were not isolated occurrences, as the latter would have had us believe. The reality, we know now, was that these open rebellions erupted with such a frequency that they were as much a part of the texture of slavery as the conditions of servitude themselves. And these revolts were only the tip of an iceberg: resistance expressed itself in other grand modes and also in the seemingly trivial forms of feigned illness and studied indolence.

If resistance was an organic ingredient of slave life, it had to be directly nurtured by the social organization that the slaves themselves improvised. The consciousness of their oppression, the conscious thrust towards its abolition, could not have been sustained without impetus from the community they pulled together through the sheer force of their own strength. Of necessity, this community would revolve around the realm which was furthermost removed from the immediate arena of domination. It could only be located in and around the living quarters, the area where the basic needs of physical life were met.

In the area of production, the slaves—pressed into the mold of beasts of burden—were forcibly deprived of their humanity. (And a human being thoroughly dehumanized has no desire for freedom) But the community gravitating around the domestic quarters might possibly permit a retrieval of the man and the woman in their fundamental humanity. We can assume that in a very real material sense, it was only in domestic life—away from the eyes and whip of the overseer—that the slaves could attempt to assert the modicum of freedom they still retained. It was only there that they might be inspired to project techniques of expanding it further by leveling what few weapons they had against the slaveholding class whose unmitigated drive for profit was the source of their misery.

Via this path, we return to the African slave woman: in the living quarters, the major responsibilities "naturally" fell to her. It was the woman who was charged with keeping the "home" in order. This role was dictated by the male supremacist ideology of white society in America; it was also woven into the patriarchal traditions of Africa. As her biological destiny, the woman bore the fruits of procreation; as her social destiny, she cooked, sewed, washed, cleaned house, raised the children. Traditionally the labor of females, domestic work is supposed to complement and confirm their inferiority.

But with the black slave woman, there is a strange twist of affairs: in the infinite anguish of ministering to the needs of the men and children around her (who were not necessarily members of her immediate family), she was performing the *only* labor of the slave community that could not be directly and immediately claimed by the oppressor. There was no compensation for work in the fields; it served no useful purpose for the slaves. Domestic labor was the only meaningful labor for the slave community as a whole (discounting as negligible the exceptional situations where slaves received some pay for their work).

Precisely through performing the drudgery that has long been a central expression of the socially conditioned inferiority of women, the black woman in chains could help to lay the foundation for some degree of autonomy, both for herself and her men. Even as she was suffering under her unique oppression as female, she was thrust by the force of circumstances into the center of the slave community. She was, therefore, essential to the *survival* of the community. Not all people have survived enslavement; hence her survival-oriented activities were themselves a form of resistance. Survival, moreover, was the prerequisite of all higher levels of struggle.

But much more remains to be said of the black woman during slavery. The dialectics of her oppression will become far more complex. It is true that she was a victim of the myth that only the woman, with her diminished capacity for mental and physical labor, should do degrading household work. Yet, the alleged benefits of the ideology of feminity did not accrue to her. She was not sheltered or protected; she would not remain oblivious to the desperate struggle for existence unfolding outside the "home." She was also there in the fields, alongside the man, toiling under the lash from sunup to sundown.

This was one of the supreme ironies of slavery: in order to approach its strategic goal—to extract the greatest possible surplus from the labor of the slaves—the black woman had to be released from the chains of the myth of femininity. In the words of W. E. B. Du Bois, " . . . our women in black had freedom contemptuously thrust upon them"[8] In order to function as slave, the black woman had to be annulled as woman, that is, as woman in her historical stance of wardship under the entire male hierarchy. The sheer force of things rendered her equal to her man.

Excepting the woman's role as caretaker of the household, male supremacist structures could not become deeply embedded in the internal workings of the slave system. Though the ruling class was male and rabidly chauvinistic, the slave system could not confer upon the black man the appearance of a privileged position vis-à-vis the black woman. The man-slave could not be the unquestioned superior within the "family" or community, for there was no such thing as the "family provided" among the slaves. The attainment of slavery's intrinsic goals was contingent upon the fullest and most brutal utilization of the productive capacities of every man, woman, and child. They all had to "provide" for the master. The black woman was therefore wholly integrated into the productive force.

> The bell rings at four o'clock in the morning and they have half an hour to get ready. Men and women start together, and the women must work as steadily as the men and perform the same tasks as the men.[9]

Even in the posture of motherhood—otherwise the occasion for hypocritical adoration—the black woman was treated with no greater compassion and with no less severity than her man. As one slave related in a narrative of his life:

> ...women who had sucking children suffered much from their breasts becoming full of milk, the infants being left at home; they therefore could not keep up with the other hands: I have seen the overseer beat them with raw hide so that the blood and the milk flew mingled from their breasts.[10]

Moses Grandy, ex-slave, continues his description with an account of a typical form of field punishment reserved for the black woman with child:

> She is compelled to lie down over a hole made to receive her corpulency, and is flogged with the whip, or beat with a paddle, which has holes in it; at every stroke comes a blister.[11]

The unbridled cruelty of this leveling process whereby the black woman was forced into equality with the black man requires no further explanation. She shared in the deformed equality of equal oppression.

But out of this deformed equality was forged quite undeliberately, yet inexorably, a state of affairs that could unharness an immense potential in the black woman. Expending indispensable labor for the enrichment of her oppressor, she could attain a practical awareness of the oppressor's utter dependence on her—for the master needs the slave far more than the slave needs the master. At the same time she could realize that while her productive activity was wholly subordinated to the will of the master, it was nevertheless proof of her ability to transform things. For "labor is the living, shaping fire; it represents the impermanence of things, their temporality ..."[12]

The black woman's consciousness of the oppression suffered by her people was honed in the bestial realities of daily experience. It would not be the stunted awareness of a woman confined to the home. She would be prepared to ascend to the same levels of resistance that were accessible to her men. Even as she performed her housework, the black woman's role in the slave community could not be identical to the historically evolved female role. Stripped of the palliative feminine veneer which might have encouraged a passive performance of domestic tasks, she was now uniquely capable of weaving into the warp and woof of domestic life a profound consciousness of resistance.

With the contributions of strong black women, the slave community as a whole could achieve heights unscalable within the families of the white oppressed or even within the patriarchal kinship groups of Africa. Latently or actively it was always a community of resistance. It frequently erupted in insurgency, but was daily animated by the minor acts of sabotage that harassed the slave master to no end. Had the black woman failed to rise to the occasion, the community of slaves could not have fully developed in this direction. The slave system would have to deal with the black woman as the custodian of a house of resistance.

The oppression of black women during the era of slavery, therefore, had to be buttressed by a level of overt ruling-class repression. Her routine oppression had to assume an unconcealed dimension of outright counterinsurgency.

III

To say that the oppression of black slave women necessarily incorporated open forms of counterinsurgency is not as extravagant as it might initially appear. The penetration of counterinsurgency into the day-to-day routine of the slave master's domination will be considered towards the end of this paper. First, the participation of black women in the overt and explosive upheavals that constantly rocked the slave system must be confirmed. This will be an indication of the magnitude of her role as caretaker of a household of resistance—of the degree to which she could concretely encourage those around her to keep their eyes on freedom. It will also confirm the objective circumstances to which the slave master's counterinsurgency was a response.

With the sole exceptions of Harriet Tubman and Sojourner Truth, black women of the slave era remain more or less enshrouded in unrevealed history. And, as Earl Conrad has demonstrated, even "General Tubman's" role has been consistently and grossly minimized. She was a far greater warrior against slavery than is suggested by the prevalent misconception that her only outstanding contribution was to make nineteen trips into the South, bringing over 300 slaves to their freedom.

[She] was head of the Intelligence Service in the Department of the South throughout the Civil War; she is the only American woman to lead troops black and white on the field of battle, as she did in the Department of the South . . . She was a compelling and stirring orator in the councils of the abolitionists and the antislavers, a favorite of the antislavery conferences. She was the fellow planner with Douglass, Martin Delany, Wendell Phillips, Gerrit Smith, and other leaders of the antislavery movement.[13]

No extensive and systematic study of the role of black women in resisting slavery has come to my attention. It has been noted that large numbers of freed black women worked towards the purchase of their relatives' and friends' freedom. About the participation of women in both the well-known and more obscure slave revolts, only casual remarks have been made. It has been observed, for instance, that Gabriel's wife was active in planning the rebellion spearheaded by her husband, but little else has been said about her.

The sketch that follows is based in its entirety on the works of Herbert Aptheker, the only resources available to me at the time of this writing.[14] These facts, gleaned from Aptheker's works on slave revolts and other forms of resistance, should signal the urgency to undertake a thorough study of the black woman as antislavery rebel. In 1971 this work is far overdue.

Aptheker's research has disclosed the widespread existence of communities of blacks who were neither free nor in bondage. Throughout the South (in South and North Carolina, Virginia, Louisiana, Florida, Georgia, Mississippi, and Alabama), Maroon communities consisting of fugitive slaves and their descendants were "an ever present feature"—from 1642 to 1864—of slavery. They provided ". . . havens for fugitives, served as bases for marauding expeditions against nearby plantations and, at times, supplied leadership to planned uprisings."[15]

Every detail of these communities was invariably determined by and steeped in resistance, for their raison d'être emanated from their perpetual assault on slavery. Only in a fighting stance could the Maroons hope to secure their constantly imperiled freedom. As a matter of necessity, the women of those communities were compelled to define themselves—no less than the men—through their many acts of resistance. Hence, throughout this brief survey the counterattacks and heroic efforts at defense assisted by Maroon women will be a recurring motif.

As it will be seen, black women often poisoned the food and set fire to the houses of their masters. For those who were also employed as domestics, these particular overt forms of resistance were especially available.

The vast majority of the incidents to be related involve either tactically unsuccessful assaults or eventually thwarted attempts at defense. In all likelihood, numerous successes were achieved, even against the formidable obstacles posed by the slave system. Many of these were probably unpublicized even at the time of their occurrence, lest they provide encouragement to the rebellious proclivities of other slaves and, for other slaveholders, an occasion for fear and despair.

During the early years of the slave era (1708), a rebellion broke out in New York. Among its participants were surely many women, for one, along with three men, was executed in retaliation for the killing of seven whites. It may not be entirely insignificant that while the men were hanged, she was heinously burned alive.[16] In the same colony, women played an active role in a 1712 uprising in the course of which slaves, with their guns, clubs, and knives, killed members of the slaveholding class and managed to wound others. While some of the insurgents—among them a pregnant woman—were captured, others—including a woman—committed suicide rather than surrender.[17]

"In New Orleans one day in 1730 a woman slave received 'a violent blow from a French soldier for refusing to obey him' and in her anger shouted 'that the French should not long insult Negroes.' "[18] As it was later disclosed, she and undoubtedly many other women, had joined in a vast plan to destroy slaveholders. Along with eight men, this dauntless woman was executed. Two years later, Louisiana pronounced a woman and four men leaders of a planned rebellion. They were all executed and, in a typically savage gesture, their heads publicly displayed on poles.[19]

Charleston, South Carolina, condemned a black woman to die in 1740 for arson,[20] a form of sabotage, as earlier noted, frequently carried out by women. In Maryland, for instance, a slave woman was executed in 1776 for having destroyed by fire her master's house, his outhouses, and tobacco house.[21]

In the thick of the Colonies' war with England, a group of defiant slave women and men were arrested in Saint Andrew's Parish, Georgia, in 1778. But before they were captured, they had already brought a number of slave owners to their death.[22]

The Maroon communities have been briefly described; from 1782 to 1784, Louisiana was a constant target of Maroon attacks. When twenty-five of this community's members were finally taken prisoner, men and women alike were all severely punished.[23]

As can be inferred from previous examples, the North did not escape the tremendous impact of fighting black women. In Albany, New York, two women were among three slaves executed for antislavery activities in 1794.[24] The respect and admiration accorded the black woman fighter by her people is strikingly illustrated by an incident that transpired in York, Pennsylvania: when, during the early months of 1803, Margaret Bradley was convicted of attempting to poison two white people, the black inhabitants of the area revolted en masse.

They made several attempts to destroy the town by fire and succeeded, within a period of three weeks, in burning eleven buildings. Patrols were established, strong guards set up, the militia dispatched to the scene of the unrest . . . and a reward of three hundred dollars offered for the capture of the insurrectionists.[25]

A successful elimination by poisoning of several "of our respectable men" (said a letter to the governor of North Carolina) was met by the execution of four or five slaves. One was a woman who was burned alive.[26] In 1810, two women and a man were accused of arson in Virginia.[27]

In 1811, North Carolina was the scene of a confrontation between a Maroon community and a slave-catching posse. Local newspapers reported that its members "had bid defiance to any force whatever and were resolved to stand their ground." Of the entire community, two were killed, one wounded, and two—both women—were captured.[28]

Aptheker's *Documentary History of the Negro People in the United States* contains a portion of the transcript of an 1812 confession of a slave rebel in Virginia. The latter divulged the information that a black woman brought him into a plan to kill their master and that yet another black woman had been charged with concealing him after the killing occurred.[29]

In 1816, it was discovered that a community of three hundred escaped slaves—men, women, children—had occupied a fort in Florida. After the United States Army was dispatched with instructions to destroy the community, a ten-day siege terminated with all but forty of the three hundred dead. All the slaves fought to the very end.[30] In the course of a similar, though smaller, confrontation between Maroons and a militia group (in South Carolina, 1826), a woman and a child were killed.[31] Still another Maroon community was attacked in Mobile, Alabama, in 1837. Its inhabitants, men and women alike, resisted fiercely—according to local newspapers, "fighting like Spartans."[32]

Convicted of having been among those who, in 1829, had been the cause of a devastating fire in Augusta, Georgia, a black woman was "executed, dissected, and exposed" (according to an English visitor). Moreover, the execution of yet another woman, about to give birth, was imminent.[33] During the same year, a group of slaves, being led from Maryland to be sold in the South, had apparently planned to kill the traders and make their way to freedom. One of the traders was successfully done away with, but eventually a posse captured all the slaves. Of the six leaders sentenced to death, one was a woman. She was first permitted, for reasons of economy, to give birth to her child.[34] Afterwards, she was publicly hanged.

The slave class in Louisiana, as noted earlier, was not unaware of the formidable threat posed by the black woman who chose to fight. It responded accordingly: in 1846, a posse of slave owners ambushed a community of Maroons, killing one woman and wounding two others. A black man was also assassinated.[35] Neither could the border states escape the recognition that slave women were eager to battle for their freedom. In 1850, in the state of Missouri, "about thirty slaves, men and women, of four different owners, had armed themselves with knives, clubs, and three guns and set out for a free state." Their pursuers, who could unleash a far more powerful violence than they, eventually thwarted their plans.[36]

This factual survey of but a few of the open acts of resistance in which black women played major roles will close with two further events. When a Maroon camp in Mississippi was destroyed in 1857, four of its members did not manage to elude capture, one of whom was a fugitive slave woman.[37] All of them, women as well as men, must have waged a valiant fight. Finally, there occurred in October, 1862, a skirmish between Maroons and a scouting party of Confederate soldiers in the state of Virginia.[38] This time, however, the Maroons were the victors, and it may well have been that some of the many women helped to put the soldiers to death.

IV

The oppression of slave women had to assume dimensions of open counter-insurgency. Against the background of the facts presented above, it would be difficult indeed to refute this contention. As for those who engaged in open battle, they were no less ruthlessly punished than slave men. It would even appear that in many cases they may have suffered penalties that were more excessive than those meted out to the men. On occasion, when men were hanged, the women were burned alive. If such practices were widespread, their logic would be clear. They would be terrorist methods designed to dissuade other black women from following the examples of their fighting sisters. If all black women rose up alongside their men, the institution of slavery would be in difficult straits.

It is against the backdrop of her role as fighter that the routine oppression of the slave woman must be explored once more. If she was burned, hanged, broken on the wheel, her head paraded on poles before her oppressed brothers and sisters, she must have also felt the edge of this counter-insurgency as a fact of her daily existence. The slave system would not only have to make conscious efforts to stifle the tendencies towards acts of the kind described above; it would be no less necessary to stave off escape attempts (escapes to Maroon country!) and all the various forms of sabotage within the system. Feigning illness was also resistance as were work slow-downs and actions destructive to the crops. The more extensive these acts, the more the slaveholder's profits would tend to diminish.

While a detailed study of the myriad modes in which this counterinsurgency was manifested can and should be conducted, the following reflections will focus on a single aspect of the slave woman's oppression, particularly prominent in its brutality.

Much has been said about the sexual abuses to which the black woman was forced to submit. They are generally explained as an outgrowth of the male supremacy of Southern culture: the purity of white womanhood could not be violated by the aggressive sexual activity desired by the white male. His instinctual urges would find expression in his relationships with his property—the black slave woman, who would have to become his unwilling concubine. No doubt there is an element of truth in these statements, but it is equally important to unearth the meaning of these sexual abuses from the vantage point of the woman who was assaulted.

In keeping with the theme of these reflections, it will be submitted that the slave master's sexual domination of the black woman contained an unveiled element of counterinsurgency. To understand the basis for this assertion, the dialectical moments of the slave woman's oppression must be restated and their movement recaptured. The prime factor, it has been said, was the total and violent expropriation of her labor with no compensation save the pittance necessary for bare existence.

Secondly, as female, she was the housekeeper of the living quarters. In this sense, she was already doubly oppressed. However, having been wrested from passive, "feminine" existence by the sheer force of things—literally by forced labor—confining domestic tasks were incommensurable with what she had become. That is to say, by virtue of her participation in production, she would not act the part of the passive female, but could experience the same need as her men to challenge the conditions of her subjugation. As the center of domestic life, the only life at all removed from the arena of exploitation, and thus as an important source of survival, the black woman could play a pivotal role in nurturing the thrust towards freedom.

The slave master would attempt to thwart this process. He knew that as a female, this slave woman could be particularly vulnerable in her sexual existence. Although he would not pet her and deck her out in frills, the white master could endeavor to reestablish her femaleness by reducing her to the level of her *biological* being. Aspiring with his sexual assaults to establish her as a female *animal*, he would be striving to destroy her proclivities towards resistance. Of the sexual relations of animals, taken at their abstract biological level (and not in terms of their quite different social potential for human beings), Simone de Beauvoir says the following:

> It is unquestionably the male who *takes* the female—she is *taken*. Often the word applies literally, for whether by means of special organs or through superior strength, the male seizes her and holds her in place; he performs the

copulatory movements; and, among insects, birds, and mammals, he pene-
trates . . . Her body becomes a resistance to be broken through . . . [39]

The act of copulation, reduced by the white man to an animal-like act,
would be symbolic of the effort to conquer the resistance the black woman
could unloose.

In confronting the black woman as adversary in a sexual contest, the
master would be subjecting her to the most elemental form of terrorism
distinctively suited for the female: rape. Given the already terroristic texture of plantation life, it would be as potential victim of rape that the slave
woman would be most unguarded. Further, she might be most conveniently manipulable if the master contrived a ransom system of sorts, forcing her to pay with her body for food, diminished severity in treatment,
the safety of her children, etc.

The integration of rape into the sparsely furnished legitimate social life
of the slaves harks back to the feudal "right of the first night," the *jus
primae noctis*. The feudal lord manifested and reinforced his domination
over the serfs by asserting his authority to have sexual intercourse with all
the females. The right itself referred specifically to all freshly married
women. But while the right to the first night eventually evolved into the
institutionalized "virgin tax,"[40] the American slaveholder's sexual domination never lost its openly terroristic character.

As a direct attack on the black female as potential insurgent, this sexual
repression finds its parallels in virtually every historical situation where the
woman actively challenges oppression. Thus, Frantz Fanon could say of
the Algerian woman: "A woman led away by soldiers who comes back a
week later—it is not necessary to question her to understand that she has
been violated dozens of times."[41]

In its political contours, the rape of the black woman was not exclusively
an attack upon her. Indirectly, its target was also the slave community as a
whole. In launching the sexual war on the woman, the master would not
only assert his sovereignty over a critically important figure of the slave
community, he would also be aiming a blow against the black man. The
latter's instinct to protect his female relations and comrades (now stripped
of its male supremacist implications) would be frustrated and violated to
the extreme. Placing the white male's sexual barbarity in bold relief, Du
Bois cries out in a rhetorical vein:

> I shall forgive the South much in its final judgment day: I shall forgive its
> slavery, for slavery is a world-old habit; I shall forgive its fighting for a well-
> lost cause, and for remembering that struggle with tender tears; I shall
> forgive its so-called pride of race, the passion of its hot blood, and even its
> dear, old, laughable strutting and posing; but one thing I shall never forgive,
> neither in this world nor the world to come: its wanton and continued and

persistent insulting of the black womanhood which it sought and seeks to prostitute to its lust.[42]

The retaliatory import of the rape for the black man would be entrapment in an untenable situation. Clearly the master hoped that once the black man was struck by his manifest inability to rescue his women from sexual assaults of the master, he would begin to experience deep-seated doubts about his ability to resist at all.

Certainly the wholesale rape of slave women must have had a profound impact on the slave community. Yet it could not succeed in its intrinsic aim of stifling the impetus towards struggle. Countless black women did not passively submit to these abuses, as the slaves in general refused to passively accept their bondage. The struggles of the slave woman in the sexual realm were a continuation of the resistance interlaced in the slave's daily existence. As such, this was yet another form of insurgency, a response to a politically tinged sexual repression.

Even E. Franklin Frazier (who goes out of his way to defend the thesis that "the master in his mansion and his colored mistress in her special house nearby represented the final triumph of social ritual in the presence of the deepest feelings of human solidarity")[43] could not entirely ignore the black woman who fought back. He notes: "That physical compulsion was necessary at times to secure submission on the part of black women ... is supported by historical evidence and has been preserved in the tradition of Negro families."[44]

The sexual contest was one of many arenas in which the black woman had to prove herself as a warrior against oppression. What Frazier unwillingly concedes would mean that countless children brutally fathered by whites were conceived in the thick of battle. Frazier himself cites the story of a black woman whose great-grandmother, a former slave, would describe with great zest the battles behind all her numerous scars—that is, all save one. In response to questions concerning the unexplained scar, she had always simply said: "White men are as low as dogs, child, stay away from them." The mystery was not unveiled until after the death of this brave woman: "She received that scar at the hands of her master's youngest son, a boy of about eighteen years at the time she conceived their child, my grandmother Ellen."[45]

An intricate and savage web of oppression intruded at every moment into the black woman's life during slavery. Yet a single theme appears at every juncture: the woman transcending, refusing, fighting back, asserting herself over and against terrifying obstacles. It was not her comrade brother against whom her incredible strength was directed. She fought alongside her man, accepting or providing guidance according to her talents and the nature of their tasks. She was in no sense an authoritarian figure; neither

her domestic role nor her acts of resistance could relegate the man to the shadows. On the contrary, she herself had just been forced to leave behind the shadowy realm of female passivity in order to assume her rightful place beside the insurgent male.

This portrait cannot, of course, presume to represent every individual slave woman. It is rather a portrait of the potentials and possibilities inherent in the situation to which slave women were anchored. Invariably there were those who did not realize this potential. There were those who were indifferent and a few who were outright traitors. But certainly they were not the vast majority. The image of black women enchaining their men, cultivating relationships with the oppressor, is a cruel fabrication that must be called by its right name. It is a dastardly ideological weapon designed to impair our capacity for resistance today by foisting upon us the ideal of male supremacy.

According to a time-honored principle, advanced by Marx, Lenin, Fanon, and numerous other theorists, the status of women in any given society is a barometer measuring the overall level of social development. As Fanon has masterfully shown, the strength and efficacy of social struggles —and especially revolutionary movements—bear an immediate relationship to the range and quality of female participation.

The meaning of this principle is strikingly illustrated by the role of the black woman during slavery. Attendant to the indiscriminate, brutal pursuit of profit, the slave woman attained a correspondingly brutal status of equality. But in practice, she could work up a fresh content for this deformed equality by inspiring and participating in acts of resistance of every form and color. She could turn the weapon of equality in struggle against the avaricious slave system that had engendered the mere caricature of equality in oppression. The black woman's activities increased the total incidence of antislavery assaults. But most important, without consciously rebellious black women, the theme of resistance could not have become so thoroughly intertwined in the fabric of daily existence. The status of black women within the community of slaves was definitely a barometer indicating the overall potential for resistance.

This process did not end with the formal dissolution of slavery. Under the impact of racism, the black woman has been continually constrained to inject herself into the desperate struggle for existence. She—like her man —has been compelled to work for wages, providing for her family as she was previously forced to provide for the slaveholding class. The infinitely onerous nature of this equality should never be overlooked. For the black woman has always also remained harnessed to the chores of the household. Yet, she could never be exhaustively defined by her uniquely "female" responsibilities.

As a result, black women have made significant contributions to struggles against the racism and the dehumanizing exploitation of a wrongly organized society. In fact, it would appear that the intense levels of resistance historically maintained by black people and thus the historical function of the black liberation struggle as harbinger of change throughout the society are due in part to the greater *objective* equality between the black man and the black woman. Du Bois put it this way:

> In the great rank and file of our five million women, we have the up-working of new revolutionary ideals, which must in time have vast influence on the thought and action of this land.[46]

Official and unofficial attempts to blunt the effects of the egalitarian tendencies as between the black man and woman should come as no surprise. The matriarch concept, embracing the clichéd "female castrator," is, in the last instance, an open weapon of ideological warfare. Black men and women alike remain its potential victims—men unconsciously lunging at the woman, equating her with the myth; women sinking back into the shadows, lest an aggressive posture resurrect the myth in themselves.

The myth must be consciously repudiated as myth, and the black woman in her true historical contours must be resurrected. We, the black women of today, must accept the full weight of a legacy wrought in blood by our mothers in chains. Our fight, while identical in spirit, reflects different conditions and thus implies different paths of struggle. But as heirs to a tradition of supreme perseverance and heroic resistance, we must hasten to take our place wherever our people are forging on towards freedom.

ENDNOTES

1. It is interesting to note a parallel in Nazi Germany: with all its ranting and raving about motherhood and the family, Hitler's regime made a conscious attempt to strip the family of virtually all its social functions. The thrust of their unspoken program for the family was to reduce it to a biological unit and to force its members to relate in an unmediated fashion to the fascist bureaucracy. Clearly the Nazis endeavored to crush the family in order to ensure that it could not become a center from which oppositional activity might originate.

2. Herbert Aptheker, ed., *A Documentary History of the Negro People in the United States* (New York: Citadel Press, 1969), 272.

3. Andrew Billingsley, *Black Families in White America* (Englewood, NJ: Prentice-Hall, 1968), 61.

4. John Henrik Clarke, "The Black Woman: A Figure in World History," *Essence* (July 1971).

5. Karl Marx, *Grundrisse der Kritik der Politischen Oekonomie* (Berlin: Dietz Verlag, 1953), 389. [Davis's translation. *Ed.*]

6. Friedrich Engels, *Origin of the Family, Private Property and the State* (New York: International Publishers, 1942), 107.

7. Frederick Douglass, *Life and Times of Frederick Douglass* (New York: Collier Books, 1962), 96.

8. W. E. B. Du Bois, *Darkwater, Voices from Within the Veil* (New York: AMS Press, 1969), 185.

9. Lewis Clarke, *Narrative of the Sufferings of Lewis and Milton Clarke, Sons of a Soldier of the Revolution* (Boston: 1846), 127 [Quoted by E. Franklin Frazier, *The Negro Family in the United States*].

10. Moses Grandy, *Narrative of the Life of Moses Grandy; Late a Slave in the United States of America* (Boston: 1844), 18 [Quoted by Frazier].

11. Ibid.

12. Marx, *Grundrisse*, 266. [Davis's translation. *Ed.*]

13. Earl Conrad, "I Bring You General Tubman," *Black Scholar* 1 nos. 3–4 (January/February 1970): 4.

14. In February, 1949, Herbert Aptheker published an essay in *Masses and Mainstream* entitled "The Negro Woman." As yet, however, I have been unable to obtain it.

15. Herbert Aptheker, "Slave Guerrilla Warfare" in *To Be Free, Studies in American Negro History* (New York: International Publishers, 1969), 11.

16. Herbert Aptheker, *American Negro Slave Revolts* (New York: International Publishers, 1970), 169.

17. Ibid., 173.

18. Ibid., 181.

19. Ibid., 182.

20. Ibid., 190.

21. Ibid., 145.

22. Ibid., 201.

23. Ibid., 207.

24. Ibid., 215.

25. Ibid., 239.

26. Ibid., 241–242.

27. Ibid., 247.

28. Ibid., 251.

29. Aptheker, *Documentary History*, 55–57.

30. Aptheker, *Slave Revolts*, 259.

31. Ibid., 277.

32. Ibid., 259.

33. Ibid., 281.

34. Ibid., 487.

35. Aptheker, "Guerrilla Warfare," 27.

36. Aptheker, *Slave Revolts*, 342.

37. Aptheker, "Guerrilla Warfare," 28.

38. Ibid., 29.

39. Simone de Beauvoir, *The Second Sex* (New York: Bantam Books, 1961), 18–19.

40. August Bebel, *Women and Socialism* (New York: Socialist Literature Co., 1910), 66–69.

41. Frantz Fanon, *A Dying Colonialism* (New York: Grove, 1967), 119.

42. Du Bois, *Darkwater*, 172.

43. E. Franklin Frazier, *The Negro Family in the United States* (Chicago: University of Chicago Press, 1966), 69.

44. Ibid., 53.

45. Ibid., 53–54.

46. Du Bois, *Darkwater*, 185.

Michele Wallace (1952–   )

Michele Wallace, born in Harlem and the daughter of feminist artist Faith Ringgold, was a founding member of the National Black Feminist Organization (1974). She is best known for the controversial feminist polemic she wrote in her twenties—*Black Macho and the Myth of the Superwoman* (1978)—which is a critique of the male-dominant civil rights and misogynistic Black Power movements, and a scathing exposé of sexual politics within the African American community. She also debunked the myth of black women as "superwomen" who have no need for feminism. *Black Macho* generated a storm of criticism within the black community, including among black feminists such as June Jordan and Gloria Joseph. In her introduction to the new edition of *Black Macho*, entitled "How I Saw It Then, How I See It Now" (London: Verso, 1990) Wallace provides her own critique of the book, which twelve years earlier sparked a major debate within the black community. "Anger in Isolation" appeared in the *Village Voice* four years before *Macho* and explains why she became a feminist and how difficult it was for a young black woman in the early years. Wallace, a prolific cultural critic, is presently a member of the faculty at CUNY where she teaches women's studies and film studies. Her recent publications include *Invisibility Blues* (1990) and *Black Popular Culture* (1992), edited by Gina Dent, the proceedings of a conference at The Studio Museum in Harlem, December 8-10, 1991, which Wallace convened.

Michele Wallace }

ANGER IN ISOLATION:
A BLACK FEMINIST'S SEARCH
FOR SISTERHOOD

When I was in the third grade I wanted to be president. I can still remember the stricken look on my teacher's face when I announced it in class. By the time I was in the fourth grade I had decided to be the president's wife instead. It never occurred to me that I could be neither because I was black. Growing up in a dreamy state of mind not uncommon to the offspring of the black middle class, I was convinced that hatred was an insubstantial emotion and would certainly vanish before it could affect me. I had the world to choose from in planning a life.

On rainy days my sister and I used to tie the short end of a scarf around our scrawny braids and let the rest of its silken mass trail to our waists. We'd pretend it was hair and that we were some lovely heroine we'd seen in the movies. There was a time when I would have called that wanting to be white, yet the real point of the game was being feminine. Being feminine *meant* being white to us.

One day when I was thirteen, on my bus ride home from school I caught a brief but enchanting glimpse of a beautiful creature—slender, honey brown, and she wore her hair natural. Very few people did then, which made her that much more striking. *This* was a look I could imitate with some success. The next day I went to school with my hair in an Afro.

On my way out of my building people stared and some complimented me, but others, the older permanent fixtures in the lobby, gaped at me in horror. Walking the streets of Harlem was even more difficult. The men on the corners who had been only moderately attentive before, now began to whoop and holler as I came into view. Becoming exasperated after a while, I asked someone why. 'They think you're a whore, sugar.' I fixed my hair and was back to normal by the next morning. Letting the world in on the secret of my native naps appealed to my proclivity for rebellion, but having people think I was not a 'nice girl' was The War already and I was not prepared for it. I pictured myself in a police station trying to

[220]

explain how I'd been raped. 'Come on, baby, you look like you know your way around,' sneered an imaginary policeman.

In 1968 when I was sixteen and the term black consciousness was becoming popular, I started wearing my hair natural again. This time I ignored my 'elders.' I was too busy reshaping my life. Blackness, I reasoned, meant that I could finally be myself. Besides recognizing my history of slavery and my African roots, I began a general housecleaning. All my old values, gathered from 'playing house' in nursery school to *Glamour* magazine's beauty tips, were discarded.

No more makeup, high heels, stockings, garter belts, girdles. I wore T-shirts and dungarees, or loose African print dresses, sandals on my feet. My dust-covered motto, 'Be a nice well-rounded colored girl so that you can get yourself a nice colored doctor husband,' I threw out on the grounds that it was another remnant of my once 'whitified' self. My mind clear now, I was starting to think about being someone again, not some*thing*— the presidency was still a dark horse but maybe I could be a writer. I dared not even say it aloud: my life was my own again. I thanked Malcolm and LeRoi—wasn't it their prescription that I was following?

It took me three years to fully understand that Stokely was serious when he'd said my position in the movement was 'prone,' three years to understand that the countless speeches that all began 'the black man . . .' did not include me. I learned. I mingled more and more with a black crowd, attended the conferences and rallies and parties and talked with some of the most loquacious of my brothers in blackness, and as I pieced together the ideal that was being presented for me to emulate, I discovered my newfound freedoms being stripped from me, one after another. No, I wasn't to wear makeup, but yes, I had to wear long skirts that I could barely walk in. No, I wasn't to go to the beauty parlor, but yes, I was to spend hours cornrolling my hair. No, I wasn't to flirt with or take shit off white men, but yes, I was to sleep with and take unending shit off black men. No, I wasn't to watch television or read *Vogue* or *Ladies' Home Journal*, but yes, I should keep my mouth shut. I would still have to iron, sew, cook, and have babies.

Only sixteen, I decided there were a lot of things I didn't know about black male/female relationships. I made an attempt to fill myself in by reading—*Soul on Ice, Native Son, Black Rage*—and by joining the National Black Theatre. In the theatre's brand of a consciousness-raising session I was told of the awful ways in which black women, me included, had tried to destroy the black man's masculinity; how we had castrated him; worked when he didn't work; made money when he made none; spent our nights and days in church praying to a jive white boy named Jesus while he collapsed into alcoholism, drug addiction, and various forms of despair; how we'd always been too loud and domineering, too outspoken.

We had much to make up for by being gentle in the face of our own humiliation, by being soft-spoken (ideally to the point where our voices could not be heard at all), by being beautiful (whatever that was), by being submissive—how often that word was shoved at me in poems and in songs as something to strive for.

At the same time one of the brothers who was a member of the theatre was also a paraprofessional in the school where my mother then taught. My mother asked him what he liked about the theatre. Not knowing that I was her daughter, he answered without hesitation that you could get all the pussy you wanted. NBT was a central institution in the black cultural movement. Much time was spent reaching for the 'godlike' in one another, the things beyond the 'flesh' and beyond all the 'whitewashing.' And what it boiled down to was that now the brother could get more pussy. If that was his revolution, what was mine?

So I was again obsessed with my appearance, worried about the rain again—the black woman's nightmare—for fear that my huge, full Afro would shrivel up to my head. (Despite blackness, black men still didn't like short hair.) My age was one thing I had going for me. 'Older black women are too hard,' my brothers informed me as they looked me up and down.

The message of the black movement was that I was being watched, on probation as a black woman, that any signs of aggressiveness, intelligence, or independence would mean I'd be denied even the one role still left open to me as 'my man's woman,' keeper of house, children, and incense burners. I grew increasingly desperate about slipping up—they, black men, were threatening me with being deserted, with being *alone*. Like any 'normal' woman, I eagerly grabbed at my own enslavement.

After all, I'd heard the horror stories of educated black women who had to marry ditchdiggers and get their behinds kicked every night. I had thought the black movement would offer me much better. In 1968 I had wanted to become an intelligent human being. I had wanted to be serious and scholarly for the first time in my life, to write and perhaps get the chance Stokely and Baldwin and Imamu Baraka (then LeRoi Jones) had gotten to change the world—that was how I defined not wanting to be white. But by 1969, I simply wanted a man.

When I chose to go to Howard University in 1969, it was because it was all black. I envisioned a super-black utopia where for the first time in life I would be completely surrounded by people who totally understood me. The problem in New York had been that there were too many white people.

Thirty pounds overweight, my hair in the ultimate Afro—washed and left to dry without combing—my skin blue-black from a summer in the sun, Howard's students, the future polite society of NAACP cocktail parties, did not exactly greet me with open arms. I sought out a new clique each day and found a home in none. Finally I found a place of revelation, if not of happiness, with other misfits in the girls' dorm on Friday and Saturday nights.

These misfits, all dark without exception, all with Afros that were too nappy, chose to stay in and watch television or listen to records rather than take advantage of the score of one-night stands they could probably achieve before being taunted into running home to their parents as 'fallen women.' They came to Howard to get husbands; if you slept around, or if it got out that you had slept with someone you weren't practically engaged to, then there would be very little possibility of a husband for you at Howard.

Such restrictions are not unique in this world, but at Howard, the scene of student takeovers just the previous year, of riots and much revolutionary talk about casting aside Western values, archaic, Victorian morals seemed curiously 'unblack.' Baffled by my new environment, I did something I've never done before—I spent most of my time with women, often turning down the inevitable humiliation or, worse, boredom of a date (a growing possibility as I shed the extra pounds) even when it was offered to me. Most of the women were from small southern and midwestern communities. They thought me definitely straitjacket material with my well-polished set of 'sophisticated' New York views on premarital sex and atheism. I learned to listen more than I spoke.

But no one talked about why we stayed in on Friday and Saturday nights on a campus that was well known for its parties and nightlife. No one talked about why we drank so much or why our hunger for Big Macs was insatiable. We talked about men—all kinds, black and white, Joe Namath, Richard Roundtree, the class president who earned quite a reputation for driving coeds out on the highway and offering them a quick screw or a long walk home. 'But girl, ain't he fine?' We talked about movie stars and singing groups into the wee hours of the morning. Guzzling gin, cheating at poker, choking on cigarettes that dangled precariously from the corners of our mouths, we'd signify. 'If we could only be woman (white) enough' was the general feeling of most of us as we trotted off to bed.

Meanwhile the males on the campus had successfully buried the old standards of light, curly-haired young men with straight noses. They sported large, unruly Afros, dashikis, and flaring nostrils. Their coal-black eyes seemed to say, 'The nights *and* days belong to me,' as we'd pass one another on the campus green, a fashionable, thin colorless little creature always on their arm.

Enough was enough. I left Howard for City College after one term, and the significance of all I'd seen there had not entirely escaped me, because I remember becoming a feminist about then. No one had been doing very well when I had left New York but now it seemed even worse—the 'new blackness' was fast becoming the new slavery for sisters.

I discovered my voice, and when brothers talked to me, I talked back. This had its hazards. Almost got my eye blackened several times. My social life was like guerrilla warfare. Here was the logic behind our grandmothers' old saying, 'A nigga man ain't shit.' It was shorthand for 'The black man has learned to hate himself and to hate you even more. Be careful. He will hurt you.'

I am reminded of a conversation I had with a brother up at City College one mild spring day. We were standing on a corner in front of the South Campus gates; he was telling me what the role of the black woman was. When a pause came in his monologue, I asked him what the role of the black man was. He membled something about, 'Simply to be a man.' When I suggested that might not be enough, he went completely ape. He turned purple. He started screaming. 'The black man doesn't have to do anything. He's a man he's a man he's a man!'

Whenever I raised the question of a black woman's humanity in conversation with a black man, I got a similar reaction. Black men, at least the ones I knew, seemed totally confounded when it came to treating black women like people. Trying to be what we were told to be by the brothers of the 'nation'—sweet and smiling—a young black woman I knew had warmly greeted a brother in passing on Riverside Drive. He responded by raping her. When she asked the brothers what she should do, they told her not to go to the police and to have the baby though she was only seventeen.

Young black female friends of mine were dropping out of school because their boyfriends had convinced them that it was 'not correct' and 'counter-revolutionary' to strive to do anything but have babies and clean house. 'Help the brother get his thing together,' they were told. Other black women submitted to polygamous situations where sometimes they were called upon to sleep with the friends of their 'husband.' This later duty was explained to me once by a 'priest' of the New York Yoruban Temple. 'If your brother has to go to the bathroom and there is no toilet in his house then wouldn't you let him use your toilet?' For toilet read black woman.

The sisters got along by keeping their mouths shut, by refusing to see what was daily growing more difficult to ignore—a lot of brothers were doing double time—uptown with the sisters and downtown with the white woman whom they always vigorously claimed to hate. Some of the bolder brothers were quite frank about it. 'The white woman lets me be a man.'

The most popular justification black women had for not becoming feminists was their hatred of white women. They often repeated this for approving black male ears. (Obviously the brother had an interest in keeping black and white women apart—'Women will chatter.') But what I figured out was that the same black man who trembled with hatred for white men found the white woman irresistible because she was not a human being but a possession in his eyes—the higher-priced spread of woman he saw on television. 'I know that the white man made the white woman the symbol of freedom and the black woman the symbol of slavery' (*Soul on Ice*, Eldridge Cleaver).

When I first became a feminist, my black friends used to cast pitying eyes upon me and say, 'That's whitey's thing.' I used to laugh it off, thinking, yes there are some slight problems, a few things white women don't completely understand, but we can work them out. In *Ebony, Jet,* and *Encore*, and even in *The New York Times*, various black writers cautioned black women to be wary of smiling white feminists. The women's movement enlists the support of black women only to lend credibility to an essentially middle-class, irrelevant movement, they asserted. Time has shown that there was more truth to these claims than their shrillness indicated. Today when many white feminists think of black women, they too often think of faceless masses of welfare mothers and rape victims to flesh out their statistical studies of woman's plight.

One unusually awkward moment for me as a black feminist was when I found out that white feminists often don't view black men as men but as fellow victims. I've got no pressing quarrel with the notion that white men have been the worst offenders, but that isn't very helpful for a black woman from day to day. White women don't check out a white man's bank account or stockholdings before they accuse him of being sexist—they confront white men with and without jobs, with and without membership in a male consciousness-raising group. Yet when it comes to the black man, it's hands off.

A black friend of mine was fired by a black news service because she was pregnant. When she proposed doing an article on this for *Ms*, an editor there turned down the proposal with these words: 'We've got a special policy for the black man.' For a while I thought that was just the conservative feminist position until I overheard a certified radical feminist explaining why she dated only black men and other nonwhite men: 'They're less of a threat to women; they're less oppressive.'

Being a black woman means frequent spells of impotent, self-consuming rage. Such a spell came upon me when I recently attended a panel discussion at a women artists' conference. One of the panel members, a museum director and a white feminist, had come with a young black man in a sweatshirt, Pro-Keds, and rag tied around the kind of gigantic Afro you don't see much anymore. When asked about her commitment to black women artists, she responded with, 'Well, what about Puerto Rican women artists, and Mexican women artists, and Indian women artists? . . .' But she doesn't exhibit Hispanic women any more than she does black women (do I have to say anything about Indian women?), which is seldom indeed, though her museum is located in an area that is predominantly black and Puerto Rican. Yet she was confident in the position she took because the living proof of her liberalism and good intentions sat in the front row, black and unsmiling, six foot something and militant-*looking*.

In the spring of 1973, Doris Wright, a black feminist writer, called a meeting to discuss 'Black Women and Their Relationship to the Women's Movement.' The result was the National Black Feminist Organization, and I was fully delighted until, true to Women's Movement form, we got bogged down in an array of ideological disputes, the primary one being lesbianism versus heterosexuality. Dominated by the myths and facts of what white feminists had done and not done before us, it was nearly impossible to come to any agreement about our position on anything; and action was unthinkable.

Many of the prime movers in the organization seemed to be representing other interest groups and whatever commitment they might have had to black women's issues appeared to take a back seat to that. Women who had initiative and spirit usually attended one meeting, were turned off by the hopelessness of ever getting anything accomplished, and never returned again. Each meeting brought almost all new faces. Overhearing an aspiring political candidate say only half-jokingly at NBFO's first conference, 'I'm gonna get me some votes out of these niggas,' convinced me that black feminists were not ready to form a movement in which I could, with clear conscience, participate.

I started a black women's consciousness-raising group around the same time. When I heard one of my friends, whom I considered the closest thing to a feminist in the room, saying at one of our sessions, 'I feel sorry for any woman who tries to take my husband away from me because she's just going to have a man who has to pay alimony and child support,' even though she was not married to the man in question, I felt a great sinking somewhere in the chest area. Here was a woman who had insisted (at least to me) upon her right to bear a child outside of marriage, trying to convince a few black women, who were mostly single and very worried about it, that she was really married—unlike them. In fact, one of the first women to leave the group was a recent graduate of Sarah Lawrence, her excuse being, 'I want to place myself in situations where I will meet more men.' The group eventually disintegrated. We had no strength to give to one another. Is that possible? At any rate, that's the way it seemed, and perhaps it was the same on a larger scale with NBFO.

Despite a sizable number of black feminists who have contributed much to the leadership of the women's movement, there is still no black women's movement, and it appears there won't be for some time to come. It is conceivable that the level of consciousness feminism would demand in black women wouldn't lead to any sort of separatist movement, anyway— despite our distinctive problems. Perhaps a multicultural women's movement is somewhere in the future.

But for now, black feminists, of necessity it seems, exist as individuals—some well known, like Eleanor Holmes Norton, Florynce Kennedy, Faith Ringgold, Shirley Chisholm, Alice Walker, and some unknown, like me. We exist as women who are black who are feminists, each stranded for the moment, working independently because there is not yet an environment in this society remotely congenial to our struggle—because, being on the bottom, we would have to do what no one else has done: we would have to fight the world.

(1975)

CHAPTER FOUR

Beyond the Margins: Black Women Claiming Feminism

Feminism is the political theory and practice that struggles to free all women: women of color, working-class women, poor women, disabled women, lesbians, old women—as well as white, economically privileged, heterosexual women. Anything less than this vision of total freedom is not feminism, but merely female self-aggrandizement.

—BARBARA SMITH, . . . *But Some of Us Are Brave*

. . . we delight in remembering that half the world is female . . . more than half the globe's female half is yellow, brown, black, and red.

—HORTENSE SPILLERS

INTRODUCTION

Though black women did not join the mainstream women's movement in large numbers, they have a long history of organizing for the purpose of improving their lives and the lives of their families. This work took place in civil rights and nationalist organizations, separate black women's organizations, and community groups. In 1973, for example, Black Women Organized for Action was initiated in San Francisco. The founding in 1973 of the National Black Feminist Organization (NBFO) in New York City a few months later signalled an important development in contemporary black women's history and modern black feminism. No longer apologetic or ambivalent about self-identifying as feminists, some black women would change the terms of the discourse on women's liberation and announce that they were no longer going to be silent about what ailed them, despite continuing charges of disloyalty within certain segments of the black community. The Statement of Purpose which NBFO released in 1973 illustrates their conception of black and women's liberation and attempts to counter media assertions that the women's movement is irrelevant to the Third World, particularly black women:

> Black women have suffered cruelly in this society from living the phenome-non of being both both black and female, in a country that is *both* racist and sexist. . . . Because we live in a patriarchy, we have allowed a premium to be put on black male suffering . . . We have been called "matriarchs" by white racists and black nationalists . . . *We,* not white men or black men, must define our own self-image . . . and not fall into the mistake of being placed upon the pedastal which is even being rejected by white women. . . . We will continue to remind the Black Liberation Movement that there can't be liberation for half the race. We must, together, as a people, work to eliminate racism, from without the black community, which is trying to destroy us as an entire people; but we must remember that sexism is destroying and crippling us from within. (Schneir, 1994, 173–174)

The publication three years earlier of Toni Cade's *The Black Woman,* Toni Morrison's *The Bluest Eye,* and Shirley Chisholm's *Unbought and Unbossed* signalled the emergence of new voices surrounding issues of race, class, and gender. Lesbian writers Audre Lorde, Barbara Smith, and Cheryl Clarke would go on to challenge heterosexist practices within the black and feminist communities, practices that threatened to silence or marginalize lesbians of color. Throughout the 1980s black feminist theory would pro-vide a corrective to the privileging of middle-class white women's voices, help to shift the discourse on women's empowerment, and articulate a transformative "humanist vision of community" (Collins, *Black Feminist Thought,* 39) which could be embraced by many communities of color.

The Combahee River Collective

The Combahee River Collective was an important black feminist group that began in 1974 as the Boston chapter of the National Black Feminist Organization (NBFO), founded in 1973. The name was inspired by a river in South Carolina where Harriet Tubman had mounted a military campaign during the Civil War to free 750 slaves. NBFO's statement of purpose emphasized the importance of the much maligned women's liberation movement to black and other Third World women and reminded the black liberation movement that "there can't be liberation for half the race" (Statement of Purpose, Schneir, 174). In 1977, three members of the collective—Barbara Smith, Beverly Smith, and Demita Frazier—wrote a statement documenting the activities of the collective and articulating their philosophy. This black feminist manifesto is a clear articulation of the evolution of contemporary black feminism and the concept of the simultaneity of oppressions that black women suffer. It also emphasized the importance of eradicating homophobia and acknowledging the role of lesbians in the development of black feminism.

Black lesbians have indeed been critical to the development of black feminism as ideology and praxis. They were active in the founding of the National Black Feminist Organization in 1973 and the National Coalition of Black Lesbians and Gay Men in 1978. They started *Azalea: A Magazine by Third World Lesbians* in 1978 and, in 1981, Kitchen Table: Women of Color Press, the only publishing collective of its kind in the United States. Despite their roles in shaping the contours of feminist discourse and liberation struggles, however, they have been denied their rightful place in African American cultural, intellectual, and political history. *An Anthology of Black Lesbian Writing* (1995), which includes writings from throughout the diaspora, is another response to these silences.

A BLACK FEMINIST STATEMENT

W e are a collective of black feminists who have been meeting together since 1974.[1] During that time we have been involved in the process of defining and clarifying our politics, while at the same time doing political work within our own group and in coalition with other progressive organizations and movements. The most general statement of our politics at the present time would be that we are actively committed to struggling against racial, sexual, heterosexual, and class oppression and see as our particular task the development of integrated analysis and practice based upon the fact that the major systems of oppression are interlocking. The synthesis of these oppressions creates the conditions of our lives. As black women we see black feminism as the logical political movement to combat the manifold and simultaneous oppressions that all women of color face.

We will discuss four major topics in the paper that follows: (1) The genesis of contemporary black feminism; (2) what we believe, i.e., the specific province of our politics; (3) the problems in organizing black feminists, including a brief herstory of our collective; and (4) black feminist issues and practice.

1. THE GENESIS OF CONTEMPORARY BLACK FEMINISM

Before looking at the recent development of black feminism, we would like to affirm that we find our origins in the historical reality of Afro-American women's continuous life-and-death struggle for survival and liberation. Black women's extremely negative relationship to the American political system (a system of white male rule) has always been determined by our membership in two oppressed racial and sexual castes. As Angela Davis points out in "Reflections on the Black Woman's Role in the Community of Slaves," black women have always embodied, if only in their physical manifestation, an adversary stance to white male rule and have actively resisted its inroads upon them and their communities in both dramatic and subtle ways. There have always been black women activists —some known, like Sojourner Truth, Harriet Tubman, Frances E. W. Harper, Ida B. Wells-Barnett, and Mary Church Terrell, and thousands upon thousands unknown—who had a shared awareness of how their sexual identity combined with their racial identity to make their whole life situation and the focus of their political struggles unique. Contemporary black feminism is the outgrowth of countless generations of personal sacrifice, militancy, and work by our mothers and sisters.

A black feminist presence has evolved most obviously in connection with the second wave of the American women's movement beginning in the late 1960s. Black, other Third World, and working women have been involved in the feminist movement from its start, but both outside reactionary forces and racism and elitism within the movement itself have served to obscure our participation. In 1973 black feminists, primarily located in New York, felt the necessity of forming a separate black feminist group. This became the National Black Feminist Organization (NBFO).

Black feminist politics also have an obvious connection to movements for black liberation, particularly those of the 1960s and 1970s. Many of us were active in those movements (civil rights, black nationalism, the Black Panthers), and all of our lives were greatly affected and changed by their ideology, their goals, and the tactics used to achieve their goals. It was our experience and disillusionment within these liberation movements, as well as experience on the periphery of the white male left, that led to the need to develop a politics that was antiracist, unlike those of white women, and antisexist, unlike those of black and white men.

There is also undeniably a personal genesis for black feminism, that is, the political realization that comes from the seemingly personal experiences of individual black women's lives. Black feminists and many more black women who do not define themselves as feminists have all experienced sexual oppression as a constant factor in our day-to-day existence.

Black feminists often talk about their feelings of craziness before becoming conscious of the concepts of sexual politics, patriarchal rule, and, most importantly, feminism, the political analysis and practice that we women use to struggle against our oppression. The fact that racial politics and indeed racism are pervasive factors in our lives did not allow us, and still does not allow most black women, to look more deeply into our own experiences and define those things that make our lives what they are and our oppression specific to us. In the process of consciousness-raising, actually life-sharing, we began to recognize the commonality of our experiences and, from that sharing and growing consciousness, to build a politics that will change our lives and inevitably end our oppression.

Our development also must be tied to the contemporary economic and political position of black people. The post–World War II generation of black youth was the first to be able to minimally partake of certain educational and employment options, previously closed completely to black people. Although our economic position is still at the very bottom of the American capitalist economy, a handful of us have been able to gain certain tools as a result of tokenism in education and employment that potentially enable us to more effectively fight our oppression.

A combined antiracist and antisexist position drew us together initially, and as we developed politically we addressed ourselves to heterosexism and economic oppression under capitalism.

2. WHAT WE BELIEVE

Above all else, our politics initially sprang from the shared belief that black women are inherently valuable, that our liberation is a necessity not as an adjunct to somebody else's but because of our need as human persons for autonomy. This may seem so obvious as to sound simplistic, but it is apparent that no other ostensibly progressive movement has ever considered our specific oppression a priority or worked seriously for the ending of that oppression. Merely naming the pejorative stereotypes attributed to black women (e.g., mammy, matriarch, Sapphire, whore, bulldagger), let alone cataloguing the cruel, often murderous, treatment we receive, indicates how little value has been placed upon our lives during four centuries of bondage in the Western Hemisphere. We realize that the only people who care enough about us to work consistently for our liberation is us. Our politics evolve from a healthy love for ourselves, our sisters, and our community, which allows us to continue our struggle and work.

This focusing upon our own oppression is embodied in the concept of identity politics. We believe that the most profound and potentially the most radical politics come directly out of our own identity, as opposed to working to end somebody else's oppression. In the case of black women this is a particularly repugnant, dangerous, threatening, and therefore revolutionary concept because it is obvious from looking at all the political movements that have preceded us that anyone is more worthy of liberation than ourselves. We reject pedestals, queenhood, and walking ten paces behind. To be recognized as human, levelly human, is enough.

We believe that sexual politics under patriarchy is as pervasive in black women's lives as are the politics of class and race. We also often find it difficult to separate race from class from sex oppression because in our lives they are most often experienced simultaneously. We know that there is such a thing as racial-sexual oppression that is neither solely racial nor solely sexual, e.g., the history of rape of black women by white men as a weapon of political repression.

Although we are feminists and lesbians, we feel solidarity with progressive black men and do not advocate the fractionalization that white women who are separatists demand. Our situation as black people necessitates that we have solidarity around the fact of race, which white women of course do not need to have with white men, unless it is their negative solidarity as racial oppressors. We struggle together with black men against racism, while we also struggle with black men about sexism.

We realize that the liberation of all oppressed peoples necessitates the destruction of the political-economic systems of capitalism and imperialism as well as patriarchy. We are socialists because we believe the work must be organized for the collective benefit of those who do the work and create the products and not for the profit of the bosses. Material resources must be equally distributed among those who create these resources. We are not convinced, however, that a socialist revolution that is not also a feminist and antiracist revolution will guarantee our liberation. We have arrived at the necessity for developing an understanding of class relationships that takes into account the specific class position of black women who are generally marginal in the labor force, while at this particular time some of us are temporarily viewed as doubly desirable tokens at white-collar and professional levels. We need to articulate the real class situation of persons who are not merely raceless, sexless workers, but for whom racial and sexual oppression are significant determinants in their working/economic lives. Although we are in essential agreement with Marx's theory as it applied to the very specific economic relationships he analyzed, we know that this analysis must be extended further in order for us to understand our specific economic situation as black women.

A political contribution that we feel we have already made is the expansion of the feminist principle that the personal is political. In our consciousness-raising sessions, for example, we have in many ways gone beyond white women's revelations because we are dealing with the implications of race and class as well as sex. Even our black women's style of talking/testifying in black language about what we have experienced has a resonance that is both cultural and political. We have spent a great deal of energy delving into the cultural and experiential nature of our oppression out of necessity because none of these matters have ever been looked at before. No one before has ever examined the multilayered texture of black women's lives.

As we have already stated, we reject the stance of lesbian separatism because it is not a viable political analysis or strategy for us. It leaves out far too much and far too many people, particularly black men, women, and children. We have a great deal of criticism and loathing for what men have been socialized to be in this society: what they support, how they act, and how they oppress. But we do not have the misguided notion that it is their maleness, per se—i.e., their biological maleness—that makes them what they are. As black women we find any type of biological determinism a particularly dangerous and reactionary basis upon which to build a politic. We must also question whether lesbian separatism is an adequate and progressive political analysis and strategy, even for those who practice it, since it so completely denies any but the sexual sources of women's oppression, negating the facts of class and race.

3. PROBLEMS IN ORGANIZING BLACK FEMINISTS

During our years together as a black feminist collective we have experienced success and defeat, joy and pain, victory and failure. We have found that it is very difficult to organize around black feminist issues, difficult even to announce in certain contexts that we are black feminists. We have tried to think about the reasons for our difficulties, particularly since the white women's movement continues to be strong and to grow in many directions. In this section we will discuss some of the general reasons for the organizing problems we face and also talk specifically about the stages in organizing our own collective.

The major source of difficulty in our political work is that we are not just trying to fight oppression on one front or even two, but instead to address a whole range of oppressions. We do not have racial, sexual, heterosexual, or class privilege to rely upon, nor do we have even the minimal access to resources and power that groups who possess any one of these types of privilege have.

The psychological toll of being a black woman and the difficulties this presents in reaching political consciousness and doing political work can never be underestimated. There is a very low value placed upon black women's psyches in this society, which is both racist and sexist. As an early group member once said, "We are all damaged people merely by virtue of being black women." We are dispossessed psychologically and on every other level, and yet we feel the necessity to struggle to change our condition and the condition of all black women. In "A Black Feminist's Search for Sisterhood," Michele Wallace arrives at this conclusion:

> We exist as women who are black who are feminists, each stranded for the moment, working independently because there is not yet an environment in this society remotely congenial to our struggle—because, being on the bottom, we would have to do what no one else has done: we would have to fight the world.[2]

Wallace is not pessimistic but realistic in her assessment of black feminists' position, particularly in her allusion to the nearly classic isolation most of us face. We might use our position at the bottom, however, to make a clear leap into revolutionary action. If black women were free, it would mean that everyone else would have to be free since our freedom would necessitate the destruction of all the systems of oppression.

Feminism is, nevertheless, very threatening to the majority of black people because it calls into question some of the most basic assumptions about our existence, i.e., that gender should be a determinant of power relationships. Here is the way male and female roles were defined in a black nationalist pamphlet from the early 1970s.

> We understand that it is and has been traditional that the man is the head of the house. He is the leader of the house/nation because his knowledge of the world is broader, his awareness is greater, his understanding is fuller and his application of this information is wiser. . . . After all, it is only reasonable that the man be the head of the house because he is able to defend and protect the development of his home. . . . Women cannot do the same things as men —they are made by nature to function differently. Equality of men and women is something that cannot happen even in the abstract world. Men are not equal to other men, i.e., ability, experience, or even understanding. The value of men and women can be seen as in the value of gold and silver— they are not equal but both have great value. We must realize that men and women are a complement to each other because there is no house/family without a man and his wife. Both are essential to the development of any life.[3]

The material conditions of most black women would hardly lead them to upset both economic and sexual arrangements that seem to represent some stability in their lives. Many black women have a good understanding of both sexism and racism, but because of the everyday constrictions of their lives cannot risk struggling against them both.

The reaction of black men to feminism has been notoriously negative. They are, of course, even more threatened than black women by the possibility that black feminists might organize around our own needs. They realize that they might not only lose valuable and hard-working allies in their struggles, but that they might also be forced to change their habitually sexist ways of interacting with and oppressing black women. Accusations that black feminism divides the black struggle are powerful deterrents to the growth of an autonomous black women's movement.

Still, hundreds of women have been active at different times during the three-year existence of our group. And every black woman who came, came out of a strongly felt need for some level of possibility that did not previously exist in her life.

When we first started meeting early in 1974 after the NBFO first eastern regional conference, we did not have a strategy for organizing, or even a focus. We just wanted to see what we had. After a period of months of not meeting, we began to meet again late in the year and started doing an intense variety of consciousness-raising. The overwhelming feeling that we had is that after years and years we had finally found each other. Although we were not doing political work as a group, individuals continued their involvement in lesbian politics, sterilization abuse, and abortion rights work, Third World Women's International Women's Day activities, and support activity for the trials of Dr. Kenneth Edelin, Joan Little, and Inez Garcia. During our first summer, when membership had dropped off considerably, those of us remaining devoted serious discussion to the possibility of opening a refuge for battered women in a black community. (There was no refuge in Boston at that time.) We also decided around that time to become an independent collective since we had serious disagreements with NBFO's bourgeois-feminist stance and their lack of a clear political focus.

We also were contacted at that time by socialist feminists, with whom we had worked on abortion rights activities, who wanted to encourage us to attend the National Socialist Feminist Conference in Yellow Springs. One of our members did attend and despite the narrowness of the ideology that was promoted at that particular conference, we became more aware of the need for us to understand our own economic situation and to make our own economic analysis.

In the fall, when some members returned, we experienced several months of comparative inactivity and internal disagreements which were first conceptualized as a lesbian-straight split but which were also the result of class and political differences. During the summer those of us who were still meeting had determined the need to do political work and to move beyond consciousness-raising and serving exclusively as an emotional support group. At the beginning of 1976, when some of the women who had not wanted to do political work and who also had voiced disagreements stopped attending of their own accord, we again looked for a focus. We decided at that time, with the addition of new members, to become a study group. We had always shared our reading with each other, and some of us had written papers on black feminism for group discussion a few months before this decision was made. We began functioning as a study group and also began discussing the possibility of starting a black feminist publication. We had a retreat in the late spring, which provided a time for both political discussion and working out interpersonal issues. Currently we are planning to gather together a collection of black feminist writing. We feel that it is absolutely essential to demonstrate the reality of our politics to other black women and believe that we can do this through writing and distributing our work. The fact that individual black feminists are living in isolation all over the country, that our own numbers are small, and that we have some skills in writing, printing, and publishing makes us want to carry out these kinds of projects as a means of organizing black feminists as we continue to do political work in coalition with other groups.

4. BLACK FEMINIST ISSUES AND PRACTICE

During our time together we have identified and worked on many issues of particular relevance to black women. The inclusiveness of our politics makes us concerned with any situation that impinges upon the lives of women, Third World, and working people. We are of course particularly committed to working on those struggles in which race, sex, and class are simultaneous factors in oppression. We might, for example, become involved in workplace organizing at a factory that employs Third-World women or picket a hospital that is cutting back on already inadequate health care to a Third World community, or set up a rape crisis center in a black neighborhood. Organizing around welfare or day-care concerns might also be a focus. The work to be done and the countless issues that this work represents merely reflect the pervasiveness of our oppression.

Issues and projects that collective members have actually worked on are sterilization abuse, abortion rights, battered women, rape, and health care. We have also done many workshops and educationals on black feminism on college campuses, at women's conferences, and most recently for high school women.

One issue that is of major concern to us and that we have begun to publicly address is racism in the white women's movement. As black feminists we are made constantly and painfully aware of how little effort white women have made to understand and combat their racism, which requires among other things that they have a more than superficial comprehension of race, color, and black history and culture. Eliminating racism in the white women's movement is by definition work for white women to do, but we will continue to speak to and demand accountability on this issue.

In the practice of our politics we do not believe that the end always justifies the means. Many reactionary and destructive acts have been done in the name of achieving "correct" political goals. As feminists we do not want to mess over people in the name of politics. We believe in collective process and a nonhierarchical distribution of power within our own group and in our vision of a revolutionary society. We are committed to a continual examination of our politics as they develop through criticism and self-criticism as an essential aspect of our practice. As black feminists and lesbians we know that we have a very definite revolutionary task to perform, and we are ready for the lifetime of work and struggle before us.

ENDNOTES

1. This statement is dated April 1977.

2. Michele Wallace. "A Black Feminist's Search for Sisterhood," *Village Voice,* 28 July 1975, 6–7.

3. Mumininas of Committee for Unified Newark, *Mwanamke Mwananchi (The Nationalist Woman),* Newark, NJ, c. 1971, 4–5.

Cheryl Clarke

Cheryl Clarke, a black lesbian feminist poet and critic, is also an administrator and doctoral student at Rutgers University in New Brunswick. Her essay "Lesbianism: An Act of Resistance" appeared in *This Bridge Called My Back: Writings by Radical Women of Color* (edited by Cherríe Moraga and Gloria Anzaldúa), and is an important black lesbian feminist manifesto. She has written angrily about homophobia in "The Failure to Transform: Homophobia in the Black Community" (*Home Girls,* 1983) in which she indicates that "it is ironic that the Black Power movement could transform the consciousness of an entire generation of black people regarding black self-determination and, at the same time, fail so miserably in understanding the sexual politics of the movement and of black people across the board" (199). She also criticizes straight black feminist writers for ignoring lesbianism in their early writings.

Cheryl Clarke }

LESBIANISM: AN ACT OF RESISTANCE

For a woman to be a lesbian in a male-supremacist, capitalist, misogynist, racist, homophobic, imperialist culture, such as that of North America, is an act of resistance. (A resistance that should be championed throughout the world by all the forces struggling for liberation from the same slave master.) No matter how a woman lives out her lesbianism—in the closet, in the state legislature, in the bedroom—she has rebelled against becoming the slave master's concubine, viz., the male-dependent female, the female heterosexual. This rebellion is dangerous business in patriarchy. Men at all levels of privilege, of all classes and colors, have the potential to act out legalistically, moralistically, and violently when they cannot colonize women, when they cannot circumscribe our sexual, productive, reproductive, creative prerogatives, and energies. And the lesbian—that woman who, as Judy Grahn says, "has taken a woman lover"[1]—has succeeded in resisting the slave master's imperialism in that one sphere of her life. The lesbian has decolonized her body. She has rejected a life of servitude implicit in Western, heterosexual relationships and has accepted the potential of mutuality in a lesbian relationship—*roles* notwithstanding.

Historically, this culture has come to identify lesbians as women who, over time, engage in a range and variety of sexual-emotional relationships with women. I, for one, identify a woman as a lesbian who says she is. Lesbianism is a recognition, an awakening, a reawakening of our passion for each (woman) other (woman) and for same (woman). This passion will ultimately reverse the heterosexual imperialism of male culture. Women, through the ages, have fought and died rather than deny that passion. In her essay "The Meaning of Our Love for Women Is What We Have Constantly to Expand," Adrienne Rich states:

> ...Before any kind of feminist movement existed, or could exist, lesbians existed: women who loved women, who refused to comply with behavior demanded of women, who refused to define themselves in relation to men.

Those women, our foresisters, millions whose names we do not know, were tortured and burned as witches, slandered in religious and later in "scientific" tracts, portrayed in art and literature as bizarre, amoral, destructive, decadent women. For a long time, the lesbian has been a personification of feminine evil.

... Lesbians have been forced to live between two cultures, both male-dominated, each of which has denied and endangered our existence ... Heterosexual, patriarchal culture has driven lesbians into secrecy and guilt, often to self-hatred and suicide.[2]

The evolving synthesis of lesbianism and feminism—two women-centered and powered ideologies—is breaking that silence and secrecy. The following analysis is offered as one small cut against that stone of silence and secrecy. It is not intended to be original or all-inclusive. I dedicate this work to all the women hidden from history whose suffering and triumph have made it possible for me to call my name out loud.*

The woman who embraces lesbianism as an ideological, political, and philosophical means of liberation of all women from heterosexual tyranny must also identify with the worldwide struggle of all women to end male-supremacist tyranny at all levels. As far as I am concerned, any woman who calls herself a feminist must commit herself to the liberation of *all* women for *coerced* heterosexuality as it manifests itself in the family, the state, and on Madison Avenue. The lesbian-feminist struggles for the liberation of all people from patriarchal domination through heterosexism and for the transformation of all socio-political structures, systems, and relationships that have been degraded and corrupted under centuries of male domination.

However, there is no one kind of lesbian, no one kind of lesbian behavior, and no one kind of lesbian relationship. Also there is no one kind of response to the pressures that lesbians labor under to survive as lesbians. Not all women who are involved in sexual-emotional relationships with women call themselves lesbians or identify with any particular lesbian community. Many women are only lesbians to a particular community and *pass* as heterosexuals as they traffic among enemies. (This is analogous to being black and passing for white with only one's immediate family knowing one's true origins.) Yet, those who hide in the closet of heterosexual presumption are sooner or later discovered. The "nigger-in-the-woodpile" story retells itself. Many women are politically active as lesbians, but may fear holding hands with their lovers as they traverse heterosexual turf. (This response to heterosexual predominance can be likened to the reaction

---

* I would like to give particular acknowledgment to the Combahee River Collective's "A Black Feminist Statement." Because this document espouses "struggling against racial, sexual, heterosexual, and class oppression," it has become a manifesto of radical feminist thought, action, and practice.

of the black student who integrates a predominately white dormitory and who fears leaving the door of her room open when she plays gospel music.) There is the woman who engages in sexual-emotional relationships with women and labels herself *bisexual.* (This is comparable to the Afro-American whose skin color indicates her mixed ancestry yet who calls herself "mulatto" rather than black.) Bisexual is a safer label than lesbian, for it posits the possibility of a relationship with a man, regardless of how infrequent or nonexistent the female bisexual's relationships with men might be. And then there is the lesbian who is a lesbian anywhere and everywhere and who is in direct and constant confrontation with heterosexual presumption, privilege, and oppression. (Her struggle can be compared to that of the civil rights activist of the 1960s who was out there on the streets for freedom, while so many of us viewed the action on the television.)

Wherever we, as lesbians, fall along this very generalized political continuum, we must know that the institution of heterosexuality is a die-hard custom through which male-supremacist institutions insure their own perpetuity and control over us. Women are kept, maintained, and contained through terror, violence, and spray of semen. It is profitable for our colonizers to confine our bodies and alienate us from our own life processes as it was profitable for the European to enslave the African and destroy all memory of a prior freedom and self-determination—Alex Haley notwithstanding. And just as the foundation of Western capitalism depended upon the North Atlantic slave trade, the system of patriarchal domination is buttressed by the subjugation of women through heterosexuality. So, patriarchs must extoll the boy-girl dyad as "natural: to keep us straight and compliant in the same way the European had to extoll caucasian superiority to justify the African slave trade. Against that historic backdrop, *the woman who chooses to be a lesbian lives dangerously.*

As a member of the largest and second most oppressed group of people of color, as a woman whose slave and ex-slave foresisters suffered some of the most brutal racist, male-supremacist imperialism in Western history, the black lesbian has had to survive also the psychic mutilation of heterosexual superiority. The black lesbian is coerced into the experience of institutional racism—like every other nigger in America—and must suffer as well the homophobic sexism of the black political community, some of whom seem to have forgotten so soon the pain of rejection, denial, and repression sanctioned by racist America. While most political black lesbians do not give a damn if white America is negrophobic, it becomes deeply problematic when the contemporary black political community (another male-dominated and male-identified institution) rejects us because of our commitment to women and women's liberation. Many black male members of that community seem still not to understand the historic connection between the oppression of African peoples in North America and the

universal oppression of women. As the women's rights activist and abolitionist, Elizabeth Cady Stanton, pointed out during the 1850s, racism and
sexism have been produced by the same animal, viz., "the white Saxon
man."

Gender oppression (i.e., the male exploitation and control of women's
productive and reproductive energies on the specious basis of a biological
difference) originated from the first division of labor, viz., that between
women and men, and resulted in the accumulation of private property,
patriarchal usurpation of "mother right" or matrilineage, and the duplici-
tous, male-supremacist institution of heterosexual monogamy (for women
only). Sexual politics, therefore, mirror the exploitative, class-bound relationship between the white slave master and the African slave—and the
impact of both relationships (between black and white and woman and
man) has been residual beyond emancipation and suffrage. The ruling-class
white man had a centuries-old model for his day-to-day treatment of the
African slave. Before he learned to justify the African's continued enslavement and the ex-slave's continued disfranchisement with arguments of the
African's divinely ordained mental and moral inferiority to himself (a
smokescreen for his capitalist greed) the white man learned, within the
structure of heterosexual monogamy and under the system of patriarchy,
to relate to black people—slave or free—as a man *relates* to a woman, viz.,
as property, as a sexual commodity, as a servant, as a source of free or cheap
labor, and as an innately inferior being.

Although counterrevolutionary, Western heterosexuality, which advances male supremacy, continues to be upheld by many black people,
especially black men, as the most desired state of affairs between men and
women. This observation is borne out on the pages of our most scholarly
black publications to our most commercial black publications, which view
the issue of black male and female relationships through the lens of heterosexual bias. But this is to be expected, as historically heterosexuality was
one of our only means of power over our condition as slaves and one of
two means we had at our disposal to appease the white man.

Now, as ex-slaves, black men have more latitude to oppress black
women, because the brothers no longer have to compete directly with the
white man for control of black women's bodies. Now, the black man can
assume the "master" role, and he can attempt to tyrannize black women.
The black man may view the lesbian—who cannot be manipulated or
seduced sexually by him—in much the same way the white slave master
once viewed the black male slave, viz., as some perverse caricature of
manhood threatening his position of dominance over the female body. This
view, of course, is a "neurotic illusion" imposed on black men by the
dictates of male supremacy, which the black man can never fulfill because
he lacks the capital means and racial privilege.

Historically, the myth in the black world is that there are only two free people in the United States, the white man and the black woman. The myth was established by the black man in the long period of his frustration when he longed to be free to have the material and social advantages of his oppressor, the white man. On examination of the myth this so-called freedom was based on the sexual prerogatives taken by the white man on the black female. It was fantasied by the black man that she enjoyed it.[3]

While lesbian-feminism does threaten the black man's predatory control of black women, its goal as a political ideology and philosophy is not to take the black man's or any man's position on top.

Black lesbians who do work within "by-for-about-black-people" groups or organizations either pass as "straight" or relegate our lesbianism to the so-called private sphere. The more male-dominated or black nationalist bourgeois the organization or group, the more resistant to change, and thus, the more homophobic and antifeminist. In these sectors, we learn to keep a low profile.

In 1979, at the annual conference of a regional chapter of the National Black Social Workers, the national director of that body was given a standing ovation for the following remarks:

> Homosexuals are even accorded minority status now . . . And white women, too. And some of you black women who call yourselves feminists will be sitting up in meetings with the same white women who will be stealing your men on the sly.

This type of indictment of women's revolution and implicitly of lesbian liberation is voiced throughout the bourgeois black (male) movement. But this is the insidious nature of male supremacy. While the black man may consider racism his primary oppression, he is hard put to recognize that sexism is inextricably bound up with the racism the black woman must suffer, nor can he see that no women (or men for that matter) will be liberated from the original "master-slave" relationship, viz., that between men and women, until we are all liberated from the false premise of heterosexual superiority. This corrupted, predatory relationship between men and women is the foundation of the master-slave relationship between white and black people in the United States.

The tactic many black men use to intimidate black women from embracing feminism is to reduce the conflicts between white women and black women to a "tug-o'-war" for the black penis. And since the black lesbian, as stated previously, is not interested in his penis, she undermines the black man's only source of power over her, viz., his heterosexuality. Black lesbians and all black women involved in the struggle for liberation must resist this manipulation and seduction.

The dyke, like every dyke in America, is everywhere—in the home, in the street, on the welfare, unemployment, and social security rolls, raising children, working in factories, in the armed forces, on television, in the public school system, in all the professions, going to college or graduate school, in middle-management, et al. The black dyke, like every other nonwhite and working-class and poor woman in America, has not suffered the luxury, privilege, or oppression of being dependent on men, even though our male counterparts have been present, have shared our lives, work, and struggle, and, in addition, have undermined our "human dignity" along the way like most men in patriarchy, the imperialist family of man. But we could never depend on them "to take care of us" on their resources alone—and, of course, it is another "neurotic illusion" imposed on our fathers, brothers, lovers, husbands that they are supposed to "take care of us" because we are women. Translate: "to take care of us" equals "to control us." Our brothers', fathers', lovers', husbands' only power is their manhood. And unless manhood is somehow embellished by white skin and generations of private wealth, it has little currency in racist, capitalist patriarchy. The black man, for example, is accorded native elite or colonial guard or vigilante status over black women in imperialist patriarchy. He is an overseer for the slave master. Because of his maleness, he is given access to certain privileges, e.g., employment, education, a car, life insurance, a house, some nice vines. He is usually a rabid heterosexual. He is, since emancipation, allowed to raise a "legitimate" family, allowed to have his piece of turf, viz., his wife and children. That is as far as his dictatorship extends for, if his wife decides that she wants to leave that home for whatever reason, he does not have the power or resources to seduce her otherwise if she is determined to throw off the benign or malicious yoke of dependency. The ruling-class white man on the other hand, has always had the power to count women among his pool of low-wage labor, his means of production. Most recently, he has "allowed" women the right to sue for divorce, to apply for AFDC, and to be neocolonized.

Traditionally, poor black men and women who banded together and stayed together and raised children together did not have the luxury to cultivate dependence among the members of their families. So, the black dyke, like most black women, has been conditioned to be self-sufficient, i.e., not dependent on men. For me personally, the conditioning to be self-sufficient and the predominance of female role models in my life are the roots of my lesbianism. Before I became a lesbian, I often wondered why I was expected to give up, avoid, and trivialize the recognition and encouragement I felt from women in order to pursue the tenuous business of heterosexuality. And I am not unique.

As political lesbians, i.e., lesbians who are resisting the prevailing culture's attempts to keep us invisible and powerless, we must become more visible (particularly black and other lesbians of color) to our sisters hidden in their various closets, locked in prisons of self-hate and ambiguity, afraid to take the ancient act of woman-bonding beyond the sexual, the private, the personal. I am not trying to reify lesbianism or feminism. I am trying to point out that lesbian-feminism has the potential of reversing and transforming a major component in the system of women's oppression, viz., predatory heterosexuality. If radical lesbian-feminism purports an antiracist, anticlassist, anti-woman-hating vision of bonding as mutual, reciprocal, as infinitely negotiable, as freedom from antiquated gender prescriptions and proscriptions, *then all people struggling to transform the character of relationships in this culture have something to learn from lesbians.*

The woman who takes a woman lover lives dangerously in patriarchy. And woe betide her even more if she chooses as her lover a woman who is not of her race. The silence among lesbian-feminists regarding the issue of lesbian relationships between black and white women in America is caused by none other than the centuries-old taboo and laws in the United States against relationships between people of color and those of the caucasian race. Speaking heterosexually, the laws and taboos were a reflection of the patriarchal slave master's attempts to control his property via controlling his lineage through the institution of monogamy (for women only) and justified the taboos and laws with the argument that purity of the caucasian race must by preserved (as well as its supremacy). However, we know that his racist and racialist laws and taboos did not apply to him in terms of the black slave woman, just as his classist laws and taboos regarding the relationship between the ruling class and the indentured servants did not apply to him in terms of the white woman servant he chose to rape. The offspring of any unions between the white ruling-class slave master and the black slave woman or white woman indentured servant could not legally inherit their white or ruling-class sire's property or name, just their mothers' condition of servitude.

The taboo against black and white people relating at any other level than master-slave, superior-inferior, has been propounded in America to keep black women and men, and white women and men, who share a common oppression at the hands of the ruling-class white man, from organizing against that common oppression. We, as black lesbians, must vehemently resist being bound by the white man's racist, sexist laws, which have endangered potential intimacy of any kind between whites and blacks.

It cannot be presumed that black lesbians involved in love, work, and social relationships with white lesbians do so out of self-hate and denial of our racial-cultural heritage, identities, and oppression. Why should a woman's commitment to the struggle be questioned or accepted on the basis of her lover's or comrade's skin color? White lesbians engaged likewise with black lesbians or any lesbians of color cannot be assumed to be acting out of some perverse, guilt-ridden racialist desire.

I personally am tired of going to events, conferences, workshops, planning sessions that involve a coming together of black and other lesbians of color for political or even social reasons and listening to black lesbians relegate feminism to white women, castigate black women who propose forming coalitions with predominantly white feminist groups, minimize the white woman's oppression and exaggerate her power, and then finally judge that a black lesbian's commitment to the liberation of black women is dubious because she does not sleep with a black woman. All of us have to accept or reject allies on the basis of politics not on the specious basis of skin color. *Have not black people suffered betrayal from our own people?*

Yes, black women's experiences of misogyny are different from white women's. However, they all add up to how the patriarchal slave master decided to oppress us. We both fought each other for his favor, approval, and protection. Such is the effect of imperialist, heterosexist patriarchy. Shulamith Firestone, in the essay, "Racism: the Sexism of the Family of Many," purports this analysis of the relationship between white and black women:

> How do the women of this racial Triangle feel about each other? Divide and conquer: Both women have grown hostile to each other, white women feeling contempt for the "sluts" with no morals, black women feeling envy for the pampered "powder puffs." The black woman is jealous of the white woman's legitimacy, privilege, and comfort, but she also feels deep contempt. . . . Similarly the white woman's contempt for the black woman is mixed with envy: for the black woman's greater sexual license, for her gutsiness, for her freedom from the marriage bind. For after all, the black woman is not under the thumb of a man, but is pretty much her own boss to come and go, to leave the house, to work (much as it is degrading work) or to be "shiftless." What the white woman doesn't know is that the black woman, not under the thumb of *one* man, can now be squashed by all. There is no alternative for either of them than the choice between being public or private property, but because each still believes that the other is getting away with something both can be fooled into mis-channeling their frustration onto each other rather than onto the real enemy, "The Man."[4]

Though her statement of the choices black and white women have under patriarchy in America has merit, Firestone analyzes only a specific relationship, i.e., between the ruling-class white woman and slave or ex-slave black woman.

Because of her whiteness, the white woman of all classes has been accorded, as the black man has because of his maleness, certain privileges in racist patriarchy, e.g., indentured servitude as opposed to enslavement, exclusive right to public assistance until the 1960s, "legitimate" offspring and (if married into the middle/upper class) the luxury to live on her husband's income, etc.

The black woman, having neither maleness nor whiteness, has always had her heterosexuality, which white men and black men have manipulated by force and at will. Further, she, like all poor people, has had her labor, which the white capitalist man has also taken and exploited at will. These capabilities have allowed black women minimal access to the crumbs thrown at black men and white women. So, when the black woman and the white woman become lovers, we bring that history and all those questions to the relationship as well as other people's problems with the relationships. The taboo against intimacy between white and black people has been internalized by us and simultaneously defied by us. If we, as lesbian-feminists, defy the taboo, then we begin to transform the history of relationships between black women and white women.

In her essay, "Disloyal to Civilization: Feminism, Racism, Gynephobia," Rich calls for feminists to attend to the complexities of the relationship between black and white women in the United States. Rich queries:

> What caricatures of bloodless fragility and broiling sensuality still imprint our psyches, and where did we receive these imprintings? What happened between the several thousand Northern white women and Southern black women who together taught in the schools founded under Reconstruction by the Freedmen's Bureau, side by side braving the Ku Klux Klan harrassment, terrorism, and the hostility of white communities? *[5]

So, all of us would do well to stop fighting each other for our space at the bottom, because there ain't no more room. We have spent so much time hating ourselves. Time to love ourselves. And that, for all lesbians, as lovers, as comrades, as freedom fighters, is the final resistance.

ENDNOTES

1. Judy Grahn, "The Common Woman," *The Work of a Common Woman* (Oakland: Diana Press, 1978), 67.

2. Adrienne Rich, *On Lies, Secrets, and Silence: Selected Prose 1966–1978* (New York: W. W. Norton, 1979), 225.

---

* One such example is the Port Royal Experiment (1862), the precursor of the Freedmen's Bureau. Port Royal was a program of relief for "freed men and women" in the South Carolina Sea Islands, organized under the auspices of the Boston Education Commission and the Freedmen's Relief Assoc. in New York and the Port Royal Relief Assoc. in Philadelphia, and sanctioned by the Union Army and the Federal Government. See *The Journal of Charolotte Forten* on the "Port Royal Experiment" (Boston: Beacon Press, 1969). Through her Northern bourgeois myopia, Forten recounts her experiences as a black teacher among the black freed men and women and her Northern white women peers.

3. Pat Robinson and Group, "Poor Black Women's Study Papers by Poor Black Women of Mount Vernon, New York," in *The Black Woman: An Anthology,* ed. Toni Cade (New York: New American Library, 1970), 194.

4. Shulamith Firestone, *The Dialectic of Sex: The Case for Feminist Revolution* (New York: Bantam Books, 1972), 113.

5. Rich, *On Lies,* 298.

Barbara Smith

Barbara Smith is one of the most important black feminist theorists and activists to emerge during the 1970s. She coedited (with Patricia Bell Scott and Gloria T. Hull) the first black women's studies anthology—*All the Women Are White, All the Blacks Are Men, But Some of Us Are Brave.* She also cofounded (with Audre Lorde) the first publishing collective by women of color, Kitchen Table: Women of Color Press. Her path-breaking essay "Toward a Black Feminist Criticism" defined black feminist literary criticism and underscored the importance of sexuality in reading black women's literature. She also taught one of the first black women writers classes in the academy at Simmons College in Boston. Her guest editorship (with Lorraine Bethel) of *Conditions Five: The Black Women's Issue* (1979) provided black lesbian feminists an outlet for their creative expression at a time when they did not have publishing outlets within the black press. The publication of *Home Girls* generated important dialogue within the mainstream feminist movement and the black community about the significance of black feminist discourse in liberation struggles. Smith is presently completing a book on the history of black lesbians.

Barbara Smith }

SOME HOME TRUTHS
ON THE CONTEMPORARY
BLACK FEMINIST MOVEMENT

In the fall of 1981, before most of *Home Girls*[1] was compiled, I was searching for a title. I'd come up with one that I knew was not quite right. At the time I was also working on the story which later became "Home" and thought that I'd like to get some of the feeling of that piece into the book. One day while doing something else entirely, and playing with words in my head, "home girls" came to me. Home Girls. The girls from the neighborhood and from the block, the girls we grew up with. I knew I was onto something, particularly when I considered that so many black people who are threatened by feminism have argued that by being a black feminist (particularly if you are also a lesbian) you have left the race, are no longer a part of the black community, in short no longer have a home.

I suspect that most of the contributors to *Home Girls* learned their varied politics and their shared commitment to black women from the same sources I did. Yet critics of feminism pretend that just because some of us speak out about sexual politics *at home,* within the black community, we must have sprung miraculously from somewhere else. But we are not strangers and never have been. I am convinced that black feminism is, on every level, organic to black experience.

Black women as a group have never been fools. We couldn't afford to be. Yet in the last two decades many of us have been deterred from identifying with a liberation struggle that might say significant things to women like ourselves, women who believe that we were put here for a purpose in our own right, women who are usually not afraid to struggle.

Although our involvement has increased considerably in recent years, there are countless reasons why black and other Third World women have not identified with contemporary feminism in large numbers.[2] The racism of white women in the women's movement has certainly been a major factor. The powers-that-be are also aware that a movement of progressive Third World women in this country would alter life as we know it.

As a result there has been a concerted effort to keep women of color from organizing autonomously and from organizing with other women around women's political issues. Third World men, desiring to maintain power over "their women" at all costs, have been among the most willing reinforcers of the fears and myths about the women's movement, attempting to scare us away from figuring things out for ourselves.

It is fascinating to look at various kinds of media from the late 1960s and early 1970s, when feminism was making its great initial impact, in order to see what black men, Native American men, Asian American men, Latino men, and white men were saying about the irrelevance of "women's lib" to women of color. White men and Third World men, ranging from conservatives to radicals, pointed to the seeming lack of participation of women of color in the movement in order to discredit it and to undermine the efforts of the movement as a whole. All kinds of men were running scared because they knew that, if the women in their midst were changing, they were going to have to change too. In 1976 I wrote:

> Feminism is potentially the most threatening of movements to black and other Third-World people because it makes it absolutely essential that we examine the way we live, how we treat each other, and what we believe. It calls into question the most basic assumption about our existence, and this is the idea that biological, i.e., sexual, identity determines all, that it is the rationale for power relationships as well as for all other levels of human identity and action. An irony is that among Third-World people biological determinism is rejected and fought against when it is applied to race, but generally unquestioned when it applies to sex.[3]

In reaction to the "threat" of such change, black men, with the collaboration of some black women, developed a set of myths to divert black women from our own freedom.

MYTHS

MYTH NO. 1: THE BLACK WOMAN IS ALREADY LIBERATED.

This myth confuses liberation with the fact that black women have had to take on responsibilities that our oppression gives us no choice but to handle. This is an insidious, but widespread, myth that many black women have believed themselves. Heading families, working outside the home, not building lives or expectations dependent on males, seldom being sheltered or pampered as women, black women have known that their lives in some ways incorporated goals that white middle-class women were striving for, but race and class privileges, of course, reshaped the meaning of those goals profoundly.

As W. E. B. Du Bois said so long ago about black women: ". . . our women in black had freedom contemptuously thrust upon them."[4] Of all the people here, women of color generally have the fewest choices about the circumstances of their lives. An ability to cope under the worst conditions is not liberation, although our spiritual capacities have often made it look like a life. Black men didn't say anything about how poverty, unequal pay, no child care, violence of every kind including battering, rape, and sterilization abuse, translated into "liberation."

Underlying this myth is the assumption that black women are towers of strength who neither feel nor need what other human beings do, either emotionally or materially. White male social scientists, particularly Daniel P. Moynihan with his "matriarchy theory," further reinforce distortions concerning black women's actual status. A song inspired by their mothers and sung by Sweet Honey in the Rock, "Oughta Be a Woman," with lyrics by June Jordan and music by Bernice Johnson Reagon, responds succinctly to the insensitivity of the myth that black women are already liberated and illustrates the home-based concerns of black feminism. Its final stanza states:

> A way outa no way is flesh outa flesh
> Courage that cries out at night
> A way outa no way is flesh outa flesh
> Bravery kept outa sight
> A way outa no way is too much to ask
> Too much of a task for any one woman.[5]

MYTH NO. 2: RACISM IS THE PRIMARY (OR ONLY) OPPRESSION BLACK WOMEN HAVE TO CONFRONT.

This myth goes hand in hand with the one that the black woman is already liberated. The notion that struggling against or eliminating racism will completely alleviate black women's problems does not take into account the way that sexual oppression cuts across all racial, nationality, age, religious, ethnic, and class groupings. Afro-Americans are no exception.

It also does not take into account how oppression operates. Every generation of black people, up until now, has had to face the reality that no matter how hard we work we will probably not see the end of racism in our lifetimes. Yet many of us keep faith and try to do all we can to make change now. If we have to wait for racism to be obliterated *before* we can begin to address sexism, we will be waiting for a long time. Denying that sexual oppression exists or requiring that we wait to bring it up until racism, or in some cases capitalism, is toppled, is a bankrupt position. A black feminist perspective has no use for ranking oppressions, but instead demonstrates the simultaneity of oppressions as they affect Third World women's lives.

MYTH NO. 3: FEMINISM IS NOTHING BUT MAN-HATING.

It is important to make a distinction between attacking institutionalized, systematic oppression (the goal of any serious progressive movement) and attacking men as individuals. Unfortunately, some of the most widely distributed writing about black women's issues has not made this distinction sufficiently clear. Our issues have not been concisely defined in these writings, causing much adverse reaction and confusion about what black feminism really is.[6]

This myth is one of the silliest and at the same time one of the most dangerous. Antifeminists are incapable of making a distinction between being critically opposed to sexual oppression and simply hating men. Women's desire for fairness and safety in our lives does not necessitate hating men. Trying to educate and inform men about how their feet are planted on our necks doesn't translate into hatred either. Centuries of antiracist struggle by various people of color are not reduced, except by racists, to our merely hating white people. If anything it seems that the opposite is true. People of color know that white people have abused us unmercifully, and it is only sane for us to try to change that treatment by every means possible.

Likewise the bodies of murdered women are strewn across the landscape of this country. Rape is a national pastime, a form of torture visited upon all girls and women, from babies to the aged. One out of three women in the United States will be raped during her lifetime. Battering and incest, those home-based crimes are pandemic. Murder, of course, is men's ultimate violent "solution." If you think that I exaggerate, please get today's newspaper and verify the facts.

If anything is going down here it's woman-hatred, not man-hatred, a veritable war against women. But wanting to end this war still doesn't equal man-hating. The feminist movement and the antiracist movement have in common trying to insure decent human life. Opposition to either movement aligns one with the most reactionary elements in American society.

MYTH NO. 4: WOMEN'S ISSUES ARE NARROW, APOLITICAL CONCERNS. PEOPLE OF COLOR NEED TO DEAL WITH THE "LARGER STRUGGLE."

This myth once again characterizes women's oppression as not particularly serious, and by no means a matter of life and death. I have often wished I could spread the word that a movement committed to fighting sexual, racial, economic, and heterosexist oppression, not to mention one that op-poses imperialism, anti-Semitism, the oppressions visited upon the physically disabled, the old and the young, at the same time that it challenges militarism and imminent nuclear destruction is the very opposite of narrow.

All segments of the women's movement have not dealt with all of these issues, but neither have all segments of black people. This myth is plausible when the women's movement is equated only with its most bourgeois and reformist elements. The most progressive sectors of the feminist movement, which includes some radical white women, have taken the above issues, and many more, quite seriously. Third World women have been the most consistent in defining our politics broadly. Why is it that feminism is considered "white-minded" and "narrow," while socialism or Marxism, from verifiably white origins, is legitimately embraced by Third World male politicos, without their having their identity credentials questioned for a minute?

MYTH NO. 5: THOSE FEMINISTS ARE NOTHING BUT LESBIANS.

This may be the most pernicious myth of all, and it is essential to understand that the distortion lies in the phrase "nothing but" and not in the identification lesbian. "Nothing but" reduces lesbians to a category of beings deserving only the most violent attack, a category totally alien from "decent" black folks, i.e., not your sisters, mothers, daughters, aunts, and cousins, but bizarre outsiders like no one you know or *ever* knew.

Many of the most committed and outspoken feminists of color have been and are lesbians. Since many of us are also radicals, our politics, as indicated by the issues merely outlined above, encompass all people. We're also as black as we ever were. (I always find it fascinating, for example, that many of the black lesbian-feminists I know still wear their hair natural, indicating that for us it was more than a "style.")

Black feminism and black lesbianism are not interchangeable. Feminism is a political movement and many lesbians are not feminists. Although it is also true that many black feminists are not lesbians, this myth has acted as an accusation and a deterrent to keep nonlesbian black feminists from manifesting themselves, for fear it will be hurled against them.

Fortunately this is changing. Personally, I have seen increasing evidence that many black women of whatever sexual preference are more concerned with exploring and ending our oppression than they are committed to being either homophobic or sexually separatist. Direct historical precedent exists for such commitments. In 1957, black playwright and activist Lorraine Hansberry wrote the following in a letter to the *Ladder,* an early lesbian periodical:

> I think it is about time that equipped women began to take on some of the ethical questions that a male-dominated culture has produced and dissect and

analyze them quite to pieces in a serious fashion. It is time that "half the human race" had something to say about the nature of its existence. Other-wise—without revised basic thinking—the woman intellectual is likely to find herself trying to draw conclusions—moral conclusions—based on accep-tance of a social moral superstructure that has never admitted to the equality of women and is therefore immoral itself. As per marriage, as per sexual practices, as per the rearing of children, etc. In this kind of work there may be women to emerge who will be able to formulate a new and possible concept that homosexual persecution and condemnation has at its roots not only social ignorance, but a philosophically active antifeminist dogma.[7]

I would like a lot more people to be aware that Lorraine Hansberry, one of our most respected artists and thinkers, was asking in a lesbian context some of the same questions we are asking today, and for which we have been so maligned.

Black heterosexual panic about the existence of both black lesbians and black gay men is a problem that they have to deal with themselves. A first step would be for them to better understand their own heterosexuality, which need not be defined by attacking everybody who is not heterosexual.

HOME TRUTHS

Above are some of the myths that have plagued black feminism. The truth is that there is a vital movement of women of color in this country. Despite continual resistance to women of color defining our specific issues and organizing around them, it is safe to say in 1985 that we have a movement of our own.

I have been involved in building that movement since 1973. It has been a struggle every step of the way, and I feel we are still in just the beginning stages of developing a workable politics and practice. Yet the feminism of women of color, particularly of Afro-American women, has wrought many changes during these years, has had both obvious and unrecognized impact upon the development of other political groupings and upon the lives and hopes of countless women.

The very nature of radical thought and action is that it has exponentially far-reaching results. But because all forms of media ignore black women, in particular black feminists, and because we have no widely distributed communication mechanisms of our own, few know the details of what we have accomplished. The story of our work and contributions remains untold.

One of the purposes of *Home Girls* was to get the word out about black feminism to the people who need it most: black people in the U.S., the Caribbean, Latin America, Africa—everywhere. It is not possible for a single essay to encompass all of what black feminism is, but there is basic information I want every reader to have about the meaning of black feminism as I have lived and understood it.

In 1977, a black feminist organization in Boston of which I was a member from its founding in 1974, the Combahee River Collective, drafted a political statement for our own use and for inclusion in Zillah Eisenstein's anthology, *Capitalist Patriarchy and the Case for Socialist Feminism*. In our opening paragraph we wrote:

> ... we are actively committed to struggling against racial, sexual, heterosexual, and class oppression and see as our particular task the development of integrated analysis and practice based upon the fact that the major systems of oppression are interlocking. The synthesis of these oppressions creates the conditions of our lives. As black women we see black feminism as the logical political movement to combat the manifold and simultaneous oppressions that all women of color face.[8]

The concept of the simultaneity of oppression is still the crux of a black feminist understanding of political reality and one of the most significant ideological contributions of black feminist thought.

We examined our own lives and found that everything out there was kicking our behinds—race, class, sex, and homophobia. We saw no reason to rank oppressions, or, as many forces in the black community would have us do, to pretend that sexism, among all the "isms," was not happening to us.

Black feminists' efforts to comprehend the complexity of our situation as it was actually occurring, almost immediately began to deflate some of the cherished myths about black womanhood, for example, that we are "castrating matriarchs" or that we are more economically privileged than black men. Although we made use of the insights of other political ideologies, such as socialism, we added an element that has often been missing from the theory of others: what oppression is comprised of on a day-to-day basis, or, as black feminist musician Linda Tillery sings, "... what it's ... really like/To live this life of triple jeopardy."[9]

MULTI-ISSUE APPROACH

This multi-issued approach to politics has probably been most often used by other women of color who face very similar dynamics, at least as far as institutionalized oppression is concerned. It has also altered the women's movement as a whole. As a result of Third World feminist organizing, the women's movement now takes much more seriously the necessity for a multi-issued strategy for challenging women's oppression. The more progressive elements of the Left have also begun to recognize that the promotion of sexism and homophobia within their ranks, besides being ethically unconscionable, ultimately undermines their ability to organize. Even a few Third World organizations have begun to include the challenging of women's and gay oppression on their public agendas.

Approaching politics with a comprehension of the simultaneity of oppressions has helped to create a political atmosphere particularly conducive to coalition building. Among all feminists, Third World women have undoubtedly felt most viscerally the need for linking struggles and have also been most capable of forging such coalitions. A commitment to principled coalitions, based not upon expediency, but upon our actual need for each other is a second major contribution of black feminist struggle. Many contributors to *Home Girls* wrote out of a sense of our ultimate interdependence. Bernice Johnson Reagon's essay, "Coalition Politics: Turning the Century," should be particularly noted. She wrote:

> You don't go into coalition because you just *like* it. The only reason you would consider trying to team up with somebody who could possibly kill you, is because that's the only way you can figure you can stay alive. . . . Most of the time you feel threatened to the core, and if you don't you're not really doing no coalescing.[10]

The necessity for coalitions has pushed many groups to rigorously examine the attitudes and ignorance within themselves that prevent coalitions from succeeding. Most notably there has been the commitment of some white feminists to make racism a priority issue within the women's movement, to take responsibility for their racism as individuals, and to do antiracist organizing in coalition with other groups.

Because I have written and spoken about racism during my entire involvement as a feminist and have also presented workshops on racism for white women's organizations for several years during the 1970s, I have not only seen that there are white women who are fully committed to eradicating racism, but that new understandings of racial politics have evolved from feminism that other progressive people would do well to comprehend.[11]

Having begun my political life in the Civil Rights movement and having seen the black liberation movement virtually destroyed by the white power structure, I have been encouraged in recent years that women can be a significant force for bringing about racial change in a way that unites oppressions instead of isolating them. At the same time the percentage of white feminists who are concerned about racism is still a minority of the movement, and even within this minority those who are personally sensitive and completely serious about formulating an *activist* challenge to racism are fewer still.

Because I have usually worked with politically radical feminists, I know that there are indeed white women worth building coalitions with, at the same time that there are apolitical, even reactionary, women who take the name of feminism in vain.

BLACK AND FEMALE

One of the greatest gifts of black feminism to ourselves has been to make it a little easier simply to *be* black and female. A black feminist analysis has enabled us to understand that we are not hated and abused because there is something wrong with us, but because our status and treatment is absolutely prescribed by the racist, misogynist system under which we live.

There is not a black woman in this country who has not, at some time, internalized and been deeply scarred by the hateful propaganda about us. There is not a black woman in America who has not felt, at least once, like "the mule of the world," to use Zora Neale Hurston's still apt phrase.[12] Until black feminism, very few people besides black women actually cared about or took seriously the demoralization of being female *and* colored *and* poor *and* hated.

When I was growing up, despite my family's efforts to explain, or at least describe, attitudes prevalent in the outside world, I often thought that there was something fundamentally wrong with me because it was obvious that I and everybody like me was held in such contempt. The cold eyes of certain white teachers in school, the black men who yelled from cars as my sister and I stood waiting for the bus, convinced me that I must have done something horrible.

How was I to know that racism and sexism had formed a blueprint for my mistreatment long before I had ever arrived here? As with most black women, others' hatred of me became self-hatred, which has diminished over the years, but has by no means disappeared. Black feminism has, for me and for so many others, given us the tools to finally comprehend that it is not something we have done that has heaped this psychic violence and material abuse upon us, but the very fact that, because of who we are, we are multiply oppressed.

Unlike any other movement, black feminism provides the theory that clarifies the nature of black women's experience, makes possible positive support from other black women, and encourages political action that will change the very system that has put us down.

The accomplishments of black feminism have been not only in developing theory, but in day-to-day organizing. Black feminists have worked on countless issues, some previously identified with the feminist movement and others that we, ourselves, have defined as priorities. Whatever issues we have committed ourselves to, we have approached them with a comprehensiveness and pragmatism that exemplify the concept "grass roots." If nothing else, black feminism deals in home truths, both in analysis and in action. Far from being irrelevant or peripheral to black people, the issues we have focused on touch the basic core of our community's survival.

Some of the issues we have worked on are reproductive rights, equal access to abortion, sterilization abuse, health care, child care, the rights of the disabled, violence against women, rape, battering, sexual harassment, welfare rights, lesbian and gay rights, educational reform, housing, legal reform, women in prison, aging, police brutality, labor organizing, anti-imperialist struggles, antiracist organizing, nuclear disarmament, and preserving the environment.

Frustratingly, it is not even possible to know all the work black and other Third World women have done, because as I've already stated, we have had no consistent means of communication, no national Third World feminist newspaper, for example, that would link us across geographic boundaries.[13] It is obvious, however, that with every passing year, more and more explicitly feminist organizing is being done by women of color. There are many signs:

Women of color have been heavily involved in exposing and combatting sterilization abuse on local, state, and national levels. Puertorriqueñas, Chicanas, Native American, and Afro-American women have been particularly active, since women in these groups are most subject to forced sterilization.

For a number of years, health issues, including reproductive freedom, have been a major organizing focus. Within the last year, a Third World women's clinic has been established in Berkeley, and a black women's Self-Help Collective has been established in Washington. The National Black Women's Health Project in Atlanta held its first conference on black women's health issues in 1983, bringing together two thousand women, many of them low-income women from the rural South.

Black and other Third World women have been centrally involved in all aspects of organizing to combat violence against women. Many women of color first became involved in the women's movement through this work, particularly working/volunteering in battered women's shelters. Because battering is so universal, shelters have characteristically offered services to diverse groups of women. There are now shelters that serve primarily Third World communities, such as Casa Myrna Vázquez in Boston.

In 1980, the First National Conference on Third World Women and Violence was held in Washington, D.C. Many precedent-setting sexual harassment cases have been initiated by black women, both because black women are disproportionately harassed in school and on their jobs, and also because it seems that they are willing to protest their harassment. A group in Washington, D.C., the African Women's Committee for Community Education, has been organizing against harassment of black women by black men on the street. In Boston, the Combahee River Collective was a mobilizing force in bringing together Third World and feminist communities when twelve black women were murdered in a three and a half month period during 1979.

Third World women are organizing around women's issues globally. Activists in the Caribbean, Latin America, Africa, India, New Zealand, England, and many other places are addressing issues which spring simultaneously from sexist, heterosexist, racist, imperialist, and economic oppression. Some of these individuals and groups specifically identify as feminist. For example, in the Virgin Islands there are a growing number of battered women's organizations on various islands. Some Afro-American women and Virgin Islanders have worked together on issues of violence against women. In Jamaica, Sistren, a community-based women's theater collective founded in 1977, organizes around basic survival issues including sexual violence and economic exploitation. In Brazil, black women are active in the women's movement and have been especially involved in neighborhood organizing among poor women. Maori, Pacific Island, and other black women in New Zealand have been doing extensive organizing on a local and national level. The first National Hui (conference) for black women was held in September, 1980 in Otara, Auckland and the first Black Dyke Hui occurred in June, 1981.

Economic exploitation, poor working conditions, inadequate health care, and anti-imperialist and antinuclear campaigns are just a few of the issues black women in New Zealand are addressing. At the same time they are challenging sexist attitudes and practices within their specific cultural groups.

Black women's organizing that is often specifically feminist has been going on in England since the mid-1970s. National black women's conferences, which include all women of color currently living in Great Britain, that is women born in England and women who have emigrated from India, Pakistan, the Caribbean, and Africa, are held annually. A Black Women's Center, which works on a wide range of community concerns, was established several years ago in the black community of Brixton, and since that time, dozens of other black women's centers have opened all over London.

Black and Indian women in South Africa, who have always been central in the struggle against Apartheid, are beginning to address specifically women's issues such as rape, which is very widespread in the cities. In the future, Third World feminists in the United States and Third World women in other countries will no doubt make increasing contact with each other and continue to build a movement that is global in both its geographic range and political scope.

A number of black and Third World lesbian organizations are addressing a variety of issues as "out" lesbians, such as Salsa Soul Sisters in New York City and Sapphire Sapphos in Washington, D.C. They are doing education and challenging homophobia in their various communities as well as working on issues that affect lesbians, women, and people of color generally. The National Coalition of Black Gays (NCBG), which has had seven chapters in various cities and currently has several thousand members, has sponsored National Third World Lesbian and Gay conferences in Washington (1979) and Chicago (1981), attended by hundreds of participants.

NCBG was also successful in the struggle to include a lesbian speaker, Audre Lorde, in the rally at the 20th Anniversary March on Washington in 1983 and was instrumental in increasing the accountability of Jesse Jackson's presidential campaign toward lesbian and gay issues.

A FLOURISHING CULTURE

Black feminist cultural work is flourishing, particularly in literature and in music. *Azalea,* a literary magazine for Third World lesbians, began publishing in 1977. The Varied Voices of Black Women concert tour featuring musicians Gwen Avery, Linda Tillery, and Mary Watkins, and poet Pat Parker appeared in eight cities in the fall of 1978. Third World women bands, singers, poets, novelists, visual artists, actors, and playwrights are everywhere creating and redefining their art from a feminist perspective.

We have done much. We have much to do. Some of the most pressing work before us is to build our own autonomous institutions. It is absolutely crucial that we make our visions real in a permanent form so that we can be even more effective and reach many more people. I would like to see ongoing multi-issued political organizations, rape crisis centers, battered women's shelters, women's centers, periodicals, publishers, buying cooperatives, clinics, and artists' collectives started and run by women of color. The Third World Women's Archives and Kitchen Table: Women of Color Press in New York, both founded in 1981, are examples of institutions controlled by women of color. We need more. I believe that everything is possible. It must be understood that black feminist organizing has *never* been a threat to the viability of the black community, but instead has enhanced the quality of life and insured the survival of every man, woman, and child in the community.

In the 1980s, every one of us faces a great deal of danger. The reign of Reagan is more blatantly opposed to people's economic, civil, human, and land rights in this country and internationally than any U.S. government for the last fifty years. We are living in a world at war, but at the same time we are also in a period of increasing politicization and conscious struggle.

If we are going to make it into the twenty-first century, it will take every last one of us pulling together. The unswerving commitment and activism of feminists of color, of home girls, are essential to making this planet truly fit for human habitation. And as Bernice Johnson Reagon explains: "We are not on the defensive.... 'Cause like it is, it is our world, and we are here to stay."[14]

ENDNOTES

1. This essay is excerpted from the introduction to *Home Girls: A Black Feminist Anthology,* ed. Barbara Smith (New York: Kitchen Table: Women of Color Press, 1983).

2. The terms Third World women and women of color are used here to designate Native American, Asian American, Latina, and Afro-American women in the U.S. and the indigenous peoples of Third World countries wherever they may live. Both the terms Third World women and women of color apply to black American women. At times in the introduction black women are specifically designated as black or Afro-American and at other times the terms women of color and Third World women are used to refer to women of color as a whole.

3. Barbara Smith, "Notes for Yet Another Paper on Black Feminism, Or Will the Real Enemy Please Stand Up?" in *Conditions: Five, The Black Women's Issue,* ed. Lorraine Bethel and Barbara Smith (Autumn 1979): 124.

4. W. E. B. Du Bois, *Darkwater, Voices from Within the Veil* (New York: AMS Press, 1969), 185.

5. June Jordan and Bernice Johnson Reagon. "Oughta Be a Woman," *Good News,* Chicago: Flying Fish Records, 1981, Songtalk Publishing Co. Quoted by permission.

6. See Linda C. Powell's review of Michele Wallace's *Black Macho and the Myth of the Superwoman* ("Black Macho and Black Feminism") in *Home Girls* and my review of bell hooks's (Gloria Watkins) *Ain't I a Woman: Black Women and Feminism in New Women's Times Feminist Review* 9 (November 1982): 10, 11, 18, 19 and 20, and in *Black Scholar* 14 (January/February 1983): 38–45.

7. Quoted from *Gay American History: Lesbians and Gay Men in the U.S.A.,* ed. Jonathan Katz (New York: T. Y. Crowell, 1976), 425. Also see Adrienne Rich's "The Problem with Lorraine Hansberry," in "Lorraine Hansberry: Art of Thunder, Vision of Light," *Freedomways* 19, no. 4, (1979): 247–255 for more material about her woman-identification.

8. "The Combahee River Collective Statement," in *Home Girls,* 272.

9. Linda Tillery, "Freedom Time," *Linda Tillery,* Oakland: Olivia Records, 1977, Tuizer Music.

10. Bernice Johnson Reagon, "Coalition Politics: Turning the Century," in *Home Girls,* 356.

11. Some useful articles on racism by white feminists are Elly Bulkin's "Racism and Writing: Some Implications for White Lesbian Critics." *Sinister Wisdom* 13 (Spring 1980): 3–22; Minnie Bruce Pratt's "Rebellion," *Feminary* 11, nos. 1 and 2, (1980): 6–20; and Adrienne Rich's "Disloyal to Civilization: Feminism, Racism, Gynephobia" in *On Lies, Secrets and Silence: Selected Prose 1966–1978* (New York: W. W. Norton, 1979), 275–310.

12. Zora Neale Hurston, *Their Eyes Were Watching God* (Urbana: University of Illinois, 1978), 29.

13. *Between Ourselves: Women of Color Newspaper,* vol. 1, no. 1, was published in February 1985, P. O. Box 1939, Washington, D.C. 20038.

14. Reagon, "Coalition Politics," 368.

bell hooks (1952–   )

bell hooks, born in Hopkinsville, Kentucky, is the most prolific, most anthologized black feminist theorist and cultural critic on the contemporary scene. Author of eleven books, her first was a groundbreaking but controversial text, *Ain't I a Woman: Black Women and Feminism* (1981). The major strengths of the text were its delineation of the impact of sexism on black women, both historically and contemporaneously; its discussion of the persistent racism of the first-wave and second-wave women's movements; and its discussion of the involvement of black women in struggles to achieve equality for women, even when they were discouraged from doing so by various segments of the white and black communities. Its major contribution was her revisionist approach to African American history, in which she advanced the thesis that slavery, a reflection of a patriarchal *and* racist social order, not only oppressed black men, but defeminized slave women. She is presently Distinguished Professor of English at City College in New York (CUNY).

The essay "Black Women: Shaping Feminist Theory" from her second book, *Feminist Theory: From Margin to Center* (1984), is a provocative critique of white feminist theory. hooks has helped to articulate the importance of feminism to a broad cross-section of the black community because of the accessibility of her writings and her attention to issues of paramount concern to African American women and men. Her most recent books are *Teaching to Transgress* (1994), *Outlaw Culture: Resisting Representations* (1994), and *Art on My Mind: Visual Politics* (1995).

Black Women:
Shaping Feminist Theory

Feminism in the United States has never emerged from the women who
are most victimized by sexist oppression; women who are daily beaten
down, mentally, physically, and spiritually—women who are powerless to
change their condition in life. They are a silent majority. A mark of their
victimization is that they accept their lot in life without visible question,
without organized protest, without collective anger or rage. Betty Friedan's
The Feminine Mystique is still heralded as having paved the way for contemporary feminist movement—it was written as if these women did not exist.
Friedan's famous phrase, "the problem that has no name," often quoted to
describe the condition of women in this society, actually referred to the
plight of a select group of college-educated, middle- and upper-class, married white women—housewives bored with leisure, with the home, with
children, with buying products, who wanted more out of life. Friedan
concludes her first chapter by stating: "We can no longer ignore that voice
within women that says: 'I want something more than my husband and
my children and my house.'" That "more" she defined as careers. She did
not discuss who would be called in to take care of the children and maintain
the home if more women like herself were freed from their house labor
and given equal access with white men to the professions. She did not
speak of the needs of women without men, without children, without
homes. She ignored the existence of all nonwhite women and poor white
women. She did not tell readers whether it was more fulfilling to be a
maid, a babysitter, a factory worker, a clerk, or a prostitute, than to be a
leisure-class housewife.

She made her plight and the plight of white women like herself synonymous with a condition affecting all American women. In so doing, she
deflected attention away from her classism, her racism, her sexist attitudes
towards the masses of American women. In the context of her book, Friedan makes clear that the women she saw as victimized by sexism were

college-educated, white women who were compelled by sexist conditioning to remain in the home. She contends:

> It is urgent to understand how the very condition of being a housewife can create a sense of emptiness, nonexistence, nothingness in women. There are aspects of the housewife role that make it almost impossible for a woman of adult intelligence to retain a sense of human identity, the firm core of self or "I" without which a human being, man or woman, is not truly alive. For women of ability, in America today, I am convinced that there is something about the housewife state itself that is dangerous.

Specific problems and dilemmas of leisure-class white housewives were real concerns that merited consideration and change but they were not the pressing political concerns of masses of women. Masses of women were concerned about economic survival, ethnic and racial discrimination, etc. When Friedan wrote *The Feminine Mystique,* more than one-third of all women were in the work force. Although many women longed to be housewives, only women with leisure time and money could actually shape their identities on the model of the feminine mystique. They were women who, in Friedan's words, were "told by the most advanced thinkers of our time to go back and live their lives as if they were Noras, restricted to the doll's house by Victorian prejudices."

From her early writing, it appears that Friedan never wondered whether or not the plight of college-educated, white housewives was an adequate reference point by which to gauge the impact of sexism or sexist oppression on the lives of women in American society. Nor did she move beyond her own life experience to acquire an expanded perspective on the lives of women in the United States. I say this not to discredit her work. It remains a useful discussion of the impact of sexist discrimination on a select group of women. Examined from a different perspective, it can also be seen as a case study of narcissism, insensitivity, sentimentality, and self-indulgence, which reaches its peak when Friedan, in a chapter titled "Progressive Dehumanization," makes a comparison between the psychological effects of isolation on white housewives and the impact of confinement on the self-concept of prisoners in Nazi concentration camps.

Friedan was a principal shaper of contemporary feminist thought. Significantly, the one-dimensional perspective on women's reality presented in her book became a marked feature of the contemporary feminist movement. Like Friedan before them, white women who dominate feminist discourse today rarely question whether or not their perspective on women's reality is true to the lived experiences of women as a collective group. Nor are they aware of the extent to which their perspectives reflect race and class biases, although there has been a greater awareness of biases in recent years. Racism abounds in the writings of white feminists, reinforcing white supremacy and negating the possibility that women will bond politically across ethnic and racial boundaries. Past feminist refusal to draw attention to and attack racial hierarchies suppressed the link between race and class. Yet class structure in American society has been shaped by the racial politic of white supremacy; it is only by analyzing racism and its function in capitalist society that a thorough understanding of class relationships can emerge. Class struggle is inextricably bound to the struggle to end racism. Urging women to explore the full implication of class in an early essay, "The Last Straw," Rita Mae Brown explained:

> Class is much more than Marx's definition of relationship to the means of production. Class involves your behavior, your basic assumptions about life. Your experience (determined by your class) validates those assumptions, how you are taught to behave, what you expect from yourself and from others, your concept of a future, how you understand problems and solve them, how you think, feel, act. It is these behavioral patterns that middle-class women resist recognizing although they may be perfectly willing to accept class in Marxist terms, a neat trick that helps them avoid really dealing with class behavior and changing that behavior in themselves. It is these behavioral patterns which must be recognized, understood, and changed.

White women who dominate feminist discourse, who for the most part make and articulate feminist theory, have little or no understanding of white supremacy as a racial politic, of the psychological impact of class, of their political status within a racist, sexist, capitalist state.

It is this lack of awareness that, for example, leads Leah Fritz to write in *Dreamers and Dealers,* a discussion of the current women's movement published in 1979:

> Women's suffering under sexist tyranny is a common bond among all women, transcending the particulars of the different forms that tyranny takes. *Suffering cannot be measured and compared quantitatively.* Is the enforced idleness and vacuity of a "rich" woman, which leads her to madness and or suicide, greater or less than the suffering of a poor woman who barely survives on welfare but retains somehow her spirit? There is no way to measure such difference, but should these two women survey each other without the screen of patriarchal class, they may find a commonality in the fact that they are both oppressed, both miserable.

Fritz's statement is another example of wishful thinking, as well as the conscious mystification of social divisions between women, that has characterized much feminist expression. While it is evident that many women suffer from sexist tyranny, there is little indication that this forges "a common bond among all women." There is much evidence substantiating the reality that race and class identity creates differences in quality of life, social status, and lifestyle that take precedence over the common experience women share—differences that are rarely transcended. The motives of materially privileged, educated, white women with a variety of career and lifestyle options available to them must be questioned when they insist that "suffering cannot be measured." Fritz is by no means the first white feminist to make this statement. It is a statement that I have never heard a poor woman of any race make. Although there is much I would take issue with in Benjamin Barber's critique of the women's movement, *Liberating Feminism,* I agree with this assertion:

> Suffering is not necessarily a fixed and universal experience that can be measured by a single rod: it is related to situations, needs, and aspirations. But there must be some historical and political parameters for the use of the term so that political priorities can be established and different forms and degrees of suffering can be given the most attention.

A central tenet of modern feminist thought has been the assertion that "all women are oppressed." This assertion implies that women share a common lot, that factors like class, race, religion, sexual preference, etc., do not create a diversity of experience that determines the extent to which sexism will be an oppressive force in the lives of individual women. Sexism as a system of domination is institutionalized, but it has never determined in an absolute way the fate of all women in this society. Being oppressed means the *absence of choices.* It is the primary point of contact between the oppressed and the oppressor. Many women in this society do have choices (as inadequate as they are), therefore exploitation and discrimination are words that more accurately describe the lot of women collectively in the United States. Many women do not join organized resistance against sexism precisely because sexism has not meant an absolute lack of choices. They may know they are discriminated against on the basis of sex, but they do not equate this with oppression. Under capitalism, patriarchy is structured so that sexism restricts women's behavior in some realms even as freedom from limitations is allowed in other spheres. The absence of extreme restrictions leads many women to ignore the areas in which they are exploited or discriminated against; it may even lead them to imagine that no women are oppressed.

There are oppressed women in the United States, and it is both appropriate and necessary that we speak against such oppression. French feminist Christine Delphy makes the point in her essay, "For a Materialist Feminism," that the use of the term oppression is important because it places feminist struggle in a radical political framework:

> The rebirth of feminism coincided with the use of the term "oppression." The ruling ideology, i.e. common sense, daily speech, does not speak about

oppression but about a "feminine condition." It refers back to a naturalist explanation: to a constraint of nature, exterior reality out of reach and not modifiable by human action. The term "oppression," on the contrary, refers back to a choice, an explanation, a situation that is political. "Oppression" and "social oppression" are therefore synonyms or rather social oppression is a redundance: the notion of a political origin, i.e., social, is an integral part of the concept of oppression.

However, feminist emphasis on "common oppression" in the United States was less a strategy for politicization than an appropriation by conservative and liberal women of a radical political vocabulary that masked the extent to which they shaped the movement so that it addressed and promoted their class interests.

Although the impulse towards unity and empathy that informed the notion of common oppression was directed at building solidarity, slogans like "organize around your own oppression" provided the excuse many privileged women needed to ignore the differences between their social status and the status of masses of women. It was a mark of race and class privilege, as well as the expression of freedom from the many constraints sexism places on working-class women, that middle-class white women were able to make their interests the primary focus of feminist movement and employ a rhetoric of commonality that made their condition synonymous with "oppression." Who was there to demand a change in vocabulary? What other group of women in the United States had the same access to universities, publishing houses, mass media, money? Had middle-class black women begun a movement in which they had labeled themselves "oppressed," no one would have taken them seriously. Had they established public forums and given speeches about their "oppression," they would have been criticized and attacked from all sides. This was not the case with white bourgeois feminists for they could appeal to a large audience of women, like themselves, who were eager to change their lot in life. Their isolation from women of other class and race groups provided no immediate comparative base by which to test their assumptions of common oppression.

Initially, radical participants in women's movement demanded that women penetrate that isolation and create a space for contact. Anthologies like *Liberation Now, Women's Liberation: Blueprint for the Future, Class and Feminism, Radical Feminism,* and *Sisterhood Is Powerful,* all published in the early 1970s, contain articles that attempted to address a wide audience of women, an audience that was not exclusively white, middle-class, college-educated, and adult (many have articles on teenagers). Sookie Stambler articulated this radical spirit in her introduction to *Women's Liberation: Blueprint for the Future:*

Movement women have always been turned off by the media's necessity to create celebrities and superstars. This goes against our basic philosophy. We cannot relate to women in our ranks towering over us with prestige and fame. We are not struggling for the benefit of the one woman or for one group of women. We are dealing with issues that concern all women.

These sentiments, shared by many feminists early in the movement, were not sustained. As more and more women acquired prestige, fame, or money from feminist writings or from gains from feminist movement for equality in the work force, individual opportunism undermined appeals for collective struggle. Women who were not opposed to patriarchy, capitalism, classism, or racism labeled themselves "feminist." Their expectations were varied. Privileged women wanted social equality with men of their class; some women wanted equal pay for equal work; others wanted an alternative life-style. Many of these legitimate concerns were easily coopted by the ruling capitalist patriarchy. French feminist Antoinette Fouque states:

The actions proposed by the feminist groups are spectacular, provoking. But provocation only brings to light a certain number of social contradictions. It does not reveal radical contradictions within society. The feminists claim that they do not seek equality with men, but their practice proves the contrary to be true. Feminists are a bourgeois avant-garde that maintains, in an inverted form, the dominant values. Inversion does not facilitate the passage to another kind of structure. Reformism suits everyone! Bourgeois order, capitalism, phallocentrism are ready to integrate as many feminists as will be necessary. Since these women are becoming men, in the end it will only mean a few more men. The difference between the sexes is not whether one does or doesn't have a penis, it is whether or not one is an integral part of a phallic masculine economy.

Feminists in the United States are aware of the contradictions. Carol Ehrlich makes the point in her essay, "The Unhappy Marriage of Marxism and Feminism: Can It Be Saved?" that "feminism seems more and more to have taken on a blind, safe, nonrevolutionary outlook" as "feminist radicalism loses ground to bourgeois feminism," stressing that "we cannot let this continue":

Women need to know (and are increasingly prevented from finding out) that feminism is *not* about dressing for success, or becoming a corporate executive, or gaining elective office; it is *not* being able to share a two-career marriage and take skiing vacations and spend huge amounts of time with your husband and two lovely children because you have a domestic worker who makes all this possible for you, but who hasn't the time or money to do it for herself; it is *not* opening a Women's Bank, or spending a weekend in an expensive workshop that guarantees to teach you how to become assertive (but not aggressive); it is most emphatically *not* about becoming a police detective or CIA agent or Marine Corps general.

But if these distorted images of feminism have more reality than ours do, it is partly our own fault. We have not worked as hard as we should have at providing clear and meaningful alternative analyses which relate to people's lives, and at providing active, accessible groups in which to work.

It is no accident that feminist struggle has been so easily coopted to serve the interests of conservative and liberal feminists since feminism in the United States has so far been a bourgeois ideology. Zillah Eisenstein discusses the liberal roots of North American feminism in *The Radical Future of Liberal Feminism,* explaining in the introduction:

> One of the major contributions to be found in this study is the role of the ideology of liberal individualism in the construction of feminist theory. Today's feminists either do not discuss a theory of individuality or they unselfconsciously adopt the competitive, atomistic ideology of liberal individualism. There is much confusion on this issue in the feminist theory we discuss here. Until a conscious differentiation is made between a theory of individuality that recognizes the importance of the individual within the social collectivity and the ideology of individualism that assumes a competitive view of the individual, there will not be a full accounting of what a feminist theory of liberation must look like in our Western society.

The ideology of "competitive, atomistic liberal individualism" has permeated feminist thought to such an extent that it undermines the potential radicalism of feminist struggle. The usurpation of feminism by bourgeois women to support their class interests has been to a very grave extent justified by feminist theory as it has so far been conceived. (For example, the ideology of "common oppression.") Any movement to resist the cooptation of feminist struggle must begin by introducing a different feminist perspective—a new theory—one that is not informed by the ideology of liberal individualism.

The exclusionary practices of women who dominate feminist discourse have made it practically impossible for new and varied theories to emerge. Feminism has its party line, and women who feel a need for a different strategy, a different foundation, often find themselves ostracized and silenced. Criticisms of or alternatives to established feminist ideas are not encouraged, e.g., recent controversies about expanding feminist discussions of sexuality. Yet groups of women who feel excluded from feminist discourse and praxis can make a place for themselves only if they first create, via critiques, an awareness of the factors that alienate them. Many individual white women found in the women's movement a liberatory solution to personal dilemmas. Having directly benefited from the movement, they are less inclined to criticize it or to engage in rigorous examination of its structure than those who feel it has not had a revolutionary impact on their lives or the lives of masses of women in our society. Nonwhite women who feel affirmed within the current structure of feminist movement (even though they may form autonomous groups) seem to also feel that their definitions of the party line, whether on the issue of black feminism or on other issues, is the only legitimate discourse. Rather than encourage a diversity of voices, critical dialogue, and controversy, they, like some white women, seek to stifle dissent. As activists and writers whose work is widely known, they act as if they are best able to judge whether other women's voices should be heard. Susan Griffin warns against this overall tendency towards dogmatism in her essay, "The Way of All Ideology":

> ...when a theory is transformed into an ideology, it begins to destroy the self and self-knowledge. Originally born of feeling, it pretends to float above and around feeling. Above sensation. It organizes experience according to itself, without touching experience. By virtue of being itself, it is supposed to know. To invoke the name of this ideology is to confer truthfulness. No one can tell it anything new. Experience ceases to surprise it, inform it, transform it. It is annoyed by any detail which does not fit into its world view. Begun as a cry against the denial of truth, now it denies any truth which does not fit into its scheme. Begun as a way to restore one's sense of reality, now it attempts to discipline real people, to remake natural beings after its own image. All that it fails to explain it records as its enemy. Begun as a theory of liberation, it is threatened by new theories of liberation; it builds a prison for the mind.

We resist hegemonic dominance of feminist thought by insisting that it is a theory in the making, that we must necessarily criticize, question, reexamine, and explore new possibilities. My persistent critique has been informed by my status as a member of an oppressed group, experience of sexist exploitation and discrimination, and the sense that prevailing feminist analysis has not been the force shaping my feminist consciousness. This is true for many women. There are white women who had never considered resisting male dominance until the feminist movement created an awareness that they could and should. My awareness of feminist struggle was stimulated by social circumstance. Growing up in a Southern, black, father-dominated, working-class household, I experienced (as did my mother, my sisters, and my brother) varying degrees of patriarchal tyranny and it made me angry—it made us all angry. Anger led me to question the politics of male dominance and enabled me to resist sexist socialization. Frequently, white feminists act as if black women did not know sexist oppression existed until they voiced feminist sentiment. They believe they are providing black women with "the" analysis and "the" program for liberation. They do not understand, cannot even imagine, that black women, as well as other groups of women who live daily in oppressive situations, often acquire an awareness of patriarchal politics from their lived experience, just as they develop strategies of resistance (even though they may not resist on a sustained or organized basis).

These black women observed white feminist focus on male tyranny and women's oppression as if it were a "new" revelation and felt such a focus had little impact on their lives. To them it was just another indication of the privileged living conditions of middle- and upper-class white women that they would need a theory to inform them that they were "oppressed." The implication being that people who are truly oppressed know it even though they may not be engaged in organized resistance or are unable to articulate in written form the nature of their oppression. These black women saw nothing liberatory in party line analyses of women's oppression. Neither the fact that black women have not organized collectively in huge numbers around the issues of "feminism" (many of us do not know or use the term) nor the fact that we have not had access to the machinery of power that would allow us to share our analyses or theories about gender with the American public negate its presence in our lives or place us in a position of dependency in relationship to those white and nonwhite feminists who address a larger audience.

The understanding I had by age thirteen of patriarchal politics created in me expectations of the feminist movement that were quite different from those of young, middle-class, white women. When I entered my first women's studies class at Stanford University in the early 1970s, white women were revelling in the joy of being together—to them it was an important, momentous occasion. I had not known a life where women had not been together, where women had not helped, protected, and loved one another deeply. I had not known white women who were ignorant of the impact of race and class on their social status and consciousness. (Southern white women often have a more realistic perspective on racism and classism than white women in other areas of the United States.) I did not feel sympathetic to white peers who maintained that I could not expect them to have knowledge of or understand the life experiences of black women. Despite my background (living in racially segregated communities), I knew about the lives of white women, and certainly no white women lived in our neighborhood, attended our schools, or worked in our homes.

When I participated in feminist groups. I found that white women adopted a condescending attitude towards me and other nonwhite participants. The condescension they directed at black women was one of the means they employed to remind us that the women's movement was "theirs"—that we were able to participate because they allowed it, even encouraged it; after all, we were needed to legitimate the process. They did not see us as equals. They did not treat us as equals. And though they expected us to provide firsthand accounts of black experience, they felt it was their role to decide if these experiences were authentic. Frequently, college-educated black women (even those from poor and working-class backgrounds) were dismissed as mere imitators. Our presence in movement activities did not count, as white women were convinced that "real" blackness meant speaking the patois of poor black people, being uneducated, streetwise, and a variety of other stereotypes. If we dared to criticize the movement or to assume responsibility for reshaping feminist ideas and introducing new ideas, our voices were tuned out, dismissed, silenced. We could be heard only if our statements echoed the sentiments of the dominant discourse.

Attempts by white feminists to silence black women are rarely written about. All too often they have taken place in conference rooms, classrooms, or the privacy of cozy living room settings, where one lone black woman faces the racist hostility of a group of white women. From the time the women's liberation movement began, individual black women went to groups. Many never returned after a first meeting. Anita Cornwall is correct in "Three for the Price of One: Notes from a Gay Black Feminist," when she states, ". . . sadly enough, fear of encountering racism seems to be one of the main reasons that so many black womyn refuse to join the women's movement." Recent focus on the issue of racism has generated discourse but has had little impact on the behavior of white feminists towards black women. Often the white women who are busy publishing papers and books on "unlearning racism" remain patronizing and condescending when they relate to black women. This is not surprising given that frequently their discourse is aimed solely in the direction of a white audience and the focus solely on changing attitudes rather than addressing racism in a historical and political context. They make us the "objects" of their privileged discourse on race. As "objects," we remain unequals, inferiors. Even though they may be sincerely concerned about racism, their methodology suggests they are not yet free of the type of paternalism endemic to white supremacist ideology. Some of these women place themselves in the position of "authorities" who must mediate communication between racist white women (naturally they see themselves as having come to terms with their racism) and angry black women whom they believe are incapable of rational discourse. Of course, the system of racism, classism, and educational elitism remain intact if they are to maintain their authoritative positions.

In 1981, I enrolled in a graduate class on feminist theory where we were given a course reading list that had writings by white women and men, one black man, but no material by or about black, Native American Indian, Hispanic, or Asian women. When I criticized this oversight, white women directed an anger and hostility at me that was so intense I found it difficult to attend the class. When I suggested that the purpose of this collective anger was to create an atmosphere in which it would be psychologically unbearable for me to speak in class discussions or even attend class. I was told that they were not angry. *I* was the one who was angry. Weeks after class ended, I received an open letter from one white female student acknowledging her anger and expressing regret for her attacks. She wrote:

> I didn't know you. You were black. In class after a while I noticed myself, that I would always be the one to respond to whatever you said. And usually it was to contradict. Not that the argument was always about racism by any means. But I think the hidden logic was that if I could prove you wrong about one thing, then you might not be right about anything at all.

And in another paragraph:

> I said in class one day that there were some people less entrapped than others by Plato's picture of the world. I said I thought we, after fifteen years of education, courtesy of the ruling class, might be more entrapped than others who had not received a start in life so close to the heart of the monster. My classmate, once a close friend, sister, colleague, has not spoken to me since then. I think the possibility that we were not the best spokespeople for all women made her fear for her self-worth and for her Ph.D.

Often in situations where white feminists aggressively attacked individual black women, they saw themselves as the ones who were under attack, who were the victims. During a heated discussion with another white female student in a racially mixed women's group I had organized, I was told that she had heard how I had "wiped out" people in the feminist theory class, that she was afraid of being "wiped out" too. I reminded her that I was one person speaking to a large group of angry, aggressive people; I was hardly dominating the situation. It was I who left the class in tears, not any of the people I had supposedly "wiped out."

Racist stereotypes of the strong, superhuman black woman are operative myths in the minds of many white women, allowing them to ignore the extent to which black women are likely to be victimized in this society and the role white women may play in the maintenance and perpetuation of that victimization. In Lillian Hellman's autobiographical work *Pentimento,* she writes, "All my life, beginning at birth, I have taken orders from black women, wanting them and resenting them, being superstitious the few times I disobeyed." The black women Hellman describes worked in her household as family servants, and their status was never that of an equal. Even as a child, she was always in the dominant position as they questioned, advised, or guided her; they were free to exercise these rights because she or another white authority figure allowed it. Hellman places power in the hands of these black women rather than acknowledge her own power over them; hence she mystifies the true nature of their relationship. By projecting onto black women a mythical power and strength, white women both promote a false image of themselves as powerless, passive victims and deflect attention away from their aggressiveness, their power (however limited in a white supremacist, male-dominated state), their willingness to dominate and control others. These unacknowledged aspects of the social status of many white women prevent them from transcending racism and limit the scope of their understanding of women's overall social status in the United States.

Privileged feminists have largely been unable to speak to, with, and for diverse groups of women because they either do not understand fully the interrelatedness of sex, race, and class oppression or refuse to take this interrelatedness seriously. Feminist analyses of woman's lot tend to focus exclusively on gender and do not provide a solid foundation on which to construct feminist theory. They reflect the dominant tendency in Western patriarchal minds to mystify woman's reality by insisting that gender is the sole determinant of woman's fate. Certainly it has been easier for women who do not experience race or class oppression to focus exclusively on gender. Although socialist feminists focus on class and gender, they tend to dismiss race or they make a point of acknowledging that race is important and then proceed to offer an analysis in which race is not considered.

As a group, black women are in an unusual position in this society, for not only are we collectively at the bottom of the occupational ladder, but our overall social status is lower than that of any other group. Occupying such a position, we bear the brunt of sexist, racist, and classist oppression. At the same time, we are the group that has not been socialized to assume the role of exploiter/oppressor in that we are allowed no institutionalized "other" that we can exploit or oppress. (Children do not represent an institutionalized other even though they may be oppressed by parents.) White women and black men have it both ways. They can act as oppressor or be oppressed. Black men may be victimized by racism, but sexism allows them to act as exploiters and oppressors of women. White women may be victimized by sexism, but racism enables them to act as exploiters and oppressors of black people. Both groups have led liberation movements that favor their interests and support the continued oppression of other groups. Black male sexism has undermined struggles to eradicate racism just as white female racism undermines feminist struggle. As long as these two groups or any group defines liberation as gaining social equality with ruling-class white men, they have a vested interest in the continued exploitation and oppression of others.

Black women with no institutionalized "other" that we may discriminate against, exploit, or oppress often have a lived experience that directly challenges the prevailing classist, sexist, racist social structure and its concomitant ideology. This lived experience may shape our consciousness in such a way that our worldview differs from those who have a degree of privilege (however relative within the existing system). It is essential for continued feminist struggle that black women recognize the special vantage point our marginality gives us and make use of this perspective to criticize the dominant racist, classist, sexist hegemony as well as to envision and create a counterhegemony. I am suggesting that we have a central role to play in the making of feminist theory and a contribution to offer that is unique and valuable. The formation of a liberatory feminist theory and praxis is a collective responsibility, one that must be shared. Though I criticize aspects of feminist movement as we have known it so far, a critique that is sometimes harsh and unrelenting, I do so not in an attempt to diminish feminist struggle but to enrich, to share in the work of making a liberatory ideology and a liberatory movement.

Audre Lorde (1934–1992)

Audre Lorde, born in Harlem to parents from Grenada, is the most revered and influential black feminist lesbian writer of the modern era. Her autobiography, *Zami: A New Spelling of My Name* (1982), describes the Greenwich Village "gay-girl" life in which she was immersed in the 1950s. Though she was to later find a home in the Harlem Writers Guild, she became disillusioned with it because of its homophobia. Her collection of essays, *Sister Outsider* (1984), includes "Age, Race, Class, and Sex: Women Redefining Difference," which is an eloquent statement of black lesbian feminism and a critique of the intolerance of difference among both white feminist and black communities.

Audre Lorde }

Age, Race, Class, and Sex: Women Redefining Difference

Much of Western European history conditions us to see human differences in simplistic opposition to each other: dominant/subordinate, good/bad, up/down, superior/inferior. In a society where the good is defined in terms of profit rather than in terms of human need, there must always be some group of people who, through systematized oppression, can be made to feel surplus, to occupy the place of the dehumanized inferior. Within this society, that group is made up of black and Third-World people, working-class people, older people, and women.

As a forty-nine-year-old black lesbian feminist socialist mother of two, including one boy, and a member of an interracial couple, I usually find myself a part of some group defined as other, deviant, inferior, or just plain wrong. Traditionally, in American society, it is the members of oppressed, objectified groups who are expected to stretch out and bridge the gap between the actualities of our lives and the consciousness of our oppressor. For in order to survive, those of us for whom oppression is as American as apple pie have always had to be watchers, to become familiar with the language and manners of the oppressor, even sometimes adopting them for some illusion of protection. Whenever the need for some pretense of communication arises, those who profit from our oppression call upon us to share our knowledge with them. In other words, it is the responsibility of the oppressed to teach the oppressors their mistakes. I am responsible for educating teachers who dismiss my children's culture in school. Black and Third-World people are expected to educate white people as to our humanity. Women are expected to educate men. Lesbians and gay men are expected to educate the heterosexual world. The oppressors maintain their position and evade responsibility for their own actions. There is a constant drain of energy, which might be better used in redefining ourselves and devising realistic scenarios for altering the present and constructing the future.

Institutionalized rejection of difference is an absolute necessity in a profit economy which needs outsiders as surplus people. As members of such an economy, we have *all* been programmed to respond to the human differences between us with fear and loathing and to handle that difference in one of three ways: ignore it, and if that is not possible, copy it if we think it is dominant, or destroy it if we think it is subordinate. But we have no patterns for relating across our human differences as equals. As a result, those differences have been misnamed and misused in the service of separation and confusion.

Certainly there are very real differences between us of race, age, and sex. But it is not those differences between us that are separating us. It is rather our refusal to recognize those differences, and to examine the distortions that result from our misnaming them and their effects upon human behavior and expectation.

Racism, the belief in the inherent superiority of one race over all others and thereby the right to dominance. Sexism, the belief in the inherent superiority of one sex over the other and thereby the right to dominance. Ageism. Heterosexism. Elitism. Classism.

It is a lifetime pursuit for each one of us to extract these distortions from our living at the same time as we recognize, reclaim, and define those differences upon which they are imposed. For we have all been raised in a society where those distortions were endemic within our living. Too often, we pour the energy needed for recognizing and exploring difference into pretending those differences are insurmountable barriers, or that they do not exist at all. This results in a voluntary isolation, or false and treacherous connections. Either way, we do not develop tools for using human difference as a springboard for creative change within our lives. We speak not of human difference, but of human deviance.

Somewhere, on the edge of consciousness, there is what I call a *mythical norm,* which each one of us within our hearts knows "that is not me." In America, this norm is usually defined as *white, thin, male, young, heterosexual, Christian, and financially secure.* It is with this mythical norm that the trappings of power reside within this society. Those of us who stand outside that power often identify one way in which we are different, and we assume that to be the primary cause of all oppression, forgetting other distortions around difference, some of which we ourselves may be practicing. By and large within the women's movement today, white women focus upon their oppression as women and ignore differences of race, sexual preference, class, and age. There is a pretense to a homogeneity of experience covered by the word *sisterhood* that does not in fact exist.

Unacknowledged class differences rob women of each others' energy and creative insight. Recently a women's magazine collective made the decision for one issue to print only prose, saying poetry was a less "rigorous" or "serious" art form. Yet even the form our creativity takes is often a class issue. Of all the art forms, poetry is the most economical. It is the one that is the most secret, that requires the least physical labor, the least material, and the one that can be done between shifts, in the hospital pantry, on the subway, and on scraps of surplus paper. Over the last few years, writing a novel on tight finances, I came to appreciate the enormous differences in the material demands between poetry and prose. As we reclaim our literature, poetry has been the major voice of poor, working-class, and colored women. A room of one's own may be a necessity for writing prose, but so are reams of paper, a typewriter, and plenty of time. The actual requirements to produce the visual arts also help determine, along class lines, whose art is whose. In this day of inflated prices for material, who are our sculptors, our painters, our photographers? When we speak of a broadly based women's culture, we need to be aware of the effect of class and economic differences on the supplies available for producing art.

As we move toward creating a society within which we can each flourish, ageism is another distortion of relationship that interferes without vision. By ignoring the past, we are encouraged to repeat its mistakes. The "generation gap" is an important social tool for any repressive society. If the younger members of a community view the older members as contemptible or suspect or excess, they will never be able to join hands and examine the living memories of the community, nor ask the all important question, "Why?" This gives rise to a historical amnesia that keeps us working to invent the wheel every time we have to go to the store for bread.

We find ourselves having to repeat and relearn the same old lessons over and over that our mothers did because we do not pass on what we have learned, or because we are unable to listen. For instance, how many times has this all been said before? For another, who would have believed that once again our daughters are allowing their bodies to be hampered and purgatoried by girdles and high heels and hobble skirts?

Ignoring the differences of race between women and the implications of those differences presents the most serious threat to the mobilization of women's joint power.

As white women ignore their built-in privilege of whiteness and define *woman* in terms of their own experience alone, then women of color become "other," the outsider whose experience and tradition is too "alien" to comprehend. An example of this is the signal absence of the experience of women of color as a resource for women's studies courses. The literature of women of color is seldom included in women's literature courses and almost never in other literature courses, nor in women's studies as a whole. All too often, the excuse given is that the literatures of women of color can only be taught by colored women, or that they are too difficult to understand, or that classes cannot "get into" them because they come out of experiences that are "too different." I have heard this argument presented by white women of otherwise quite clear intelligence, women who seem to have no trouble at all teaching and reviewing work that comes out of the vastly different experiences of Shakespeare, Molière, Dostoyevski, and Aristophanes. Surely there must be some other explanation.

This is a very complex question, but I believe one of the reasons white women have such difficulty reading black women's work is because of their reluctance to see black women as women and different from themselves. To examine black women's literature effectively requires that we be seen as whole people in our actual complexities—as individuals, as women, as human—rather than as one of those problematic but familiar stereotypes provided in this society in place of genuine images of black women. And I believe this holds true for the literatures of other women of color who are not black.

The literatures of all women of color recreate the textures of our lives, and many white women are heavily invested in ignoring the real differences. For as long as any difference between us means one of us must be inferior, then the recognition of any difference must be fraught with guilt. To allow women of color to step out of stereotypes is too guilt-provoking, for it threatens the complacency of those women who view oppression only in terms of sex.

Refusing to recognize difference makes it impossible to see the different problems and pitfalls facing us as women.

Thus, in a partriarchal power system where white skin privilege is a major prop, the entrapments used to neutralize black women and white women are not the same. For example, it is easy for black women to be used by the power structure against black men, not because they are men, but because they are black. Therefore, for black women, it is necessary at all times to separate the needs of the oppressor from our own legitimate conflicts within our communities. This same problem does not exist for white women. Black women and men have shared racist oppression and still share it, although in different ways. Out of that shared oppression we have developed joint defenses and joint vulnerabilities to each other that are not duplicated in the white community, with the exception of the relationship between Jewish women and Jewish men.

On the other hand, white women face the pitfall of being seduced into joining the oppressor under the pretense of sharing power. This possibility does not exist in the same way for women of color. The tokenism that is sometimes extended to us is not an invitation to join power; our racial "otherness" is a visible reality that makes that quite clear. For white women there is a wider range of pretended choices and rewards for identifying with patriarchal power and its tools.

Today, with the defeat of ERA, the tightening economy, and increased conservatism, it is easier once again for white women to believe the dangerous fantasy that if you are good enough, pretty enough, sweet enough, quiet enough, teach the children to behave, hate the right people, and marry the right men, then you will be allowed to coexist with patriarchy in relative peace, at least until a man needs your job or the neighborhood rapist happens along. And true, unless one lives and loves in the trenches it is difficult to remember that the war against dehumanization is ceaseless.

But black women and our children know the fabric of our lives is stitched with violence and with hatred, that there is no rest. We do not deal with it only on the picket lines, or in dark midnight alleys, or in the places where we dare to verbalize our resistance. For us, increasingly, violence weaves through the daily tissues of our living—in the supermarket, in the classroom, in the elevator, in the clinic and the school yard, from the plumber, the baker, the saleswoman, the bus driver, the bank teller, the waitress who does not serve us.

Some problems we share as women, some we do not. You fear your children will grow up to join the patriarchy and testify against you; we fear our children will be dragged from a car and shot down in the street, and you will turn your backs upon the reasons they are dying.

The threat of difference has been no less blinding to people of color. Those of us who are black must see that the reality of our lives and our struggle does not make us immune to the errors of ignoring and misnaming difference. Within black communities, where racism is a living reality, differences among us often seem dangerous and suspect. The need for unity is often misnamed as a need for homogeneity, and a black feminist vision mistaken for betrayal of our common interests as a people. Because of the continuous battle against racial erasure that black women and black men share, some black women still refuse to recognize that we are also oppressed as women, and that sexual hostility against black women is practiced not only by the white racist society, but implemented within our black communities as well. It is a disease striking the heart of black nationhood, and silence will not make it disappear. Exacerbated by racism and the pressures of powerlessness, violence against black women and children often becomes a standard within our communities, one by which manliness can be measured. But these woman-hating acts are rarely discussed as crimes against black women.

As a group, women of color are the lowest paid wage earners in America. We are the primary targets of abortion and sterilization abuse, here and abroad. In certain parts of Africa, small girls are still being sewed shut between their legs to keep them docile and for men's pleasure. This is known as female circumcision, and it is not a cultural affair as the late Jomo Kenyatta insisted, it is a crime against black women.

Black women's literature is full of the pain of frequent assault, not only by a racist patriarchy, but also by black men. Yet the necessity for and history of shared battle have made us, black women, particularly vulnerable to the false accusation that anti-sexist is anti-black. Meanwhile, womanhating as a recourse of the powerless is sapping strength from black communities, and our very lives. Rape is on the increase, reported and unreported, and rape is not aggressive sexuality, it is sexualized aggression. As Kalamu ya Salaam, a black male writer points out, "As long as male domination exists, rape will exist. Only women revolting and men made conscious of their responsibility to fight sexism can collectively stop rape."*

Differences between ourselves as black women are also being misnamed and used to separate us from one another. As a black lesbian feminist comfortable with the many different ingredients of my identity, and a woman committed to racial and sexual freedom from oppression, I find I am constantly being encouraged to pluck out some one aspect of myself and present this as the meaningful whole, eclipsing or denying the other parts of self. But this is a destructive and fragmenting way to live. My fullest concentration of energy is available to me only when I integrate all the parts of who I am, openly, allowing power from particular sources of my living to flow back and forth freely through all my different selves, without the restrictions of externally imposed definition. Only then can I bring myself and my energies as a whole to the service of those struggles which I embrace as part of my living.

A fear of lesbians, or of being accused of being a lesbian, has led many black women into testifying against themselves. It has led some of us into destructive alliances, and others into despair and isolation. In the white women's communities, heterosexism is sometimes a result of identifying with the white patriarchy, a rejection of that interdependence between women-identified women that allows the self to be, rather than to be used in the service of men. Sometimes it reflects a die-hard belief in the protective coloration of heterosexual relationships, sometimes a self-hate, which all women have to fight against, taught us from birth.

Although elements of these attitudes exist for all women, there are particular resonances of heterosexism and homophobia among black women. Despite the fact that woman-bonding has a long and honorable history in the African and African American communities, and despite the knowledge and accomplishments of many strong and creative women-identified black women in the political, social and cultural fields, heterosexual black women often tend to ignore or discount the existence and work of black lesbians. Part of this attitude has come from an understandable terror of black male attack within the close confines of black society, where the punishment for any female self-assertion is still to be accused of being

---

* From "Rape: A Radical Analysis, an African-American Perspective" by Kalamu ya Salaam in *Black Books Bulletin,* vol. 6, no. 4 (1980).

a lesbian and therefore unworthy of the attention or support of the scarce black male. But part of this need to *misname and ignore black lesbians comes from a very real fear that openly women-identified black women who are no longer dependent upon men for their self-definition may well reorder our whole concept of social relationships.*

Black women who once insisted that lesbianism was a white woman's problem now insist that black lesbians are a threat to black nationhood, are consorting with the enemy, are basically unblack. These accusations, coming from the very women to whom we look for deep and real understanding, have served to keep many black lesbians in hiding, caught between the racism of white women and the homophobia of their sisters. Often, their work has been ignored, trivialized, or misnamed, as with the work of Angelina Grimké, Alice Dunbar-Nelson, Lorraine Hansberry. Yet women-bonded women have always been some part of the power of black communities, from our unmarried aunts to the amazons of Dahomey.

And it is certainly *not black lesbians who are assaulting women and raping children and grandmothers on the streets of our communities.*

Across this country, as in Boston during the spring of 1979 following the unsolved murders of twelve black women, black lesbians are spearheading movements against violence against black women.

What are the particular details within each of our lives that can be scrutinized and altered to help bring about change? How do we redefine difference for all women? It is not our differences that separate women, but our reluctance to recognize those differences and to deal effectively with the distortions that have resulted from the ignoring and misnaming of those differences.

As a tool of *social control,* women have been encouraged to recognize only one area of human difference as legitimate, those differences that exist between women and men. And we have learned to deal across those differences with the urgency of all oppressed subordinates. All of us have had to learn to live or work or coexist with men, from our fathers on. We have recognized and negotiated these differences, even when this recognition only continued the old dominant/subordinate mode of human relationship, where the oppressed must recognize the masters' difference in order to survive.

But our future survival is predicated upon our ability to relate within equality. As women, we must root out internalized patterns of oppression within ourselves if we are to move beyond the most superficial aspects of social change. Now we must recognize differences among women who are our equals, neither inferior nor superior, and devise ways to use each others' difference to enrich our visions and our joint struggles.

The future of our earth may depend upon the ability of all women to identify and develop new definitions of power and new patterns of relating across difference. The old definitions have not served us, nor the earth that supports us. The old patterns, no matter how cleverly rearranged to imitate progress, still condemn us to cosmetically altered repetitions of the same old exchanges, the same old guilt, hatred, recrimination, lamentation, and suspicion.

For we have, built into all of us, old blueprints of expectation and response, old structures of oppression, and these must be altered at the same time as we alter the living conditions which are a result of those structures. For the master's tools will never dismantle the master's house.

As Paulo Freire shows so well in *The Pedagogy of the Oppressed,* * the true focus of revolutionary change is never merely the oppressive situations that we seek to escape, but that piece of the oppressor that is planted deep within each of us, and that knows only the oppressors' tactics, the oppressors' relationships.

Change means growth, and growth can be painful. But we sharpen self-definition by exposing the self in work and struggle together with those whom we define as different from ourselves, although sharing the same goals. For black and white, old and young, lesbian and heterosexual women alike, this can mean new paths to our survival.

---

* Seabury Press, New York, 1970.

Deborah K. King

Deborah King, associate professor of sociology at Dartmouth College, is completing a book on the enforcement of affirmative action policies in American higher education. Her groundbreaking essay, "Multiple Jeopardy: The Context of a Black Feminist Ideology" (*Signs,* August 1988), is an important contribution to black feminist theory, which goes beyond the triple jeopardy thesis to describe the nature of black womanhood. She argues that the oppressions black women experience are not additive but intersecting, so that "multiple jeopardy" is a more useful metaphor to describe the black female experience.

Deborah K. King }

Multiple Jeopardy, Multiple Consciousness: The Context of a Black Feminist Ideology

Black women have long recognized the special circumstances of our lives in the United States: the commonalities that we share with all women, as well as the bonds that connect us to the men of our race. We have also realized that the interactive oppressions that circumscribe our lives provide a distinctive context for black womanhood. For us, the notion of double jeopardy is not a new one. Near the end of the nineteenth century, Anna Julia Cooper, who was born a slave and later became an educator and earned a Ph.D., often spoke and wrote of the double enslavement of black women and of our being "confronted by both a woman question and a race problem."[1] In 1904, Mary Church Terrell, the first president of the National Association of Colored Women, wrote, "Not only are colored women ... handicapped on account of their sex, but they are almost everywhere baffled and mocked because of their race. Not only because they are women, but because they are colored women."[2]

The dual and systematic discriminations of racism and sexism remain pervasive, and, for many, class inequality compounds those oppressions. Yet, for as long as black women have known our numerous discriminations, we have also resisted those oppressions. Our day-to-day survival as well as our organized political actions have demonstrated the tenacity of our struggle against subordination. In the mid-nineteenth-century, Sojourner Truth, an antislavery activist and women's rights advocate, repeatedly pronounced the strength and perseverance of black women.[3] More than one hundred years later, another black woman elaborated on Truth's theme. In addressing the National Association for the Advancement of Colored People (NAACP) Legal Defense Fund in 1971, Fannie Lou Hamer, the daughter of sharecroppers and a civil rights activist in Mississippi, commented on the special plight and role of black women over 350 years: "You know I work for the liberation of all people because when I liberate myself, I'm liberating other people ... her [the white woman's] freedom is shackled in chains to mine, and she realizes for the first time that she is not free until I am free."[4] The necessity of addressing all oppressions is one of the hallmarks of black feminist thought.

THE THEORETICAL INVISIBILITY
OF BLACK WOMEN

Among the first and perhaps most widely used approaches for understanding women's status in the United States has been the race-sex analogy. In essence, the model draws parallels between the systems and experiences of domination for blacks and those for women, and, as a result, it assumes that political mobilizations against racism and sexism are comparable. In 1860, Elizabeth Cady Stanton observed, "Prejudice against color, of which we hear so much, is no stronger than that against sex."[5] Scholars in various disciplines have drawn similar analogies between racism and sexism. Sociologist Helen Hacker and historian William Chafe have both noted that, unlike many ethnic groups, women and blacks possess ineradicable physical attributes that function "systematically and clearly to define from birth the possibilities to which members of a group might aspire."[6] In the first formal typology of the race-sex analogy, Helen Hacker identifies four additional dimensions on which the castelike status of blacks and women are similar: (1) ascribed attributes of emotionality, immaturity, and slyness; (2) rationalizations of status as conveyed in the notions of appropriate "place" and the contented subordinate; (3) accommodating and guileful behaviors and (4) economic, legal, educational, and social discriminations.[7] Feminist theorists, including Simone de Beauvoir, Kate Millett, Mary Daly, and Shulamith Firestone have all drawn extensively on this analogy in their critiques of the patriarchy.[8]

This analogy has served as a powerful means of conveying an image of women's subordinate status, and of mobilizing women and men for political action. The social movements for racial equality in the United States, whether the abolitionist movement in the nineteenth century or the Civil Rights movement in the mid-twentieth-century, were predecessors, catalysts, and prototypes for women's collective action. A significant segment of feminist activists came to recognize and understand their own oppression, as well as to develop important organizing skills through their participation in efforts for racial justice.[9] In sum, the race-sex correspondence has been used successfully because the race model was a well-established and effective pedagogical tool for both the theoretical conceptualization of and the political resistance to sexual inequality.

We learn very little about black women from this analogy.[10] The experience of black women is apparently assumed, though never explicitly stated, to be synonymous with that of either black males or white females; and since the experiences of both are equivalent, a discussion of black women in particular is superfluous. It is mistakenly granted that either there is no difference in being black and female from being generically black (i.e., male) or generically female (i.e., white). The analogy obfuscates or denies what Chafe refers to as "the profound substantive differences" between blacks and women. The scope, both institutionally and culturally, and the intensity of the physical and psychological impact of racism is qualitatively different from that of sexism. The group experience of slavery and lynching for blacks, genocide for Native Americans, and military conquest for Mexi-can-Americans and Puerto Ricans, is not substantively comparable to the physical abuse, social discrimination, and cultural denigration suffered by women. This is not to argue that those forms of racial oppressions are greater or more unjust but that the substantive differences need to be identified and to inform conceptualizations. Althea Smith and Abigail Stewart point out that "the assumption of parallelism led to research that masked the differences in these processes [i.e., racism, sexism, and their effects on self-image] for different groups."[11] A similar point has been forcefully made by bell hooks: "no other group in America has so had their identity socialized out of existence as have black women. We are rarely recognized as a group separate and distinct from black men, or a present part of the larger group 'women' in this culture. . . . When black people are talked about the focus tends to be on black men; and when women are talked about the focus tends to be on white women."[12] It is precisely those differences between blacks and women, between black men and black women, between black women and white women, that are crucial to under-standing the nature of black womanhood.

THE PROMISE AND LIMITATIONS
OF DOUBLE JEOPARDY

In 1972, Frances Beale, a founding member of the Women's Liberation Committee of the Student Nonviolent Coordinating Committee (SNCC) and, later, a member of the Third World Women's Alliance, introduced the term "double jeopardy" to describe the dual discriminations of racism and sexism that subjugate black women. Concerning black women, she wrote, "As blacks they suffer all the burdens of prejudice and mistreatment that fall on anyone with dark skin. As women they bear the additional burden of having to cope with white and black men."[13] Beale also astutely observed that the reality of dual discriminations often entailed economic disadvantage; unfortunately she did not incorporate that understanding into the conceptualization. Perhaps she viewed class status as a particular consequence of racism, rather than as an autonomous source of persecution;

but such a preponderant majority of black women have endured the very lowest of wages and very poorest conditions of rural and urban poverty that some scholars have argued that economic class oppression must necessarily constitute a third jeopardy.[14] Still others have suggested that heterosexism or homophobia represents another significant oppression and should be included as a third or perhaps fourth jeopardy.[15] The triple jeopardy of racism, sexism, and classism is now widely accepted and used as the conceptualization of black women's status. However, while advancing our understanding beyond the erasure of black women within the confines of the race-sex analogy, it does not yet fully convey the dynamics of multiple forms of discrimination.

Unfortunately, most applications of the concepts of double and triple jeopardy have been overly simplistic in assuming that the relationships among the various discriminations are merely additive. These relationships are interpreted as equivalent to the mathematical equation, racism plus sexism plus classism equals triple jeopardy. In this instance, each discrimination has a single, direct, and independent effect on status, wherein the relative contribution of each is readily apparent. This simple incremental process does not represent the nature of black women's oppression but, rather, I would contend, leads to nonproductive assertions that one factor can and should supplant the other. For example, class oppression is the largest component of black women's subordinate status, therefore the exclusive focus should be on economics. Such assertions ignore the fact that racism, sexism, and classism constitute three, interdependent control systems. An interactive model, which I have termed multiple jeopardy, better captures those processes.[16]

The modifier "multiple" refers not only to several, simultaneous oppressions but to the multiplicative relationships among them as well. In other words, the equivalent formulation is racism multiplied by sexism multiplied by classism. The sexual exploitation of black women in slavery is a historical example. While black women workers suffered the same demanding physical labor and brutal punishments as black men, as females, we were also subject to forms of subjugation applicable only to women. Angela Davis, in *Women, Race, and Class,* notes, "If the most violent punishments of men consisted in floggings and mutilations, women were flogged and mutilated, as well as raped."[17] At the same time, our reproductive and child-rearing activities served to enhance the quantity and quality of the "capital" of a slave economy. Our institutionalized exploitation as the concubines, mistresses, and sexual slaves of white males distinguished our experience from that of white females' sexual oppression because it could only have existed in relation to racist and classist forms of domination.

The importance of any one factor in explaining black women's circumstances thus varies depending on the particular aspect of our lives under consideration and the reference groups to whom we are compared. In some cases, race may be the more significant predictor of black women's status; in others, gender or class may be more influential.

In the interactive model, the relative significance of race, sex, or class in determining the conditions of black women's lives is neither fixed nor absolute but, rather, is dependent on the socio-historical context and the social phenomenon under consideration. These interactions also produce what to some appears a seemingly confounding set of social roles and political attitudes among black women. Sociologist Bonnie Thornton Dill has discussed the importance of scholars' recognizing, incorporating, and interpreting the complex variety of social roles that black women have performed in reaction to multiple jeopardies. She argues that the constellation of "attitudes, behaviors, and interpersonal relationships ... were adaptations to a variety of factors, including the harsh realities of their environment, Afro-American cultural images of black womanhood, and the sometimes conflicting values and norms of the wider society."[18]

A black woman's survival depends on her ability to use all the economic, social, and cultural resources available to her from both the larger society and within her community. For example, black women historically have had to assume economically productive roles as well as retain domestic ones, and until recently our labor force participation rate well exceeded that of white women.[19] Labor, whether unpaid and coerced (as under slavery) or paid and necessary employment, has been a distinctive characteristic of black women's social roles. It has earned us a small but significant degree of self-reliance and independence that has promoted egalitarian relations with black men and active influence within the black family and community.[20] But it also has had costs. For instance, black women have most often had to work in low-status and low-paying jobs since race and sex discrimination have historically limited our employment options. The legacy of the political economy of slavery under capitalism is the fact that employers, and not black women, still profit the most from black women's labor. And when black women become the primary or sole earners for households, researchers and public analysts interpret this self-sufficiency as pathology, as deviance, as a threat to black family life.[21] Yet, it is black women's well-documented facility to encompass seemingly contradictory role expectations of worker, homemaker, and mother that has contributed to the confusion in understanding black womanhood.[22] These competing demands (each requiring its own set of resistances to multiple forms of oppression) are a primary influence on the black woman's definition of her womanhood, and her relationships to the people around her. To reduce this complex of negotiations to an addition problem (racism + sexism = black women's experience) is to define the issues, and indeed black womanhood itself, within the structural terms developed by Europeans and especially white males to privilege their race and their sex unilaterally. Sojourner's declaration, "ain't I a woman?" directly refutes this sort of conceptualization of womanhood as one-dimensional rather than dialectical.

MULTIPLE JEOPARDY WITHIN THE POLITICS OF LIBERATION

In order to understand the concept of multiple jeopardy, it is necessary to look beyond the social structure and process of the dominant society that insidiously pervade even the movements for race, gender, and class liberation. Thus, the confrontations among blacks about sexism and classism, among women about racism and classism, and among the various economic classes about racism and sexism compose a second feature of the context of black feminist ideology. A formidable impediment in these battles is the "monist" approach of most liberation ideologies. In *Liberating Theory,* monism is described as a political claim "that one particular domination precipitates all really important oppressions. Whether Marxist, anarchist, nationalist, or feminist, these 'ideal types' argue that important social relations can all be reduced to the economy, state, culture, or gender."[23] For example, during the suffrage debates, it was routinely asserted that only one group might gain voting privileges—either blacks or women, that is black men or white women. For black women, the granting of suffrage to either group would still mean our disenfranchisement because of either our sex or our race. Faced with this dilemma, many black women and most black men believed that the extension of suffrage to black males was imperative in order to protect race interests in the historical period of postbellum America. But because political empowerment for black women would require that both blacks and women gained the right to vote, some of these same black women also lobbied strenuously for women's suffrage.[24]

The contemporary efforts of black women to achieve greater equal opportunity and status present similar dilemmas, whether in the areas of reproductive rights, electoral politics, or poverty. Our history of resistance to multiple jeopardies is replete with the fierce tensions, untenable ultimatums, and bitter compromises between nationalism, feminism, and class politics. In a curious twist of fate, we find ourselves marginal to both the movements for women's liberation and black liberation irrespective of our victimization under the dual discriminations of racism and sexism. A similar exclusion or secondary status typifies our role within class movements. Ironically, black women are often in conflict with the very same subordinate groups with which we share some interests. The groups in which we find logical allies on certain issues are the groups in which we may find opponents on others. To the extent that we have found ourselves confronting the exclusivity of monistic politics, we have had to manage ideologies and activities that did not address the dialectics of our lives. We are asked to decide with whom to ally, which interests to advance. Should black women's primary ideological and activist commitment be to race, sex, or class-based social movements? Can we afford to be monist? Can we afford not to be?

In the following consideration of the dialectics within each of three liberation movements, I hope to describe the tensions and priorities that influence the construction of a black feminist ideology. To the extent that any politic is monistic, the actual victims of racism, sexism, or classism may be absent from, invisible within, or seen as antagonistic to that politic. Thus, prejudicial attitudes and discriminatory actions may be overt, subtle, or covert; and they may have various manifestations through ideological statements, policies and strategies, and interpersonal relations. That is, black and/or poor women may be marginal to monistic feminism, women's concerns may be excluded from nationalistic activism, and indifference to race and gender may pervade class politics. This invisibility may be due to actual exclusion or benign neglect, while marginality is represented in tokenism, minimization, and devalued participation. Antagonism involves two subordinate groups whose actions and beliefs are placed in opposition as mutually detrimental. From this conceptual framework, the following discussion highlights the major aspects of multiple jeopardy within liberation politics.

INTRARACIAL POLITICS

Racial solidarity and race liberation have been and remain a fundamental concern for black Americans. Historically and currently, slavery, segregation, and institutional as well as individual discrimination have been formative experiences in most blacks' socialization and political outlook. The inerasable physical characteristics of race have long determined the status and opportunities of black women in the United States. Since race serves as a significant filter of what blacks perceive and how blacks are perceived, many black women have claimed that their racial identity is more salient than either their gender or class identity.[25] Diane Lewis, an anthropologist, has remarked that when racism is seen as the principal cause of their subordinate status, "their interests as blacks have taken precedence over their interests as women."[26] This political importance of race is evident for other reasons as well. Certainly, the chronological order of the social movements for racial, gender, and class justice in part explains the priority given to racial interests. In both the nineteenth and twentieth centuries, the abolition and Civil Rights movements predate women's suffrage and the women's movement. Similarly, collective efforts that addressed economic deprivation and exploitation, such as trade unionism beginning in the late 1800s, communist organizing in the 1920s and 1930s, and the anti-imperialist activism of the 1960s were preceded by or simultaneous with race-oriented movements. Considering the order of events, it is reasonable to expect that most black women would have made commitments to and investments in the race movements such that they would not or could not easily abandon those for later movements.

Furthermore, through the necessity of confronting and surviving racial oppression, black women have assumed responsibilities atypical of those assigned to white women under Western patriarchy. Black women often held central and powerful leadership roles within the black community and within its liberation politics. We founded schools, operated social welfare services, sustained churches, organized collective work groups and unions, and even established banks and commercial enterprises. That is, we were the backbone of racial uplift, and we also played critical roles in the struggle for racial justice.[27] Harriet Tubman led slaves to freedom on the underground railroad; Ida Wells-Barnett led the crusade against lynching; Fannie Lou Hamer and Ella Baker were guiding political spirits of the Southern black efforts that gave birth to SNCC and the Mississippi Freedom Democratic Party; the "simple" act of Rosa Parks catapulted Martin Luther King to national prominence. Black women, therefore, did not experience sexism within the race movement in quite the ways that brought many white women to feminist consciousness within either civil rights or New Left politics.[28]

All together this history constitutes a powerful impetus toward a monistic race approach as the means of liberation for black women. Michele Wallace concludes that black women simply lack a feminist consciousness as a matter of choice, out of ignorance, misguided beliefs, or an inability to recognize sexual domination both within and without the black community.[29] Since the 1800s, however, the writings of such prominent black women as Sojourner Truth, Maria Stewart, Anna Julia Cooper, Josephine St. Pierre Ruffin, Frances Watkins Harper, Pauli Murray, Frances Beale, Audre Lorde, and Angela Davis have described a broader view of black consciousness.[30] Even among those black women who expressed grave reservations about participating in the women's movement, most recognized sexism as a factor of their subordination in the larger society and acknowledged sexual politics among blacks. They could identify the sexual inequities that resulted in the images of black women as emasculating matriarchs; in the rates of sexual abuse and physical violence; and in black men assuming the visible leadership positions in many black social institutions, such as the church, the intelligentsia, and political organizations.[31] During the Civil Rights and black nationalist movements of the 1960s and 1970s, men quite effectively used the matriarchy issue to manipulate and coerce black women into maintaining exclusive commitments to racial interests and redefining and narrowing black women's roles and images in ways to fit a more traditional Western view of women. Black feminists Pauli Murray and Pauline Terrelonge Stone both agree that the debates over this issue became an ideological ploy to heighten guilt in black women over their supposed collusion with whites in the oppression of black men.[32] Consequently, these intraracial tensions worked against the public articulations of a feminist consciousness by most black women. Nevertheless, a point of concern and contention within the black community was how sexual inequalities might best be addressed, not whether they existed. A few black women responded by choosing monistic feminism, others sought a distinct black feminist activism. While many organized feminist efforts within race-oriented movements, some also adopted a strict nationalist view. Over time, there were also transformations of perspectives. For example, the black women of SNCC created within it a women's liberation group which later became an independent feminists-of-color organization, the Third World Women's Alliance, which is today the only surviving entity of SNCC.

The politics of race liberation have rarely been exclusively race-based. Because so many blacks historically have been economically oppressed, race liberation has out of necessity become more pluralistic through its incorporation of economic interests. Whether civil rights or a nationalist activism, the approach to class injustice generally promotes greater economic opportunities and rewards within the existing capitalist order. At the turn of the century, for instance, the collective action known as racial uplift involved the efforts of educated, middle-class blacks to elevate the moral, physical, social, and economic conditions of lower-income blacks. The National Association of Wage Earners was established in the 1920s by women like Nannie Burroughs, Maggie Wallace, and Mary McCleod Bethune to assist black female domestic and factory workers.[33]

The Civil Rights movement initially seemed to avoid the value-laden implications of this pattern of middle-class beneficence toward those with fewer economic resources. Both Aldon Morris, a sociologist, and Clayborne Carson, a historian, have written of the genuine grass roots orientation of the black southern strategy in the 1950s and early 1960s.[34] The majority of the participants were rural, poorly educated, and economically disadvantaged, but more important, these same individuals set the priorities and the strategies of the movement. The legacy was an affirmation of the strength of seemingly powerless people, and particularly of the black women who were among the principal organizers and supporters.[35]

Despite these auspicious beginnings, Cornel West, a black theologian, described the 1960s as a time when the interest of poor blacks were often betrayed.[36] Middle-class blacks were better able to take advantage of the relatively greater opportunities made possible through the race-oriented, legal liberalism of equal opportunity and affirmative action policies and electoral politics. Only such groups as the Nation of Islam and the League of Revolutionary Black Workers, like Marcus Garvey's United Negro Improvement Association earlier in this century, continued to represent the interests of working-class and impoverished blacks. The contemporary controversy over class polarization in the black community is a consequence of the movement's not effectively addressing the economic status of all blacks. Given the particularly precarious economic status of black women, this neglect and marginalization of class is especially problematic for them. The National Welfare Rights Organization, founded in 1967, was one of the few successful, though short-lived, efforts to address the class divisions. Only recently have race-focal groups, including the Urban League and the National Association for the Advancement of Colored People, addressed the plight of impoverished black women.

Racial solidarity has been a fundamental element of black women's resistance to domination. However, the intraracial politics of gender and class have made a strictly nationalistic approach overly restrictive and incalculably detrimental to our prospects for full liberation. Given a social condition that is also compounded by other oppressions, black women have necessarily been concerned with affecting, at the very least, an amelioration of economic and gender discriminations. Consequently, some black women have sought an association with feminism as one alternative to the limitations of monistic race politics.

POLITICS AMONG WOMEN

At one level, black women, other women of color, and white women, share many common contemporary concerns about their legal status and rights, encounters with discrimination, and sexual victimization. It is on these shared concerns that feminists have sought to forge a sense of sisterhood and to foster solidarity. This effort is manifest in a variety of ways, but the slogan, "sisterhood is powerful," best exemplifies the importance and the hoped for efficacy of such solidarity in the achievement of women's equality and liberation. For example, all-female restrictions for consciousness-raising sessions, intellectual and artistic programs and publications, organizations, businesses, and communities reflect this singular orientation; and lesbian feminist separatism represents the absolute ideological expression of the monistic tendencies in feminism.

Presumably, black women are included in this sisterhood, but, nonetheless, invisibility and marginality characterize much of our relationship to the women's movement. The assertion of commonality, indeed of the universality and primacy of female oppression, denies the other structured inequalities of race, class, religion, and nationality, as well as denying the diverse cultural heritages that affect the lives of many women. While contending that feminist consciousness and theory emerged from the personal, everyday reality of being female, the reality of millions of women was ignored. The phrase, "the personal is the political" not only reflects a phenomenological approach to women's liberation—that is, of women defining and constructing their own reality—but it has also come to describe the politics of imposing and privileging a few women's personal lives over all women's lives by assuming that these few could be prototypical. For black women, the personal is bound up in the problems peculiar to multiple jeopardies of race and class, not the singular one of sexual inequality. This has not necessarily meant that black women rejected feminism, but merely that they were not single-mindedly committed to the organizations and some of the agenda that have come to be called the women's movement, that is, the movement of white, often protestant, middle-class women.

Feminism has excluded and devalued black women, our experiences, and our interpretations of our own realities at the conceptual and ideological level. Black feminists and black women scholars have identified and critically examined other serious flaws in feminist theorizing. The assumption that the family is by definition patriarchal, the privileging of an individualistic worldview, and the advocacy of female separatism are often antithetical positions to many of the values and goals of black women and thus are hindrances to our association with feminism.[37] These theoretical blinders obscured the ability of certain feminists first to recognize the multifaceted nature of women's oppressions and then to envision theories that encompass those realities. As a consequence, monistic feminism's ability to foresee remedies that would neither abandon women to the other discriminations, including race and class, nor exacerbate those burdens is extremely limited. Without theories and concepts that represent the experiences of black women, the women's movement has and will be ineffectual in making ideological appeals that might mobilize such women. Often, in fact, this conceptual invisibility has led to the actual strategic neglect and physical exclusion or nonparticipation of black women. Most black women who have participated in any organizations or activities of the women's movement are keenly aware of the racial politics that anger, frustrate, and alienate us.

The case of the struggle for suffrage in the nineteenth century again is an instructive example of the complexity of multiple jeopardy and its politics. Initially, there was an alliance of blacks and women for universal suffrage. However, as the campaign ensued, opponents of universal suffrage, and of any extension of voting privileges, were successful in transforming the debate into one of who should receive the vote—women or black males. Many prominent white suffragists, including Elizabeth Cady Stanton, Susan B. Anthony, and Carrie Chapman Catt abandoned the alliance and demanded a "women only" enfranchisement. The question of black women's suffrage should have been especially problematical for them. In fact, it was never seriously considered. More damning, however, were their politics of expediency. They cooperated with avowed racists in order to gain the southern vote and liberally used racial slurs and epithets arguing that white women's superior character and intellect made them more deserving of the right to vote than blacks, Native Americans, and Eastern European and Asian immigrants.

As Angela Davis observes in her examination of race and class in the early women's rights campaign, even the Seneca Falls Declaration "all but ignored the predicament of white working-class women, as it ignored the condition of black women in the South and North alike."[38] Barbara Andolsen, in one of the most comprehensive studies of racism in the woman suffrage movement observed: "[it] had a bold vision and noble principles ... but this is a story of a vision betrayed. For the white women who led this movement came to trade upon their privilege as the daughters (sisters, wives, and mothers) of powerful white men in order to gain for themselves some share of the political power those men possessed. They did not adequately identify ways in which that political power would not be accessible to poor women, immigrant women, and black women."[39] Yet despite the blatant racism and class bias of the women's suffrage movement, black women, discouraged and betrayed, continued to work for their right to vote, both as blacks and as women, through their own suffrage organizations.

This history of racism in the early women's movement has been sustained by contemporary white feminists. Within organizations, most twentieth-century black women encounter myriad experiences that deny their reality. In some instances, it is the absence of materials, information, speeches, readings, or persons representing black women. When present at all, women of color are underrepresented and have marginal and subordinate roles. Recently, Paula Giddings has reported that the National Organization for Women (NOW) remains insensitive to such problematic issues as rape, abortion, sterilization, poverty, and unions. Women of color are rarely elected as officers or appointed to major positions, and NOW has actually encouraged minority women's chapters rather than the incorporation of their concerns into the "regular" chapters.[40] Lawyer and educator Mary Frances Berry, in her analysis of the politics of amending the constitution, has argued that one reason for the defeat of the Equal Rights Amendment was the failure of its proponents to campaign, educate, and mobilize the black community, and especially black women.[41]

Many white feminist activists have often assumed that their antisexism stance abolished all racial prejudice or discriminatory behaviors. At best, this presumption is naive and reflects a serious ignorance of the pervasiveness of racism in this society. Many blacks, women and men alike, see such postures as arrogant, racist, and dangerous to their own interests.

Diane Lewis concluded that the status of black women and our interests within the women's movement and its organizations essentially replicates our structurally subordinate position to white women in the larger society.[42] Different opportunity structures and life options make interracial alliances and feminist solidarity problematic. Conceptually invisible, interpersonally misunderstood and insulted, and strategically marginal, black women have found that much in the movement has denied important aspects of our history and experience. Yet, despite the critical obstacles and limitations, the imperatives of multiple jeopardy necessitate recognizing and resisting sexism.

Beyond the race politics in feminism, many black women share concerns of impoverished and working-class women about class politics. What has become mainstream feminism rests on traditional, liberal economic aspirations of equal employment opportunities for women. In practice, however, the emphasis is often on the professional careers of those women who are already economically privileged and college educated. It could be argued, for instance, that equal access to all types of vocational training and jobs may not be desirable as a necessary or primary goal. While it is true that men on average earn more than women, all men do not have equally attractive jobs in terms of working conditions, compensation and benefits, prestige, and mobility. Those male jobs may represent, at best, only a minimal improvement over the jobs of many working women. White feminist economic concerns have concentrated on primary sector employment, but these are not the positions that are most critical and accessible to lower- or no-income women. Referring to the equal opportunity approach, Karen Kollias points out that "the majority of nonwhite, lower- and working-class women don't have the power to utilize these benefits because their primary, objective economic conditions haven't changed."[43] . . .

This lack of attention to economic issues has significant implications for the participation of black women. Many of the differences of priorities between black and white women are related to class. Issues of welfare, hunger, poor housing, limited health care, and transportation are seldom seen as feminist interests and are rarely the subject of feminist social policies. As Brenda Eichelberger maintains, "the black woman's energy output is more often directed toward such basic survival issues, while the white woman's is more often aimed at fulfillment."[44] The economic concerns of women from lower-income backgrounds are relatively ignored and distorted in the contemporary women's movement. The feminist interpretation of the "feminization" of poverty is a case in point. While noting that some women, again middle class, have indeed experienced a recent drastic decline in life circumstances as a consequence of divorce, the feminization analysis has misrepresented many of the causes of female poverty. For example, most impoverished women have been poor throughout their lives as a consequence of their class position or of racial oppression. Linda Burnham writes that race and class are more significant causative factors in black women's impoverishment than is gender. In the thesis of the feminization of poverty, she contends, "The vulnerability of white women to impoverishment is overstated; the impoverishment of black men is ignored or underestimated; and the fundamental basis in working-class exploitation for the continual regeneration of poverty is abandoned for a focus on gender."[45]

In summary, feminism's neglect, misunderstanding, or de-emphasis of the politics of race and class have direct implications for the actions of black women in relationship to the movement. Often, our response has been to avoid participation in white female, middle-class dominated organizations and to withhold our support from policies that are not in our race and class interests. Nevertheless, just as the importance of race led many black women to commitments to racially based politics, and gender interests compelled our feminist efforts, economic injustices have brought many to consider class politics as a major avenue of liberation.

CLASS POLITICS

Economic exploitation is the third societal jeopardy constraining the lives of black women. Historically, the three major movements to address the deprivations of class in the United States have been trade unionism and the anticapitalist politics of the 1930s and 1960s, which are colloquially referred to as the Old and the New Left. Having their origins in responses to the degradations that accompanied urbanization and industrialization, labor unionists and leftists organized to address the problems of wage labor and economic stratification in a capitalistic society, including the excessive working hours in poor, unsafe conditions, low pay and limited job security, fluctuations in the labor demand, the decline in work satisfaction, the loss of worker autonomy, and poverty. Each movement, although monistic, possessed different objectives. Unionism was reformist in orientation, seeking to ameliorate the worst of the above conditions. In contrast, the socialist and communist ideologies of the Left were revolutionary in that they aspired to eradicate capitalism and ostensibly to establish a classless society.

Into the first quarter of this century, organized labor's approach to economic disadvantage held little promise for blacks or women, and thus no promise for black women. Samuel Gompers, the leading force of trade unionism and president of the American Federation of Labor (AFL, founded in 1886), believed that the best means of improving wages for Anglo males was to restrict the labor supply. His strategy was to advocate the return of women to the home and the banning of blacks and Asians from the unions. Although the AFL never formally adopted these restrictions at the national level, many local chapters did so through both formal rules and informal practices.[46] Trade unionists cultivated a cultural image of the worker as a married male who required a family wage to support a wife and children. Labor actively supported protective labor legislation, which effectively excluded women from the jobs that would provide them with sufficient incomes to support themselves and their families. These efforts against women were coupled with the exclusion of blacks, other racial minorities, and, initially, southern and eastern European immigrant males from the most economically rewarding labor in the unionized crafts and the closed shops. Blacks, in particular, were specifically denied union membership or else relegated to the unskilled, low-paying jobs. Consequently, the denial of a family wage to black males exacerbated the circumstances of already economically distressed black families and individuals. In occupations where blacks were well represented, unionization often meant their forceable expulsion. Many of the race riots in the early 1900s were related to the tensions between black laborers and white laborers in competition for employment. So, an effective two-prong strategy for improving white men's income required the demand for a family wage and the restriction of labor competition from women and racial minorities.

In response to union discrimination, white women and black women and men organized. The Working Women's Association, formed in 1868, was one of the earlier attempts at synthesizing feminist and white female workers' concerns; the Women's Trade Union League, established in 1903, allied white working- and middle-class women, while the International Ladies' Garment Workers' Union publicized the conditions of white working women, demanded equal pay, demanded female representation in the national labor unions, formed female unions, and organized strikes.[47] Ironically, most of the women's trade union organizations as well as many socialist feminists supported protective legislation, but with the mistaken belief that involving the state would ensure safer work environments and reasonable labor requirements for both women and men. However, an unintended consequence of this strategy was that many women's economic situations declined because protective legislation could be used to reinforce occupational segregation and thus limit women's wage-earning opportunities.

As the wives and daughters of men who did not earn a family wage, black women's participation in the labor market was crucial to the survival of themselves and their families. Yet, black women benefited little from the unionization efforts among white women. First, they were disproportionately situated in those occupations least likely to be unionized, such as domestic and nonhousehold service and agricultural labor. In large industrial workplaces, they were segregated from white female workers, where the organizing took place, and were often pawns in the labor-management contests.[48] Second, white trade unionists failed actively to recruit black females, and they often were denied membership because of their race. The protective legislation further hampered their opportunities by closing off numerous employment opportunities simply on the basis of sex. Black women wanted better-paying jobs, but they often had to settle for the jobs that were considered too hazardous, dirty, or immoral for white women, and for which they were not fairly compensated. During the Depression, race-gender discrimination was so pervasive that employment in federal work-relief projects often was closed to them. Thus, significant numbers of black women were unemployed and/or underemployed and, therefore, untouched by union activism.

Despite their exclusion from the major unions, black women and men organized caucuses within predominantly white unions and formed their own unions, such as the Urban League's Negro Workers Councils, African Blood Brotherhood, Negro American Labor Council, National Negro Labor Council, and Dodge Revolutionary Union Movement (DRUM). A. Philip Randolph, founder of the Brotherhood of Sleeping Car Porters, called for a march on Washington in the 1940s to demand the end of wage and job discrimination, the desegregation of schools and public accommodations, protection of immigrant workers, cessation of lynching, and the unionization of black women. During the Depression, trade unions and unemployed councils held demonstrations demanding immediate cash relief and unemployment compensation, as well as advocating race solidarity. For blacks in the first half of this century, class and race interests were often inseparable. Black women benefited indirectly from black men's labor activism, and they often supported those efforts by participating on picket lines, providing food and clothing for strikers and their families, and, most important, making financial contributions to the households from their own paid labor. Black women also engaged in labor organizing directly, both through existing predominantly white unions and through their own activism. Black domestics, tobacco workers, garment workers, and others organized strikes and fought for union representation.[49]

The political Left, in general, supported black women and men and white working women during the Progressive Era. In fact, leading intellectuals, including Emma Goldman, Margaret Sanger, Charlotte Perkins Gilman, Elizabeth Gurley Flynn, Langston Hughes, Paul Robeson, W. E. B. Du Bois, and C. L. R. James saw socialism as the route for liberation. Two black women, Lucy Parsons and Claudia Jones, were among the early labor activists and Socialists of the Old Left.

At the same time, women active in the New Left became increasingly frustrated with the theoretical and strategic indifference to the woman question. The sexual politics within the movement subjected women to traditional gender role assignments, sexual manipulation, male leadership and domination, plus a concentration on an essentially male issue, the draft.[50] Once again, invisibility typifies the role of black women in New Left radical politics. Black women responded by incorporating class interests into their race and gender politics. In the founding documents of various black feminist organizations, scathing critiques of the political economy are a cornerstone of the analysis of domination. For example, the *Combahee River Collective Statement* pointedly declared that "the liberation of all oppressed peoples necessitates the destruction of the political-economic systems of capitalism and imperialism as well as partriarchy. . . . We are not convinced, however, that a socialist revolution that is not also a feminist and antiracist revolution will guarantee our liberation."[51] This excerpt clearly articulates an understanding of multiple jeopardy and its function in the dominant society and within liberation politics. Out of necessity, black women have addressed both narrow labor and broad economic concerns.

Political theorist Manning Marable has argued that progressive forces must uproot racism and patriarchy in their quest for a socialist democracy through a dedication to equality.[52] Yet a major limitation of both unionism and radical class politics is their monist formulations, wherein economics are exaggerated at the expense of understanding and confronting other oppressions such as racism and sexism. Despite the historical examples of black women and men and white women as union activists and socialists and the examples of the sporadic concern of organized labor and leftists with race and gender politics, class politics have not provided the solution to black women's domination because they continue to privilege class issues within a white male framework. Given the inability of any single agenda to address the intricate complex of racism, sexism, and classism in black women's lives, black women must develop a political ideology capable of interpreting and resisting that multiple jeopardy.

MULTIPLE CONSCIOUSNESS IN BLACK FEMINIST IDEOLOGY

Gloria Joseph and Jill Lewis have suggested that black women face a dilemma analogous to that of Siamese twins, each of whom have distinct and incompatible interests.[53] Black women cannot, they argue, be wholeheartedly committed and fully active in both the black liberation struggle and the women's liberation movement, because of sexual and racial politics within each respectively. The authors recognize the demands of multiple jeopardy politics and the detrimental effect of neglecting these dual commitments. But what they fail to consider are the multiple and creative ways in which black women address their interdependent concerns of racism, sexism, and classism.

Black women have been feminists since the early 1800s, but our exclusion from the white woman's movement and its organizations has led many incorrectly to assume that we were not present in the (white) women's movement because we were not interested in resisting sexism both within and without the black community. What appears recently to be a change in black women's position, from studied indifference to disdain and curiosity to cautious affirmation of the women's movement, may be due to structural changes in relationships between blacks and whites that have made black women "more sensitive to the obstacles of sexism and to the relevance of the women's movement."[54] Black women's apparent greater sensitivity to sexism may be merely the bolder, public articulation of black feminist concerns that have existed for well over a century. In other words, black women did not just become feminists in the 1970s. We did, however, grant more salience to those concerns and become more willing to organize primarily on that basis, creating the Combahee River Collective, the National Black Feminist Organization, and Sapphire Sapphos. Some black women chose to participate in predominantly white women's movement activities and organizations, while others elected to develop the scholarship and curriculum that became the foundation of black women's studies, while still others founded black feminist journals, presses, and political organizations.[55]

Several studies have considered the relevance of black women's diverse characteristics in understanding our political attitudes; these reports seem fairly inconsistent, if not contradictory.[56] The various findings do suggest that the conditions that bring black women to feminist consciousness are specific to our social and historical experiences. For black women, the circumstances of lower socioeconomic life may encourage political, and particularly feminist, consciousness.[57] This is in contrast to feminist as well as traditional political socialization literature that suggests that more liberal, that is, feminist, attitudes are associated with higher education attainment and class standing. Many of the conditions that middle-class, white feminists have found oppressive are perceived as privileges by black women, especially those with low incomes. For instance, the option not to work outside of the home is a luxury that historically has been denied most black women. The desire to struggle for this option can, in such a context, represent a feminist position, precisely because it constitutes an instance of greater liberty for certain women. It is also important to note, however, that the class differences among black women regarding our feminist consciousness are minimal. Black women's particular history thus is an essential ingredient in shaping our feminist concerns.

Certainly the multifaceted nature of black womanhood would meld diverse ideologies, from race liberation, class liberation, and women's liberation. The basis of our feminist ideology is rooted in our reality. To the extent that the adherents of any one ideology insist on separatist organizational forms, assert the fundamental nature of any one oppression, and demand total cognitive, affective, and behavioral commitment, that ideology and its practitioners exclude black women and the realities of our lives.

A black feminist ideology, first and foremost, thus declares the visibility of black women. It acknowledges the fact that two innate and inerasable traits, being both black and female, constitute our special status in American society. Second, black feminism asserts self-determination as essential. Black women are empowered with the right to interpret our reality and define our objectives. While drawing on a rich tradition of struggle as blacks and as women, we continually establish and reestablish our own priorities. As black women, we decide for ourselves the relative salience of any and all identities and oppressions, and how and the extent to which those features inform our politics. Third, a black feminist ideology fundamentally challenges the interstructure of the oppressions of racism, sexism, and classism both in the dominant society and within movements for liberation. It is in confrontation with multiple jeopardy that black women define and sustain a multiple consciousness essential for our liberation, of which feminist consciousness is an integral part.

Finally, a black feminist ideology presumes an image of black women as powerful, independent subjects. By concentrating on our multiple oppressions, scholarly descriptions have confounded our ability to discover and appreciate the ways in which black women are not victims. Ideological and political choices cannot be assumed to be determined solely by the historical dynamics of racism, sexism, and classism in this society. Although the complexities and ambiguities that merge a consciousness of race, class, and gender oppressions make the emergence and praxis of a multivalent ideology problematical, they also make such a task more necessary if we are to work toward our liberation as blacks, as the economically exploited, and as women.

ENDNOTES

1. Gerda Lerner, ed., *Black Women in White America: A Documentary History* (New York: Vintage, 1973), 573.

2. Mary Church Terrell, "The Progress of Colored Women," *Voice of the Negro* 1, no. 7 (July 1904): 292.

3. See Lerner, *Black Women,* especially 566–72; and Bert James Loewenberg and Ruth Bogin, eds., *Black Women in Nineteenth-Century American Life* (University Park: Pennsylvania State University Press, 1976), 234–42.

4. See Lerner, *Black Women,* 609–11.

5. Elizabeth Cady Stanton as quoted by William Chafe, *Women and Equality: Changing Patterns in American Culture* (New York: Oxford University Press, 1977), 44. Some eighty years after Stanton's observation, Swedish social psychologist Gunnar Myrdal, in an appendix to his *An American Dilemma: The Negro Problem and Modern Democracy* (New York: Harper & Row, 1962), also saw the woman problem as parallel to the Negro problem.

6. Chafe, *Women and Equality,* 77.

7. Helen Hacker, "Women as a Minority Group," *Social Forces* 30 (1951): 60–69.

8. For examples of feminist writings using the race-sex analogy or the master-slave model, see Simone de Beauvoir, *The Second Sex,* trans. and ed. H. M. Parshley (New York: Random House, 1974); Kate Millett, *Sexual Politics* (New York: Avon, 1969); Shulamith Firestone, *The Dialectics of Sex* (New York: William Morrow, 1970); and Mary Daly, *Beyond God the Father: Toward a Philosophy of Women's Liberation* (Boston: Beacon Press, 1973).

9. See Sara Evans, *Personal Politics: The Roots of Women's Liberation in the Civil Rights Movement and the New Left* (New York: Vintage, 1980); Catharine Stimpson, "Thy Neighbor's Wife, Thy Neighbor's Servants: Women's Liberation and Black Civil Rights," in *Woman in Sexist Society: Studies in Power and Powerlessness,* ed. Vivian Gornick and Barbara Moran (New York: Basic Books, 1971), 452–79; and Angela Davis, *Women, Race, and Class* (New York: Random House, 1981). Recently, there has been some debate concerning precisely what lessons, if any, women learned from their participation in the abolitionist and Civil Rights movements. For an argument against the importance of race-oriented movements for feminist politics, see E. C. DuBois, *Feminism and Suffrage* (Ithaca, NY: Cornell University Press, 1978).

10. Other limitations have been noted by Linda La Rue, who contends that the analogy is an abstraction that falsely asserts a common oppression of blacks and women for rhetorical and propagandistic purposes ("The Black Movement and Women's Liberation," in *Female Psychology: The Emerging Self,* ed. Sue Cox [Chicago: Science Research Association, 1976). In *Ain't I a Woman* (Boston: South End Press, 1981), bell hooks questions whether certain women, particularly those self-identified feminists who are white and middle class, are truly oppressed as opposed to being discriminated against. Simpson bluntly declares that the race-sex analogy is exploitative and racist. See also Margaret A. Simons, "Racism and Feminism: A Schism in the Sisterhood," *Feminist Studies* 5 (1979): 384–401, for a critical review of this conceptual approach in feminist theorizing.

11. Chafe, *Women and Equality,* 76; Althea Smith and Abigail J. Stewart, "Approaches to Studying Racism and Sexism in Black Women's Lives," *Journal of Social Issues* 39 (1983): 1–15.

12. hooks, *Ain't I a Woman,* 7.

13. Frances Beale, "Double Jeopardy: To Be Black and Female," in *The Black Woman: An Anthology,* ed. Toni Cade (New York: New American Library, 1979), 90–100.

14. See, e.g., Beverly Lindsay, "Minority Women in America: Black American, Native American, Chicana, and Asian American Women," in *The Study of Woman: Enlarging Perspectives of Social Reality,* ed. Eloise C. Synder (New York: Harper & Row, 1979), 318–63. She presents a paradigm wherein whiteness, maleness, and money are advantageous; a poor, black woman is triply disadvantaged. Lindsay argues that triple jeopardy, the interaction of sexism, racism, and economic oppression, is "the most realistic perspective for analyzing the position of black American women; and this perspective will serve as common linkage among the discussions of other minority women" (328).

15. See Barbara Smith, ed., *Home Girls: A Black Feminist Anthology* (New York: Kitchen Table Press, 1983), especially section 3; and Audre Lorde, "Scratching the Surface: Some Notes on Barriers to Women and Loving," *Black Scholar* 13 (Summer 1982): 20–24, and *Sister Outsider: Essays and Speeches* (Trumansburg, NY: Crossing Press, 1984).

16. For other attempts at nonadditive models, see Smith and Stewart "Approaches to Studying Racism"; Elizabeth M. Almquist, "Untangling the Effects of Race and Sex: The Disadvantaged Status of Black Women," *Social Science Quarterly*

56 (1975): 129–42; and Margaret L. Andersen, *Thinking about Women: Sociological and Feminist Perspectives* (New York: Macmillan, 1983). The term "ethnogender" is introduced in Vincent Jeffries and H. Edward Ransford, *Social Stratification: A Multiple Hierachy Approach* (Boston: Allyn & Bacon, 1980); and Edward Ransford and Jon Miller, "Race, Sex, and Feminist Outlook," *American Sociological Review* 48 (1983): 46–59.

17. Davis, *Women, Race, and Class,* 7.

18. Bonnie Thornton Dill, "The Dialectics of Black Womanhood," *Signs: Journal of Women in Culture and Society* 4 (1979): 543–55, especially 547. Smith and Stewart, "Approaches to Studying Racism," 1, make a similar point.

19. In slavery, there was 100 percent labor force participation by black women. In 1910, thirty-four percent were in the official labor force. In 1960, the figure was forty percent, and by 1980, it was over fifty percent. Comparable figures for white women are eighteen percent in 1890, twenty-two percent in 1910, thirty-seven percent in 1960, and fifty-one percent in 1980. For a more detailed discussion, see Phyllis A. Wallace, *Black Women in the Labor Force* (Cambridge: MIT Press, 1980).

20. Angela Davis, "Reflections of the Black Woman's Role in the Community of Slaves," *Black Scholar* 3 (December 1971): 2–16, offers an enlightening discussion of the irony of independence out of subordination. See also Deborah Gray White, *Ar'n't I a Woman? Female Slaves in the Plantation South* (New York: W. W. Norton, 1985), for a more detailed analysis of the contradictions of the black female role in slavery. For a discussion of the role of black women in the family, see Robert Staples, *The Black Woman in America* (Chicago: Nelson Hall, 1973); Robert Hill, *The Strengths of Black Families* (New York: Emerson Hall, 1972); Herbert Guttman, *The Black Family in Slavery and Freedom, 1750 to 1925* (New York: Random House, 1976); Carol Stack, *All Our Kin: Strategies for Survival in a Black Community* (New York: Harper & Row, 1974); and Charles Willie, *A New Look at Black Families* (New York: General Hall, 1976). For a discussion of black women's community roles, see Bettina Aptheker, *Woman's Legacy: Essays on Race, Sex, and Class in American History* (Amherst: University of Massachusetts Press, 1982); Paula Giddings, *When and Where I Enter: The Impact of Black Women on Race and Sex in America* (New York: William Morrow, 1983); Lerner, *Black Women;* Sharon Harley and Rosalyn Terborg-Penn, eds., *The Afro-American Woman: Struggles and Images* (Port Washington, NY: Kennikat Press, 1978); Linda Perkins, "The Impact of the 'Cult of True Womanhood' on the Education of Black Women," *Journal of Social Issues* 39 (1983): 17–28; and the special issue, "The Impact of Black Women in Education," *Journal of Negro Education* 51, no. 3 (Summer 1982).

21. See Robert Staples, "The Myth of the Black Matriarchy," in his *The Black Family: Essays and Studies* (Belmont, CA: Wadsworth, 1971), and *The Black Woman in America.* Also see hooks, *Ain't I a Woman* and Cheryl T. Gilkes, "Black Women's Work as Deviance: Social Sources of Racial Antagonism within Contemporary Feminism," (working paper no. 66, Wellesley, MA: Wellesley College, Center for Research on Women, 1979). However, more recently Robert Staples has argued that black women who are too independent will be unable to find black mates and that black men are justified in their preference for a more traditionally feminine partner ("The Myth of Black Macho: A Response to Angry Black Feminists," *Black Scholar* 10 [March–April 1979]: 24–32).

22. See White, *Ar'n't I a Woman?* and Jacqueline Jones, *Labor of Love, Labor of Sorrow: Black Women, Work and the Family, From Slavery to the Present* (New York: Basic Books, 1985).

23. Michael Albert et al., *Liberating Theory* (Boston: South End Press, 1986), 6.

24. For further discussion of suffrage and racism, see Davis, *Women, Race, and Class;* Giddings, *When and Where I Enter;* Harley and Terborg-Penn, *The*

Afro-American Woman, and Barbara H. Andolsen, *"Daughters of Jefferson, Daughters of Bootblacks": Racism and American Feminism* (Macon, GA: Mercer University Press, 1986).

25. See Gloria Joseph and Jill Lewis, *Common Differences: Conflicts in Black and White Feminist Perspectives* (New York: Avon, 1981); Diane K. Lewis, "A Response to Inequality: Black Women, Racism, and Sexism," *Signs* 3 (1977): 399–61; and bell hooks, *Feminist Theory: From Margin to Center* (Boston: South End Press, 1984), for extended discussions of the dynamics of structural subordination to and social conflict with varying dominant racial and sexual groups.

26. Lewis, "A Response to Inequality," 343.

27. Giddings, *When and Where I Enter;* Harley and Terborg-Penn, *The Afro-American Woman;* and Davis, "Reflections on the Black Woman's Role in the Community of Slaves."

28. See Evans, *Personal Politics;* and Clayborne Carson, *In Struggle: SNCC and the Black Awakening of the 1960s* (Cambridge: Harvard University Press, 1981).

29. Michele Wallace, *Black Macho and the Myth of the Superwoman* (New York: Dial, 1979). See also Linda C. Powell, "Black Macho and Black Feminism," in Smith, *Home Girls,* 283–92, for a critique of Wallace's thesis.

30. For statements by Truth, Stewart, Cooper, Ruffin, and Harper, see Loewenberg and Bogin, *Black Women in Nineteenth-Century American Life;* and Lerner, *Black Woman;* for Lorde, see Lorde, *Sister Outsider;* for Davis, see Davis, *Women, Race, and Class;* for Beale, see Frances Beale, "Double Jeopardy," and "Slave of a Slave No More: Black Women in the Struggle," *Black Scholar* 12, no. 6 (November/December 1981): 16–24; and for Murray, see Pauli Murray, "The Liberation of Black Women," in *Women: A Feminist Perspective,* ed. Jo Freeman (Palo Alto, CA: Mayfield, 1975), 351–63.

31. Regarding the church, see Pauline Terrelonge Stone, "Feminist Consciousness and Black Women," in Freeman, ed., 575–88; Joseph and Lewis, *Common Differences;* Jacqueline Grant, "Black Women and the Church," in *But Some of Us Are Brave: Black Women's Studies,* ed. Gloria T. Hull et al. (Old Westbury, NY: Feminist Press, 1982), 141–52; and Cheryl Townsend Gilkes, " 'Together and in Harness'; Women's Traditions in the Sanctified Church," *Signs* 10 (Summer 1985): 678–99. Concerning politics, see La Rue, *The Black Movement;* Mae C. King,, "The Politics of Sexual Stereotypes," *Black Scholar* 4 (March/April 1973): 12–22; and Manning Marable, *How Capitalism Underdeveloped Black America* (Boston: South End Press, 1983), especially chapter 3. For a discussion of sexual victimization, see Barbara Smith, "Notes for Yet Another Paper on Black Feminism, or Will the Real Enemy Please Stand Up," *Conditions* 5 (1979): 123–27, as well as Joseph and Lewis, *Common Differences.* For a critique of the notion of the matriarch, see Stone, *Feminist Consciousness;* and Staples, "The Myth of the Black Matriarchy."

32. See Murray, "The Liberation of Black Women"; and Stone, *Feminist Consciousness.*

33. Evelyn Brooks Bennett, "Nannie Burroughs and the Education of Black Woman," in Harley and Terborg-Penn, *The Afro-American Woman,* 97–108.

34. Aldon Morris, *The Origins of the Civil Rights Movement: Black Communities Organizing for Change* (New York: Free Press, 1984); and Carson, *In Struggle.*

35. See the recent publication by Jo Ann Gibson Robinson, *The Montgomery Bus Boycott and the Women Who Started It* (Knoxville: University of Tennessee Press, 1987).

36. Cornel West, "The Paradox of the Afro-American Rebellion," in *The Sixties without Apology,* ed. Sohnya Sayres, Anders Stephanson, Stanley Aronowitz, and Fredric Jameson (Minneapolis: University of Minnesota Press, 1984).

37. Lorde, *Sister Outsider,* especially 66–71; hooks, *Feminist Theory;* Linda Burnham, "Has Poverty Been Feminized in Black America?" *Black Scholar* 16, no. 2 (March/April 1985): 14–24; and Maria C. Lugones and Elizabeth V. Spelman, "Have We Got a Theory for You! Feminist Theory, Cultural Imperialism and the Demand for 'The Woman's Voice,' " *Women's Studies International Forum* 6, no. 6 (1983): 573–81.

38. Davis, *Women, Race, and Class,* 53–54.

39. Andolsen, *"Daughters of Jefferson,"* 78.

40. Giddings, *When and Where I Enter,* 348.

41. Mary Frances Berry, *Why ERA Failed: Politics, Women's Rights, and the Amending Process of the Constitution* (Bloomington: Indiana University Press, 1986).

42. Lewis, "A Response to Inequality."

43. Karen Kollias, "Class Realities: Create a New Power Base," in *Building Feminist Theory: Essays from Quest,* ed. *Quest* staff (New York: Longman, 1981), 125–38, especially 134.

44. Brenda Eichelberger, "Voices on Black Feminism," *Quest: A Feminist Quarterly* 4 (1977): 16–28, especially 15.

45. Burnham, "Has Poverty Been Feminized?" 15.

46. For discussion of women, employment, and the labor movement, see Diane Balser, *Sisterhood and Solidarity: Feminism and Labor in Modern Times* (Boston: South End Press, 1987); Carol Groneman and Mary Beth Norton, eds., *"To Toil the Livelong Day": America's Women at Work, 1780–1980* (Ithaca, NY: Cornell University Press, 1987); Philip S. Foner, *Women and the American Labor Movement: From World War I to the Present* (New York: Free Press, 1980); Bettina Berch, *The Endless Day: The Political Economy of Women and Work* (New York: Harcourt Brace Jovanovich, 1982); and Mary Frank Fox and Sharlene Hesse-Biber, *Women at Work* (Palo Alto, CA: Mayfield, 1984). For blacks, see Marable, *How Capitalism Underdeveloped;* Richard Polenberg, *One Nation Divisible: Class, Race, and Ethnicity in the United States since 1938* (New York: Penguin, 1980); Philip S. Foner, *Organized Labor and the Black Worker, 1619–1973* (New York: International Publishers, 1976); and Dorothy K. Newman et al., *Protest, Politics, and Prosperity; Black Americans and White Institutions, 1940–75* (New York: Pantheon, 1978).

47. See Balser, *Sisterhood and Solidarity,* for a detailed consideration of the contemporary union activities of women, especially their efforts to organize clerical and other pink collar-workers.

48. See Jones, *Labor of Love;* Giddings, *When and Where I Enter;* and Davis, *Women, Race, and Class,* for an examination of black women's work roles and labor activism.

49. See Delores Janiewski, "Seeking 'a New Day and a New Way': Black Women and Unions in the Southern Tobacco Industry"; and Elizabeth Clark-Lewis, " 'This Work Had a End': African-American Domestic Workers in Washington, D.C., 1910–1940," both in Groneman and Norton, *"To Toil the Livelong Day."*

50. Heidi Hartmann and Zillah Eisenstein provide theoretical critiques of monist Marxism as an adequate avenue for women's liberation. Both Lydia Sargent and Sara Evans detail the sexual politics of the Left (see Heidi Hartmann, "The Unhappy Marriage of Marxism and Feminism," in Sargent, *Woman and Revolution;* Eisenstein, "Reform and/or Revolution: Toward a Unified Women's Movement," in Sargent, *Woman and Revolution,* 339–62; Sargent, "New Left Women and Men: The Honeymoon Is Over," in Sargent, *Woman and Revolution,* xi–xxxii; and Evans, *Personal Politics*).

51. See Combahee River Collective, *Combahee River Collective Statement: Black Feminist Organizing in the Seventies and Eighties* (New York: Kitchen Table Press, 1986), 12–13.

52. Marable, *How Capitalism Underdeveloped.*

53. Joseph and Lewis, *Common Differences,* 38.

54. Lewis, "A Response to Inequality," 341.

55. For information on the development of black feminist scholarship and academic programs, see Patricia Bell Scott, "Selective Bibliography on Black Feminism" in Hull et al., *But Some of Us Are Brave;* Black Studies/Women's Studies Faculty Development Project, "Black Studies/Women's Studies: An Overdue Partnership" (Women's Studies, University of Massachusetts, Amherst, 1983, mimeographed); Nancy Conklin et al., "The Culture of Southern Black Women: Approaches and Materials" (University: University of Alabama Archives of American Minority Cultures and Women's Studies Program, Project on the Culture of Southern Black Women, 1983); the premiere issue *SAGE: A Scholarly Journal on Black Women* 1, no. 1 (Spring 1984); and the establishment of Kitchen Table: A Women of Color Press, New York. The Center for Research on Women at Memphis State University, the Women's Research and Resource Center at Spelman College, and the Minority Women's Program at Wellesley College are among the academic centers.

56. See Andrew Cherlin and Pamela Waters, "Trends in United States Men's and Women's Sex-Role Attitudes: 1972–1978," *American Sociological Review* 46 (1981): 453–60. See also, Janice Gump, "Comparative Analysis of Black Women's and White Women's Sex-role Attitudes," *Journal of Consulting and Clinical Psychology* 43 (1975): 858–63; and Marjorie Hershey, "Racial Difference in Sex-Role Identities and Sex Stereotyping: Evidence against a Common Assumption," *Social Science Quarterly* 58 (1978): 583–96. For various opinion polls, see "The 1972 Virginia Slims American Women's Opinion Poll" and "The 1974 Virginia Slims American Women's Opinion Poll," conducted by the Roper Organization (Williamstown, MA: Roper Public Opinion Research Center, 1974). See Barbara Everitt Bryant, "American Women: Today and Tomorrow," National Commission on the Observance of International Women's Year (Washington, D.C.: GPO, March 1977). Gloria Steinem, "Exclusive Louis Harris Survey: How Women Live, Vote and Think," *Ms.* 13 (July 1984): 51–54.

57. For analyses of the influence of socioeconomic class and race on feminist attitudes, see Willa Mae Hemmons, "The Women's Liberation Movement: Understanding Black Women's Attitudes," in *The Black Woman,* ed. LaFrances Rodgers-Rose (Beverly Hills, CA: Sage Publications, 1980), 285–99; and Ransford and Miller, "Race, Sex, and Feminist Outlook."

Jacquelyn Grant

Jacquelyn Grant is among a small group of "womanist" scholars doing pioneering work in theology. She teaches systematic theology at the Interdenominational Theological Center in Atlanta, Georgia, and is founding director of Black Women in Church and Society, a program that focuses on black women's leadership development and the enhancement of participation of black women in the church. "Black Theology and the Black Woman," which appeared in *Black Theology: A Documentary History* (1979), is an early essay on sexism in the black church. Grant's most significant publication is *White Women's Christ and Black Women's Jesus: Feminist Christology and Womanist Response* (1989), in which she articulates her own womanist theology.

Jacquelyn Grant }

BLACK THEOLOGY AND THE
BLACK WOMAN

Liberation theologies have arisen out of the contexts of the liberation struggles of black Americans, Latin Americans, American women, black South Africans, and Asians. These theologies represent a departure from traditional Christian theology. As a collective critique, liberation theologies raise serious questions about the normative use of Scripture, tradition and experience in Christian theology. Liberation theologians assert that the reigning theologies of the West have been used to legitimate the established order. Those to whom the church has entrusted the task of interpreting the meaning of God's activity in the world have been too content to represent the ruling classes. For this reason, say the liberation theologians, theology has generally not spoken to those who are opposed by the political establishment.

Ironically, the criticism that liberation theology makes against classical theology has been turned against liberation theology itself. Just as most European and American theologians have acquiesced in the oppression of the West, for which they have been taken to task by liberation theologians, some liberation theologians have acquiesced in one or more oppressive aspects of the liberation struggle itself. Where racism is rejected, sexism has been embraced. Where classism is called into question, racism and sexism have been tolerated. And where sexism is repudiated, racism and classism are often ignored.

Although there is a certain validity to the argument that any one analysis —race, class, or sex—is not sufficiently universal to embrace the needs of all oppressed peoples, these particular analyses, nonetheless, have all been well presented and are crucial for a comprehensive and authentic liberation theology. In order for liberation theology to be faithful to itself, it must hear the critique coming to it from the perspective of the black woman— perhaps the most oppressed of all the oppressed.

I am concerned in this essay with how the experience of the black woman calls into question certain assumptions in liberation theology in general, and black theology in particular. In the Latin American context, this has already been done by women such as Beatriz Melano Couch and Consuelo Urquiza. A few Latin American theologians have begun to respond. Beatriz Couch, for example, accepts the starting point of Latin American theologians, but criticizes them for their exclusivism with respect to race and sex. She says:

> ...we in Latin America stress the importance of the starting point, the praxis, and the use of social science to analyze our political, historical situation. In this I am in full agreement with my male colleagues... with one qualitative difference. I stress the need to give importance to the different cultural forms that express oppression; to the ideology that divides people not only according to class, but to race, to sex. Racism and sexism are oppressive ideologies, which deserve a specific treatment in the theology of liberation.[1]

More recently, Consuelo Urquiza called for the unification of Hispanic American women in struggling against their oppression in the church and society. In commenting on the contradiction in the Pauline Epistles that undergird the oppression of the Hispanic American woman, Urquiza said: "At the present time all Christians will agree with Paul in the first part of [Galatians 3:28] about freedom and slavery that there should not be slaves. ...However, the next part of this verse... has been ignored, and the equality between man and woman is not accepted. They would rather skip that line and go to the epistle to Timothy [2:9–15]."[2] Women theologians of Latin background are beginning to do theology and to sensitize other women to the necessity of participating in decisions that affect their lives and the life of their communities. Latin American theology will gain from these inputs, which women are making to the theological process.

Third World and black women[3] in the United States will soon collaborate in an attack on another aspect of liberation theology—feminist theology. Black and Third World women have begun to articulate their differences and similarities with the feminist movement, which is dominated by white American women who until now have been the chief authors of feminist theology. It is my contention that the theological perspectives of black and Third World women should reflect these differences and similarities with feminist theology. It is my purpose, however, to look critically at black theology as a black woman in an effort to determine how adequate is its conception of liberation for the total black community. Pauli Murray and Theressa Hoover have in their own ways challenged black theology. Because their articles appear in this section (documents 39 and 37), it is unnecessary for me to explain their point of view. They have spoken for themselves.

I want to begin with the question: "Where are black women in black theology?" They are, in fact, invisible in black theology, and we need to know why this is the case. Because the black church experience and black experience in general are important sources for doing black theology, we need to look at the black woman in relation to both in order to understand the way black theology has applied its conception of liberation. Finally, in view of the status of the black woman vis-à-vis black theology, the black church and the black experience, a challenge needs to be presented to black theology. This is how I propose to discuss this important question.

THE INVISIBILITY OF BLACK WOMEN IN BLACK THEOLOGY

In examining black theology, it is necessary to make one of two assumptions: (1) either black women have no place in the enterprise, or (2) black men are capable of speaking for us. Both of these assumptions are false and need to be discarded. They arise out of a male-dominated culture, which restricts women to certain areas of the society. In such a culture, men are given the warrant to speak for women on all matters of significance. It is no accident that all of the recognized black theologians are men. This is what might be expected, given the status and power accorded the discipline of theology. Professional theology is done by those who are highly trained. It requires, moreover, mastery of that power most accepted in the definition of manhood, the power or ability to "reason." This is supposedly what opens the door to participation in logical, philosophical debates and discussions presupposing rigorous intellectual training, for most of history, outside the "woman's sphere." Whereas the nature of men has been defined in terms of reason and the intellect, that of women has to do with intuition and emotionalism. Women were limited to matters related to the home while men carried out the more important work, involving the use of the rational faculties.[4] These distinctions were not as clear in the slave community.[5] Slaves and women were thought to share the characteristics of emotionality and irrationality. As we move further away from the slave culture, however, a dualism between black men and women increasingly emerges. This means that black males have gradually increased their power and participiation in the male-dominated society, while black females have continued to endure the stereotypes and oppressions of an earlier period.

When sexual dualism has fully run its course in the black community (and I believe that it has), it will not be difficult to see why black women are invisible in black theology. Just as white women formerly had no place in white theology—except as the receptors of white men's theological interpretations—black women have had no place in the development of black theology. By self-appointment, or by the sinecure of a male-dominated society, black men have deemed it proper to speak for the entire black community, male and female.

In a sense, black men's acceptance of the patriarchal model is logical and to be expected. Black male slaves were unable to reap the benefits of patriarchy. Before emancipation they were not given the opportunity to serve as protector and provider for black women and children, as white men were able to do for their women and children. Much of what was considered "manhood" had to do with how well one could perform these functions. It seems only natural that the post-emancipation black men would view as of primary importance the reclaiming of their property— their women and their children. Moreover, it is natural that black men would claim their "natural" right to the "man's world." But it should be emphasized that this is logical and natural only if one has accepted without question the terms and values of patriarchy—the conept of male control and supremacy.

Black men must ask themselves a difficult question. How can a white society characterized by black enslavement, colonialism, and imperialism provide the normative conception of women for black society? How can the sphere of the woman, as defined by white men, be free from the evils and oppressions that are found in the white society? The important point is that in matters relative to the relationship between the sexes, black men have accepted without question the patriarchal structures of the white society as normative for the black community. How can a black minister preach in a way that advocates St. Paul's dictum concerning women while ignoring or repudiating his dictum concerning slaves? Many black women are enraged as they listen to "liberated" black men speak about the "place of women" in words and phrases similar to those of the very white oppressors they condemn.

Black women have been invisible in theology because theological scholarship has not been a part of the woman's sphere. The first of the above two assumptions results, therefore, from the historical orientation of the dominant culture. The second follows from the first. If women have no place in theology it becomes the natural prerogative of men to monopolize theological concerns, including those relating specifically to women. Inasmuch as black men have accepted the sexual dualisms of the dominant culture, they presume to speak for black women.

Before finally dismissing the two assumptions, a pertinent question should be raised. Does the absence of black women in the circles producing black theology necessarily mean that the resultant theology cannot be in the best interest of black women? The answer is obvious. Feminist theologians during the past few years have shown how theology done by men in male-dominated cultures has served to undergird patriarchal structures in society.[6] If black men have accepted those structures, is there any reason to believe that the theology written by black men would be any more liberating of black women than white theology was for white women? It would seem that in view of the oppression that black people have suffered, black men would be particularly sensitive to the oppression of others.

James Cone has stated that the task of black theology "is to analyze the nature of the gospel of Jesus Christ in the light of oppressed black people so they will see the gospel as inseparable from their humiliated condition, bestowing on them the necessary power to break the chains of oppression. This means that it is a theology of and for the black community, seeking to interpret the religious dimensions of the forces of liberation in that community."[8] What are the forces of liberation in the black community and the black church? Are they to be exclusively defined by the struggle against racism? My answer to that question is No. There are oppressive realities in the black community that are related to, but independent of, the fact of racism. Sexism is one such reality. Black men seek to liberate themselves from racial stereotypes and the conditions of oppression without giving due attention to the stereotypes and oppressions against women, which parallel those against blacks. Blacks fight to be free of the stereotype that all blacks are dirty and ugly, or that black represents evil and darkness.[9] The slogan "Black is Beautiful" was a counterattack on these stereotypes. The parallel for women is the history of women as "unclean," especially during menstruation and after childbirth. Because the model of beauty in the white male-dominated society is the "long-haired blonde," with all that goes along with that mystique, black women have an additional problem with the Western idea of "ugliness," particularly as they encounter black men who have adopted this white model of beauty. Similarly, the Christian teaching that woman is responsible for the fall of *mankind* and is, therefore, the source of evil has had a detrimental effect in the experience of black women.

Like all oppressed peoples, the self-image of blacks has suffered damage. In addition they have not been in control of their own destiny. It is the goal of the black liberation struggle to change radically the socioeconomic and political conditions of black people by inculcating self-love, self-control, self-reliance, and political power. The concepts of self-love, self-control, self-reliance, and political participation certainly have broad significance for black women, even though they were taught that, by virtue of their sex, they had to be completely dependent on *man;* yet while their historical situation reflected the need for dependence, the powerlessness of black men made it necessary for them to seek those values for themselves.

Racism and sexism are interrelated just as all forms of oppression are interrelated. Sexism, however, has a reality and significance of its own because it represents that peculiar form of oppression suffered by black women at the hands of black men. It is important to examine this reality of sexism as it operated in both the black community and the black church.

We will consider first the black church and secondly the black community to determine to what extent black theology has measured up to its defined task with respect to the liberation of black women.[10]

THE BLACK CHURCH AND THE BLACK WOMAN

I can agree with Karl Barth as he describes the peculiar function of theology as the church's "subjecting herself to a self-test." "She [the church] faces herself with the question of truth, i.e., she measures her action, her language about God, against her existence as a church."[11]

On the one hand, black theology must continue to criticize classical theology and the white church. But on the other hand, black theology must subject the black church to a "self-test." The task of the church, according to James Cone, is threefold: (1) "It proclaims the reality of divine liberation. . . . It is not possible to receive the good news of freedom and also keep it to ourselves; it must be told to the whole world. . . ." (2) "It actively shares in the liberation struggle." (3) It "is a visible manifestation that the gospel is a reality. . . . If it [the church] lives according to the old order (as it usually has), then no one will believe its message."[12] It is clear that black theology must ask whether or not the black church is faithful to this task. Moreover, the language of the black church about God must be consistent with its action.[13] These requirements of the church's faithfulness in the struggle for liberation have not been met as far as the issue of women is concerned.

If the liberation of women is not proclaimed, the church's proclamation cannot be about divine liberation. If the church does not share in the liberation struggle of black women, its liberation struggle is not authentic. If women are oppressed, the church cannot possibly be "a visible manifestation that the gospel is a reality"—for the gospel cannot be real in that context. One can see the contradictions between the church's language or proclamation of liberation and its action by looking both at the status of black women in the church as laity and black women in the ordained ministry of the church.

It is often said that women are the "backbone" of the church. On the surface this may appear to be a compliment, especially when one considers the function of the backbone in the human anatomy. Theressa Hoover prefers to use the term "glue" to describe the function of women in the black church. In any case, the telling portion of the word backbone is "back." It has become apparent to me that most of the ministers who use this term have reference to location rather than function. What they really mean is that women are in the "background" and should be kept there. They are merely support workers. This is borne out by my observation that in many churches women are consistently given responsibilities in the kitchen, while men are elected or appointed to the important boards and leadership positions. While decisions and policies may be discussed in the kitchen, they are certainly not made there. Recently I conducted a study in one conference of the African Methodist Episcopal Church, which indicated that women are accorded greater participation on the decision-making boards of smaller rather than larger churches.[14] This political maneuver helps to keep women "in their place" in the denomination as well as as in the local congregations. The conspiracy to keep women relegated to the background is also aided by the continuous psychological and political strategizing that keeps women from realizing their own potential power in the church. Not only are they rewarded for performance in "backbone" or supportive positions, but they are penalized for trying to move from the backbone to the head position—the leadership of the church. It is by considering the distinction between prescribed support positions and the policy-making, leadership positions that the oppression of black women in the black church can be seen more clearly.

For the most part, men have monopolized the ministry as a profession. The ministry of women as fully ordained clergypersons has always been controversial. The black church fathers were unable to see the injustices of their own practices, even when they paralleled the injustices in the white church against which they rebelled.

In the early nineteenth century, the Rev. Richard Allen perceived that it was unjust for blacks, free and slaves, to be relegated to the balcony and restricted to a special time to pray and kneel at the communion table; for this he should be praised. Yet because of his acceptance of the patriarchal system, Allen was unable to see the injustice in relegating women to one area of the church—the pews—by withholding ordination from women as he did in the case of Mrs. Jarena Lee.[15] Lee recorded Allen's response when she informed him of her call to "go preach the Gospel":

> He replied by asking in what sphere I wished to move in? I said, among the Methodists. He then replied, that a Mrs. Cook, a Methodist lady, had also some time before requested the same privilege; who it was believed, had done much good in the way of *exhortation,* and *holding prayer meetings;* and who had been permitted to do so by the *verbal license* of the preacher in charge at the time. But as to women preaching, he said that our Discipline knew nothing at all about it—that *it did not call* for women preachers.[16]

Because of this response, Jarena Lee's preaching ministry was delayed for eight years. She was not unaware of the sexist injustice in Allen's response. "Oh how careful ought we be, lest through our by-laws of church government and discipline, we bring into disrepute even the word of life. For as unseemly as it may appear nowadays for a woman to preach, it should be remembered that nothing is impossible with God. And why should it be thought impossible, heterodox, or improper for a woman to preach, seeing the Saviour died for the woman as well as the man?"[17]

Another "colored minister of the gospel," Elizabeth, was greatly troubled over her call to preach, or more accurately, over the response of men to her call to preach. She said: "I often felt that I was unfit to assemble with the congregation with whom I had gathered.... I felt that I was despised on account of this gracious calling, and was looked upon as a speckled bird by the ministers to whom I looked for instruction ... some [of the ministers] would cry out, 'you are an enthusiast,' and others said, 'the Discipline did not allow of any such division of work.'"[18] Sometime later when questioned about her authority to preach against slavery and her ordination status, she responded that she preached "not by the commission of men's hands: if the Lord had ordained me, I needed nothing better."[19] With this commitment to God rather than to a male-dominated church structure, she led a fruitful ministry.

Mrs. Amanda Berry Smith, like Mrs. Jarena Lee, had to conduct her ministry outside the structures of the A.M.E. Church. Smith described herself as a "plain Christian woman" with "no money" and "no prominence."[20] But she was intrigued with the idea of attending the General Conference of 1872 in Nashville, Tennessee. Her inquiry into the cost of going to Nashville brought the following comments from some of the A.M.E. brethren:

> "I tell you, Sister, it will cost money to go down there; and if you ain't got plenty of it, it's no use to go"; ... another said:
> "What does she want to go for?"
> "Woman preacher; they want to be ordained," was the reply.
> "I mean to fight that thing," said the other.
> "Yes, indeed, so will I," said another.[21]

The oppression of women in the ministry took many forms. In addition to not being granted ordination, the authenticity of "the call" of women was frequently put to the test. Lee, Elizabeth, and Smith spoke of the many souls they had brought to Christ through their preaching and singing in local black congregations, as well as in white and mixed congregations. It was not until Bishop Richard Allen heard Jarena Lee preach that he was convinced that she was of the Spirit. He, however, still refused to ordain her. The "brethren," including some bishops of the 1872 General Conference of the A.M.E. Church, were convinced that Amanda Berry Smith was blessed with the Spirit of God after hearing her sing at a session held at Fisk University. Smith tells us that "... the Spirit of the Lord seemed to fall on all the people. The preachers got happy...." This experience brought invitations for her to preach at several churches, but it did not bring an appointment to a local congregation as pastor or the right of ordination.

She summed up the experience in this way: "... after that many of my brethren believed in me, especially as the question of ordination of women never was mooted in the Conference."[22]

Several black denominations have since begun to ordain women.[23] But this matter of women preachers having the extra burden of proving their call to an extent not required of men still prevails in the black church today. A study in which I participated at Union Theological Seminary in New York City bears this out. Interviews with black ministers of different denominations revealed that their prejudices against women, and especially women in the ministry, resulted in unfair expectations and unjust treatment of women ministers whom they encountered.[24]

It is the unfair expectations placed upon women and blatant discrimination that keeps them "in the pew" and "out of the pulpit." This matter of keeping women in the pew has been carried to ridiculous extremes. At the 1971 Annual Convocation of the National Conference of Black Churchmen,[25] held at the Liberty Baptist Church in Chicago, I was slightly amused when, as I approached the pulpit to place my cassette tape recorder near the speaker, Walter Fauntroy, as several brothers had already done, I was stopped by a man who informed me that I could not enter the pulpit area. When I asked why not, he directed me to the pastor who told me that women were not permitted in the pulpit, but that he would have a man place the recorder there for me. Although I could not believe that explanation a serious one, I agreed to have a man place it on the pulpit for me and returned to my seat in the sanctuary for the continuation of the convocation. The seriousness of the pastor's statement became clear to me later at that meeting when Mary Jane Patterson, a Presbyterian Church executive, was refused the right to speak from the pulpit.[26] This was clearly a case of sex discrimination in a black church—keeping women "in the pew" and "out of the pulpit."

As far as the issue of women is concerned, it is obvious that the black church described by C. Eric Lincoln has not fared much better than the Negro church of E. Franklin Frazier.[27] The failure of the black church and black theology to proclaim explicitly the liberation of black women indicates that they cannot claim to be agents of divine liberation. If the theology, like the church, has no word for black women, its conception of liberation is inauthentic.

THE BLACK EXPERIENCE AND THE BLACK WOMAN

For the most part, black church*men* have not dealt with the oppression of black women in either the black church or the black community. Frederick Douglass was one notable exception in the nineteenth century. His active advocacy for women's rights was a demonstration against the contradiction between preaching "justice for all" and practicing the continued oppression of women. He, therefore, "dared not claim a right [for himself] which he would not concede to women."[28] These words describe the convictions of a man who was active both in the church and in the larger black community. This is significant because there is usually a direct relationship between what goes on in the black church and the black secular community.

The status of black women in the community parallels that of black women in the church. Black theology considers the black experience to be the context out of which its questions about God and human existence are formulated. This is assumed to be the context in which God's revelation is received and interpreted. Only from the perspective of the poor and the oppressed can theology be adequately done. Arising out of the Black Power movement of the 1960s, black theology purports to take seriously the experience of the larger community's struggle for liberation. But if this is, indeed, the case, black theology must function in the secular community in the same way as it should function in the church community. It must serve as a "self-test" to see whether the rhetoric or proclamation of the black community's struggle for liberation is consistent with its practices. How does the "self-test" principle operate among the poor and the oppressed? Certainly black theology has spoken to some of the forms of oppression that exist within the community of the oppressed. Many of the injustices it has attacked are the same as those that gave rise to the prophets of the Old Testament. But the fact that black theology does not include sexism specifically as one of those injustices is all too evident. It suggests that the theologians do not understand sexism to be one of the oppressive realities of the black community. Silence on this specific issue can only mean conformity with the status quo. The most prominent black theologian, James Cone, has recently broken this silence. "The black church, like all other churches, is a male-dominated church. The difficulty that black male ministers have in supporting the equality of women in the church and society stems partly from the lack of a clear liberation-criterion rooted in the gospel and in the present struggles of oppressed peoples.... It is truly amazing that many black male ministers, young and old, can hear the message of liberation in the gospel when related to racism but remain deaf to a similar message in the context of sexism...."[29] It is difficult to understand how black men manage to exclude the liberation of black women from their interpretation of the liberating gospel. Any correct analysis of the poor and oppressed would reveal some interesting and inescapable facts about the situation of women within oppressed groups. Without succumbing to the long and fruitless debate of "who is more oppressed than whom?" I want to make some pointed suggestions to black male theologians.

It would not be very difficult to argue that since black women are the poorest of the poor, the most oppressed of the oppressed, their experience provides a most fruitful context for doing black theology. The research of Jacquelyne Jackson attests to the extreme deprivation of black women. Jackson supports her claim with statistical data that "in comparison with black males and white males and females, black women yet constitute the most disadvantaged group in the United States, as evidenced especially by their largely unenviable educational, occupational, employment, and income levels, and availability of marital partners."[30] In other words, in spite of the "quite insignificant" educational advantage that black women have over black men, they have "had the greatest access to the worst jobs at the lowest earnings."[31] It is important to emphasize this fact in order to elevate to its rightful level of concern the condition of black women, not only in the world at large, but in the black community and the black church. It is my contention that if black theology speaks of the black community as if the special problems of black women do not exist, it is no different from the white theology it claims to reject precisely because of its inability to take account of the existence of black people in its theological formulations.

It is instructive to note that the experience of black women working in the Black Power movement further accented the problem of the oppression of women in the black community. Because of their invisibility in the leadership of the movement they, like women of the church, provided the "support" segment of the movement. They filled the streets when numbers were needed for demonstrations. They stuffed the envelopes in the offices and performed other menial tasks. Kathleen Cleaver, in a *Black Scholar* interview, revealed some of the problems in the movement that caused her to become involved in women's liberation issues. While underscoring the crucial role played by women as Black Power activists, Kathleen Cleaver, nonetheless, acknowledged the presence of sex discrimination.

> I viewed myself as assisting everything that was done.... The form of assistance that women give in political movements to men is just as crucial as the leadership that men give to those movements. And this is something that is never recognized and never dealt with. *Because women are always relegated to assistance,* and this is where I became interested in the liberation of women. Conflicts, constant conflicts came up, conflicts that would rise as a result of the fact that I was married to a member of the Central Committee and I was also an officer in the Party. Things that I would have suggested myself would be implemented. But if I suggested them the suggestion might be rejected. If they were suggested by a man, the suggestion would be implemented.
>
> It seemed throughout the history of my working with the Party, I always had to struggle with this. The suggestion itself was never viewed objectively. *The fact that the suggestion came from a woman gave it some lesser value.* And it seemed that it had something to do with the egos of the men involved. I know that the first demonstration that we had at the courthouse for Huey Newton I was very instrumental in organizing; the first time we went out on

the soundtrucks, I was on the soundtrucks; the first leaflet we put out, I wrote; the first demonstration, I made up the pamphlets. And the members of that demonstration for the most part were women. I've noticed that throughout my dealings in the black movement in the United States, that the *most anxious, the most eager, the most active, the most quick to understand the problem and quick to move are women.*[32]

Cleaver exposed the fact that even when leadership was given to women, sexism lurked in the wings. As executive secretary of the Student Nonviolent Coordinating Committee (SNCC), Ruby Doris Robinson was described as the "heartbeat of SNCC." Yet there were "the constant conflicts, the constant struggles that she was subjected to because she was a woman."[33]

Notwithstanding all the evidence to the contrary, some might want to argue that the central problem of black women is related to their race and not their sex. Such an argument then presumes that the problem cannot be resolved apart from the black struggle. I contend that as long as the black struggle refuses to recognize and deal with its sexism, the idea that women will receive justice from that struggle alone will never work. It will not work because black women will no longer allow black men to ignore their unique problems and needs in the name of some distorted view of the "liberation of the total community." I would bring to the minds of the proponents of this argument the words of President Sekou Toure as he wrote about the role of African women in the revolution. He said, 'If African women cannot possibly conduct their struggle in isolation from the struggle that our people wage for African liberation, African freedom, conversely, is not effective unless it brings about the liberation of African women."[34] Black men who have an investment in the patriarchal structure of white America and who intend to do Christian theology have yet to realize that if Jesus is liberator of the oppressed, all of the oppressed must be liberated. Perhaps the proponents of the argument that the cause of black women must be subsumed under a larger cause should look to South African theologians Sabelo Ntwasa and Basil Moore. They affirm that "black theology, as it struggles to formulate a theology of liberation relevant to South Africa, cannot afford to perpetuate any form of domination, not even male domination. If its liberation is not human enough to include the liberation of women, it will not be liberation."[35]

A CHALLENGE TO BLACK THEOLOGY

My central argument is this: black theology cannot continue to treat black women as if they were invisible creatures who are on the outside looking into the black experience, the black church, and the black theological enterprise. It will have to deal with the community of believers in all aspects as integral parts of the whole community. Black theology, therefore, must speak to the bishops who hide behind the statement, "Women don't want women pastors." It must speak to the pastors who say, "My church isn't ready for women preachers yet." It must teach the seminarians who feel that "women have no place in seminary." It must address the women in the church and community who are content and complacent with their oppression. It must challenge the educators who would reeducate the people on every issue except the issue of the dignity and equality of women.

Black women represent more than fifty percent of the black community and more than seventy percent of the black church. How then can an authentic theology of liberation arise out of these communities without specifically addressing the liberation of the women in both places? Does the fact that certain questions are raised by black women make them any less black concerns? If, as I contend, the liberation of black men and women is inseparable, then a radical split cannot be made between racism and sexism. Black women are oppressed by racism *and* sexism. It is therefore necessary that black men and women be actively involved in combating both evils.

Only as black women in greater numbers make their way from the background to the forefront will the true strength of the black community be fully realized. There is already a heritage of strong black women and men upon which a stronger nation can be built. There is a tradition that declares that God is at work in the experience of the black woman. This tradition, in the context of the total black experience, can provide data for the development of a holistic black theology. Such a theology will repudiate the God of classical theology who is presented as an absolute Patriarch, a deserting father who created black men and women and then "walked out" in the face of responsibility. Such a theology will look at the meaning of the total Jesus Christ Event; it will consider not only how God through Jesus Christ is related to the oppressed men, but to women as well. Such a theology will "allow" God through the Holy Spirit to work through persons without regard to race, sex, or class. This theology will exercise its prophetic function, and serve as a "self-test" in a church characterized by the sins of racism, sexism, and other forms of oppression. Until black women theologians are fully participating in the theological enterprise, it is important to keep black male theologians and black leaders cognizant of their dereliction. They must be made aware of the fact that black women are needed not only as Christian educators, but as theologians and church leaders. It is only when black women and men share jointly the leadership in theology and in the church and community that the black nation will become strong and liberated. Only then will there be the possibility that black theology can become a theology of divine liberation.

One final word for those who argue that the issues of racism and sexism are too complicated and should not be confused. I agree that the issues should not be "confused." But the elimination of both racism and sexism is so crucial for the liberation of black persons that we cannot shrink from facing them together. Sojourner Truth tells us why this is so. In 1867, she spoke out on the issue of suffrage, and what she said at that time is still relevant to us as we deal with the liberation of black women today.

> I feel that if I have to answer for the deeds done in my body just as much as a man, I have a right to have just as much as a man. There is a great stir about colored men getting their rights, but not a word about the colored women; and if colored men get their rights, and not colored women theirs, you see the colored men will be masters over the women, and it will be just as bad as it was before. So I am for keeping the whole thing going while things are stirring: because if we wait till it is still, it will take a great while to get it going again....[36]

Black women have to keep the issue of sexism "going" in the black community, in the black church, and in black theology until it has been eliminated. To do otherwise means that they will be pushed aside until eternity. Therefore, with Sojourner Truth, I'm for "keeping things going while things are stirring...."

ENDNOTES

1. Beatriz Melano Couch, remarks on the feminist panel of Theology in the Americas Conference in Detroit in August 1975, printed in *Theology in the Americas,* ed. Sergio Torres and John Eagleson (Maryknoll, NY: Orbis Books, 1976), 375.

2. Consuelo Urquiza, "A Message from a Hispanic American Woman," *The Fifth Commission: A Monitor for Third World Concerns* IV (June-July 1978), insert. The Fifth Commission is a commission of the National Council of the Churches of Christ in the USA (NCC), 475 Riverside Drive, New York, N.Y.

3. I agree with the Fifth Commission that "the Third World is not a geographic entity, but rather the world of oppressed peoples in their struggle for liberation." In this sense, black women are included in the term "Third World." However, in order to accent the peculiar identity, problems, and needs of black women in the First World or the Third World contexts, I choose to make the distinction between black and other Third World women.

4. For a discussion of sexual dualisms in our society, see Rosemary Ruether, *New Women/New Earth* (New York: Seabury Press, 1975), chapter 1; and *Liberation Theology* (New York: Paulist Press, 1972), 16 ff. Also for a discussion of sexual (social) dualisms as related to the brain hemispheres, see Sheila Collins, *A Different Heaven and Earth* (Valley Forge: Judson Press, 1974), 169–70.

5. Angela Davis, "Reflections on the Black Woman's Role in the Community of Slaves," *Black Scholar* 4, no. 3 (December 1971): 3–15. I do take issue with Davis's point, however. The black community may have experienced "equality in inequality," but this was forced on them from the dominant or enslaving community. She does not deal with the inequality within the community itself.

6. See Sheila Collins, *A Different Heaven;* Rosemary Ruether, *New Woman;* Letty Russell, *Human Liberation in the Feminist Perspective* (Philadelphia:

Westminster Press, 1974); and Mary Daly, *Beyond God the Father* (Boston: Beacon Press, 1973).

7. Surely the factor of race would be absent, but one would have to do an in-depth analysis to determine the possible effect on the status of black women.

8. James Cone, *A Black Theology of Liberation* (Philadelphia: J. B. Lippincott, 1970), 23.

9. Eulalio Baltazar discusses color symbolism (white is good; black is evil) as a reflection of racism in the white theology that perpetuates it. *The Dark Center: A Process Theology of Blackness* (New York: Paulist Press, 1973).

10. One may want to argue that black theology is not concerned with sexism but with racism. I will argue in this essay that such a theology could speak only half the truth, if truth at all.

11. Karl Barth, *Church Dogmatics,* vol. 1, part 1, 2.

12. Cone, *A Black Theology,* 230–32.

13. James Cone and Albert Cleage do make this observation of the contemporary black church and its response to the struggles against racism. See Cleage, *The Black Messiah* (New York: Sheed and Ward, 1969); and Cone, *A Black Theology.*

14. A study that I conducted in the Philadelphia Conference of the African Methodist Episcopal Church, May 1976. It also included sporadic samplings of churches in other conferences in the First Episcopal District. As for example, a church of 1,660 members (500 men and 1,160 women) had a trustee board of 8 men and 1 woman and a steward board of 13 men and 6 women. A church of 100 members (35 men and 65 women) had a trustee board of 5 men and 4 women and a steward board of 5 men and 4 women.

15. Jarena Lee, *The Life and Religious Experiences of Jarena Lee: A Colored Lady Giving an Account of Her Call to Preach the Gospel* (Philadelphia, 1836), in *Early Negro Writing 1760–1837,* ed. Dorothy Porter (Boston: Beacon Press, 1971), 494–514.

16. Ibid., 503 (italics added): Carol George in *Segregated Sabbaths* (New York: Oxford University Press, 1973) presents a very positive picture of the relationship between Jarena Lee and Bishop Richard Allen. She feels that by the time Lee approached Allen, he had "modified his views on women's rights" (129). She contends that since Allen was free from the Methodist Church he was able to "determine his own policy" with respect to women under the auspices of the A.M.E. Church. It should be noted that Bishop Allen accepted the Rev. Jarena Lee as a woman preacher and not as an ordained preacher with full rights and privileges thereof. Even Carol George admitted that Lee traveled with Bishop Allen only "as an unofficial member of their delegation to conference sessions in New York and Baltimore," "to attend," not to participate in them. I agree that this does represent progress in Bishop Allen's view as compared to Lee's first approach; on the second approach, he was at least encouraging. Then he began "to promote her interests" (129)—but he did not ordain her.

17. Ibid.

18. "Elizabeth: A Colored Minister of the Gospel," in *Black Women in Nineteenth-Century American Life,* ed. Bert James Loewenberg and Ruth Bogin (University Park, PA: Pennsylvania State University Press, 1976), 132. The denomination of Elizabeth is not known to this writer. Her parents were Methodists, but she was separated from her parents at the age of eleven. However, the master from whom she gained her freedom was Presbyterian. Her autobiography was published by the Philadelphia Quakers.

19. Ibid., 133.

20. Amanda Berry Smith, *An Autobiography: The Story of the Lord's Dealings with Mrs. Amanda Berry Smith, the Colored Evangelist* (Chicago, 1893), in Loewenberg and Bogin, *Black Women,* 157.

21. Ibid.

22. Ibid., 159.

23. The African Methodist Episcopal Church started ordaining women in 1948, according to the Rev. William P. Foley of Bridgestreet A.M.E. Church in Brooklyn, New York. The first ordained woman was Martha J. Keys.

 The African Methodist Episcopal Zion Church ordained women as early as 1884. At that time, Mrs. Julia A. Foote was ordained Deacon in the New York Annual Conference. In 1894, Mrs. Mary J. Small was ordained Deacon, and in 1898, she was ordained Elder. See David Henry Bradley, Sr., *A History of the A.M.E. Zion Church,* vol. 2 *1872–1968* (Nashville: Parthenon Press, 1970), 384, 393.

 The Christian Methodist Episcopal Church enacted legislation to ordain women in the 1970 General Conference. Since then approximately seventy-five women have been ordained. See the Rev. N. Charles Thomas, general secretary of the C.M.E. Church and director of the Department of Ministry, Memphis, Tennessee.

 Many Baptist churches still do not ordain women. Some churches in the Pentecostal tradition do not ordain women. However, in some other Pentecostal churches, women are founders, pastors, elders, and bishops.

 In the case of the A.M.E.Z. Church, where women were ordained as early as 1884, the important question would be, what happened to the women who were ordained? In addition, all of these churches (except for those that do give leadership to women) should answer the following questions: Have women been assigned to pastor "class A" churches? Have women been appointed as presiding elders? (There is currently one woman presiding elder in the A.M.E. Church.) Have women been elected to serve as bishop of any of these churches? Have women served as presidents of conventions?

24. Yolande Herron, Jacquelyn Grant, Gwendolyn Johnson, and Samuel Robers, "Black Women and the Field Education Experience at Union Theological Seminary: Problems and Prospects" (New York: Union Theological Seminary, May 1978).

25. This organization continues to call itself the National Conference of Black Churchmen despite the protests of women members.

26. NCBC has since made the decision to examine the policies of its host institutions (churches) to avoid the recurrence of such incidents.

27. E. Franklin Frazier, *The Negro Church in America;* C. Eric Lincoln, *The Black Church Since Frazier* (New York: Schocken Books, 1974).

28. Printed in Phillip S. Foner, ed., *Frederick Douglass on Women's Rights* (Westport, Conn.: Greenwood Press), 51.

29. Cone, "Black Ecumenism and the Liberation Struggle," delivered at Yale University, February 16–17, 1978, and Quinn Chapel A.M.E. Church, May 22, 1978. In two other recent papers he has voiced concern on women's issues, relating them to the larger question of liberation. These papers are: "New Roles in the Ministry: A Theological Appraisal" and "Black Theology and the Black Church: Where Do We Go From Here?"

30. Jacquelyne Jackson, "But Where Are the Men?" *Black Scholar,* op. cit., 30.

31. Ibid., 32.

32. Kathleen Cleaver was interviewed by Sister Julia Herve. Ibid., 55–56.

33. Ibid., 55.

34. Sekou Toure, "The Role of Women in the Revolution," *Black Scholar,* vol. 6, no. 6 (March 1975), 32.

35. Sabelo Newasm and Basil Moore, "The Concept of God in Black Theology," in *The Challenge of Black Theology in South Africa,* ed. Basil Moore (Atlanta, Ga.: John Knox Press, 1974), 25–26.

36. Sojourner Truth, "Keeping the Things Going While Things Are Stirring," printed in Miriam Schneir, ed., *Feminism: The Essential Historical Writings* (New York: Random House, 1972), 129–30.

Patricia Hill Collins

Patricia Hill Collins, professor of Afro-American studies and sociology at the University of Cincinnati, has helped to transform feminist theory with her ground-breaking monograph *Black Feminist Thought* (1990), which has become one of the most widely used texts in women's studies curricula. "The Social Construction of Black Feminist Thought" appeared in *Signs* 4 (Summer 1989), a major outlet for the publication of black feminist discourse in the late 1970s and 1980s, particularly in sociology. Diane K. Lewis's "A Response to Inequality: Black Women, Racism, and Sexism (*Signs* 3, Winter 1977) was the first of these essays to appear in *Signs* followed by Bonnie Dill's "The Dialectics of Black Womanhood," *Signs* 4 (Spring 1979), 543–55

Patricia Hill Collins }

The Social Construction of
Black Feminist Thought

Sojourner Truth, Anna Julia Cooper, Ida Wells-Barnett, and Fannie Lou Hamer are but a few names from a growing list of distinguished African American women activists. Although their sustained resistance to black women's victimization within interlocking systems of race, gender, and class oppression is well known, these women did not act alone.[1] Their actions were nurtured by the support of countless, ordinary African American women who, through strategies of everyday resistance, created a powerful foundation for this more visible black feminist activist tradition.[2] Such support has been essential to the shape and goals of black feminist thought.

The long-term and widely shared resistance among African American women can only have been sustained by an enduring and shared standpoint among black women about the meaning of oppression and the actions that black women can and should take to resist it. Efforts to identify the central concepts of this black women's standpoint figure prominently in the works of contemporary black feminist intellectuals.[3] Moreover, political and epistemological issues influence the social construction of black feminist thought. Like other subordinate groups, African American women not only have developed distinctive interpretations of black women's oppression, but have done so by using alternative ways of producing and validating knowledge itself.

A BLACK WOMEN'S STANDPOINT

THE FOUNDATION OF BLACK FEMINIST THOUGHT

Black women's everyday acts of resistance challenge two prevailing approaches to studying the consciousness of oppressed groups.[4] One approach claims that subordinate groups identify with the powerful and have no valid independent interpretation of their own oppression.[5] The second approach assumes that the oppressed are less human than their rulers and, therefore, are less capable of articulating their own standpoint.[6] Both approaches see any independent consciousness expressed by an oppressed group as being not of the group's own making and/or inferior to the perspective of the dominant group.[7] More important, both interpretations suggest that oppressed groups lack the motivation for political activism because of their flawed consciousness of their own subordination.

Yet African American women have been neither passive victims of nor willing accomplices to their own domination. As a result, emerging work in black women's studies contends that black women have a self-defined standpoint on their own oppression.[8] Two interlocking components characterize this standpoint. First, black women's political and economic status provides them with a distinctive set of experiences that offers a different view of material reality than that available to other groups. The unpaid and paid work that black women perform, the types of communities in which they live, and the kinds of relationships they have with others suggest that African American women, as a group, experience a different world than those who are not black and female.[9] Second, these experiences stimulate a distinctive black feminist consciousness concerning that material reality.[10] In brief, a subordinate group not only experiences a different reality than a group that rules, but a subordinate group may interpret that reality differently than a dominant group.

Many ordinary African American women have grasped this connection between what one does and how one thinks. Hannah Nelson, an elderly black domestic worker, discusses how work shapes the standpoints of African American and white women: "Since I have to work, I don't really have to worry about most of the things that most of the white women I have worked for are worrying about. And if these women did their own work, they would think just like I do—about this, anyway."[11] Ruth Shays, a black inner city resident, points out how variations in men's and women's experiences lead to differences in perspective: "The mind of the man and the mind of the woman is the same. But this business of living makes women use their minds in ways that men don't even have to think about."[12] Finally, elderly domestic worker Rosa Wakefield assesses how the standpoints of the powerful and those who serve them diverge: "If you eats these dinners and don't cook 'em, if you wears these clothes and don't buy or iron them, then you might start thinking that the good fairy or some spirit did all that.... Blackfolks don't have no time to be thinking like that.... But when you don't have anything else to do, you can think like that. It's bad for your mind, though."[13]

While African American women may occupy material positions that stimulate a unique standpoint, expressing an independent black feminist consciousness is problematic precisely because more powerful groups have a vested interest in suppressing such thought. As Hannah Nelson notes, "I have grown to womanhood in a world where the saner you are, the madder you are made to appear."[14] Nelson realizes that those who control the schools, the media, and other cultural institutions are generally skilled in establishing their view of reality as superior to alternative interpretations. While an oppressed group's experiences may put them in a position to see things differently, their lack of control over the apparatuses of society that sustain ideological hegemony makes the articulation of their self-defined standpoint difficult. Groups unequal in power are correspondingly unequal in their access to the resources necessary to implement their perspectives outside their particular group.

One key reason that standpoints of oppressed groups are discredited and suppressed by the more powerful is that self-defined standpoints can stimulate oppressed groups to resist their domination. For instance, Annie Adams, a southern black woman, describes how she became involved in civil rights activities.

> When I first went into the mill we had segregated water fountains. . . . Same thing about the toilets. I had to clean the toilets for the inspection room and then, when I got ready to go to the bathroom, I had to go all the way to the bottom of the stairs to the cellar. So I asked my boss man, "What's the difference? If I can go in there and clean them toilets, why can't I use them?" Finally, I started to use that toilet. I decided I wasn't going to walk a mile to go to the bathroom.[15]

In this case, Adams found the standpoint of the "boss man" inadequate, developed one of her own, and acted upon it. In doing so, her actions exemplify the connections between experiencing oppression, developing a self-defined standpoint on that experience, and resistance.

THE SIGNIFICANCE OF BLACK FEMINIST THOUGHT

The existence of a distinctive black women's standpoint does not mean that it has been adequately articulated in black feminist thought. Peter Berger and Thomas Luckmann provide a useful approach to clarifying the relationship between a black women's standpoint and black feminist thought with the contention that knowledge exists on two levels.[16] The first level includes the everyday, taken-for-granted knowledge shared by members of a given group, such as the ideas expressed by Ruth Shays and Annie Adams. Black feminist thought, by extension, represents a second level of knowledge, the more specialized knowledge furnished by experts who are part of a group and who express the group's standpoint. The two levels of knowledge are interdependent; while black feminist thought articulates the taken-for-granted knowledge of African American women, it also encourages all black women to create new self-definitions that validate a black women's standpoint.

Black feminist thought's potential significance goes far beyond demonstrating that black women can produce independent, specialized knowledge. Such thought can encourage collective identity by offering black women a different view of themselves and their world than that offered by the established social order. This different view encourages African American women to value their own subjective knowledge base.[17] By taking elements and themes of black women's culture and traditions and infusing them with new meaning, black feminist thought rearticulates a consciousness that already exists.[18] More important, this rearticulated consciousness gives African American women another tool of resistance to all forms of their subordination.[19]

Black feminist thought, then, specializes in formulating and rearticulating the distinctive, self-defined standpoint of African American women. One approach to learning more about a black women's standpoint is to consult standard scholarly sources for the ideas of specialists on black women's experiences.[20] But investigating a black women's standpoint and black feminist thought requires more ingenuity than that required in examining the standpoints and thought of white males. Rearticulating the standpoint of African American women through black feminist thought is much more difficult since one cannot use the same techniques to study the knowledge of the dominated as one uses to study the knowledge of the powerful. This is precisely because subordinate groups have long had to use alternative ways to create an independent consciousness and to rearticulate it through specialists validated by the oppressed themselves.

THE EUROCENTRIC MASCULINIST KNOWLEDGE-VALIDATION PROCESS[21]

All social thought, including white masculinist and black feminist, reflects the interests and standpoint of its creators. As Karl Mannheim notes, "If one were to trace in detail . . . the origin and . . . diffusion of a certain thought-model, one would discover the affinity it has to the social position of given groups and their manner of interpreting the world."[22] Scholars, publishers, and other experts represent specific interests and credentialing processes and their knowledge claims must satisfy the epistemological and political criteria of the contexts in which they reside.[23]

Two political criteria influence the knowledge-validation process. First, knowledge claims must be evaluated by a community of experts whose members represent the standpoints of the groups from which they originate. Second, each community of experts must maintain its credibility as defined by the larger group in which it is situated and from which it draws its basic, taken-for-granted knowledge.

When white males control the knowledge-validation process, both political criteria can work to suppress black feminist thought. Since the general culture shaping the taken-for-granted knowledge of the community of experts is one permeated by widespread notions of black and female inferiority,[24] new knowledge claims that seem to violate these fundamental assumptions are likely to be viewed as anomalies.[25] Moreover, specialized thought challenging notions of black and female inferiority is unlikely to be generated from within a white-male-controlled academic community because both the kinds of questions that could be asked and the explanations that would be found satisfying would necessarily reflect a basic lack of familiarity with black women's reality.[26]

The experiences of African American women scholars illustrate how individuals who wish to rearticulate a black women's standpoint through black feminist thought can be suppressed by a white-male-controlled knowledge-validation process. Exclusion from basic literacy, quality educational experiences, and faculty and administrative positions has limited black women's access to influential academic positions.[27] Thus, while black women can produce knowledge claims that contest those advanced by the white male community, this community does not grant that black women scholars have competing knowledge claims based in another knowledge-validation process. As a consequence, any credentials controlled by white male academicians can be denied to black women producing black feminist thought on the grounds that it is not credible research.

Those black women with academic credentials who seek to exert the authority that their status grants them to propose new knowledge claims about African American women face pressures to use their authority to help legitimate a system that devalues and excludes the majority of black women.[28] One way of excluding the majority of black women from the knowledge-validation process is to permit a few black women to acquire positions of authority in institutions that legitimate knowledge and to encourage them to work within the taken-for-granted assumptions of black female inferiority shared by the scholarly community and the culture at large. Those black women who accept these assumptions are likely to be rewarded by their institutions, often at significant personal cost. Those challenging the assumptions run the risk of being ostracized.

African American women academicians who persist in trying to rearticulate a black women's standpoint also face potential rejection of their knowledge claims on epistemological grounds. Just as the material realities of the powerful and the dominated produce separate standpoints, each group may also have distinctive epistemologies or theories of knowledge. It is my contention that black female scholars may know that something is true but be unwilling or unable to legitimate their claims using Eurocentric masculinist criteria for consistency with substantiated knowledge and Eurocentric masculinist criteria for methodological adequacy.

For any particular interpretive context, new knowledge claims must be consistent with an existing body of knowledge that the group controlling the interpretive context accepts as true. The methods used to validate knowledge claims must also be acceptable to the group controlling the knowledge-validation process.

The criteria for the methodological adequacy of positivism illustrate the epistemological standards that black women scholars would have to satisfy in legitimating alternative knowledge claims.[29] Positivist approaches aim to create scientific descriptions of reality by producing objective generalizations. Since researchers have widely differing values, experiences, and emotions, genuine science is thought to be unattainable unless all human characteristics except rationality are eliminated from the research process. By following strict methodological rules, scientists aim to distance themselves from the values, vested interests, and emotions generated by their class, race, sex, or unique situation and in so doing become detached observers and manipulators of nature.[30]

Several requirements typify positivist methodological approaches. First, research methods generally require a distancing of the researcher from her/his "object" of study by defining the researcher as a "subject" with full human subjectivity and objectifying the "object" of study.[31] A second requirement is the absence of emotions from the research process.[32] Third, ethics and values are deemed inappropriate in the research process, either as the reason for scientific inquiry or as part of the research process itself.[33] Finally, adversarial debates, whether written or oral, become the preferred method of ascertaining truth—the arguments that can withstand the greatest assault and survive intact become the strongest truths.[34]

Such criteria ask African American women to objectify themselves, devalue their emotional life, displace their motivations for furthering knowledge about black women, and confront, in an adversarial relationship, those who have more social, economic, and professional power than they. It seems unlikely, therefore, that black women would use a positivist epistemological stance in rearticulating a black women's standpoint. Black women are more likely to choose an alternative epistemology for assessing knowledge claims, one using standards that are consistent with black women's criteria for substantiated knowledge and with black women's criteria for methodological adequacy. If such an epistemology exists, what are its contours? Moreover, what is its role in the production of black feminist thought?

THE CONTOURS OF AN AFROCENTRIC
FEMINIST EPISTEMOLOGY

Africanist analyses of the black experience generally agree on the fundamental elements of an Afrocentric standpoint. In spite of varying histories,
black societies reflect elements of a core African value system that existed
prior to and independently of racial oppression.[35] Moreover, as a result of
colonialism, imperialism, slavery, apartheid, and other systems of racial
domination, blacks share a common experience of oppression. These similarities in material conditions have fostered shared Afrocentric values that
permeate the family structure, religious institutions, culture, and community life of blacks in varying parts of Africa, the Caribbean, South America,
and North America.[36] This Afrocentric consciousness permeates the shared
history of people of African descent through the framework of a distinctive
Afrocentric epistemology.[37]

Feminist scholars advance a similar argument. They assert that women
share a history of patriarchal oppression through the political economy of
the material conditions of sexuality and reproduction.[38] These shared material conditions are thought to transcend divisions among women created by
race, social class, religion, sexual orientation, and ethnicity and to form the
basis of a women's standpoint with its corresponding feminist consciousness
and epistemology.[39]

Since black women have access to both the Afrocentric and the feminist
standpoints, an alternative epistemology used to rearticulate a black
women's standpoint reflects elements of both traditions.[40] The search for
the distinguishing features of an alternative epistemology used by African
American women reveals that values and ideas that Africanist scholars
identify as being characteristically "black" often bear remarkable resemblance to similar ideas claimed by feminist scholars as being characteristically "female."[41] This similarity suggests that the material conditions of
oppression can vary dramatically and yet generate some uniformity in the
epistemologies of subordinate groups. Thus, the significance of an Afrocentric feminist epistemology may lie in its enrichment of our understanding
of how subordinate groups create knowledge that enables them to resist
oppression.

The parallels between the two conceptual schemes raise a question: Is
the worldview of women of African descent more intensely infused with
the overlapping feminine/Afrocentric standpoints than is the case for either
African American men or white women?[42] While an Afrocentric feminist
epistemology, reflects elements of epistemologies used by blacks as a group
and women as a group, it also paradoxically demonstrates features that may
be unique to black women. On certain dimensions, black women may more
closely resemble black men, on others, white women, and on still others,

black women may stand apart from both groups. Black feminist sociologist Deborah K. King describes this phenomenon as a "both/or" orientation, the act of being simultaneously a member of a group and yet standing apart from it. She suggests that multiple realities among black women yield a "multiple consciousness in black women's politics" and that this state of belonging yet not belonging forms an integral part of black women's oppositional consciousness.[43] Bonnie Thornton Dill's analysis of how black women live with contradictions, a situation she labels the "dialectics of black womanhood," parallels King's assertions that this "both/or" orientation is central to an Afrocentric feminist consciousness.[44] Rather than emphasizing how a black women's standpoint and its accompanying epistemology are different from those in Afrocentric and feminist analyses, I use black women's experiences as a point of contact between the two.

Viewing an Afrocentric feminist epistemology in this way challenges analyses claiming that black women have a more accurate view of oppression than do other groups. Such approaches suggest that oppression can be quantified and compared and that adding layers of oppression produces a potentially clearer standpoint. While it is tempting to claim that black women are more oppressed than everyone else and therefore have the best standpoint from which to understand the mechanisms, processes, and effects of oppression, this simply may not be the case.[45]

African American women do not uniformly share an Afrocentric feminist epistemology since social class introduces variations among black women in seeing, valuing, and using Afrocentric feminist perspectives. While a black women's standpoint and its accompanying epistemology stem from black women's consciousness of race and gender oppression, they are not simply the result of combining Afrocentric and female values —standpoints are rooted in real material conditions structured by social class.[46]

CONCRETE EXPERIENCE AS A CRITERION OF MEANING

Carolyn Chase, a thirty-one-year-old inner city black woman, notes, "My aunt used to say, 'A heap see, but a few know.' "[47] This saying depicts two types of knowing, knowledge and wisdom, and taps the first dimension of an Afrocentric feminist epistemology. Living life as black women requires wisdom since knowledge about the dynamics of race, gender, and class subordination has been essential to black women's survival. African American women give such wisdom high credence in assessing knowledge.

Allusions to these two types of knowing pervade the words of a range of African American women. In explaining the tenacity of racism, Zilpha Elaw, a preacher of the mid-1800s, noted: "The pride of a white skin is a bauble of great value with many in some parts of the United States, who readily sacrifice their intelligence to their prejudices, and possess more knowledge than wisdom."[48] In describing differences separating African American and white women, Nancy White invokes a similar rule: "When you come right down to it, white women just *think* they are free. Black women *know* they ain't free."[49] Geneva Smitherman, a college professor specializing in African American linguistics, suggests that "from a black perspective, written documents are limited in what they can teach about life and survival in the world. Blacks are quick to ridicule 'educated fools,' ... they have 'book learning,' but no 'mother wit,' knowledge, but not wisdom."[50] Mabel Lincoln eloquently summarizes the distinction between knowledge and wisdom: "To black people like me, a fool is funny—you know, people who love to break bad, people you can't tell anything to, folks that would take a shotgun to a roach."[51]

Black women need wisdom to know how to deal with the "educated fools" who would "take a shotgun to a roach." As members of a subordinate group, black women cannot afford to be fools of any type, for their devalued status denies them the protections that white skin, maleness, and wealth confer. This distinction between knowledge and wisdom, and the use of experience as the cutting edge dividing them, has been key to black women's survival. In the context of race, gender, and class oppression, the distinction is essential since knowledge without wisdom is adequate for the powerful, but wisdom is essential to the survival of the subordinate.

For ordinary African American women, those individuals who have lived through the experiences about which they claim to be experts are more believable and credible than those who have merely read or thought about such experiences. Thus, concrete experience as a criterion for credibility frequently is invoked by black women when making knowledge claims. For instance, Hannah Nelson describes the importance that personal experience has for her: "Our speech is most directly personal, and every black person assumes that every other black person has a right to a personal opinion. In speaking of grave matters, your personal experience is considered very good evidence. With us, distant statistics are certainly not as important as the actual experience of a sober person."[52] Similarly, Ruth Shays uses her concrete experiences to challenge the idea that formal education is the only route to knowledge: "I am the kind of person who doesn't have a lot of education, but both my mother and my father had good common sense. Now, I think that's all you need. I might not know how to use thirty-four words where three would do, but that does not mean that I don't know what I'm talking about ... I know what I'm talking about because I'm talking about myself. I'm talking about what I have lived."[53] Implicit in Shays's self-assessment is a critique of the type of knowledge that obscures the truth, the "thirty-four words" that cover up a truth that can be expressed in three.

Even after substantial mastery of white masculinist epistemologies, many black women scholars invoke their own concrete experiences and those of other black women in selecting topics for investigation and methodologies used. For example, Elsa Barkley Brown subtitles her essay on black women's history, "how my mother taught me to be a historian in spite of my academic training."[54] Similarly, Joyce Ladner maintains that growing up as a black woman in the South gave her special insights in conducting her study of black adolescent women.[55]

Henry Mitchell and Nicholas Lewter claim that experience as a criterion of meaning with practical images as its symbolic vehicles is a fundamental epistemological tenet in African American thought-systems.[56] Stories, narratives, and Bible principles are selected for their applicability to the lived experiences of African Americans and become symbolic representations of a whole wealth of experience. For example, Bible tales are told for their value to common life, so their interpretation involves no need for scientific historical verification. The narrative method requires that the story be "told, not torn apart in analysis, and trusted as core belief, not admired as science."[57] Any biblical story contains more than characters and a plot—it presents key ethical issues salient in African American life.

June Jordan's essay about her mother's suicide exemplifies the multiple levels of meaning that can occur when concrete experiences are used as a criterion of meaning. Jordan describes her mother, a woman who literally died trying to stand up, and the effect that her mother's death had on her own work:

> I think all of this is really about women and work. Certainly this is all about me as a woman and my life work. I mean I am not sure my mother's suicide was something extraordinary. Perhaps most women must deal with a similar inheritance, the legacy of a woman whose death you cannot possibly pinpoint because she died so many, many times and because, even before she became your mother, the life of that woman was taken.... I came too late to help my mother to her feet. By way of everlasting thanks to all of the women who have helped me to stay alive, I am working never to be late again.[58]

While Jordan has knowledge about the concrete act of her mother's death, she also strives for wisdom concerning the meaning of that death.

Some feminist scholars offer a similar claim that women, as a group, are more likely than men to use concrete knowledge in assessing knowledge claims. For example, a substantial number of the 135 women in a study of women's cognitive development were "connected knowers" and were drawn to the sort of knowledge that emerges from firsthand observation. Such women felt that since knowledge comes from experience, the best way of understanding another person's ideas was to try to share the experiences that led the person to form those ideas. At the heart of the procedures used by connected knowers is the capacity for empathy.[59]

In valuing the concrete, African American women may be invoking not only an Afrocentric tradition, but a women's tradition as well. Some feminist theorists suggest that women are socialized in complex relational nexuses where contextual rules take priority over abstract principles in governing behavior. This socialization process is thought to stimulate characteristic ways of knowing.[60] For example, Canadian sociologist Dorothy Smith maintains that two modes of knowing exist, one located in the body and the space it occupies and the other passing beyond it. She asserts that women, through their child-rearing and nurturing activities, mediate these two modes and use the concrete experiences of their daily lives to assess more abstract knowledge claims.[61]

Amanda King, a young black mother, describes how she used the concrete to assess the abstract and points out how difficult mediating these two modes of knowing can be:

> The leaders of the ROC [a labor union] lost their jobs too, but it just seemed like they were used to losing their jobs. . . . This was like a lifelong thing for them, to get out there and protest. They were like, what do you call them—intellectuals. . . . You got the ones that go to the university that are supposed to make all the speeches, they're the ones that are supposed to lead, you know, put this little revolution together, and then you got the little ones . . . that go to the factory everyday, they be the ones that have to fight. I had a child, and I thought I don't have the time to be running around with these people. . . . I mean I understand some of that stuff they were talking about, like the bourgeoisie, the rich and the poor and all that, but I had surviving on my mind for me and my kid.[62]

For King, abstract ideals of class solidarity were mediated by the concrete experience of motherhood and the connectedness it involved.

In traditional African American communities, black women find considerable institutional support for valuing concrete experience. Black extended families and black churches are two key institutions where black women experts with concrete knowledge of what it takes to be self-defined black women share their knowledge with their younger, less experienced sisters. This relationship of sisterhood among black women can be seen as a model for a whole series of relationships that African American women have with each other, whether it is networks among women in extended families, among women in the black church, or among women in the African American community at large.[63]

Since the black church and the black family are both woman-centered and Afrocentric institutions, African American women traditionally have found considerable institutional support for this dimension of an Afrocentric feminist epistemology in ways that are unique to them. While white women may value the concrete, it is questionable whether white families, particularly middle-class nuclear ones, and white community institutions provide comparable types of support. Similarly, while black men are supported by Afrocentric institutions, they cannot participate in black women's sisterhood. In terms of black women's relationships with one another then, African American women may indeed find it easier than others to recognize connectedness as a primary way of knowing, simply because they are encouraged to do so by black women's tradition of sisterhood.

EPISTEMOLOGY AND BLACK FEMINIST THOUGHT

Living life as an African American woman is a necessary prerequisite for producing black feminist thought because within black women's communities thought is validated and produced with reference to a particular set of historical, material, and epistemological conditions.[64] African American women who adhere to the idea that claims about black women must be substantiated by black women's sense of their own experiences, and who anchor their knowledge claims in an Afrocentric feminist epistemology, have produced a rich tradition of black feminist thought.

Traditionally, such women were blues singers, poets, autobiographers, storytellers, and orators validated by the larger community of black women as experts on a black women's standpoint. Only a few unusual African American feminist scholars have been able to defy Eurocentric masculinist epistemologies and explicitly embrace an Afrocentric feminist epistemology. Consider Alice Walker's description of Zora Neale Hurston: "In my mind, Zora Neale Hurston, Billie Holiday, and Bessie Smith form a sort of unholy trinity. Zora *belongs* in the tradition of black women singers, rather than among 'the literati.' . . . Like Billie and Bessie she followed her own road, believed in her own gods, pursued her own dreams, and refused to separate herself from 'common' people."[65]

Zora Neale Hurston is an exception for, prior to 1950, few black women earned advanced degrees, and most of those who did complied with Eurocentric masculinist epistemologies. While these women worked on behalf of black women, they did so within the confines of pervasive race and gender oppression. Black women scholars were in a position to see the exclusion of black women from scholarly discourse, and the thematic content of their work often reflected their interest in examining a black women's standpoint. However, their tenuous status in academic institutions led them to adhere to Eurocentric masculinist epistemologies so that their work would be accepted as scholarly. As a result, while they produced black feminist thought, those black women most likely to gain academic credentials were often least likely to produce black feminist thought that used an Afrocentric feminist epistemology.

As more black women earn advanced degrees, the range of black feminist scholarship is expanding. Increasing numbers of African American women scholars are explicitly choosing to ground their work in black women's experiences, and, by doing so, many implicitly adhere to an Afrocentric feminist epistemology. Rather than being restrained by their "both/and" status of marginality, these women make creative use of their outsider-within status and produce innovative black feminist thought. The difficulties these women face lie less in demonstrating the technical components of white male epistemologies than in resisting the hegemonic nature of these patterns of thought in order to see, value, and use existing alternative Afrocentric feminist ways of knowing.

In establishing the legitimacy of their knowledge claims, black women scholars who want to develop black feminist thought may encounter the often conflicting standards of three key groups. First, black feminist thought must be validated by ordinary African American women who grow to womanhood "in a world where the saner you are, the madder you are made to appear."[66] To be credible in the eyes of this group, scholars must be personal advocates for their material, be accountable for the consequences of their work, have lived or experienced their material in some fashion, and be willing to engage in dialogues about their findings with ordinary, everyday people. Second, if it is to establish its legitimacy, black feminist thought also must be accepted by the community of black women scholars. These scholars place varying amounts of importance on rearticulating a black women's standpoint using an Afrocentric feminist epistemology. Third, black feminist thought within academia must be prepared to confront Eurocentric masculinist political and epistemological requirements.

The dilemma facing black women scholars engaged in creating black feminist thought is that a knowledge claim that meets the criteria of adequacy for one group and thus is judged to be an acceptable knowledge claim may not be translatable into the terms of a different group. Using the example of Black English, June Jordan illustrates the difficulty of moving among epistemologies: "You cannot 'translate' instances of Standard English preoccupied with abstraction or with nothing/nobody evidently alive into Black English. That would warp the language into uses antithetical to the guiding perspective of its community of users. Rather you must first change those Standard English sentences themselves into ideas consistent with the person-centered assumptions of Black English."[67] While both worldviews share a common vocabulary, the ideas themselves defy direct translation.

Once black feminist scholars face the notion that, on certain dimensions of a black women's standpoint, it may be fruitless to try to translate ideas from an Afrocentric feminist epistemology into a Eurocentric masculinist epistemology, then the choices become clearer. Rather than trying to uncover universal knowledge claims that can withstand the translation from one epistemology to another, time might be better spent rearticulating a black women's standpoint in order to give African American women the tools to resist their own subordination. The goal here is not one of integrating black female "folk culture" into the substantiated body of academic knowledge, for that substantiated knowledge is, in many ways, antithetical to the best interests of black women. Rather, the process is one of rearticulating a preexisting black women's standpoint and recentering the language of existing academic discourse to accommodate these knowledge claims. For those black women scholars engaged in this rearticulation process, the social construction of black feminist thought requires the skill and sophistication to decide which knowledge claims can be validated using the epistemological assumptions of one but not both frameworks, which claims can be generated in one framework and only partially accommodated by the other, and which claims can be made in both frameworks without violating the basic political and epistemological assumptions of either.

Black feminist scholars offering knowledge claims that cannot be accommodated by both frameworks face the choice between accepting the taken-for-granted assumptions that permeate white-male-controlled academic institutions or leaving academia. Those black women who choose to remain in academia must accept the possibility that their knowledge claims will be limited to their claims about black women that are consistent with a white male worldview. And yet those African American women who leave academia may find their work is inaccessible to scholarly communities.

Black feminist scholars offering knowledge claims that can be partially accommodated by both epistemologies can create a body of thought that stands outside of either. Rather than trying to synthesize competing worldviews that, at this point in time, defy reconciliation, their task is to point out common themes and concerns. By making creative use of their status as mediators, their thought becomes an entity unto itself that is rooted in two distinct political and epistemological contexts.[68]

Those black feminists who develop knowledge claims that both epistemologies can accommodate may have found a route to the elusive goal of generating so-called objective generalizations that can stand as universal truths. Those ideas that are validated as true by African American women, African American men, white men, white women, and other groups with distinctive standpoints, with each group using the epistemological approaches growing from its unique standpoint, thus become the most objective truths.[69]

Alternative knowledge claims, in and of themselves, are rarely threatening to conventional knowledge. Such claims are routinely ignored, discredited, or simply absorbed and marginalized in existing paradigms. Much more threatening is the challenge that alternative epistemologies offer to the basic process used by the powerful to legitimate their knowledge claims. If the epistemology used to validate knowledge comes into question, then all prior knowledge claims validated under the dominant model become suspect. An alternative epistemology challenges all certified knowledge and opens up the question of whether what has been taken to be true can stand the test of alternative ways of validating truth. The existence of an independent black women's standpoint using an Afrocentric feminist epistemology calls into question the content of what currently passes as truth and simultaneously challenges the process of arriving at that truth.

ENDNOTES

1. For analyses of how interlocking systems of oppression affect black women, see Frances Beale, "Double Jeopardy: To Be Black and Female," in *The Black Woman,* ed. Toni Cade (New York: Signet, 1970); Angela Y. Davis, *Women, Race, and Class* (New York: Random House, 1981); Bonnie Thornton Dill, "Race, Class, and Gender: Prospects for an All-Inclusive Sisterhood," *Feminist Studies* 9, no. 1 (1983): 131–50; bell hooks, *Ain't I a Woman? Black Women and Feminism* (Boston: South End Press, 1981); Diane Lewis, "A Response to Inequality: Black Women, Racism, and Sexism," *Signs: Journal of Women in Culture and Society* 3, no. 2 (Winter 1977): 339–61; Pauli Murray, "The Liberation of Black Women," in *Voices of the New Feminism,* ed. Mary Lou Thompson (Boston: Beacon Press, 1970), 87–102; and the introduction in Filomina Chioma Steady, *The Black Woman Cross-Culturally* (Cambridge, MA: Schenkman, 1981), 7–41.

2. See the introduction in Steady for an overview of black women's strengths. This strength-resiliency perspective has greatly influenced empirical work on African American women. See, e.g., Joyce Ladner's study of low-income black adolescent girls, *Tomorrow's Tomorrow* (New York: Doubleday, 1971); and Lena Wright Myers's work on black women's self-concept, *Black Women: Do They Cope Better?* (Englewood Cliffs, NJ: Prentice-Hall, 1980). For discussions of black women's resistance, see Elizabeth Fox-Genovese, "Strategies and Forms of Resistance: Focus on Slave Women in the United States," in *In Resistance: Studies in African, Caribbean and Afro-American History,* ed. Gary Y. Okihiro (Amherst: University of Massachusetts Press, 1986), 143–65; and Rosalyn Terborg-Penn, "Black Women in Resistance: A Cross-Cultural Perspective," in Okihiro, *In Resistance,* 188–209. For a comprehensive discussion of everyday resistance, see James C. Scott, *Weapons of the Weak: Everyday Forms of Peasant Resistance* (New Haven, CT: Yale University Press, 1985).

3. See Patricia Hill Collins's analysis of the substantive content of black feminist thought in "Learning from the Outsider Within: The Sociological Significance of Black Feminist Thought," *Social Problems* 33, no. 6 (1986): 14–32.

4. Scott describes consciousness as the meaning that people give to their acts through the symbols, norms, and ideological forms they create.

5. This thesis is found in scholarship of varying theoretical perspectives. For example, Marxist analyses of working-class consciousness claim that "false consciousness" makes the working class unable to penetrate the hegemony of ruling-class ideologies. See Scott's critique of this literature.

6. For example, in Western societies, African Americans have been judged as being less capable of intellectual excellence, more suited to manual labor, and therefore less human than whites. Similarly, white women have been assigned roles as emotional, irrational creatures ruled by passions and biological urges. They too have been stigmatized as being less than fully human, as being objects. For a discussion of the importance that objectification and

dehumanization play in maintaining systems of domination, see Arthur Brittan and Mary Maynard, *Sexism, Racism and Oppression* (New York: Basil Blackwell, 1984).

7. The tendency for Western scholarship to assess black culture as pathological and deviant illustrates this process. See Rhett S. Jones, "Proving Blacks Inferior: The Sociology of Knowledge," in *The Death of White Sociology,* ed. Joyce Ladner (New York: Vintage, 1973), 114–35.

8. The presence of an independent standpoint does not mean that it is uniformly shared by all black women or even that black women fully recognize its contours. By using the concept of standpoint, I do not mean to minimize the rich diversity existing among African American women. I use the phrase "black women's standpoint" to emphasize the plurality of experiences within the overarching term "standpoint." For discussions of the concept of standpoint, see Nancy M. Hartsock, "The Feminist Standpoint: Developing the Ground for a Specifically Feminist Historical Materialism," in *Discovering Reality,* ed. Sandra Harding and Merrill Hintikka (Boston: D. Reidel, 1983), 283–310; *Money, Sex, and Power* (Boston: Northeastern University Press, 1983); and Alison M. Jaggar, *Feminist Politics and Human Nature* (Totowa, NJ: Rowman & Allanheld, 1983), 377–89. My use of the standpoint epistemologies as an organizing concept in this essay does not mean that the concept is problem-free. For a helpful critique of standpoint epistemologies, see Sandra Harding, *The Science Question in Feminism* (Ithaca, NY: Cornell University Press, 1986).

9. One contribution of contemporary black women's studies is its documentation of how race, class, and gender have structured these differences. For representative works surveying African American women's experiences, see Paula Giddings, *When and Where I Enter: The Impact of Black Women on Race and Sex in America* (New York: William Morrow, 1984); and Jacqueline Jones, *Labor of Love, Labor of Sorrow: Black Women, Work, and the Family from Slavery to the Present* (New York: Basic Books, 1985).

10. For example, Judith Rollins, *Between Women: Domestics and Their Employers* (Philadelphia: Temple University Press, 1985); and Bonnie Thornton Dill, " 'The Means to Put My Children Through': Child-Rearing Goals and Strategies among Black Female Domestic Servants," in *The Black Woman,* ed. LaFrances Rodgers-Rose (Beverly Hills, CA: Sage Publications, 1980), 107–23, report that black domestic workers do not see themselves as being the devalued workers that their employers perceive and construct their own interpretations of the meaning of their work. For additional discussions of how black women's consciousness is shaped by the material conditions they encounter, see Ladner, *Tomorrow's Tomorrow;* Myers, *Black Women;* and Cheryl Townsend Gilkes, " 'Together and in Harness': Women's Traditions in the Sanctified Church," *Signs* 10, no. 4 (Summer 1985): 678–99. See also Marcia Westkott's discussion of consciousness as a sphere of freedom for women in "Feminist Criticism of the Social Sciences," *Harvard Educational Review* 49, no. 4 (1979): 422–30.

11. John Langston Gwaltney, *Drylongso: A Self-Portrait of Black America* (New York: Vintage, 1980), 4.

12. Ibid., 33.

13. Ibid., 88.

14. Ibid., 7.

15. Victoria Byerly, *Hard Times Cotton Mill Girls: Personal Histories of Womanhood and Poverty in the South* (New York: ILR Press, 1986), 134.

16. See Peter L. Berger and Thomas Luckmann, *The Social Construction of Reality* (New York: Doubleday, 1966), for a discussion of everyday thought and the role of experts in articulating specialized thought.

17. See Michael Omi and Howard Winant, *Racial Formation in the United States* (New York: Routledge & Kegan Paul, 1986), especially 93.

18. In discussing standpoint epistemologies, Hartsock, in *Money, Sex, and Power,* notes that a standpoint is "achieved rather than obvious, a mediated rather than immediate understanding" (132).

19. See Scott, *Weapons of the Weak;* and Hartsock, *Money, Sex, and Power.*

20. Some readers may question how one determines whether the ideas of any given African American woman are "feminist" and "Afrocentric." I offer the following working definitions. I agree with the general definition of feminist consciousness provided by black feminist sociologist Deborah K. King: "Any purposes, goals, and activities that seek to enhance the potential of women, to ensure their liberty, afford them equal opportunity, and to permit and encourage their self-determination represent a feminist consciousness, even if they occur within a racial community" (in "Race, Class and Gender Salience in Black Women's Womanist Consciousness" [typescript, Dartmouth College, Department of Sociology, Hanover, NH, 1987], 22). To be black or Afrocentric, such thought must not only reflect a similar concern for the self-determination of African American people, but must in some way draw upon key elements of an Afrocentric tradition as well.

21. The Eurocentric masculinist process is defined here as the institutions, paradigms, and any elements of the knowledge-validation procedure controlled by white males and whose purpose is to represent a white male standpoint. While this process represents the interests of powerful white males, various dimensions of the process are not necessarily managed by white males themselves.

22. Karl Mannheim, *Ideology and Utopia: An Introduction to the Sociology of Knowledge* (1936; reprint, New York: Harcourt, Brace & Co., 1954), 276.

23. The knowledge-validation model used in this essay is taken from Michael Mulkay, *Science and the Sociology of Knowledge* (Boston: Allen & Unwin, 1979). For a general discussion of the structure of knowledge, see Thomas Kuhn, *The Structure of Scientific Revolutions* (Chicago: University of Chicago Press, 1962).

24. For analyses of the content and functions of images of black female inferiority, see Mae King, "The Politics of Sexual Stereotypes," *Black Scholar* 4, nos. 6–7 (1973): 12–23; Cheryl Townsend Gilkes, "From Slavery to Social Welfare: Racism and the Control of Black Women," in *Class, Race, and Sex: The Dynamics of Control,* ed. Amy Smerdlow and Helen Lessinger (Boston: G. K. Hall, 1981), 288–300; and Elizabeth Higginbotham, "Two Representative Issues in Contemporary Sociological Work on Black Women," in *All the Women Are White, All the Blacks Are Men, But Some of Us Are Brave,* ed. Gloria T. Hull, Patricia Bell Scott, and Barbara Smith (Old Westbury, NY: Feminist Press, 1982).

25. Kun, *The Structure.*

26. Evelyn Fox Keller, *Reflections on Gender and Science* (New Haven, CT: Yale University Press, 1985), 167.

27. Maxine Baca Zinn, Lynn Weber Cannon, Elizabeth Higginbotham, and Bonnie Thornton Dill, "The Cost of Exclusionary Practices in Women's Studies," *Signs* 11, no. 2 (Winter 1986): 290–303.

28. Berger and Luckmann (in *The Social Construction of Reality*) note that if an outsider group, in this case African American women, recognizes that the insider group, namely, white men, requires special privileges from the larger society, a special problem arises of keeping the outsiders out and at the same time having them acknowledge the legitimacy of this procedure. Accepting a few "safe" outsiders is one way of addressing this legitimation problem. Collins's discussion (in "Learning from the Outsider Within") of black women as "outsiders within" addresses this issue. Other relevant works include Frantz

Fanon's analysis of the role of the national middle class in maintaining colonial systems, *The Wretched of the Earth* (New York: Grove, 1963); and William Tabb's discussion of the use of "bright natives" in controlling African American communities, *The Political Economy of the Black Ghetto* (New York: W. W. Norton, 1970).

29. While I have been describing Eurocentric masculinist approaches as a single process, there are many schools of thought or paradigms subsumed under this one process. Positivism represents one such paradigm. See Harding, *The Science Question,* for an overview and critique of this literature. The following discussion depends heavily on Jaggar, *Feminist Politics,* 355–58.

30. Jaggar, *Feminist Politics,* 356.

31. See Keller, *Reflections on Gender,* 67–126, especially her analysis of static autonomy and its relation to objectivity.

32. Ironically, researchers must "objectify" themselves to achieve this lack of bias. See Arlie Russell Hochschild, "The Sociology of Feeling and Emotion: Selected Possibilities," in *Another Voice: Feminist Perspectives on Social Life and Social Science,* ed. Marcia Millman and Rosabeth Kanter (Garden City, NY: Anchor, 1975), 280–307. Also, see Jaggar, *Feminist Politics.*

33. See Norma Haan, Robert Bellah, Paul Rabinow, and William Sullivan, eds., *Social Science as Moral Inquiry* (New York: Columbia University Press, 1983), especially Michelle Z. Rosaldo's "Moral/Analytic Dilemmas Posed by the Intersection of Feminism and Social Science," 76–96; and Robert Bellah's "The Ethical Aims of Social Inquiry," 360–81.

34. Janice Moulton, "A Paradigm of Philosophy: The Adversary Method," in Harding and Hintikka, *Discovering Reality,* 149–64.

35. For detailed discussions of the Afrocentric worldview, see John S. Mbiti, *African Religions and Philosophy* (London: Heinemann, 1969); Dominique Zahan, *The Religion, Spirituality, and Thought of Traditional Africa* (Chicago: University of Chicago Press, 1979); and Mechal Sobel, *Trabelin' On: The Slave Journey to an Afro-Baptist Faith* (Westport, CT: Greenwood Press, 1979), 1–76.

36. For representative works applying these concepts to African American culture, see Niara Sudarkasa, "Interpreting the African Heritage in Afro-American Family Organization," in *Black Families,* ed. Harriette Pipes McAdoo (Beverly Hills, CA: Sage Publications, 1981); Henry H. Mitchell and Nicholas Cooper Lewter, *Soul Theology: The Heart of American Black Culture* (San Francisco: Harper & Row, 1986); Robert Farris Thompson, *Flash of the Spirit: African and Afro-American Art and Philosophy* (New York: Vintage, 1983); and Ortiz M. Walton, "Comparative Analysis of the African and the Western Aesthetics," in *The Black Aesthetic,* ed. Addison Gayle (Garden City, NY: Doubleday, 1971), 154–64.

37. One of the best discussions of an Afrocentric epistemology is offered by James E. Turner, "Foreword: Africana Studies and Epistemology; a Discourse in the Sociology of Knowledge," in *The Next Decade: Theoretical and Research Issues in Africana Studies,* ed. James E. Turner (Ithaca, NY: Cornell University Africana Studies and Research Center, 1984), v–xxv. See also Vernon Dixon, "World Views and Research Methodology," summarized in Harding, *The Science Question,* 170.

38. See Hester Eisenstein, *Contemporary Feminist Thought* (Boston: G. K. Hall, 1983). Nancy Hartsock's *Money, Sex, and Power,* 145–209, offers a particularly insightful analysis of women's oppression.

39. For discussions of feminist consciousness, see Dorothy Smith, "A Sociology for Women," in *The Prism of Sex: Essays in the Sociology of Knowledge,* ed. Julia A. Sherman and Evelyn T. Beck (Madison: University of Wisconsin Press, 1979); and Michelle Z. Rosaldo, "Women, Culture, and Society: A Theoretical Overview," in *Woman, Culture, and Society,* ed. Michelle Z. Rosaldo and

Louise Lamphere (Stanford, CA: Stanford University Press,1974), 17–42. Feminist epistemologies are surveyed by Jaggar, *Feminist Politics.*

40. One significant difference between Afrocentric and feminist standpoints is that much of what is termed womens culture is, unlike African American culture, treated in the context of and produced by oppression. Those who argue for a women's culture are electing to value, rather than denigrate, those traits associated with females in white patriarchal societies. While this choice is important, it is not the same as identifying an independent, historical culture associated with a society. I am indebted to Deborah K. King for this point.

41. Critiques of the Eurocentric masculinist knowledge-validation process by both Africanist and feminist scholars illustrate this point. What one group labels "white" and "Eurocentric," the other describes as "male-dominated" and "masculinist." Although he does not emphasize its patriarchal and racist features, Morris Berman's *The Reenchantment of the World* (New York: Bantam Books, 1981) provides a historical discussion of Western thought. Afrocentric analyses of this same process can be found in Molefi Kete Asante, "International/Intercultural Relations," in *Contemporary Black Thought,* ed. Molefi Kete Asante and Abdulai S. Vandi (Beverly Hills, CA: Sage Publications, 1980), 43–58; and Dona Richards, "European Mythology: The Ideology of 'Progress,' " in Asante and Vandi, *Contemporary Black Thought,* 59–79. For feminist analyses, see Hartsock, *Money, Sex, and Power.* Harding also discusses this similarity (see Chap. 7, "Other 'Others' and Fractured Identities: Issues for Epistemologists," 63–96).

42. Harding, *The Science Question,* 166.

43. D. King, "Race, Class and Gender Salience."

44. Bonnie Thornton Dill, "The Dialectics of Black Womanhood," *Signs* 4, no. 3 (Spring 1979): 543–55.

45. One implication of standpoint approaches is that the more subordinate the group, the purer the vision of the oppressed group. This is an outcome of the origins of standpoint approaches in Marxist social theory, itself a dualistic analysis of social structure. Because such approaches rely on quantifying and ranking human oppressions—familiar tenets of positivist approaches—they are rejected by blacks and feminists alike. See Harding, *The Science Question,* for a discussion of this point. See also Elizabeth V. Spelman's discussion of the fallacy of additive oppression in "Theories of Race and Gender: The Erasure of Black Women," *Quest* 5, no. 4 (1982): 36–62.

46. Class differences among black women may be marked. For example, see Paula Giddings's analysis (in *When and Where I Enter*) of the role of social class in shaping black women's political activism; or Elizabeth Higginbotham's study of the effects of social class in black women's college attendance in "Race and Class Barriers to Black Women's College Attendance," *Journal of Ethnic Studies* 13, no. 1 (1985): 89–107. Those African American women who have experienced the greatest degree of convergence of race, class, and gender oppression may be in a better position to recognize and use an alternative epistemology.

47. Gwaltney, *Drylongso,* 83.

48. William L. Andrews, *Sisters of the Spirit: Three Black Women's Autobiographies of the Nineteenth Century* (Bloomington: Indiana University Press, 1986), 85.

49. Gwaltney, *Drylongso,* 147.

50. Geneva Smitherman, *Talkin and Testifyin: The Language of Black America* (Detroit: Wayne State University Press, 1986), 76.

51. Gwaltney, *Drylongso,* 68.

52. Ibid., 7.

53. Ibid., 27, 33.

54. Elsa Barkley Brown, "Hearing Our Mothers' Lives" (paper presented at the Fifteenth Anniversary Faculty Lecture Series, African American and African Studies, Emory University, Atlanta, 1986).

55. Ladner, *Tomorrow's Tomorrow.*

56. Mitchell and Lewter, *Soul Theology.* The use of the narrative approach in African American theology exemplifies an inductive system of logic alternately called "folk wisdom" or a survival-based, need-oriented method of assessing knowledge claims.

57. Ibid., 8.

58. June Jordan, *On Call: Political Essays* (Boston: South End Press, 1985), 26.

59. Mary Belenky, Blythe Clinchy, Nancy Goldberger, and Jill Tarule, *Women's Ways of Knowing* (New York: Basic Books, 1986), 113.

60. Hartsock, *Money, Sex, and Power,* 237; and Nancy Chodorow, *The Reproduction of Mothering* (Berkeley and Los Angeles: University of California Press, 1978).

61. Dorothy Smith, *The Everyday World as Problematic* (Boston: Northeastern University Press, 1987).

62. Byerly, *Hard Times Cotton Mill Girls,* 198.

63. For black women's centrality in the family, see Steady, *The Black Woman;* Ladner, *Tomorrow's Tomorrow;* Brown, "Hearing Our Mothers' Lives"; and McAdoo, *Black Families.* See Gilkes, " 'Together and in Harness,' " for black women in the church; and chapter 4 of Deborah Gray White, *Ar'n't I a Woman? Female Slaves in the Plantation South* (New York: W. W. Norton, 1985). See also Gloria Joseph, "Black Mothers and Daughters: Their Roles and Functions in American Society," in *Common Differences: Conflicts in Black and White Feminist Perspectives,* ed. Gloria Joseph and Jill Lewis (Garden City, NY: Anchor, 1981), 75–126. Even though black women play essential roles in black families and black churches, these institutions are not free from sexism.

64. Black men, white women, and members of other race, class, and gender groups should be encouraged to interpret, teach, and critique the black feminist thought produced by African American women.

65. Walker, *In Search of Our Mothers' Gardens* (New York: Harcourt Brace Jovanovich, 1974), 91.

66. Gwaltney, *Drylongso.*

67. Jordan, *On Call,* 130.

68. Collins, "Learning from the Outsider Within."

69. This point addresses the question of relativity in the sociology of knowledge and offers a way of regulating competing knowledge claims.

CHAPTER FIVE

The Body Politic:
Sexuality, Violence,
and Reproduction

... black women are the beached whales of the sexual universe, un-voiced, misseen, not doing, awaiting their verb. Their sexual experiences are depicted, but not often by them.... they have had long experience with the brutalizations of male power, are subject to rape, know their womanhood and sexual being as crucially related and decisively timed moments in the creation and nurture of human life....

—HORTENSE SPILLERS,
"Interstices: A Small Drama of Words"

INTRODUCTION

Black women's bodies have been sites of contestation since Europeans first set foot on African soil to appropriate free labor for the brutal system of slavery. Myths about black female sexuality, born on the African continent, would follow black women to the "New World" and help to justify their sexual exploitation for generations thereafter.

Contemporary black feminists concern themselves with a broader discourse on sexuality and reproduction. They write about abortion, incest, lesbianism, homophobia, rape, domestic violence, and sexual harassment. Their concerns transcend geographical boundaries because of their global perspective on the oppression of women. Their African diasporan or Pan-African perspective demands that they be in solidarity with women of African descent throughout the world and that they struggle with them around issues of particular concern to women. This includes the elimination of poverty and disease and barriers to women's emancipation. It also includes issues around reproductive health, including the controversial practice of female genital mutilation. Ultimately, issues surrounding the body politic, in all their complexity, will profoundly impact the well-being and survival of black women and their families.

Barbara Omolade

Barbara Omolade, an activist, writer, and professor, grew up in New York City and participated in both the civil rights and women's movements. While a senior in college, she worked in the New York SNCC offices where she became a nationalist, an intellectual, and serious about political matters and African culture. While on welfare as a single mother, she read Gerda Lerner's *Black Women in White America* and decided to pursue graduate study. A job at a battered women's shelter (after welfare) inspired her to read (*The Rising Song,* xii) and in 1970 she returned to the academy and taught a course on black women. In the late 1970s she worked at Women's Action Alliance and Women's Survival Space and volunteered with The Black United Front and The Sisterhood of Black Single Mothers.

"Hearts of Darkness," which appeared in *Powers of Desire: The Politics of Sexuality* (1983), is a historical essay dealing with the neglected topic of black female sexuality in which Omalade critiques the myth of black women as mainly victims. The essay is also a black feminist rendering of the complex sexual history of the United States.

Her book, *The Rising Song of African American Women* (1994), a provocative collection of autobiographical/political essays, chronicles her development as a "race woman" and black feminist activist/teacher. It includes her previously published essay on black feminist pedagogy, analyses of the Central Park jogger case, black women troops in the Gulf War, and the Tawana Brawley saga. Omolade works at City College at the Center for Worker Education in New York.

Barbara Omolade }

HEARTS OF DARKNESS

The sexual history of the United States began at the historical moment when European men met African women in the "heart of darkness"[1] —Mother Africa. They faced each other as conqueror and conquered: African women captives were considered the sexual property of the European conquerors.[2]

The African sexuality confronted by European men was an integral part of a sensuality that permeated music, dance, and religion. West African women often performed dances such as the "crotch dance, an improvised folk drama enacted by the women at the height of the birth celebration, in which women strike their crotches firmly with both their hands."[3] However tactile, pleasurable, and comfortable these daily creative art forms, they were not necessarily indicative of sexual promiscuity. Rather, African cultures taught men and women to use their bodies in fluid, rhythmic ways, within a sexual code of behavior that frequently countenanced murdering women who committed adultery and often practiced female clitoridectomy.[4] The African woman who faced the European man was a wife, a mother, a daughter, a sister, nestled in tribal societies and protected by fathers, husbands, and brothers who upheld the sanctity and primacy of marriage and motherhood for women.

Nevertheless, in the hip-shaking, bare-breasted women with sweating bodies who danced to drums played by intense black men, in the market women and nursing mothers wrapped in African cloth, in the scantily clad farming women, the European man saw a being who embodied all that was evil and profane to his sensibilities. He perceived the African's sensual ways according to his own cultural definitions of sex, nudity, and blackness as base, foul, and bestial. He did not attempt to understand how Africans defined their own behavior.[5] He made assumptions and invented knowledge about their behavior as he created the conditions for this "knowledge" to become the reality. He viewed the African expression of sensuality through public rites, rituals, and dances as evidence of the absence of any sexual codes of behavior, an idea that both fascinated and repelled him and also provided him with a needed rationale for the economic exploitation of African men and women.

As historian Richard Hofstadter explains:

Naked and libidinous: for the white man's preoccupation with Negro sexuality was there at the very beginning, an outcome not only of his own guilt at sexual exploitation—his easy access to the black woman was immediately blamed on *her* lasciviousness—but also of his envious suspicion that some extraordinary potency and ecstatic experience were associated with primitive lust.[6]

Within the strange "commingling of desire and hate,"[7] white men would continue to penetrate and plunder Mother Africa for five centuries while creating a worldview centered around the myth of race and racism that upheld white supremacy and the total domination of black people.

The sexual history of the United States became fused with contradiction and duality, with myth and distortion, with the white man's hate and desire for the black woman, with competition and jealousy between white and black women for white men, with love and struggle between black men and black women. American sexual history reflects the development of patriarchal control stretched to its maximum extent by European men operating within a racial caste system supported by state power in which white maleness becomes the only definition of being. Simultaneously, the extremes of American patriarchy, particularly under slavery, pushed black women outside traditional patriarchal protection, thereby transforming all previous definitions of womanhood, particularly the idea that woman requires male protection because of her innate weakness and inferiority.[8] Black women were oppressed and exploited labor and as such were forced to redefine themselves as women outside of and antagonistic to the racial patriarch, who denied their being. Most black women refused to accept the traditional notions of subordination of woman to man. The black woman resisted racial patriarchy by escaping, stealing, killing, outsmarting, and bargaining with her white master while she had sex with him, had babies by him, ministered to his needs, growing "to know all there was to know about him."[9] At the same time, most black women accepted traditional notions of patriarchy from black men because they viewed the Afro-Christian tradition of woman as mother and wife as personally desirable and politically necessary for black people's survival.

The racial patriarchy of the white man enabled him to enact his culture's separation between the goodness, purity, innocence, and frailty of woman with the sinful, evil strength, and carnal knowledge of woman by having sex with white women, who came to embody the former, and black women, who came to embody the latter.[10] The white man's division of the sexual attributes of women based on race meant that he alone could claim to be sexually free: he was free to be sexually active within a society that upheld the chastity and modesty of white women as the "repositories of white civilization."[11] He was free to be irresponsible about the consequences of his sexual behavior with black women within a culture that placed a great value on the family as a sacred institution protecting women, their progeny, and his property. He was free to use violence to eliminate his competition with black men for black or white women, thus breaking the customary allegiance among all patriarchs. He was also free to maintain his public hatred of racial mixing while privately expressing his desire for black women's bodies. Ultimately, white men were politically empowered to dominate all women and all black men and women; this was their sexual freedom.

From the beginning, the founding fathers assumed the patriarchal right to regulate and define the sexual behavior of their servants and slaves according to a fusion of Protestantism, English Common Law, and personal whim. During the early colonial period the distinctions between indentured servant and slave were blurred and relative: most workers, black and white, male and female, worked without direct payment or without control over their labor. These laborers shared enough common experiences to jointly attack their masters and to have sex with each other.[12] The master's racial attitudes of antipathy toward black people and his fears of a unified antagonistic force of all workers, including Indian women and men, demanded that the category "white" be expanded to give political power and freedom to all white men (theoretically and potentially, if not at that actual historical time) and patriarchal protection and white privilege to all white women. Thus, during the later colonial period, black men and white women who had sex, married, and/or had children were punished and persecuted as American society denied them the right to choose each other as mates.[13] The category "white" would also mean that the people designated "black" could be held in perpetual slavery.[14] Therefore, laws were passed and practices instituted to regulate the sexual and social behavior of white and black, servants and slaves. The legal and actual distinction between slave and servant was widened with "slavery reflecting lifelong power relationships, while servitude became a more temporary relationship of service."[15] In other words, in spite of the common experiences of black and white workers in colonial America, indentured servants were whitened as slaves became black.

Though black people were less than five percent of the population in the later part of the seventeenth century, a 1662 Virginia statute stipulated that "all offspring follow the condition of the mother in the event of a white man getting a Negro with child."[16] A 1664 statute prohibited all unions between the races.[17] In 1665, the first English slave code in New York provided that slavery was for life.[18] Colonial law and custom reflected the parameters that would continue to govern American sexual behavior: regardless of who impregnated black women, any offspring would be slave. As Hofstadter puts it, this "guaranteed in a society where interracial sex usually involved the access of white men to black women, that without other provisions to the contrary, the mulatto population would be slave."[19] Well before the institution of slavery was firmly established in the antebellum South during the nineteenth century, these laws and others prohibiting black political participation, ownership of land, and the right to carry arms[20] were aimed at creating a black population in perpetual servitude.

Slavery and slaveholders dominated American political and economic life for about two hundred years. As Carl Degler describes it:

> The labor of slaves provided the wherewithal to maintain lawyers and actors, cotton factors and publishers, musicians in Charleston, senators in Washington, and gamblers on the Mississippi river boats. Slaveholders were agricultural entrepreneurs in a capitalistic society: their central importance as a class resided not in their numbers, which were admittedly small, but in their ability to accumulate surplus for investment.[21]

Degler's phrase "ability to accumulate surplus for investment" tends to obscure all traces of the inhumanity of slavery: black women's bodies were a primary means of accumulating the surplus: "My mother was young— just fifteen or sixteen years old. She had fourteen chillen and you know that meant a lots of wealth."[22] New slave owners with one or two slaves attempting to "construct an initial labor force" and establish an economic base in order to realize profits broke up slave communities or African clans by obtaining individual slaves through purchase, gift, or marriage. The fecundity of black women was key to the slave owner's goal. Gutman documents that as one planter said, "An owner's labor force doubled through natural increase every 15 years."[23] A slave, looking back, agrees:

> They would buy a fine girl and a fine man and just put them together like cattle; they would not stop to marry them. If she was a good breeder, they was proud of her. I was stout and they were saving me for a breeding woman, but by the time I was big enough I was free. I had an aunt in Mississippi and she had about 20 children by her marster.[24]

"Natural increase" meant that the black woman was encouraged and sometimes forced to have sex frequently in order to have babies whether by black men or white men, in stable or unstable relationships.

But as early as 1639, black women resisted forced sex:

[O]ne source . . . tells of a Negro woman being held as a slave on Noddles Island in Boston harbor. Her master sought to mate her with another Negro, but, the chronicler reported, she kicked her prospective lover out of bed, saying that such behavior was "beyond her slavery."[25]

But though it was beyond *her* concept of enslavement, it was not beyond her master's, for every part of the black woman was used by him. To him she was a fragmented commodity whose feelings and choices were rarely considered: her head and her heart were separated from her back and her hands and divided from her womb and vagina. Her back and muscle were pressed into field labor where she was forced to work with men and work like men. Her hands were demanded to nurse and nurture the white man and his family as domestic servant whether she was technically enslaved or legally free. Her vagina, used for his sexual pleasure, was the gateway to the womb, which was his place of capital investment—the capital investment being the sex act, and the resulting child the accumulated surplus, worth money on the slave market.

The totalitarian system of slavery extended itself into the very place that was inviolable and sacred to both African and European societies—the sanctity of the woman's body and motherhood within the institution of marriage. Although all women were slaves under patriarchy, the particular enslavement of black women was also an attack on all black people. All sexual intercourse between a white man and a black woman irrespective of her conscious consent became rape, because the social arrangement assumed the black woman to be without any human right to control her own body.[26] And the body could not be separated from its color.

Racial oppression tends to flow from the external to the internal: from political institutions, social structures, the economic system, and military conquest, into the psyche and consciousness and culture of the oppressed and the oppressor. In contrast, sexual oppression tends to direct itself directly to the internal, the feeling and emotional center, the private and intimate self, existing within the external context of power and social control. Black women fused both racial and sexual oppression in their beings and movements in both black and white worlds.

Black women moved through the white man's world: through his space, his land, his fields, his streets, and his woodpiles.

The Negro woman carried herself like a queen, tall and stately in spite of her position as a slave. The overseer, the plantation owner's son, sent her to the house on some errand. It was necessary to pass through a wooded pasture to reach the house, and the overseer intercepted her in the woods and forced her to put her head between the rails in an old stake and rider fence, and there in that position, my great, great grandfather was conceived.[27]

In the white man's world, black women would have a place: "I know at least fifty places in my small town were white men are positively raising two families—a white family in the 'Big House' in front, and a colored family in a 'Little House' in the backyard."[28] In the white man's world, black women were separated from black men: "When I left the camp my wife had had two children by some one of the white bosses, and she was living in fairly good shape in a little house off to herself."[29] They became the teachers of sex to white boys. "Testimony seems to be quite widespread to the fact that many if not most southern boys begin their sexual experiences with Negro girls."[30]

White men tortured and punished black women who refused them: For fending off the advances of an overseer on a Virginia plantation, Minnie Falkes's mother was suspended from a barn rafter and beaten with a horsewhip "nekkid" til blood run down her back to her heels.[31] Madison Jefferson adds:

> Women who refused to submit themselves to the brutal desires of their owners, are repeatedly whipt to subdue their virtuous repugnance, and in most instances this hellish practice is but too successful—when it fails, the women are frequently sold off to the south.[32]

The black woman worked in the white man's home, both before and after formal emancipation. She knew her master/lover as a man; she was intimate with his humanity; she fed him and she slept with him; she ministered to his needs.[33] One slave remarked, "Now mind you all of the colored women didn't have to have white men, some did it because they wanted to and some were forced. They had a horror of going to Mississippi and they would do anything to keep from it."[34]

Black women and white women were sisters under the oppression of white men in whose houses they both lived as servants. In the antebellum South, Mary Chestnut wrote, "There is no slave after all like a wife."[35] A white woman married to the planter/patriarch endured, suffered, and submitted to him in all things. White women, though viewed as pure and delicate ladies by Southern myth, had to serve their husband/masters as did the female servants and slaves; managing the household, entertaining the guests, overseeing the feeding and clothing of both slaves and relatives.[36]

Both white and black women were physically weakened and often died from birthing too many of the master's children. White men often had several wives in succession because many died in childbirth. While white wives visited relatives for long periods of time to have space between pregnancies,[37] exercising a much-needed control over childbearing, black women all too often filled the gap for both recreational and procreational sex. Ann Firor Scott writes of one South Carolinian who thought, "The availability of slave women for sex avoided the horrors of prostitution. He pointed out that men could satisfy their sexual needs while increasing their slave property."[38] To be a white woman in the antebellum South meant accepting the double standard; brothers, fathers, and mates could enjoy sex with her sisters in bondage, black women. White women however, were prevented from enjoying sex because they were viewed as "pure women incapable of erotic feeling."[39]

Many southern white women privately disliked the double standard and the horrors of the sexual life it implied: "Under slavery we lived surrounded by prostitutes like patriarchs of old, our men live in one house with their wives and concubines."[40] An ex-slave woman agreed:

> Just the other day we were talking about white people when they had slaves. You know when a man would marry, his father would give him a woman for a cook, and she would have children right in the home by him, and his wife would have children too. Sometimes the cook's children favored him so much that the wife would be mean to them and make him sell them.[41]

Yet for all the private outrage of white women at the "injustice and shame" to all womanhood of the sexual activities of white men, black women stood alone without the support of their sisters. Most white women sadistically and viciously punished the black women and her children for the transgressions of their white men. One study states:

> To punish black women for minor offenses, mistresses were likely to attack with any weapon available—a fork, butcher knife, knitting needle, pan of boiling water. Some of the most barbaric forms of punishment resulting in the mutilation and permanent scarring of female servants were devised by white mistresses in the heat of passion.[42]

White women used the social relationship of supervisor of black women's domestic labor to act out their racial superiority, their emotional frustrations, and their sexual jealousies. Black women slaves and domestic servants were useful buffers between white men and white women, pulling them together, resolving their conflicts, maintaining continuity and structure for the white family whose physical and emotional needs they fulfilled.[43]

When the daughter and son of the white man and the black woman faced the father, they reflected the fruits of his passion as well as the duplicity of his life. Their light skin or light eyes, their straight hair or nose reflected himself to himself, and yet he still refused to acknowledge paternity. The exceptional white father/master/lover who cared would often free his black children and wife, hustle them out of town, educating and supporting them from afar, helping them rise within black society while hoping for silence and anonymity. But in spite of traditional patriarchal concerns for fatherhood, most white fathers did nothing for their colored children. Most colored children shared the experience of this ex-slave: "My grandfather was an Irishman, and he was a foreman, but he had to whip his children and grandchildren just like the others."[44] Those few slaveholders who loved and respected their slave wives were limited by societal criticism and the law from formally marrying them.[45]

Though she had no privacy, away from the view of all, could the black woman have ever desired and loved her master/lover? Could she have separated the hands that whipped her body from the hands that gripped her body in lovemaking? After all, the master/lover was only a man who desired the slave woman and had the power to take her as a woman. Patriarchal society would define the perfect man as the perfect master, and it was the submissiveness of the slave woman that made her the perfect slave and the perfect woman. After all, a man's power over a woman was like the master's power over a slave. It came from "innate superiority."[46] But the ultimate place of desire and fulfillment of the submissive and perfected woman was in violent conflict with the rage and humiliation and forced labor of being a slave woman forced to lie in the arms of the enslaver, the enemy ultimately responsible for her humiliation and her suffering. Yet the woman could not be separated from the color. One black woman remembers:

> One mark in particular stands out in my memory, one she bore just above her right eye. As well as she liked to regale me with stories of her scars, this one she never discussed with me. Whenever I would ask a question concerning it, she would simply shake her head and say "White men are as low as dogs, child. Stay from them." It was only after her death, and since I became a woman that I was told by my own mother that she received that scar at the hands of her master's youngest son, a boy of about eighteen years, at the time she conceived their child, my grandmother, Ellen.[47]

Though mulattoes were "common as blackberries,"[48] most black women resisted white men's sexual advances and resented being a convenient scapegoat for the white women's sexual suppression. Black women were often unwilling participants in the sexual lives of white men and women. In spite of close contact, many did not necessarily admire or identify with white families. They often longed to go home to the black world to care for their own men and children.

As she crossed the tracks to the black world, she could breathe a little easier, soften, and slow up her steps. She could smile at her neighbors and kin along the road or warn them away with her stern and tired face. They understood that her day had been rough. The care of her children, her men, and her sisters would occupy her time now. She would find private space in cleaning her house, tending her garden, fixing her room with doilies and trinkets. She would sew sister's dress, braid her baby girl's hair, and fix that hat for Sunday's church meeting. In this world there was space for her to pull herself together. The space was contained and narrow, but it did give her easement from the white man's world and his desire for her body.

Against the white man's animal panting and arbitrary carnal desires that stalked their daughters, the old ones' harsh words and demands of modesty emphasized with a slap or a hard look forced the girls to hide and conserve the precious darkness between their legs. The old ones would frequently frustrate and confuse their daughters' sexual desires, for though their rage originated from the sexual abuses of white men, they extended taboos against all sexual expression.

African cultural values taught deference and respect to the elderly, who set parameters for sexual, romantic, and marital relationships within tribal rituals and rites. Within slave and rural black communities away from the interferences of white men, the deference continued.[49] Young black men courted and romanced young women with African-like ritual and respect, always under the watchful eyes of the old ones.

> When this courting process proceeded naturally and freely, the couple might eventually have a child, or if the girl had already had her first baby (often by a different man) they might marry and settle into a long-lasting monogamous union.[50]

The old ones in the new world were consulted for their approval and consent to marital plans or pregnancies by their daughters and sons. Sometimes, mothers and grandmothers (fathers and grandfathers also) were unmoved by romance or youthful passion and clamped down on their daughters' sexual desires for any but the most stable mates with the firmness of an iron chastity belt.

Though black women were mothers, midwives, and farmers, with daughters growing up close to them, frequently in crowded homes with many siblings and relatives, most young black women learned little explicit information about sex.[51] Thus, in spite of and because of the historical sexual abuse of black women, both black men and black women lived sexually conservative lives characterized by modesty and discretion. In fact, most black women were reluctant to openly discuss specific sexual abuses against their person by white men, even within their own families.[52]

The black man moved toward the black woman, clothing her raped and abused body with the mantle of respectable womanhood, giving protection and sometimes claiming ownership of her. Many black men agreed with white men that "wives should submit themselves to their husbands in all things."[53] As the dominant institution within the black community, the black church reinforced and supported the traditional patriarchal views of men claiming wardship over women.

Protecting black women was the most significant measure of black manhood and the central aspect of black male patriarchy. Black men felt outrage and shame at their frequent inability to protect black women, not merely from the whippings and hard work, but also from the master/lover's touch. During and after slavery, black men spoke out angrily against the harsh treatment of black women, many vowing never to allow black women to be sexually abused and economically exploited again.[54] Their methods often became rigidly patriarchal; however, they did in many instances keep black women from becoming the open prey of the white man. W. E. B. Du Bois summed up the feelings of many black men:

> . . . but one thing I shall never forgive, neither in this world nor in the world to come: it's [the white South's] wanton and continued and persistent insulting of the black womanhood which it sought and seeks to prostitute to its lust.[55]

After the Civil War, black men and black women married each other in droves, giving their unions legitimacy and validating their right to choose and love each other.[56] Many felt that the slave master could no longer come between black men and black women for the law connected them. Yet in their successful attempts to recapture political and economic power, white men claimed a glorified past of total domination over black people, continuing to enter the "heart of darkness" as their right.

Although, during Reconstruction, terror and hunger forced black men and black women into peonage and sharecropping, the black community resisted the new chains of white male domination. Women vowed to stand by their men, never to return to the fields, to the kitchens, or to the beds of white men. As the white community attacked and extended its dominion, black women carved out new ways to survive as well as uphold their marriages and the implied sanctity of their bodies.

Black men struggled to farm their own land in order to provide for their families, keeping wives and daughters away from white men's farms and arms. Many asserted as one ex-slave did to his white father/master who doubted his ability to provide for his family. "I am going to feed and clothe them, and I can do it on bare rock."[57] Black women withdrew from farm labor for the white man, and when they had to work, they insisted on day work rather than sleep-in domestic work.[58] Black women also sewed, dressed hair, washed clothes, and cooked meals in their own homes for wages in order to keep out of the white men's homes.

In the context of the black community of resistance, "heterosexual privilege usually became the only privilege black women had. For without racial or sexual privilege, marriage and motherhood become the last resort."[59] The very traditional experiences of motherhood and sex within marriage were not necessarily viewed as oppressive to black women, for they were the literal and symbolic weapons she could utilize to assure the biological and social reproduction of black people. Marriage and motherhood were humanizing experiences that gave her life meaning, purpose and choice. These experiences were denied within the racist milieu where her humanity was questioned and her human rights and privileges to love and be loved were denied.

The African values retained within the black community in combination with its learned Christian values reinforced sexual loyalty and monogamy for black women. Although white society described her as an insatiable animal with no feelings of love and commitment, in one way or another, and with a variety of consequences, black women have been monogamous, serially monogamous, and sexually loyal partners to black men (and sometimes white men also).

Black men held a wide range of views about black women from those that reinforced female subordination to those that reinforced equal social relations between the sexes. Many black men, moving away from traditional patriarchal views, supported and encouraged independence in their wives, and more often in their daughters.[60] Black women were supported by black men in building black elementary schools and community institutions and in encouraging their daughters to become educated as teachers to escape the "abominations" of the white man. As teachers, black women could be kept within the black community away from the sexual advances of white men and under the watchful protecting eyes of male principals and ministers as well. Teaching required of black women an even more rigorous adherence to a sex code enjoining chastity and model womanhood than that guiding other black women.[61]

Sex codes upholding the values of monogamy and sexual loyalty were part of the extended kinship networks that provided valuable emotional, physical, and economic support for black women. Kin accepted children sired by white men into the family. There was no such thing as "illegitimacy," for each child was considered part of the community, where its mother might be stigmatized by rarely ostracized. Women abandoned by their husbands were viewed with sympathy. To a great extent, black women forced into sexual relations with white men were still considered suitable mates by black men. There was the widespread practice of black men parenting children not sired by them, even when a child's father was white. Nearly every black family had a white absentee father or grandfather and a wide range of skin colors. Only those women who continued to live outside the sexual code, which condemned adultery and promiscuity with white or black men, were viewed as sinful.[62] Both during and after slavery, black women and men have had a complex history of struggling together to maintain stable, monogamous families, transmuting the destructive forces from without, cooperating and supporting each other from within.

The historical oppression of black women and men should have created social equality between them, but even after the end of slavery when the white patriarch receded, maleness and femaleness continued to be defined by patriarchal structures, with black men declaring wardship over black women. In the black community, the norm of manhood was patriarchal power; the norm of womanhood was adherence to it, though both black men and women selected which aspects of these norms they would emphasize.

Many black women became enraged at the thought of being owned and taken by any man, even if he had black skin. The whippings, the work, the penetration by the whipper and the white master/lover left them with rage and rebellion against the traditional roles of wife and mother. They would resist as Rose Williams resisted when

> forced to live with a man named Rufus because the master wanted them "to bring forth portly children" warned the slave to stay away from her "fore I busts yous brains out and stomp on dem." She finally relented when threatened with a whipping, but she never married, explaining, "after what I done for de massa I's never wants no truck with any man—de lawd forgive dis cullud woman, but he have to 'scuse me and look for some others for to 'plenish de earth."[63]

Black women within the rural black community often defied the restrictions on their womanhood and sexuality by living alone (near family and kin) and working their own farms, running their own lives without men as mates and protectors, frequently sojourning for truth and God. Many of these women learned these independent ways from their fathers and brothers. Women often lived with women as both emotional and sexual companions. Women in urban black communities had several male lovers and companions but did not submit to them in traditional ways because they maintained an independent life as community workers, political and social activists, and workers within the paid labor force.

At the beginning of the twentieth century, both rural and urban black women followed the role models of black female artists, singers, dancers, and actresses who expressed and reinforced the sensuality of African traditions by shaking and shimmying on stages and in clubs and roadhouses. Black women leaving the restrictions of the rural South agreed with Bessie Smith:

> I'm a young woman and ain't done runnin' roun'...
> Some people call me a hobo, some call me a bum.
> Nobody knows my name, nobody knows what I've done.
> See that long, lonesome road? Lord you know it's gotta end.
> And I'm a good woman and I can get plenty men.[64]

These black women lived lives of explicit sexuality and erotic excitement with both men and women. As they broke away from the traditional paternal restraints within the black community, they were castigated for seeming to reflect the truth of the white man's views of black women as whorish and loose. But these "wild women"[65] did not care, modeling for Southern rural black women a city life full of flashy clothes, fast cars, and access to sophisticated men.

However, most black women did not have access to the mobility of a freer sexual life even within marriage until the 1960s, when large-scale urbanization, a shift from domestic to clerical jobs, and the breakup of the traditional kinship networks of the rural South took place. Even then, black women's sexuality was still contained within a white male patriarchy that continued to view her as already sexually liberated.

Black woman could not be completely controlled and defined by her own men, for she had already learned to manage and resist the advances of white men, earning and internalizing a reputation for toughness and strength, for resiliency and resolve, that enhanced the myth of her as both matriarch and wild woman. Her political resistance increased her potential to become a woman of power, capable of defining herself and rising to protect herself and her children, frequently throwing the mantle of protection over black men as well.

Slavery and womanhood remained interconnected long after the formal bondage of black people was over. Being a black woman with a black man could still mean slavery. And the woman could not be separated from the color. Being a black woman without a black man could also still mean slavery. And the color could not be separated from the woman.

These contradictions have been fully explored by only a few black women, for black women and black men continue to be engaged in a community of struggle to create a space in which to live and to survive:

> Black women speaking with many voices and expressing many individual opinions, have been nearly unanimous in their insistence that their own emancipation cannot be separated from the emancipation of their men. Their liberation depends on the liberation of the race and the improvement of life in the black community.[66]

Sex between black women and black men, between black men and black men, between black women and black women, is meshed within complex cultural, political, and economic circumstances. All black sexuality is underlined by a basic theme: where, when, and under what circumstances could/ would black men and black women connect with each other intimately and privately when all aspects of their lives were considered the dominion of the public, white master/lover's power?

If the sexual act between white men and black women was a ritual reenactment of domination, the oppression failed to completely dampen the sexual expression of black women within the black community, which often became a ritual enactment of affirmation of her freedom and happiness within intense emotional connections with her men, her sisters, her children, her gods, and more often with herself. In spite of centuries of personal and political rape, black women could still say, "i found god in myself/and i loved her/i loved her fiercely."[67]

History, traditionally written as a record of public events, has obscured and omitted the relationship between public events and private acts. Therefore, sex has always been in the closet of American history, hidden away from and kept outside the public realm of political and economic events. White men used their power in the public sphere to construct a private sphere that would meet their needs and their desire for black women, which if publically admitted would have undermined the false construct of race they needed to maintain public power. Therefore, the history of black women in America reflects the juncture where the private and public spheres and personal and political oppression meet.

The master/lover ruled over the world; he divided it up and called everyone out of their name. During the day, he would call her "wench," "negress," "Sable Venus," "dusky Sal," and "Auntie." He described and wrote about her endurance, ate her biscuits, and suckled her breasts. At night he would chant false endearments and would feel engulfed within her darkness. He would accuse her of raping herself, naming his lesser brothers as the fathers of his and her children. He would record every battle, keep every letter, document each law, building monuments to himself, but he would never tell the true story, the complete story, of how he used to rape to make the profit, of how he used the bodies of women to satisfy his needs. He would never tell how he built a society with the aid of dark-skinned women, while telling the world he did it alone.

He would cover the tracks between his house and hers, he would deny the semen-stained sheets she was forced to wash. History would become all that men did during the day, but nothing of what they did during the night. He would forget her children. He would deny his love or lust for her. He would deny his failure to obey his own laws. He refused to listen to the logical extension of his argument for the massacres, the slave raids, the genocide, the lynch mobs, the Ku Klux Klan. He could not live up to his own fears and arguments against mongrelization of the race, the separation of black from white. He built an exterior world that reflected his fragmented insides.

But the woman learned to face him, the rapist who hated and loved her with such passion. She learned to use her darkness to create light. She would make the divided, white and black, external and internal world into wholeness. She would "lean on Jesus," reaching out to help and for help, and would gather around her children and kin to help them make the world whole and livable. She would mother all the children—black and white—and serve both men—conqueror and conquered—knowing "all there was to know," for she could not separate the color from the woman.

Only a few daring men, mostly black ones, would recognize that only she understood what it had taken for white men to dominate the world and what it would mean, finally, to be free. But some black women who voiced what they knew did not survive:

> A slave woman ain't allowed to respect herself, if she would. I had a pretty sister, she was whiter than I am, for she took more after her father. When she was sixteen years old, her master sent for her. When he sent for her again, she cried and didn't want to go. She told mother her troubles, and she tried to encourage her to be decent and hold up her head above such things if she could. Her master was so mad, to think she had complained to her mother, that he sold her right off to Louisiana, and we heard afterward that she died there of hard usage.[68]

But others sold down river survived and remembered their mothers and fathers, remembered the white master/lover, the black master/lover, and the black brother/lover. They, in their turn, gave their daughters and sons the gifts of determination and freedom, the will to love and the strength to have faith. Some would accept these gifts, some would reject them. History, however, would obliterate the entire story, occasionally giving it only a false footnote. But deep within the daughters' hearts and minds it would be remembered, and this memory would become the historical record everything had to be measured by.

ENDNOTES

1. Joseph Conrad, *Heart of Darkness* (New York: Dell Publishing, 1960).

2. See Susan Brownmiller, *Against Our Will* (New York: Simon and Schuster, 1975).

3. T. Obinkaram Echewa, "African Sexual Attitudes," *Essence* 2, no. 9 (January 1981): 56.

4. Sarah La Forey, "Female Circumcision" (manuscript).

5. Winthrop Jordan, *White over Black* (Chapel Hill: University of North Carolina Press, 1968), 3–43.

6. Richard G. Hofstadter, *America at 1750: A Social Portrait* (New York: Vintage, 1973), 108.

7. Conrad, *Heart of Darkness,* 116.

8. Angela Davis, "Reflections on the Black Woman's Role in the Community of Slaves," *Black Scholar* 3, no. 4 (December 1971): 7.

9. Barbara Chase-Riboud, *Sally Hemings* (New York: Viking, 1979), 284.

10. Jordan, *White over Black,* 3–43.

11. Ibid., 148.

12. Gary Nash, *Red, White, and Black: The Peoples of Early America,* 2d ed. (Englewood Cliffs, NJ: Prentice-Hall, 1983), 115–26.

13. A Leon Higgenbotham, Jr., *In the Matter of Color: Race and the American Legal Process—The Colonial Period* (Oxford: Oxford University Press, 1978), 43–47.

14. Jordan, *White over Black,* 138–39.

15. Ibid.

16. Cited in Carl Degler, *Out of Our Past: Forces That Shaped Modern America* (New York: Harper & Row, 1959), 32.

17. Ibid., 83.

18. Hofstadter, *America at 1750,* 111.

19. Ibid., 115.

20. Ibid., 116.

21. Degler, *Out of Our Past,* 163.

22. ———, *Autobiographical Accounts of Negro Ex-Slaves* (Nashville: Fisk University Press, 1968), 2.

23. Herbert Gutman, *The Black Family in Slavery and Freedom, 1750–1925* (New York: Pantheon, 1976), 76, 138.

24. Degler, *Autobiographical Accounts,* 1.

25. Degler, *Out of Our Past,* 34.

26. Davis, "Black Woman's Role."

27. E. Franklin Frazier, *The Negro Family in the United States,* rev. ed. (Chicago: University of Chicago Press, 1948), 53.

28. Gerda Lerner, ed., *Black Women in White America* (New York: Vintage, 1973), 156.

29. Ibid., 154.

30. John Dollard, *Caste and Class in a Southern Town,* rev. ed. (Garden City, NY: Doubleday/Anchor, 1949), 139.

31. Jacqueline Jones, "My Mother Was Much of a Woman: Black Women, Work, and the Family Under Slavery" (manuscript, 1980).

32. Quoted in John Blassingame, ed., *Slave Testimony: Two Centuries of Letters, Speeches, Interviews, and Autobiographies* (Baton Rouge: Louisiana State University Press, 1977), 221.

33. Chase-Riboud, *Sally Hemings,* 284.

34. *Autobiographical Accounts,* 1–2.

35. Quoted in Anne Firor Scott, *Southern Lady: From Pedestal to Politics, 1830–1930* (Chicago: University of Chicago Press, 1970), 50.

36. Ibid., 34–36.

37. Ibid., 37.

38. Ibid., 52.

39. Jordan, *White over Black,* 148.

40. Scott, *Southern Lady,* 52.

41. *Autobiographical Accounts,* 1.

42. Jones, "My Mother Was Much of a Woman," 41–42.

43. David Katzman, "Domestic Service: Women's Work," in *Women Working: Theories and Facts in Perspective,* ed. Ann Stromberg and Shirley Harkness (Palo Alto, CA: Mayfield, 1978), 381–83.

44. *Autobiographical Accounts,* 1.

45. Frazier, *Negro Family,* 67.

46. Chase-Riboud, *Sally Hemings,* 40.

47. Frazier, *Negro Family,* 47.

48. Scott, *Southern Lady,* 53.

49. Barbara Omolade, "African and Slave Motherhood" (masters thesis, Goddard College, 1979).

50. Jones, "My Mother Was Much of a Woman," 36.

51. Results of Oral History Class Projects—Black Women's History Courses, 1975–1982—comp. and ed. Barbara Omolade.

52. Frazier, *Negro Family,* 73–124.

53. Joanne Grant, *Black Protest: History Documents and Analysis from 1619 to the Present* (New York: Fawcett, 1968), 33.

54. Blassingame, *Slave Testimony.*

55. W. E. B. Du Bois, *Darkwater* (New York: Schocken Books, 1925), 172.

56. Gutman, *Black Family,* 17.

57. Lerner, *Black Women in White America,* 291.

58. David Katzman, *Seven Days a Week: Women and Domestic Service in Industrializing America* (New York: Oxford University Press, 1978), 85–90.

59. Barbara Smith, "Toward a Black Feminist Criticism," *Conditions: Two* 1, no. 2 (October 1977): 25–52.

60. Lerner, *Black Women in White America,* 79, 220.

61. See, for example, Franklin Frazier, *Black Bourgeoisie* (Glencoe, IL: Free Press, 1957), 71–78.

62. Frazier, *Negro Family;* oral history survey, cited in n. 51.

63. Gutman, *Black Family,* 85.

64. Lawrence Levine, *Black Culture and Black Consciousness* (Oxford: Oxford University Press, 1977), 275.

65. Ida Cox, "Wild Women Don't Have the Blues" (Northern Music Co., 1924).

66. Lerner, *Black Women in White America,* xxv.

67. Ntozake Shange, quoted in Carol P. Christ, *Diving Deep and Surfacing: Women Writers on Spiritual Quest* (Boston: Beacon Press, 1980), 117.

68. Blassingame, *Slave Testimony,* 256.

Darlene Clark Hine (1947–   )

Darlene Clark Hine, John A. Hanna Professor of American history at Michigan State University, is one of the most influential scholars in the new field of black women's studies. She has played a pioneering role in the rewriting of African American and women's history because of her important scholarly and editorial work with two mammoth publishing projects—the sixteen-volume series *Black Women in United States History: From Colonial Times to the Present,* and the two-volume historical encyclopedia, *Black Women in America.* She has also published widely on black nursing history and black women in the Midwest. Her pioneering essay on "the culture of dissemblance" among African American women is a major contribution to the largely unwritten history of sexuality among black Americans. In a recent essay in Gerald Early's *Lure and Loathing* (1994), a collection of essays about Du Bois's concept of double consciousness, Hines speculates about how Du Bois might have responded to black women's "'fiveness': Negro, American, woman, poor, black woman" (338). She also argues that studying black women provides "greater illumination of the power relations that operate along the interlocking grid of race, sex, and class in America."

Darlene Clark Hine }

Rape and the Inner Lives of Black Women in the Middle West: Preliminary Thoughts on the Culture of Dissemblance

One of the most remarked upon but least analyzed themes in black women's history deals with black women's sexual vulnerability and powerlessness as victims of rape and domestic violence. Author Hazel Carby put it baldly when she declared: "The institutionalized rape of black women has never been as powerful a symbol of black oppression as the spectacle of lynching. Rape has always involved patriarchal notions of women being, at best, not entirely unwilling accomplices, if not outwardly inviting a sexual attack. The links between black women and illicit sexuality consolidated during the antebellum years had powerful ideological consequences for the next hundred and fifty years."[1] I suggest that rape and the threat of rape influenced the development of a culture of dissemblance among black women. By dissemblance I mean the behavior and attitudes of black women that created the appearance of openness and disclosure, but actually shielded the truth of their inner lives and selves from their oppressors.

To be sure, themes of rape and sexual vulnerability have received considerable attention in the recent literary outpourings of black women novelists. Of the last six novels I have read and reread, for example, five contained a rape scene or a graphic description of domestic violence.[2] Moreover, this is not a recent phenomenon in black women's writing.

Virtually every known nineteenth-century female slave narrative contains a reference to, at some juncture, the ever present threat and reality of rape. Two works come immediately to mind: Harriet Jacob's *Incidents in the Life of a Slave Girl* (1861) and Elizabeth Keckley's *Behind the Scenes, or Thirty Years a Slave, and Four Years in the White House* (1868). Yet there is another thread running throughout these slave narratives—one that concerns these captive women's efforts to resist the misappropriation and to maintain the integrity of their own sexuality.[3] The combined influence of rape (or the threat of rape), domestic violence, and economic oppression is key to understanding the hidden motivations informing major social protest and migratory movements in Afro-American history.

Second only to black women's concern for sexual preservation is the pervasive theme of the frustration attendant to finding suitable employment. Oral histories and autobiographical accounts of twentieth-century migrating black women are replete with themes about work. Scholars of black urban history and black labor history agree that black women faced greater economic discrimination and had fewer employment opportunities than did black men. Black women's work was the most undesirable and least remunerative of all work available to migrants.

As late as 1930 a little over three thousand black women, or fifteen percent, of the black female labor force in Chicago were unskilled and semiskilled factory operatives. Thus, over eighty percent of all employed black women continued to work as personal servants and domestics. Historian Alan H. Spear pointed out that "Negro women were particularly limited in their search for desirable positions. Clerical work was practically closed to them and only a few could qualify as school teachers. Negro domestics often received less than white women for the same work and they could rarely rise to the position of head servant in large households"[4]

Given that many black women immigrants were doomed to work in the same kinds of domestic service jobs they held in the South, one wonders why they bothered to move in the first place. There were some significant differences that help explain this phenomenon. A maid earning seven dollars a week in Cleveland perceived herself to be, and probably was, much better off than a counterpart receiving two dollars and fifty cents a week in Mobile, Alabama. A factory worker, even one whose work was dirty and low status, could and did imagine herself better off than domestic servants who endured the unrelenting scrutiny, interference, and complaints of household mistresses and the untoward advances of male family members.

I believe that in order to understand this historical migratory trend we need to understand the noneconomic motives propelling black female migration. I believe that many black women quit the South out of a desire to achieve personal autonomy and to escape both from sexual exploitation from inside and outside of their families and from the rape and threat of rape by white as well as black males. To focus on the sexual and the personal impetus for black women's migration in the first several decades of the twentieth century neither dismisses nor diminishes the significance of economic motives. Rather, as historian Lawrence Levine cautioned, "As indisputably important as the economic motive was, it is possible to overstress it so that the black migration is converted into an inexorable force and Negroes are seen once again not as actors capable of affecting at least some part of their destinies, but primarily as beings who are acted upon—Southern leaves blown North by the winds of destitution."[5] It is reasonable to assume that some black women were indeed "Southern leaves blown North" and that there were many others who were self-propelled actresses seeking respect, control over their own sexuality, and access to well-paying jobs.

My own research on the history of black women in the Middle West had led me to questions about how, when, and under what circumstances the majority of them settled in the region. These questions have led to others concerning the process of black women's migration across time, from the flights of runaway slaves in the antebellum period to the great migrations of the first half of the twentieth century. The most common, and certainly the most compelling, motive for running, fleeing, migrating was a desire to retain or claim some control and ownership of their own sexual beings and the children they bore. In the antebellum period hundreds of slave women risked their lives and those of their loved ones to run away to the ostensibly free states of the Northwest Territory, in quest of an elusive sexual freedom for themselves and freedom from slavery for their children.

Two things became immediately apparent as I proceeded with researching the history and reading the autobiographies of late nineteenth- and early twentieth-century migrating, or fleeing, black women. First, that these women were sexual hostages and domestic violence victims in the South (or in other regions of the country) did not reduce their determination to acquire power to protect themselves and to become agents of social change once they settled in midwestern communities. Second, the fundamental tension between black women and the rest of the society—referring specifically to white men, white women, and, to a lesser extent, black men —involved a multifaceted struggle to determine who would control their productive and reproductive capacities and their sexuality. At stake for black women caught up in this ever-evolving, constantly shifting, but relentless war was the acquisition of personal autonomy and economic liberation. Their quest for autonomy, dignity, and access to opportunity to earn an adequate living was (and still is) complicated and frustrated by the antagonisms of race, class, and gender conflict and by differences in regional economies. At heart though, the relationship between black women and the larger society has always been, and continues to be, adversarial.

Because of the interplay of racial animosity, class tensions, gender role differentiation, and regional economic variations, black women, as a rule, developed and adhered to a cult of secrecy, a culture of dissemblance, to protect the sanctity of inner aspects of their lives. The dynamics of dissemblance involved creating the appearance of disclosure, or openness about themselves and their feelings, while actually remaining an enigma. Only with secrecy, thus achieving a self-imposed invisibility, could ordinary black women accrue the psychic space and harness the resources needed to hold their own in the often one-sided and mismatched resistance struggle.

The inclination of the larger society to ignore those considered "marginal" actually enabled subordinate black women to craft the veil of secrecy and to perfect the art of dissemblance. Yet it could also be argued that their secrecy or "invisibility" contributed to the development of an atmosphere inimical to realizing equal opportunity or a place of respect in the larger society. There would be no room on the pedestal for the Southern black lady. Nor could she join her white sisters in the prison of "true womanhood." In other words, stereotypes, negative images, and debilitating assumptions filled the space left empty due to inadequate and erroneous information about the true contributions, capabilities, and identities of black women.

This line of analysis is not without problems. To suggest that black women deliberately developed a culture of dissemblance implies that they endeavored to create, and were not simply reacting to, widespread misrepresentations and negative images of themselves in white minds. Clearly, black women did not possess the power to eradicate negative social and sexual images of their womanhood. Rather, what I propose is that in the face of the pervasive stereotypes and negative estimations of the sexuality of black women, it was imperative that they collectively create alternative self-images and shield from scrutiny these private, empowering definitions of self. A secret, undisclosed persona allowed the individual black woman to function, to work effectively as a domestic in white households, to bear and rear children, to endure the frustration-born violence of frequently under- or unemployed mates, to support churches, to found institutions, and to engage in social service activities, all while living within a clearly hostile white, patriarchal, middle-class America.

The problem this penchant for secrecy presents to the historian is readily apparent. Deborah Gray White has commented about the difficulty of finding primary source material for personal aspects of black female life: "Black women have also been reluctant to donate their papers to manuscript repositories. That is in part a manifestation of the black woman's perennial concern with image, a justifiable concern born of centuries of vilification. Black women's reluctance to donate personal papers also stems from the adversarial nature of the relationship that countless black women have had with many public institutions, and the resultant suspicion of anyone seeking private information."[6]

White's allusion to "resultant suspicion" speaks implicitly to one important reason why so much of the inner life of black women remains hidden. Indeed, the concepts of "secrets" and "dissemblance," as I employ them, hint at those issues that black women believed better left unknown, unwritten, unspoken except in whispered tones. Their alarm, their fear, or their Victorian sense of modesty implies that those who broke the silence provided grist for detractors' mills and, even more ominously, tore the protective cloaks from their inner selves. Undoubtedly, these fears and suspicions contribute to the absence of sophisticated historical discussion of the impact of rape (or threat of rape) and incidences of domestic violence on the shape of black women's experiences.

However, the self-imposed secrecy and the culture of dissemblance, coupled with the larger society's unwillingness to discard tired and worn stereotypes, has also led to ironic incidences of misplaced emphases. Until quite recently, for example, when historians talked of rape in the slavery experience, they often bemoaned the damage this act did to the black male's sense of esteem and respect. He was powerless to protect his woman from white rapists. Few scholars probed the effect that rape, the threat of rape, and domestic violence had on the psychic development of the female victims. In the late nineteenth and early twentieth centuries, as Carby has indicated, lynching, not rape, became the most powerful and compelling symbol of black oppression. Lynching, it came to be understood, was one of the major noneconomic reasons why Southern black men migrated North.

The culture of dissemblance assumed its most institutionalized form in the founding, in 1896, of the National Association of Colored Women's clubs (NACW). This association of black women quickly became the largest and most enduring protest organization in the history of Afro-Americans. Its size alone should have warranted the same degree of scholarly attention paid to Marcus Garvey's Universal Negro Improvement Association. Not surprisingly, the primary objects of NACW attack were the derogatory images and negative stereotypes of black women's sexuality. By 1914, it had a membership of fifty thousand, far surpassing the membership of every other protest organization of the time, including the National Association for the Advancement of Colored People and the National Urban League. In 1945, in Detroit, for example, the Detroit Association of Colored Women's Clubs, federated in 1921, boasted seventy-three member clubs with nearly three thousand individual members.[7]

Mary Church Terrell, the first president of the NACW, declared in her initial presidential address that there were objectives of the black women's struggle that could be accomplished only by the "mothers, wives, daughters, and sisters of this race." She proclaimed, "We wish to set in motion influences that shall stop the ravages made by practices that sap our strength and preclude the possibility of advancement." She boldly announced, "We proclaim to the world that the women of our race have become partners in the great firm of progress and reform. . . . We refer to the fact that this is an association of colored women, because our peculiar status in this country . . . seems to demand that we stand by ourselves."[8]

At the core of essentially every activity of NACW's individual members was a concern with creating positive images of black women's sexuality. To counter negative stereotypes, many black women felt compelled to downplay, even deny, sexual expression. The twin obsessions with naming and combating sexual exploitation tinted and shaped black women's support even of the woman's suffrage movement. Nannie H. Burroughs, famed religious leader and founder of the National Training School for Women and Girls at Washington, D.C., cajoled her sisters to fight for the ballot. She asserted that with the ballot black women could ensure the passage of legislation to win legal protection against rapists. Calling the ballot a "weapon of moral defense" she exploded, "when she [a black woman] appears in court in defense of her virtue, she is looked upon with amused contempt. She needs the ballot to reckon with men who place no value upon her virtue."[9]

Likewise, determination to save young unskilled and unemployed black women from having to bargain sex in exchange for food and shelter motivated some NACW members to establish boarding houses and domestic service training centers, such as the Phillis Wheatley Homes, and Burroughs's National Training School. This obsession with providing black women with protection from sexual exploitation and with dignified work inspired other club members in local communities around the country to support or to found hospitals and nursing training schools.

At least one plausible consequence of this heightened mobilization of black women was a decline in black urban birth rates. As black women became more economically self-sufficient, better educated, and more involved in self-improvement efforts, including participation in the flourishing black women's club movement in midwestern communities, they had greater access to birth control information. As the institutional infrastructure of black women's clubs, sororities, church-based women's groups, and charity organizations sunk roots into black communities it encouraged its members to embrace those values, behaviors, and attitudes traditionally associated with the middle classes. To urban black middle-class aspirants, the social stigma of having many children did, perhaps, inhibit reproduction. To be sure, over time the gradually evolving male-female demographic imbalance meant that increasingly significant numbers of black women, especially those employed in the professions, in urban midwestern communities would never marry. The point stressed here, however, is that not having children was, perhaps for the very first time, a choice enjoyed by large numbers of black women.

There were additional burdens placed upon and awards granted to the small cadre of single, educated, professional black women who chose not to marry or to bear children. The more educated they were, the greater the sense of being responsible, somehow, for the advance of the race and for the elevation of black womanhood. They held these expectations of themselves and found a sense of racial obligation reinforced by the demands of the black community and its institutions. In return for their sacrifice of sexual expression, the community gave them respect and recognition. Moreover, this freedom and autonomy represented a socially sanctioned, meaningful alternative to the uncertainties of marriage and the demands of child rearing. The increased employment opportunities, whether real or imagined, and the culture of dissemblance enabled many migrating black women to become financially independent and simultaneously to fashion socially useful and autonomous lives, while reclaiming control over their own sexuality and reproductive capacities.

This is not to say that black women, once settled into midwestern communities, never engaged in sex for pay or occasional prostitution. Sara Brooks, a black domestic servant from Alabama who migrated to Cleveland, Ohio, in the 1930s ill-disguised her contempt for women who bartered their bodies. She declared, while commenting on her own struggle to pay the mortgage on her house, "Some women woulda had a man to live in the house and had an outside boyfriend, too, in order to get the house paid for and the bills." She scornfully added, "They meet a man and if he promises em four or five dollars to go to bed, they's grab it. That's called sellin' your own body, and I wasn't raised like that."[10] What escapes Brooks, in this moralizing moment, is that her poor and powerless black female neighbors were extracting value from the only thing the society now allowed them to sell. As long as they occupied an enforced subordinate position within American society, this "sellin' your own body" as Brooks put it, was, I submit, Rape.

In sum, at some fundamental level all black women historians are engaged in the process of historical reclamation. But it is not enough simply to reclaim those hidden and obscure facts and names of black foremothers. Merely to reclaim and to narrate past deeds and contributions risks rendering a skewed history focused primarily on the articulate, relatively well-positioned members of the aspiring black middle class. In synchrony with the reclaiming and narrating must be the development of an array of analytical frameworks that allow us to understand why black women behave in certain ways and how they acquired agency.

The migration of hundreds of thousands of black women out of the South between 1915 and 1945, and the formation of thousands of black women's clubs and the NACW, are actions that enabled them to put into place, to situate, a protest infrastructure and to create a self-conscious black women's culture of resistance. Most significant, the NACW fostered the development of an image of black women as being supermoral women. In particular, the institutionalization of women's clubs embodied the shaping and honing of the culture of dissemblance. This culture, grounded as it was on the twin prongs of protest and resistance, enabled the creation of positive alternative images of their sexual selves and facilitated black women's mental and physical survival in a hostile world.

ENDNOTES

1. Hazel V. Carby, *Reconstructing Womanhood: The Emergence of the Afro-American Woman Novelist* (New York: Oxford University Press, 1987), 39.

2. See Terry McMillan, *Mam* (Boston: Houghton Mifflin, 1987); Grace Edwards-Yearwood, *In the Shadow of the Peacock* (New York: McGraw-Hill, 1988); Alice Walker, *The Color Purple* (New York: Harcourt Brace Jovanovich, 1982); Toni Morrison, *The Bluest Eye* (New York: Washington Square Press, 1972); and Gloria Naylor, *The Women of Brewster Place* (New York: Penguin, 1983).

3. Harriet A. Jacobs, *Incidents in the Life of a Slave Girl Written by Herself,* ed. Jean Fagan Yellin (Cambridge: Harvard University Press, 1987); and Elizabeth Keckley, *Behind the Scenes, or Thirty Years a Slave, and Four Years in the White House* (New York: Oxford University Press, 1988). See also Rennie Simson, "The Afro-American Female: The Historical Construction of Sexual Identity," in *The Powers of Desire: The Poltics of Sexuality,* ed. Ann Snitow, Sharon Thompson, and Christine Stansell (New York: Monthly Review Press, 1983), 229–35.

4. Alan H. Spear, *Black Chicago: The Making of a Negro Ghetto, 1890–1920* (Chicago: University of Chicago Press, 1967), 34.

5. Lawrence W. Levine, *Black Culture and Black Consciousness: Afro-American Folk Thought from Slavery to Freedom* (New York: Oxford University Press, 1977), 274.

6. Deborah Gray White, "Mining the Forgotten: Manuscript Sources for Black Women's History," *Journal of American History* 74 (June 1987): 237–42, especially 237–38.

7. Robin S. Peebles, "Detroit's Black Women's Clubs," *Michigan History* 70 (January/February 1986): 48.

8. Darlene Clark Hine, "Lifting the Veil, Shattering the Silence: Black Women's History in Slavery and Freedom," in *The State of Afro-American History: Past, Present, and Future,* ed. Darlene Clark Hine (Baton Rouge: Louisiana State University Press, 1986), 223–49, especially 236–37.

9. Rosalyn Terborg-Penn, "Woman Suffrage: 'First because We Are Women and Second because We Are Colored Women,'" *Truth: Newsletter of the Association of Black Women Historians* (April 1985), 9; Evelyn Brooks Barnett, "Nannie Burroughs and the Education of Black Women, in *The Afro-American Woman,* ed. Rosalyn Terborg-Penn and Sharon Harley (Port Washington, N.Y.: Kennikat Press, 1978), 97–108.

10. Thordis Simonsen, ed., *You May Plow Here: The Narrative of Sara Brooks* (New York: Simon and Schuster, 1987), 219.

Shirley Chisholm (1924–   )

Shirley Chisholm, born in Brooklyn, New York, to Barbadian parents, was the first black woman to be elected to Congress (1968). She was also the first African American to seek nomination for the presidency of the United States (1972), a process that she chronicled in *The Good Fight* (1973). Following the 1984 Democratic Convention, she provided the catalyst for the founding of the National Political Congress of Black Women. She stunned audiences by revealing in her autobiography, *Unbossed and Unbought* (1970), that being a woman had been more disadvantageous than being black. Outspoken in her defense of black and women's liberation, she was also one of the first black women to advocate publicly for the legalization of abortion and wrote eloquently in her autobiography about her pro-choice position. "Facing the Abortion Question," written when she was President of the National Association for the Repeal of Abortion Laws (NARAL) and before *Roe v. Wade* (1973), chronicles her involvement with the controversial issue of abortion rights and responds to persons in the black community who are anti-choice. She argues about the importance of black women's ability to get safe, legal abortions and is especially sensitive to the plight of poor women who are more negatively impacted by unwanted pregnancies.

Shirley Chisholm }

Facing the Abortion Question

In August of 1969 I started to get phone calls from NARAL, the National Association for the Repeal of Abortion Laws, a new organization based in New York City that was looking for a national president. In the New York State Assembly I had supported abortion reform bills introduced by Assemblyman Albert Blumenthal, and this had apparently led NARAL to believe I would sympathize with its goal: complete repeal of all laws restricting abortion. As a matter of fact, when I was in the Assembly I had not been in favor of repealing all abortion laws, a step that would leave the question of having or not having the operation entirely up to a woman and her doctor. The bills I had tried to help pass in Albany would only have made it somewhat easier for women to get therapeutic abortions in New York State, by providing additional legal grounds and simplifying the procedure for getting approval. But since that time I had been compelled to do some heavy thinking on the subject, mainly because of the experiences of several young women I knew. All had suffered permanent injuries at the hands of illegal abortionists. Some will never have children as a result. One will have to go to a hospital periodically for treatment for the rest of her life.

It had begun to seem to me that the question was not whether the law should allow abortions. Experience shows that pregnant women who feel they have compelling reasons for not having a baby, or another baby, will break the law and, even worse, risk injury and death if they must to get one. Abortions will not be stopped. It may even be that the number performed is not being greatly reduced by laws making an abortion a "criminal operation." If that is true, the question becomes simply that of what kind of abortions society wants women to have—clean, competent ones performed by licensed physicians or septic, dangerous ones done by incompetent practitioners.

So when NARAL asked me to lead its campaign, I gave it serious thought. For me to take the lead in abortion law repeal would be an even more serious step than for a white politician to do so, because there is a deep and angry suspicion among many blacks that even birth control clinics are a plot by the white power structure to keep down the numbers of blacks, and this opinion is even more strongly held by some in regard to legalizing abortions. But I do not know any black or Puerto Rican *women* who feel that way. To label family planning and legal abortion programs "genocide" is male rhetoric, for male ears. It falls flat to female listeners, and to thoughtful male ones. Women know, and so do many men, that two or three children who are wanted, prepared for, reared amid love and stability, and educated to the limit of their ability will mean more for the future of the black and brown races from which they come than any number of neglected, hungry, ill-housed, and ill-clothed youngsters. Pride in one's race, as well as simple humanity, supports this view. Poor women of every race feel as I do, I believe. There is objective evidence of it in a study by Dr. Charles F. Westhoff of the Princeton Office of Population Research. He questioned 5,600 married persons and found that twenty-two percent of their children were unwanted. But among persons who earned less than $4,000 a year, forty-two percent of the children were unwanted. The poor are more anxious about family planning than any other group.

Why then do the poor keep on having large families? It is not because they are stupid or immoral. One must understand how many resources their poverty has deprived them of, and that chief among these is medical care and advice. The poor do not go to doctors or clinics except when they absolutely must; their medical ignorance is very great, even when compared to the low level of medical knowledge most persons have. This includes, naturally, information about contraceptives and how to get them. In some of the largest cities, clinics are now attacking this problem; they are no-where near to solving it. In smaller cities and in most of the countryside, hardly anything is being done.

Another point is this: not only do the poor have large families, but also large families tend to be poor. More than one-fourth of all the families with four children live in poverty, according to the federal government's excessively narrow definition; by humane standards of poverty, the number would be much larger. The figures range from nine percent of one-child families that have incomes below the official poverty line, up to forty-two percent of the families with six children or more. Sinking into poverty, large families tend to stay there because of the educational and social handicaps that being poor imposes. It is the fear of such a future for their children that drives many women, of every color and social stratum, except perhaps the highest, to seek abortions when contraception has failed.

Botched abortions are the largest single cause of death of pregnant women in the United States, particularly among nonwhite women. In 1964, the president of the New York County Medical Society, Dr. Carl Goldmark, estimated that eighty percent of the deaths of gravid women in Manhattan were from this cause.

Another study by Edwin M. Gold, covering 1960 through 1962, gave lower percentages, but supplied evidence that women from minority groups suffer most. Gold said abortion was the cause of death in twenty-five percent of the white cases, forty-nine percent of the black ones, and sixty-five percent of the Puerto Rican ones.

Even when a poor woman needs an abortion for the most impeccable medical reasons, acceptable under most states' laws, she is not likely to succeed in getting one. The public hospitals to which she must go are far more reluctant to approve abortions than are private, voluntary hospitals. It's in the records: private hospitals in New York City perform 3.9 abortions for every 1,000 babies they deliver, public hospitals only 1 per 1,000. Another relevant figure is that ninety percent of the therapeutic abortions in the city are performed on white women. Such statistics convinced me that my instinctive feeling was right: a black woman legislator, far from avoiding the abortion question, was compelled to face it and deal with it.

But my time did not permit me to be an active president of NARAL, so I asked to be made an honorary president. My appearances on television in September 1969, when the association's formation was announced, touched off one of the heaviest flows of mail to my Washington office that I have experienced. What surprised me was that it was overwhelmingly in favor of repeal. Most of the letters that disagreed with me were from Catholics, and most of them were temperate and reasoned. We sent those writers a reply that said in part, "No one should be forced to have an abortion or to use birth control methods which for religious or personal reasons they oppose. But neither should others who have different views be forced to abide by what they do not and cannot believe in." Some of the mail was from desperate women who thought I could help them. "I am forty-five years old," one wrote, "and have raised a family already. Now I find that I am pregnant and I need help. Please send me all the information." A girl wrote that she was pregnant and did not dare tell her mother and stepfather: "Please send me the name of a doctor or hospital that would help. You said if my doctor wouldn't do it to write to you. Where can I turn?" We sent the writers of these letters a list of the names and addresses of the chapters of the Clergy Consultation Service on Abortion and suggested that they find a local family planning or birth control clinic.

The reaction of a number of my fellow members of Congress seemed to me a little strange. Several said to me, "This abortion business . . . my God, what are you doing? That's not politically wise." It was the same old story; they were not thinking in terms of right or wrong, they were considering only whether taking a side of the issue would help them stay in office—or in this case, whether taking a stand would help me get reelected. They concluded that it would not help me, so it was a bad position for me to take. My advisers were, of course, all men. So I decided to shake them up a little with a feminist line of counterattack. "Who told you I shouldn't do this?" I asked them. "Women are dying every day, did you know that? They're being butchered and maimed. No matter what men think, abortion is a fact of life. Women will have them; they always have and always will. Are they going to have good ones or bad ones? Will the good ones be reserved for the rich while poor women have to go to quacks? Why don't we talk about real problems instead of phony ones?"

One member asked the question that was on the minds of all the others: "How many Catholics do you have in your district?" "Look," I told him, "I can't worry about that. That's not the problem." Persons who do not deal with politicians are often baffled by the peculiarly simple workings of their minds. Scientists and scholars in particular are bewildered by the political approach. When a member of Congress makes a statement, the scholar's first thought is "Is what he said true? Is he right or wrong?" The falseness or validity of an officeholder's statement is almost never discussed in Washington, or anyplace where politics sets the tone of discourse. The question political people ask is seldom "Is he right?" but "Why did he say that?" Or they ask, "Where does he expect that to get him?" or "Who put him up to that?"

But returning to abortion, the problem that faced me was what action I should take in my role as a legislator, if any; naturally, I intend to be as active as possible as an advocate and publicist for the cause, but was there any chance of getting a meaningful bill through Congress? Some NARAL officials wanted me to introduce an abortion repeal bill as a gesture. This is very common; probably a majority of the bills introduced in all legislative bodies are put in for the sake of effect, to give their sponsor something to talk about on the stump. That was never my style in Albany, and I have not adopted it in Washington. When I introduce legislation, I try to draft it carefully and then look for meaningful support from people who have the power to help move the bill.

So I looked for House members, in both parties and of all shades of conservatism and liberalism, who might get together on abortion repeal regardless of party. I wrote letters to a number of the more influential House members. It would have been easy to get three or four, or even ten or twelve, liberal Democrats to join me in introducing a bill, but nothing would have happened. A majority of House members would have said, "Oh, that bunch again," and dismissed us. But just a few conservative Republican sponsors, or conservative Democratic ones, would change all that. The approach I took was eminently sound, but it didn't work. A few members replied that they would support my bill if it ever got to the floor, but could not come out for it publicly before then or work for it. I did not doubt their sincerity, but it was a safe thing to say because the chances of a bill's reaching the floor seemed slim. Several others answered with longish letters admiring my bold position and expressing sympathy, but not agreement. "I am not ready to assume such a position," one letter said. Another said, in almost these words, "This kind of trouble I don't need." So I put my roughly drafted bill in a drawer and decided to wait. There is no point in introducing it until congressmen can be persuaded to vote for it, and only one thing will persuade them. If a congressman feels he is in danger of losing his job, he will change his mind—and then try to make it look as though he had been leading the way. The approach to Congress has to be through the arousal and organization of public opinion.

The question will remain "Is abortion *right?*" and it is a question that each of us must answer for himself. My beliefs and my experience have led me to conclude that the wisest public policy is to place the responsibility for that decision on the individual. The rightness or wrongness of an abortion depends on the individual case, and it seems to me clearly wrong to pass laws regulating all cases. But there is more to it than that. First, it is my view, and I think the majority's view, that abortion should always remain a last resort, never a primary method of limiting families. Contraceptive devices are the first choice: *devices,* because of their established safety compared to the controversial oral contraceptives. The weight of responsible medical opinion, by which I mean the opinions of qualified persons who have never been in the pay of the drug industry, seems to be that the question of the Pill's safety is not proven and that there are clear warnings that much more study is needed. So Pill research should continue, and meanwhile the emphasis—particularly in a publicly supported family planning program—should be on proven, safe and effective methods. Beyond that, still from the standpoint of public policy, there must be far more stress on providing a full range of family planning services to persons of all economic levels. At present, the full gamut of services, from expert medical advice to, as a last resort, safe "legal" abortions, is available for the rich. Any woman who has the money and the sophistication about how things are done in our society can get an abortion within the law. If she is from a social stratum where such advice is available, she will be sent to a sympathetic psychiatrist, and he will be well paid to believe her when she says she is ready to kill herself if she doesn't get rid of her pregnancy. But unless a woman has the $700 to $1000 minimum it takes to travel this route, her only safe course in most states is to have the child.

This means that, whether it was so intended, public policy as expressed in American abortion laws (excepting the handful of states where the repeal effort has succeeded) is to maximize illegitimacy. Illegitimate children have always been born and for the foreseeable future they will continue to be. Their handicap is not some legal blot on their ancestry; few intelligent persons give any thought to that today. The trouble is that illegitimate children are usually the most unwanted of the unwanted. Society has forced a woman to have a child in order to punish her. Our laws were based on the puritan reaction of "You've had your pleasure—now pay for it." But who pays? First, it is the helpless woman, who may be a girl in her early teens forced to assume the responsibility of an adult; young, confused, partially educated, she is likely to be condemned to society's trash heap as a result. But the child is often a worse loser. If his mother keeps him, she may marry or not (unmarried mothers are even less likely to marry than widows or divorcées). If she does not, she will have to neglect him and work at undesirable jobs to feed him, more often than not. His home life will almost certainly be abnormal; he may survive it and even thrive, depending on his mother's personal qualities, but the odds have to be against him.

Of course, there should be no unwanted children. Whether they are legitimate or illegitimate is not of the first importance. But we will not even approach the ideal of having every child wanted, planned for, and cherished, until our methods of contraception are fully reliable and completely safe, and readily available to everyone. Until then, unwanted pregnancies will happen, in marriage and out of it. What is our public policy to be toward them? There are very few more important questions for society to face; this question is one that government has always avoided because it did not dare intrude on the sanctity of the home and marriage. But the catastrophic perils that follow in the train of overpopulation were not well known in the past and those perils were not imminent, so the question could be ducked. It cannot be any longer.

For all Americans, and especially for the poor, we must put an end to compulsory pregnancy. The well-off have only one problem when an unwanted pregnancy occurs; they must decide what they want to do and what they believe is right. For the poor, there is no such freedom. They started with too little knowledge about contraception, often with none except street lore and other misinformation. When trapped by pregnancy, they have only two choices, both bad—a cheap abortion or an unwanted child to plunge them deeper into poverty. Remember the statistics that show which choice is often taken: forty-nine percent of the deaths of pregnant black women and sixty-five percent of those of Puerto Rican women . . . due to criminal, amateur abortions.

Which is more like genocide, I have asked some of my black brothers— this, the way things are, or the conditions I am fighting for in which the full range of family planning services is freely available to women of all classes and colors, starting with effective contraception and extending to safe, legal termination of undesired pregnancies, at a price they can afford?

Beth E. Richie

Beth Richie is one of the earliest and most outspoken black women activists in the domestic violence movement and is presently a faculty member in the program in community health education at Hunter College. Her doctoral dissertation was "An Exploratory Study of the Link between Gender Identity Development, Violence against Women, and Crime among African American Battered Women" (CUNY, 1985). She is former cochair of the Women of Color Task Force of the National Coalition Against Domestic Violence, and founding member of the Women of Color Organizing Project, Leadership Institute for Women.

This essay, which appeared in the *Black Scholar* in 1985, admonishes African Americans to break the silence about male violence against black women within our communities, which she analyzes from an explicitly Third-World, feminist perspective. She argues that a narrow racial analysis positing that black men batter their women because they've been battered by whites is problematic and overlooks the broader context of institutionalized sexism, which perpetuates violence against women. In a recent essay (coauthored with Valli Kanuhua), "Battered Women of Color in Public Health Care Systems: Racism, Sexism, and Violence" *(Wings of Gauze),* Richie expands her discussion by critiquing the differential treatment that battered women of color experience in the health care system. She also provides an analysis of the complex dynamics at play within communities of color—dynamics that tend to silence women with respect to the abuse they suffer from men of color,—a phenomenon labeled "split loyalties." She also discusses the problems that activist women of color in the domestic violence movement experience with white feminists who continue to believe that sexism (not racism or classism) is the primary source of women's oppression.

See also Evelyn C. White's *Chain, Chain, Change: For Black Women Dealing with Physical and Emotional Abuse* (1985) and *The Speaking Profits Us: Violence Against Women of Color,* edited by Mary Violet Burns for the Center of Domestic and Sexual Violence, in Seattle.

Beth E. Richie }

BATTERED BLACK WOMEN: A CHALLENGE FOR THE BLACK COMMUNITY

O ver the past decade, the question of domestic violence against women —including black women—has emerged as a major concern in the fight against women's oppression. This is a controversial subject because, unlike other aspects of the subjugation of black women that target racism and economic exploitation, the burgeoning problem of battered women at first appears as an individual problem: a man beating a woman.

Too many blacks still think this is a divisive issue that should not be aired in public. However, the problem of battered women is a social phenomenon, not an individual one, and combatting this expression of social malaise must be approached with as much vigor as those rooted in the vagaries of a racial and class society.

The purpose of this article is to trace some of the obstacles I have encountered as a young black woman who calls herself a feminist working in the battered women's movement. My experiences have led me to some conclusions, which I offer for consideration.

I was introduced to the battered women's movement while working in New York City. It is a rare privilege to be associated with a multicultural, Third World-controlled agency with strong roots in the community. I had such a privilege for two years as I joined with dedicated workers in service to a predominantly black and Hispanic population.

The goal of our multidimensional involvement with community families was empowerment to assist families in the development of skills and the accumulation of resources necessary to overcome the cultural, racial, economic, and political oppression that smothered the community. We saw the family as the only institution truly able to meet and nourish individual needs. The agency was designed to foster independence in the community and to support families fighting back against exploitation, while maintaining their cultural and racial identities. In sharp contrast, most educational, social-service, and health-care systems in the community discourage autonomy and self-determination. Being an enthusiast and sharing the commitment to community and individual empowerment, I joined in the work and began to call the community my home.

After a period of time, I gradually realized that some of these strong, culturally-identified families, which we had been supporting so vehemently, were dangerous places for some women to live in. Furthermore, the political machine at the forefront of the grassroots community movement was, in fact, subtly exploiting women by denying the reality of sexual oppression. As I began to look closely, the incidences of battering, I have since learned, may have been intentionally set for me. I can now recognize that this "trap" is analogous to the "trap" in which many battered women find themselves. It is the trap of silence. Because of the scarcity of agencies such as mine, I hesitated to disclose my observations. I was immobilized by denial and sadness. Fear of being cast out by the community silenced me in the beginning. Loyalty and devotion are enormous barriers to overcome.

The world is so hostile to Third World people that it seems much less painful to remain quietly ambivalent. I struggled with how to illuminate this dark secret about our homes and ourselves. Disclosure is so easily confused with treason!

After a few false starts, I found a way to break the silence. I began to hold regular meetings for women in the community to talk together about positive issues: community strength and survival techniques. Discussions ranged from cultural rituals, such as holidays, to practical skills, such as living on an inadequate income. As the passage of time built trust, so it certified alliances, and women began to talk about problems in the community and finally about incidents of violence in their homes. Survival techniques and community concerns were expanded to include violence against women. The acknowledgement of the problem brought great joy and many tears. Women freed themselves from the trap of silence.

These triumphant women developed a mighty support network, as all through history black women have done so well. They set out to create an arena in which battered women could meet the community in full voice. A great deal of progress was made in the eighteen months I knew these women. Certainly, there is a long way to go. My point is not to extol their virtues, but rather to relate the message about the trap.

Black women, be forewarned. It is a painful, unsettling task to call attention to violence in our community. You may find yourselves feeling caught by the trap called loyalty. There is already so much negative information about our families that a need to protect ourselves keeps us quiet. Yet, we must not allow our voices to be silenced. Instead, we must strengthen and speak the truths about our families; we must support each other; but we must hear the cries of our battered sisters and let them be heard by others!

BATTERED MINORITY WOMEN

In an effort to verify my experience, I looked to other Third World communities. My quest led me to sixteen vivacious women who refer to themselves as "Battered Minority Women" (BMW). Despite the inaccessibility
of mainstream educational systems to members of BMW, these women are
extremely well-educated, particularly in terms of political strategies. Their
life experiences have afforded them keen insight and expert technique.
Their alliance is built upon: (1) a history of being physically battered by
men in their homes; (2) the experience of having survived the trauma of a
lifetime of poverty; and (3) a strong allegiance to various Third World
community groups. Most significantly, however, BMW shares a common
analysis of the causes of battering, and they agree about the most appropriate response.

BMW believes that domestic violence is not a problem in black communities. Its occurrence, like substance abuse, crime, and unwanted adolescent
pregnancy, is a symptom of living systematically deprived in a society that
is designed to dominate and control Third World people. (On this point, I
concur with their analysis.)

They define battering as the "systematic deprivation inflicted upon Third
World men by society, which, in turn, is inflicted upon Third World
women." That is, black women are beaten solely because their men are
deprived. The response they advocate lies herein.

According to the BMW, black women should involve themselves in the
struggle for racial justice in order to end battering in their homes. They
consider the only real issue to be racial liberation; the concept of sexual
oppression does not exist for them. They assert that there is no inequality
of power between men and women, and they reject the notion that they
are being mistreated by the men who beat them. Complete responsibility
lies with white society. (This summary of their analysis has been confirmed
by BMW as accurate.)

BMW members do not consider themselves feminist and negate the need
to be part of a larger movement for sexual equality. They provide temporary refuge for the battered women in their community through a safe-
home model, demonstrating once again stalwart support for one another.
Most of the women they protect return home after the violent episode.
BMW proudly acknowledges a high return rate of women to the BMW
safe-homes.

BMW is associated with groups in Boston, Los Angeles, Detroit, and
Atlanta, who share a similar philosophy. I have heard their sentiments
expressed frequently in quite convincing terms, and suspect that many
women are lured by their analysis of racial oppression, just as I am.

I find this disturbing because if the argument is taken one step further, it approaches the theory of the black matriarch. This well-popularized myth suggests the notion of the "strong black woman," willing and able to accept beating in the support of her man. The implication is that the role of black women in our families is to receive regular whippings in order to alleviate black men's stress. Clearly, this is a dangerous betrayal.

Undoubtedly, the stress black men must endure is cruel and often overwhelming. The connection this has to black women's accepting beatings puzzles me. Who is responsible? And where is the strength in acceptance? It is true that black women have historically been able to secure employment at times when black men could not. Does this make us any less oppressed? Why are we arguing whose oppression is worse?

We must cease this senseless debate. To be black in this society is bad; it's bad for men, women, and children. While it remains critical that black people continue actively struggling against racism and discrimination, it must not be done at the physical and psychological expense of black women. We have paid our dues, and black men must be held responsible for every injury they cause. Yes, experience has taught black women to be strong and resilient. We must learn that on occasion we must use our strength for ourselves.

The position that BMW advocates concerning sexist oppression is problematic. To negate the notion of feminism in our lives is to deny a critical component of our personhood. There is no such thing as partial liberation. We must demand our share of equality, too-long denied.

CONFRONTING THE ISSUE

Thus, once we choose to speak out against the violence in our families, we may be confronted with serious challenges to our work based on differences in political understanding of women-battering. To meet these challenges we must take time to carefully talk, to construct and refine our analysis of violence against women, especially against black women. Even more, we must consider how to work side by side with those who disagree with our conclusions.

THE ROLE OF POLICE . . .

While we study and deliberate about women abuse, it is important for black women working in the battered women's movement to address the special problems associated with having to depend upon the criminal justice system as a vehicle for protection and problem resolution. The criminal justice and law enforcement systems have been the worst offenders in perpetuating violence against black people.

How can blacks in the domestic violence movement reconcile the reality of police brutality and blatant racism in the criminal justice system with the need for police and court intervention on behalf of battered women?

I cannot offer answers to these questions, but I suggest that black women confront these issues directly. As a movement, we must work within the system to assure that justice is available to our families. All the while, we must remain alert to the fact that the police may not necessarily respond consistently or responsibly. We must cultivate alternative methods of protecting black women in our communities.

. . . And the Issue of Homophobia

Black women also need to candidly confront the issue of homophobia in society, particularly within our communities. Hatred of homosexuals and fear of being associated with lesbian women are both commonly expressed reasons that black women do not identify with the feminist movement. We continue to negate the valuable contributions made by black lesbian women to our culture as well as our struggle for racial liberation. By doing so, we have alienated steadfast allies. Black women must assume a leadership role in challenging our communities to put in check institutional and individual homophobic behavior. Currently, it is a decided barrier in our struggle.

To learn of rampant homophobia and deep-seated hatred of homosexuals startled me. To realize that oppressed people sometimes oppress others curiously disturbed me. However, it has helped allay my confusion and guilt about holding black men responsible for their violent behavior. Black women must be held accountable for the homophobia within our ranks.

Women of Color Institute

The meaning of violence against women in our communities is different from that in white or other Third-World communities. We need to create time and space for researching a new, more meaningful analysis that is relevant to our lives. This is work we must do alone with no apologies for not including others. (No one apologized for the long years we have been excluded.) Our community needs something that the white women's movement has not given us, and we should know better than to expect to be *given* anything. We must do our own work.

This concept was dramatically illustrated at the Women of Color Institute of the 1982 National Coalition Against Domestic Violence meeting and conference. The one-day Institute, "Building a Colorful Coalition," provided the occasion for assembling our vision and building our voice. By acknowledging our differences, we affirmed our union.

Nearly 100 Asian, Hispanic, Native American, black, and other Third World women gathered in Milwaukee, Wisconsin, to attend the Institute, a true celebration of sisterhood. Certainly, every participant considered it the highlight of the conference. For me it was the highlight of my work in the battered women's movement.

The brilliant organizers of the Institute created an arena where we could strength our spirit as Third World women and clarify our dream for a violence-free world. The Institute and the Women of Color Caucus emerged in a leadership role of the conference, confirming my belief that Third World women will be catalysts in bringing about positive change in the struggle for the liberation of all people.

THE CHALLENGES AHEAD

Black women must also work on the direction for the struggle of the racial justice movement. Let us not be distracted by the progress we have made. Although we have won some critical battles, I have a troubling sense that some of the victories may be leading some of us astray. As we surround ourselves with objects rumored to bring happiness and success, we often forget that most black people do not have adequate resources with which to control their lives. It is tempting to push on for our individual advancement without regard for those we are leaving behind.

Black women must more critically analyze this system to which we have demanded access. We must reject those components that suggest exploitation. Too many individuals have been lost to an image of being free. The struggle against racial oppression must continue to be of utmost importance in our lives. The younger we are, the higher the risk of forgetting how far we have come and of limiting our vision of how far we will be able to go.

In conclusion, I have a sense that the lonely, isolating experiences of a black feminist in the battered women's movement can be over. I can soon recover from the exhaustion I feel at having to constantly make a place for myself in a society that negates my existence. It is clumsy and burdensome to live in constant defense against simultaneous racial and sexual oppression. I find it empowering to be sharing my journey with you.

The ideas I have discussed represent only a part of the agenda for our future. We must begin in our homes, our heads, and mostly our hearts to identify "traps" of loyalty. We must demand equality in our communities and in our relationships with black men. Homophobic behavior must become unacceptable in our lives. As black women we must rededicate ourselves to the struggle for racial equality and ending violence in the justice system. Finally, we must study together and plan our future in the battered women's and feminist movements in ways that are meaningful to our lives.

Clearly, we have a great task before us. Let's join together and use our spirit to move us towards our dream of peace.

I take full responsibility for the views expressed in this article, but I would like to acknowledge those who helped in their formation: The Committee to End Violence in the Lives of Women and Women of Color Caucus of the National Coalition Against Domestic Violence. I am most indebted to the Third World women of the communities I know, who taught me the meaning of survival and support.

June Jordan (1936–   )

June Jordan, writer, activist, and presently professor of black studies and women's studies at the University of California, Berkeley, has written three volumes of poetry, several plays, three collections of essays, a biography of Fannie Lou Hamer, and one novel, *His Own Where,* for young adults. She gained national prominence as one of the radical poets of the sixties and continues to be one of the most insightful political writers of this era on a variety of issues, including sexuality. One of her earliest statements on the subject "Where Is the Love?" (originally published in *Essence*) occurred at the 1978 National Black Writers Conference at Howard University during a historic and controversial session on "Feminism and the Black Woman Writer," whose panelists also included Barbara Smith, Sonia Sanchez, and Acklyn Lynch. In this essay she described herself as a feminist, which has much the same meaning to her as her blackness: "It means that I must everlastingly seek to cleanse myself of the hatred and the contempt that surrounds and permeates my identity, as a woman, and as a black human being" (*Civil Wars,* 142). As a black feminist she is both hurt and angered by the pain of her sisters: "the bitter sufferings of hundreds of thousands of women who are the sole parents, the mothers of hundreds of thousands of children, the desolation and the futility of women trapped by demeaning, lowest-paying occupations, the unemployed, the bullied, the beaten, the battered, the ridiculed, the slandered, the trivialized, the raped, and the sterilized, the lost millions . . . of beautiful, creative, and momentous lives turned to ashes on the pyre of gender identity" (144–45).

"A New Politics of Sexuality" appeared in *Technical Difficulties* (1992) and was adapted from her keynote address at the Bisexual, Gay, and Lesbian Student Association at Stanford University in April 1991. It attacks heterosexism and espouses a new politics of bisexuality. For an analysis of the history of bisexuality, see Lillian Faderman's *Odd Girls and Twilight Lovers: A History of Lesbian Life in Twentieth-Century America* (1991), in which she also discusses homosexuality and the existence of a black lesbian subculture during the Harlem Renaissance of the 1920s.

In "A Weaponry of Choice: Black American Women Writers and the Essay," which recalls Jordan's foreword to *Civil Wars* (her first collection of essays), Pamela Mittlefehldt analyzes the use of the essay as a powerful tool for black feminist resistance. Since black women's voices have been "traditionally obliterated in Western thought and literature" (*The Politics of the Essay,* 1993), the revolutionary essays of Jordan and others underscore the importance of fighting with words.

June Jordan }

A New Politics of Sexuality

As a young worried mother, I remember turning to Dr. Benjamin Spock's *Common Sense Book of Baby and Child Care* just about as often as I'd pick up the telephone. He was God. I was ignorant, but striving to be good: a good Mother. And so it was there, in that best-seller pocketbook of do's and don't's, that I came upon this doozie of a guideline: Do not wear miniskirts or other provocative clothing because that will upset your child, especially if your child happens to be a boy. If you give your offspring "cause" to think of you as a sexual being, he will, at the least, become disturbed; you will derail the equilibrium of his notions about your possible identity and meaning in the world.

It had never occurred to me that anyone, especially my son, might look upon me as an asexual being. I had never supposed that "asexual" was some kind of positive designation I should, so to speak, lust after. I was pretty surprised by Dr. Spock. However, I was also, by habit, a creature of obedience. For a couple of weeks I actually experimented with lusterless colors and dowdy tops and bottoms, self-consciously hoping thereby to prove myself as a lusterless and dowdy and, therefore, excellent female parent.

Years would have to pass before I could recognize the familiar, by then, absurdity of a man setting himself up as the expert on the subject that presupposed women as the primary objects for his patriarchal discourse—on motherhood, no less! Years passed before I came to perceive the perversity of dominant power assumed by men, and the perversity of self-determining power ceded to men by women.

A lot of years went by before I understood the dynamics of what anyone could summarize as the Politics of Sexuality.

I believe the Politics of Sexuality is the most ancient and probably the most profound arena for human conflict. Increasingly, it seems clear to me that deper and more pervasive than any other oppression, than any other bitterly contested human domain, is the oppression of sexuality, the exploitation of the human domain of sexuality for power.

When I say sexuality, I mean gender: I mean male subjugation of human beings because they are female. When I say sexuality, I mean heterosexual institutionalization of rights and privileges denied to homosexual men and women. When I say sexuality I mean gay or lesbian contempt for bisexual modes of human relationship.

The Politics of Sexuality therefore subsumes all of the different ways in which some of us seek to dictate to others of us what we should do, what we should desire, what we should dream about, and how we should behave ourselves, generally. From China to Iran, from Nigeria to Czechoslovakia, from Chile to California, the politics of sexuality—enforced by traditions of state-sanctioned violence plus religion and the law—reduces to male domination of women, heterosexist tyranny, and, among those of us who are in any case deemed despicable or deviant by the powerful, we find intolerance for those who choose a different, a more complicated—for example, an interracial or bisexual—mode of rebellion and freedom.

We must move out from the shadows of our collective subjugation—as people of color/as women/as gay/as lesbian/as bisexual human beings.

I can voice my ideas without hesitation or fear because I am speaking, finally, about myself. I am black and I am female and I am a mother and I am bisexual and I am a nationalist and I am an antinationalist. And I mean to be fully and freely all that I am!

Conversely, I do not accept that any white or black or Chinese man—I do not accept that, for instance, Dr. Spock—should presume to tell me, or any other woman, how to mother a child. He has no right. He is not a mother. My child is not his child. And, likewise, I do not accept that anyone —any woman or any man who is not inextricably part of the subject he or she dares to address—should attempt to tell any of us, the objects of her or his presumptuous discourse, what we should do or what we should not do.

Recently, I have come upon gratuitous and appalling pseudoliberal pronouncements on sexuality. Too often, these utterances fall out of the mouths of men and women who first disclaim any sentiment remotely related to homophobia, but who then proceed to issue outrageous opinions like the following:

· That it is blasphemous to compare the oppression of gay, lesbian, or bisexual people to the oppression, say, of black people, or of the Palestinians.

· That the bottom line about gay or lesbian or bisexual identity is that you can conceal it whenever necessary and, so, therefore, why don't you do just that? Why don't you keep your deviant sexuality in the closet and let the rest of us —we who suffer oppression for reasons of our ineradicable and always visible components of our personhood such as race or gender—get on with our more necessary, our more beleaguered struggle to survive?

Well, number one: I believe I have worked as hard as I could, and then harder than that, on behalf of equality and justice—for African Americans, for the Palestinian people, and for people of color everywhere.

And no, I do not believe it is blasphemous to compare oppressions of sexuality to oppressions of race and ethnicity: Freedom is indivisible or it is nothing at all besides sloganeering and temporary, shortsighted, and short-lived advancement for a few. Freedom is indivisible, and either we are working for freedom or you are working for the sake of your self-interests and I am working for mine.

If you can finally go to the bathroom wherever you find one, if you can finally order a cup of coffee and drink it wherever coffee if available, but you cannot follow your heart—you cannot respect the response of your own honest body in the world—then how much of what kind of freedom does any one of us possess?

Or, conversely, if your heart and your honest body can be controlled by the state, or controlled by community taboo, are you not then, and in that case, no more than a slave ruled by outside force?

What tyranny could exceed a tyranny that dictates to the human heart, and that attempts to dictate the public career of an honest human body?

Freedom is indivisible; the Politics of Sexuality is not some optional "special-interest" concern for serious, progressive folk.

And, on another level, let me assure you: if every single gay or lesbian or bisexual man or woman active on the Left of American politics decided to stay home, there would be *no* Left left.

One of the things I want to propose is that we act on that reality: that we insistently demand reciprocal respect and concern from those who cheerfully depend upon our brains and our energies for their, and our, effective impact on the political landscape.

Last spring, at Berkeley, some students asked me to speak at a rally against racism. And I did. There were four or five hundred people massed on Sproul Plaza, standing together against that evil. And, on the next day, on that same plaza, there was a rally for bisexual and gay and lesbian rights, and students asked me to speak at that rally. And I did. There were fewer than seventy-five people stranded, pitiful, on that public space. And I said then what I say today: That was disgraceful! There should have been just one rally. One rally: freedom is indivisible.

As for the second, nefarious pronouncement on sexuality that now enjoys mass-media currency: the idiot notion of keeping yourself in the closet—that is very much the same thing as the suggestion that black folks and Asian Americans and Mexican Americans should assimilate and become as "white" as possible—in our walk/talk/music/food/values—or else. Or else? Or else we should, deservedly, perish.

Sure enough, we have plenty of exposure to white everything, so why would we opt to remain our African/Asian/Mexican selves? The answer is that suicide is absolute, and if you think you will survive by hiding who you really are, you are sadly misled: there is no such thing as partial or intermittent suicide. You can only suvive if you—who you really are—do survive.

Likewise, we who are not men and we who are not heterosexist—we, sure enough, have plenty of exposure to male-dominated/heterosexist this and that.

But a struggle to survive cannot lead to suicide: suicide is the opposite of survival. And so we must not conceal/assimilate/integrate into the would-be dominant culture and political system that despises us. Our survival requires that we alter our environment so that we can live and so that we can hold each other's hands and so that we can kiss each other on the streets, and in the daylight of our existence, without terror and without violent and sometimes fatal reactions from the busybodies of America.

Finally, I need to speak on bisexuality. I do believe that the analogy is interracial or multiracial identity. I do belive that the analogy for bisexuality is a multicultural, multiethnic, multiracial world view. Bisexuality follows from such a perspective and leads to it, as well.

Just as there are many men and women in the United States whose parents have given them more than one racial, more than one ethnic iden- tity and cultural heritage to honor; and just as these men and women must deny no given part of themselves except at the risk of self-deception and the insanities that must issue from that; and just as these men and women embody the principle of equality among races and ethnic communities; and just as these men and women falter and anguish and choose and then falter again and then anguish and then choose yet again how they will honor the irreducible complexity of their God-given human being—even so, there are many men and women, especially young men and women, who seek to embrace the complexity of their total, always-changing social and political circumstance.

They seek to embrace our increasing global complexity on the basis of the heart and on the basis of an honest human body. Not according to ideology. Not according to group pressure. Not according to anybody's concept of "correct."

This is a New Politics of Sexuality. And even as I despair of identity politics—because identity is given and principles of justice/equality/free- dom cut across given gender and given racial definitions of being, and because I will call you my brother, I will call you my sister, on the basis of what you *do* for justice, what you *do* for equality, what you *do* for freedom, and *not* on the basis of who you are, even so I look with admiration and respect upon the new, bisexual politics of sexuality.

This emerging movement politicizes the so-called middle ground: Bisexuality invalidates either/or formulation, either/or analysis. Biexuality means I am free and I am as likely to want and to love a woman as I am likely to want and to love a man, and what about that? Isn't that what freedom implies?

If you are free, you are not predictable and you are not controllable. To my mind, that is the keenly positive, politicizing significance of bisexual affirmation:

To insist upon complexity, to insist upon the validity of all of the components of social/sexual complexity, to insist upon the equal validity of all of the components of social/sexual complexity.

This seems to me a unifying, 1990s mandate for revolutionary Americans planning to make it into the twenty-first century on the basis of the heart, on the basis of an honest human body, consecrated to every struggle for justice, every struggle for equality, every struggle for freedom.

Paula Giddings (1947–   )

Paula Giddings, born in Yonkers, New York, wrote the first contemporary feminist history of African American women—*When and Where I Enter* (1984)—after a career as an editor with Random House and journalist with *Encore America*. Her involvement with a project on black women's history based in South Carolina provided the catalyst for her lifelong commitment to writing black women's history. She has also written a history of Delta Sigma Theta, Inc., entitled *In Search of Sisterhood*. "The Last Taboo," which appeared in Toni Morrison's collection of essays on the Clarence Thomas/Anita Hill saga, is a cogent analysis of the impact of persistent silences within the black community on issues relating to sexuality. She is presently completing a biography of Ida Wells-Barnett.

Paula Giddings }

THE LAST TABOO

The agonizing ordeal of the Clarence Thomas nomination should have taught us a valuable lesson: racial solidarity is not always the same as racial loyalty. This is especially true, it seems to me, in a postsegregation era, in which solidarity so often requires suppressing information about any African American of standing regardless of their political views or character flaws. Anita Hill's intervention in the proceedings should have told us that when those views or flaws are also sexist, such solidarity can be especially destructive to the community.

As the messenger for this relatively new idea, Anita Hill earned the antipathy of large segments of the African American community. More at issue than her truthfulness—or Clarence Thomas's character or politics —was whether she *should* have testified against another black person, especially a black man, who was just a hairsbreadth away from the Supreme Court. Of course, Anita Hill was not the only black person who testified against the nomination of Clarence Thomas, nor even the only woman to do so. But the nature of her complaint went further. It forced a mandate on gender: "the cultural definition of behavior defined as appropriate to the sexes in a given society at a given time," to borrow historian Gerda Lerner's definition. For many, what was *inappropriate* was that a black woman's commitment to a gender issue superseded what was largely perceived as racial solidarity. Still others, I think, reacted to an even greater taboo, perhaps the last and most deeply set one. This was to disclose not only a gender but a sexual discourse, unmediated by the question of racism. What Hill reported to the world was a black-on-black sexual crime involving a man of influence in the mainstream community.

The issues of gender and sexuality have been made so painful to us in our history that we have largely hidden them from ourselves, much less the glaring eye of the television camera. Consequently, they remain largely unresolved. I am convinced that Anita Hill, by introducing the issues in a way that could not be ignored, offered the possibility of a modern discourse on these issues that have tremendous, even lifesaving import for us.

I.

It is our historical experience that has shaped or, perhaps more accurately, misshaped the sex/gender issues and discourse in our community. That history was broached by Clarence Thomas himself when he used the most remembered phrase of the hearing: "high-tech lynching." Thus, he evoked the image of the sexually laden nineteenth-century lynching—often announced several days in advance to assure a crowd—after which the body was hanged, often burned, mutilated, and body parts, including genitals, were fought over for souvenirs. These were low-tech lynchings. Interestingly, it was almost exactly a century ago, in 1892, when the number of African Americans being lynched, 241, reached a peak after steadily escalating since the decade before. Then the epidemic of mob murder against blacks continued with impunity because of the perception that black men, no longer constrained by the "civilizing influence" of slavery, had regressed to a primitive state and were routinely raping white women. At that time "rape, and the rumors of rape, [were] a kind of acceptable folk pornography in the Bible Belt," observed historian Jacquelyn Dowd Hall.

Although Thomas's application of this phenomenon to his own situation was highly questionable, even ironic, in one way he was substantially correct. Now, as a century ago, white men, regardless of their own moral standing, still exercise the power to judge blacks on the basis of their perceived sexuality. However, what many failed to take into account with Thomas's evocation was that it was a black woman, Ida B. Wells, who initiated the nation's first anti-lynching campaign. For lynching was also a woman's issue: it had as much to do with ideas of gender as it had with race.

Often overlooked is the fact that black men were thought capable of these sexual crimes *because* of the lascivious character of the women of the race in a time when women were considered the foundation of a group's morality. Black men raped, it was widely believed, because black men's mothers, wives, sisters, and daughters were seen as "morally obtuse," "openly licentious," and had "no immorality in doing what nature prompts," as Harvard-educated Phillip A. Bruce, brother-in-law of writer Thomas Nelson Page, observed in his influential *Plantation Negro as Freeman* (1889). As one offer of proof, the author noted that black women never complained about being raped by black men. Other observers such as the following southern female writer to the popular periodical the *Independent* confirmed:

Degeneracy is apt to show most in the weaker individuals of any race; so Negro women evidence more nearly the popular idea of total depravity than the men do. They are so nearly lacking in virtue that the color of a Negro woman's skin is generally taken (and quite correctly) as a guarantee of her immorality.... And they are evidently the chief instruments of the degradation of the men of their race.... I sometimes read of a virtuous Negro woman, hear of them, but the idea is absolutely inconceivable to me...I cannot imagine such a creation as a virtuous black woman.

The status of black women had been dramatically etched into the annals of science earlier in the century. It was in fact personified in the figure of a single South African woman by the name of Sara Bartmann, aka the "Hottentot Venus." In 1810, when England was in the throes of debate about the slave trade, Ms. Bartmann was first exhibited in London "to the public in a manner offensive to decency," according to observers at the time (Gilman, 1985).

What made Ms. Bartmann such a subject of interest was the extraordinary size and shape of her buttocks, which served as a displacement of the fascination with female genitalia at the time. Sara Bartmann was displayed for five years, until she died, in Paris, at the age of twenty-five. Her degradation by what was defined as science and civilization did not end there. An autopsy was performed, preparing her genitalia "in such a way as to allow one to see the nature of the labia." Her organs were studied and reported upon by Dr. George Cuvier in 1817, coolly comparing Ms. Bartmann's genitalia with that of orangutans. Her sexual organs were then given to the Musée de l'Homme in Paris—where they are still on display.

Sara Bartmann's sexual parts, her genitalia and her buttocks, serve as the central image for the black female throughout the nineteenth century, concludes Gilman. It was also the image, he notes, that served as an icon for black sexuality throughout the century.

It is no coincidence that Sara Bartmann became a spectacle in a period when the British were debating the prohibition of slavery. As historian Barbara Fields and others have pointed out, there, as in North America, race took on a new significance when questions arose about the entitlement of nonenslaved blacks to partake of the fruits of Western liberty and citizenship. In North America, Euro-Americans had to resolve the contradictions between their own struggle for political freedom and that of the black men and women they still enslaved. This contradiction was resolved (by both pro- and antislavery whites) by racialism: ascribing certain inherited characteristics to blacks, characteristics that made them unworthy of the benefits of first-class citizenship. At the core of those characteristics was the projection of the dark side of sexuality, now literally embodied by black females. The use of a broad racial tarbrush, in turn, meant looking at race through the veneer of ideology: an institutionalized set of beliefs through which one interprets social reality. By the nineteenth century, then, race had become an ideology, and a basis of that ideology had become sexual difference. If there was a need for racialism in the late eighteenth century, it became an absolute necessity by the late nineteenth century, when lynching reached its peak. For after the Civil War, the Thirteenth, Fourteenth, and Fifteenth Amendments granted freedmen suffrage and black men and women many of the privileges of citizenship. In a state like Mississippi, which had some of the strongest black political organizations of any state, this translated into the kind of empowerment that saw, in the 1870s, two black men serve as United States senators, and blacks as secretaries of state and education, among other high offices. Throughout the South, especially, there was also dramatic evidence of African Americans gaining an economic foothold as the numbers of black-owned businesses and black landowners increased.

Additionally, unprecedented numbers of African American men and women were attending both predominantly white and predominantly black colleges, and aspiring to professional positions deemed out of reach just a generation before. This was even true of black women. By the 1880s the first black women were passing state bar exams to become attorneys, and were the first women of any race to practice medicine in the South. By the turn of the century, Booker T. Washington's National Business League reported that there were "160 black female physicians, seven dentists, ten lawyers, 164 ministers, assorted journalists, writers, artists, 1,185 musicians and teachers of music, and 13,525 school instructors." The period saw a virtual renaissance among black women artists and writers. The Philadelphia-born sculptor Meta Warwick Fuller was under the tutelage of Auguste Rodin; Frances Ellen Harper and Pauline Hopkins published two of the earliest novels by black women; Oberlin-educated Anna Julia Cooper published *A Voice from the South* (1892), a treatise on race and feminism that anticipated much of the later work of W. E. B. Du Bois; and journalist Ida B. Wells, in 1889, was elected as the first woman secretary of the Afro-American Press Association.

Ironically, such achievements within a generation of slavery did not inspire an ideology of racial equality but one of racial difference, the latter being required to maintain white supremacy. That difference would be largely based on perceptions of sexual difference, and as noted before, the foundation of sexual difference lay in attitudes about black women.

II.

By the late nineteenth century, however, difference would be characterized at its most dualistic: as binary opposition—not just in terms of race and sexuality, but of gender and class as well. Such oppositions were effective means of social control at a time when the country was losing its sociosexual mooring in the face of radical and fundamental changes driven (as now) by a technological revolution. For if the late twentieth century was shaped by advances like the computer, the late nineteenth was adjusting itself around innovations such as the typewriter, the gasoline-driven car, the internal-combustion airplane, the sewing machine, the incandescent light, the phonograph, and the radio. Such innovations bring on new systems of marketing and financing them, and thus new possibilities of wealth, as the late-nineteenth-century emergence of the Rockefellers, Morgans, Du Ponts, and Carnegies attest. In addition, new corporate cultures increased urbanization, made sex outside of the family more possible, and contributed to the increased commodification of sex in forms of pornography and brothels, as it became more associated with pleasure rather than merely reproduction. At the same time, money and the labor-saving devices allowed middle-class women to spend less time doing domestic housework and more time seeking education and reform outside of the home. Add to this growing numbers of immigrants from eastern and southern Europe, the increasing disparity between the haves and the have-nots (by 1890, the poorest one-half of families received one-fifth of all wages and salaries), labor unrest and unemployment that reached thirty percent in some years during the decade, and the need for control becomes obvious. That control was effectively handled through creating categories of difference through binary opposition. For example, maleness was defined by its opposition to female-ness; whiteness by its opposition to blackness. The same dualism applied to the concepts of civilization and primitivity, purity and pollutedness, goodness and evil, public and private. The nineteenth-century paradigm regarding sexuality tied all of these oppositions together, which operated to the detriment of blacks and women in general, and black women in particular.

For example, in the late nineteenth century, men were believed to have a particularly rapacious sexual drive that had to be controlled. The last thing needed at home was a woman who had the same sexual drive that men had; what was needed was in binary opposition to perceived male sexuality. What was needed was a woman who did not tempt, and was thus synonymous with "good." And so, although in another period women were thought to have strong, even the more ungovernable, sexual drives, by the late nineteenth century, they were thought to have hardly any libido at all. Furthermore, female sexuality was now considered pathological (Gilman, 1985). That meant, of course, that good women did not have erotic feelings, and those who might have had inappropriate urges were recommended to see physicians like J. Marion Sims or Robert Battey, who employed radical gynecological surgery, including clitoridectomies, to "correct" masturbation and other forms of sexual passion (D'Emilio, Freedman, 1988). Such severe methods were necessary to sustain diametrically opposed identities to "bad" women: lower-class women, and especially black women.

Economically lower-class women fell under the "bad" column by virtue of the fact that they worked outside the home and thus were uninsulated from the sexual aggression of the society. Certainly, it was the former group of women who made up the growing numbers of prostitutes, a label that could fall even on women more drawn to casual sex than to remuneration, and were of great interest to scientists as well as white middle-class female reformers and repressed men. With Sara Bartmann as a model and basis of comparison, their sexual organs were studied, codified, and preserved in jars. Anthropologists such as Cesare Lombrosco, coauthor of the major study of prostitution in the late nineteenth century, *The Prostitute and the Normal Woman* (1893), wrote that the source of their passion and pathology lay in the labia, which reflected a more primitive structure than their upper-class counterparts. One of Lombrosco's students, Abele de Blasio, focused on the buttocks. His specialty was steatopygia (excessive fat on the buttocks), which was also deemed to be a special characteristic of whores —and, of course, black women. They would represent the very root of female eroticism, immorality, and disease.

In the medical metaphors of the day, the sexual organs of sexual women were not only hotbeds of moral pathology, but of disease. In the nineteenth century the great fear was of a sexually transmitted disease that was spreading among the population, was incurable, and after invading the body, disfigured and decomposed it in stages. The name of the disease was syphilis, and it was the era's metaphor for the retribution of sexual sin. Despite evidence to the contrary, it was seen as a disease that affected not only persons, but groups perceived as both licentious and deviant. Prostitutes of course fell into this category, but it did not seem to affect business. Science even abandoned long-held views to accommodate the paradigm. Formerly, it was believed that Christopher Columbus's sailors had introduced the disease to Europe. Now the new wisdom traced it to a form of leprosy that had long been present in Africa and had spread into Europe during the Middle Ages. At the wellspring of this plague were the genital organs of black women (Gilman, 1985).

As the epitome of the immorality, pathology, and impurity of the age, black women were seen in dualistic opposition to their upper-class, pure, and passionless white sisters. It was this binary opposition of women (black men's sex drives were not seen as inherently different than those of white men, only less controlled) that was the linchpin of race, class, and even gender difference. It was this opposition, furthermore, that also led to lynching. For it was the white women's qualities so profoundly missing in black women, that made black men find white women irresistible, and "strangely alluring and seductive," in the words of Phillip Bruce.

III.

Categorizing women through binary opposition had a devastating impact. Even the relatively privileged middle-class white women were subjected to the sexual tyrannies of the age. The opposition of public, a male sphere, and private, a female one, led to conclusions that imprisoned women in the home. The eminent Harvard-trained physician Dr. Edward Clarke, for example, wrote in his influential book *Sex in Education* (1873) that education could ruin a woman's sexual organs. Ideas about male sexual irrepressibility in opposition to women's passionlessness were largely responsible for the fact that "rape in marriage was no crime, nor even generally disapproved," "wife beating was only marginally criminal," and "incest was common enough to require skepticism that it was tabooed," according to historians Linda Gordon and Ellen Carol DuBois (1983). Women would have to untangle and rework paradigms in order to protect themselves and, as DuBois and Gordon note, exercise their right to enjoy the pleasure of sex. Toward this end, white feminists began challenging the oppositional frameworks concerning the sexuality of men and women. For example, Dr. Elizabeth Blackwell, a physician, offered the startling counteropinion that men and women had equal sexual urges, thus providing a rationale for consensual sex in marriage—and for "free lovers" outside of marriage as well. They also regulated the torrent of male sexuality by insisting that women should only be required to have sex when they wanted to get pregnant. Called "voluntary motherhood," it was a "brilliant" tactic, says Gordon, for it "insinuated a rejection of male sexual domination into a politics of defending and improving motherhood." And at a time when they still had little power or even identity outside of the home, women disdained abortion and contraception, insisting—in a world of depersonalized sex—on maintaining the link between sexual intercourse and reproduction. Consequently, say the authors, the principle of marital mutuality and women's right to say no was established among white middle-class couples in the late nineteenth century. This is perhaps evidenced by the fact that although birth control methods were not widely approved, the birthrate among white native-born women declined by 1900 to an average of 3.54—fifty percent below the level of the previous century!

Despite their enlightened views on such issues as a single standard of sexuality for men and women, as well as others, white feminists fell short on issues like nonmarital rape, probably because of its interracial implications. Although they could bring themselves to counter gender oppositions, those that involved race, and, to a lesser extent class, seemed to be beyond their reach. This would be left to black feminists like Ida B. Wells and others who constantly challenged the dualism between good and bad, black and white, and its implications especially as it affected African American women.

Ida Wells simply turned this paradigm on its head, with her own empirical evidence gathered from her investigation of the circumstances of 728 lynchings that had taken place over the previous decade. Her meticulously documented findings would not only challenge the assumption of rape—which also exonerated black women to a significant extent—but also included findings about the lynching of black women as well as their sexual exploitation at the hands of whites. It was black women who needed protection, Wells insisted, as "the rape of helpless Negro girls and women, which began in slavery days, still continued without reproof from church, state, or press," thus changing their representation to that of victims. Her most dramatic challenge to the paradigm, of course, was her questioning of the passionless purity of Southern white women. There *were* interracial liaisons between black men and white women, Wells published in her findings, but they were consensual and often initiated by white women. In May of 1892, Wells would publish the editorial that got her exiled from the South: "If Southern white men are not careful . . . ," she challenged, "a conclusion will be reached which will be damaging to the moral reputation of their women" (Wells, *On Lynchings* [New York: Arno Press, 1969]). Wells, perhaps the first leader to broach the subject of black sexual oppression after slavery, had now completely challenged the period's assumptions. Black men weren't rapists, white men were; black women weren't doing what "nature prompted," white women were; Wells's framework actually rescued both black and white women from their dehumanized objectification.

When, in reaction to Wells's ideas, the president of the Missouri Press Association, John Jacks, wrote a letter calling all black women "prostitutes, thieves and liars," it was the proverbial straw for nascent regional clubs to come together under a national umbrella in 1896. "Read the letter carefully, and use it discriminately" (it was "too indecent for publication"), challenged Boston activist and editor Josephine St. Pierre Ruffin, and "decide if it be not the time to stand before the world and declare ourselves and our principles." Formed as the National Association for Colored Women (NACW), with a membership that would reach 50,000 by 1916, it would act not only as a means to realize suffrage, education, and community development, but the vessel through which black women challenged, in public, the beliefs that were getting black men lynched and black women raped and exploited. Sexual exploitation was so pervasive that it drove black women north in search of safer climes. "It is a significant and shameful fact that I am constantly in receipt of letters from still unprotected women in the South," complained the nineteenth-century Chicago activist Fannie

Barrier Williams, "begging me to find employment for their daughters . . . to save them from going into the homes of the South as servants as there is nothing to save them from dishonor and degradation." In 1893, before the predominantly white Congress of Representative Women, Williams challenged that black women shouldn't be disparaged but protected, adding that "I do not want to disturb the serenity of this conference by suggesting why this protection is needed and the kind of man against whom it is needed."

IV.

Nevertheless, despite their extraordinary boldness in bringing this issue before the white public, black women activists were precluded from presenting another kind of critique, one which was also important. The brutal concept of binary opposition prevented them from a frank public discourse concerning intraracial gender relations and sexuality, with which white feminists had been relatively successful. This void was a potentially life-threatening one in a time of adjustment to nonslavery; a time when gender roles, altered first by slavery and then by rapid social and economic changes, were in chaos; a time when the sexuality of both black men and women had to have been twisted by sexism and racism, and now by numbing poverty. Ghettos were congealing, families were in disarray, domestic violence was on the increase, cocaine and alcohol were being abused, and venereal diseases were increasing at an alarming rate. But in this social-Darwinistic environment, where blacks were judged harshly, even murderously, by their perceived difference from the white middle-class ideal, where it was believed that the poor deserved to be poor because of moral and character flaws, where a man, as Wells reported, could be lynched under the pretense of beating his wife, how could there be a public discourse about such things? How was one going to explain the higher rates of venereal disease such as syphilis among blacks? And how was one to explain before a hostile white public that the higher rates of infant mortality were largely due to children's inheriting "enfeebled constitutions and congenital diseases, inherited from parents suffering from the effects of sexual immorality and debauchery" (25), as an 1897 report, *Proceedings of the Second Conference for the Study of Problems Concerning Negro City Life,* under the general direction of W. E. B. Du Bois, then at Atlanta University, stated?

Publicly voicing such concerns in a society defined by binary opposition could leave blacks in general and black women in particular vulnerable to the violent whims of whites. It is no wonder that the issues of intraracial sexuality and gender have long been tabooed in public discourse. At the same time, not voicing these concerns have left the community, especially women, bereft of the help and protection so needed. As an anonymous black women writer, one of the few who dared break the silence of intraracial sexuality, wrote to the *Independent* in 1904, "We poor colored wage earners of the South are fighting a terrible battle, on the one hand, we are assailed by white men, and on the other hand, we are assailed by black men who should be our natural protectors." There are sexist backlashes within our community, too.

For black women, the accumulated effects of assault and the inability to "eradicate negative social and sexual images of their womanhood" had "powerful ideological consequences," concludes historian Darlene Hine. To protect themselves, she observes, black women created what she calls "a culture of dissemblance." Hine defines this as "the behavior and attitudes of black women that created the appearance of openness and disclosure but actually shielded the truth of their inner lives and selves from their oppressors" (292)—and I would add, even from ourselves. This is the reason, I think, why we have not forced such sex/gender discourses, seen primarily as disclosures, in our community. It is why feminist issues, though not women's rights issues, are more problematic for us. Not only is feminism specifically associated with our historic binary opposites—middle-class white women—it demands an analysis of sexual issues. This is why to break through the silence and traditional sense of racial solidarity is such a controversial act for us. This, in turn, largely accounts for the vitriol earned by those who indicate a public discourse on sexuality in their work, such as Alice Walker in *The Color Purple* or Ntozake Shange in *For Colored Girls*. ...I think these traditional notions are also the reason why Anita Hill's appearance was so controversial in the black community. Those who publicly supported her, namely black scholars and the National Coalition of 100 Black Women—formed in 1970 when the women's movement was making an impact—were those in touch with gender issues and their role in the needed transformation of our institutions and communities. This is the window black women writers have pointed toward but that Anita Hill, in her first-person, clear, unswervingly direct testimony before the public, has actually opened. It was an act of great inner courage and conviction, to turn back the veil of our Du Boisian double consciousness. It was an act that provided clarity about our new status in the late twentieth century.

V.

There would be some that would argue that that status is no more empowered than it was a hundred years ago, thus requiring that we use the same strategies of solidarity. There is no question that, in some ways, the essential aspects of racism and sexism still affect us. This was evident in the statement "African American Women in Defense of Ourselves," first appearing in the *New York Times* as a paid ad on November 17, signed by 1,603 black women, most of them scholars, in response to the treatment of Anita Hill during the hearings. Insisting that the "malicious defamation of Professor Hill insulted all women of African American descent," it concluded that "throughout U.S. history, black women have been stereotyped as immoral, insatiable, perverse; the initiators in all sexual contacts—abusive or otherwise.... As Anita Hill's experience demonstrates, black women who speak of these matters are not likely to be believed...." The words sound very much like those that led women to organize the NACW almost exactly a century ago, and in fact, the similar conditions that previously made us want to wrap ourselves in that protective skin have come back around with a vengeance. Certainly, the late twentieth century, with its dislocating technological revolution, rapacious money-making, excesses of sex, guilt, and consumption, and incurable diseases viewed as Old Testament warnings should give us pause. For when such a confluence occurs, there are cultural reflexes to create categories of difference, including sexual difference, with all of its murderous Willie Horton, Bensonhurst, David Duke, and Central Park gang-rape implications. And although we may have passed the era that could take a Hottentot Venus seriously, we cannot rest assured that advances in science will save us from such folly. That respectable journals would make connections between green monkeys and African women, for example, or trace the origin of AIDS to African prostitutes— the polluted sexual organs of black women—reveals our continued vulnerability to racist ideology. It tells us that concepts of racial difference (in this situation, sexual practices) can still be used as weapons of degradation, and that the idea of difference turns on sexuality, and sexuality, in this culture, is loaded with concepts of race, gender, and class. This explains in part why the backlashes against women, black and nonblack, as well as race, carry a virulence that goes beyond the fear of competition or the sharing of power once so handily monopolized by others.

On the other hand, there have been some fundamental, dramatic changes, largely realized by our own struggle for equality and empowerment, that allow us, in fact demand, a new strategy. For although racism still exists, our situation has changed since the sixties in spite of it. It has changed because of two interrelated developments: the sexual revolution and de jure desegregation. They are interrelated because sex was the principle around which wholesale segregation and discrimination was organized with the ultimate objective of preventing intermarriage (D'Emilio, Freedman, 1988). The sexual revolution, however, separated sexuality from reproduction, and so diluted the ideas about purity—moral, racial, and physical.

Both desegregation and the sexual revolution make dissemblance and suppression in the name of racial solidarity anachronistic, for they were prescribed to divert perceptions of difference, based on sexual difference between black women and white. Despite the tenacity about ideas of difference, recent sociopolitical developments—further codified by feminist theory as well as black studies—make binary opposition as a sole indicator of meaning passé.

In the meantime, increasing sexual aggression, including date rape on college campuses that tend to be underreported by black women; the number of "children having children"; the plague of domestic violence; the breakup of families; and the spread of fatal venereal disease among African Americans at a time when we have more "rights" than ever before tells us that gender issues are just as important—if not more so—in the black community as racial issues have always been. More than ever before it is essential that we advance a discourse on sexuality that is liberating for those who engage in it and truncating to the souls of those who don't. As Naima Major, former director of the National Black Women's Health Project (NBWHP)—one of the few black institutions that regularly engages in sexuality issues—said to me, most of the black women she sees "seem to cut themselves off at the waist," even when they are coming to talk specifically about sexuality.

This is particularly alarming in view of the fact that we are in a sexually aggressive era, one where sex is commodified and often depersonalized, especially for young women. Their worlds were the subject of a study of adolescents aged fifteen to seventeen, conducted by Pat McPherson and Michelle Fine, and their observations were disturbing. From the stories of these young women, the authors surmised that their generation is more likely to "be aware of, witness to, and victim of" male sexual abuse among both peers and family. Their sexual experiences with peers are not characterized by learning the meaning or enjoyment of sex, or even making choices about engaging in it, but in protecting themselves from what is viewed (as in the past) as the irrepressible sexual drives of the men in their lives. A black adolescent in this interracial group spoke about not her own sexual preferences but the need to satisfy, indeed mollify, men quickly through cunnilingus so that the evening could end early, and hassle-free. And the authors noted that female adolescents also protect themselves by suppressing signs of their gender: by becoming "one of the boys" through not only dress, but through even misogynist behavior and attitudes. These are issues that were addressed a century ago, under similar sociosexual conditions, but the solutions have not been passed on through families or social institutions. We must begin to do it.

The analysis of how sex/gender systems apply to us in the 1990s becomes urgent when we see that *fifty-eight percent* of black women beyond the age of eighteen *never* use any form of birth control, according to a 1991 study conducted by the National Council of Negro Women (NCNW). Yet only one percent of those women said that they wanted to get pregnant, and only two percent said that they did not know how to use birth control. Does this finding indicate ambivalence about separating sexuality from reproduction despite not wanting a child? Does it indicate the desire, however sublimated, to become pregnant? Or, as I suspect, is the finding a reflection of the fact that their male partners look down on birth control?

One thing we know, there seems to be what one might call a cult of motherhood in our community. How else might one interpret the finding of journalist Leon Dash in his book *When Children Want Children* (1988), that nearly a fourth of all unmarried teenage mothers intentionally become pregnant? What does motherhood mean to these youngsters? The ability to exercise maternal authority in lieu of other avenues of self-esteem and empowerment? rebellion against the depersonalization of sex? or perhaps, as a century ago, does this finding represent the effort to control male sexuality? The answers to these questions are important, as the babies of teenagers are more apt to be underweight and thus have learning and other physical disabilities. There is also tragedy in another statistic: forty-eight percent of the teenagers who intentionally got pregnant later regretted their decision.

Even college students, according to a report by the Black Women's Health Project, indicated a conflict about delaying childbearing in the face of "women's traditional and proper role as mother"—"indeed as a respected 'matriarch' in a community beset by failing family structures." Of course, there is also male pressure insinuated in some of these findings. The college students said that they felt intense pressure from male partners who wanted to be fathers—one of the few avenues toward manhood?—as well as from cultural and religious leaders not to have abortions. Although one has to respect religious and/or moral views about this, one has to wonder if young women are making rational, informed decisions about these things —lives depend on it.

Another issue not engaged adequately is one that Leon Dash discovered after hours of interviews with teenagers over the course of an entire year —the time it takes to get beyond their personal dissemblance strategies. Many of the motives behind sexual decisions—for better sometimes, but often for worse—were shaped by the fact that their families had a tremendous amount of sexual abuse within them, sometimes traced through two, three, or more generations. Ironically, Dash's decision to publicly reveal such information caused more consternation among self-conscious middle-class blacks than the dire implications of the information itself.

If all of this sounds very nineteenth-century, there is a reason for it. Black men and women have not had their own sexual revolution—the one we couldn't have before. We need a discourse that will help us understand modern ideas about gender and sex/gender systems, about male privilege, and about power relations; about the oppressive implications of pornography—something even at least one Harvard professor seems not to understand.

In our considerations of Anita Hill, it is important to understand that she spoke not of a physical transgression on the part of Clarence Thomas, but a verbal one masked in pornographic language. Pornography, "a fantasy salvation that inspires nonfantasy acts of punishment for uppity females," as one historian put it, speaks specifically to power relations between men and women. For African Americans these relations remain unanalyzed in the light of the empowerment of black male elites like those represented by Thomas, who, since the seventies, have emerged as gatekeepers for the upward mobility of all blacks in the newly accessible corporate, political, academic, and business spheres of influence. It is men, not women, who control the sociosexual and professional relationships in the black community. Among other notions that must be dispensed with is the weak male/strong female patriarchal paradigm that clouds so much of our thinking about ourselves.

Implicit in Hill's testimony is the challenge to transcend a past that once protected, but now twists, the deepest sense of ourselves and our identities. The silences and dissemblance in the name of a misguided solidarity must end. A modern and transformative discourse must begin. Anita Hill has broken through. Let us follow.[1]

ENDNOTES

1. In this essay, Gerda Lerner's definition of gender can be found in *The Creation of Patriarchy* (New York: Oxford University Press, 1987). Secondary sources regarding Phillip A. Bruce can be found in Herbert G. Gutman, *The Black Family in Slavery and Freedom, 1750–1925* (New York: Pantheon, 1976); and Jacquelyn Dowd Hall explores lynching and rape in *Revolt Against Chivalry: Jessie Daniel Ames and the Women's Campaign Against Lynching* (New York: Columbia University Press, 1971). The issue of the *Independent* referred to is dated March 17, 1904; and explications of Sara Bartmann, the Hottentot Venus, can be found in Sander L. Gilman's essay "Black Bodies, White Bodies: Toward an Iconography of Female Sexuality in Late Nineteenth-Century Art, Medicine and Literature," in *"Race," Writing and Difference,* ed. Henry Louis Gates (Chicago: University of Chicago Press, 1985, 1986). Analysis of sexuality during different periods in American history can be found in John D'Emilio and Estelle Freedman, *Intimate Matters: The History of Sexuality in America* (New York: Harper & Row, 1988). Discussions of the National Association of Colored Women, black women's status in the nineteenth century, and Fannie B. Williams's and Ida B. Wells's anti-lynching campaign can be found in Paula Giddings, *When and Where I Enter: The Impact of Black Women on Race and Sex in America* (New York: William Morrow, 1984). The article by Barbara Fields is entitled "Ideology and Race in American History" and is found in J. Kousser and James M. McPherson, eds., *Race, Region and Reconstruction* (New York: Oxford University Press, 1982). The references to Gordon and DuBois are found in Ellen DuBois and Linda Gordon, "Seeking Ecstasy on the Battlefield: Danger and Pleasure in Nineteenth Century Feminist Sexual Thought," *Feminist Studies,* vol. 9.,

no. 1 (Spring 1983). The quote by Anna Julia Cooper is in her *Voice from the South* (1892), reprinted by Negro Universities Press (New York, 1969), 68–69. The report cited under the direction of W. E. B. Du Bois, about blacks' health and sexuality in the late nineteenth century, is entitled *Proceedings of the Second Conference for the Study of Problems Concerning Negro City Life,* originally published by Atlanta University Publications. See vol. I, reprinted by Octagon Books,1968. The explanation of the culture of dissemblance is found in Darlene Clark Hine, "Rape and the Inner Lives of Black Women in the Middle West: Preliminary Thoughts on the Culture of Dissemblance," in *Unequal Sisters: A Multicultural Reader in U.S. Women's History,* ed. Ellen Carol DuBois and Vicki L. Ruiz (New York: Routledge & Kegan Paul, 1990). The study on contemporary adolescents is "Hungry for an Us: Our Girl Group Talks About Sexual and Racial Identities," by Pat McPherson and Michelle Fine. It was published in Janice M. Irvine, ed., *Sexual Cultures: Adolescence, Community and the Construction of Identity* (Philadelphia: Temple University Press, 1993). The women-of-color study was underwritten by the National Council of Negro Women with the Communications Consortium Media Center and is entitled "Women of Color Reproductive Health Poll," August 29, 1991. The book in which Leon Dash published his findings on pregnant teenagers is entitled *When Children Want Children: The Urban Crisis of Teenage Childbearing* (New York: William Morrow, 1989). The report issued in 1991 by the National Black Women's Health Project is entitled "Report: Reproductive Health Program of the National Black Women's Health Project."

Pearl Cleage

Pearl Cleage, Atlanta playwright and performance artist, edits *Catalyst,* a literary magazine, and is the author of two books—*Mad at Miles,* which focuses on violence against black women, and *Deals with the Devil,* a collection of personal essays.

"What Can I Say" is a black feminist response to the highly publicized O. J. Simpson case, which involves domestic violence and the double murder of his former wife, Nicole Simpson, and her friend Ronald Goldman. This unfortunate saga provides an opportunity, yet again, for Cleage's exposure of the insensitivity of male politicians to the widespread social evil of violence against women. She offers as a last resort a disturbing solution —women arming themselves—and recalls Ida Wells-Barnett's admonishment to blacks at the turn of the century to defend themselves in the face of unrestrained racist attacks.

What Can I Say?

I have been trying to think of something sensible to say about the murder of Nicole Brown Simpson and Ronald Goldman. But I can't, because this is nothing new. Men kill and torture and slap and stab and beat and abuse their wives and ex-wives and girlfriends and ex-girlfriends and lovers and ex-lovers every day. Nicole Brown Simpson is more real to us only because we heard her terrified sobbing on the recording of the 911 call where O. J. can be heard clearly in the background, screaming, threatening, cursing...

She is more real because so many of us thought we knew and loved her ex-husband, although all we ever saw was his football skill and his smiling public face, which seems to have very little to do with the rampaging maniac kicking in her door at midnight, secure in the knowledge that the police were unlikely to restrain or arrest him.

But this isn't news to me. Nicole Simpson's death doesn't really provide any new information about male violence toward women and, so far, it hasn't given us the impetus to develop any new strategies to confront the problem either. The media is still filled with pictures of angry, sign-carrying women marching on Congress, or picketing the state legislature or appealing to the president.

There we are, asking the powerful men who make the laws that govern our lives to pretty please focus on this issue for a minute if they can take a second from their busy schedules because, hey, we're dying out here. Well, that's just not enough. We've done all that asking and picketing and being indignant on the six o'clock news before, and there are still more animal shelters in this country than there are facilities for battered women on the run from their abusers.

And even though the most common advice given to women who are victims of nonstranger male violence is to leave him/move out/cut him loose, statistics show that a woman who leaves is seventy-five percent more likely to be killed by her abuser than a woman who stays.

So we've got a couple of options, it seems to me. We can sit around and bemoan the fact that this horrible thing happened, and is happening, make our picket signs, and head for City Hall; or we can decide to think about all of it differently. Having long ago lost my willingness to place my fate and the fate of my sisters in the hands of any men, the decision to think about it differently is my clear first choice. Let's not try to take on the whole subject at first. Let's start with two obvious things: self-definition and self-defense.

Generally, male crimes against women with whom they are, or have been, intimate, are grouped together under the term "domestic violence." Notice how the phrase sounds somehow less horrible because of that word "domestic" in it? Just the word "domestic" calls up images of lovely little homes, presided over by a strong, generous dad and a smiling, well-organized mom. Things that happen in such an environment might be a little unpleasant from time to time, but that's about as bad as it gets. The word violence tacked on the end seems almost benign.

So let's redefine our terms and call things by their proper names. Instead of saying O. J. Simpson was guilty of "domestic violence" back in October of 1993 when Nicole Simpson made the 911 call we've all heard, what if we charged him with breaking and entering? How about assault and battery? How about attempted murder? How about rape? (I know, I know . . . but you don't think men terrorize women the way O. J. Simpson was terrorizing Nicole Simpson and then wait to be invited to have sex, do you?)

These itemized crimes sound a lot more serious than the catchall of "domestic violence." We're used to people who commit these terrible crimes being punished severely. Sent to jail. Electrocuted. Hanged by the neck until dead. Sometimes these perpetrators are even killed in self-defense by their intended victims who were able to protect themselves when called upon to do so.

All of these punishments for these terrible crimes are societally sanctioned and community condoned. Nobody goes to prison for shooting somebody who kicked in the back door of the house and is coming up the steps, probably armed, and certainly intending to do bodily harm to the home owner. Unless the person doing the breaking and entering is an ex-husband. In that case, the woman is supposed to call 911 and hope for the best.

Well, I heard one of Nicole Brown Simpson's many 911 calls, and I heard O. J. screaming and raging in the background, and 911 is not enough. Which brings us to the question of self-defense. I think she should have been armed. I think she should have bought herself a gun and learned how to use it. I think she should have gotten comfortable with her ability to use that gun and defended herself and her children by any means necessary. Period.

I am afraid as I write those words. Afraid that my brothers will read it and be angry with me. Afraid that I will be accused of male bashing, of judging O. J. too harshly before he's even had a trial. Of being a part of bringing down another good brother. Even worse, I can hear the howls of outrage that I could even think of advocating that black women arm themselves when our community is already an armed camp.

But as you think about the whole idea of self-defense for women who are experiencing male violence in their homes, I ask you to remember the words of crusading African American woman journalist and anti-lynching activist Ida B. Wells. Wells was distraught and terrified after the murderous turn-of-the-century riot in Memphis, Tennessee, where two of her friends were killed and black folks were dragged from their houses by white mobs and beaten in the streets. But she channeled that horror into a renewed determination to take personal responsibility for her own safety.

"A Winchester rifle should have a place of honor in every home," Wells told her community. "When the white man knows he runs as great a risk of biting the dust every time his Afro-American victim does, he will have a greater respect for Afro-American life."

What if we substitute gender for race? "When the male knows he runs as great a risk of biting the dust every time his female victim does, he will have a greater respect for female life."

It sounds so terrible to me even as I write the words. So angry and vengeful. I don't want to write about female self-defense. I want to write about love and healing and black nationalism and wholeness. But then a voice whispers deep inside me: What would I be writing about if Nicole Brown Simpson had been my daughter?

Or yours.

Evelynn Hammonds

Evelynn Hammonds, professor in the program in science, technology, and society at the Massachusetts Institute of Technology, is one of the few black women historians of science in the country. She attributes the development of her feminist consciousness to the racism and sexism she experienced as a graduate student in MIT's physics department, which she describes in Sandra Harding's anthology *The "Racial" Economy of Science* (1993) during an interview with Aimee Sands. She is one of the few black academics doing feminist critiques of science, and writing about the situation of black women scientists from a feminist perspective. One of her major research interests has been blacks and AIDS. She, along with Robin Kilson, convened the historic conference "Black Women in the Academy: Defending Our Name, 1894–1994," which brought over two thousand mostly black women academics to MIT, January 13–15, 1994. Hammonds reminded the audience at the opening plenary session that there were parallels between 1894, when black women's morality was being maligned, and 1994, when black women, such as Anita Hill and Lani Guinier, were being demonized in the media. Hammonds is on leave from MIT with a post-doctoral fellowship at Princeton University's School for Advanced Studies.

Evelynn Hammonds }

MISSING PERSONS:
AFRICAN AMERICAN WOMEN, AIDS,
AND THE HISTORY OF DISEASE

*Nobody is ever in to see me or hear my complaints. They are never
there when I try to make an appointment to get anything done.
Nobody cares. I continue to get sick over and over again, and nobody
listens to what I have to say. I don't think that's fair, because I feel I
deserve better, because not only am I a woman, I am also a human
being; and it's hard enough for me to deal with the issue of having
AIDS, dying a day at a time and to have to live under the circumstances that I am under.*[1]

In 1990, every two hours a black person died from HIV disease.[2] Needless
to say, in 1992 the situation is worsening. Between 1981 (when the first
cases of the acquired immunodeficiency syndrome (AIDS) were reported
in the United States) and 1991, 15,493 cases in women have been reported.
The number of cases in women increased from 6.6 percent of the total in
1985, to 11.5 percent of the total reported cases by the end of 1990.[3]

Fifty-two percent of these women are African American; twenty-seven
percent are white; twenty-one percent are Hispanic; and one percent are
classified as unknown. Under the category "unknown" are the cases of
AIDS among Native American and Asian American women. By 1987,
AIDS had become the eighth leading cause of death in women of reproductive age in the United States. Today, it is the leading cause of death for
black women 15–44 years old in New York and New Jersey.[4]

WHY DO AFRICAN AMERICAN WOMEN
DISPROPORTIONATELY GET AIDS?

In spite of the fact that the majority of women with AIDS are African
American, the devastating toll that AIDS is taking on the lives of these
women has yet to be perceived as a national crisis. Neither scientific, epide-
miological, nor historical or cultural studies about AIDS have addressed

the question of why African American women are at such greater risk for HIV infection and why their survival rates are so abysmally low. Now that the percentages for women with AIDS have more than doubled in the last two years (in some cities women make up twenty-five percent of the AIDS cases), research on women is in process. One might wonder, however, whether the government's recent focus on women is not mainly directed at their reproductive lives, that is, women become the risk factor for HIV in children. In this essay I want to look at a number of factors that have supported the invisibility of African American women with AIDS. First, I look at examples of the representation of these women in the media, in particular focusing on how media reports shape and reflect the social context of the epidemic with regard to African American women with AIDS. Secondly, I discuss how AIDS is affecting the lives of poor, African American women. Many analyses of the AIDS epidemic have noted that much of our contemporary response, both in terms of methods of controlling the epidemic and confronting the stigma associated with this disease, is linked to earlier practices and responses to the epidemic of sexually transmitted diseases (STDs) in the first half of the twentieth century. In the final section, I raise a number of questions about how African American women were viewed with regard to this history of sexually transmitted diseases. In sum, I argue that African American women are disproportionately vulnerable to the ravages of AIDS in part because of the long-term and persistent failure of public health practices to control sexually transmitted diseases in the African American community.

It goes without saying that gender has not been at the center of discussions or research about AIDS. The way in which AIDS was first conceptualized as a disease of gay men, then a disease of various "risk groups," e.g., intravenous drug users, foreclosed the recognition of women as potentially a significant proportion of the AIDS caseload.[5] This is even more apparent when examining gender within racial categories. In the broadest sense, little attention has been paid to the plight of African American women with AIDS because they are women. Overall, the medical establishment and most activist groups have focused on men, who make up the larger numbers of people with AIDS.[6] And as feminists and other activists have documented, women have historically received unequal treatment in the United States health care system. African American women, as evidenced by their higher rates of many diseases, have long been among the least served by the health care system. AIDS appears in African American communities at the end of a long trail of neglect in the Reagan-Bush years —including the cut-off of federal funds for abortion, jobs, housing, and the failure to control *sexually transmitted diseases*. The conditions that African American women live under in their communities, their roles as mothers, wives, workers, and lovers, all shape their responses to AIDS.

MEDIA IMAGES: "MOST ARE POOR, MANY ARE RECKLESS"

The impact of HIV infection on African American women and other women of color has received an odd sort of coverage in the media. On the one hand when the threat of AIDS to women is discussed, no mention is made of African American women. When African American women are discussed, they are relegated to the drug abuser category or partners of drug abusers or bad mother category for passing AIDS onto their children. A good example of this appeared in August 1987 in an article by Jane Gross, which appeared on the front page of the *New York Times*. The headline read: "Bleak Lives: Women Carrying AIDS," followed by "Women Who Carry the AIDS Virus: Most Are Poor, Many Are Reckless."[7] I refer to this article in part to underline how little has changed since it appeared in 1987 and because it so clearly lays out the assumptions about women who become infected with HIV.

First, the article stated the grim statistics; in New York City in August 1987 there were 50,000 women infected with HIV; eighty percent were black and Hispanic. The first paragraph of the article announced:

> They are the primary carriers of the disease from the world of drug abuse to the larger community, making their education an increasingly urgent task.

The identification of women as "carriers" was stated without supporting scientific data. Perhaps the writer was unaware of the scientific data but, by 1987, studies showed that women were at greater risk of infection from infected men than the other way around. Or, in the rhetoric of the medical literature, female to male transmission of HIV is "less efficient."[8] The women in this article are portrayed as passive victims in abusive relationships with men who are most often drug abusers. Their lives are described as "unruly," "chaotic," "despairing." The most demeaning attack is made on African American women who, through HIV positive, become pregnant and choose to continue their pregnancies rather than have an abortion. Gross reported that

> ... Women explain that they want to have another child to leave something behind in the face of death, that they view a fifty-fifty chance of having a healthy baby acceptable odds. But counselors say these explanations usually do not surface until a pregnancy has proceeded past the point when abortion is possible. They wind up having babies more by default than intent.[9]

The behaviors highlighted by these experts' comments, suggest that these African American women are not responsible to themselves or to the children they bear. The prevalence of such attitudes is attested to by reports from women of color who are HIV positive, who are, in many cities, being subjected to hostility from hospital staff and counselors because they want to have their babies. Gross, like other writers, portrays African American women largely from the perspective of neonatal infection, which implies that the women themselves are not patients but only vectors of disease, or put another way, the risk factor for their children.

The article goes on to quote a social worker who commented that from her experience running a counseling group, only the middle-class women in her group expressed concern about their health. "Among the poorest women, who are often indifferent or ignorant about health care, there is no demonstrated concern about their physical well-being..." The sense of powerlessness that African American women who are HIV positive experience is used to emphasize their irresponsibility. Such comments leave unexamined the personal and economic difficulties that these women face in their attempts to get access to good health care and counseling. Gross does not present a portrait of women who are fighting a disease, and the reader is not drawn to be sympathetic toward them. Instead, it is a portrait of the by now classic stereotype of black women who are unstable and irresponsible, even more so because they now carry a deadly disease. They are blamed for not having control over their lives.

The article does not report that these women are being diagnosed at later stages in the disease. We are not told about the different opportunistic infections in women that could possibly mask early diagnosis. We are not told how many of these women have lost their homes and custody of children when their HIV status is made known, nor that their opportunities for anonymous testing, good counseling, or access to drug treatment programs are severely limited. There have now been recommendations to implement testing of all pregnant women. African American women are likely to become the first nonincarcerated, civilian United States citizens to confront mass screening for HIV. And I would suggest, in the wake of this recommendation, there is also the possibility that some might call for mandatory abortions or, given that Medicaid monies are not allowed to cover abortion in most states, preemptive sterilization for these same HIV-infected pregnant women.

QUICK: NAME ONE BLACK WOMAN WITH AIDS

Gross's article is not atypical. I have read few stories in the mainstream media detailing the emotional trauma that HIV infection causes for African American women; nothing about survival strategies; no stories of daily life —how living with AIDS affects jobs, family relationships, or friendships. On Sunday, June 17, 1990, the *New York Times* ran a full page of profiles of black and white gay people living with AIDS. One woman was interviewed though no picture of her was printed. She said, "You want so much for someone to hold you, and no one wants to touch you." Her response only hints at the emotional trauma such women are facing. So many questions remain unasked in such accounts—how are these women dealing with the stigma associated with a disease that is perceived to be associated largely with white gay males? How are they dealing with the loss of their children or how are they preparing their children for their own impending deaths? What is happening to women who don't have children or extended families? Perhaps the problem is that, to date, no "famous" black woman has died of AIDS for the media to create a symbol that would garner support for African American women with the disease.

The tactics used by the media to make the American public aware of the various dimensions of the AIDS epidemic have been troubling. One tactic has been to take one person's story and transform it into a symbol for some particular aspect of the epidemic that needs to be addressed. For example, Ryan White epitomized the "innocent" child, made a victim of the bigoted attitudes of parents who barred him from his local school and town. White's story became the vehicle to educate the public about the small risk of AIDS's being transmitted casually and the plight of "innocent" children who are stigmatized because of their infection. Similarly, the story of Kimberly Bergalis, alleged to have been infected by her dentist, has been the centerpiece of the debate over whether there should be restrictions on dentists, physicians, and health care workers who are HIV positive. White gay male artists, entertainers, and writers suffering and dying from AIDS are featured in articles that eloquently reveal to the larger heterosexual world the emotional toll that AIDS has taken in gay communities while breaking down stereotypes about gay life. These articles serve to reveal the junctures and disjunctures in our beliefs about sexuality and sexual practices as well as the anxieties in American life about sex and morality.

In each of these cases, in some way the media has used such symbols to subtly urge the public to embrace people with AIDS. African American women with AIDS are constantly represented with respect to drug use—either their own or their partner's. They are largely poor or working class. They are single mothers. Media portrayals of these people with AIDS allude to the spectre of drug abuse and uncontrolled sexuality coupled with welfare "dependency" and irresponsibility. Such allusions undermine any representations of African American women with AIDS that would allow them to be embraced by the larger public.

Public health educators have been challenged to deal with the issue of cultural sensitivity in AIDS prevention and education material, and thus have created advertising campaigns displaying African American women in a positive light. This advertising often presents nameless figures who may look more like the average black woman, and thus encourage other African American women to identify with the ads' message on AIDS prevention; but these ads may not be able to elevate the threat AIDS poses to African American women, or the plight of those already infected, to the levels of recognition that could dethrone the more prevalent negative imagery.

C. J.: VENGEFUL BLACK WOMAN

Unfortunately, unless active criticism of current media images of African American women with AIDS is made, other more negative imagery may arise as the numbers rise within African American communities. A case in point is the recent article in the *New York Times* (this story was also covered on television) on the case of a black woman with AIDS in Dallas, who is reportedly, ". . . trying to spread the virus out of revenge on the man who infected her."[10] While admitting that the veracity of the story is in question, the article reports that a woman known only by the initials "C. J." apparently first wrote to *Ebony* magazine in September, 1991, that ". . . since contracting the AIDS virus she had become compulsively promiscuous, frequently picking up men in nightclubs." She is quoted as writing, "I feel if I have to die of a horrible disease I won't go alone."[11] This same woman, or someone claiming to be the same woman, is reported to have called a local Dallas black radio show telling of meeting men, some of them married, and having unprotected sex with them in "revenge."[12] She is further reported to have said, "I blame it on men, period . . . I'm doing it to all the men because it was a man that gave it to me."[13] It is notable that the radio host is said to have encouraged the woman to seek counseling. The episode apparently has resulted in an increased number of heterosexual men in the Dallas area seeking information about AIDS. Public health experts in that city commented on this as a positive aspect of a sad story: "This woman's announcement has been the most powerful reinforcement of that message I've ever seen in Dallas." The more general comments about C. J.'s story in the article are from men who assert that the incident has changed people's attitudes about high-risk behavior, while another characterizes C. J.'s behavior as "serial killing."

As I read this article, I was struck by how quickly C. J. leaves the narrative. The story ultimately does not center around her plight, but only on the threat she poses to heterosexual men. There are no comments reported from African American women. Little of the commentary reported suggests that public discussion of the trauma AIDS engenders for women who are infected occurred. But I also see as a subtext in this article the image invoked by Gross and others of the woman as the vector of infection to men—in this case, not the prostitute or the out-of-control drug abuser, but the dangerous, scorned woman, consciously exacting her revenge against men (and this before Anita Hill). Men are portrayed to be at risk by the reckless behavior of this woman. Attention is turned away from the circumstances that might drive a woman to such vengeful behavior. In the absence of a discussion of those circumstances, little is revealed to the reader about the complexity of male-female relationships in the African American communities, and specifically the tensions in those relationships that are coming to light as AIDS spreads in these communities.

Facts about the transmission of HIV in African American communities are obscured as well. For example, African American men are disproportionately infected with AIDS, and most African American women have sexual relationships with men of their race. In the absence of the factor of female drug use, this means that these women are at greater risk because of the behaviors of men. C. J.'s behavior, regardless of whether or not her story is true, is believable because it can be read as the rage of many heterosexual African American women about the lack of power they feel in their relationships with men. That such rage exists is no secret in the black community as the debates over Shaharazad Ali's book make clear.[14] C. J.'s story also reveals the way in which infidelity, betrayal, and loneliness have shaped the emotional landscape many African American women live with. As AIDS spreads in African American communities, more explosive reactions can be expected. It is hardly conceivable that the white-dominated media will portray such reactions with any degree of complexity or sensitivity about African American lifestyles.

THE FACE OF AIDS FOR AFRICAN AMERICAN WOMEN

The average age of African American women with AIDS at the time of diagnosis is thirty-six years. A significant number of the women were diagnosed when they were in their twenties and thus would have been infected as adolescents.[15] Most of these young women live in urban areas in the Northeast. The fact that many of the African American women with AIDS are so young is a startling statistic. It suggests that they were infected at an age when they had the least control over their sexual lives. They were at an age when they were vulnerable to the demands not just of partners of their own age, but older men as well. In contrast to a picture of women in their twenties aware of the consequences of their actions, instead some number of African American women contracted AIDS at an age when their ideas about sex were just being formed. Many of these young women also live in urban communities where few support systems exist to protect them and allow them to grow unmolested to adulthood. Additionally, it is reported that few HIV-infected individuals in communities of color with high rates of infection, such as in sections of New York City, know their infection status.[16] Many African American women and men simply do not know that they are in danger. Far too many are only found to have AIDS upon autopsy.

Though fifty-one percent of women with AIDS were infected through intravenous (IV) drug use, twenty-nine percent were infected through heterosexual contact.[17] As Ernest Drucker notes, in New York City, "... even those women who did have histories of IV drug use were, almost universally, *also* the sexual partners of men (sometimes many men) who were IV drug users ... Thus, it becomes extremely difficult to attribute these women's infection to one exposure or the other, since they were dually exposed for sustained periods of time to both risks of infection."[18] It is obvious then that African American women in such contexts are both dually exposed and dually victimized in a social setting now being ravaged by an incurable disease.

Every aspect of family life is touched by the presence of AIDS. "As AIDS cuts a swath through family after family, some have four or five members already sick with the disease and more infected."[19] Few people are aware of what these families face. Suki Ports, of the Minority Task Force on Aids, reported the following story:

> Frances worked. She had difficulty after the birth of her six-year-old and needed many transfusions. She had a second child, who is fourteen months old. This baby was diagnosed with AIDS, so Frances quit work to take care of her ... She then had to make a choice. She could move into an SRO, with two children, one sick, no cooking facilities except a hot plate, and get full benefits, or move in with her mother and receive no benefits, because her mother works ... Her choice was made. It is difficult, and it's straining the mothers' resources and good nature. Family benefits to assist the whole family are not available without creating a new precedent for payments in an already strained financial outlook.[20]

Many women are also hiding the fact that members of their family have AIDS. Long-practiced and familiar cultural beliefs are breaking down in the face of AIDS in African American communities. There is little evidence that fear or stigma is decreasing. Anecdotal reports suggest that some families who have relatives die of AIDS are refusing to have public funerals or indicate the cause of death in obituary notices. I found Frances's story as the debate was being waged in Congress on the bill that would mandate that businesses protect the jobs of workers who had to take leave to care for family members who are ill. I heard no one speak to the need for this bill because of the spread of the AIDS epidemic.

THE GENDER OF AIDS

African American women have also been caught in the matrix of the construction of AIDS as a disease. As the discussion in "Searching for Women," the excellent literature review on women and HIV in the United States, compiled by the College of Public and Community Service at the University of Massachusetts, Boston, and the Multicultural AIDS Coalition indicates, the Centers for Disease Control case definition of AIDS was first formulated in 1982. This case definition was based on clinical information from the groups of white gay men who had been studied. The natural history of AIDS in low-income men or in women was not included.[21] There is a great deal of debate as to whether there are female-specific manifestations of HIV infection. Cervical dysplasia, cervical cancer, pelvic inflammatory disease, and vaginal candidiasis are most commonly mentioned.

The problem for women though is that these diseases also occur among uninfected women. Therefore, any specifically female manifestations of HIV would be difficult to see clinically against the background noise of these other more common infections in women. This situation is even more complicated for African American women because they have higher rates of some of the infections mentioned. Reported gonorrhea is 10 times higher in blacks; black women report 1.8 times the rate of ambulatory or hospitalized treatment of pelvic inflammatory disease than do whites; herpes simplex virus is 3.4 times higher; syphilis rates are higher, and cervical cancer is 2.3 times more common in African American women.[22]

These data suggest that the medical establishment has historically failed to deal with the prevalence of sexually transmitted diseases in African American women. As late as 1989, after almost a century of study of syphilis in this country, the authors of a 1989 paper wrote,

> While the present study demonstrates the significantly greater prevalence of syphilis seroreactivity among blacks than among whites, we do not yet know enough about racial differences in sexual behavior through which infection is acquired, or about racial differences in ways in which infection is eliminated to explain persisting differences in prevalence.[23]

Venereal disease control programs that have been touted as successfully diminishing the impact of these diseases on the larger United States population have broken down in urban communities of color. The failure of these programs is related to the AIDS epidemic in one very crucial way. The professional background of CDC (Centers for Disease Control) officials most responsible for formulating AIDS policy was in venereal disease control.[24] These are the same people who must now try and understand ques-

tions with respect to AIDS that they have failed to answer in their attempts
to control other sexually transmitted diseases in African American communities.

MISSING PERSONS: BLACK WOMEN AND
THE HISTORY OF STDs

It is at this point that I realized that the silence around the issues of AIDS,
sexually transmitted disease and African American women was not a new
phenomenon, indeed its roots are very old. The impact of the failure to
control sexually transmitted diseases on African American women has
never been evaluated. Historical studies of the history of sexually transmitted disease have not placed black women at the center of the historical
reconstruction of these diseases. For example, in rereading James Jones's
book, *Bad Blood,* on the history of the infamous Tuskegee syphilis experiment, it occurred to me that many of the men in this study were married.
Given that these men did not know they had syphilis, they must have
continued to have sexual relationships with women. What happened to
these women? In 1972 the study ended, and in 1973, compensation of the
survivors began. Not until 1975 did the government agree to compensate
treatment of the subject's wives and their children with congenital syphilis.
In a footnote, Jones notes that health care for the surviving spouses could
cost as much as $12 million, while medical care for the surviving children
might cost as much as $127 million. As of May 1980, approximately fifty
surviving wives and twenty surviving children were receiving full medical
care after examinations revealed that they had syphilis that was directly
attributable to the government's failure to treat the men. Why the government had to debate the issue of compensation to the wives and children of
these men is unclear and unexplained. But this is perhaps not unusual;
there are a number of long-unanswered historical questions about the role
of African American women in the history of sexually transmitted diseases.

For example, historians note that "prostitutes" were specifically singled
out as the source of venereal disease in the period between 1900 and 1930,
when national attention was first focused on the issue of venereal disease.
In the early decades of this century, immigrant and native-born working-class white women were targeted by physicians and public health experts
attempting to control outbreaks of syphilis. Historians of medicine have
failed to mention that African American women were targeted as well.
And few explore the meaning of the term "prostitute," particularly with
regard to black women. Since slavery, as historians of African American
history have shown, the label is often used against *all* African American
women irrespective of class, education, and most importantly behavior.

Racial theories that ascribed to African American women an inherent immorality were buttressed by physicians and social reformers when the incidence of venereal disease among African American women began to rise in the twentieth century.

While the source and use of statistics on the incidence of venereal disease in the African American community was hotly debated, most observers agreed that the incidence was high in these communities throughout the country. One source notes that syphilis rates among African American women were as much as fifteen times those of white women, particularly for women in their childbearing years. Deaths from gonorrhea were also high.[25] Statistics collected by physicians at the Syphilis Division of the Medical Clinic of the Johns Hopkins Hospital in Baltimore show that African American women had the highest rates of syphilis from 1916 until 1928. And while rates among black males and white males and females began to decrease after 1925, the rate among African American women seemed to be rising.[26]

No study that I know of goes beyond merely reporting that African American women were the most common sufferers of venereal disease to explore the meanings and uses that were made of this disparity by physicians, public health experts, and other social reformers in the past. I would argue that the historical record must be rewritten to illustrate how race influenced practices designed to control venereal disease, if we are to understand how the legacy of such practices affects current efforts to control AIDS.

Historians note that many repressive tactics were invoked by public health experts attempting to control venereal disease before World War II. Yet little is known as to how imposition of quarantines, detention, and internment were shaped by the racial and ethnic composition of the groups of women labelled prostitutes when the very possibility of infection could be used as a sufficient cause for incarceration. What was happening to African American women when physicians were simultaneously claiming that. "... ninety-five percent of the negro race are likely to contract syphilis or other venereal disease including those of the educated classes," and "... the worn-out prostitute of today may be the woman you employ as your maid tomorrow?"[27] African American physicians, sociologists, educators, and club women vigorously protested the view that the presence of venereal disease gave credence to the racist assertion that all African American women were inherently immoral.[28] They pointed to socioeconomic factors and the exploitation of young black women in the cities by unscrupulous white and black men as important factors. In urban areas the increased visibility of African American women became a source of anxiety for whites. The interwar years were times of intense racial strife and severe economic crisis for African American women, who by the hundreds stood in unemployment lines on the streets of many cities.[29] How and in what context were public health experts in their concern about venereal disease, supplying a new scientific justification to the existing process of policing so-called dangerous working women of color and white women?

Sexually transmitted diseases are highly stigmatized in this culture. How do we examine the impact of the stigma associated with these diseases on women's lives? In article after article in this period, white physicians echo the themes: that all African American people had syphilis; and that the immorality of African American women could be measured by the numbers of illegitimate infants and the numbers of those born with congenital syphilis. Black women as source, cause, and victims of venereal disease had to contend with both the stigma and the severe effect of venereal disease on their reproductive health. In 1924, a study by the Association for Improving the Condition of the Poor in New York City found:

> Negro women suffering from syphilis but receiving neither adequate prenatal instruction nor medical treatment lost an average of fifty-four percent of their babies through miscarriage, still-birth, or death during the first two years . . . twenty-nine percent of surviving children of syphilitic mothers were diagnosed as syphilitic.[30]

As it is with AIDS today, commentary on the impact of syphilis as experienced by African American women is absent from this literature. In addition, physicians' views of African American women were further diminished because they often failed to return to clinics for the expensive treatment of their disease during and after pregnancy, giving further "evidence" of their irresponsibility. Few of the white physicians and nurses who staffed these clinics showed any awareness that their attitudes and behavior toward African American women bore any relation to failure of these women to return for treatment.

The discovery that syphilis had a serious impact on maternal health and fetal death received a good deal of attention in the 1920s. Physicians at Johns Hopkins Hospital, who conducted a three-year study of the significance of syphilis in prenatal development and the causation of fetal death, argued increasingly for the need for complete medical control of pregnant women suffering from the disease. Their reports consistently articulate different methods of control for white women of the "intelligent classes," described more as "innocent" victims, versus all black women, who are cited as "ignorant," "unmoral," and "unmanageable."[31] Social workers enlisted to encourage follow-up care for women with syphilis also reported that native-born white women took an intelligent interest in learning the facts about syphilis and accepted that they should not have more children, while black women and immigrant women were censured for their refusal to submit to the control of medical and welfare authorities.[32] Given such facts, we might ask how the stigma associated with venereal disease affected the kind of support given to efforts to provide infant and maternal care for African American women as the rates of sexually transmitted diseases and infant mortality rates fell among middle-class white women.[33]

The incidence of venereal disease among African American women and the practices they were subjected to served as powerful ideological weapons to control the sexual and reproductive behavior of white women. African American women were punished because they suffered from disease associated with immoral behavior and for their so-called refusal to submit to medical authority. When physicians came to the defense of women who had a venereal disease, it was to a sentimental, objectified ideal, one that arguably bore little resemblance to most white women and hardly applied to African American women.[34] Programs for middle-class white women were designed to reduce the stigma associated with having syphilis and seeking treatment. African American women's options for treatment were limited by economic resources and the necessity of exposing themselves to censure by white professionals on an issue inextricably related to sex, in a context where their privacy and dignity could not be and never had been preserved. It is not surprising that programs that successfully treated African American women were largely staffed by African American physicians and nurses.[35]

From 1945 to 1964, syphilis rates among all groups fell in the United States. In 1945, syphilis rates among nonwhites were thirteen times higher than among whites. By 1964, they were still ten times higher than for whites. Total expenditures for venereal disease control fell steadily throughout that same period of time.

CONCLUSION

I believe that the invisibility and objectification of African American women in the AIDS epidemic is tied to the historical treatment of African American women with respect to sexually transmitted disease. The Tuskegee syphilis experiment is just one example of the legacy of danger and death that sexually transmitted diseases represent for African American communities. For a black woman to expose that she had a sexually transmitted disease was, for much of this century, to render herself multiply stigmatized, bringing up older images of immorality and uncontrolled sexuality that neither class nor educational privilege could protect her from. It possibly meant that pregnancy carried more risks; it often precipitated long-term health problems and even early death. That physicians and public health experts have long accepted higher rates of sexually transmitted diseases among African American women is a sign that somehow this had quietly become a norm. That overt racial comments from white health care providers on the cause of this higher incidence of sexually transmitted disease and the attendant problems for fetal and maternal health are less evident today than in the 1920s is not necessarily a sign that attitudes have changed or that the stigma associated with these diseases has diminished.

Current public health efforts must address the long term stigma that African American women continue to experience with respect to sexually transmitted diseases. As the uninterrupted disparity in the incidence of these diseases within this community over the last fifty years indicates, those efforts have largely failed. Bringing to the fore the historical treatment and experience of African American women, their children, and their partners with respect to sexually transmitted diseases in the past is a necessary step.

In addition, most of all, what is needed is a viable black feminist movement. African American feminists need to intervene in the public and scientific debates about AIDS, making plain the impact that medical and public health policy will have on African American women. An analysis of gender is desperately needed to frame the discussion of sexual relations in the black community. Sexism lies behind the disempowerment and lack of control that African American women experience in the face of AIDS. African American women are multiply stigmatized in the AIDS epidemic —only a multifaceted African American feminist analysis attentive to issues of race, sex, gender, and power can adequately expose the impact of AIDS on our communities and formulate just policies to save women's lives.

ENDNOTES

1. Testimony of Margaret Rivera, Report of the Public Hearing, "AIDS: Its Impact on Women, Children and Families." (New York State Division for Women, 12 June 1987), 21.

2. Victoria A. Cargill and Mark Smith, "HIV Disease and the African American Community," *New England Journal of Medicine,* 1990.

3. Tedd V. Ellerbrock et al., "Epidemiology of Women With AIDS in the United States, 1981 Through 1990; A Comparison With Heterosexual Men With AIDS," *Journal of the American Medical Association* 265, no. 22 (12 June 1991): 2971.

4. Ibid.

5. IV drug users were constructed as male in the mass media before the spectacle of "crack babies." Moreover, drug treatment models and facilities continue to favor male clients while the despair of women's addiction to crack disappears quickly behind our image of them as monsters for "delivering drugs" to their babies.

6. By using the term "attention," it is not my intent in this essay to disparage or belittle the heroic efforts of the many health care workers, activists, and others who *have* labored to bring the plight of African American women and other women with AIDS to light. By using the term "attention," I only mean to address the fact that the deaths of African American women with AIDS have not garnered the kind of front-page headlines or other prominent popular media attention given to other people with AIDS, as will be discussed more fully later in the essay.

7. Jane Gross, "Bleak Lives, Women Carrying AIDS," *New York Times,* 27 August 1987.

8. N. S. Padian, "Heterosexual Transmission of Acquired Immunodeficiency Syndrome: International Perspectives and National Projections," *Review of Infectious Diseases* 9 (1987): 947–960.

9. Gross, "Bleak Lives."

10. "Tale of Revenge Stirs AIDS Furor: Woman Claims She's Trying to Infect Men, Prompting a Surge of Concern," *New York Times,* 1 October 1991.

11. Ibid.

12. Ibid.

13. Ibid.

14. Shaharazad Ali, *The Blackman's Guide to Understanding the Blackwoman* (1990). This is a very controversial and widely discussed book in the black community, which points to the tensions in heterosexual relationships

15. Ellerbrock, "Epidemiology," 2973.

16. Ernest Drucker, "Epidemic in the War Zone: AIDS and Community Survival in New York City," *International Journal of Health Services* 20, no. 4 (1990): 605. Drucker notes that fewer than ten percent of the estimated 150 to 250 thousand people infected with HIV in New York City know their HIV status.

17. Ellerbrock, "Epidemiology," 2974.

18. Drucker, "Epidemic," 609.

19. Drucker, "Epidemic," 613.

20. "AIDS: Its Impact on Women, Children and Families," 51.

21. "Searching for Women: A Literature Review on Women and HIV in the United States" (Working Group at the College of Public and Community Service, University of Massachusetts, Boston, and the Multicultural AIDS Coalition, April 1991), 54.

22. Robert A. Hahn et al., "Race and the Prevalence of Syphilis Seroreactivity in the United States Population: A National Sero-Epidemiologic Study," *American Journal of Public Health* 79, no. 4 (1989): 469.

23. Ibid., 469.

24. Ronald Bayer, "AIDS and the Future of Reproductive Freedom," in *A Disease of Society: Cultural and Institutional Responses to AIDS,* ed. D. Nelkin, D. Willis, and S. Parris (Cambridge: Cambridge University Press, 1991), 202.

25. Charles S. Johnson, "Public Opinion and the Negro," *Opportunity: A Journal of Negro Life* 1, no. 7 (1923): 127.

26. Thomas B. Turner, "The Race and Sex Distribution of the Lesions of Syphilis in 10,000 Cases," *Bulletin of the Johns Hopkins Hospital* 46, no. 2, 159–185.

27. Thomas Murrell, "Syphilis and the American Negro: A Medico-Sociologic Study," *Journal of the American Medical Association* 54 (1910): 846–849.

28. Johnson, "Public Opinion," 204.

29. Paula Giddings, *When and Where I Enter: The Impact of Black Women on Race and Sex in America* (New York: Bantam Books, 1984), 146.

30. John C. Gebhart, "Syphilis as a Prenatal Problem," *Journal of Social Hygiene* 10, no. 4 (April 1924): 208–217.

31. J. W. Williams, "The Significance of Syphilis in Prenatal Care and in the Causation of Fetal Death," *Bulletin of the Johns Hopkins Hospital* 31, no. 351 (May 1920): 141–145.

32. Mable Mildred Galt, "The Medical-Social Aspects of Pre-Natal Work as Related to Syphilis: A Study of the South Medical Clinic of the Massachusetts General Hospital, Boston, MA" (Ph.D. diss. Smith College School of Social Work, 1923).

33. See Molly Ladd Taylor, "Women's Health and Public Policy," in *Women, Health & Medicine in America,* ed. Rima Apple (New York: Garland Publishing, Co. 1990), 403.

34. Allan Brandt, *No Magic Bullet: A Social History of Venereal Disease in the United States Since 1880* (New York: Oxford University Press, 1987), 17.

35. Gebhart, "Syphilis."

CHAPTER SIX

Reading the Academy

*To be black and female in the academy has its own particular frustra-
tion because it was never intended for us to be here. We are in spaces
that have been appropriated for us. But I consider every course I
teach a course in black feminism. Whether I am teaching William
Faulkner or Henry James, by speaking out on my position as a black
woman, the course becomes a black feminism course.*

—NELLIE McKAY

INTRODUCTION

African American women have been passionate about education and
consummate institution builders for over a century both here and
elsewhere. Despite racist and sexist treatment in a variety of institutional
contexts, they have continued to struggle for equal access, fair treatment,
and images of themselves within the academy. Their contemporary battles
include transforming higher education to make it more responsive to the
needs of black women, establishing black women's studies, and revamping
both black studies and women's studies because of their insensitivity to
gender on the one hand and race on the other. Since many contemporary
black feminists find themselves within the academy, much of their discourse has been ignored or maligned because of its seeming irrelevance to
the lives of black people.

A major challenge for feminists as we approach the twenty-first century
is generating theory that is useful in liberating the black community from
a host of ills. The continued development of our intellects, devalued by the
larger community and frequently unappreciated or ignored within our own
communities, is critical for both self-understanding and the survival of the
group.

Margaret Walker Alexander
(1915–   )

Margaret Walker Alexander, poet, novelist, and teacher, is professor emerita, Jackson State University, where she taught for nearly forty years. She also directed their Institute for the Study of the History, Life, and Culture of Black People, beginning in 1986, and hosted the first national conference on black women writers. The daughter of educators, Walker grew up on a college campus surrounded by books—the poetry of Paul Laurence Dunbar, Shakespeare, and the Bible. Her publications include her first collection of poetry, the award-winning *For My People* (1942); *Jubilee* (1966), a historical novel inspired by the story of her enslaved great-grandmother, Vyry; *Prophets for a New Day* (1970); *Richard Wright: Daemonic Genius*; and *How I Wrote* Jubilee (1972), which includes an auto-biographical essay on the sexism that black women, including family members, experience within the academy. This painful account of her own struggles as an academic underscores the importance of gender analyses of higher education, which have been sorely lacking in the literature on histor-ically black colleges. In an essay, "On Being Female, Black and Free," included in *The Writer and Her Work*, edited by Janet Steinburg, Walker reveals that she didn't notice sexism growing up in the South because of the blatant nature of racism, but after she returned to graduate school for the doctorate, she began to notice discrimination against women. She concludes: "As a woman, I have come through the fires of hell because I am a black woman, because I am poor, because I live in America, and because I am determined to be both a creative artist and maintain my inner integrity and my instinctive need to be free."

Margaret Walker Alexander }

BLACK WOMEN IN ACADEMIA

The first woman in my family to experience discrimination in academia was my mother. She was the first woman in her family to get a college degree and to teach school. Her father and uncle taught school, but her mother did not get an education. My mother was the youngest of seven children, and her older sisters, like her mother, had done washing and ironing and cooking for white folks. They wanted my mother, a talented musician, to have an opportunity to get an education to be a lady. So they sent her from Pensacola, Florida, to Washington, D.C., to boarding school. Although she received a scholarship to Howard University for her college training, she did not accept it. She was homesick for Florida. After three years scrubbing floors to help pay for her schooling, she wanted nothing so much as to go home.

Completing high school, she returned to Pensacola, where she met my father and became engaged to be married. That next school term she taught country school in Greenville, Alabama, making only a few dollars a month. The first year she lived with her grandmother, and the next September she married my father and went to Birmingham, Alabama, to live.

Six weeks after I was born she was asked to teach music in the small Methodist church school, Central Alabama Institute, which was located close to the church my father pastored in Mason City. After a brief year at Central, my father was moved to a church in Marion, Alabama. In the middle of the year, my mother received a letter asking her to return to Central Alabama Institute. She wrote she would very much like that, but she had to stay with her husband, and added that she could only accept the work if they offered my father a job as well. They hired my father and thus began twenty years of teaching in church schools for my mother and father. In all that time my mother's salary never was as much as a hundred dollars a month.

My mother finished college in New Orleans by going to school at night for four years while working in the day. Obviously this would not have been possible had not my grandmother lived with us and done all the cooking, washing, ironing, and housecleaning. When my father received his master's degree at Northwestern, after going six summers, my mother was offered a scholarship to complete her graduate work in music, but could not accept because of her children and family. I was a teenager, and she said it was the wrong time for her to leave me as well as my sisters and brother. Her teaching job grew so impossible that she suddenly quit while I was in the middle of college. The day I graduated from college, my father also ended his teaching career and went back to the ministry as a pastor. My mother said she worked around the clock teaching private pupils, music classes, conducting the singing, playing the organ, conducting the orchestra, arranging music, and traveling with the singing male group, all for a pittance plus harassment. She had no rank or tenure, and she was reduced to receiving a few dollars (about thirty-five) in a small bank envelope. This was during the Depression. Soon afterward she began working on the WPA, where she made more than she had teaching.

I also graduated to the WPA, but unlike my mother, I had gone uninterrupted through Northwestern, getting my degree in English when I was nineteen. After three years I went to graduate school in order to get a master's degree and teach. Getting my master's in one school year nearly killed me. I was on NYA (National Youth Association, a government-supported agency) and had so little money I ate lunch only once a week when a friend bought it. When I went home in August, my father lifted me from the train and I was in a state of collapse. For eighteen months I was unable to work.

Meanwhile, one of my sisters had graduated from music college and had taken a job teaching music at a small school in Mississippi. Her salary was forty dollars a month, and like my mother, she worked seven days a week. This included playing for vespers and church on Sunday and leading the choir practices. She said the only time she had for herself was at night from close to midnight until dawn. After teaching two years in Mississippi, she went to Knoxville, Tennessee, for a larger salary but the same backbreaking schedule. Then she taught at Tuskegee; after two years she went back to Chicago to get her master's degree, then moved to Paducah, Kentucky. Throughout these eight years her salary remained less than two hundred dollars per month.

In disgust she left the South, saying she would never teach in a black college again, that she could not take the humiliations heaped upon her by the college administration while nearly killing herself with work and making so little money. She went to New York City and plunged herself into the concert field, only to discover that the hardest thing in the world for a black woman to do is make a living playing on the classical concert stage. After several grueling years of playing with a symphony orchestra, town hall recitals, on radio and television, and touring the South and Midwest, she gave up and went into the public schools of New York City, where at least the pay was good, although the work was neither stimulating nor rewarding.

My second younger sister, meanwhile, had graduated from college and was substituting in the public schools of New Orleans. For many years, no woman teacher was allowed to marry, and many women kept their marriage a secret. Until she retired, she taught in the same school where she began teaching during World War II. She, too, went summers to graduate school, taking her master's degree in child psychology from the University of Chicago. For fifteen years she served on every curriculum committee for primary instruction established by the Board of Education, New Orleans Parish. In the late fifties she took a sabbatical and went to Columbia to study for a year, taking primary supervision and curriculum building. She has suffered a triple discrimination. In addition to being black and female, she was an early victim of polio, and for a long time there was a question about whether she could be appointed to teach. It so happened at that time that Franklin Delano Roosevelt was president, and we argued if the President of the United States could be president in a wheelchair, surely she could teach. She uses neither a crutch nor a cane and never has been in a wheelchair. Just the same she has endured much with constant reminders that she is handicapped. Some years ago she went back to school and received another master's degree from Loyola University, with special emphasis on teaching mathematics and science to elementary schoolchildren. She drives her car and is rated as an excellent teacher. And, although she has no wish to be a principal, she has thrice been denied the job of primary supervisor.

As for myself, my teaching career has been fraught with conflict, insults, humiliations, and disappointments. In every case where I have attempted to make a creative contribution and succeeded, I have immediately been replaced by a man. I began teaching thirty years ago at Livingstone College in Salisbury, North Carolina, for the handsome sum of one hundred and thirty dollars a month. I was very happy to get it. I had a master's degree but no teaching experience. I arrived in Salisbury at two-thirty one cold February morning, and although I was expected, there was no one at the station to meet me. I finally found a taxi to take me to the campus, and banged on the door of the girls' dormitory for fully a half an hour before anyone opened it. Less than three hours after I went to bed, the matron ordered me out for breakfast at six o'clock and told me I had an eight o'clock class. My life was arranged for me hour after hour and controlled by a half-dozen people. I was resented in the town and by some faculty and staff people because I was replacing one of their favorite people. (And I didn't know this person from Adam's cat.) I had absolutely no social life and spent most of my afternoons and evenings in my room, writing. That summer I had to move out of the dormitory into a private home and then back again to the dormitory in the fall. I won the Yale Award for Younger Poets that summer and began getting job offers from everywhere. I felt strong pressure to stay at Livingstone, but when I went home, my parents had accepted a job for me at West Virginia State College. It paid the grand sum of two hundred dollars a month, and my dear mother felt it was her duty to grab it before somebody else did. Meanwhile at Livingstone, I went to my first College Language Association[1] (CLA) meeting at Hampton Institute. As I observed then, men were completely in control of the CLA, and only recently did the organization get a woman president.

At West Virginia State College I never had a stable living situation. The night I arrived I had no place to go. The dean had leaned out of his bedroom window to tell the driver to take me to so-and-so's house for the time being. The next day they moved me to another place where I was clearly unwanted. I slept there but had to get up cold mornings and walk through the snow to the dining hall. After Christmas I moved into an apartment I expected to share with another young woman, and found myself in a threesome. That didn't work, and again my dear mother solved it by arriving and putting all my stuff outdoors. Next I moved in with a crazy woman. Finally the administration let me go where I had been told all year I could not stay, to a dormitory. Five places in one school year. I had had it! Had I been a man, no one would have dared move me around like that.

When the National Concert and Artists Corporation offered me a contract to lecture and read poetry for the next five years, guaranteeing me three times as much as my nine months salary at West Virginia, I took it. I had suffered constant embarrassments from my immediate supervisor, who declared that it looked as if I were the head of the department instead of an instructor. "All you can hear is Margaret Walker!" she said disapprovingly. I would arrive in my classroom to be told by my students that the head of the department had begged them to leave because I was late. They replied they would wait because they learned more from me in fifteen minutes than they learned from some people in an hour. That did not help my situation. I was hissed at when I arrived at the chairman's office and was told he was too busy to see me. When I insisted, I was told, "I thought you were a student," as if that was the way to talk to a dog much less a student. But the real harrowing experience of my life came at Jackson State College. In September 1949, when I began teaching in Jackson, Mississippi, I was married and the mother of three children. My youngest was nine weeks old the day I began. For nine months everything went well and members of the administration kept saying they were honored to have me, until I moved my family and furniture. They saw that my husband was sick and disabled from the war, that I had three children under six years of age, that I was poor and had to work; I was no longer their honored poet, but a defenseless black woman to be harassed.

That summer the president openly attacked me in a faculty meeting by accusing me of talking about the low standards of education in Mississippi. He told me in so many words that if I didn't like what went on in Mississippi I could find myself another job. He ranted and raved so, I was close to tears, and a neighbor nudged me and said, "Let's go home, Mrs. Alexander." Had I been single, I would have quit that day, but I had three children and a husband, and I had just moved. So I bowed my head and decided to stay on. Perhaps I should have taken another job. That faculty meeting put me on ice for a year. Almost nobody darkened my door except my housekeeper and my family. A year later, I was ordered to produce a literary festival for the seventy-fifth anniversary of the college and was told to write some occasional poetry and write and produce a pageant for the occasion. I said then that if I succeeded I would have to leave here, and if I failed, I would also have to leave. I succeeded through much stress and strain and public embarrassment, and then by the hardest effort, I secured a Ford Fellowship and left. I stayed away for fifteen months, and when I returned to a substantial raise, I also had another child.

From 1954 until 1960, at Jackson State in Mississippi, my salary remained well under $6,000 each year. Meanwhile I had devised a humanities program to suit the needs of black students in Mississippi. We not only raised the cultural level seventy-five percent, but among other things, we also provided a unit on race in the modern world and the great contributions of black people to the modern world. Trouble over the humanities program nearly drove me out of my mind. I was replaced by a man who openly said he was hired to get rid of me. Words cannot express the hell that man put me through with consent of the administration. Finally the administration decided it had enough evidence against me to fire me from the college, at a time when my husband was recuperating in the hospital from his third operation and could not work any longer at the job he had been doing for seven years. I was called into the president's office, and in the presence of the dean, I was vilified and castigated and told that if I would just resign, everybody would be happy. Knowing it had already been announced that I was going to be fired, I replied, "Why should I resign a job that I have done well every day for thirteen years and that I like? You fire me!" The president changed the subject. I knew I was entitled not only to tenure but also to an appeal and that my contract said I could not be fired except for moral turpitude and insubordination. I stood up and insisted that he tell me one thing: "Gentlemen, do I understand that I am fired?"

"Now Mrs. Alexander, you know we have not said anything about firing you."

"I just wanted to know."

The dean said, "I knew it would end like this. I knew this would be it."

I said, "Well, you know, we live till we die, don't we? Regardless, we live till we die."

Then began the death struggle for me to return to graduate school. I contended that I was no longer willing to be classified as the equivalent of the Ph.D. because I was a poet. My salary was not equivalent, and so I was determined to go back and get that degree that everybody worshipped so much and that brought more salary to the holder. My children were growing up and getting ready for college. My husband was disabled, and I absolutely needed the money. I was tired of living on borrowed money from one month to the next.

I had difficulty getting another appointment with the president. Finally he consented to see me. I told him I felt insecure, and I was worried about my future. I needed more money, and I felt the best way to ensure a raise was to go back to graduate school. He informed me that I wasn't going to get any more money. I was doing well enough. I had a house and a car, and he was sure I was doing better than I ever had done in my life. Besides, he said, you are too old to go back to school, and you have been so sick you are not even a good risk for a loan. I got into my car and went out to the edge of the town. I got out where nobody could see or hear me, and I screamed at the top of my voice. Then I went back to plan my strategy.

I borrowed five hundred dollars from the credit union and got another three hundred from the college as salary, plus additional money from my husband. I took my two younger children, ages six and eleven, and I went back to the University of Iowa to summer school. There I inquired about my chances of returning for the doctorate degree, of using my Civil War novel for my dissertation, and of getting financial assistance.

I went back to Jackson State College for another hellish year, but in September 1962, I managed to get away. I put pressure on the administration, and I managed to get half of my salary for two years, while I taught freshman English at Iowa for the other half. I signed a note to borrow my salary for the third year. My mother kept my children. Had she not been living, I could not have gone back to graduate school. (I had two children in college during those three years. One graduated a week before I did.)

When I returned to Jackson with my degree, I asked not to be involved with humanities. Instead, I tried to formulate a new freshman English program modeled on the Iowa Rhetoric Program for writing themes with a relevant reading list. After a year the college administration did not so much as give me the courtesy of saying they would not require my services in that capacity the next year. They simply replaced me with a man: not a man with superior training, rank, or ability, just a man.

I turned again to my interest in creative writing, which I had first started at the college, and taught courses in literary criticism, the Bible as literature, and black literature. After another so-so year, I devised a black studies program that was funded under Title III. My years with that program were the happiest of my teaching career at Jackson State College. As I told the late dean, I had worked for over twenty years at Jackson State, and, although it may have been profitable enough to meet my bills for the barest necessities, it had not been pleasant for a single day.

ENDNOTE

1. The College Language Association is the primary organization of black language and literature professionals, founded during the days when the Modern Language Association and the National Council of Teachers of English did not encourage black membership or participation.

Gloria Joseph

Gloria Joseph, writer, activist, and "black revolutionary spirited feminist of West Indian parents," returned to her home in the Virgin Islands after retiring from the School of Social Science at Hampshire College in Amherst, Massachusetts. She coedited with Jill Lewis *Common Differences* (1981) in which she wrote a pioneering essay on mothers and daughters within the black community. Her essay "The Incompatible Menage À Trois: Marxism, Feminism and Racism," which appeared in *Women and Revolution* (1981), refers to racism as the "incestuous child of patriarchy and capitalism" that white feminists frequently ignore in Marxist analyses of the woman question. She also argues that Marxists and feminists do a poor job of analyzing the experiences of black women. Her essay "Black Feminist Pedagogy and Schooling in Capitalist White America" is an early critique of the academy and an important contribution to black feminist discourse on education in the United States. Joseph, along with Alexis de Veaux, is completing a biography of Audre Lorde.

Gloria Joseph }

Black Feminist Pedagogy
and Schooling in
Capitalist White America

Schools and schooling in capitalist America are very little different from other institutions and their methodological processes in capitalist America. Institutions operate from a well-programmed blueprint, which is designed to serve the people in an unequal and hierarchical manner. To "serve the people" can be readily translated into "to serve the devil." The heinous nature of capitalist America gives easy rise to a feeling of existing in a living hell for the majority of the exploited, who indeed exist for the benefit of those with and in power. The educational system orchestrates an internecine relationship between teachers and students. This relationship, which results in miseducated, misguided, misinformed youth, and adults (leaders) who use "disinformation" tactics and chicanery, operates today with maximum success in keeping the inequalities and hierarchies that characterize capitalist America.

In *Schooling in Capitalist America*, Bowles and Gintis state: "The major characteristics of the educational system in the United States today flow directly from its role in producing a work force willing and able to staff occupational positions in the capitalist system. We conclude that the creation of an equal and liberating school system requires a revolutionary transformation of economic life."[1] That was written in 1976. In 1903, the great scholar and Afro-American leader, W. E. B. Du Bois, stated: "The problem of the twentieth century is the problem of the color-line, the relation of the darker to the lighter races . . . in Africa and Asia, in America and in the islands of the sea."[2]

The integration of Du Bois's prophetic words with the quote from Bowles and Gintis, gives a greater sense of realism and accuracy to the current educational system in capitalist America.

The exclusion of the race question as a distinct entity, in any theoretical discussion of capitalist America, is a serious omission, and any analysis that does not specifically address the racial dimension is incomplete and inadequate. Racial relations and the United States educational system have an extremely inglorious past, which presently demands acute attention. It could be argued that every relationship is unique, and race relations have no patent on uniqueness; that no general theories are adequate, and from this point of view, most theories are too general. However, there is ample evidence to indicate that relations between races have a long and important history that is not reducible to relations between the sexes or classes.

The American dream has never worked for blacks, and that is a truism that must be remembered whenever analysis and discussion concerning the future of the nation's population are in progress. To say that "... the creation of an equal and liberating school system requires a revolutionary transformation of economic life" is to disregard the dynamics of the racial dimension. The absence of a sharp focus on racism inhibits the social change desired. I am in agreement with the statement that the role of the educational system in America today is to produce a work force willing and able to staff occupational positions in the capitalist system. However, this statement is basically applicable to the white population in America. There exists a significantly large body of blacks and Latinos who are not in the economic work force at all. A most radical approach to dealing with the problems of radical educational change would be to focus on the blacks, Latinos, Native Americans—the domestic Third World people—as the vanguard. Historically in the United States of America, those fighting racism have been in the vanguard of social movements. The struggle for racial equality, which serves as a generational linkage, provides the nation with a focus that is the antithesis of the avaricious, necrophilic, aggressive, materialistic, selfish, attitudes that characterize the dominant Western perspective. The history of nonwhites in the United States of America, a history that is grounded in a spirituality that places interpersonal relations among people, as opposed to the acquisition of objects, as being of highest value, should be a major focus of education. Education has always been central in antiracist struggle, for education—or the denial of it—has been integral to the maintenance of a racist society. In Puerto Rico and among native people in North America, education was used by the United States to force children to speak English, to learn United States history, to adopt "American" culture, all part of an effort to destroy the fabric of traditional culture and society, in order to better control subjugated peoples. For similar reasons, it was made illegal in the south to teach African people held in slavery to read or write. I am arguing for and advocating an educational system that uses the history of blacks, Latinos, and Native Americans. In America, their values, struggles, exploitation as building blocks towards developing revolutionary education that equals "truthful history!" "An understanding of history is critical in shaping an awareness of the present and the vision for a viable future."[3]

In the struggle to ensure that the young be allowed to learn accurate and inclusive history of African Americans, Asian Americans, Chicanos, Native Americans, Puerto Ricans, women of all groups, and the history of menial-jobs-working-class people, we will necessarily be informing ourselves and others of what that history is, how it shaped our present, and how those who came before us have struggled to create necessary change. Learning that history will help to shatter the prevailing mythology that inhibits so many from acting more decisively for social change and to create a more just society and viable future for all.

Schooling in white capitalist America reproduces capitalist social relations of production, and this system of education is, and has been, detrimental to the livelihood of blacks. My participation in this educational system is done within the degrees of contradiction that I have allowed myself. That is to say that since morally I cannot contribute to the continuation of the exploitation of blacks, in my role as educator I view the educational system as a system in its own right constituted by intrinsic imperatives, and capable of creating building blocks for radical changes in the structure of American capitalist society. It is in this spirit that I introduce the black feminist pedagogy that I feel complements and goes beyond the Marxist sociology of education.

The economic and political status of Afro-American women, as an oppressed group in the United States of America provides its members with a distinctive experiential reality, and disparate explanations of that reality as well. As a subordinate group (subordinate to the dominant Eurocentric masculine corporate powerhouse), Afro-American women have a well developed alternative way of producing and validating knowledge about their experienced reality. The validations of their experienced realities differ markedly from explanations offered by the dominant Eurocentric masculine viewpoint.

Afro-American women's lives have been greatly affected by the intersection of systems of racial, sexual, and class oppressions. However, they have developed a unique black female culture whose purpose is to foster authentic black female self-definition and self-valuation that counters and transcends the multiple structures of oppressions that they face.[4]

Literature on black women reveals that Afro-American women do not see themselves as objects; do not identify with those in power; and have produced an independent black women's point of view about their specific experiences with oppression. By and large, the literature tells us that Afro-American women have a realistic, commonsense, rational view of their relationship to the dominant society and do not operate on false illusions about their chances for survival or success.

The existence of a functional black women's point of view assumes that there is an extant body of specialized knowledge that can be identified as black feminist thought, and this existing body of knowledge is an authentic representation of a black women's viewpoint. In other words it can be assumed that a unique, self-defined black women's consciousness exists concerning black women's material reality and that this point of view on reality has been authentically articulated in a body of knowledge that can be labeled BLACK FEMINIST THOUGHT.[5]

The feminist sociologist, Chandra Talapado Mohanty, in a brilliant paper on *The Social Construction of Black Feminist Thought*, concludes that there are four criteria that appear to characterize an alternative epistemology (how we know what we know) used by Afro-American women in evaluating and validating their point of view/perspectives. They are (i) the use of dialogue in assessing knowledge claims; (ii) the centrality of personal expressiveness; (iii) the ethic of personal accountability; and (iv) concrete experience as a criterion of meaning.[6] These criteria will be demonstrated in the section of this chapter where classroom examples of black feminist pedagogy are presented. The practice of black feminist pedagogy embodies these four criteria.

Black feminist pedagogy is designed to raise the political consciousness of students by introducing a worldview with an Afrocentric orientation to reality, and the inclusion of gender and patriarchy as central to an understanding of all historical phenomena. The presence of an independent black women's point of view using an alternative epistemology is fundamentally significant because its existence challenges not only the content of what currently passes as "truth," but simultaneously challenges the process of arriving at that truth. Specifically I am presenting a pedagogy with a structure of an underlying philosophy that will generate a new political consciousness. This is akin to the philosophical structure, the ideology, of the great Brazilian educator, Paulo Freire, who developed a unique method of teaching reading, which was formulated on his discovery that adults can begin to read in a matter of forty hours if the first words they decipher are charged with political meaning.

Similarly political, social, and economic concepts, from a curriculum planned and taught by teachers possessing a black feminist perspective/consciousness, would introduce a radical educational methodological imperative.

The introduction of a black feminist perspective as the radical construct in the pedagogy that I am discussing regards gender and patriarchy as critical in the constructing of society (and that patriarchy reflects white men's worldviews, perspectives, and interests).

Black feminist pedagogy embodies a philosophy that is a philosophy of liberation. Black feminism's major premise is the active engagement in the struggle to overcome the oppressions of racism, heterosexism, and classism, as well as sexism. It encompasses a worldview with the inclusion of gender and patriarchy as central to an understanding of all historical phenomena, and addresses Third World women at home and abroad. The black feminist perspective of which I speak intrinsically encompasses the application of an Afrocentric orientation to reality that is rooted in history, a reality that is informed by an understanding of the structures of African culture.

In discussing the black feminist perspective, it is important to be mindful of the fact that we are simultaneously talking about a conceptual system. A conceptual system refers to those philosophical constructs we use to define and structure reality, and is therefore basic to the way in which we perceive and interpret. It is the basis of our worldview. All people have a conceptual system usually shaped for the most part by the culture with which they identify. The relationship of one's conceptual system worldview and behavior, are internally consistent.[7] Tragically, the American school system has systematically and deliberately denied its nonwhite clientele the right to identify with their cultures. Rather, we have students "thinking white" as a result of the white, male studies programs that have dominated education throughout its beleaguered history.

The Afrocentric conceptual system is not exclusively black or exclusively African. It is a journey toward wholeness that requires seeing the world not black or white, but in its full spectrum.

The curriculum in our schools today can correctly be called a "white studies" and a "male studies" program, focusing on the achievements, cultures, experiences, and perspectives of white men and omitting or distorting the histories, experiences, cultures, and perspectives of people of color, and women of all colors. There have been some changes since the 1960s, but much of its has been superficial. A few great men of color and a few women of various colors are now referred to, but little is said of the great movements for social change that countless and nameless women and men have taken part in in the United States of America. There are occasional mentions of discrimination, but students are led to believe it results from the prejudiced attitudes of some misguided folks rather than from the deliberate policies and practices of white- and male-dominated institutions. Sex-biased language such as "the pioneer took his wife and family west" has been changed to "the pioneer family moved West," but the different experiences of "pioneer" women in a patriarchal society are no more considered today than are the experiences of native women and men whose lands are being invaded.

"In order for students, male and female, to understand and be prepared to change this patriarchal capitalist society, they must learn the history of women's experiences in this land, from the Cherokee grandmother on the Trail of Tears to the black mother in slavery's chains, from the Chicana fighting her people's dispossession to the Puertoriqueña fighting for her nation's independence, from the young white woman newly working in Lowell's mills in the early 1900s, from the middle-class "lady" to that unsurpassable Sojourner Truth! They must learn the similarities and differences among women's experiences and between women and men's experiences."[8] And they must learn about the black experience in America as experienced by blacks, and not as interpreted from a perspective based on Eurocentric ideological constructs and values.

Black feminist pedagogy as a philosophy of liberation for humankind, is designed to enable students, through the social, economic, cultural, moral, and religious history of Third World people, to reexamine and see the world through a perspective that would instill a revolutionary, conscious, liberating ideology. Black feminist pedagogy will be the medium for the message. The art and science of teaching as advocated by black feminist philosophy involves direct schooling for the future that holds viable options other than slave-slave master, or corporate giant-woeful worker, relationships. Students will be the building blocks, the true agents for radical change. The teaching of history from the black feminist perspective is not to imply a one-sided view of history, for as Raya Dunayevskaya so eloquently states in her essay, "Women as Thinkers and Revolutionaries," "There is no such thing as black history that is not also white history. There is no such thing as women's history that is not the actual history of humanity's struggle toward freedom."[9]

In discussing social relations in capitalist America, it is of critical importance to begin to examine the minds of the slave captor, power makers, or corporate monsters (however you wish to call those who control capitalist America) from the Afrocentric perspective. If the conceptual system has any validity, any value, it will be important to be able to compare and contrast for people two conceptual systems, that of the oppressed and that of the oppressors, because the two systems have different and very real consequences for their adherents. . . .

Black feminist philosophy incorporates a conceptual system capable of being measured against other conceptual systems, and black feminist pedagogy will examine the capitalist mentality as well as the history and philosophy of the Native American Indians who believed that one can no more own the land that is a source of provision for humans and animals than one can own the air above the land. Teachers applying black feminist techniques do not view students as passive recipients. We need only to review the history of student uprisings worldwide to realize their revolutionary potential. What has been lacking in most of their social movements has been a well formulated ideology—one that has been instilled and internalized from an early age. Schooling in capitalist America has indeed instilled an ideology, but one designed to maintain the status quo. The black feminist pedagogy will supply students with an ideology that will provide the necessary materials for creating conditions needed for radical change.

Black feminist theory is a theory of change with black feminist pedagogy being the change agent in and outside of the classrooms—wherever education takes place. Black feminist theory does not see class as the primary contradiction with the working class being the agents for change. Rather it sees the primary contradiction to be power relations between blacks and whites, males and females, with black women being the change agents. Black feminist theory and Marxism both function on the premise that you have to look at specific historical forms of oppression, and that power has to be reconstituted, reconstructed, to help find a weak link. Black feminist theory challenges Marxist theory to consider race as a primary contradiction, and it challenges feminists (white feminist theorists) to recognize the automatic dual oppression of sexism and racism that Afro-American and all women of color in the United States face with a routineness akin to breathing. Black feminists ask Marxist and white feminists, "Is our liberation going to be a part of your revolution? And if so why is it not a major topic in your theory building—in your literature—in your consciousness?"

Classroom illustrations of black feminist pedagogy in practise will be helpful at this point. Students bring certain basic assumptions into the classrooms, and these assumptions reveal the power of ideology—the American-dream ideology. For example, black students will frequently describe experiences of blatant racial discrimination, then in Yuppie tones declare that "every one is equal, racial differences don't really matter, you can make it if you try hard enough." Black and white female students will readily relate humiliating examples of sexist treatment, then, contradictory to their assertions, proclaim, "I think that with the proper qualifications women can make it in society today. Things have changed—look at Indira Gandhi, Geraldine Ferraro, and Corazon Aquino." These students, black and white female and male, desperately want to believe in the American ideology that America is the land of opportunity and you can become anything you want if you try and work hard enough—what Bowles and Gintis refer to as the meritocratic ideology. Introduce to these students the more truthful belief that wealth in America is not the result of hard work, but rather the result of graft, corruption, and protected crime, and the resistance will be overwhelming. Teaching style and radicalized students are of great importance in overcoming such resistance.

The first classroom illustration occurs in a college course on Third-World women and feminism.[10] The topic of women and resistance led to the mentioning of Eleanor Bumpers, the black woman killed by a squad of policemen in SWAT gear. They were evicting her for being behind in her rent by approximately $98.

After explaining to the class who Eleanor Bumpers was, the statement was made that negligence in paying her rent had very little to do with her death. The students, predominantly white women, initially could not understand what was meant by such a statement. Using the Socratic method, the students soon understood that Eleanor Bumpers's death was an illustration of the general treatment of blacks and poor people in our society.

It spoke of police brutality and racism in its worse form, that of seeing an individual as less than human because that person is nonwhite, poor, and elderly. It spoke of putting material wealth and value over human life. Further discussion concerned the inability of white feminists to identify and express national outrage over this incident. The shared historical experience of the black feminist instructor informed her/him that Eleanor Bumpers was fighting the same war of resistance against dehumanization and dominance that our ancestors in slavery fought. Later in the course the question of capital punishment came up. . . .

The second illustration of the implementation of thinking black in the classroom is in a course on domestic violence. In a small Eastern college the students were asked to compile lists of adjectives that they associated with the black ghetto, suburbia, and Appalachia. The purpose was to compare similarities and differences in perceptions and then discuss the commonality of wife battering. The composition of the class was fifteen white females and three white males, six black and three Puerto Rican females, and one black male. Interestingly enough the white students glibly offered ghetto characteristics. These included: overcrowding, drugs, muggings, slum areas, poverty, and multiplicity of sexual partners. The last characteristic elicited a perceptible gasp of indignation from a black student. As the instructor heard the list grow, automatically she knew that accepting these responses was to accept a conceptual system that was inherently blaming the victim. That is to say that it was buying into an ideology that attributes defects and inadequacy to the malignant nature of poverty, injustice, slum life, and racial difficulties. The stigma that marks the victim and accounts for her/his victimization is an acquired stigma of social origin. But the stigma, though derived in the past from environmental forces is still located in the victim, inside her/his skin. Within this formation, the liberal humanitarian can have it both ways. She/he can concentrate her/his charitable interests on the defects of the victim, condemn the vague social and environmental stresses that produced the defect, and ignore the continuing effect of victimizing social forces. It justifies a perverse form of social action designed to change not society, but rather society's victim. It is this type of thinking that the Afrocentric conceptual system aims to undermine. Armed with such a scintillating weapon for change, the black feminist teacher artfully and skillfully interprets classroom interaction while never veering from the goals of liberation for humankind through the process of an analysis of oppressions. . . .

This analysis of oppression stresses racial, sexual, and heterosexual oppression, as well as class. The critical importance of the racial dimension was illustrated in the classroom example being discussed. The black and Puerto Rican students were asked for their lists of characteristics that they associate with the black ghetto. Leading the list was police brutality, followed by exploitation, slum landlords, worst quality of food in the neighborhood stores with the highest prices, corruption, and insensitive city officials. The discussion that followed concerned reality beginning with experience, and how divergent assumptions about the world leads to contrary references on the same event. It is noteworthy that despite the differences in economic backgrounds of the black and Puerto Rican students, and despite the fact that some were gay others not, inevitably their responses to black feminist pedagogy intimated that the black dimension is and has been critically significant in their lives and to their survival in capitalist America.

Comments from white students after exposure to black feminist pedagogy were uniform: the majority showed visible signs of being uncomfortable, but remained silent in their discontent and amazement. Slowly but surely, after mustering up much courage, they stated that they felt taken aback, silenced, afraid that they would be challenged with questions they were unable to answer because they had never "thought that way" before (that way being Afrocentric thought or "thinking black"). In response to their comments, the domestic Third World students countered, with assurance and conviction in their voices, expressions such as, "This is the first time in my school career that I feel comfortable, really comfortable, in a class, because I feel like the teacher understands where I'm coming from"; "I feel good about the class because all sides of a question are discussed. For once the white way is not the only way or the right way." Eventually the vast majority of students realize and appreciate the value of being exposed to the consistency of a perspective that gives credence and respect to all peoples of different cultures. . . .

Black feminist pedagogy has its roots in Africa, the mother of civilization. The philosophy and practice is applicable and beneficial to people throughout the world. That it holds specific relevancy for racism worldwide is extremely appropriate at this time in the 1980s. Racist mobs of young whites hurling insults and assaulting blacks, and white police regularly beating and brutalizing blacks with near impunity, are endemic to male violence and racist mentalities that distinguish the American landscape. White racist violence is flourishing under the Reagan administration, which has gutted civil rights enforcement and slashed social service spending while pouring hundreds of billions of dollars into militarization and his pestiferous pet—nuclear star wars. . . .

Schooling in white capitalist America nourishes a system that helps to train/teach young white children to carry out their racist violence. It instills its white students with a cultural imperialism and intellectual ethnocentricism, which fuels them with a white superiority that implicitly and explicitly encourages racism, sexism, and heterosexism. This same educational system fails to educate nonwhites, who attend classes with regularity or irregularity.

Black feminist pedagogy has as an end result the development of generations of black, white, Puerto Rican, Chicano, Asian American, and Native American people prepared to radically change capitalist white America. It is fitting to have black feminist pedagogy as the theoretical construct for educational change. Black women historically have been central to educational change as teachers, survival technicians, administrators, and revolutionary thinkers. It is politically sound to listen to the reason and intellect of our ancestral educational role models. A social movement led by black women—the vanguard—is in order. If and when persons with vision in America have sufficient power to radically change the social relations, black feminist pedagogy should be the prime blueprint for the task.

ENDNOTES

1. S. Bowles and H. Gintis, *Schooling in Capitalist America* (London: Routledge & Kegan Paul, 1976), 265.

2. A famous quote by Dr. W. E. B. Du Bois, which appears in his *Souls of Black Folks*. The quote also appears on posters and postcards and has become a popular adage.

3. Unpublished essay by Dr. Robert Moore from a speech delivered in Toronto, Canada, in 1985 at an education conference.

4. C. T. Mohanty, *The Social Construction of Black Feminist Thought; An Essay in the Sociology of Knowledge* (paper), 5.

5. Ibid, 14.

6. Ibid, 15.

7. For a full discussion of this literature, see L. Myers, *Contributions in Black Studies, How to Think Black: Toni Cade Bambara's* The Salt Eaters, 6, 1983–84, 39–44.

8. Unpublished essay by R. Moore, Panel on Education—Third National Convention of Women for Racial and Economic Equality, May 1984, 6.

9. R. Dunayevskaya, from the essay, "Women as Thinkers and Revolutionaries," *Women's Liberation and the Dialectics of Revolution*, 80.

10. The classroom illustrations are based on actual experiences of the author.

Elizabeth Higginbotham

Elizabeth Higginbotham is associate professor of sociology and associate director of the Center for Research on Women at Memphis State University. Her current research is the upward mobility of women of color, and she is currently completing a book on educated black women. She has published widely on race, class, and gender in the lives of women, and is highly sought after in colleges and universities throughout the country because of her work at Memphis State, designing faculty development workshops on incorporating women of color into the college curriculum. Her essay "Designing an Inclusive Curriculum: Bringing All Women into the Core" (1990) grows out of this important work.

Elizabeth Higginbotham }

Designing an Inclusive Curriculum: Bringing All Women into the Core

To be successful, transforming the curriculum involves three interrelated tasks. The first is to gain information about the diversity of the female experience. The second task is to decide how to teach this new material, a process that typically involves reconceptualizing one's discipline in light of a race, class, and gender-based analysis. Often this means learning to move typically marginal groups into the core of the curriculum. Furthermore, efforts can be made to present issues on people of color in their complexity, rather than in stereotypic ways. The third task is to structure classroom dynamics that ensure a safe atmosphere to support learning for *all* the students. This paper will discuss each of these tasks. It begins with a critique of the traditional curriculum in light of its treatment of people of color.

MARGINAL IN THE TRADITIONAL CURRICULUM

When I consistently see many bright and respected scholars failing to take steps to bring women of color into their teaching and research, I look for social, structural explanations. A sociological perspective can help us to understand the roots of racist thinking and the many forms it takes in traditional disciplines and women's studies. This approach is more productive than blaming these scholars—or simply attacking them as racists. The search for the social, structural roots of the marginalization of people of color in scholarship and education takes me back to my early schooling.

As a black person in a society dominated by whites, I was always an outsider—a status—that Patricia Hill Collins argues has advantages and costs.[1] I was cognizant even as a young child that the experiences of black people were missing in what I was taught in elementary school. This pattern was later replicated in junior high and high school, then in college, and later in graduate school. But while I had been critical all along, not until I entered graduate school could I debate with others about the content of courses.

Throughout my whole educational career, agents of the dominant group attempted to teach me the "place" of black people in the world. What was actively communicated to me was that black people and other people of color are on the periphery of society. They are marginal. I learned that what happens to people of color has little relevance for members of the dominant group and for mainstream thinking.

Early in school, when we were studying the original thirteen North American colonies, I was exposed to the myths about who we were and are as a nation. One of the first lessons was that America is a land that people entered in search of freedom—religious freedom, the freedom to work as independent farmers, freedom from the privileged nobility and the hierarchical stratification of Europe, and freedom from the rapid industrialization of Europe. Colonists, and later white immigrants, wanted change in their lives, and they took the risk to begin life anew in this budding but already glorious nation. The fact that they were seeking their "freedom" while enslaving others (principally Native Americans and Africans) was not viewed as a contradictory activity, but just "one of those things" the United States had to do to build a great and prosperous nation.

New York, where I grew up and received much of my education, prided itself on being a progressive state, and required schools to devote time to the Negro experience (as it was called). We discussed slavery in the South, and during Negro History Week we learned about Harriet Tubman, Booker T. Washington, Frederick Douglass, and George Washington Carver. We were explicitly taught that black people did not share the same history as whites. African people had been forced to come to North America against their will, and instead of finding freedom, they had had to work as slaves.

The experiences of Afro-Americans never informed the standard characterizations of the society: even the slave experience of Africans and Afro-Americans did not alter the image that America was a land in which people found freedom. As a student, I had to master the myths and accept them as part of my socialization into the political system. I also learned that the information I accumulated about black people—and later other people of color—was nice to know for "cultural enrichment." Exposure to the experiences of Afro-Americans, Puerto Ricans, and others was useful to develop tolerance for difference and make us better citizens, but this information was never meant to identify concepts, to develop perspectives, or to generate images or theories about the society as a whole.

I was in school to learn the experiences of the dominant group which was also very male, as well as white and affluent—and that would be the basis for an understanding of the system. If I learned that, I could go to college and perhaps do more interesting work than my parents did.

In spite of the intended message, it was hard for me to understand why the experiences of black people were not incorporated into our images of who we are as a nation. At the time there was no mention of Asian Americans, Chicanos, or Native Americans. But I came to understand the practice. Whatever happened to black people was an exception to the rule —we were a deviant case—just like using "i" before "e" except after "c." Since the experiences of black people did not have to be included in our search for the truth, they were not the material from which theories and frameworks were derived.

As I reflect on my early educational experiences, I see that the messages I received as a child, an adolescent, and an adult blamed the victim. For example, we were taught that the African people who "came" to America were not civilized; therefore, they could not pursue the American dream as initial settlers and white immigrants had been able to do. The lack of black participation in mainstream American society was attributed to lesser abilities, defective cultures, lack of motivation, and so forth. To make a "victim-blaming" attribution, teachers did not actually have to say that black Americans were lazy, ignorant, or savage—although that would surely do the trick. Instead, victim-blaming was subtly encouraged in classes where images of America as the land of freedom and opportunity were juxtaposed with the black experience, without any reconciling of the contradictions through a structural explanation. Students then relied on prevailing myths and stereotypes to explain the black "anomaly."

As a young black girl, I found these messages problematic, and throughout my life I have sought answers to questions about the experiences of black people at different historic moments. As a scholar, I still struggle with how best to use the knowledge I have gained. Thus, I approach the issue of curriculum integration with a fundamental critique of the traditional curriculum. I did not begin by discovering that women were missing from the curriculum—instead I have always perceived schools as foreign institutions. The information taught in schools was alien to me, to my family, to my neighborhood, and in a certain respect to the city, New York, in which I lived. Yet, in order to move to the next educational level and succeed in society, I had to master this information and pass tests. In my view, you were smart if you could pass the tests, but you had to look elsewhere for information to help you survive in the real world.

Today's wave of curriculum reforms presents an opportunity to restructure education, to alter the environment that was alien to me and many others. Such a remedy would include in the curriculum all the people in the classroom and the nation. Instead of focusing solely on the experiences of dominant group members, faculty members would teach students to use and value many different experiences in order to develop conceptions of life in this country and around the world.

I began by discussing my early experiences, because these experiences are common to many. Although we learn these lessons as members of either privileged or oppressed groups, they are similar lessons. If we are clear about the origins of practices that exclude people of color, we can dispense with blaming ourselves and each other for the difficulties we face in trying to change the curriculum. We are swimming upstream against the intellectual racism that flows through American ideology. The *disregard* for the experiences of black people and other people of color is part of the American creed. To create a multicultural curriculum we must "unlearn" the ideology that marginalizes all but a tiny elite of American citizens.

Curriculum transformation has the potential for changing our traditional visions of education in American society. Yet, it can also replicate old biases. This is especially likely to occur in situations where the integration process is envisioned as a minor tune-up to an educational system that is fundamentally solid. From my perspective, however, our curriculum needs a major overhaul. It needs much more than the addition of women. It must incorporate the men who are omitted—especially working-class men and men of color. Elizabeth Minnich reminds us that fundamental change is not possible unless we first understand why these groups were excluded.[2] Enlightened by such a critique, we can decide how we want to change and what we will teach. We can then select the path that leads to a restructuring of the curriculum toward inclusiveness across many dimensions of human experience.

CURRICULUM CHANGE STARTS WITH FACULTY DEVELOPMENT

Integrating the diversity among women into the curriculum is difficult. Most faculty members are just learning about women through recent exposure to feminist scholarship; few of them are knowledgeable about and at ease with material on women of color. This is understandable. No one mentioned women of color when most contemporary college faculty pursued their degrees, yet the lack of correct information is a major contributor to the limited and inadequate treatment of women of color in courses and in research projects.

As the products of educational experiences that relegated people of color and women to the margins of their fields, faculty members need to compensate for the institutionalized biases in the educational system. They can work to eliminate this bias by gaining familiarity with the historical and contemporary experiences of racial-ethnic groups, the working class, middle-class women, and other groups traditionally restricted to the margins. The first step is to acknowledge one's lack of exposure to these histories.

Structural difficulties make learning new information about women and people of color problematic. It is often hard for faculty members to compensate for the gaps in their knowledge when they are faced with heavy teaching responsibilities and the pressure to publish. College administrators can encourage efforts with release time, financial support for workshops and institutes, and the like. Even without such resources. faculty members can develop long- and short-term strategies—for example, by organizing seminars to explore the new scholarship. All that is needed is a commitment and a shared reading list.

Another difficulty is the interdisciplinary nature of women's studies. Most faculty members are trained to research a specific discipline. Fortunately, over the years, more resources and tools have become available to help navigate this interdisciplinary field. The Center for Research on Women at Memphis State University has been a pioneer in this area; other research centers and curriculum projects have produced bibliographies, collections of syllabi, essays, and resources to assist with curriculum change. Some resources specifically include race, class, and gender as dimensions of analysis.

Institutionalized racism and sexism are structured into both the commercial and academic publishing markets, thus making it more difficult for scholars studying women and people of color to publish their work. Women's studies centers have initiated projects to help faculty identify relevant citations and locate new research, and the development of women's studies and racial-ethnic studies journals has helped a great deal, but structural barriers persist that impede access to research on certain populations, particularly women of color, working-class women, and women in the southern and western regions of this nation. Thus, the very resources college faculty need about women of color are difficult to locate.

Learning to identify myth and misinformation about people of color is a critical task in course and curriculum revision. It is a process that alters teaching content and classroom dynamics. For example, with new knowledge faculty members can teach students in ways that appreciate human diversity. Faculty members will also be better prepared to interrupt and challenge racist, sexist, class-bias, and homophobic remarks made in the classroom.

My own areas of specialization have given me information on the experiences of different racial and ethnic groups in this society. I often forget that everyone is not familiar with how most of the Southwest became part of the United States; with the Chinese Exclusion Act of 1882; with the implications of the Immigration Act of 1924 for people of color; with the internment of Japanese American citizens during World War II; and with the fact that Puerto Ricans are citizens, not immigrants, and cannot be considered undocumented workers. One has to remember that most dominant-group faculty and students are not nearly as familiar with these histories as are students who belong to specific ethnic and racial-ethnic groups. This history of oppression is part of the oral traditions in ethnic and racial-ethnic communities as well as religious groups. Afro-American, Latino, Asian American, and Native American students enter our classrooms with at least a partial awareness of the historic struggles of their people. They frequently feel alienated in educational settings where their teachers and other students relate to them without any awareness of their group's history. For example, a faculty member or a student who talks about how Japanese Americans have *always* done well in this country denies the reality that racism has severely marred the lives of both Japanese immigrants and Japanese Americans. For much of this century Japanese aliens were denied the opportunity to become citizens. During World War II they were removed from the West Coast and placed in internment camps, primarily because Anglos resented their economic success. Non-Japanese American faculty and students may be unaware of this history. The lack of correct information on the part of faculty members has consequences for what happens in the classroom: to the Japanese American student, Anglo ignorance of these issues is symptomatic of the persistent denial that racism is an issue for this group.[3]

With new information, faculty can challenge myths and begin to interrupt racism in the classroom. The mastering of new information is a key ingredient in combatting the feelings of powerlessness many faculty members experience in the face of the racist and sexist attitudes of their students. Once we acknowledge our lack of information, we can use the many resources available to learn about the experiences of women, people of color, working-class people, and other traditionally marginalized groups.

WHAT DO I DO WITH NEW INFORMATION?

A key issue faced by faculty is finding a "place" for working-class women, black women, and other women of color in the curriculum. How do we challenge established practices of marginalizing these populations and truly develop a different educational process? How do we weave this new information on women and specifically women of color into a course on the family, the labor market, the sociology of education, the introduction to political science, and so forth? This is where many faculty learn by trial and error.

Revising the content of one's course requires the clarification of personal goals and educational aims.[4] This is not an issue that faculty approach lightly. One cannot introduce a reading or a lecture where minority women are covered and then merely assume that the goal has been achieved. Curriculum transformation requires much more. Yet, as we move toward that goal, our individual educational philosophy and commitment to our discipline will play a key role in how we resolve these issues.

It is common practice to begin initial integration efforts with one or two lectures on women of color. Faculty who stop at that level of inclusion find that their course is not transformed and that this addition has little impact on students. In fact, this approach can generate new problems. An instructor who performs the obligatory lecture often encounters opposition from students. For example, a black woman colleague of mine taught a traditional course on the family and included a unit on the black family. A few vocal students were quick to remind her that they had signed up for a course on the family, not the "black family." Had she incorporated material on the black family in every unit throughout the course, the "black family" would not have appeared to be anomalous, but an integral part of the study of the family.

Yet, this additive approach is problematic. If faculty introduce material on black women or women of color as interesting variations on womanhood, such actions indicate that readings and lecture materials on these populations are not part of the "core" knowledge covered in the class. Students can tolerate a certain amount of cultural enrichment, but if this material exceeds more than one or two lectures, they lose their patience because they think the instructor is deviating from the core. This reaction can be avoided if material on white working-class women, black women, and other women of color (as well as men of color and working-class people) is integrated throughout the course. The diversity of experiences should be presented as knowledge that students are responsible for learning and will be evaluated for covering.

Approaches that keep women of color on the margins or peripheral to the course materials fail to address critical issues of racism, sexism, and classism. Faculty who use such approaches tend to introduce material on white middle-class people as the norm, and then later ask for a discussion on the variations found among working-class whites and people of color. This approach does a great deal to foster ideas that blame the victim. Students may even use such discussions as opportunities to verbalize the racism they have learned from the media and other sources. Such interactions tend to polarize a class, and then the faculty member has an additional battle to wage.

In sociology, where attention is given to norms, ideal types, and the like, women of color are often incorporated as deviant cases. Peripheral treatments of groups are obvious to students; furthermore, these approaches complement students' previous learning about racial-ethic groups. Often when an instructor is about to begin the one obligatory lecture on the black family, the black woman, Latinas, working-class women in the labor market or whomever, a student will ask the question all the students want answered, "Are we going to be tested on this?" This also tends to happen when a guest speaker who is a racial minority or a female is invited to class. Students may listen politely but not feel compelled to write anything down or remember what was said.

Students carry old lessons into the classroom. They have already learned that what happens to people of color (or to women) does not count. This has been evident in their learning prior to college and continues in most college courses. Learning about different groups is treated as cultural enrichment, not as a part of the basic scholarship of a field. These are essentially correct impressions on the part of students. The core material is still about affluent white men: the historical experiences, social conditions, and scholarly contributions of people of color and women are marginal to the disciplines.

Beyond a Universal Model of Gender

In many curriculum integration efforts in social science teaching, the marginalization of women of color takes two forms. Women of color are addressed either as tangents to the "generic" woman or as the "exceptional" woman of color. In the first case, African American, Asian American, and Native American women and Latinas are present, but their experiences are not critical to the development of theory or paradigms. This teaching strategy is often linked with the view that gender relations are the foundation for universal experiences. Within this framework, other sources of inequality, particularly race and class, might be acknowledged, but they are clearly less important than gender. As a result, scholarship on women of color in both women's studies and curriculum integration efforts is marginalized.[5] Faculty tend to rely upon the experiences of white, middle-class, heterosexual Americans as the norm and view all others are merely exceptions to the rule.

Sandra Morgen is very critical of this universalist stance. She identifies how looking at the experiences of women of color expands our understanding of critical issues for women and gives a feminist perspective greater depth.[6] Morgen examines how we can develop deeper appreciations of motherhood, the feminization of poverty, and women and resistance by examining the historical and current situations of women of color.

With regard to motherhood, Morgen identifies the way that most white, middle-class feminist scholars see the nuclear family as normative. In a discussion of Dinnerstein's *Mermaid and the Minotaur* (1976), Adrienne Rich's *Of Woman Born* (1976), and Nancy Chodorow's (1978) *The Reproduction of Mothering,* Morgen argues that much feminist scholarship about "the" family

> presumes that working women are a relatively recent phenomenon, and that working mothers are even newer, and that the normative family is mom, dad, and the kids, and that mothers live with their children and are the

primary, if not near exclusive, force in their socialization. These assumptions are problematic when explaining the historical and contemporary experiences of many poor and working-class women, and of many women of color. These women have as a group been in the labor force for a much longer period of time, and in situations like slavery, sharecropping, domestic work, or unregulated industrial production that did not allow for the kind of full-time motherhood, or the specific mother-child relations which are presumed in Chodorow, Dinnerstein, and Rich.[7]

The impact of racial oppression on the mothering behavior of women of color in the nineteenth century is a theme in the work of Bonnie Thornton Dill.[8] She describes how racial oppression not only shaped the productive roles of African American, Latina, and Asian immigrant women, but also influenced the reproductive labor of these women. Dill's and Morgen's works demonstrate that much can be gained by using the experiences of women of color to develop new theories about women's experiences. Such approaches sharply contrast with those that fit the experiences of women of different classes and races into a universal model.

Morgen also describes how an analysis of the feminization of poverty can be informed by looking at the circumstances of women who are not new to poverty.[9] She is joined by other scholars who have discovered that not all women are a husband away from poverty. While many middle-class white women experience a significant decline in their social status when they sever their attachment to a middle-class white male, many working-class women and women of color find themselves attached to men and still poor.[10] Their poverty is not only a gender issue but is related to a legacy of class and racial discrimination.[11]

We can also see beyond approaches that focus on women as victims by learning how working-class women and women of color resist class and racial oppression.[12] Rather than a continuum from accommodation to rebellion, Morgen sees diverse personal and protracted struggles against oppression. These women actively resist the limitations placed on their lives by gender, class, and racial oppression. Denied access to many public spheres, they do not protest by voting or writing letters to congressmen; instead, they are involved in grass-roots organizing, efforts to improve public schools and other neighborhood institutions, jobs actions, and the like. Morgen's book (coedited with Ann Bookman) *Women and the Politics of Empowerment* incorporates much of the new research on women and resistance, research that is primarily on working-class women.[13] Rich examples of resistance are also found in the new scholarship on women in domestic work.[14]

If we abandon the practice of keeping working-class women and women of color on the margins in our teaching and our research, and seek ways to incorporate the diversity of women's experiences, we are more likely to involve students and challenge their racist assumptions. We can also move students beyond seeing women of color and working-class women as victims.

ADDRESSING THE LIVES OF ORDINARY WOMEN OF COLOR

A second way that women of color are introduced into the curriculum is by a brief look at a few "exceptional" examples. This method is very common in history and the social sciences, where "exceptional" black women such as Sojourner Truth, Harriet Tubman, Ida B. Wells, and Mary McLeod Bethune are discussed. In contrast to marginal treatments of women of color, described above, where the population of women of color is seen as an undifferentiated mass, this approach holds up a few models— nonvictims—for admiration. In the case of black women, this is often done under the guise that racism has not been terribly difficult for them. The subtle message to students is that if successful black women could achieve in the face of obstacles, other black women failed to attain the same heights because of faulty culture, lack of motivation, and other individual deficits. A faculty member might not intend to reinforce the individualistic lessons of the American ideology, but students interpret the material in this way because it is a common theme in our history. The "exceptions" approach fails to depict the larger social system in which the struggles of women of color, whether successful or not, take place.

In "The Politics of Black Women's Studies," by Barbara Smith and Gloria Hull, which is the introductory essay in *But Some of Us Are Brave: Black Women's Studies,* the authors warn of this practice:

> A descriptive approach to the lives of black women, a "great black women" in history or literature approach, or any traditional male-identified approach will not result in intellectually groundbreaking or politically transforming work. We cannot change our lives by teaching solely about "exceptions" to the ravages of white-male oppression. Only through exploring the experiences of supposedly "ordinary" black women whose "unexceptional" actions enabled us and the race to survive, will we be able to begin to develop an overview and analytic framework for understanding the lives of Afro-American women.[15]

To do otherwise is to deceive ourselves. The experiences of a few exceptional black women, as typically portrayed in the classroom, serve to deny the reality of oppressive structures. This approach does not help students develop an appreciation for the role of race, class, and gender in people's lives. As we attempt to bring women of color out of the margins, we must be prepared to challenge students' tendency to romanticize a few heroines.

These two practices, teaching about women of color as tangents to the "generic" woman and examining the lives of exceptional women of color, work to justify and perpetuate the marginalization of women of color in women's studies scholarship. Approaches such as these retard the field of women's studies and complicate the task of integrating women into the high school and college curricula. While these approaches might represent a step or phase in the process of changing the curriculum, we must also remain clear on the larger goals and objectives of curriculum transformation. As pointed out earlier, each step in transformation brings its own set of problems and contradictions into the classroom. If we are not clear about our ultimate goal, we may become discouraged and retreat before new problems. In the end, we seek a curriculum that teaches an awareness and appreciation of the diversity of human experiences as well as the commonality of the human condition.

If a course is structured around the dominant-group experience and people of color are marginalized, faculty members lose the opportunity to critically address social structure—that is, the ways in which the institutions of society shape our options and influence our behavior. Transforming the curriculum requires explicit discussions of the roles of gender, race, and class in shaping the lives of everybody. This is accomplished by exploring the diversity of the experiences of men and women in the United States and around the world. For example, being female means privileges and the accompanying restrictions of dependency for some women, while for others it means poverty and the burden of supporting themselves and dependents.

Within this framework, no norm or modal case is taken for granted. If one teaches the sociology of the American family, it is with an eye on examining the diversity of family forms and lives. In family studies, only a minority of today's families fit the supposed norm of the 1950s and 1960s, of a full-time-employed father and a mother at home with the children. Therefore, it is easier and more accurate to look at the variations of family forms and discuss which factors obstruct or support specific types of family structures. Faculty members might even find that students, who are well aware of the variety of families, might be motivated to explore the factors behind this diversity. This perspective is the core of a recent textbook about the sociology of the family, *Diversity in American Families,* by Maxine Baca Zinn and D. Stanley Eitzen.[16] The book, which elaborates how race and class, major structures of inequality, affect specific family forms, is well received by students because it does not hold up any single type as the norm by which all other families are judged.

RACISM, DIVERSITY, AND CLASSROOM DYNAMICS

Racism is a pervasive classroom problem that has to be addressed. One approach is to inform students that racism often takes the form of misinformation about racial-ethnic groups. Discussions of how misinformation is systematically taught in the schools and the media, and in informal ways from friends, parents, and the like, may relieve individual students from feeling guilty for holding racist notions. Students should be encouraged to think critically about the information they get regarding their own group and others' groups, so that they will learn to question broad generalizations like "All whites are middle class" and "All blacks are poor." Information that sheds light on the diversity within a group is more likely to be correct.

Students should be encouraged to think critically about information that devalues or dehumanizes members of specific groups. For example, any idea that some people (usually blacks, Latinos, or Native Americans) are more comfortable with hunger, poverty, and the like than other groups (usually white Americans) implies that the former are "less than human." Any information that students received that has the effect of dehumanizing a group can be identified as racist and therefore not a fact of the social world.

These are just a few ideas to help faculty think about combatting racism in the classroom. Correct information and changing teaching methods will do a great deal to challenge the racism embedded in our educational system —where there are a limited number of legitimate lines of inquiry and where "inquirers are only allowed to ask certain questions."[17] . . .

The routes individual faculty members take to enhance classroom dynamics will vary widely, but there can be some goals we all share. Part of the task of the college instructor is to create an environment where there can be an honest and open exchange about the material and where students can do what they are rarely asked to do—learn from each other.

CONCLUSION

Curriculum transformation is a challenge in which all faculty can participate. As we pursue short- and long-term goals, it is important to be mindful of the several tasks involved in the process: securing information, integrating material into our teaching, and establishing a supportive classroom. Do not become discouraged by the slow progress. Establishing support for faculty can be critical in the success of projects. Join with other colleagues in learning new materials and experimenting in the classroom. The presence of support groups can help faculty members reflect on their progress and motivate them to take new risks. Faculty who accept this new challenge may find a rejuvenated interest in teaching their students.

ENDNOTES

1. Patricia Hill Collins, "Learning from the Outsider Within: The Sociological Significance of Black Feminist Thought," *Social Problems* 33 (December 1986): 14–32.

2. Elizabeth K. Minnich, *Transforming Knowledge* (Philadelphia: Temple University Press, 1990).

3. Eugene F. Wong, "Asian American Middleman Minority Theory: The Framework for an American Myth," *Journal of Ethnic Studies* 13 (Spring 1985): 51–88.

4. Margaret Andersen, "Curriculum Change in Higher Education," *Signs: Journal of Women and Culture in Society* 12 (Winter 1987): 222–54.

5. Maxine Baca Zinn, Lynn Weber Cannon, Elizabeth Higginbotham, and Bonnie Thornton Dill, "On the Costs of Exclusionary Practices in Women's Studies," *Signs: Journal of Women and Culture in Society* 11 (Winter 1986): 290–303.

6. Sandra Morgen, "To See Ourselves, To See Our Sisters: The Challenge of Re-envisioning Curriculum Change" (publication from the Research Clearinghouse and Curriculum Integration Project, Center for Research on Women, Memphis State University, 1986).

7. Morgen, "To See Ourselves," 12.

8. Bonnie Thornton Dill, "Our Mothers' Grief: Racial-Ethnic Women and the Maintenance of Families," *Journal of Family History* 13: 412–31.

9. Morgen, "To See Ourselves."

10. Linda Burnham, "Has Poverty Been Feminized in Black America?" in *For Crying Out Loud: Women and Poverty in the United States,* ed. Ann Withorn and Rochelle Lefkowitz (New York: Pilgrim Press, 1986), 69–83.

11. Elizabeth Higginbotham, "We Were Never on a Pedestal: Women of Color Continue to Struggle with Poverty, Racism and Sexism," in *For Crying Out Loud: Women and Poverty in the United States,* ed. Ann Withorn and Rochelle Lefkowitz (New York: Pilgrim Press, 1986). 97–109.

12. Morgen, "To See Ourselves."

13. Ann Bookman and Sandra Morgen, eds., *Women and the Politics of Empowerment* (Philadelphia: Temple University Press, 1988).

14. Ellizabeth Clark-Lewis, " 'This Work Had an End': The Transition from Live-in to Day Work" (working paper no. 2, Southern Women: The Intersection of Race, Class and Gender, Center for Research on Women, Memphis State University, 1985); and Judith Rollins, *Between Women: Domestics and Their Employers* (Philadelphia: Temple University Press, 1985).

15. Gloria T. Hull and Barbara Smith, "The Politics of Black Women's Studies," in *All the Women Are White, All the Blacks Are Men, But Some of Us Are Brave: Black Women's Studies,* ed. Gloria T. Hull, Patricia Bell Scott, and Barbara Smith (Old Westbury, NY: Feminist Press, 1982), xxi–xxii.

16. Maxine Baca Zinn and D. Stanley Eitzen, *Diversity in American Families* (New York: Harper & Row, 1987).

17. Vicky Spelman, "Combatting the Marginalization of Black Women in the Classroom," *Women's Studies Quarterly* 10 (Summer 1982): 15–16.

CHAPTER SEVEN

Discourses of Resistance: Interrogating Mainstream Feminism and Black Nationalism

By and large within the women's movement . . . white women focus upon their oppression as women and ignore differences of race, sexual preference, class, and age. There is a pretense to a homogeneity of experience covered by the word sisterhood *that does not in fact exist. . . . As white women ignore their built-in privilege of whiteness and define* woman *in terms of their own experience alone, then women of color become "other," the outsider whose experience is too "alien" to comprehend.*

— A U D R E   L O R D E , *Sister Outsider*

. . . there is a dangerous trend observable in some quarters of the movement to program [black women] out of their "evil" ways into a cover-up, shut-up, lay-back-and-be-cool obedience role. . . . She is being encouraged—in the name of the revolution no less—to cultivate "virtues" that if listed would sound like the personality traits of slaves. . . . We rap about being correct but ignore the danger of having one-half of our population regard the other with such condescension and perhaps fear that that half finds it necessary to "reclaim his manhood" by denying her her peoplehood. We have much, alas, to work against. . . . [we must] face the task of creating a new identity, a self, perhaps an androgynous self, via commitment to the struggle.

— T O N I   C A D E , *The Black Woman*

INTRODUCTION

Black feminist discourse is inherently oppositional because it runs counter to mainstream points of view both within and without African American communities. Being oppositional, especially if you're black and female, requires courage and tenacity. Being feminist exposes you to criticism, hostility, and even outright misogyny. Feminist ideologies also provide you with a particular worldview that is useful for negotiating the difficult terrain of North America. They help you understand the seemingly inexplicable and rage against the evil that all oppressed people suffer. They enable you to imagine a world that does not exist but should. And, finally, they connect you to particular women throughout the globe who share your commitment to a better world, and to women throughout history who dreamed, kept the faith, and passed their sisterly wisdom on.

Pauline Terrelonge

Pauline Terrelonge's essay "Feminist Consciousness and Black Women" is a response to the widely held belief within the black community that racism rather than sexism is the major burden of African American women. She also discusses male privilege within the black community, a concept that is at odds with the myth of the powerless black male and the liberated black woman. One of the questions she explores in great detail is why large numbers of black women, given their material reality, have not developed a feminist consciousness. Her embrace of feminism provides a counterdiscourse to the many voices in the black community that discourage black women from becoming feminists.

Pauline Terrelonge }

Feminist Consciousness and Black Women

Like the Populist movement at the turn of the century, and the Prohibition and Antiwar movements of subsequent decades, the contemporary feminist movement is having an enormous impact on black America. It is not so much that black people have embraced the feminist movement, or that they have even begun to identify with it. Rather its effect is seen in the controversy it has engendered within the race concerning the exact status of black males and females, and what the ideal role of each should be. A common (and, some would argue, the dominant) view within the black community at the present time is that blacks have withstood the long line of abuses perpetrated against them ever since their arrival in this country mainly because of the black woman's fortitude, inner wisdom, and sheer ability to survive. As a corollary to this emphasis on the moral, spiritual, and emotional strength of the black woman in offsetting the potential annihilation of the race, proponents of this view stress the critical role that she plays in keeping the black family together and in supporting black males. Indeed, many blacks regard the role of uniting all blacks to be the primary duty of the black woman, one that should supersede all other roles that she might want to perform, and certainly one that is essentially incompatible with her own individual liberation.[1] Pursuit of the latter is generally judged to be a selfish goal, detrimental to the overall welfare of the race. In short, sexism is viewed by many blacks, both male and female, to be a factor of minimal importance in the overall oppression of the black woman. The brunt of culpability for her unequal condition is accorded to racism.[2]

The object of this essay is to challenge this point of view. It is my belief that the foregoing view of black female subordination expresses a narrow perspective on the nature of social oppression in American society, and because of this, the solutions that are commonly proposed—e.g., correcting the imbalance in the black sex ratio, or building stronger black families— are doomed to serve as only partial palliatives to the problems facing black women.

The first fact that must be grasped is that the black female condition in America has developed in a society where the dominant economic form is the market economy and the sole purpose of economic activity is the making of a profit on the part of large corporations. Because profit maximization is the superordinate goal to which all other social goals are merely subsidiary, labor is a premium. Labor must not only be made as highly productive as possible, but also be obtained at the cheapest possible cost. The manipulation of the labor market is essential to attain these dual goals and provide for the effective functioning of the American economic order.

A major strategy for manipulating labor has been the maintenance of a sexual division of labor, i.e., a situation where certain roles are designated as male, others as female. The allocation of societal functions according to gender has been based on certain biological factors that objectively differentiate the sexes and the way those factors are interpreted through the ideology of sexism. The fact that women bear children has been used to justify their relegation to the domestic sphere. Their ability to reproduce has been made a duty, to which have been added the responsibilities of nurturing the offspring, serving the spouse, and performing or supervising all domestic-related chores. It is easy to see how the pattern of female responsibility for the domestic sphere is useful to the economic system; it has allowed certain critical societal functions to be performed without the need of providing monetary remuneration.[3]

It is generally recognized that the ideology of racism has functioned to maintain blacks in a subordinate economic state.[4] Less readily recognized, however, are the similarities of the process of racial subordination to that of female subordination. In both cases the rationale for subordination resides in characteristics ascribed by the large capitalist interests, which are almost totally white male. Moreover, both forces—sexism and racism—create an occupationally segregated labor market, thereby giving rise to a situation where there are male jobs and female jobs, white jobs and black jobs.

From a cursory view, the white female has appeared historically to enjoy a privileged status; after all, as a result of sharing the bedrooms of white males, to her fall many of the material privileges and benefits of the society. But it is essential to recognize that rarely has she achieved these amenities on her own merit; nearly always it has been through the efforts and good graces of her spouse. The apparent freedoms and material well-being enjoyed by many white women depend not on women earning them but on women fulfilling a nurturant and supportive role and, of course, maintaining a distinctive sexual identity through a socially defined image of female attractiveness. Thus, beauty and sexual attractiveness are essential to woman's economic survival, and maintaining these assets has become a major concern, second only to fulfillment of her domestic functions.

The cult of the home, like so many other aspects of white America, has unfortunately permeated the culture of Afro-America. While the cult in black society has been subjected to indigenous permutations,[5] in essence it bears close similarities to the white pattern, as would be expected in view of the fact that the economic forces affecting the larger society also impinge on the black subculture. Thus, within Afro-American culture (and I emphasize within), maleness creates privileges—that is, certain freedoms and rights are attached to being male. Certain sexually specific behaviors are part of the black socialization process. The result is that marriage among blacks is just as much a union of unequals as it is in the larger society; child rearing, domestic chores, and custody of children are largely female concerns. Hence, it is erroneous to argue that the domestic patterns of white society are not replicated in the black community. The "housewife" model may not fit completely, but it is closely approximated in the sense that black women must bear the brunt of the domestic-related chores, even when they also work outside the home.

What has historically differentiated black women from most white women is the peculiar way in which the racial and sexual caste systems have interfaced. Throughout their history in America, black women have had to face a condition of double dependency—(1) on their spouses or mates, and (2) on their employers. Although these dependencies have also been the lot of many employed white women, proportionately fewer of the latter faced both of them. Double dependency has practically always been the onus of black women. Moreover, because of the racial caste system, a significant proportion of black married women, both historically and contemporaneously, have not had the economic support of their husbands —because their husbands are either absent or underemployed or unable to find employment. What is significant about the fact that so many black women have had to contribute to their families' financial support is that society's reaction to their plight has been sexist. Because they are more economically independent of a male breadwinner than is the societal norm, many black women have been made to feel that they usurped the male role, as though they—and not society—were ultimately responsible for the black man's inability to be the main breadwinner.

It is sometimes argued that the black woman's lack of choice over whether she should or should not work renders her condition totally dissimilar to that of a white woman. While it is true that black men have had a more difficult time providing for their families than white men, and that this has forced more black women to be in the labor force than white women, it must be recognized that the roles of both groups of women were ultimately conditioned by larger economic forces: White women were conditioned not to work in the productive sector; black women were conditioned to work. Those white women who were forced by economic circumstances to work outside the home were made to feel that their behavior was somehow deviant, and in most cases they abandoned their occupational participation when it was no longer absolutely necessary to their families' financial well-being. Thus, neither group of women, white or black, had an option. Consequently, the behavior of both groups of women was a direct consequence of economic forces over which they exercised little or no control.

The foregoing picture of the different though mutually consistent roles played by black and white women has not remained static over the years. In the last twenty-five years, dramatic changes have taken place in the composition of the female labor force. Increasing numbers of married white women have sought paid employment, and black women have made major gains in earnings. In short, the labor-force profiles of both groups of women have become more and more similar, especially for young women.[6]

The movement of white females into the labor sphere has been partially caused by inflation, which has made it increasingly difficult for white males to maintain a middle-class standard of living solely from their earnings. This situation bears stark similarity to the one that has traditionally prevailed in black society, where familial economic survival—in both the working and the middle classes—generally depends on both spouses' income.

For white women, like black women, labor-force participation has not relieved them of performing traditional female domestic chores. For both groups of women, this has had a significant impact on the nature of their occupational participation, as it is generally interpreted by employers as a sign of the inherent unreliability of female labor—i.e., as a source of potential absenteeism and turnover—and is used as an added rationale for relegating women to the least prestigious, least financially remunerative, and most menial tasks. Even working women who are not wives or mothers find their occupational destinies affected by employer expectations that they do or will perform dual roles.

The entrance of more women into the productive sphere of the society has not brought about the demise of occupational segregation based on sex; indeed, economists reveal that occupational segregation based on sex is highly resistant to change.[7] Thus, women continue to predominate in those jobs that are least secure; least subject to unionization; least lucrative in terms of compensation, working conditions, and fringe benefits; and least conducive to career advancement.[8] So the influx of women into the labor market has not appreciably reduced the chances of males to find employment in a labor market that continues to be occupationally segregated. Women can be absorbed by the economy as a result of the fact that in the past thirty years there has been a phenomenal increase in some traditional female jobs, primarily in the clerical and service sectors of the economy.

Women are judged by employers to be particularly suited for clerical and service jobs for three basic reasons: (1) because of their socialization, they are assumed to prefer these jobs despite the low wages;[9] (2) female socialization trains them to display the attitudes of docility and compliance essential to the functioning of bureaucracies; and (3) because women are assumed to be ultimately supported by men, employers think they will not resist being shunted into or out of the economy according to its boom and bust cycle. The latter is particularly detrimental to black women, since a considerable proportion of them are the sole or major suppliers of family income.

What is interesting about most female-dominated jobs is that they increasingly demand two credentials that are more difficult for black women than white to attain. One is a relatively high level of education, at least a high-school diploma. The other is the facility to read, write, and communicate verbally in mainstream English. Although it is not readily acknowledged, jobs such as telephone operator, typist, and secretary, commonly require an ability to use the language of white middle-class society. Because of their subcultural status and the low quality of education they receive, black women historically have been at a distinct disadvantage in manipulating the cultural symbols of the larger society. Thus, the deprecatory societal evaluation of black linguistic patterns and the institutional racism of the nation's educational system have worked to black women's disadvantage in the competition between black and white female workers for clerical jobs. In 1987 the proportions of black and white working women in administrative-support and clerical jobs were 26.4 and 29.5 percent respectively.[10] Nonetheless, the rapid infiltration of black women into the clerical sphere in recent years seems to indicate that the discrimination against black women holding clerical jobs is declining. Whether they are actually achieving total equality with white women in this sphere, or whether white women hold relatively more prestigious jobs, is a question that needs further investigation. What is clear is that the wage levels of black and white women workers have now almost completely converged.

Although black men are also victims of white ethnocentrism and poor education, their chances of earning higher pay than do black women are enhanced as racial barriers fall, because many high-paying male occupations —e.g., in craft unions, municipal services, and the military—do not place such demand on the communication skills that are the sine qua non for advancement in clerical jobs. Indeed, the military offers many black men the chance of making up the deficiencies they incurred in the nation's educational system, as well as the opportunity to gain significant social benefits that are, for many, the route to upward occupational mobility. The continued sexual stereotyping of positions in those areas that have belatedly opened up to blacks reduces the chances for black women to move out of the traditionally female, clerical jobs. Thus, the erosion of racial barriers in employment is working more to the advantage of black men than black women.[11]

It is important to recognize this point, because it contradicts the commonly held view that the black woman fares infinitely better in American society than does the black man. Those who advance this claim generally rest their arguments on two facts. First, a greater proportion of black women than men hold jobs that are designated *professional* in the Bureau of the Census classification schema, and, second, historically, black women were more likely to have graduated from high school and college than black men.

Yet is must be recognized that black women have never held high-status professional jobs in any great numbers. This is because, even in the professional occupational category, rigid sex segregation persists. Black women are able to find relatively easy access to such female occupations as nursing and teaching, but have a hard time, particularly in comparison to black men, gaining access to higher-status occupations such as law, medicine, and dentistry.[12] The latter are just as much male fields among blacks as among whites.

Black women's greater educational attainment is similarly misleading. First, in the society at large, women are more likely to have graduated from high school than are men, so that this is not an aberration among blacks. Moreover, although the number of black female college graduates has historically exceeded that of black male graduates,[13] this was not the case in all parts of the nation.[14] Since the advent of a whole gamut of minority programs designed to boost black college enrollment in the 1970s, black males have made strides in attaining a college education and are now 43.6 percent of all black students attending college.[15] Nor does attending college necessarily have the same impact on women as on men. A study of historically black colleges in the 1960s, containing half of all black college students, showed that the women significantly lowered their aspirations for professional achievement by the time they were seniors, whereas the men maintained or increased theirs.

> These black college-educated women appeared to be significantly limited by sexual constraints in their career aspirations. They consistently chose traditionally feminine occupations and very few planned to venture into occupations dominated by men. Even more significantly, perhaps, the women saw the "feminine" jobs they selected as having lower status and demanding less ability than the "masculine" occupations—a telling comment on how they viewed what they had to offer in the job world.[16]

The association of femaleness with a distinctive economic function transcends racial lines. This fact is often obscured by certain racial differences in female labor force participation, such as the higher unemployment rate of black women than of white women, as well as the tendency of black women to begin their careers in jobs lower in status, their greater expectations of working, and their tendency to value higher wages above job satisfaction.[17] Although these differences should not be underestimated, it is myopic to focus on them exclusively in assessing the black female condition. The observation by Gump and Rivers, based on an extensive review of the literature on black/white differences in labor force participation, is particularly poignant here:

> Much data has been presented portraying the black women as more likely to enter the labor force, more interested in doing so, more likely to work full-time and continuously, and more necessary to the financial welfare of her family.... While such facts suggest a woman much less constricted by the traditional role than her white counterpart, it is equally true that black women choose occupations traditional for women, are motivated perhaps more by a sense of responsibility than by achievement need, are much more traditional in their sex-role attitudes than are young white women, and to some extent seem burdened by the responsibility they carry.
>
> Thus it appears that black women have *not* escaped many of the constraints imposed upon white women, though they are free of some of them.... There are those who would assert too quickly the freedom of black women, and they must be reminded of her bondage.[18]

If there is much in the objective condition of black women that warrants the development of a black feminist consciousness, why have so many black women failed to recognize the patterns of sexism that directly impinge on their everyday lives? Why have they failed to address a social force that unremittingly thwarts their ability to compete on an equal basis in the society?

Five factors have contributed to this situation. The most formidable is that many black intellectuals and spokespeople have ignored the issue of sexism, largely because it has been viewed as a racially divisive issue. That is, a feminist consciousness has been regarded as a force that could generate internal conflict between black males and black females. It is this writer's firm conviction that, far from being a source of internecine conflict, a feminist consciousness would contribute to the welfare of the race in a variety of ways:

1. It would enable black men and women to attain a more accurate and deeper level of understanding of many of the social problems that are currently undermining the viability of the race. Such problems as the black male unemployment rate, the absence of the black male in the family, the large representation of black women among those on welfare, and the high black "illegitimacy" rate are just a few of the many social problems afflicting blacks that are, in part at least, attributable to the operation of sexism in our society.

2. Elimination of sexism on the interpersonal level within black culture would result in each sex developing its individual talents and capacities unhindered by societal definitions of appropriate sexual behavior, thus increasing the general pool of black abilities.

3. A feminist consciousness, in ridding black males and females of their socially conditioned anxieties concerning masculinity and feminity, would foster greater psychological well-being and thereby strengthen the interpersonal bonds that are constantly being eroded and loosened by the impact of interpersonal sexism.

A second factor that helps to explain the absence of feminist consciousness among black women is the ideology of racism. Racism is so ingrained in American culture, and so entrenched among many white women, that black females have been reluctant to admit that anything affecting the white female could also affect them. Indeed, many black women have tended to see all whites, regardless of sex, as sharing the same objective interest, and clearly the behavior of many white women vis-à-vis blacks has helped to validate this reaction.

A third factor is the message that emerged in the black social movement of the sixties. In one sense, this movement worked to the detriment of black women, because they were told in many different ways that the liberation of the black man was more important than was their own liberation. In fact, they were often given to believe that any attempt on their part to take an equal place with the black man in the movement would contribute to his emasculation.[19]

The idea of black matriarchy, another ideological ploy commonly introduced to academicians and policymakers, is a fourth factor that has suppressed the development of a feminist consciousness among black women. In a nutshell, this view holds that in their conjugal and parental relationships black women are more dominant than black men, and so black and white women relate to their mates in altogether different ways.[20] It is easy to see how this view of black women could be used by some to negate the fact of black female oppression: If the black woman were indeed found to be more dominant than is the black man, this could be construed as meaning that she is not dependent on him and thus not in need of liberation. In fact, scholarly exploration of the issue has revealed the idea of black matriarchy to be mythical and has shown that the relationship of black and white women to their mates is fundamentally similar. And even if a black matriarchy did exist, it would be fallacious to infer from this that the black woman is not sexually oppressed, for her subordination is a derivative of both her family-related role and her position in the productive sphere of the economy. Thus, single and married black women are both placed in positions of subservience whenever they seek employment. Both are subjected to the manipulative tactics that are used to keep all female laborers —white and black, married and unmarried—in a low economic state compared to male laborers.

What the participants in the debate on black matriarchy fail to recognize is the white bias of their viewpoints. Implicit in their arguments is the idea that any matriarchy is unnatural and deviant. To attach such a pejorative label to matriarchy, and to view the patriarchal form as a positive good or an index of normality, is to accept the normative standard of the larger white society. Given the role that the family plays in supporting and perpetuating existing unequal economic arrangements, it may be fitting for us to question whether it would not be in the best interests of blacks to work out familial relationships that deviate from the conventional patriarchal norm and approximate a more egalitarian pattern, thereby challenging the racial and sexual status quo.

A final factor that has inhibited the development of a feminist consciousness among women in American society in general, and black females in particular, has been the church. Biblical support for sexual inequality is as strong today as it ever was, and the Christian church has played a preeminent role in validating the patriarchal nature of Western culture.[21] This is as true in black churches as it is in white ones, although the role of black religion in enchaining black women has been little subject to discussion.[22] The persistence of patriarchal views in black churches is undoubtedly due in some measure to the fact that most of our noted black theologians are men. But a more important point is that it persists because of the deep religiosity of black people today and the fact that most black religions are basically Christian despite some deviations and modifications. For whatever reason, it is significant that the church is the most important social institution in the black community and the one in which black women (in contrast to black men) spend most of their time and energy. This dedication undoubtedly has contributed in no small part to the black female's passive acceptance of her subservient societal role. Even so-called black nationalist religions, which proffer a different view of the world and a substitute for the teachings of Christianity, have failed to come to terms with the subordination of black women in our society. Indeed, some have even adopted theological preachments designed to stultify the development of female talents and to push women yet further into the traditional servile roles of mother and wife.[23]

In sum, black women in America have been placed in a dependent position vis-à-vis men. The source of their dependence is dual: It originates in the role they have been socialized to play in the family and the discrimination they face when they seek remunerative employment outside the home. Because sexual dependence works to the detriment of the entire race —both male and female—all blacks, regardless of sex, need to recognize the way in which their behavior, be it familial, marital, occupational, or otherwise, is subject to social control. From this realization they need to develop alternative behavioral norms for themselves and socialization patterns for their offspring that will challenge the distribution of power in America.

The view that racism is the sole cause of black female subordination in America today exhibits a very simplistic view of the black female condition. The economic processes of the society subordinate different groups of workers in different ways, but always for the same end. Because white supremacy and male chauvinism are merely symptoms of the same economic imperatives, it is facile to argue that white pigmentation is the sine qua non for the attainment of power in America, that white women share the same objective interests as white men, and that white women thus have nothing in common with black women. Although whiteness may be a contributory condition for the attainment of social privilege, sex and socioeconomic status are contingent conditions. Because color, gender, and wealth are at the present time collective determinants of power and privilege in America, it is almost impossible to disentangle their individual effects. Thus, those who would assert that the elimination of one type of social discrimination should have priority over all others display a naive conceptualization of the nature of power in American society and the multifaceted character of social oppression.

ENDNOTES

1. Examples of literature supporting this perspective are Mae King, "Oppression and Power: The Unique Status of the Black Woman in the American Political System," *Social Science Quarterly* 56 (1975): 116–28; Linda La Rue, "The Black Movement and Women's Liberation," *Black Scholar* 1 (May 1970): 36–42; and Julia Mayo, "The New Black Feminism: A Minority Report," in *Contemporary Sexual Behavior: Critical Issues in the 1970s*, ed. Joseph Zubin and John Money (Baltimore: Johns Hopkins University Press, 1973), 175–86.

2. Notable exceptions are Barbara Sizemore, "Sexism and the Black Male," *Black Scholar* 4 (March/April 1973): 2–11; Aileen Hernandez, "Small Change for Black Women," *Ms.* 3 (August 1974): 16–18; Elizabeth Almquist, "Untangling the Effects of Race and Sex: The Disadvantaged Status of Black Women," *Social Science Quarterly* 56 (1975): 129–42; Charmeyne D. Nelson, "Myths about Black Women Workers in Modern America," *Black Scholar* 6 (March 1975): 11–15; and William A. Blakey, "Everybody Makes the Revolution: Some Thoughts on Racism and Sexism," *Civil Rights Digest* 6 (Spring 1974): 11–19.

3. Margaret Bentsen, "The Political Economy of Women's Liberation," *Monthly Review* 21 (September 1970); Juliet Mitchell, *Women's Estate* (New York: Random House, 1971), 99–158; Paul Baran and Paul Sweezy, *Monopoly Capital* (New York: Monthly Review Press, 1966); Gayle Rubin, "The Traffic in Women: Notes on the 'Political Economy' of Sex," in *Toward an Anthropology of Women,* ed. Rayna Reiter (New York: Monthly Review Press, 1975), 3; Jean Gardiner, "Women's Domestic Labor," *New Left Review* 89 (January/February 1975): 47–59; and Sheila Rowbotham, *Woman's Consciousness, Man's World* (Baltimore: Penguin, 1974).

4. See, among others, Harold Baron, "The Demand for Black Labor: Historical Notes on the Political Economy of Racism," *Radical America* 5 (March/April 1971): 1–46.

5. For further discussion of black sex-role socialization see, among others, Diane K. Lewis, "The Black Family: Socialization and Sex Roles," *Phylon* 34 (Fall 1975): 221–37; Carlfred Broderick, "Social Heterosexual Development among Urban Negroes and Whites," *Journal of Marriage and the Family* 27 (May 1965): 200–3; Alice R. Gold and M. Carol St. Ange, "Development of Sex-Role Stereotypes in Black and White Elementary Girls," *Developmental Psychology* 10 (May 1974): 461; and Boone E. Hammond and Joyce Ladner, "Socialization into Sexual Behavior in a Negro Slum Ghetto,"in *The Individual, Sex, and Society*, ed. Carlfred B. Broderick and Jesse Bernard (Baltimore: Johns Hopkins University Press, 1969), 41–52.

6. See Almquist's article for more data on this point.

7. See Blau and Winkler.

8. Ibid.

9. Edward A. Nicholson and Roger D. Roderick, *Correlates of Job Attitudes among Young Women* (Columbus: Ohio State University Research Foundation, 1973), 10.

10. *Employment and Earnings*, January 1988, 180.

11. Stuart H. Garfinkle, "Occupation of Women and Black Workers, 1962–74," *Monthly Labor Review* 98 (November 1975): 25–35.

12. Almquist, "Untangling the Effects of Race and Sex;" Marion Kilson, "Black Women in the Professions, 1890–1970." *Monthly Labor Review* 100 (May 1977): 38–41: and Diane Nilsen Westcott, "Blacks in the 1970s: Did They Scale the Job Ladder?" *Monthly Labor Review* 105 (June 1982): 29–38.

13. Women are 54.7 percent of all black college graduates. Bureau of Labor Statistics, unpublished data from the March 1987 Current Population Survey. Part of the reason for this is that until recently blacks were basically a rural people, and it is generally the case for farmer families to withdraw males from school to work the farm, but not females, since farming is considered to be a male occupation. For further discussion of how this has contributed to present-day disparities in black male and female occupational status, see E. Wilbur Bock, "Farmer's Daughter Effect: The Case of the Negro Female Professionals," *Phylon* (Spring 1969): 17–26.

14. Andrew Billingsley, *Black Families in White America* (Englewood Cliffs, NJ: Prentice-Hall, 1968), 79–82.

15. Bureau of Labor Statistics, unpublished data from the March 1987 Current Population Survey.

16. Patricia Gurin and Carolyn Gaylord, "Educational and Occupational Goals of Men and Women at Black Colleges," *Monthly Labor Review* 99 (June 1976): 13–14.

17. Patricia Cayo Sexton, *Women and Work*, Employment and Training Administration, R. & D. Monograph no. 46 (Washington, D.C.: Department of Labor, 1977). 15; and Joyce O. Beckett, "Working Wives: A Racial Comparison," *Social Work* 21 (November 1976): 463–71.

18. Janice Porter Gump and L. Wendell Rivers, *The Consideration of Race in Efforts to End Sex Bias* (Washington, D.C.: Department of Health, Education and Welfare, National Institute of Education 1973), 24–25.

19. Joyce A. Ladner, *Tomorrow's Tomorrow: The Black Woman* (Garden City, NY: Doubleday, 1971), 284; Robert Staples, *The Black Woman in America* (Chicago: Nelson Hall, 1975), 174–76; Janice Gump, "Comparative Analysis of Black Women's and White Women's Sex Role Attitudes," *Journal of Consulting and*

Clinical Psychology 43 (1975), 862–63; and Cellestine Ware, *Woman Power: The Movement for Women's Liberation* (New York: Tower Publications, 1970), 75–99.

20. S. Parker and R. J. Kleiner, "Social and Psychological Dimensions of Family Role Performance of the Negro Male," *Journal of Marriage and the Family* 31 (1969): 500–6; John H. Scanzoni, *The Black Family in Modern Society* (Boston: Allyn & Bacon, 1971); Katheryn Thomas Dietrich, "A Re-examination of the Myth of Black Matriarchy," *Journal of Marriage and the Family* 37 (May 1975): 367–74; H. H. Hyman and J. S. Reed, "Black Matriarchy Reconsidered: Evidence from Secondary Analysis of Sample Surveys," *Public Opinion Quarterly* 33 (1969): 346–54; Robert Staples, "The Myth of the Black Matriarchy," in *The Black Family,* ed. Robert Staples (Belmont, CA: Wadsworth, 1971), 149–59; Alan Berger and William Simon, "Black Families and the Moynihan Report: A Research Evaluation," *Social Problems* 33 (December 1974): 145–61.

21. Simone de Beauvoir, *The Second Sex* (New York: Vintage, 1974); Susan Bell, *Women, from the Greeks to the French Revolution* (Belmont, CA: Wadsworth, 1973); and Alan Cuming, "Women in Greek and Pauline Thought," *Journal of the History of Ideas* 34 (December 1973): 517–28.

22. Notable exceptions are Rosemary Reuther, "Crisis in Sex and Race: Black vs. Feminist Theology," *Christianity and Crisis* 34 (15 April 1974): 67–73; and Reuther, "Continuing the Discussion: A Further Look at Feminist Theology," *Christianity and Crisis* 34 (24 June 1974): 139–43.

23. Barbara Sizemore, "Sexism and the Black Male," *Black Scholar* 4 (March/April 1973): 2–11; and Harry Edwards, "Black Muslim and Negro Christian Family Relationships," *Journal of Marriage and the Family* 30 (November 1968): 604–11.

E. Frances White

E. Frances White's "Africa on My Mind: Gender, Counter Discourse and African American Nationalism" appeared in the Spring 1990 issue of *Journal of Women's History* and is one of the first essays written from a black feminist perspective that analyzes in a comprehensive manner black nationalist discourse. White is associate professor of history and black studies at Hampshire College. Her essay "Listening to the Voices of Black Feminism" (*Radical America,* 1984) discusses the evolution of her own "incipient feminism" which was fanned by her frustration with black nationalist movements in the 1960s. The essay also critiques several contemporary black feminists.

E. Frances White }

Africa on My Mind: Gender, Counterdiscourse, and African American Nationalism

Equality is false; it's the devil's concept. Our concept is complementarity. Complementarity means you complete or make perfect that which is imperfect.

The man has the right that does not destroy the collective needs of his family.

The woman has the two rights of consultation and then separation if she isn't getting what she should be getting.

—M. Ron Karenga, *The Quotable Karenga*

The African past lies camouflaged in the collective African American memory, transformed by the middle passage, sharecropping, industrialization, urbanization. Few material goods from Africa survived this difficult history, but Africans brought with them a memory of how social relations should be constructed that has affected African American culture to the present. Although the impact of these African roots are difficult to assess, few historians today deny the importance of this past to African American culture.

But the memories I seek to interrogate in this essay have little to do with "real" memories or actual traditions that African Americans have passed along through blood or even practices. Rather, I am concerned with the way African Americans in the late twentieth century construct and reconstruct collective political memories of African culture to build a cohesive group that can shield them from racist ideology and oppression. In particular it is the political memories of African gender relations and sexuality that act as models for African American social relations that will serve as this paper's focus.

Below I will focus on black nationalism as an oppositional strategy that both counters racism and constructs conservative utopian images of African

American life. I will pay close attention to the intertwined discussions on the relationship of the African past to present-day culture and to attempts to construct utopian and repressive gender relations. After situating my work theoretically in the next section, I return to an examination of Afrocentric paradigms that support nationalist discourse on gender and the African past. Finally I look at the emergence of a black feminist discourse that attempts to combine nationalist and feminist insights in a way that counters racism but tries to avoid sexist pitfalls.

Throughout the essay, I choose examples from across the range of nationalist thinking. Some of this writing is obviously narrow and sexist. Other works have influenced my thinking deeply and have made significant contributions to understanding African American women's lives. I argue, however, that all fail to confront the sexist models that ground an important part of their work. I imagine that my criticisms will be read by some as a dismissal of all Afrocentric thinking. Nothing could be further from my intentions. It is because I value the contributions of nationalists that I want to engage them seriously. Yet it is the kind of feminism that demands attention to internal community relations that leads me to interrogate this discourse even while acknowledging its ability to undermine racist paradigms. This kind of black feminism recognizes the dangers of criticizing internal relations in the face of racist attacks but also argues that we will fail to transform ourselves into a liberated community if we do not engage in dialogue on the difficult issues that confronts us.[1]

African American nationalists have taken the lead in resurrecting and inventing African models for the African diaspora in the United States. They recognize that dominant, negative images of Africa have justified black enslavement, segregation, and continuing impoverishment.[2] Accordingly, nationalists have always argued persuasively that African Americans deny their connections to Africa at the peril of allowing a racist subtext to circulate without serious challenge. At the same time, nationalists have recognized that counterattacks on negative portrayals of Africa stimulate political mobilization against racism in the United States. The consciously identified connections between African independence and the United States Civil Rights movements and, more recently, between youth rebellion in South Africa and campus unrest in the United States stand out as successful attempts to build a Pan-African consciousness.

The construction of Pan-African connections can have its problems, however. At times it depends on the search for a glorious African past while accepting dominant European notions of what that past should look like. As I have argued elsewhere,[3] proving that Africans created "civilizations" as sophisticated as those in Europe and the Near East has concerned nationalists too much.[4] In the process of elevating Egypt, for example, they have often accepted as uncivilized and even savage primitives the majority of Africans who lived in stateless societies, but whose past deserves respect for its complex relationship to the world around it.[5]

Perhaps more importantly, the nationalist or Afrocentric construction of a political memory attempts to set up standards of social relations that can be both liberating and confining. The quotation at the beginning of this essay by the "inventor" of Kwanza traditions, Ron Karenga, illustrates this point. Building off conservative concepts of "traditional" African gender relations before colonial rule, he argues that the collective needs of black families depend on women's complementary and unequal roles. As I shall make clear below, Karenga has significantly modified his sexist ideas about gender relations, but the ideology of complementarity and collective family needs continues to work against the liberation of black women.

In addition, many nationalists, both male and female, remain openly hostile to any feminist agenda. In a paper arguing that black people should turn to African polygamous and extended family forms to solve the "problem" of female-headed households, Larry Delano Coleman concludes:

> The "hyperliberated" black woman is in fact so much a man that she has no need for men, however wimpish they may be; and the "hyperemasculated" black man is so much a woman, that he has no need for women. May each group of these hyper-distorted persons find homosexual heaven among the whites, for the black race would be better served without them.[6]

Coleman defines "the race" in a way that excludes feminists, lesbians, and gay men from community support—a terrifying proposition in this age of resurgent racism.[7]

In advocating polygamous families, Nathan and Julia Hare, the influential editors of *Black Male/Female Relationships,* link homosexuality with betrayal of the race:

> Just as those black persons who disidentify with their race and long to alter their skin color and facial features to approximate that of the white race may be found to suffer a racial identity crisis, the homosexual individual who disidentifies with his/her biological body to the point of subjecting to the surgery of sex-change operations similarly suffers a gender identity confusion, to say the least.[8]

Both the Hares' and Coleman's standards of appropriate gender relations depends on a misguided notion of African culture in the era before "the fall"—that is, before European domination distorted African traditions. These nationalists have idealized polygamous and extended families in a way that stresses both cooperation among women and male support of wives but ignores cross-generational conflict and intrafamily rivalry also common in extended, polygamous families. They have invented an African past to suit their conservative agenda on gender and sexuality.

In making appeals to conservative notions of appropriate gender behavior, African American nationalists reveal their ideological ties to other nationalist movements, including European and Euro-American bourgeois nationalists over the past 200 years. These parallels exist despite the different class and power bases of these movements. European and Euro-American nationalists turned to the ideology of respectability to help them impose the bourgeois manners and morals that attempted to control sexual behavior and gender relations. This ideology helped the bourgeoisie create a "private sphere" that included family life, sexual relations, and leisure time. Respectability set standards of proper behavior at the same time that it constructed the very notion of private life. Nationalism and respectability intertwined as the middle class used the nation-state to impose its notions of the private sphere's proper order on the upper and lower classes. Through state-run institutions, such as schools, prisons, and census bureaus, the bourgeoisie disciplined people and collected the necessary information to identify and control them.[9]

Often African Americans have served as a model of abnormality against which nationalism in the United States was constructed. White bourgeois nationalism has often portrayed African Americans as if they threatened respectability. Specifically, white nationalists have described both black men and women as hypersexual. Moreover, black family life has consistently served as a model of abnormality for the construction of the ideal family life. Black families were matriarchal when white families should have been male-dominated. Now they are said to be female-headed when the ideal has become an equal heterosexual pair.[10]

As I have suggested, black people have developed African American nationalism as an oppositional discourse to counter such racist images. Ironically, though not surprisingly, this nationalism draws on the ideology of respectability to develop a cohesive political movement. The African American ideology of respectability does not always share the same moral code with western nationalism. Some Afrocentric thinkers, such as Larry Coleman, turn to Africa for models of gender relations and call for polygamy as an appropriate form of marriage between black men and women. More crucially, black nationalists did not and cannot call on state power to enforce their norms. Their opposition to abortion carries very different weight from the campaign of the Christian right, whose agenda includes making a bid for control of state institutions.

It is this lack of access to state power and African American nationalists' advocacy of an oppressed people that gives Afrocentric ideology its progressive, radical edge and ultimately distinguishes it from European and Euro-American bourgeois nationalism. Paradoxically then, Afrocentric ideology can be radical and progressive in relation to white racism and conservative and repressive in relation to the internal organization of the black community. Clearly, nationalists struggle in a way that can deeply threaten white racism. Both the open repression and the ideological backlash against nationalists indicate that their discourse strikes at the heart of black oppression. Yet I often find too narrow black nationalist efforts to define what the community or nation should be. In particular many nationalists attempt to construct sexist and heterosexist ideal models for appropriate behavior.

THE DIALECTICS OF DISCURSIVE STRUGGLE

How does one prove strength in oppression without overstating the case, diluting criticism of the system and absolving the oppressor in the process? Likewise, the parallel dilemma is how does one critique the system and state of things without contributing to the victimology school, which thrives on litanies of lost battles and casualty lists, while omitting victories and strengths and the possibilities for change inherent in both black people and society? [11]

Karenga has identified a key dilemma facing black scholarship: how do black scholars take into account the possibilities of liberation at the same time that they balance a sense of strength against the realities of victimization? One strategy for moving beyond this dilemma to what Karenga calls an "emancipatory Black science" is to examine the ideological battles in which black people engage, exploring both the racist discourse that they struggle against and the oppositional language constructed in the process of this struggle. As a site of ideological battles, discourses intertwine with the material conditions of our lives. They help organize our social existence and social reproduction through the production of signs and practices that give meaning to our lives.[12] Closely tied to the socioeconomic and political institutions that enable oppressive relations, discourses are often reflected in a variety of forms. For example, the dominant discourse on Africa includes multilayered interventions that are knitted together from scholarly literature, fiction, art, movies, television, media, travel books, government documents, folklore, jokes, and more. The discourse that relies on these interventions creates an image of Africa that reinforces the continent's subordinate power relations to the West. Dominant discursive practice depends on more than lies and myths, although misrepresentation and deception do have roles to play in its strategy. Instead, the West's will to knowledge about Africa has been inextricably bound up with imperialist relations.

It is impossible for people's thoughts on Africa to be unencumbered by this discourse. None of us—not even Africans—can come to the study of Africa without being influenced by its negative image. Accordingly, dominant discourse attempts to blind both the oppressor and the oppressed by setting up smokescreens between people and reality. As Said argues for the Middle East, "... for a European or American studying the Orient there can be no disclaiming the main circumstance of his actuality: that he comes up against the Orient as a European or American first, as an individual second."[13] One way that dominant discourse sets up a smokescreen is to make arbitrary categories appear natural and normal. For example, it makes us think that race is a natural category by taking minor biological differences and infusing them with deep symbolic meanings that affect all our lives. Race, then, is a social construction that feels real to us and has significant consequences....

The very nature of dominant discourse leads it to be contested by subordinate groups whose daily experiences help penetrate and demystify its hegemony.[14] This "dialectic of discursive struggle" reveals the vulnerabilities of hegemonies.[15] As part of the same dialectic, counterdiscourses operate on the same ground as dominant ideology. Scott argues:

> The crucial point is rather that the very process of attempting to legitimate a social order by idealizing it always provides its subjects with the means, the symbolic tools, the very ideas for a critique that operates entirely within the hegemony. For most purposes, then, it is not at all necessary for subordinate classes to set foot outside the confines of the ruling ideals in order to formulate a critique of power.[16]...

The writings of certain feminists of color reveal the Janus-faced nature of counterdiscourse as these women search for allies among the male-dominated nationalist and white-dominated feminist movements. For example, women of color offered challenges within the feminist movement that forced women to acknowledge the problems with an undifferentiated category, Woman. Many of these theorists highlighted the complexities of human identity in recognition of the reality that women have ethnic/race and class positions, inter alia, that interact with gender and sexuality to influence their lives. Accordingly, feminists of color pushed for a movement whose discursive practices opposed sexism and racism simultaneously[17] For example, Audre Lorde has asked, how does horizontal hostility keep women from ending their oppression? She argued that women need to celebrate their differences and use difference for creative dialogue[18] Outside a narrow band of bourgeois or separatist-feminists, few United States white feminists today write without giving at least token acknowledgment to Lorde's call to recognize difference.[19]

At the same time, women of color challenged their various ethnic communities to become conscious of sexism at home. Cherrie Moraga problematizes the meaning of home and community as she sensitively explores the way her education and light skin pushed her away from other Chicanos.

"I grew white," she acknowledged.[20] But she also stressed that her community forced her to leave home because of her feminism and lesbianism. feeling betrayed by a mother who accepted the ideology that males were better than females, she fled from those who told her, you are a traitor to your race if you do not put men first. She watched the rise of the Chicano nationalist movement, La Raza, alienated on the sidelines. Yet she found herself increasingly uncomfortable in her nearly all-white surroundings.

Ultimately, she concluded that to be critical of one's race is not to betray it. She joined with other Chicana feminists to turn around the traditional interpretation of Malinche's life, which traces the birth of the Mexican people to Malinche's betrayal of her people. Instead, Moraga and others expose a prior betrayal of Malinche, who had been sold into slavery by her own people.[21] By refusing to accept the terms of a Chicago nationalist movement that brands her a traitor because she publicly criticizes gender relations, Moraga demands a place for herself and other lesbians within Chicano communities.

It is not surprising that feminists such as Audre Lorde and Cherríe Moraga challenge both feminists and nationalist communities. As women with strong lesbian political consciences, they confront homophobia in nationalist movements. Locked in struggle against heterosexism in their own communities, it is very difficult for them to maintain an image of their communities as harmonious. Cheryl Clarke has specifically accused nationalists of increasing the level of homophobia in African American communities during the 1960s and 1970s. She argues persuasively that homophobia limits the political struggle of African Americans:

> The expression of homophobic sentiments, the threatening political postures assumed by black radicals and progressives of the nationalist/communist ilk, and the seeming lack of any willingness to understand the politics of gay and lesbian liberation collude with the dominant white male culture to repress not only gay men and lesbians, but also to repress a natural part of all human beings, namely the bisexual potential in us all. Homophobia divides black people as political allies, it cuts off political growth, stifles revolution, and perpetuates patriarchal domination.[22]

In *Reconstructing Womanhood,* Hazel Carby goes even further when she finds fault with some African American feminists for failing to recognize that even their writings form part of a multiaccented counterdiscourse. She cautions black feminist literary critics to be historically specific when they write about black women's fiction and to recognize competing interests among African American women. She asserts, "in these terms black and feminist cannot be absolute, transhistorical forms (or form) of identity."[23] Black feminists do not have an essential, biologically-based claim on understanding black women's experience since we are divided by class, region, and sexual orientation. Even we have multiple identities that create tensions and contradictions among us. We need not all agree nor need we all speak with one voice. As with all counterdiscourses, the assumption that there exists one essential victim suppresses internal power divisions. To Terdiman's "no discourse is ever a monologue," we should add, the site of counterdiscourse is itself contested terrain.

INVENTING AFRICAN TRADITION

The contemporary African American woman must recognize that, in keeping with her African heritage and legacy, her most important responsibilities are to the survival of the home, the family, and its children.[24]

It is out of the feminist tradition of challenging the oppositional discourses that are meaningful to women of color that I interrogate the significance of black nationalism for African American women's lives. Like Sylvia Yanagisako, "I treat tradition as a cultural construction whose meaning must be discovered in present words no less than past acts."[25] As I have suggested, the traditions revealed in nationalist discursive practices are Janus-faced—turned toward struggle with oppressive forces and contesting for dominance within black communities.

This discourse can be represented by Molefi Kete Asante's writings and the journal he edits, *Journal of Black Studies*. Asante recognizes the importance of developing a counterdiscourse within the privileged arena of academia and has consistently published a high quality journal. He is also responsible for developing the first Ph.D. program in African American studies at Temple University.

The focus of his work and his journal is an Afrocentric one because it places "Africans and the interest of Africa at the center of our approach to problem solving."[26] By African, he means both people from the African continent and its diaspora. Although he has collapsed the distinction between African Americans and Africans, he avoids the traps many nationalists fall into when they posit a simplistic, mystical connection between African and African Americans. Unlike earlier nationalists who appealed to a natural, essential element in African culture, he argues that culture "is the product of the material and human environment in which people live."[27] In an editor's note introducing a special issue of the *Journal of Black Studies,* "African Cultural Dimensions," he continues:

As editor I seek to promulgate the view that all culture is cognitive. The manifestations of culture are the artifacts, creative solutions, objects, and rituals that are created in response to nature. Thus, the manuscripts which have been scrupulously selected for this issue are intended to continue the drama of cultural discussion of African themes.[28]

Africans, he argues, have constructed a culture that stands in opposition to Eurocentric culture. He develops a convincing critique of a Eurocentric worldview. For Asante, Eurocentric culture is too materialistic, and the social science that has evolved from this culture in academe too often assumes an objective, universal approach that ultimately suffers from positivism. He argues that neither Marxism nor Freudianism escape from this shortcoming though he acknowledges that the Frankfurt School's criticisms of positivism has influenced his work.

According to Asante, the task for African Americans is to move beyond the Eurocentric idea to a place where transcultural, Afrocentric analysis becomes possible. He cautions against using a Eurocentric mode that accepts oppositional dichotomies as a reflection of the real world.[29] His critique of the positivist tendency to split mind and body is cogent. Unfortunately, his theory also relies on a false dichotomy. Essentially, his categories, Afrocentric and Eurocentric, form an untenable binary opposition: Europeans are materialistic while Africans are spiritual; Europeans abort life while Africans affirm it.

He is quite right to recognize the existence of a protest discourse that counters racist ideology. But he denies the way that these discourses are both multivocal and intertwined. As suggested above, the dialectic nature of discursive struggle requires that counter- and dominant discourses contest the same ideological ground.

This point can be better understood by examining the roots of Asante's Afrocentric thought. He consciously builds off Negritude and authenticity, philosophies devised explicitly to counter racist ideology and develop nationalist cohesion. V. Y. Mudimbe (1988) has exposed the nature of the binary opposition used by cultural nationalists of the 1930s and 1940s who explored their difference as blacks. Leopold Senghor and Aimé Césaire and other Francophone Africans and African Caribbeans relied on the spiritual/materialistic dichotomy. Turned on its head, this is the opposition used against Africans during the late nineteenth century. As many have pointed out, this reversal of paradigms owed much to the celebration of the "noble savage" by such interwar European writers as Jean-Paul Sartre. Ironically, Western anthropologists, whom nationalists often disparage, also took an active role in this ideological "flip." It was anthropologists such as Michel Griaule and Melville J. Herskovits who revealed to Western-educated intellectuals the internal coherence of African systems of thought.[30] Equally important was the cross-fertilization of ideas between Africans, African Caribbeans, and African Americans. As a result of these three influences, "African experiences, attitudes, and mentalities became mirrors of a spiritual and cultural richness."[31] Far from cultureless savages, Africans had built the essence of spiritual culture.

This reversal of the racist paradigms on Africa accompanied and contributed to the growth of the nationalist movements that ultimately freed the continent from formal colonial rule. The nature of African independence reflects the double-edged character of this nationalism. On the one hand, nationalism helped build the political coherence necessary to threaten European rule; on the other hand, it obscured class and gender divisions in a way that prevented them from being addressed fairly. Clearly, this nationalism shared much with a European brand of nationalism that envisioned a culture unequally divided along gender and class lines.

Similarly, Asante does little to take us beyond the positivism that he criticizes, and his schema assumes a universality as broad as the Eurocentric discourse he shuns. Moreover, the Afrocentric ideology he uses depends on an image of black people as having a culture that has little or nothing to do with white culture. This is one of its major contradictions. On the one hand, nationalists like Asante have to prove to African Americans that Afrocentric ways are different from and better than Euro-American ways. Nationalists try to convince black people that they should begin to live their lives by this Afrocentric ideology. For example, some nationalists argue that African Americans should turn away from materialism to focus on the spiritual needs of the black community. Yet on the other hand, Asante and others argue that black culture is already based on an Afrocentric worldview that distinguishes it from Euro-American culture. Rather than being an ideology that African Americans must turn to, Afrocentric thought becomes inherent in black culture, and black people already live by these ways in opposition to dominant culture.

I would argue instead that African American culture constantly interacts with dominant culture. Of course, black people do have their own ways not only because they protect themselves from penetration by white culture but also because they are creative. Nonetheless, blacks and whites all live together in the same society, and culture flows in both directions. Like the dominant culture, most African Americans believe that spirituality has a higher value than materialism at the same time that most of these people pursue material goals. If materialism were not considered crass by dominant society, Afrocentric critique would have little value. It is also important to note the extent to which white culture is influenced by African Americans. At an obvious level, we see black influence on white music with the most recent appearance of rap music on television and radio commercials. At a less obvious level, Afrocentric critiques compel hegemonic forces to work at covering the reality of racist relations. Far from being an ideology that has no relationship to Eurocentric thought, nationalist ideology is dialectically related to it.

What I find most disturbing about Asante's work is his decision to collapse differences among black people into a false unity that only a simplistic binary opposition would allow. The focus on similarities between

Africans and African Americans at the expense of recognizing historical differences can only lead to a crisis once differences are inevitably revealed. Moreover, his binary opposition cannot account for differences among Africans. Many eloquent African writers have warned us about the problems that came from accepting a false unity during the decolonization phase that has led to the transfer of local power from an expatriate elite to an indigenous one. Ngugi wa Thiongo, Sembene Ousmane, and Chinua Achebe would all warn us against such pitfalls.

And, of course, we cannot face sexism with this false unity, as Buchi Emecheta, Sembene Ousmane, and Mariama Bâ movingly show. Asante does tell us that along with the move beyond the Eurocentric idea, we can develop a post-male ideology as we unlock creative human potential."[32] Yet he has nothing more to say about gender in the entire book. It is hard to believe that this gesture toward black feminists needs to be taken seriously. It is to other Afrocentric thinkers that we must turn to understand more clearly what this discourse has to say about women.

Among the most important nationalists the *Journal of Black Studies* publishes is Ron Karenga, the founder of *Us*. Some readers will remember him for his leadership role among cultural nationalists in ideological battles against the Black Panthers in the 1960s and 1970s and for this pamphlet, *The Quotable Ron Karenga*. In *Black Awakening in Capitalist America,* Robert Allen quoted a critical excerpt from Karenga's book, exposing its position on women and influencing many young black women (including myself) to turn away from this nationalist position.[33]

Perhaps the key word in Karenga's early analysis of utopian gender relations is complementarity. In this theory, women should complement male roles and, therefore, share the responsibilities of nation building. Of course, in this formulation, complementary did not mean equal. Instead, men and women were to have separate tasks and unequal power. Indeed, in much of Africa today, women give more to men than they get in return in their complementary labor exchange. This is not to suggest that African women are only victims in their societies; nonetheless, sexism based on a complementary model severely limits the possibilities of many women's lives.

It is important to note that Karenga has reformed his position on women. Apparently, he used the time he spent in jail during the 1970s effectively by spending much of his time studying. It is from his jail cell that he published influential pieces in *Black Scholar* and the *Journal of Black Studies*. He began to articulate more clearly a critique of hegemonic culture, showing the impact of reading Lukacs, Gramsci, Cabral, and Touré. And though he does not say so explicitly, he begins to respond to black feminist critics of his work. Indeed, I find the change in his position on women impressive. Although he remains mired in heterosexist assumptions and never acknowledges his change of heart, he drops his explicit arguments supporting the subordination of women. The new Ron Karenga argues for equality in the heterosexual pair despite his continued hostility to feminists.[34]

Unfortunately, too few nationalists have made this transition with him. Male roles remain defined by conventional, antifeminist notions that fail to address the realities of black life. For example, articles in Nathan and Julia Hare's journal, *Black Male/Female Relationships,* consistently articulate such roles. Charlyn A. Harper-Bolton begins her contribution, "A Reconceptualization of the African American Woman" by examining "traditional African philosophy, the nature of the traditional African woman, and the African American slave woman."[35] She uses African tradition as her starting point because she assumes an essential connection between the African past and African American present:

> The contemporary African American woman carries within her very essence, within her very soul, the legacy that was bequeathed to her by the traditional African woman and the African American slave woman.[36]

She leaves unproblematic the African legacy to African Americans as she presents an ahistorical model of African belief systems that ignores the conflict and struggle over meaning so basic to the making of history. This model assumes a harmonious spirituality versus conflicting materialism dichotomy that grounds the work of Asante and her major sources, John Mbiti and Wade Nobles.[37]

It is a peculiarly Eurocentric approach that accepts conflict and competing interests in a Western context but not in an African one. Harper-Bolton never moves beyond the mistaken notion that Africans lived simply and harmoniously until the evil Europeans upset their happy life. Ironically, as I have been arguing, such an image of Africans living in static isolation from historical dynamics supports racist ideals and practices and conveniently overlooks the power dynamics that existed in precolonial Africa like anywhere else in the world. In addition, her model portrays African women as a monolithic and undifferentiated category with no competing interests, values, and conflicts. The power of older women over younger women that characterizes so many African cultures becomes idealized as a vision of the elders' wisdom in decision making. It accepts the view of age relations presented by more powerful older women whose hidden agenda often is to socialize girls into docile daughters and daughters-in-law.

When Harper-Bolton turns to the legacy of slave women for contemporary life she owes a large, but unacknowledged, debt to the social science literature on African survivals in African American culture. In particular, her work depends on the literature that explores the African roots of African American family patterns. Writers such as Gutman, Blassingame, and Kullikoff have attempted to build off Melville J. Herskovits's early work on African survivals. This literature has been crucial for forming our understanding of black women's roles during slavery with particular reference to the African roots of these roles.

Unfortunately, this literature also shares certain problems that have clouded our understanding of this African heritage. What concerns me most are the sources that these historians use to compare African and African American slave families. Two major sources have been used uncritically that are particularly problematic when studying African women's roles in the precolonial era. First, historians have relied on precolonial travellers' accounts written by Westerners exploring the African continent. These accounts are important sources to turn to—and I have used them myself. But they must be used with great care because it is precisely at the point of describing African women and gender relations that these accounts are most problematic. Often these travellers' debates over whether or not African women were beasts of burden and whether or not African women were sexually loose spoke to debates in Europe. Rosalind Coward has explored the obsession of eighteenth- and nineteenth-century Westerners with gender relations around the world, assuming as they did that these relations were a measure of civilization.[38] Needless to say, these travellers brought the sexist visions of their own society to bear on African gender relations, and, therefore, their writings must be used carefully.

But I am more troubled by the second major source used by historians looking for African legacies, that is, anthropological reports written between the 1930s and 1950s. My interest here is not in being a part of "anthropology bashing"—accusing it of being the most racist of the Western disciplines. (Historians, after all, did not believe that Africa even had a history; they rarely turned their attention to its study until the 1960s.) But the use of anthropological accounts in the study of African history is very troubling to me. Used uncritically, as they most often are, these accounts lead historians into the trap that assumes a static African culture. Anthropology can give us hints about the past; but given the dynamic cultures that I assume Africa had in the past, these hints must be treated carefully.

Moreover, there is a particular problem in the use of these accounts for understanding African women's history. Most of the reports relied on were written in the mid-twentieth century, a time when anthropologists and the colonial rulers for whom they worked were seeking to uncover "traditional" African social relations. They were responding to what they saw as a breakdown in these relations, leaving the African colonies more unruly and, most importantly, more unproductive than they hoped. Young men and young women ran off from the rural areas to towns, escaping the control of their elders. Divorce soared in many areas. The elders, too, were concerned with what they saw as a breakdown in their societies. Both elders and colonial rulers worried that young people made marriages without their elders' approval and then, finding that they had chosen partners with whom they were no longer compatible, the uncontrollable youth divorced without approval and made new, short-term marriages.

The anthropologists set out to find out what led to this "breakdown" and to discover the customary rules that they felt had restricted conflict in "traditional" Africa. Once again we see the concept of a harmonious Africa before colonial rule emerging. In his introduction to the seminal collection, *African Systems of Kinship and Marriage,* A. R. Radcliffe-Brown expressed this concern.

> African societies are undergoing revolutionary changes, as the result of European administrators, missions, and economic factors. In the past the stability of social order in African societies has depended much more on the kinship system than on anything else.... The anthropological observer is able to discover new strains and tensions, new kinds of conflict, as Professor [Meyer] Fortes has done for the Ashanti and Professor Daryll Forde shows for the Yakö.[39]

In part, Radcliffe-Brown and his coeditor, Daryll Forde, offered this set of essays as a guideline to colonial administrators so that the colonialists could counteract the destabilizing influences of Westernization. Such anthropologists obviously felt the need for a better understanding of people under colonial rule.

Not surprisingly, it was the male elders whom the anthropologists asked about these customary laws, not the junior women and men who now divorced at an increased rate. Martin Chanock points out in "Making Customary Law: Men, Women, and Courts in Colonial Northern Rhodesia" that customary law was developed out of this alliance between the colonial rulers and the elders' interests. Of course, African elders were unequal partners in this alliance. Yet since both elders and colonial rulers viewed the increasing rates of divorce and adultery as signs of moral decline, they collaborated to develop customary laws that controlled marriages. "For this purpose claims about custom were particularly well-suited as they provided the crucial and necessary legitimation for the control of sexual behavior."[40] Chanock shows the way customary laws in Northern Rhodesia represented increased concern with punishing women to keep them in control. Therefore, in many cases such as adultery, what got institutionalized as "tradition" or "custom" was more restrictive for women than in the past.

It is with this concern of maintaining male control over women and elders' control over their juniors that many anthropologists of the 1940s and 1950s explored "traditional" African culture. To read their sources into the past could lead us to very conservative notions of what African gender relations were about. Yet Harper-Bolton accepts these views uncritically when she presents as unproblematic a model of gender relations that fails to question women's allocation to a domestic life that merely complements male roles.[41] And, by extension, she buys into an antifeminist ideology. She warns that rejection of African tradition leads women into two directions that are antithetical to healthy developments in African American family life. In one direction, women can fall into loose sexual behavior by accepting Euro-American conceptions of woman and beauty. In the other direction, women become trapped in aggressiveness in the work place and rejection of motherhood. Harper-Bolton argues:

> What happened to this African American woman is that she accepted, on the one hand, the Euro-American definition of "woman" and attempts, on the other hand, to reject this definition by behaving in an opposite manner. Her behavior becomes devoid of an African sense of womanness. In her dual acceptance/rejection of the Euro-American definition of woman, this African American woman, in essence, becomes a "white man".[42]

CAN NATIONALISM AND FEMINISM MERGE?

Not all Afrocentric thinkers need be so blatantly antifeminist. Some African American women have attempted to combine nationalism and feminism. As black feminists have sought an independent identity from dominant white, bourgeois feminism, some have explicitly turned to Afrocentric ideology for their understanding of these gender relations. These efforts stressed that African American women grew up in families that had roots in African experiences and, therefore, were fundamentally different from the ones described by white feminists. Such arguments recognized the need to search for solutions to sexism in black families that are based on their own experiences and history.

One of the most successful attempts to rely on Afrocentric thinking comes from a newly evolving school of thought known as African women's diaspora studies. This school of thought is represented best by *Black Woman Cross-Culturally* edited by Filomina Chioma Steady and *Women in Africa and the African Diaspora,* edited by Rosalyn Terborg-Penn, Andrea Benton Rushing, and Sharon Harley and tries to reclaim the African past for African American women. These works have significantly raised the level of understanding of the connections among women in Africa and its diaspora. A number of the scholars published in these books have read extensively about black women around the world and have drawn bold comparisons. For them, women from Africa and the African diaspora are united by a history of "economic exploitation and marginalization manifested through slavery and colonization and . . . [in the contemporary period] through neocolonialism in the United States."[43] Influenced by nationalist impulses, they criticize much of the earlier literature on black women for using a white filter to understand African culture. Further, they persuasively argue that too often black women are presented as one-dimensional victims of patriarchy or racism.[44] Instead, these women use African feminist theory as described by Steady to remove this white filter on African American lives and to identify "the cosmology common to traditional African women who lived during the era of the slave trade" and who provided a common cultural source for all black women today.[45]

Steady is careful to point out that she does not want to romanticize African history as she acknowledges that tensions and conflicts existed in Africa as it did elsewhere. Unfortunately, none of these authors explores any of these tensions and conflicts, and, thus, they present an overwhelmingly harmonious picture. Nor do they clearly articulate the ways that they will unearth the cosmology of Africans living in the era of the Atlantic slave trade. Their footnotes do not reveal any sources on this cosmology that go beyond the problematic anthropological reports that give a male-biased view of the past.

While African women's diaspora studies take us a long way, they reveal some of the same shortcomings I have criticized in the nationalist writings of Asante and Harper-Bolton. These feminists accept the ideology of complementarity as if it signified equal. They rely on a notion of African culture that is based on biased anthropological reports of a static, ahistorical Africa. Finally, they construct a dichotomy between African feminism and Western feminism that depends on the Afrocentric spirituality/materialism dichotomy. Clearly, these women advocate women's equality, but they find it much easier to address racism in the women's movement than sexism in black liberation struggles. In their attempt to combine Afrocentric and feminist insights, they recognize the importance of nationalist discourse for countering the hegemonic ideology that seeks to confine African American lives. But I would go beyond the conservative agenda that nationalists have constructed and, thus, strengthen their advocacy of a feminist discourse.

In the fine special issue of *Signs* on women of color, Patricia Hill Collins has produced one of the most persuasive attempts to combine Afrocentric thought and feminism. In the tradition of Molefi Asante, she recognizes the need to struggle for increased space within the academy for African American scholars. Although she does not say so explicitly, I read her article in the light of the narrow-minded failure of many academic departments to take Afrocentric scholars seriously and to give African Americans tenure. In recognition of the serious work many women's studies programs must do to make their classrooms appeal to more than white middle-class students, she tries to sensitize feminists to the worldview that their black students may bring with them to classes but that may be at odds with narrow academic training.

She may have gone too far, however, when she tries to identify an essential black women's standpoint. For Collins, the black women's standpoint has evolved from the experiences of enduring and resisting oppression. Black feminist thought is interdependent with this standpoint as it formulates and rearticulates the distinctive, self-defined standpoint of African American women.[46] At the same time, black feminist theory intersects with Afrocentric and feminist thought.

For Collins, both Afrocentric and female values emerge out of concrete experience:

> Moreover, as a result of colonialism, imperialism, slavery, apartheid, and other systems of racial domination, blacks share a common experience of oppression. These similarities in material conditions have fostered shared Afrocentric values that permeate the family structure, religious institutions, culture, and community life of blacks in varying parts of Africa, the Caribbean, South America, and North America.[47]

Similarly:

> Women share a history of patriarchal oppression through the political economy of the material conditions of sexuality and reproduction. These shared material conditions are thought to transcend divisions among women created by race, social class, religion, sexual orientation, and ethnicity and to form the basis of a women's standpoint with its corresponding feminist consciousness and epistemology.[48]

Thus, the contours of Afrocentric feminist epistemology include black women's material conditions and a combination of Afrocentric and female values. Collins's Afrocentric feminist values shares much with the essentialist cultural feminism of Carol Gilligan, including the ethic of caring and the ethic of personal accountability.[49]

Collins builds from the black feminist insight that black women experience oppressions simultaneously. Unfortunately, she remains mired in a false dichotomy that limits the value of this insight. For example, while she recognizes the importance of discussing class, she is unable to keep class as a variable throughout her analysis. At times, she assumes that all white women are middle class and all black women are working class. She sets up working-class black women to comment on the lives of privileged white women:

> Elderly domestic Rosa Wakefield assesses how the standpoints of the powerful [white middle-class women] and those who serve them [poor black women] diverge: "If you eats these dinners and don't cook 'em, if you wears

these clothes and don't buy or iron them, then you might start thinking that the good fairy or some spirit did all that. . . . Blackfolks don't have no time to be thinking like that. . . . But when you don't have anything else to do, you can think like that. It's bad for your mind, though."[50]

Missing in such accounts is the position of middle-class black women and working-class white women. In Collins's view, all white women have class privilege, although she does recognize that some black women have obtained middle-class status. She admits that "African American women do not uniformly share an Afrocentric feminist epistemology since social class introduces variations among black women in seeing, valuing, and using Afrocentric feminist perspectives."[51] She even acknowledges that black women's experiences do not place them in a better position than anyone else to understand oppression.[52] Yet the quintessential black woman is one who has "experienced the greatest degree of convergence of race, class, and gender oppression. . . ."[53] Collins certainly does not raise the possibility that class differences may create tensions within the black sisterhood that she takes as unproblematic.

Ultimately, she falls prey to the positivist social science that she seeks to critique. She links positivist methodology to a Eurocentric masculinist knowledge-validation process that seeks to objectify and distance itself from the "objects" of study.[54] Like Asante, she recognizes many of the shortcomings with mainstream social science research such as the tendency to create false objectivity. Yet also like Asante, she falls into a positivist trap. In her case, she brings her readers back to the possibility of universal truths.

> Those black feminists who develop knowledge claims that both [Afrocentric and feminist] epistemologies can accommodate may have found a route to the elusive goal of generating so-called objective generalizations that can stand as universal truths.[55]

Like most positivists, she never asks, "whose universal truths are these anyway?" Collins's quest for universal truth will be doomed to failure as long as she accepts as unproblematic an Afrocentric sisterhood across class, time, and geography. Her truths depend on an Afrocentric ideology that suppresses differences among African Americans.

Like all oppositional discourses, the Afrocentric feminism of Collins, Steady, and Terhog-Penn have multisided struggles. They compete for ideological space against the dominant discourse on Africa, its diaspora, and within feminist and nationalist movements. The dialectics of discursive struggle links their work to dominant discourse and other competing oppositional voices. Both dominant and counterdiscourses occupy contested terrain. Afrocentric feminists may reveal an almost inescapable tendency in nationalist discourse that ties it to conservative agendas on gender and sexuality. At the same time, they reveal the strengths of nationalist ideology in its counterattack against racism.

ENDNOTES

1. See Cheryl Clarke, "The Failure to Transform: Homophobia in the Black Community," in *Home Girls: A Black Feminist Anthology,* ed. Barbara Smith (New York: Kitchen Table Press, 1983), 197–208; and Audre Lorde, *Sister Outsider: Essays and Speeches* (Trumansburg, NY: Crossing Press, 1984).

2. They only need point to the racist scientific theories that AIDS began in Central Africa from people who ate [subtext: had sex with] green monkeys to prove this point. Spread by the popular and scientific media, this theory appealed to a white culture that still believes that black sexuality is out of control and animalistic. The scientific evidence contributed to the racist subtext of the anti-AIDS hysteria. See Evelynn Hammonds, "Race, Sex, AIDS: The Construction of 'Other,' " *Radical America* 20, no. 6 (1986); and Evelynn Hammonds and Margaret Cerullo, "AIDS in Africa: The Western Imagination and the Dark Continent," *Radical America* 21, nos. 2–3 (1987).

3. E. Frances White, "Civilization Denied: Questions on *Black Athena,"* *Radical America* 18, nos. 2–3 (1987): 5.

4. See, for example, Cheikh Anta Diop, *The African Origins of Civilization: Myth or Reality,* trans. Mercer Cook (New York: Lawrence Hill, 1974).

5. Chancellor Williams, *The Destruction of African Civilization: Great Issues of a Race from 4500 B.C. to 200 A.D.* (Chicago: Third World Press, 1974).

6. Larry Delano Coleman, "Black Man/Black Woman: Can the Breach Be Healed?" *Nile Review* 2, no. 7: 6.

7. Cheryl Clarke, "The Failure to Transform," has raised similar objections in this thoughtful essay. She argues that leftist male intellectuals have helped to institutionalize homophobia in the black community. I refer to this essay in more detail below.

8. Nathan Hare and Julia Hare, "The Rise of Homosexuality and Other Diverse Alternatives," *Black Male/Female Relationships* 5 (1981): 10.

9. George Mosse, *Nationalism and Sexuality, Respectability and Abnormal Sexuality in Modern Europe* (New York: H. Fertig Publishers, 1985).

10. According to George Mosse, ibid., German nationalists label certain people as "outsiders" who did not live up to the norms set up by nationalism and respectability. By labeling homosexuals, prostitutes, Jews, etc. as perverts who lived outside the boundaries of acceptable behavior, nationalists helped build cohesion. Jewish men, for example, were said to epitomize all that was unmanly and unvirile. By contrast, a good, manly German looked suspiciously at Jewish men. Many of the newly evolving negative identities and classifications fused with the stereotypes of Jews. In this way the rise of National Socialism was inextricably tied to the increase in anti-Semitism.

11. Ron M. Karenga. *Introduction to Black Studies* (Los Angeles: Kawaida Publications, 1982), 213.

12. See Richard Terdiman, *Discourse/Counter-Discourse: The Theory and Practice of Symbolic Resistance in Nineteenth-Century France* (Ithaca: Cornell University Press, 1985).

13. Edward W. Said, *Orientalism* (New York: Vintage, 1978), 11.

14. See James C. Scott, *Weapons of the Weak: Everyday Forms of Peasant Resistance* (New Haven: Yale University Press, 1985). Scott, however, may underemphasize the extent to which people are influenced by dominant hegemonies.

15. Terdiman, *Discourse/Counter-Discourse,* 68.

16. Scott, *Weapons of the Weak,* 338.

17. For further exploration of these ideas, see E. Frances White, "Racisme et sexisme: La confrontation des féministes noires aux formes conjointes de l'oppression," *Les Temps Modernes* 42, no. 485 (December 1986): 173–84.

18. See Lorde, *Sister Outsider.*

19. For examples of white feminists who have been influenced by Audre Lorde's insights, see Barbara Johnson, *A World of Difference* (Baltimore and London: Johns Hopkins University Press, 1987); Teresa de Lauretis, "Feminist Studies/ Critical Studies: Issues, Terms and contexts," in *Feminist Studies/Critical Studies,* ed. T. de Lauretis (Bloomington: Indiana University Press, 1986), 1–19; and de Lauretis, *Technologies of Gender: Essays on Theory, Film, and Fiction* (Bloomington: Indiana University Press, 1987).

20. Cherríe Moraga, *Loving in the War Years: lo que nunca pasa por sus labios* (Boston: South End Press, 1983), 99.

21. See also Gloria Anzaldúa, *Borderlands/La Frontera: The New Mestiza* (San Francisco: Spinster/Aunt Lite, 1987); and Norma Alarcón, "Chicana's Feminist Literature: A Re-vision Through Malintzin or Malintzin: Putting Flesh Back on the Object," in *This Bridge Called My Back: Writings by Radical Women of Color,* ed. Cherríe Moraga and Gloria Anzladúa (Watertown, MA: Persephone Press, 1981), 182–90.

22. Clarke, "The Failure to Transform," 207.

23. Carby, *Reconstructing Womanhood,* 17.

24. Charlyn A. Harper-Bolton, "A Reconceptualization of the Black Woman," *Black Male/Female Relationships* 6 (1982): 42.

25. Sylvia Junko Yanagisako, *Transforming the Past: Traditions and Kinship Among Japanese Americans* (Stanford: Stanford University Press, 1985), 18.

26. Molefi Kete Asante, *The Afrocentric Idea* (Philadelphia: Temple University Press, 1987), 8, note 3.

27. Molefi Kete Asante, "Editor's Note," *Journal of Black Studies* 8, no. 2 (1977): 123.

28. Ibid., 123.

29. See Asante, *The Afrocentric Idea.*

30. V. Y. Mudimbe, *The Invention of Africa: Gnosis, Philosophy, and the Order of Knowledge* (Bloomington: Indiana University Press, 1985), 75–92.

31. Ibid., 89.

32. Asante, *Afrocentric Idea,* 8.

33. Allen, *Black Awakening in Capitalist America.*

34. See Karenga, *Introduction to Black Studies.*

35. Harper-Bolton, "A Reconceptualization of the Black Woman," 32.

36. Ibid., 40.

37. See John Mbiti, *African Religion and Philosophy* (Garden City, NY: Doubleday 1970) and Wade Nobles, "Africanity: Its Role in Black Families," *Black Scholar* 5, no. 9 (1974).

38. Rosalind Coward, *Patriarchal Precedents: Sexuality and Social Relations* (London: Routledge & Kegan Paul, 1983).

39. A. R. Radcliffe-Brown and Daryll Forde, *African Systems of Kinship and Marriage* (London: Oxford University Press, 1950), 84–85.

40. Martin Chanock, "Making Customary Law: Men, Women, and Courts in Colonial Northern Rhodesia," in *African Women and the Law: Historical Perspective,* ed. Margaret Jean Hay and Marcia Wright (Boston: Boston University Press, 1982).

41. See Harper-Bolton, "Reconceptualization of the Black Woman," 38.

42. Ibid., 41.

43. Filomina Chioma Steady, "African Feminism: A Worldwide Perspective," in *Women in Africa and the African Diaspora,* ed. Rosalyn Terborg-Penn, Andrea Rushing, and Sharon Harley (Washington, D.C.: Howard University Press, 1987).

44. Rosalyn Terborg-Penn, "African Feminism: A Theoretical Approach to the History of Women in the African Diaspora," in *Women in Africa and the African Diaspora,* 49.

45. Ibid., 49; see also Filomena Steady, "African Feminism," and Filomena Steady, "The Black Woman Cross-Culturally: An Overview," in *The Black Woman Cross-Culturally* (Cambridge: Schenkman, 1981), 7–48.

46. Patricia Hill Collins, "The Social Construction of Black Feminist Thought," *Signs: Journal of Women in Culture and Society* 14, no. 4 (1989): 750.

47. Ibid., 755.

48. Ibid.

49. See Carol Gilligan, *In a Different Voice* (Cambridge: Harvard University Press, 1982).

50. Collins, "Social Construction of Black Feminist Thought," 748–49.

51. Ibid., 758.

52. Ibid., 757.

53. Ibid., 758.

54. Ironically, she shows how difficult it is to separate out knowledge-validation processes when she argues that we have to use different techniques to study black women than to study the powerful at the same time that much of her analysis depends on the insights of white men such as Peter L. Berger and Thomas Luckmann, *The Social Construction of Reality* (New York: Doubleday, 1966).

55. Collins, "Social Construction of Black Feminist Thought," 773.

Barbara Ransby and Tracye Matthews

Barbara Ransby is a member of the department of history at De Paul University, Chicago, and is a community activist and cofounder of the Ella Baker-Nelson Mandela Center. She is completing a biography on the life and political thought of civil rights activist Ella Baker and guest editing a special issue of *Race and Class* on "Black Women: A Global View for the 21st Century." She is also one of the founders of the black feminist collective African American Women in Defense of Ourselves, which emerged in response to attacks on Anita Hill in 1991, when she accused Supreme Court justice nominee Clarence Thomas of having sexually harassed her a decade earlier.

Tracye Matthews, former director of the Ella Baker-Nelson Mandela Center, is completing a dissertation on the role of women in the Black Panther Party at the University of Michigan.

Ransby and Matthews are among a cadre of young black feminist scholars who are writing in the tradition of Anna Julia Cooper. Their essay, "Black Popular Culture and the Transcendence of Patriarchal Illusions," which appeared in a 1993 issue of *Race and Class,* is a much needed critique of the misogyny of some segments of black popular culture. It also analyzes black nationalist discourse as patriarchal and insensitive to gender.

Barbara Ransby and Tracye Matthews }

Black Popular Culture and the Transcendence of Patriarchal Illusions

Over the past decade in African American communities throughout the United States, there has been a visible resurgence of various forms of black cultural nationalism. This has partly occurred in response to some of the crises currently facing African Americans, and partly reflects the sense of frustration and desperation many people, especially black youth, feel about the prospects for our collective future, and their hunger for some hopeful alternative.

There are three major components of this resurgence which have triggered heated debates within the halls of academia and on the streets of black America. They are: first, the cultural and intellectual movement known as Afrocentrism; second, a growing interest in and commercialization of the memory of Malcolm X; and third, the provocative and popular lyrics of certain subgenres of rap music, which have emerged within the larger context of what is termed Hip Hop culture. All three of these trends share two characteristics: they all contain an oppositional edge, which offers respite from the oppressive realities of daily life in a hostile dominant culture. At the same time, however, each trend represents a very male-centered definition of the problems confronting the black community and proposes pseudosolutions that further marginalize and denigrate black women. A masculinized vision of black empowerment and liberation resonates through the literature on Afrocentrism, the lyrics of male rappers, and the symbolic imagined homogeneous black community, the class biases in the rhetoric of the Afrocentric behaviorists is obvious. This racialized class discourse is painfully similar to the racist and sexist theory of the black matriarchy promoted by Daniel P. Moynihan in the 1960s to explain the reputed cultural inferiority, that is pathology, of "the matriarchal Negro family." The solution, of course, is to celebrate and re-create artificially the "greatness" and "authenticity" of a mythical and generic ancient African family.

An important corollary to discussions of the breakdown of the black family is the cry for black male role models. The underlying assumption here is that we need strong black patriarchs to give moral direction to the floundering female-headed households that have destabilized the black community. This dialogue has been framed even more specifically within a discussion of the crisis of the black male. Clearly, there is a legitimate cause for concern and action to address the specific ways in which black men are victimized in our society. The statistics on black male incarceration, homicide, and unemployment are both frightening and familiar. Yet, aside from some weak and ineffectual calls for an end to racism and creation of jobs for black youth, many cultural nationalists emphasize the recognition and visibility of more black male role models, whether historical or contemporary, as the key to black community empowerment. The struggle is defined as one to reclaim and redefine black manhood. Ironically, this is also the point at which the politics and positions of some cultural nationalists, liberals, and right-wing conservatives seem to converge. Consistent with the view that the problem with black people is culturally based, and centered around an alleged crisis in black manhood, their arguments are again framed by the use of certain race-, class- and gender-coded terms that blame poor people for their own oppression. Personal characteristics such as low self-esteem, lack of self-awareness and pride and, most of all, lack of discipline are cited as the sources of many of the larger social problems confronting the black community, from drugs and gangs to teenage pregnancy.

In addition, the gendered nature of this discussion of the "problem with black people" becomes very obvious when one examines who is generally targeted, implicitly or explicitly, as its root cause. African American women, especially single mothers, are routinely vilified as the culprit. For example, regular attacks on our black women in the media, most often disguised as an attack on the admittedly inadequate welfare system, portray them as lazy, unfit mothers, members of a morally bankrupt underclass, who should be punished for their inability to sustain a middle-class family life-style on a subpoverty income. Programs are proposed and implemented that penalize black women and their children for the crime of being poor —for example, actions are being taken, at the local and national level, to make the surgical implant of the Norplant five-year contraceptive mandatory for women who receive welfare. In several states, funding restrictions have been imposed that will further impoverish women receiving public assistance by not affording women who have additional children any additional welfare benefits with which to feed and clothe the child. These women will have to stretch their meager allocations to accommodate the new family member or be forced to not have children. This type of anti-black woman victim blaming is echoed in the popular media—black and white—in some of the new black films being produced, such as on Malcolm X, in music lyrics, and in the theoretical debates about poverty.

MALCOLM X AND POPULAR CULTURE

Rap music and Malcolm X are two mainstays of popular black youth culture in the 1990s. Images of Malcolm are ubiquitous in African American communities from Harlem to South Central Los Angeles, and virtually every major city in between. In fact, the extensive commodification of Malcolm's profile and his quotes in the form of T-shirts, tennis shoes, posters, backpacks, baseball caps, and even underwear, is testimony to the ability of capitalism to exploit just about anything, including dead black revolutionaries. Similarly, the rap music industry, including rappers with explicitly political messages, has enjoyed considerable commercial success. But a careful scrutiny suggests that the more commercially successful artists are the ones whose music—like the pervasive images of Malcolm—has been sanitized and diluted, or at least sufficiently jumbled, as to be safe for mass consumption. (Even lyrical brews concocted with a distinctly militant flavor are frequently laced with enough counterproductive and counterrevolutionary messages, especially with regard to gender and the status of women, to dull their potentially radical edge.)

Just as rap artists have been labeled the "new black prophets," Malcolm has been crowned our "shining black prince," because both symbolize an uncompromising opposition to racism and cultural imperialism. Unfortunately, however, few critics have seriously interrogated the masculine imagery associated with these personas or the gender politics they represent. At a time when single black mothers are being ruthlessly maligned for contributing to the alleged moral decay of the larger black community, enter two types of black saviors, personified by Malcolm X, on the one hand, and rapper Ice Cube, on the other. Malcolm is the strong, powerful, dignified black patriarch standing at the head of his family, acting as protector and provider. Ice Cube, conversely, is, as he proudly proclaims in his recent album, "the pimp," an angry macho, oversexed character, who, above all, is not soft. He doesn't take insults from his enemies or back talk from his women. Thus, Malcolm is the redemptive black patriarch, and Ice Cube is the warrior black pimp. In all cultures, the authority of patriarchs and the power of pimps rests squarely on the backs of the women whom they control or exploit.

Discussions about the alleged breakdown of the black family and the need for strong African American male role models serve as an important backdrop to the resurgent interest in and celebration of Malcolm X. Spike Lee's *X,* which has, unfortunately, become the final word on Malcolm X for millions of Americans, is but an expensive Hollywood ending to a much longer period of reconstructing his memory. One of the many distortions and omissions surrounding the retrospective of Malcolm's life and times has been the conspicuous inattention to gender politics. Malcolm's own view of women, as well as the implications of a largely masculinized version of the black freedom movement, is uncritically accepted by many who invoke his memory.

In this revisionist reconstruction of the past, and especially in Lee's film, Malcolm has been amputated from the larger social and political context of the 1960s to stand on his own as representative of an entire movement and era. We rarely see the problematic dichotomy of Malcolm versus Martin anymore—even that has been glossed over in an attempt to give an essentialist veneer of "race" as thicker than "politics." What we are also left with is an erasure of the grassroots component of the Black Power and Civil Rights movements, especially the role of grassroots women organizers, who were the very backbone of groups like SNCC (the Student Nonviolent Coordinating Committee), MFDP (Mississippi Freedom Democratic Party) and, in a different way, the Black Panther Party. Organizers like Fannie Lou Hamer and Ella Baker have been literally "X'd" out of the popular— and, unfortunately, most academic—histories, African American youth and others are left with the disempowering misperception that only larger-than-life great men can make or change history, and that this process is an individual rather than a collective venture. The struggle for black liberation is thus equated solely with the struggle to redeem black manhood, and with individual triumph over adversities and indignities. Moreover, black manhood is redeemed by militant posturing heroes, not by the arduous and often unrewarding task of daily organizing and struggle. The deified persona of Malcolm X, a strong black male who overcame a life of poverty, immorality, and crime to become a critic of American injustice, a steadfast and manly defender of black people and a paragon of puritanical morality, fits neatly into this scenario. Thus, the prescription for solving the problems and dilemmas facing the African American community today is—add strong black men and stir.

This Hollywood image of Malcolm X readily lends itself to the current political agendas of the various and disparate groups who seek opportunistically to lay claim to his legacy—from Nation of Islam leader and former Malcolm adversary, Louis Farrakhan, to ultraconservative Supreme Court Justice Clarence Thomas. What has been created in popular culture, according to historian Robin D. G. Kelley, is a "Malcolm safe for democracy." While most portrayals of Malcolm, even twenty-second sound bites, display his incisive critique of racism, they systematically exclude any reference to his positions on other crucial issues such as imperialism, colonialism, capitalism, and, of course, gender. In one of the rare published critiques of

Malcolm's gender politics, black feminist sociologist Patricia Hill Collins argues that "masculinist assumptions pervade Malcolm X's thinking, and these beliefs, in turn, impoverished his version of black nationalism... [his] views on women reflected dominant views of white manhood and womanhood applied uncritically to the situation of African Americans."[1] In most accounts, however, Malcolm's patriarchal and sexist ideas, which regrettably remained static through most of his life, are either ignored, downplayed, or reinforced. For example, in the movie *X,* Betty Shabazz is portrayed uncritically as "the strong woman behind the great man." No mention is made of the fact that she left Malcolm after the birth of each of their five children, or of her subordinate status within the context of their male-headed family. Furthermore, no mention is made of Malcolm's own effort to grapple with and challenge the sexism that characterized most of his adult life. In a correspondence to his cousin-in-law, Hakim Jamal, in January 1965, Malcolm himself confronts this issue:

> I taught brothers not only to deal unintelligently with the devil or the white woman, but I also taught many brothers to spit acid at the sisters. They were kept in their places—you probably didn't notice this in action, but it is a fact. I taught these brothers to spit acid at the sisters. If the sisters decided a thing was wrong, they had to suffer it out. If the sister wanted to have her husband at home with her for the evening, I taught the brothers that the sisters were standing in their way; in the way of the Messenger, in the way of progress, in the way of God Himself. I did these things brother. I must undo them.[2]

Although Paul Lee, one of the few researchers who has attempted to address Malcolm's gender politics, was a consultant to Spike Lee (no relation) during the making of the movie, Spike opted to ignore this aspect of Paul Lee's insightful work. It did not fit, apparently, with the type of Malcolm the filmmaker was attempting to fabricate. The hero worship of Malcolm as great black father and the uncritical acceptance of his retrograde views on gender, a weakness that he himself recognized, is quite consistent with the new culture of poverty theorists, who blame African American people—women, in particular—for perpetuating our own oppression, and who propose strong male-dominated families as the solution.

RAP MUSIC AND HIP HOP CULTURE

While the celebration of Malcolm as a cult hero offers us a stifled and restricted ideal of black womanhood safely relegated to the footnotes of a self-consciously masculine text, many male rappers project a different, although equally problematic, set of gender roles. The Nation of Islam's position on male-female relationships, and one that Malcolm endorsed most of his life, suggests that black women should be "respected and protected," confined to a domestic sphere, and serve a subordinate role relative to their husbands. In contrast, a significant amount of the gender imagery in rap, especially in the subgenre of gangsta rap, simultaneously celebrates and condemns the kind of black woman who is presumably undeserving of either respect or protection, the bad girl, Jezebel, whore, bitch. The oversexed black woman who is only relevant to the extent that she serves as a source of male entertainment and pleasure. This prototype is described as a possession, a thing, like a car, jewelry, and clothes. And if she dares to overstep her bounds, assert her humanity, and demand something in return, she is characterized as a deserving recipient of violence. The imagery is graphically reinforced in the music videos and on stage, where back-up dancers gyrate, almost naked, and in some cases simulate sex acts. At the same time, they are taunted with insults and derogatory names by the male rappers. The women are usually smiling with welcoming approval at this abusive and degrading treatment. This is certainly not a liberatory vision, but one, sadly, quite consistent with the racist and sexist stereotypes we have endured for centuries. Moreover, it feeds directly into a public discourse in which the criminalization of poor black women is linked to their sexuality. For example, in the current debate about welfare reform, African American women have been scapegoated as the undeserving recipients of public aid because of their alleged sexual irresponsibility and immoral behavior.

The cultural and ideological assault upon black women not only helps to justify reactionary public policies that compromise the lives of poor black women and their children, it also helps to justify direct acts of physical violence. The real life case of Dee Barnes—the New York City talk show host who was publicly beaten into submission by rapper Dr. Dre in a Manhattan nightclub for allegedly making critical comments about him on the air—is one clear example of the relationship between art and real life. This incident illustrates the extent to which some male rappers actually believe and internalize the misogynist messages they put forth in song. The believability of Dr. Dre's recent public service announcement against battering is undermined by the lyrics of his new single, "Nothin But a Thang," in which he once again advocates "puttin' the slap down" on a ho that doesn't know her place.

At the same time, coexisting alongside these sexist lyrics are some that are very positive and progressive. Groups like Public Enemy and Arrested Development call for "revolution" and for "poor whites and blacks [to] bum rush the system." Furthermore, an alternative to the antiwoman messages of other artists is offered by rap groups like Digable Planets, Disposable Heroes of Hiphoprisy, and Arrested Development. A few songs actually identify fighting sexism as a priority for the black freedom movement. Still, while some of these groups consciously reject the verbal slander and sexual objectification of black women, most do not advocate total gender equality or feminist/womanist empowerment. Rather, a number of these artists idealize traditional nuclear families with strong patriarchal father figures as the ultimate salvation of the race. But, in addition, female rappers from Queen Latifah to M. C. Lyte and Salt 'n Peppa also speak in a different and distinct voice with regard to gender politics. Although these women rappers have been reluctant to criticize fellow rappers in public for fear that such criticism might fuel racist biases against the genre as a whole, they have created a counterdiscourse through their own music. For example, in her song, "The Evil that Men Do," Queen Latifah challenges white male patriarchal power and outlines the ways in which it targets poor black women, especially those trapped by the welfare system. This type of lyrical content not only offers an alternative to the sexism of many male rappers, but is an indirect challenge to their authority to articulate the black experience in exclusive male terms.

Many critics have had a difficult time reconciling the positive and progressive messages of rap with the often sexist and misogynist references to African American women. For example, how do we reconcile the call for reparations, the freeing of political prisoners, and self-defense against police brutality with slanderous references to black women as bitches, hoes, freaks, and sack chasers? On one level, the ability of some (not all) rap artists to merge the call for black empowerment with the call for black female subjugation seems like a glaring inconsistency, yet, on another level, it is not incongruous at all. In fact, this issue reflects the ongoing and long-standing contradictions of cultural nationalism with regard to gender and, by extension, the gender dilemma that the African American freedom movement has yet fully to address or resolve. As E. Frances White points out in her brilliant article on nationalism and gender, there is a precedent, in the cultural nationalist movements of the 1960s, for "an oppositional strategy that both counters racism and constructs conservative utopian images of African American life . . . (especially) utopian and repressive gender roles."[3] The reconciliation of sexism and antiracism is typical of a particular strain of cultural black nationalism. This vision of black struggle and empowerment equates black liberation with black male liberation only; uncritically accepts the dominant society's patriarchal model of gender and family relations; sees the sexual objectification and sexual manipulation of black women as a male prerogative; and defines political militancy as a part of some exclusive male domain.

These flawed and erroneous assumptions about gender and liberation provide a perfect rationale for the continued subjugation of black women, almost as a matter of principle. That is, if Black Power is defined as redeeming black manhood, and black manhood is defined uncritically as the right to be the patriarchal heads of black families, and the exclusive defenders of the black community, black women are, by definition, relegated to a marginal status. The point here is to suggest that the type of political radicalism defined by some male rap artists is not antithetical to their promotion of antiwomanist messages, but, rather, is quite consistent, and goes to the core of the contradictions and limitations of the political framework itself.

To paraphrase the radical intellectual and activist Ella Baker, even dissidents are products of the societies we seek to transform. That is, it is part of the dialectical nature of popular protest that groups and individuals can and do oppose certain modes of oppression, while they simultaneously reinforce others. Therefore, while rap artists express a just and righteous rage against the myriad of forces poised to undermine the survival of black men, it is often an undirected rage and one in which black women get caught in the crossfire of a war to defend black manhood. In essence, some rappers embrace a political vision that uncritically accepts and internalizes the dominant society's narrow and patriarchal definition of manhood, and then defines liberation as the extent to which black men meet those criteria: the acquisition of money, violent military conquest, and the successful subjugation of women as domestic and sexual servants. This is, ultimately, not a revolutionary praxis, but an assimilationist one dressed up in black face.

Criticism of the negative, particularly sexist, tendencies within rap has often met with a defensive response. While, on the one hand, some observers have romanticized rap music as the authentic and uncensored voice of black protest, other scholars and activists have been reluctant to criticize certain rap artists for fear of being perceived as divisive, or of "airing the dirty laundry" of the black community to a mixed audience. These reservations are not without merit. It is true that part of the attack on black musicians by censors of various brands reflects a racial double standard, which exempts racist rock groups and sexually explicit performers like Madonna. Nevertheless, this fact alone does not explain away or excuse the negative and abusive verbal assaults made upon black women.

By and large, critics have either tried to dismiss or ignore the sexual politics of rap music, or, in a few cases, attempted to legitimize the macho and misogynist stance of black male rappers as an affirmation of their manhood: on occasion, this has even been elevated to the level of a distinct mode of resistance. For example, without mentioning black women, critic Jon Michael Spencer describes the sexism of male rappers as an "insurrection of subjugated sexualities," citing Foucault, Fanon, and white fears of black male sexuality to underscore his point. He writes: "Male rappers, flaunting exaggerated perceptions of their sexual capacities, tease white fears of alleged black illicit sexualities...rap's insurgence of subjugated sexualities is radical because there is no secret, no confession, no self-interrogation."[4] What this critic fails to recognize is that the aggressive assertion of male sexuality does not get expressed in a social vacuum, but that the aggression has a target, and that target is black women. And since when has black male hypersexuality been insurrectionary relative to racist stereotypes of black sexuality? And since when has sexual violence against and manipulation of black women been of any concern to the dominant society? Rappers who promote misogynist images of women are aiming those attacks point blank at black women.* This is not a militant assertion of black manhood; it is a militant debasement of black womanhood and, by extension, black personhood. Moreover, the black community has a right to, and should, expect something from its native sons that it does not expect —and certainly has never gotten—from white entertainers: a recognition of the humanity of all black people, men and women.

The popularity of rap music, commercialized Afrocentrism, and what David Maurrasse has termed Malcolmania are all testimony to the legitimate rage and disaffection from American society that millions of black youth feel. These trends also evidence the inability of traditional, or even ostensibly radical or revolutionary, black leaders to offer a serious political program that channels that rage into constructive political strategies. Political weaknesses notwithstanding, the appeal of Malcolm X and the popularity of militant rappers do represent a limited form of resistance to racial oppression. Wearing the symbolic "X" or blasting the lyrics to "Fight the Power," while not the most effective political strategy and not without contradictions, do represent defiant statements of opposition against a system that has deemed them powerless, subhuman, and expendable. The obvious problem, of course, is that such a male-centered definition of oppression and liberation leaves out more than half of the African American population. The representation of those symbols in exclusively male form, the class bias and essentialism of Afrocentricity and, in the case of rap, the accompanying denigration of black women, dull the radical edge that these modes of cultural expression might otherwise represent. African American youth, male and female, are clearly searching for viable outlets for their pent-up, and potentially political, energy, anger, and creativity. This is, if nothing else, a hopeful sign and cause for optimism. Possibly the most profound political impact of both the celebration of Malcolm and the popularity of political rap has been to give legitimacy and international visibility to the rage and the humanity of a whole generation of disenfranchised black urban youth. Perhaps these searching young minds will find answers and political solutions, not on MTV or BET [Black Entertainment Television], or in the speeches of immortal prophets, but within themselves. It is

---

* The whole argument is painfully reminiscent of Eldridge Cleaver's misogynist assertion, twenty years ago, that rape is a political act, and Norman Mailer's contention that black men were more in touch with their sexuality than whites.

a complex journey from consciousness to the concrete politics of empowerment, and one that is, by definition, full of contradictions and detours. It is perhaps most important, individually and collectively, simply to stay on the right road, and to resist the temptation to gloss over and silence our contradictions. The words of the radical Trinidadian intellectual, C. L. R. James, are inspiring in this regard. He writes:

> A revolution is first and foremost a movement from the old to the new, and needs, above all, new words, new verses, new passwords—all the symbols in which ideas and feelings are made tangible. The mass creation and appropriation of what is needed is a revealing picture of a whole people on their journey into the modern world, sometimes pathetic, sometimes vastly comic, ranging from the sublime to the ridiculous, but always vibrant with the life that only a mass of ordinary people can give.[5]

ENDNOTES

1. Patricia Hill Collins, "Learning to Think for Ourselves," in *Malcolm X: In Our Image,* ed. J. Wood (New York, 1991), 74.

2. Paul Lee, "Malcolm X's Evolved Views on the Role of Women in Society" (manuscript, 1991).

3. E. Frances White, "Africa on My Mind: Gender Counter Discourse and African American Nationalism," *Journal of Women's History* (Spring 1990): 73.

4. Jon Michael Spencer, "Rhapsody in Black: Utopian Aspirations," *Theology Today* 48, no. 4 (1992).

5. C. L. R. James, in *Race Today* 6, no. 5 (1974): 144.

Alice Walker (1944–   )

Alice Walker, born in Eatonton, Georgia, helps to reclaim the creative legacy of black women in her landmark essay, "In Search of Our Mothers' Gardens," by celebrating the anonymous artists among us, like her mother, who gardened and quilted and made life more beautiful. A civil rights activist and teacher, Alice Walker taught the first course on black women writers, at Wellesley College in the 1970s. She has published five novels, two collections of short stories, five collections of poetry and two collections of essays. She also edited the first collection of writings on Zora Neale Hurston. Her most recent publication is *Warrior Marks* (with Pratibha Parmar), a narrative of her involvement with the making of a film on female genital mutilation.

Walker's counterdiscourse on "womanism" provided an alternative terminology for black feminists during a time when many women of color were raising angry voices about their marginalization or erasure within mainstream white feminist discourse. Her essay "In the Closet of the Soul" (*Living by the Word,* 1988) provides a counterargument to those angry voices within the black community, in particular, who raged against her Pulitzer Prize–winning novel, *The Color Purple* (1983), because of its alleged negative treatment of black men. It was originally a letter she wrote in 1986 in response to a question about her reaction to criticism of the character Mister. Walker is completing a collection of essays in response to *The Color Purple.*

Alice Walker }

In the Closet of the Soul

[At a reading of my work at the University of California at Davis in 1986 I met an African American couple, both of whom had African names. The wife asked for a copy of the poem to Winnie Mandela I had read, which I gave her. She then asked about my reaction to criticism of the character Mister in *The Color Purple*. She was very intense, beautiful, and genuine, and I wanted to give her an answer worthy of her inquiry. I wrote this essay, which I sent to her.]

.   .   .

Dear Mpinga,

You asked if I was shocked at the hostile reaction of some people, especially some black men, to the character of Mister in the book and more particularly in the movie *The Color Purple*. I believe I replied only half-jokingly that no, I was beyond shock. I was saddened by the response, disappointed certainly, but I have felt better as I've tried to put myself in the place of the men (and some women) and tried to understand the source of what appears to be in many a genuine confusion, yes (as you say), but also a genuine pain.

An early disappointment to me in some black men's response to my work—to *The Third Life of Grange Copeland* and *Meridian,* for instance—is their apparent inability to empathize with black women's suffering under sexism, their refusal even to acknowledge our struggles; indeed, there are many black men who appear unaware that sexism exists (or do not even know what it is), or that women are oppressed in virtually all cultures, and if they do recognize there is abuse, their tendency is to minimize it or to deflect attention from it to themselves. This is what happened, to a large extent, with the movie. A book and movie that urged us to look at the oppression of women and children by men (and, to a lesser degree, by women) became the opportunity by which many black men drew attention to themselves—not in an effort to rid themselves of the desire or tendency to oppress women and children, but, instead, to claim that inasmuch as a "negative" picture of them was presented to the world, they were, in fact, the ones *being* oppressed. The people responsible for the picture became, ironically, "outside agitators." We should just go back to the sickness we came from.

It has been black men (as well as black women and Native Americans) who have provided in this culture the most inspiring directions for every-one's freedom. As a daughter of these men I did not hear a double standard when they urged each person to struggle to be free, even if they intended to impart one. When Malcolm said, Freedom, by any means necessary, I thought I knew what he meant. When Martin said, Agitate nonviolently against unjust oppression, I assumed he also meant in the home, if that's where the oppression was. When Frederick Douglass talked about not expecting crops without first plowing up the ground, I felt he'd noticed the weeds in most of our backyards. It is nearly *crushing* to realize there was an assumption on *anyone's* part that black women would not fight injustice except when the foe was white.

I was saddened that, in their need to protect their egos from already well-known-to-be-hostile-and-indifferent white racists (who have made plain for centuries that how they treat us has little to do with the "positive" or "negative" image we present), many black men missed an opportunity to study the character of Mister, a character that I deeply love—not, obvi-ously, for his meanness, oppression of women, and general early boor-ishness, but because he went deeply enough into himself to find the courage to change. To grow.

It is a mistake to assume that Celie's "meekness" makes her a saint and Mister's brutality makes him a devil. The point is, neither of these people is healthy. They are, in fact, dreadfully ill, and they manifest their dis-ease according to their culturally derived sex roles and the bad experiences early impressed on their personalities. They proceed to grow, to change, to be-come whole, i.e., well, by becoming more like each other, but stopping short of taking on each other's illness. Celie becomes more self-interested and aggressive; Albert becomes more thoughtful and considerate of others.

At the root of the denial of easily observable and heavily documented sexist brutality in the black community—the assertion that black men don't act like Mister, and if they do, they're justified by the pressure they're under as black men in a white society—is our deep, painful refusal to accept the fact that we are not only the descendants of slaves, but we are also the descendants of slave *owners*. And that just as we have had to struggle to rid ourselves of slavish behavior, we must as ruthlessly eradicate any desire to be mistress or "master." I have not, by any means, read or even seen all the negative reviews of Mister's character and its implications for blacks in America. However, in the ones I have read, I've been struck by the absence of any analysis of who, in fact, Mister is. Nobody, no critic, that is, has asked this character, "Boy, who your peoples?"

In the novel and in the movie (even more so in the movie, because you can *see* what color people are), it is clear that Mister's father is part white; this is how Mister comes by his run-down plantation house. It belonged to his grandfather, a white man and a slave owner. Mister learns how to treat women and children from his father, Old Mister. Who did old Mister learn from? Well, from Old Master, his slave-owning father, who treated Old Mister's mother and old Mister (growing up) as slaves, *which they were.** Old Mister is so riddled with self-hatred, particularly of his black "part," the "slave" part (totally understandable, given his easily imagined suffering during a childhood among blacks and whites who despised each other), that he spends his life repudiating, denigrating, and attempting to dominate anyone blacker than himself, as is, unfortunately, his son. The contempt that Old Mister's father/owner exhibited for his black slave "woman" (Old Mister's mother) is reflected in Old Mister's description of Shug Avery, who, against all odds, Albert loves: "She black as tar, she nappy headed. She got legs like baseball bats." *This is a slave owner's description of a black woman.* But Albert's ability to genuinely love Shug, and find her irresistibly beautiful—black as she is—is a major sign of mother love, the possibility of health; and, since she in her blackness reflects him, an indication that he is at least capable of loving himself. No small feat.

We have been slaves *here* and we have been slaves *there.* Our white great-grandfathers abused and sold us *here,* and our black great-grandfathers abused and sold us *there.* This means—should mean—that we are free now. We don't owe them anything but our example of how not to be like them in that way. Slavery forced us to discontinue relating to each other as tribes: we were all in it together. Freedom should force us to stop relating as owner and owned. *If it doesn't, what has it all been for?* What the white racist thinks about us, about anything, is not as important as this question.

But crucial to our development, too, it seems to me, is an acceptance of our actual as opposed to our mythical selves. We are the mestizos of North America. We are black, yes, but we are "white," too, and we are red. To attempt to function as only one, when you are really two or three, leads, I believe, to psychic illness: "white" people have shown us the madness of that. (Imagine the psychic liberation of white people if they understood that

---

* This is not to imply that all sexist cruelty among black people was inherited from white slave owners. On the contrary, in the sections of *The Color Purple* that are set in Africa there is an exploration of the historical oppression of women that is endemic to many traditional African cultures and that continues today.

probably no one on the planet is genetically "white.") Regardless of who will or will not accept us, including perhaps, our "established" self, we must be completely (to the extent it is possible) who we are. And who we are becomes more obvious to us, I think, as we grow older and more open to the voices of suffering from our own souls.

For instance, I know about Old Mister's father—that he was a slave owner—because he was also my great-great-grandfather. But I didn't begin to *feel* him, *let* myself feel him, until I was in my late thirties. I discovered his very real presence in an odd way: I began to hear him pleading to be let in. I wrote a poem about this called "Family Of"*

> Sometimes I feel so bad
> I ask myself
> Who in the world
> Have I murdered?
>
> It is a Wasichu's voice
> That asks this question,
> Coming from nearly inside of me.
>
> It is asking to be let in, of course.
>
> I am here too! he shouts,
> Shaking his fist.
> Pay some attention to me!
>
> But if I let him in
> What a mess he'll make!
> Even now asking who
> He's murdered!
> Next he'll complain
> Because we don't keep a maid!
>
> He is murderous and lazy
> And I fear him,
> This small, white man;
> Who would be neither courteous
> Nor clean
> Without my help.
> By the hour I linger
> On his deficiencies
> And his unfortunate disposition,
> Keeping him sulking
> And kicking
> At the door.

---

* The poems in this essay are from *Horses Make a Landscape Look More Beautiful* by Alice Walker (San Diego: Harcourt Brace Jovanovich, 1984).

There is the mind that creates
Without loving, for instance,
The childish greed;
The boatloads and boatloads of tongues...

Besides, where would he fit
If I did let him in?
No sitting at round tables
For him!

I could be a liberal
And admit one of his children;
Or be a radical and permit two.
But it is *he* asking
To be let in, alas.

Our mothers learned to receive him occasionally,
Passing as Christ. But this did not help us much.
Or perhaps it made all the difference.

But there. He is bewildered
And tuckered out with the waiting.
He's giving up and going away.
Until the next time.

And murdered quite sufficiently, too, I think,
Until the next time.

I used to read this poem occasionally to my students, but stopped.
The young white men present always thought "This small, white man"
meant them, and that they were being "murdered" and excluded even
in the classroom; the black men and women seemed to think the same
thing, and that the "murder" was both literal and justified. They may
all have had a point, and the poem does work on that level. However,
the impetus for the poem came out of my struggle with my great-great-
grandfather, the slave owner and rapist (what *else* was he? I've often
racked my brains!) whom I had no intention of admitting into my self.
The more I heard him plead, like a damned soul, to be let into my
psyche (and it occurred to me that karmic justice being as exact as it is,
I might be the only one of his descendants in whom his voice still
exists), the more I denounced him as a white man, a killer, destroyer of
the planet, a Wasichu, naturally no part of me. Get lost, you old bastard,
is essentially what I said. Being a part of me already, however, he
couldn't.

I dreamed of him. My image of him at the time—and over a period of
years, and still—was of a small, white, *naked,* pale-eyed, pale-haired, oldish
white man. Weak-looking; weak, near-sighted eyes, weak limbs. Ineffec-

tual. Hard to imagine him raping anyone—but then, she, my great-great-grandmother, was only eleven.

That is what I learned from relatives when I began to ask questions about "this small, white man," wringing his hands and crying and begging outside my psyche (on his knobby knees) all alone. Already I had found my Indian great-great-grandmother, and she was safely smoking inside my heart.

It took the death of John Lennon to squeeze the old man through. John had been Irish, too (though born in Liverpool). And when he was murdered (and I *loved* him, "white" as he was, for there is no denying the beauty and greatness of his spirit), I felt the price we pay for closing anyone off. To cut anyone out of the psyche is to maim the personality; to suppress any part of the personality is to maim the soul.

And so, I opened the heart of my soul, and there, with the Africans, are the Indian great-great-grandmother and the old white child molester and rapist. Lately I have been urging him to enlarge his personality to include singing or making music on the fiddle. And to stop shouting!

But when I wrote a poem about the peaceful coming together racially, at last, of my psyche, a black male critic wrote the following:

. . . So as I receive Alice Walker's eleventh book (she has edited an additional one as well) and her fourth volume of poetry, I face my usual decision: Given my disdain for what she and her work represent, in too large a part, should I assess her work? I know I can count on having to cut through her whimpering, half-balanced neurosis and wonder how on earth to avoid an exercise in negativity. And, of course, all of this contemplation begins before I even open her latest book.

After I open it, the worst slaps at me almost before I can take another breath. Her poem-dedication reads:

for two who
slipped away
almost
entirely:
my "part" Cherokee
great-grandmother
Tallulah
(Grandmama Lula)
on my mother's side
about whom
only one
agreed-upon
thing
is known:
her hair was so long
she could sit on it;

and my white (Anglo-Irish?)
great-great-grandfather
on my father's side;
nameless
(Walker, perhaps?),
whose only remembered act
is that he raped
a child:
my great-great-grandmother,
who bore his son,
my great-grandfather,
when she was eleven . . .

So again, here we go with the old Negro refrain of: *me ain't really a nigger
. . . no, no . . . me really an injin;* and *let me point out the rapist in my bloodline
to you.* The Negro is the only species who goes around advertising he or she
was raped and has a rapist in his or her bloodline. It is the kind of twisted
pathology that black psychology is still trying to unravel.

Yet none of this can be taken lightly because Alice Walker is being pushed
by the liberal mainstream as *the* black writer in season—while they seek to
remove Toni Morrison—with her incessant searching for truth and healing
in black life—from that pedestal. But the truth is Mrs. Morrison won't go
for the bone of divide-and-conquer that the liberals especially like to see
black people gnawing at. One can see their dribble-laden glee when they can
find a black man who through his actions or words attacks a black woman
and vice versa. So, of course, they love Ms. Walker, lover of queer bourgeois
liberal affectations and deep-down hater of black.

These comments, by black poet and writer K. T. H. Cheatwood, appeared in a review of my collection of poems *Horses Make a Landscape Look
More Beautiful* in the *Richmond* (Virginia) *News Leader,* in the winter of
1984. Unfortunately, in quoting my poem-dedication to my white and
Indian ancestors, he left off the most important section:

Rest in peace.
The meaning of your lives
is still
unfolding.

Rest in peace.
In me
the meaning of your lives
is still
unfolding.

Rest in peace, in me.
The meaning of your lives
is still
unfolding.

Rest. In me
the meaning of your lives
is still
unfolding.

Rest. In peace
in me
the meaning
of our lives
is still
unfolding.

Mr. Cheatwood thinks, apparently, that I should be ashamed to mention, to "advertise," my great-great-grandmother's rape. He assumes an interest, on my part, in being other than black, of being "white." I, on the hand, feel it is my blackness (not my skin color so much as the culture that nurtured me) that causes me to open myself, acknowledge my soul and its varied components, take risks, affirm everyone I can find (for I, too, have been called everything but a child of God), and that inasmuch as my great-great-grandmother was forced to endure rape *and* the birth of a child she couldn't have wanted, as well, the least I *can* do is mention it. In truth, this is all the herstory of her that I know. But if I affirm *that,* then I can at least *imagine* what the rest of her life must have been like. And this, I believe, has some importance for us all.

We are the African and the trader. We are the Indian and the settler. we are the slaver and the enslaved. We are oppressor and oppressed. We are the women and we are the men. We are the children. The ancestors, black and white, who suffered during slavery—and I've come to believe they *all* did; you need only check your own soul to imagine how—grieve, I believe, when a black man oppresses women, and when a black woman or man mistreats a child. They've paid those dues. Surely they bought our gentleness toward each other with their pain.

So, these are my thoughts. Mpinga. I love that, though born in America, you have chosen an African name. I can remember when such an expression of psychic and cultural duality would have been but vaguely understood. But times change, and people do, too. Now such affirmations are almost routine. The infinite faith I have in people's ability to understand anything that makes sense has always been justified, finally, by their behavior. In my work and in myself I reflect black people, women *and* men, as I reflect others. One day even the most self-protective ones will look into the mirror I provide and not be afraid.

Your sister,
Alice

1986

POSTSCRIPT

In my response to Mpinga I did not touch on what I consider the egregious hypocrisy of many of the critics of the novel and the movie. In letters sent to the producers of the film while it was being shot (letters threatening picket lines, boycotts, and worse if the script was not submitted to them, prior to filming, for approval), members of the group Blacks Against Black Exploitation of Blacks in the Media made it clear that a primary concern of theirs was not merely the character of Mister, but a fear of the "exposure" of lesbianism "in the black community." One of the letters expressed the fear that, just as the use of cocaine skyrocketed in the black community after the showing of *Superfly,* a movie about a racially mixed, black-ghetto hustler, pimp, and dope dealer that many black audiences identified with in the seventies, lesbianism, apparently in their view another "plague," would race through the black community in the eighties. It was also stated that homosexuality was "subject to control" by the community, and that love between black women was okay as long as it wasn't publicly expressed. (This brought to mind the sentiment of white supremacists that they don't mind black people being free, as long as they confine their freedom to some other planet.)

If the concern of critics had sincerely been the depiction of the cruel black male character Mister, as played by Danny Glover (in a film that is, after all, about a black woman, whose struggle is precisely that of overcoming abuse by two particularly unsavory men), they were late in sounding the alarm. What of black actors, men and women, who play CIA agents? United States spies? Members of COINTELPRO? These characters are used to legitimize real organizations that are involved in assassinating our leaders and heroes around the world and destabilizing and destroying whole Third World *countries* besides. Yet, because they're middle class, speak Standard English, are never permitted to sleep with anybody at all, they are considered decent models for us to have.

In my opinion, it is not the depiction of the brutal behavior of a black male character that is the problem for the critics; after all, many of us have sat in packed theaters where black men have cheered (much as white racists have cheered at images depicting blacks being abused) when a black woman was being terrorized or beaten, or, as in one of Prince's films, thrown in a garbage dumpster. Rather, it is the behavior of the women characters that is objectionable; because whatever else is happening in the novel and the film (and as is true more and more in real life), women have their own agenda, and it does not include knuckling under to abusive men. Women loving women, and expressing it "publicly," if they so choose, is part and parcel of what freedom for women means, just as this is what it means for anyone else. If you are not free to express your love, you are a slave; and anyone who would demand that you enslave yourself by not freely expressing your love is a person with a slaveholder's mentality.

Rather than be glad that the ability to love has not been destroyed altogether in us, some critics complain about the "rightness" of its direction, hiding behind such shockingly transparent defenses as "but what will white people think of us?" Since "white people" are to a large extent responsible for so much of our worst behavior, which is really their behavior copied slavishly, it is an insult to black people's experience in America to make a pretense of caring what they think.

Much of the criticism leveled against me and my work by black men (and some women) has been delivered in arrogance ("I haven't read the book or seen the movie, but. . . ."), ignorance ("I don't think any black people back then had wallpaper. . . ."), bad faith ("I think the author just doesn't like black men; after all, she was married to a white one. . . ."), and without love.* In the end, this simple injustice will be an undeserved burden and worrisome puzzle to our children, our next generation of rebels and poets (dare they create from the heart? think with their own brain? make decisions that in a treacherous world inevitably involve risk or invite attack?), many of whom write to me frequently about both the film and the book and exhibit a generosity of heart and a tolerance of spirit sadly lacking in some of their parents.

---

* One shining example of criticism by a black man offered *with* love is the review of *The Color Purple*, the movie, by Carl Dix that appeared in the *Revolutionary Worker*. He expressed concern over the way so many of Celie's problems seemed to be solved by her receiving a house and business left to her by her father (who had been lynched when she was a child). He correctly argues that the inheritance of private property is not a viable solution in terms of the masses of poor people and wishes that this aspect of Celie's existence could have been more progressive. I understand this criticism and feel it does indeed project our thoughts forward into the realm of better solutions for the landless, jobless, and propertyless masses. However, I also feel that for Celie's time— the post–Reconstruction era in the South, whose hallmark was the dispossession of blacks—this solution was in fact progressive; it spoke eloquently of the foresight of her father in his attempt to provide for her in a society where black people's attempts to provide for their coming generations were brutally repressed.

Epilogue

Johnnetta B. Cole

"Sticks and stones may break my bones, but names will never hurt me." I remember well that childhood saying, a saying that, even as an adult, I have had more than one occasion to use. I think that my mother taught it to me when I was three years old, when for the first time that I was conscious of, I was called a "nigger." There is no confusion in my head about that incident when a little white boy called me that name; and perhaps it does not matter if my mother taught me that saying on that occasion or on some other. The point is that I, like all folks who are cast in the state of "the other," was told early on to stay there; and the message was delivered by many means, including name-calling. Declaring that "names will never hurt me" was just one of several defenses that I was taught to deal with being black and female in America.

What is the relevance of that childhood saying to this brief comment on Beverly Guy-Sheftall's collection of the writings of African American feminists? In the most obvious sense, it has everything to do with the long and ongoing struggle of African American women who have used multiple ways of saying (using another expression that I grew up with): "Don't be calling me out of my name." Or, put another way, I speak here of the struggle of we African American women to "name ourselves."

In offering an epilogue on this book, I turn our attention to the very title, which places together the terms "African American" and "feminist." In this pathbreaking collection of articles, Dr. Guy-Sheftall has taken us from the early 1830s to contemporary times. Only since the seventies have black women used the term "feminism." And yet, it is that concept that she uses to bring into the same frame the ideas and analyses of Maria Stewart, Sojourner Truth, and Frances E. W. Harper of the early nineteenth century, and the work of women such as the late Audre Lorde, Barbara Smith, and bell hooks, who stand on the threshold of the twenty-first century.

Once again, I think of that childhood saying in recalling that the word, the term, "feminism," is one that large numbers of African American women believe will hurt them. How often I hear a black woman say that she strongly believes in the equality of women and men, *but* she adds, she is not a feminist. At Spelman College, it is not uncommon for one of our students to speak of her deep commitment to a full professional life in which she is paid as well as any man who does a similar job. *But,* adds the young sister, I am not a feminist.

Why is it that among so many contemporary African American women there is a dread of being called feminist? It seems to me that it is not at all because of what a feminist perspective can do for black women, but because of what black women falsely assume that feminism will demand of them. Fueled by media misrepresentations and exaggerations of what feminism is and what feminists do, black women, and indeed many women of color, assume that in order to be a feminist, one must put the struggle against racism after the struggle against sexism. This notion of either/or, the assumption that you must choose only one form of oppression against which you will struggle, is neither necessary nor helpful. Racism, sexism—sometimes we African American women cannot clearly tell where one ends and the other begins. But given the multiple ways in which racism and sexism are "cut from the same cloth," we cannot afford to fight the oppressions to which we are subjected on only one front. I like to make the analogy that if both of your arms were tied behind your back as you prepared to swim, would you choose to have only one released?

Another factor, not totally unrelated, which continues to prevent the involvement of large numbers of black women in the feminist movement is the extent to which white women have not dealt with their racism. Black women argue that they cannot participate in a movement in which they are devalued because of their race. A corollary is when white women assume that their own realities of what it means to be a woman are the only realities in existence.

Surely the single most tenacious misconception about feminism is that to be a feminist is to hate men. Black women, like white women, know what it is to be the victim of male chauvinism, by black men as well as white men. But an enormous difference in the experiences of black and white women is that black women also witness countless ways in which their fathers, brothers, sons, husbands, lovers—indeed every black man they know, is also victimized by racism. And so African American women feel a bond with black men, which comes from being called that same name, from being denied access to similar opportunities, from so often receiving the poorest of what America has to offer in terms of jobs, education, health care, and housing.

And then there is the question of lesbianism. African American women are certainly not immune to the extensive presence of homophobia in

American society, and indeed with African American communities. With the media and certain fundamentalist groups still implying that feminism and lesbianism are synonymous, large numbers of women of every racial and ethnic group turn away from a movement that is in their interest because they assume it was created by, and is currently dominated by, lesbians.

With such resistance to being associated with feminism, what choices do African American women have, especially when the very issues that feminism addresses are not the exclusive possession of white women? White women do not have a monopoly on the issues of equal pay for equal work; of men sharing with women the responsibilities of nurturing children and "keeping house"; of women's being in charge of their own bodies and their reproductive powers; of bringing to an end the physical and sexual abuse of women. These are the issues of all of us women folks of all racial and ethnic groups, of every sexual orientation, of various ages and economic conditions, of women who are fully abled and those who are differently abled.

One response of African American women has been to insist on defining their struggle for gender equality through the use of words other than feminism. This is the approach taken by Alice Walker in using the word "womanist" and asserting that womanist is to purple as feminist is to lavender.

The alternative approach for black women who see the relevance to their lives of issues associated with the term feminism is the one Beverly Guy-Sheftall has taken in this volume. She has boldly and convincingly illustrated a long history of feminist thought among African American women. She has claimed the name. She has refused to cut off contemporary African American women from the long line of sisters who have righteously struggled for the liberation of African American women from the dual oppressions of racism and sexism. This is the extraordinary value of this book. It is the very first collection of readings on the evolution of black feminism in the United States.

As each African American woman brings closure on reading this volume, having felt the enormous courage, insight, and tenacity of early black feminists of the 1830s, down to the writings of sisters of these very days in which she lives, perhaps it will be possible for each to say, "Sticks and stones may break my bones, but names will never hurt me."

Selected
Bibliography

ALBERT, JUDITH CLAVIR and STEWART ALBERT, eds. *The Sixties Papers.* New York: Praegar, 1984.

ALBRECHT, LISA and ROSE M. BREWER. *Bridges of Power: Women's Multicultural Alliances.* Philadelphia: New Society Publishers, 1990.

ALLEN, ROBERT and PAMELA L. ALLEN. *Reluctant Reformers: The Impact of Racism on American Social Reform Movements.* Washington, D.C.: Howard University Press, 1974.

ALTBACH, HOSHINO. *From Feminism to Liberation.* Cambridge, Mass.: Schenkman, 1971.

ANDOLSEN, BARBARA HILKERT. *"Daughters of Jefferson, Daughters of Bootblacks": Racism and American Feminism.* Macon, Ga.: Mercer University Press, 1986.

ANDREWS, WILLIAM. *Sisters of the Spirit: Three Black Women's Autobiographies of the Nineteenth Century.* Bloomington: Indiana University Press, 1986.

APTHEKER, BETTINA. *Woman's Legacy: Essays on Race, Sex, and Class in American History.* Amherst: University of Massachusetts Press, 1982.

BABCOX, DEBORAH and MADELINE BELKIN, eds. *Liberation Now: The Writings of the Women's Liberation Movement.* New York: Dell, 1971.

BAIR, BARBARA and SUSAN E. CAYLEFF, eds. *Wings of Gauze: Women of Color and the Experience of Health and Illness.* Detroit: Wayne State University Press, 1993.

BAKER, HOUSTON A. JR. *Workings of the Spirit: The Poetics of Afro-American Women's Writing.* Chicago: University of Chicago Press, 1991.

BARTLETT, KATHARINE T. and ROSEANNE KENNEDY, eds. *Feminist Legal Theory: Readings in Law and Gender.* Boulder, Colo.: Westview Press, 1991.

BEALE, FRANCES. "Slave of a Slave No More." *Black Scholar* 6 (March 1975), 2–10.

BEAUVOIR, SIMONE DE. *The Second Sex.* New York: Knopf, 1953.

BELL, ROSEANN, BETTYE PARKER, and BEVERLY GUY-SHEFTALL, eds. *Sturdy Black Bridges: Visions of Black Women in Literature.* Garden City, N.Y.: Anchor, 1979.

BELL SCOTT, PATRICIA. *Life Notes: Personal Writings by Contemporary Black Women.* New York: W. W. Norton, 1994.

Birth Control Review (September 1919). Special Issue, "The Negroes' Need for Birth Control."

"Black Feminism: A New Mandate." *Ms.* (May 1974), 99.

"Black Scholar Interviews Kathleen Cleaver." *Black Scholar* 3 (December 1971), 54–59.

Black Scholar 10 (May/June 1979).

Black Scholar 16 (March/June 1985).

BLAIR, KAREN J. *The Clubwoman as Feminist: True Womanhood Redefined, 1868–1914.* New York: Holmes and Maier, 1980.

BLANSFORD, VIRGINIA. *Black Women and Liberation Movements.* Washington, D.C.: Institute for the Arts and Humanities, n.d.

BOBO, JACQUELINE and ELLEN SEITER. "Black Feminism and Media Criticism." *Screen 32* (Fall 1991), 286–302.

BONTEMPS, ARNA ALEXANDER, ed. *Forever Free: Art by African American Women, 1862–1980.* Alexandria, Va.: Stephenson, 1980.

BORIS, EILEEN. "The Power of Motherhood: Black and White Activist Women Redefine the 'Political.'" *Yale Journal of Law and Feminism* 2 (1989), 25–49.

BOURNE, JENNY. "Towards an Anti-Racist Feminism." *Race and Class* 25 (Summer 1983), 1–22.

BOYD, MELBA JOYCE. *Discarded Legacy: Politics and Poetics in the Life of Frances E. W. Harper, 1825–1911.* Detroit: Wayne State University Press, 1994.

BREEN, WILLIAM J. "Black Women and the Great War: Mobilization and Reform in the South." *Journal of Southern History* 44 (August 1978), 421–40.

BROUGHTON, VIRGINIA. *Twenty Years Experience of a Missionary.* Chicago: Pony Press Publishers, 1907.

BROWN, CYNTHIA STOKES, ed. *Ready From Within: Septima Clark and the Civil Rights Movement.* Navarro, Calif.: Wild Trees Press, 1986.

BROWN, ELAINE. *A Taste of Power: A Black Woman's Story.* New York: Pantheon, 1993.

BROWN, ELSA BARKLEY. "Womanist Consciousness: Maggie Lena Walker and the Independent Order of Saint Luke." *Signs* 14 (Spring 1989), 610–33.

———. "African-American Women's Quilting: A Framework for Conceptualizing and Teaching African-American Women's History." *Signs* 13 (1989), 921–29.

BROWN, HALLIE QUINN. *Homespun Heroines and Other Women of Distinction.* Xenia, Ohio: Aldine Printing House, 1926.

BROWN, IRA. "Racism and Sexism: The Case of Pennsylvania Hall." *Phylon* 37 (1976), 126–36.

BUCK, PEARL. *American Argument with Eslanda Goode Robeson.* New York: John Day, 1949.

BURROUGHS, NANNIE. "Minutes, the Women's Missionary Convention." *Journal of the Twentieth Annual Session of the National Baptist Convention Held in Richmond, Virginia, September 12–17, 1990.* Vol. 1. Nashville: National Baptist Publishing Board, 1990, 197.

———. "Not Color But Character." *Voice of the Negro* 1 (July 1904), 294–98.

CADE, TONI, ed. *The Black Woman: An Anthology.* New York: Signet, 1970.

CANNON, KATIE S. *Black Womanist Ethics.* Atlanta: Scholars Press, 1988.

———. "The Emergence of a Black Feminist Consciousness." *Feminist Interpretations of the Bible,* ed. Lett M. Russell. Philadelphia: Westminster Press, 1985.

CARAWAY, NANCIE. *Segregated Sisterhood: Racism and the Politics of American Feminism.* Knoxville: University of Tennessee Press, 1991.

CARBY, HAZEL. *Reconstructing Womanhood: The Emergence of the Afro-American Woman Novelist.* New York: Oxford University Press, 1987.

————. "It Jus Be's Dat Way Sometime: The Sexual Politics of Women's Blues," *Unequal Sisters,* ed. Ellen Carol Du Bois and Vicki L. Ruiz. New York: Routledge, 1990, 238–49.

————. " 'On the Threshold of Woman's Era': Lynching, Empire, and Sexuality in Black Feminist Theory." *Critical Inquiry* 12 (Autumn 1985), 262–77.

————. "White Woman Listen! Black Feminism and the Boundaries of Sisterhood." *The Empire Strikes Back: Race and Racism in '70's Britain.* London: Hutchinson and Company, 1982.

CARSON, CLAYBORNE. *In Struggle: SNCC and the Black Awakening of the 1960s.* Cambridge: Harvard University Press, 1981.

CHISOLM, SHIRLEY. "Race, Revolution and Women." *Black Scholar* 7 (December 1971), 17–21.

————. "Racism and Anti-Feminism." *Black Scholar* 1 (January/February 1970), 17–21.

————. *Unbought and Unbossed.* New York: Avon, 1970.

CHRISMAN, ROBERT and ROBERT L. ALLEN, eds. *Court of Appeal: The Black Community Speaks Out on the Racial and Sexual Politics of Clarence Thomas vs. Anita Hill.* New York: Ballantine Books, 1992.

CHRISTIAN, BARBARA. "A Race for Theory." *Cultural Critique* 6 (Spring 1987), 51–63.

————. *Black Feminist Criticism: Perspectives on Black Women Writers.* New York: Pergamon, 1985.

————. *Black Women Novelists.* Westport, Conn.: Greenwood Press, 1984.

CLARK, SEPTIMA POINSETTE. *Echo in My Soul.* New York: E. P. Dutton, 1962.

COLE, JOHNNETTA. *Conversations: Straight Talk with America's Sister President.* New York: Doubleday, 1993.

COLLIER-THOMAS, BETTYE. *Frances Ellen Watkins Harper: Abolitionist and Feminist Reformer.* Chapel Hill: University of North Carolina Press, forthcoming.

COLLINS, PATRICIA HILL. *Black Feminist Thought: Knowledge, Consciousness, and the Politics of Empowerment.* Boston: Unwin Hyman, 1990.

Conditions Five (1979). The Black Woman's Issue.

COOK, JOANNE, CHARLOTTE BUNCH-WEEKS, and ROBIN MORGAN, eds. *The New Women: An Anthology of Women's Liberation.* Greenwich, Conn.: Fawcett, 1970.

COOPER, ANNA JULIA. *A Voice from the South: By a Black Woman of the South.* Xenia, Ohio: Aldine Printing House, 1892.

————. *Slavery and the French Revolutionists, 1788–1805.* Trans. Frances Richardson Keller. Lewiston, Maine: Edwin Mellen Press, 1988.

COPPIN, FANNIE JACKSON. *Reminiscences of School Life, and Hints on Teaching.* Philadelphia: African Episcopal Concern, 1913.

COTT, NANCY F. *The Grounding of Modern Feminism.* New Haven: Yale University Press, 1987.

CRAWFORD, VICKI L., JACQUELINE ROUSE, and BARBARA WOODS, eds. *Women in the Civil Rights Movement: Trailblazers and Torchbearers, 1941–1965*. Brooklyn, N.Y.: Carlson, 1990.

CULP, D. ed. *Twentieth-Century Negro Literature: Or a Cyclopedia of Thought on the Vital Topics Relating to the American Negro*. Toronto: J. L. Nichols, 1902.

DALY, MARY. *Gyn/Ecology: The Metaethics of Radical Feminism*. Boston: Beacon Press, 1979.

THE DAMNED. *Lessons From the Damned: Class Struggle in the Black Community*. Ojai, Calif.: Times Change Press, 1973.

DANDRIDGE, RITA B. *Black Women's Blues: A Literary Anthology, 1934–1988*. New York: G. K. Hall & Co., 1992.

DANIEL, SADIE. *Women Builders*. Washington, D.C.: Associated Publishers, 1931.

DANNETT, SYLVIA. *Profiles of Negro Womanhood*. New York: Educational Heritage, 1964.

DAVIES, CAROLE BOYCE. *Black Women, Writing and Identity: Migrations of the Subject*. London and New York: Routledge, 1994.

DAVIS, ANGELA. "Reflections on the Black Woman's Role in the Community of Slaves." *Black Scholar* 3 (December 1971), 4–15.

———. *Women, Culture, and Politics*. New York: Random House, 1989.

———. *Women, Race, and Class*. New York: Random House, 1981.

DAVIS, BEVERLY. "To Seize the Moment: A Retrospective on the National Black Feminist Organization." *SAGE: A Scholarly Journal on Black Women* 5 (Fall 1988), 43–46.

DAVIS, ELIZABETH. *Lifting as They Climb: The National Association of Colored Women*. Washington, D.C.: National Association of Colored Women, 1833.

DAVIS, FLORA. *Moving the Mountain: The Women's Movement in America Since 1960*. New York: Simon and Schuster, 1991.

DAVIS, MARIANNA, ed. *Contributions of Black Women to America*, 2 vols. Columbia, S.C.: Kenday Press, 1982.

DECKARD, BARBARA SINCLAIR. *The Women's Movement: Political, Socioeconomic, and Psychological Issues*. New York: Harper & Row, 1979.

DECOSTA-WILLIS, MIRIAM, ed. *The Memphis Diary of Ida B. Wells*. Boston: Beacon Press, 1995.

DENT, GINA, ed. *Black Popular Culture: A Project by Michele Wallace*. Seattle: Bay Press, 1992.

DILL, BONNIE. "Race, Class, and Gender: Prospects for an All-Inclusive Sisterhood." *Feminist Studies* 9 (Spring 1983): 131–50.

DUBEY, MADHU. *Black Women Novelists and the Nationalist Aesthetic*. Bloomington: Indiana University Press, 1994.

DuBOIS, ELLEN CAROL and VICKI L. RUIZ, eds. *Unequal Sisters: A Multicultural Reader in U.S. Women's History*. New York: Routledge & Kegan Paul, 1990.

DU BOIS, WILLIAM E. B. *Darkwater: Voices from Within the Veil*. New York: Harcourt, Brace & Howe, 1920.

DuCILLE, ANN. *The Coupling Convention: Sex, Text, and Tradition in Black Women's Fiction*. New York: Oxford University Press, 1993.

DUNBAR-NELSON, ALICE. "Women's Most Serious Problems." *Messenger* (March 1927), 73.

DUSTER, ALFREDA M., ed. *Crusade for Justice: The Autobiography of Ida B. Wells.* Chicago: University of Chicago Press, 1970.

EARLY, GERALD, ed. *Lure and Loathing.* New York: Penguin, 1993.

ECHOLS, ALICE. *Daring to Be Bad: Radical Feminism in America, 1967–1975.* Minneapolis: University of Minneapolis Press, 1989.

EICHELBERGER, B. "Voices of Black Feminism." *Quest: A Feminist Quarterly* 3 (Spring 1977), 16–28.

"Eldridge Cleaver on Women's Liberation." *Guardian,* 2 August, 1969, 5.

EVANS, MARI, ed. *Black Women Writers.* Garden City, N.Y.: Anchor, 1984.

EVANS, SARAH. *Personal Politics: The Roots of Women's Liberation in the Civil Rights Movement and the New Left.* New York: Knopf, 1979.

FADERMAN, LILLIAN. *Odd Girls and Twilight Lovers: A History of Lesbian Life in Twentieth-Century America.* New York: Penguin, 1991.

FIRESTONE, SHULAMITH and ANNE KOEDT, eds. *Notes from the Second Year: Women's Liberation, the Major Writings of the Radical Feminists.* New York: New York Radical Women, 1970.

FLEXNER, ELEANOR. *Century of Struggle: The Woman's Rights Movement in the United States.* Cambridge: Harvard University Press, 1959.

FLYNN, JOYCE and JOYCE OCCOMY, eds. *The Collected Works of Marita Bonner.* Boston: Beacon Press, 1987.

FONER, ERIC, ed. *Major Speeches by Negroes in the U.S., 1797–1971.* New York: Simon and Schuster, 1972.

FONER, PHILIP S., ed. *Frederick Douglass on Women's Rights.* Westport, Conn.: Greenwood Press, 1976.

FOSTER, FRANCES. "Changing Concepts of the Black Woman." *Journal of Black Studies* (June 1973), 433–52.

———, ed. *A Brighter Coming Day: A Frances Ellen Watkins Harper Reader.* New York: Feminist Press, 1989.

FREEMAN, JO. *The Politics of Women's Liberation.* New York: David McKay, 1975.

———, ed. *Women: A Feminist Perspective.* Palo Alto, Calif.: Mayfield, 1984.

GABEL, LEONA C. *From Slavery to the Sorbonne and Beyond: The Life and Writings of Anna J. Cooper.* Northampton, Mass.: Smith College, 1982.

GARROW, DAVID, ed. *The Montgomery Bus Boycott and the Women Who Started It: The Memoir of Jo Ann Gibson Robinson.* Knoxville: University of Tennessee Press, 1987.

GARVEY, AMY JACQUES. *Garvey and Garveyism.* New York: Collier Books, 1970.

GATES, HENRY LOUIS JR., ed. *The Schomburg Library of Nineteenth-Century Black Women Writers.* 30 vols. New York: Oxford University Press, 1988.

———, ed. *Reading Black, Reading Feminist: A Critical Anthology.* New York: Meridian Books, 1990.

GIDDINGS, PAULA. "Black Feminism Takes Its Rightful Place." *Ms.* (October 1985).

———. *When and Where I Enter: The Impact of Black Women on Sex and Race in America.* New York: William Morrow, 1984.

GILBERT, OLIVE. *Narrative of Sojourner Truth: A Northern Slave.* Boston: O. Gilbert, 1850.

GILMAN, SANDER L. "Black Bodies, White Bodies: Toward an Iconography of Female Sexuality in Late Nineteenth-Century Art, Medicine, and Literature." *"Race," Writing, and Difference,* ed. Henry Louis Gates Jr. Chicago: University of Chicago Press, 1985.

GOLDEN, MARITA, ed. *Wild Women Don't Wear No Blues: Black Women Writers on Love, Men and Sex.* New York: Doubleday, 1993.

GORDON, LINDA. *Woman's Body, Woman's Right: A Social History of Birth Control in America.* New York: Grossman, 1976.

GORNICK, VIVIAN and BARBARA K. MORAN, eds. *Woman in Sexist Society: Studies in Power and Powerlessness.* New York: New American Library, 1972.

GRANT, JACQUELYN. "Black Theology and the Black Woman." *Black Theology: A Documentary History, 1966–1979,* ed. Gayrand S. Wilmore and James H. Cove. Maryknoll, N.Y.: Orbis, 1979.

———. *White Women's Christ and Black Women's Jesus: Feminist Christology and Womanist Response.* Atlanta, Ga.: Scholars Press, 1989.

GUY-SHEFTALL, BEVERLY. *Daughters of Sorrow: Attitudes Toward Black Women, 1880–1920.* Brooklyn, N.Y.: Carlson, 1990.

HALL, JACQUELYN DOWD. *Revolt Against Chivalry.* Rev. ed. New York: Columbia University Press, 1993.

HAMMONDS, EVELYNN. "Missing Persons: African American Women, AIDS and the History of Disease." *Radical America* 20, No. 6 (1986), 7–23.

HAMPTON, ROBERT, ed. *Violence in the Black Family: Correlates and Consequences.* Lexington, Mass.: Lexington Books, 1987.

HANSBERRY, LORRAINE, "Simone de Beauvoir and *The Second Sex:* An American Commentary," unpublished manuscript. Croton, N.Y.: Hansberry Papers, 1957.

HANSEN, DEBRA GOLD. *Strained Sisterhood: Gender and Class in the Boston Female Anti-Slavery Society.* Amherst: University of Massachusetts Press, 1993.

HARDING, SANDRA, ed. *"The "Racial" Economy of Science.* Bloomington: Indiana University Press, 1993.

HARLEY, SHARON and ROSALYN TERBORG-PENN, eds. *The Afro-American Woman: Struggles and Images.* Port Washington, N.Y.: Kennikat Press, 1978.

HAWKS, JOANNE V. and SHEILA L. SKEMP, eds. *Sex, Race, and the Role of Women in the South.* Jackson: University of Mississippi Press, 1983.

HEDGEMAN, ANNA ARNOLD. *The Trumpet Sounds: A Memoir of Negro Leadership.* New York: Holt, Rinehart & Winston, 1964.

HEIGHT, DOROTHY. "To Be Black and a Woman." *Women's Role in Contemporary Society, the Report of the New York Commission on Human Rights, September 21–25, 1970.* New York: Avon, 1972.

HERNANDEZ, AILEEN. "Small Change for Black Woman." *Ms.* (August 1974), 16.

HERSH, BLANCHE GLASSMAN. *The Slavery of Sex: Feminist-Abolitionists in America.* Urbana: University of Illinois Press, 1978.

HEWITT, NANCY A. and SUZANNE LEBSOCK, eds. *Visible Women: New Essays on American Activism.* Urbana: University of Illinois Press, 1993.

HIGGINBOTHAM, EVELYN BROOKS. *Righteous Discontent, The Women's Movement in the Black Baptist Church, 1880–1920.* Cambridge: Harvard University Press, 1993.

HILL, GEORGE H. *Black Women in Television: An Illustrated History and Bibliography.* New York: Garland Publishing, 1990.

HINE, DARLENE CLARK, ed. *Black Women in U.S. History,* 8 vols. Brooklyn, N.Y.: Carlson, 1990.

HIRSCH, MARIANNE and EVELYN FOX KELLER, eds. *Conflicts in Feminism.* New York: Routledge & Kegan Paul, 1990.

HOLE, JUDITH and ELLEN LEVINE. *Rebirth of Feminism.* New York: Quadrangle, 1971.

———. *Women Power: The Movement for Women's Liberation.* New York: Tower Publications, 1970.

HOLLAND, SHARON PATRICIA. "Which Me Will Survive?: Audre Lorde and the Development of a Black Feminist Ideology." *Critical Matrix* 1 (1988), 2–30.

HOOD, ELIZABETH. "Black Women, White Women: Separate Paths to Liberation." *Black Scholar* 4 (April 1978), 8–13.

HOOKS, BELL. *Ain't I a Woman: Black Women and Feminism.* Boston: South End Press, 1981.

———. *Black Looks: Race and Representation.* Boston: South End Press, 1992.

———. *Feminist Theory: From Margin to Center.* Boston: South End Press, 1984.

———. *Talking Back: Thinking Feminist, Thinking Black.* Boston: South End Press, 1989.

———. *Yearning: Race, Gender, and Cultural Politics.* Boston: South End Press, 1990.

HORTON, JAMES O. "Freedom's Yoke: Gender Conventions Among Antebellum Free Blacks." *Feminist Studies* 12 (1986), 51–76.

HULL, GLORIA T. *Color, Sex and Poetry: Three Women Writers of the Harlem Renaissance.* Bloomington: Indiana University Press, 1987.

———, ed. *Give Us Each Day: The Diary of Alice Dunbar-Nelson.* New York: W. W. Norton, 1984.

———, ed. *The Collected Works of Alice Dunbar-Nelson.* The Schomburg Library of Nineteenth-Century Black Women Writers, Vol. 2, ed. Henry Louis Gates Jr. New York: Oxford University Press, 1988.

HULL, GLORIA, PATRICIA BELL SCOTT, and BARBARA SMITH. *All the Women Are White, All the Blacks Are Men, But Some of Us Are Brave: Black Women's Studies.* Old Westbury, N.Y.: Feminist Press, 1982.

HUNTER, CHARLAYNE. "Many Blacks Wary of 'Women's Liberation' Movement." *New York Times,* 17 November 1970, 60.

ISAACS, SAYLER COOK. "Black Women and Feminism." *TransAfrica Forum* 2 (Summer 1983), 3–7.

JACKSON, JACQUELYN. "Black Women in a Racist Society." *Racism and Mental Health,* ed. Charles Willie et al. Pittsburgh: University of Pittsburgh Press, 1972.

JAMES, STANLIE and ABENA P. A. BUSIA, eds. *Theorizing Black Feminisms.* New York: Routledge & Kegan Paul, 1994.

JAY, KARLA, "Double Trouble for Black Women: An Interview with Margaret Sloan," *The Tide* 3 (July 1974), 3, 22–24.

JOERS, RUTH-ELLEN BOETCHER and ELIZABETH MITTMAN, eds. *The Politics of the Essay: Feminist Perspectives.* Bloomington: Indiana University Press, 1993.

JOHNSON, BUZZ. *"I Think of My Mother": Notes on the Life and Times of Claudia Jones.* London: Karia Press, 1985.

JOHNSON, WILLA D. and THOMAS L. GREEN. *Perspectives on Afro-American Women.* Washington, D.C.: ECCA Publications, 1973.

JONES, JACQUELINE. *Labor of Love, Labor of Sorrow: Black Women, Work, and the Family: From Slavery to the Present.* New York: Random House, 1985.

JORDAN, JUNE. "Second Thoughts of a Black Feminist." *Ms.* 5 (February 1977), 113–15.

———. *Civil Wars.* Boston: Beacon Press, 1981.

———. *Technical Difficulties.* New York: Pantheon, 1992.

JOSEPH, GLORIA, "Black Feminist Pedagogy and Schooling in Capitalist White America." *Bowles and Gintis Revisited: Correspondence and Contradiction in Educational Theory,* ed., Mike Cole. London and New York: The Falmer Press, 1988.

JOSEPH, GLORIA and JILL LEWIS. *Common Differences: Conflicts in Black and White Feminist Perspectives.* Garden City, N.Y.: Anchor, 1981.

JOYCE, JOYCE ANN. *Warriors, Conjurers and Priests: Defining African-centered Literary Criticism.* Chicago: Third World Press, 1994.

KATZ, JONATHAN NED. *Gay American History: Lesbians and Gay Men in the U.S.A.* Rev. ed. New York: Meridian Books, 1992.

KENNEDY, FLORYNCE. *Color Me Flo: My Hard Life and Good Times.* Englewood Cliffs, N.J.: Prentice-Hall, 1976.

KING, MAE. "Oppression and Power: The Unique States of the Black Woman in the American Political System." *Social Science Quarterly* 56 (1975): 1–16.

KING, MARY. *Freedom Song: A Personal Story of the 1960s Civil Rights Movement.* New York: William Morrow, 1977.

———. "The Politics of Sexual Stereotypes." *Black Scholar* 4 (March/April 1973), 12–23.

KLETZING, H. F. and W. H. CROGMAN. *Progress of a Race.* Atlanta, Ga.: J. L. Nichols, 1897.

KOEDT, ANNE, ELLEN LEVINE, and ANITA RAPONE, eds. *Radical Feminism.* New York: Quadrangle, 1973.

KRADITOR, AILEEN. *The Ideas of the Woman Suffrage Movement, 1890–1920.* New York: W. W. Norton, 1981.

LADNER, JOYCE. *Tomorrow's Tomorrow.* Garden City, N.Y.: Doubleday, 1972.

LAPSANSKY, EMMA J. "Feminism, Freedom and Community: Charlotte Forten and Women Activists in Nineteenth-Century Philadelphia." *Pennsylvania Magazine of History and Biography* 113 (1989), 3–19.

LA RUE, LINDA. "The Black Movement and Women's Liberation." *Black Scholar* 1 (May 1970), 36–42.

LAWSON, L. *Woman of Distinction: Remarkable in Works and Invincible in Character.* Raleigh, N.C.: L. A. Scruggs, 1893.

LERNER, GERDA, ed. *Black Women in White America: A Documentary History.* New York: Vintage, 1972.

LEWIS, DIANE. "A Response to Inequality: Black Women, Racism and Sexism." *Signs* 2 (Winter 1977), 339–61.

LEWIS, SAMELLA. *The Art of Elizabeth Catlett.* Claremont, Calif.: Hancraft Studios, 1984.

LINDSAY, BEVERLY, ed. *Comparative Perspectives of Third World Women: The Impact of Race, Sex, and Class.* New York: Praeger, 1980.

LOEWENBERG, BERT J. and RUTH BOGIN, eds. *Black Women in Nineteenth-Century American Life.* University Park: Pennsylvania State University Press, 1976.

LOMAX, PEARL [CLEAGE]. "Black Women's Lib?" *Essence* (August 1972), 68.

LORDE, AUDRE. *Sister Outsider: Essays and Speeches.* Trumansburg, N.Y.: Crossing Press, 1984.

———. *Zami: A New Spelling of My Name.* Watertown, Mass.: Persephone Press, 1982.

LYNN, SUSAN. *Progressive Women in Conservative Times: Racial Justice, Peace, and Feminism, 1945–1960s.* New Brunswick, N.J.: Rutgers University Press, 1992.

MABEE, CARLETON. *Sojourner Truth: Slave, Prophet, Legend.* New York: New York University Press, 1993.

MACBRADY, J., ed. *A New Negro for a New Century.* Chicago: American Publishing House, 1900.

MAJORS, MONROE. *Noted Negro Women, Their Triumphs and Activities.* Chicago: Donohue & Henneberry, 1893.

MALCOLM, SHIRLEY, et al., eds. *The Double Bind: The Price of Being a Minority Woman in Science.* Washington, D.C.: American Association for the Advancement of Science, 1976.

MALSON, MICHELINE, et al., eds. *Black Women in America: Social Science Perspectives.* Chicago: University of Chicago Press, 1988.

MARABLE, MANNING. *How Capitalism Underdeveloped Black America.* Boston: South End Press, 1983.

McDOWELL, DEBORAH E. *"The Changing Same": Black Women's Literature, Criticism and Theory.* Bloomington: Indiana University Press, 1995.

MORAGA, CHERRíE and GLORIA ANZALDUA, eds. *This Bridge Called My Back: Writings by Radical Women of Color.* Watertown, Mass.: Persephone Press, 1981.

MORGAN, ROBIN, ed. *Sisterhood Is Powerful: An Anthology of Writings from the Women's Movement.* New York: Random House, 1970.

MORRIS, ALTON D. *The Origins of the Civil Rights Movement: Black Communities Organizing for Change.* New York: Free Press, 1984.

MORRISON, TONI, ed. *Race-ing Justice, En-gendering Power: Essays on Anita Hill, Clarence Thomas and the Construction of Social Reality.* New York: Pantheon, 1992.

———. "What the Black Woman Thinks About Women's Lib." *New York Times Magazine,* 22 August 1971, 15.

MORTON, PATRICIA. *Disfigured Images: The Historical Assault on Afro-American Women.* New York: Praeger, 1991.

MOSES, WILSON. *The Golden Age of Black Nationalism, 1850–1925.* New York: Oxford University Press, 1978.

MOSSELL, N. F. *The Work of the Afro-American Woman.* Philadelphia: Geo. S. Ferguson, 1908.

MURRAY, PAULI. *Proud Shoes: The Story of an American Family.* New York: Harper & Row, 1956.

———. *Song in a Weary Throat.* New York: Harper & Row, 1987.

NEVERDON-MORTON, CYNTHIA. *Afro-American Women of the South and the Advancement of the Race, 1895–1925.* Knoxville: University of Tennessee Press, 1989.

NICHOLS, J. and W. CROGMAN, eds. *Progress of a Race.* Chicago: American Publishing House, 1900.

NOBLE, JEANNE. *Beautiful, Also, Are the Souls of My Black Sisters: A History of Black Women in America.* Englewood Cliffs, N.J.: Prentice-Hall, 1978.

OMOLADE, BARBARA. *The Rising Song of African American Women.* New York: Routledge, 1994.

PAINTER, NELL IRVIN. "Sojourner Truth in Life and Memory: Writing the Biography of an American Exotic." *Gender and History* 2 (1990), 3–19.

"Panther Sisters on Women's Liberation." *Off the Pigs! The History and Literature of the Black Panther Party,* ed. G. Louis Heath. Metuchen, N.J.: Scarecrow Press, 1976.

PERKINS, KATHY A. *Black Female Playwrights.* Bloomington: Indiana University Press, 1990.

PETERSON, ELIZABETH A. *African American Women: A Study in Success.* Jefferson, N.C.: McFarland, 1992.

PETTIGREW, L. EUDORA. "Women's Liberation and the Black Woman." *Journal of Social and Behavioral Sciences* 23 (Spring 1971), 146–61.

PORTER, DOROTHY. "The Organized Educational Activities of Negro Literary Societies, 1828–1846." *Journal of Negro Education* 54 (1930): 556–76.

PRYSE, MARJORIE and HORTENSE J. SPILLERS, eds. *Conjuring: Black Women, Fiction, and Literary Tradition.* Bloomington: Indiana University Press, 1985.

QUARLES, BENJAMIN. *Black Abolitionists.* New York: Collier, 1969.

REED, EVELYN. *Problems of Women's Liberation.* New York: Pathfinder Press, 1969.

REID, INEZ. *"Together" Black Women.* New York: Emerson-Hall, 1971.

REUTHER, R. "Crisis in Sex and Race: Black Theology vs. Feminist Theology." *Christianity and Crisis* 34 (1974), 67.

RICHARDSON, MARILYN, ed. *Maria W. Stewart: America's First Black Woman Political Writer: Essays and Speeches.* Bloomington: Indiana University Press, 1987.

ROBERTS, J. R., ed. *Black Lesbians: An Annotated Bibliography.* Tallahassee, Fla.: Naiad, 1981.

ROBINSON, PATRICIA, et al. *Poor Black Women.* New England Free Press, n.d.

RODGERS-ROSE, LA FRANCES, ed. *The Black Woman.* Beverly Hills, Calif.: Sage Publications, 1980.

RODRIQUE, JESSIE M. "The Black Community and the Birth Control Movement." *Passion and Power: Sexuality in History,* eds. Kathy Peiss and Christina Simmons. Philadelphia: Temple University Press, 1989.

ROUSE, JACQUELINE ANNE. *Lugenia Burns Hope: Black Southern Reformer.* Athens: University of Georgia Press, 1989.

ROSE, TRICIA. *Black Noise: Rap Music and Black Culture in Contemporary America.* Hanover, N.H.: Wesleyan University Press, 1994.

ROSENBERG, ROSALIND. *Divided Lives: American Women in the Twentieth Century.* New York: Hill & Wang, 1992.

RUCHANES, LOUIS. "Race, Marriage and Abolition in Massachusetts." *Journal of Negro History* 40 (1955), 250–73.

RUPP, LEILA and VERTA TAYLOR. *Survival in the Doldrums: The American Women's Rights Movement, 1945 to the 1960s.* New York: Oxford University Press, 1987.

RUSSELL, LETTY M., ed. *Feminist Interpretation of the Bible.* Philadelphia: Westminster Press, 1895.

SAGE: A Scholarly Journal on Black Women. Vol. 1–9.

SALAAM, KALAMU YA. *Our Women Keep Our Skies from Falling: Six Essays in Support of the Struggle to Smash Sexism, Develop Women.* New Orleans: Mkombo, 1980.

SALEM, DOROTHY C. *To Better Our World: Black Women in Organized Reform, 1890–1920.* Brooklyn, N.Y.: Carlson, 1990.

———. *African American Women: A Biographical Dictionary.* New York: Garland Publishing, 1993.

SALES, RUBY. "In Our Own Words: An Interview with Ruby Sales." *Women's Review of Books* 7 (February 1990), 24.

SANCHEZ-EPPLER, KAREN. *Touching Liberty: Abolition, Feminism, and the Politics of the Body.* Berkeley: University of California Press, 1993.

SARGENT, LYDIA, ed. *Women and Revolution: A Discussion of the Unhappy Marriage of Marxism and Feminism.* Boston: South End Press, 1981.

SCHNEIR, MIRIAM, ed. *Feminism in Our Time: The Essential Writings, World War II to the Present.* New York: Vintage, 1994.

SCOTT, ANNE FIROR. "Most Invisible of All: Black Women's Voluntary Associations." *Journal of Southern History* 56 (1900), 3–22.

———. *Feminism: The Essential Historical Writings.* New York: Vintage, 1972.

SCOTT, JOYCE HOPE. "From Foreground to Margin: Female Configurations and Masculine Self-Representation in Black Nationalist Fiction." *Nationalisms and Sexualities,* ed. Andrew Parker et al. New York: Routledge, 1992.

SCOTT, KESHO YVONNE. *The Habit of Surviving: Black Women's Strategies for Life.* New Brunswick, N.J.: Rutgers University Press, 1991.

———. "Sexism and Racism: One Battle to Fight." *Personnel and Guidance Journal* 51 (October 1972), 123–216.

SCRUGGS, LAWSON. *Women of Distinction: Remarkable in Works and Invincible in Character.* Raleigh, N.C.: L. A. Scruggs, 1893.

SEWALL, M., ed. *World's Congress of Representative Women.* Chicago: Rand McNally, 1894.

SHAW, STEPHANIE J. "Black Club Women and the Creation of the National Association of Colored Women." *Journal of Women's History* 3 (Fall 1991), 10–25.

SIMMS. MARGARET C. and JULIANNE MALVEAUX, eds. *Slipping Through the Cracks: The Status of Black Women.* New Brunswick, N.J.: Transaction Books, 1986.

SIMONS, MARGARET A., "Racism and Feminism: A Schism in the Sisterhood," *Feminist Studies* 5 (Summer 1979), 384–401.

SIZEMORE, BARBARA. "Sexism and the Black Male." *Black Scholar* 4 (March/April 1973), 2–11.

SKEETER, SHARYN. "Black Women Writers: Levels of Identity." *Essence* 4 (May 1973), 3–10.

SLOAN, MARGARET. "Black Feminism: A New Mandate." *Ms.* (May 1974), 98.

SMYTHE, MABEL. "Feminism and Black Liberation." *Women in Higher Education,* ed. W. Furniss and P. Graham. Washington, D.C.: American Council on Education, 1974.

SNITOW, ANN, ed. *Powers of Desire: The Politics of Sexuality.* New York: Monthly Review Press, 1983.

SOLOMON, IRVIN D. *Feminism and Black Activism in Contemporary America: An Ideological Assessment.* Westport, Conn.: Greenwood Press, 1989.

SPELMAN, ELIZABETH. *Inessential Woman: Problems of Exclusion in Feminist Thought.* Boston: Beacon Press, 1988.

———. "Theories of Race and Gender: The Erasure of Black Women." *Quest* 5 (1979).

SPILLERS, HORTENSE. "Interstices: A Small Drama of Words." *Pleasure and Danger: Exploring Female Sexuality,* ed. Carole S. Vance. New York: Routledge & Kegan Paul, 1984.

STANTON, ELIZABETH CADY, et al., eds. *The History of Woman Suffrage,* 6 vols. Rochester and New York: Fowler & Wells, 1889–1922.

STEADY, FILOMINA CHIOMA, ed. *The Black Woman Cross-Culturally.* Cambridge, Mass.: Schenkman, 1981.

STERLING, DOROTHY. *Black Foremothers: Three Lives.* Old Westbury, N.Y.: Feminist Press, 1979.

———, ed. *We Are Your Sisters: Black Women in the Nineteenth Century.* New York: W. W. Norton, 1984.

STETSON, ERLENE. "Black Feminism in Indiana, 1893–1933." *Phylon* 44 (December 1983), 292–98.

STEWART, MARIA. *Productions of Mrs. Maria W. Stewart.* Boston: W. Lloyd Garrison & Knapp, 1832.

STIMPSON, CATHERINE. "Conflict Probable, Coalition, Possible: Feminism and the Black Movement." *Women in Higher Education,* ed. W. Furniss and P. Graham. Washington, D.C.: American Council on Education, 1974.

SWERDLOW, AMY and HANNA LESSINGER, eds. *Class, Race, and Sex: The Dynamics of Contro.* Boston: G. K. Hall, 1983.

TANNER, LESLIE, ed. *Voices from Women's Liberation.* New York: Signet, 1970.

TATE, CLAUDIA. *Domestic Allegories of Political Desire: The Black Heroine's Text at the Turn of the Century.* New York: Oxford University Press, 1992.

TERBORG-PENN, ROSALYN. "Discontented Black Feminists: Prelude and Postscript to the Passage of the Nineteenth Amendment." *Decades of Discontent: The Women's Movement, 1920–1940,* ed. Lois Scharf and Joan M. Jensen. Westport, Conn.: Greenwood Press, 1983.

TERRELL, MARY CHURCH. *Colored Woman in a White World.* Washington, D.C.: Ransdell Publishing, 1940.

TESFAGIORGIS, FREIDA HIGH W. "Afrofemcentrism: The Art of Elizabeth Catlett and Faith Ringgold." *SAGE* 4 (Spring 1987), 25–32.

THISTLETHWAITE, SUSAN. *Sex, Race and God: Christian Feminism in Black and White.* New York: Crossroad, 1991.

THOMPSON, MARY LOU, ed. *Voices of the New Feminism*. Boston: Beacon Press, 1970.

TOWNES, EMILE M. *Womanist Justice, Womanist Hope*. Atlanta: Scholars Press, 1993.

TOWNS, SAUNDRA. "The Black Woman as Whore: Genesis of the Myth." *The Black Position* 3 (1974), 39–59.

UMANSKY, LAURI. " 'The Sisters Reply': Black Nationalist Pronatalism, Black Feminism, and the Quest for a Multiracial Women's Movement, 1965–1974," *Critical Matrix* 2 (1994), 19–50.

VANCE, CAROLE S., ed. *Pleasure and Danger: Exploring Female Sexuality*. Boston: Routledge & Kegan Paul, 1984.

VAN DEBURG, WILLIAM. *New Day in Babylon: The Black Power Movement and American Culture, 1965–1975*. Chicago: University of Chicago Press, 1992.

VAN DEBURG, WILLIAM and JOHN C. VAN HORNE, eds. *The Abolitionist Sisterhood: Women's Political Culture in Antebellum America*. Ithaca, N.Y.: Cornell University Press, 1994.

VAZ, KIM MARIE, ed. *Black Women in America*. Thousand Oaks, Calif.: Sage Publications, 1995.

VITALE, SYLVIA WITTS. "Black Sisterhood." *National Black Feminist Organization Newsletter* 1 (September 1975), 2.

Voice of the Negro 1 (July 1904).

WADE-GAYLES, GLORIA. *No Crystal Stair: Visions of Race and Sex in Black Women's Fiction*. New York: Pilgrim Press, 1984.

WALKER, ALICE. *In Search of Our Mothers' Gardens: Womanist Prose*. San Diego: Harcourt Brace Jovanovich, 1983.

———. *Living by the Word: Selected Writings, 1973–1987*. San Diego: Harcourt Brace Jovanovich, 1988.

WALKER, ALICE and PRATHIBHA PARMAR. *Warrior Marks: Female Genital Mutilation and the Sexual Blinding of Women*. New York: Harcourt Brace and Company, 1993.

WALKER, MARGARET. *How I Wrote* Jubilee. Old Westbury, N.Y.: Feminist Press, 1972.

WALKER, ROBBIE JEAN. *The Rhetoric of Struggle: Public Address by African American Women*. New York: Garland Publishing, 1992.

WALL, CHERYL. *Changing Our Own Words: Essays on Writing by Black Women*. New Brunswick, N.J.: Rutgers University Press, 1989.

WALLACE, MICHELE. *Black Macho and the Myth of the Superwoman*. New York: Dial, 1979.

———. *Invisibility Blues: From Pop to Theory*. London: Verso, 1990.

———. "On the National Black Feminist Organization." *Redstockings Feminist Revolution*. New York: Random House, 1975, 174.

WALTERS, RONALD G. *The Anti-Slavery Appeal: American Abolitionists After 1830*. Baltimore: 1976.

WARE, CELLESTINE. *"Black Feminism," Notes from the Third Year*, ed. Anne Koedt. 1973, 25.

———. *Woman Power*. New York: Tower Publications, 1970.

WARE, SUSAN. *Beyond Suffrage: Women in the New Deal*. Cambridge: Harvard University Press, 1981.

WASHINGTON, MARY HELEN. *Invented Lives: Narratives of Black Women, 1860–1960.* Garden City, N.Y.: Anchor, 1987.

WEEMS, RENITA. *I Asked for Intimacy: Stories, Blessings, Betrayals, and Birthings.* San Diego: LuraMedia, 1993.

———. *Just a Sister Away: A Womanist Vision of Women's Relationships in the Bible.* San Diego: LuraMedia, 1988.

WELLS, DIANA. *Getting There: The Movement Toward Gender Equality.* New York: Carroll & Graf Publishers, 1994.

WELLS-BARNETT, IDA. *Southern Horrors.* Ida Wells-Barnett, 1892.

WELTER, BARBARA. "The Cult of True Womanhood." *American Quarterly* 18 (Summer 1966), 151–74.

WHITE, DEBORAH GRAY. *Ar'n't I a Woman: Female Slaves in the Plantation South.* New York: W. W. Norton, 1985.

WHITE, EVELYN. *Chain, Chain, Change: For Black Women Dealing with Physical and Emotional Abuse.* Seattle: Seal Press, 1985.

WHITE, FRANCES. "Listening to the Voices of Black Feminism." *Radical America* 18, Nos. 2 and 3 (March–June 1984), 7–25.

WILLIAMS, DELORES S. *Sisters in the Wilderness: The Challenge of Womanist God-Talk.* New York: Orbis Books, 1993.

WILLIAMS, PATRICIA J. *The Alchemy of Race and Rights: Diary of a Law Professor.* Cambridge: Harvard University Press, 1991.

WILLIS, ELLEN. "Sisters Under the Skin? Confronting Race and Sex." *Village Voice Literary Supplement,* 8 June 1982, 12.

WILMORE G. and J. CONE, eds. *Black Theology: A Documentary History, 1966–1979.* Maryknoll, N.Y.: Orbis Books, 1979.

The Women's Era. Vols. 1–3, 1873–1875.

YEE, SHIRLEY J. *Black Women Abolitionists: A Study in Activism, 1828–1860.* Knoxville: University of Tennessee Press, 1992.

YELLIN, JEAN FAGAN, ed. *Incidents in the Life of a Slave Girl Written by Herself.* Cambridge: Harvard University Press, 1987.

———. *Women and Sisters: The Antislavery Feminists in American Culture.* New Haven: Yale University Press, 1989.

Index